Big Data Management and Processing

Chapman & Hall/CRC
Big Data Series

SERIES EDITOR
Sanjay Ranka

AIMS AND SCOPE

This series aims to present new research and applications in Big Data, along with the computational tools and techniques currently in development. The inclusion of concrete examples and applications is highly encouraged. The scope of the series includes, but is not limited to, titles in the areas of social networks, sensor networks, data-centric computing, astronomy, genomics, medical data analytics, large-scale e-commerce, and other relevant topics that may be proposed by potential contributors.

PUBLISHED TITLES

BIG DATA MANAGEMENT AND PROCESSING
Kuan-Ching Li, Hai Jiang, Albert Y. Zomaya

BIG DATA COMPUTING: A GUIDE FOR BUSINESS AND TECHNOLOGY MANAGERS
Vivek Kale

BIG DATA IN COMPLEX AND SOCIAL NETWORKS
My T. Thai, Weili Wu, and Hui Xiong

BIG DATA OF COMPLEX NETWORKS
Matthias Dehmer, Frank Emmert-Streib, Stefan Pickl, and Andreas Holzinger

BIG DATA : ALGORITHMS, ANALYTICS, AND APPLICATIONS
Kuan-Ching Li, Hai Jiang, Laurence T. Yang, and Alfredo Cuzzocrea

NETWORKING FOR BIG DATA
Shui Yu, Xiaodong Lin, Jelena Mišić, and Xuemin (Sherman) Shen

Big Data Management and Processing

Edited by

Kuan-Ching Li

Guangzhou University, China

Providence University, Taiwan

Hai Jiang

Arkansas State University, USA

Albert Y. Zomaya

University of Sydney, Australia

CRC Press

Taylor & Francis Group

Boca Raton London New York

CRC Press is an imprint of the

Taylor & Francis Group, an **informa** business

CRC Press
Taylor & Francis Group
6000 Broken Sound Parkway NW, Suite 300
Boca Raton, FL 33487-2742

Printed on acid-free paper

International Standard Book Number-13: 978-1-4987-6807-8 (Hardback)

Library of Congress Cataloging-in-Publication Data

Names: Li, Kuan-Ching, editor. | Jiang, Hai, editor. | Zomaya, Albert Y., editor.
Title: Big data management and processing / compiled by Kuan-Ching Li, Hai Jiang, Albert Y. Zomaya.
Description: Boca Raton : Taylor & Francis, CRC Press, 2017. | Series: Chapman & Hall/CRC big data series ; 3 | Includes bibliographical references.
Identifiers: LCCN 2016051834 | ISBN 9781498768078 (hardback : alk. paper)
Subjects: LCSH: Big data. | Data mining. | Information storage and retrieval systems.
Classification: LCC QA76.9.B45 B556 2017 | DDC 005.7- -dc23
LC record available at https://lccn.loc.gov/2016051834

Visit the Taylor & Francis Web site at
http://www.taylorandfrancis.com

and the CRC Press Web site at
http://www.crcpress.com

Contents

Foreword

Big Data Management and Processing (edited by Li, Jiang, and Zomaya) is a state-of-the-art book that deals with a wide range of topical themes in the field of Big Data. The book, which probes many issues related to this exciting and rapidly growing field, covers processing, management, analytics, and applications.

The many advances in Big Data research that we witness today are brought about because of the many developments we see in algorithms, high-performance computing, databases, datamining, machine learning, and so on. These developments are discussed in this book. The book also showcases some of the interesting applications and technologies that are still evolving and that will lead to some serious breakthroughs in the coming few years.

I believe that *Big Data Management and Processing* is a very valuable addition to the literature. It will serve as a source of up-to-date research in this continuously developing area. The book also provides an opportunity for researchers to explore the use of advanced computing technologies and their impact on enhancing our capabilities to conduct more sophisticated studies.

I expect that *Big Data Management and Processing* will be well received by the research and development community. It should prove very beneficial for researchers and graduate students focusing on Big Data and will serve as a very useful reference for practitioners and application developers.

Sartaj Sahni
University of Florida

Preface

The scope of *Big Data* today spans many aspects and it is not limited to main computing components (e.g., processors, storage devices, and visualization facilities) alone, but it expands into a much larger range of issues related to management and policy. Also, "Big Data" can mean "Big Energy," because of the pressure that data places on a variety of infrastructures needed to host, manage, and transport data. This in turn raises various monetary, environmental, and system performance concerns.

Recent advances in software hardware technologies have improved the handling of big data. However, there still remain many issues that are pertinent to the overloading that happens due to the processing of massive amounts of data, which calls for the development of various software and hardware solutions as well as new algorithms that are more capable of processing of data.

This book, *Big Data Management and Processing*, seeks to provide an opportunity for researchers to explore a range of big data-related issues and their impact on the design of new computing systems. The book is quite timely, since the field of big data computing as a whole is undergoing rapid changes on a daily basis. Vast literature exists today on such data processing paradigms and frameworks and their implications for a wide range of distributed platforms.

The book is intended to be a virtual roundtable of several outstanding researchers that one might invite to attend a conference on big data computing systems. Of course, the list of topics that is explored here is by no means exhaustive, but most of the conclusions provided here should be extended to the other computing platforms that are not covered here. There was a decision to limit the number of chapters while providing more pages for contributed authors to express their ideas, so that the book remains manageable within a single volume.

It is also hoped that the topics covered will get the readers to think of the implications of such new ideas on the developments in their own fields. The book endeavors to strike a balance between theoretical and practical coverage of innovative problem-solving techniques for a range of platforms. The book is intended to be a repository of paradigms, technologies, and applications that target the different facets of big data computing systems.

The 21 chapters are carefully selected to provide a wide scope with minimal overlap between the chapters so as to reduce duplications. Each contributor was asked that his/her chapter should cover review material as well as current developments. In addition, the choice of authors was made so as to select authors who are leaders in the respective disciplines.

Acknowledgments

First and foremost we would like to thank and acknowledge the contributors to this volume for their support and patience, and the reviewers for their useful comments and suggestions that helped in improving the earlier outline of the book and presentation of the material. Also, we extend our deepest thanks to Randi Cohen from CRC Press (USA) for his collaboration, guidance, and most importantly, patience in finalizing this handbook. Finally, we would like to acknowledge the efforts of the team from CRC Press's production department for their extensive efforts during the many phases of this project and the timely fashion in which the book was produced.

Editors

Kuan-Ching Li is a professor with appointments at the Guangzhou University, China and Providence University, Taiwan. He is a recipient of awards from Nvidia and support from a number of industrial companies. He has also received guest and distinguished chair professorships from universities in China and other countries. He has been actively involved in numerous conferences and workshops in program/general/steering conference chairman positions and as a program committee member, and has organized numerous conferences related to high-performance computing and computational science and engineering.

Professor Li is the Editor-in-Chief of technical publications such as International Journal of Computational Science and Engineering (IJCSE), International Journal of Embedded Systems (IJES), and International Journal of High Performance Computing and Networking (IJHPCN), all published by Inderscience. He also serves as an editorial board member and a guest editor for a number of journals. In addition, he is the author or editor of several technical professional books published by CRC Press, Springer, McGraw-Hill, and IGI Global. His topics of interest include GPU/manycore computing, big data, and cloud. He is a Member of the AAAS, a Senior Member of the IEEE, and a Fellow of the IET.

Hai Jiang is a professor in the Department of Computer Science at Arkansas State University, USA. He received his BS degree from Beijing University of Posts and Telecommunications, China, and his MA and PhD degrees from Wayne State University, Detroit, Michigan, USA. His current research interests include parallel and distributed systems, computer and network security, high-performance computing and communication, big data, and modeling and simulation. He has published one book and several research papers in major international journals and conference proceedings. He has served as a U.S. National Science Foundation proposal review panelist and a U.S. DoE (Department of Energy) Smart Grid Investment Grant (SGIG) reviewer multiple times.

Professor Jiang serves as the executive editor of *International Journal of High Performance Computing and Networking* (IJHPCN). He is an editorial board member of *International Journal of Big Data Intelligence* (IJBDI), *The Scientific World Journal* (TSWJ), *Open Journal of Internet of Things* (OJIOT), and *GSTF Journal on Social Computing* (JSC) and a guest editor of *IEEE Systems Journal, International Journal of Ad Hoc and Ubiquitous Computing, Cluster Computing*, and *The Scientific World Journal* for multiple special issues. He has also served as a general or program chair for some major conferences/workshops (CSE, HPCC, ISPA, GPC, ScaleCom, ESCAPE, GPU-Cloud, FutureTech, GPUTA, FC, SGC). He has been involved in more than 90 conferences and workshops as a session chair or program committee member, including major conferences such as AINA, ICPP, IUCC, ICPADS, TrustCom, HPCC, GPC, EUC, ICIS, SNPD, TSP, PDSEC, SECRUPT, and ScalCom. He is a professional member of ACM and IEEE Computer Society and a representative of the U.S. NSF XSEDE (Extreme Science and Engineering Discovery Environment) Campus Champion for Arkansas State University.

Albert Y. Zomaya is the chair professor of high-performance computing and networking in the School of Information Technologies, University of Sydney, Australia and also serves as the director of the Centre for Distributed and High Performance Computing. He has published more than 600 scientific papers and articles and is the author, coauthor, or editor of more than 20 books. He is the founding editor-in-chief of *IEEE Transactions on Sustainable Computing* and serves as an associate editor for more than 20 leading journals. He served as the editor-in-chief of *IEEE Transactions on Computers* from 2011 to 2014.

Professor Zomaya is the recipient of the IEEE Technical Committee on Parallel Processing Outstanding Service Award (2011), the IEEE Technical Committee on Scalable Computing Medal for Excellence in Scalable Computing (2011), and the IEEE Computer Society Technical Achievement Award (2014). He is a chartered engineer and a fellow of AAAS, IEEE, and IET. His research interests are in the areas of parallel and distributed computing and complex systems.

Contributors

Syedmeysam Abolghasemi
Department of Computer Science
Old Dominion University
Norfolk, Virginia

Antonio Juarez Alencar
The Tércio Pacitti Institute
Federal University of Rio de Janeiro
Brazil

Guillaume Aupy
School of Engineering
Vanderbilt University
Nashville, Tennessee

Paolo Balboni
Tilburg Institute for Law, Technology, and Society
Tilburg, The Netherlands
and
ICT Legal Consulting
Milan, Italy
and
European Privacy Association
Brussels, Belgium

Mauro Penha Bastos
The Tércio Pacitti Institute
Federal University of Rio de Janeiro
Brazil

Anne Benoit
LIP, ENS Lyon
Lyon, France

Angelos Bilas
Institute of Computer Science (ICS)
Foundation for Research and Technology—Hellas (FORTH)
and
Department of Computer Science
University of Crete, Greece

Vito Giovanni Castellana
High Performance Computing
Pacific Northwest National Laboratory
Richland, Washington

Huaming Chen
School of Computing and Information Technology
University of Wollongong
Wollongong, NSW, Australia

Jianguo Chen
College of Computer Science and Electronic Engineering
Hunan University
Changsha, Hunan, China

Jinjun Chen
Swinburne Data Science Research Institute
Swinburne University of Technology
Australia

Min Chen
Department of Computer Science
State University of New York
New Paltz, New York

Alfredo Cuzzocrea
DIA Department
University of Trieste and ICAR-CNR
Trieste, Italy

Monica Ferreira da Silva
The Tércio Pacitti Institute
Federal University of Rio de Janeiro
Brazil

Miyuru Dayarathna
WSO2 Inc.
Mountain View, California

Theodora Dragan
European Privacy Association
Brussels, Belgium

Fabrizio Ferrandi
Dipartimento di Elettronica, Informazione e Bioingegneria
Politecnico di Milano
Milano, Italy

Ryan Florin
Department of Computer Science
Old Dominion University
Norfolk, Virginia

Paul Fremantle
WSO2 Inc.
Mountain View, California

Pilar González-Férez
Department of Computer Engineering
Technology University of Murcia
Murcia, Spain

and

Institute of Computer Science (ICS)
Foundation for Research and Technology—Hellas (FORTH)
Greece

Chonglin Gu
Department of Computer Science and Technology
Harbin Institute of Technology
Shenzhen, China

Hejiao Huang
Department of Computer Science and Technology
Harbin Institute of Technology
Shenzhen, China

Xiaohua Jia
Department of Computer Science and Technology
Harbin Institute of Technology
Shenzhen, China

Fan Jiang
Department of Computer Science
University of Manitoba
Winnipeg, MB, Canada

Junwhan Kim
CSIT
University of the District of Columbia
Washington, DC

Marco Lattuada
Dipartimento di Elettronica, Informazione e Bioingegneria
Politecnico di Milano
Milano, Italy

Carson Kai-Sang Leung
Department of Computer Science
University of Manitoba
Winnipeg, MB, Canada

Boyang Li
Department of Electrical and Computer Engineering
Clarkson University
Potsdam, New York

Kenli Li
College of Computer Science and Electronic Engineering
Hunan University
and
National Supercomputing Center in Changsha
Changsha, Hunan, China

Keqin Li
College of Computer Science and Electronic Engineering
Hunan University
Changsha, Hunan, China

and

Department of Computer Science
State University of New York
New Paltz, New York

Norman Lim
Department of Systems and Computer Engineering
Carleton University
Ottawa, ON, Canada

Nam Ling
Department of Computer Engineering
Santa Clara University
Santa Clara, California

Chen Liu
Department of Electrical and Computer Engineering
Clarkson University
Potsdam, New York

Yuhong Liu
Department of Computer Engineering
Santa Clara University
Santa Clara, California

Simone A. Ludwig
Department of Computer Science
North Dakota State University
Fargo, North Dakota

Richard Kyle MacKinnon
Department of Computer Science
University of Manitoba
Winnipeg, MB, Canada

Shikharesh Majumdar
Department of Systems and Computer Engineering
Carleton University
Ottawa, Ontario, Canada

Marco Minutoli
High Performance Computing
Pacific Northwest National Laboratory
Richland, Washington

Rim Moussa
LaTICE Lab
University of Tunis and ENICarthage
Tunis, Tunisia

Surya Nepal
CSIRO Data61
Australia

Stephan Olariu
Department of Computer Science
Old Dominion University
Norfolk, Virginia

Roberto Palmieri
ECE, Virginia Tech
Blacksburg, Virginia

Srinath Perera
WSO2 Inc.
Mountain View, California

Florin Pop
Department of Computer Science
University Politehnica of Bucharest
Bucharest, Romania

Loic Pottier
LIP, ENS Lyon
Lyon, France

Deepak Puthal
School of Computing and Communications
University of Technology
Sydney, Australia

Xiongpai Qin
Information School
Renmin University of China
Beijing, China

Padma Raghavan
School of Engineering
Vanderbilt University
Nashville, Tennessee

Rajiv Ranjan
School of Computing Science
Newcastle University
United Kingdom

Binoy Ravindran
ECE, Virginia Tech
Blacksburg, Virginia

Yves Robert
LIP, ENS Lyon
Lyon, France

and

University of Tennessee
Knoxville

Soror Sahri
LIPADE Lab
University Rene Descartes
Paris, France

Eber Assis Schmitz
The Tércio Pacitti Institute
Federal University of Rio de Janeiro
Brazil

Manu Shantharam
Computational Research Scientist
San Diego Supercomputer Center
San Diego, California

Jun Shen
School of Computing and Information Technology
University of Wollongong
Wollongong, NSW, Australia

Jiangning Song
Department of Biochemistry and Molecular Biology
Monash University
Clayton, Victoria, Australia

Petros Sotirios Stefaneas
Department of Mathematics
School of Applied Mathematics and Physical Sciences
National Technical University of Athens
Athens, Greece

Sriskandarajah Suhothayan
WSO2 Inc.
Mountain View, California

Zhuo Tang
College of Computer Science and Electronic Engineering
Hunan University
Changsha, Hunan, China

Antonino Tumeo
High Performance Computing
Pacific Northwest National Laboratory
Richland, Washington

Mihaela-Andreea Vasile
Department of Computer Science
University Politehnica of Bucharest
Bucharest, Romania

Lei Wang
School of Computing and Information Technology
University of Wollongong
Wollongong, NSW, Australia

Yu Wang
Department of Computer Engineering
Santa Clara University
Santa Clara, California

Chengwen Wu
Department of Computer Science and Technology
Tsinghua University
Beijing, China

Aida Ghazi Zadeh
Department of Computer Science
Old Dominion University
Norfolk, Virginia

Guangyan Zhang
Department of Computer Science and Technology
Tsinghua University
Beijing, China

Weimin Zheng
Department of Computer Science and Technology
Tsinghua University
Beijing, China

1 Big Data*

Legal Compliance and Quality Management

Paolo Balboni and Theodora Dragan

CONTENTS

ABSTRACT

The overlap between big data and personal data is becoming increasingly relevant in today's society, in light of the technological developments and, in particular, of the increased use of personal data as currency for purchasing "free" services. The global nature of big data, coupled with recently developed data analytics and the interest of companies in predicting trends and consumer preferences, makes it necessary to analyze how personal data and big data are connected. With a focus on the quality of data as fundamental prerequisite for ensuring that outcomes are accurate and relevant, the authors explore the ways in which traditional and modern personal data protection principles apply to the big data context.

It is not about the quantity of the data, but about the quality of it!

* All websites were last accessed on August 19, 2016.

1.1 INTRODUCTION

It is 2016 and big data is everywhere: in the newspapers, on TV, in research papers, and on the lips of every IT specialist. This is not only due to its catchy name, but also due to the sheer quantity of data available—according to IBM, we create 2.5 quintillion (2.5 times 10^{18}) bytes of data every day.* But what is the big deal with big data and, in particular, to what extent does it affect, or overlap with, personal data?

1.1.1 Topic, Approach, and Methodology

By way of introduction, the first step is to provide a definition of the concept that runs through this chapter. Various attempts at defining big data have been made in recent years, but no universal definition has been agreed upon yet. This is likely due to the constant evolution of this concept, which makes it difficult to describe without risking that the definition is either too generic or that it becomes inadequate within a short period of time.

One attempt at a universal definition was made by Gartner, a leading information technology research and advisory company, that defines big data as "high-volume, high-velocity and/or high-variety information assets that demand cost-effective, innovative forms of information processing that enable enhanced insight, decision making, and process automation."† In this case, data are regarded as assets, which attaches an intrinsic value to it. On the other hand, the Article 29 Data Protection Working Party defines big data as "the exponential growth both in the availability and in the automated use of information: it refers to gigantic digital datasets held by corporations, governments and other large organisations, which are then extensively analysed using computer algorithms."‡ This definition regards big data as a phenomenon composed of both the process of collecting information and the subsequent step of analyzing it. The common elements of the different definitions are therefore the size of the database and the analytical aspect, which together are expected to lead to better, more focused services and products, as well as more efficient business operations and more targeted approaches.

Big data can be (and has been) used in an incredibly diverse range of situations. It was employed to help athletes of Great Britain's rowing team achieve superior performance levels at the 2016 Olympic Games in Rio de Janeiro, by analyzing relevant information about their predecessors' performance.§ Predictive analytics were used in order to deal with traffic in highly congested cities, paving the way for the creation of the smart cities of the future.¶ Further, big data can have a great impact on medical sciences, and has already helped boost obesity research results by enabling researchers to identify links between obesity and depression that were previously unknown.**

Although big data does not always consist of personal data and could, for example, relate to technical information or to information about objects or natural phenomena, the European Data Protection Supervisor (EDPS) pointed out in its Opinion 7/2015 that "one of the greatest values of big data for businesses and governments is derived from the monitoring of *human* behaviour, collectively and

* IBM—What Is Big Data? 2016. *IBM—Bringing Big Data to the Enterprise*. https://www-01.ibm.com/software/data/bigdata/what-is-big-data.html.

† What Is Big Data?—Gartner IT Glossary—Big Data. 2012. *Gartner IT Glossary*. http://www.gartner.com/it-glossary/big-data/.

‡ Article 29 Data Protection Working Party. 2013. *Opinion 03/2013 on Purpose Limitation*.

§ Marr, Bernard. 2016. How Can Big Data and Analytics Help Athletes Win Olympic Gold in Rio 2016? *Forbes.com*. http://www.forbes.com/sites/bernardmarr/2016/08/09/how-big-data-and-analytics-help-athletes-win-olympic-gold-in-rio-2016/#12bedc444205.

¶ Toesland, Finbarr. 2016. Smart-from-the-Start Cities Is the Way Forward. *Raconteur*. http://raconteur.net/technology/smart-from-the-start-cities-is-the-way-forward.

** Big Data Boosts Obesity Research Results | The New York Academy of Sciences. 2016. *Nyas.Org*. http://www.nyas.org/AboutUs/AcademyNews.aspx?cid=d7d7b0bd-7eb5-411c-8fcf-0c60296e152f.

individually."* Analyzing and predicting human behavior enables decision makers in many areas to make decisions that are more accurate, consistent, and economical, thereby enhancing the efficiency of society as a whole. A few fields of application that immediately come to mind when thinking of big data analytics based on personal data are university admissions, job recruitment, customer profiling, targeted marketing, or health services. Analyzing the information about millions of previous applicants, candidates, customers, or patients makes it easy to establish common threads and to predict all sorts of things, such as whether a specific person is fit for the job or is likely to develop a certain disease in the future.

An interesting study was recently conducted by the University of Cambridge Psychometrics Centre: by analyzing the social networking "likes" of 58,000 users, researchers found that they were able to predict ethnic origin with an accuracy of 95% and religious or political orientation with an accuracy of over 80%.† Even more dramatically perhaps, they were able to predict psychological traits such as intelligence or emotional stability. The research was conducted using openly available data provided by the study subjects themselves (Facebook likes). Its results can be fine-tuned even further when cross-referencing them with data about the same subjects drawn from other sources, such as other social networking profiles or Internet usage habits. This is the point where big data starts overlapping with personal data, being separated only by a blurry border: "liking" a specific rock band does not constitute personal data as such, but the ability of linking this information directly to an individual or to other information makes it possible to identify what the person actually likes; furthermore, it enables to draw inferences about their personality, possibly revealing even sensitive political or religious preference (as was the case in the Cambridge study). "Companies may consider most of their data to be non personal data sets, but in reality it is now rare for data generated by user activity to be completely and irreversibly anonymised," stated the EDPS in a recent Opinion.‡ The availability of massive amounts of data from different sources combined with the desire to learn more about people's habits therefore poses a serious challenge regarding the right to privacy of the individual and requires that the data protection principles are carefully taken into consideration.

A fundamental part of big data analytics, however, is that the raw data must be accurate in order to lead to accurate results; massive quantities of inaccurate data can lead to skewed results and poor decision making. Bruce Schneier, an internationally renowned security technologist, refers to this as the "pollution problem of the information age."§ There is a risk that analytical applications find patterns in cases where the individual facts are not directly correlated, which may lead to unfair conclusions and may adversely affect the persons involved. Another risk is that of being trapped in an "information bubble," with people only being shown certain information that has been predicted to be of interest to them (but may not be in reality). In an article published in 2015 by *TIME* magazine, Facebook's newsfeed algorithm was explained: whereas users have access to an average of 1,500 posts per day, they only see about 300 of them, which have been preselected by an algorithm in order to correspond as much as possible with the interests and preferences of each user.¶ The author of the article concludes that "by structuring the environment, Facebook is training people implicitly to behave in a particular way in that algorithmic environment." Therefore, data quality is paramount

---

* European Data Protection Supervisor. 2015. *Opinion 7/2015—Meeting the Challenges of Big Data: A Call for Transparency, User Control, Data Protection by Design and Accountability*. Available at: https://secure.edps.europa.eu/EDPSWEB/webdav/site/mySite/shared/Documents/Consultation/Opinions/2015/15-11-19_Big_Data_EN.pdf.

† Kosinski, M., D. Stillwell, and T. Graepel. 2013. Private Traits and Attributes Are Predictable from Digital Records of Human Behavior. *Proceedings of the National Academy of Sciences* 110 (15): 5802–5805. doi: 10.1073/pnas.1218772110.

‡ European Data Protection Supervisor. 2014. *Preliminary Opinion of the European Data Protection Supervisor Privacy and Competitiveness in the Age of Big Data: The Interplay between Data Protection, Competition Law and Consumer Protection in the Digital Economy*. https://secure.edps.europa.eu/EDPSWEB/webdav/site/mySite/shared/Documents/Consultation/Opinions/2014/14-03-26_competitition_law_big_data_EN.pdf.

§ Schneier, Bruce. 2015. *Data and Goliath*. New York: W.W. Norton.

¶ Here's How Your Facebook News Feed Actually Works. 2015. *TIME.Com*. http://time.com/3950525/facebook-news-feed-algorithm/.

to ensuring that the algorithms and analytical procedures are carried out successfully and that the predicted results correspond with the reality.

This chapter is aimed at analyzing the personal data protection legal compliance aspects of big data from a modern perspective, in order to identify the main challenges and to make adequate recommendations for the more efficient and lawful use of data as an asset. Few considerations are also made on the connection between big personal data analytics and competition law. The methodology is straightforward: the observations made throughout the chapter are based on the research conducted by regulatory and advisory bodies, as well as on the empirical research and practical experience of the authors. One of the chapter's focal points is data quality. Owing to the nature of big data, raw data that are not of adequate quality (accurate, relevant, consistent, and complete) represent an obstacle in harnessing the value of the data. It is hoped that the chapter will enable the reader to gain a better understanding that a correct legal compliance management can make a fundamental difference between simply collecting vast amount of data, on the one hand, and effectively using the power of big data, on the other hand.

1.1.2 Structure and Arguments

This chapter is organized into two main sections: the first one addresses the personal data aspects of big data from a business perspective and is aimed at identifying the benefits and challenges of using big data analytics on massive personal datasets. The second part deals in detail with how the traditional data protection principles should be applied to big data analytics, while also tackling modern data protection principles. Overall, the chapter aims to serve as a good basis for understanding both the positive and the negative implications of deploying big data analytics on personal datasets. In addition, the chapter will focus on the importance of the quality of the data analyzed, on the different ways in which good levels of data quality can be achieved, and on the negative consequences that may ensue when they are not.

1.2 BUSINESS OF BIG DATA

It is by now clear: big data means big business. Data are frequently called "the oil of the 21st century" or "the fuel of the digital economy," and the era we live in has been referred to as the "data gold rush" by Neelie Kroes, the vice president of the European Commission responsible for the Digital Agenda.* This is true not only at the theoretical level but also in practice. A report by the leading consulting firm McKinsey found that "the intensity of big data varies across sectors but has reached critical mass in every sector" and that "we are on the cusp of a tremendous wave of innovation, productivity, and growth, as well as new modes of competition and value capture—all driven by big data as consumers, companies, and economic sectors exploit its potential."†

With so much importance being given to data, it is not surprising that new business models are emerging, companies are being created, and apps and games are being designed with data collection as one of the main purposes. The most recent and compelling example is that of the Pokémon Go mobile game, which was designed to allow users to collect characters in specific places around the city.‡ Niantic Labs, the developer of the game that has practically gone viral in only a couple of weeks, has access to data about the whereabouts of players, their connections, and other data such as area, climate, time of the day, and so on. It collects data from roughly 9.5 million daily active

* European Commission—Press Release—Speech: The Data Gold Rush. 2014. *Europa.Eu*. http://europa.eu/rapid/press-release_SPEECH-14-229_en.htm.

† McKinsey Global Institute. 2011. *Big Data: The Next Frontier for Innovation, Competition, and Productivity*. http://file:///Users/theodoradragan/Downloads/MGI_big_data_full_report%20(1).pdf.

‡ See, Hautala, Laura. 2016. *Pokemon Go: Gotta Catch All Your Personal Data*. CNET. http://www.cnet.com/news/pokemon-go-gotta-catch-all-your-personal-data/.

users, a number that is growing exponentially by the day at the moment.* This is a clear example of how apps and games are starting to develop around the business of data, but also of how the data can be collected in "fun" ways without the users necessarily being aware of how and what data are gathered—the privacy policy is however very vague on these aspects.†

1.2.1 Connection between Big Data and Personal Data

The business of big data requires conducting a careful balancing exercise between the importance of harvesting the value of the data to foster innovation and evolution on the one hand, and the powerful impact that big data can have on many business sectors on the other hand. The manner in which personal data are collected and subsequently analyzed affects competition policy, antitrust policy, and consumer protection. In a paper published by the World Economic Forum, attention has been drawn to the fact that, "as ecosystem players look to use (mobile-generated) data, they face concerns about violating user trust, rights of expression, and confidentiality."‡ Big data and business are very much intertwined, and even more so when the big data in question is personal data, in particular because "for many online offerings which are presented or perceived as being 'free', personal information operates as a sort of indispensable currency used to pay for those services: 'free' online services are 'paid for' using personal data which have been valued in total at over EUR 300 billion and have been forecast to treble by 2020."§

The concept of personal data is defined by Regulation 679/2016 as "any information relating to an identified or identifiable natural person ('data subject'); an identifiable natural person is one who can be identified, directly or indirectly, in particular by reference to an identifier such as a name, an identification number, location data, an online identifier or to one or more factors specific to the physical, physiological, genetic, mental, economic, cultural or social identity of that natural person."¶ While the list of factors specific to the identity of the person has been enriched from the previous definition of personal data that was contained in Directive 95/46/EC, the main elements remain the same. These elements have been discussed and elaborated by the Article 29 Working Party in its Opinion 4/2007, which establishes that there are four fundamental elements to establish whether an information is to be considered personal data.**

According to the Opinion, these elements are: "any information," "relating to," "identified or identifiable," and "natural person."

1.2.1.1 Any Information

All information relevant to a person is included, regardless of the "position or capacity of those persons (as consumer, patient, employee, customer, etc.)."†† In this case, the information can be objective or subjective and does not necessarily have to be true or proven.

---

* Wagner, Kurt. 2016. How Many People Are Actually Playing Pokémon Go? *Recode*. http://www.recode.net/2016/7/13/12181614/pokemon-go-number-active-users.

† Pokémon GO Privacy Policy. 2016. *Nianticlabs.Com*. https://www.nianticlabs.com/privacy/pokemongo/en.

‡ World Economic Forum. 2012. *Big Data, Big Impact: New Possibilities for International Development*. http://www3.weforum.org/docs/WEF_TC_MFS_BigDataBigImpact_Briefing_2012.pdf.

§ European Data Protection Supervisor. 2014. *Preliminary Opinion of the European Data Protection Supervisor Privacy and Competitiveness in the Age of Big Data: The Interplay between Data Protection, Competition Law and Consumer Protection in the Digital Economy*. https://secure.edps.europa.eu/EDPSWEB/webdav/site/mySite/shared/Documents/Consultation/Opinions/2014/14-03-26_competitition_law_big_data_EN.pdf.

¶ Article 4(1), Regulation (Eu) 2016/679 of the European Parliament and of the Council of 27 April 2016 on the protection of natural persons with regard to the processing of personal data and on the free movement of such data, and repealing Directive 95/46/EC (General Data Protection Regulation), *Official Journal of the European Union*, L 119/3, 4/5/2016.

** Article 29 Data Protection Working Party. 2007. *Opinion 4/2007 on the Concept of Personal Data*. http://ec.europa.eu/justice/policies/privacy/docs/wpdocs/2007/wp136_en.pdf.

†† Idem, p. 7.

The words "any information" also imply information of any form, audio, text, video, images, etc. Importantly, the manner in which the information is stored is irrelevant. The Working Party expressly mentions biometric data as a special case,* as such data can be considered as information content as well as a link between the individual and the information. Because biometric data are unique to an individual, they can also be used as an identifier.

1.2.1.2 Relating to

Information related to an individual is information about that individual. The relationship between data and an individual is often self-evident, an example of which is when the data are stored in an individual employee's files or in a medical record. This is, however, not always the case, especially when the information regards objects. Such objects belong to individuals, but additional meanings or information are required to create the link to the individual.†

At least one of the following three elements should be present in order to consider information to be related to an individual: "content," "purpose," or "result." An element of "content" is present when the information is in reference to an individual, regardless of the (intended) use of the information. The "purpose" element instead refers to whether the information is used or is likely to be used "with the purpose to evaluate, treat in a certain way or influence the status or behavior of an individual."‡ A "result" element is present when the use of the data is likely to have an impact on a certain person's rights and interests.§ These elements are alternatives and are not cumulative, implying that one piece of data can relate to different individuals based on diverse elements.

1.2.1.3 Identified or Identifiable

"A natural person can be 'identified' when, within a group of persons, he or she is 'distinguished' from all other members of the group."¶ When identification has not occurred but is possible, the individual is considered to be "identifiable."

In order to determine whether those with access to the data are able to identify the individual, all reasonable means likely to be used either by the controller or by any other person should be taken into consideration. The cost of identification, the intended purpose, the way the processing is structured, the advantage expected by the data controller, the interest at stake for the data subjects, and the risk of organizational dysfunctions and technical failures should be taken into account in the evaluation.**

1.2.1.4 Natural Person

Directive 95/46/EC is applicable to the personal data of natural persons, a broad concept that calls for protection wholly independent from the residence or nationality of the data subject.

The concept of personality is understood as "the capacity to be the subject of legal relations, starting with the birth of the individual and ending with his death."†† Personal data thus relate to identified or identifiable living individuals. Data concerning deceased persons or unborn children falling in principle outside the application of personal data protection legislation (Recital 20 of Regulation (EU) 679/2016) may, however, indirectly be subject to protection in particular cases. When the data relate to other living persons, or when a data controller makes no differentiation in their documentation between living and deceased persons, it may not be possible to ascertain whether the person the data relate to is living or deceased; additionally, some national laws consider deceased or

* Idem, p. 8.
† Idem, p. 9.
‡ Idem, p. 10.
§ Idem, p. 11.
¶ Idem, p. 12.
** Idem, p. 15.
†† Idem, p. 22.

unborn persons to be protected under the scope of Directive 95/46/EC.* Legal persons are excluded from the protection provided under Regulation (EU) 679/2016 and Directive 95/46/EC. However, some provisions of Directive 2002/58/EC† (amended by Directive 2009/136/EC‡) extend the scope of Directive 95/46/EC to legal persons.§

In conclusion, in some cases, the data may not be personal in nature, but may become personal data as a result of cross-referencing it with other sources and databases containing information about specific users, therefore shrinking the circle of potential persons to "identifiable persons" and ultimately even to specifically identified individuals. The 2013 *MIT Technology Review* raised the question of whether big data has made anonymity impossible, arguing that "as the amount of data expands exponentially, nearly all of it carries someone's digital fingerprints."¶ Big *personal* data is becoming more and more the norm, rather than the exception, calling for the adoption of specific safeguarding measures with regard to the individual's right to privacy.

1.2.2 Competition Aspects

The development of the digital market has made it clear that in the business of big data, personal data is a particularly important asset, especially regarding gaining (and maintaining) a strong market position. This is why personal data are also being used as a competitive advantage by some digital businesses. The EDPS addressed the ever-increasing connection between big personal data analytics and competition law in the workshop on "Privacy, Consumers, Competition and Big Data" that it held in 2014 with the aim of discussing the themes explored in its Preliminary Opinion published earlier that same year.**

Given the lack of a "unifying objective" with regard to competition law at the EU level, authorities evaluate each situation (such as mergers between companies having a dominant market position) on a case-by-case basis, based on very specific parameters of competition. The parameters have been established by Commission Guidelines and are the following: price, output, product quality, product variety, and innovation.†† However, applying these criteria in relation to companies whose business model is centered around big data is difficult, especially considering, for example, the challenge of measuring the probability of the merged entity to raise the price in case of services offered "for free" in exchange of the personal data of the users. Therefore, the report recommended increasing vigilance with regard to such issues and monitoring the market to establish whether an abuse of dominant market position is being carried out using personal data as a "weapon."

---

* Idem, pp. 22–23.

† Directive 2002/58/EC of the European Parliament and of the Council of 12 July 2002 concerning the processing of personal data and the protection of privacy in the electronic communications sector (Directive on privacy and electronic communications) [2002] OJL 201, 31/07/2002 P. 0037–0047.

‡ Directive 2009/136/EC of the European Parliament and of the Council of 25 November 2009 amending Directive 2002/22/EC on universal service and users' rights relating to electronic communications networks and services, Directive 2002/58/EC concerning the processing of personal data and the protection of privacy in the electronic communications sector and Regulation (EC) No. 2006/2004 on cooperation between national authorities responsible for the enforcement of consumer protection laws (Text with EEA relevance). [2006] OJ L 337, 18/12/2009 P. 0011–0036.

§ In the EDPS Preliminary Opinion on Big Data, it is also expected that: "[c]ertain national jurisdictions (Austria, Denmark, Italy and Luxembourg) extend some protection to legal persons." European Data Protection Supervisor. 2014. *Preliminary Opinion of the European Data Protection Supervisor Privacy and Competitiveness in the Age of Big Data: The Interplay between Data Protection, Competition Law and Consumer Protection in the Digital Economy*, p. 13, footnote 31. Available at https://secure.edps.europa.eu/EDPSWEB/webdav/site/mySite/shared/Documents/Consultation/Opinions/2014/14-03-26_competitition_law_big_data_EN.pdf.

¶ MIT Technology Review. 2013. *Big Data Gets Personal*. https://www.technologyreview.com/business-report/big-data-gets-personal/.

** European Data Protection Supervisor. 2014. *Report of Workshop of Privacy, Consumers, Competition and Big Data*. https://secure.edps.europa.eu/EDPSWEB/webdav/site/mySite/shared/Documents/Consultation/Big%20data/14-07-11_EDPS_Report_Workshop_Big_data_EN.pdf.

†† Commission Guidelines on the application of Article 81(3) of the Treaty (2004/C 101/08).

Given these market conditions, it appears useful to consider using privacy and personal data protection compliance as a competitive advantage in order to harness the full value of the data held by a company. Privacy and personal data protection compliance can ensure that the data, even when it is massive in quantity, is collected, stored, and processed according to the relevant rules. As mentioned earlier in the chapter, the principle of data quality plays a particularly important role in this matter, as it helps ensure that only accurate, relevant, and up-to-date data are processed, helping with compliance but also with making sure that the outcomes of the data analysis are relevant and useful. A research conducted by the consulting firm Deloitte points out the "epistemological fallacy that more bytes yield more benefits," arguing that it is "an example of what philosophers call a 'category error'. Decisions are not based on raw data; they are based on relevant information. And data volume is at best a rough proxy for the value and relevance of the underlying information."* Therefore, it is not about the quantity of data collected, but about the quality of the information contained in it.

The best approach to ensure consistent data quality within a database is to start from the point of collection and to implement measures or procedures along the chain of processing. When data are collected responsibly, consumer trust could improve and users could therefore provide more accurate data. In a recent survey by SDL, 79% of respondents said they are more likely to provide personal information to brands that they "trust."† Having an adequate, transparent, and easy-to-understand privacy policy is the first step in that direction, as it would contribute to balance out the information asymmetry between companies and consumers. Another step would be the implementation of regular reviewing procedures, aimed at identifying the data that are still relevant, rectifying the data that are out of use or incorrect, and deleting the data that are no longer of use. It would also constitute an opportunity for "cleaning up" the database periodically, in order to ensure that there is no "dead data" from so-called zombie accounts.‡

Taking such steps would ensure that the database consists of reliable, good-quality data that not only comply with the relevant laws and regulations, but whose analysis can provide more detailed and accurate outcomes. Companies that care about the quality of the data they process are therefore more likely to have a real market advantage over the ones that do not take any steps in this respect. Academic research corroborates the theoretical assumptions and the practical observations: Erik Brynjolfsson, the director of the MIT Initiative on the Digital Economy studied a sample of publicly traded firms and concluded that the firms in the sample that had adopted a data-driven decision-making approach enjoyed 5%–6% higher output and productivity than would be expected given their other investments and level of information technology usage.§

1.3 RECONCILING TRADITIONAL AND MODERN DATA PROTECTION PRINCIPLES

The most recent Opinion on topics related to big data issued by the EDPS discussed whether, and how, traditional data protection principles should be applied to big data analytics that involve

* Guszcza, James and Bryan Richardson. 2014. Two Dogmas of Big Data: Understanding the Power of Analytics for Predicting Human Behavior. *Deloitte Review*, 15. http://dupress.com/articles/behavioral-data-driven-decision-making/#end-notes.

† SDL. 2014. *New Privacy Study Finds 79 Percent of Customers Are Willing to Provide Personal Information to a 'Trusted Brand'*. http://www.sdl.com/about/news-media/press/2014/new-privacy-study-finds-customers-are-willing-to-provide-personal-information-to-trusted-brands.html.

‡ European Data Protection Supervisor. 2014. *Report of Workshop of Privacy, Consumers, Competition and Big Data*. https://secure.edps.europa.eu/EDPSWEB/webdav/site/mySite/shared/Documents/Consultation/Big%20data/14-07-11_EDPS_Report_Workshop_Big_data_EN.pdf.

§ Brynjolfsson, Erik, Lorin M. Hitt, and Heekyung Hellen Kim. Strength in Numbers: How Does Data-Driven Decisionmaking Affect Firm Performance? *SSRN Electronic Journal*. doi: 10.2139/ssrn.1819486. http://papers.ssrn.com/sol3/papers.cfm?abstract_id=1819486.

personal data.* The underlying consideration that transpired from the document was that "we need to protect more dynamically our fundamental rights in the world of big data." It was argued that the "traditional" data protection principles (i.e., those established before the era of big data) such as *transparency*, *proportionality*, and *purpose limitation* have to be modernized and strengthened, but also complemented by "new principles," that have been developed more recently in response to the challenges brought about by big data itself—*accountability*, *privacy by design*, and *privacy by default*. In the following sections, the application of these principles will be discussed with reference to the overarching principle of *data quality* that the authors have advocated throughout the chapter. Data quality is considered to be closely linked to each of these principles. Ensuring that the data are relevant, accurate, and up-to-date is fundamental for the successful application of the principles, while also representing the bridge between compliance and revenue, enabling thus the *return of investment* (ROI).

1.3.1 Traditional Data Protection Principles

The EDPS refers to transparency, proportionality, and purpose limitation as "traditional" data protection principles. Although these principles were identified since before the era of big data analytics, they remain just as essential nowadays. They have been upgraded to fit the context, so it is important to gain an understanding of how big data has changed the way that they are applied.

1.3.1.1 Transparency

The principle of transparency regards the information given to the data subject about the use made of the data by the data controller. Transparency is one of the basic principles of data protection and lies at the core of data quality: if the practices of the data controller are transparent, then the users know what they can expect and are more likely to provide accurate data about themselves; therefore, the dataset created is more likely to be relevant. One way to ensure transparency used to be by giving information notices to users to let them know how their data are processed. However, in the era of big data, more proactivity on the part of the data controller is required, so that it can be ensured that the information given to the users is easy to read and understand.

Too often, privacy policies consist of texts written in "legalese" that are not understood by users. A study conducted by Pew Research Center found that 52% of respondents did not know what a privacy policy was, erroneously believing that it meant an assurance that their data would be kept confidential by the company.† This could also be the result of the fact that privacy policies are often long and complex texts that would simply take too much time to read carefully. According to a study carried out by two researchers from Carnegie Mellon, it would take a person an average of 76 work days to read the privacy policy of every website visited throughout a year.‡ The study was conducted in 2008 and, considering the dynamic expansion of the use of Internet, it may well be that nowadays an individual would not even have enough time in a year to read all the privacy policies of the websites visited within that same year.

Privacy policies are, at the moment, the main tool that is considered to ensure transparency and yet, they are inefficient at achieving that purpose. Some options for improving privacy policies were

* European Data Protection Supervisor. 2015. *Opinion 7/2015—Meeting the Challenges of Big Data: A Call for Transparency, User Control, Data Protection by Design and Accountability*. https://secure.edps.europa.eu/EDPSWEB/webdav/site/mySite/shared/Documents/Consultation/Opinions/2015/15-11-19_Big_Data_EN.pdf.

† Pew Research Center. 2014. *Half of Online Americans Don't Know What a Privacy Policy Is*. http://www.pewresearch.org/fact-tank/2014/12/04/half-of-americans-dont-know-what-a-privacy-policy-is/.

‡ Cranor, Lorrie Faith and Aleecia McDonald. 2008. *Reading the Privacy Policies You Encounter in a Year Would Take 76 Work Days*. http://www.theatlantic.com/technology/archive/2012/03/reading-the-privacy-policies-you-encounter-in-a-year-would-take-76-work-days/253851/.

suggested by a group of professors from Carnegie Mellon at PrivacyCon held in January this year.* They proposed extracting and highlighting data practices that do not match users' expectations, using visual formats to display privacy policies, and highlighting in different colors the practices that correspond to common expectations and the ones that do not.

These ideas could help users decipher the privacy policies and understand how their data are being used, increasing transparency and contributing to balancing out the information asymmetry between data controllers and data subjects.

The authors support these suggestions and agree with the idea that visually enhanced privacy policies would be more effective and would transmit information quickly, grabbing users' attention. Using different colors to identify the privacy-level compliance would render the privacy policy, as a tool, more efficient in communicating the information. As a positive side effect, easier-to-understand privacy policies would enhance user trust in the data controller and contribute to data quality, as users tend to provide more accurate data about themselves when they trust the company that is the controller of that data.

1.3.1.2 Proportionality and Purpose Limitation

The sheer volume of personal data that each single user leaves behind while browsing the Internet or using an app on their mobile phone is enormous. Computational social scientist Alex Pentland refers to these data as "breadcrumbs": "I believe that the power of big data is that it is information about people's behaviour instead of information about their beliefs. It's about the behaviour of customers, employees, and prospects for your new business. It's not about the things you post on Facebook, and it's not about your searches on Google, which is what most people think about, and it's not data from internal company processes and RFIDs. This sort of big data comes from things like location data off of your cell phone or credit card: It's the little data breadcrumbs that you leave behind you as you move around in the world."† A real-life example of how these breadcrumbs of data can be used is that of Netflix, that used big data analytics to find out whether the online series "House of Cards" would be a hit, based on the information it gathered from its customer base of over 30 million users worldwide.‡

The principles of proportionality and purpose limitation are closely tied to the Netflix example. Incredible amounts of data are gathered each day, but it is not always clear how the data will be used in the future, and that is precisely what the value of data resides in: the potential of using it over and over, for different purposes, without diminishing its overall value. Therefore, the traditional data protection principles of proportionality and purpose limitation find application in the big data sector too.

In this respect, on April 2, 2013, the Article 29 Data Protection Working Party published an opinion on the principle of purpose limitation.§ The concept of purpose limitation has two primary building blocks:

- Personal data must be collected for specified, explicit, and legitimate purposes (the so-called purpose specification).¶

---

* PrivacyCon Organised by the Federal Trade Commission. 2016. *Expecting the Unexpected: Understanding Mismatched Privacy Expectations Online.* https://www.ftc.gov/system/files/documents/videos/privacycon-part-2/part_2_privacycon_slides.pdf.

† Edge. 2012. *Reinventing Society in the Wake of Big Data—A Conversation with Alex (Sandy) Pentland.* https://www.edge.org/conversation/reinventing-society-in-the-wake-of-big-data.

‡ Carr, David. 2014. Giving Viewers What They Want: For 'House Of Cards,' Using Big Data to Guarantee Its Popularity. *NYTimes.com.* http://www.nytimes.com/2013/02/25/business/media/for-house-of-cards-using-big-data-to-guarantee-its-popularity.html?pagewanted=all&_r=0.

§ Article 29 Data Protection Working Party. 2013. Opinion 03/2013 on purpose limitation. Adopted on April 2, 2013. Available at: http://ec.europa.eu/justice/data-protection/article-29/documentation/opinion-recommendation/files/2013/wp203_en.pdf.

¶ Ibid. p. 11.

- Personal data must not be further processed in a way incompatible with those purposes (the so-called compatible use).*

Compatible or incompatible use needs are to be assessed—"compatibility assessment"—on a case-by-case basis, according to the following key factors (see also Article 6.4 Regulation (EU) 679/2016):

- The relationship between the purposes for which the personal data have been collected and the purposes of further processing†
- The context in which the personal data have been collected and the reasonable expectations of the data subjects as to their further use‡
- The nature of the personal data and the impact of the further processing on the data subjects§
- The safeguards adopted by the controller to ensure fair processing and to prevent any undue impact on the data subjects¶

In this opinion, the Article 29 Data Protection Working Party deals with Big Data.** More precisely, Article 29 Data Protection Working Party specifies that, in order to lawfully process Big Data, in addition to the four key factors of the compatibility assessment to be fulfilled, additional safeguards must be assessed to ensure fair processing and to prevent any undue impact. Article 29 Data Protection Working Party considers two scenarios to identify such additional safeguards:

1. "[i]n the first one, the organizations processing the data want to detect trends and correlations in the information.
2. In the second one, the organizations are interested in individuals (...) [as they specifically want] to analyse or predict personal preferences, behaviour and attitudes of individual customers, which will subsequently inform 'measures or decisions' that are taken with regard to those customers."††

In the first scenario, the so-called functional separation plays a major role in deciding whether further use of data may be considered compatible. Examples of "functional separation" are: "full or partial anonymisation, pseudonymsation, or aggregation of the data, privacy enhancing technologies, as well as other measures to ensure that the data cannot be used to take decisions or other actions with respect to individuals"‡‡

In the second scenario, prior customers/data subjects consent (i.e., free, specific, informed, and unambiguous "opt-in") would be required for further use to be considered compatible. In this respect, Article 29 Data Protection Working Party specifies that "such consent should be required, for example, for tracking and profiling for purposes of direct marketing, behavioural advertisement, data-brokering, location-based advertising or tracking-based digital market research."§§ Furthermore, access for data subjects: (i) to their "profiles," (ii) to the algorithm that develops the profiles, and (iii) to the source of data that led to the creation of the profiles is regarded as prerequisite for consent to be informed and to ensure transparency.¶¶ Moreover, data subjects should be effectively granted the right to correct or update their profiles. Last but not least, Article 29 Data Protection

---

* Ibid. p. 12.
† Ibid. p. 23.
‡ Ibid. p. 24.
§ Ibid. p. 25.
¶ Ibid. p. 26.
** Ibid. pp. 45ss.
†† Ibid. p. 46.
‡‡ Ibid. p. 27.
§§ Ibid. p. 46.
¶¶ Ibid. p. 47.

Working Party recommends allowing "data portability": "safeguards such as allowing data subjects/customers to have access to their data in a portable, user-friendly and machine readable format [as a way] to enable businesses and data-subjects/consumers to maximise the benefit of big data in a more balanced and transparent way."*

1.3.2 Modern Data Protection Principles

The EDPS has identified "four essential elements for the responsible and sustainable development of big data:

- Organisations must be much more transparent about how they process personal data;
- Afford users a higher degree of control over how their data is used;
- Design user friendly data protection into their products and services; and
- Become more accountable for what they do."†

It is evident from the above list that, of the four essential elements, only the first one relates to a traditional data protection principle (transparency). The other three of the four essential elements are all related to modern data protection principles, such as accountability, privacy by default and by design, and increased users' control of their own data. In that sense, big personal data processing is very different from traditional personal data processing, since it requires additional principles to be followed—principles that have been designed specifically to respond to the challenges of big data.

1.3.2.1 Accountability

The (by now *cliché*) popular saying "with great power comes great responsibility" perfectly captures the essence of accountability in big personal data processing (see also Article 5.2 Regulation (EU) 679/2016). The accountability is related not only to how the data are processed (how transparent the procedures are, how much access the data subject has to its own data, etc.) but also to issues of algorithmic decision making, which is the direct result of big personal data processing in the twenty-first century.‡ Processing the personal data at a high level is only a means to an end, the final purpose being reaching the ability to make informed decisions on a high scale based on the information collected and stored in big databases. As the EDPS points out in its Opinion 7/2015, "one of the most powerful uses of big data is to make predictions about what is likely to happen but has not yet happened."§ This is, again, closely tied to the quality of data that the authors have been emphasizing throughout this chapter: if data quality is high, related decisions are likely to have positive results, whereas, if the data are of poor quality, decisions are likely to have a negative impact on the affected population, leading to potentially unfair and/or discriminatory conclusions. In any case, data controllers have to take responsibility and be accountable for the decisions they make based on the processing of big datasets of personal data.

Proactive steps, such as disclosing the logic involved in big data analytics or giving clear and easily understandable information notices to the data subjects, are needed to establish accountability. This is so especially since the information contained in the datasets is not always collected directly from

---

* Ibid. p. 47. For example, access to information about energy consumption in a user-friendly format could make it easier for households to switch tariffs and get the best rates on gas and electricity, as well as enabling them to monitor their energy consumption and modify their lifestyles to reduce their bills as well as their environmental impact.

† European Data Protection Supervisor. 2015. *Opinion 7/2015—Meeting the Challenges of Big Data: A Call for Transparency, User Control, Data Protection by Design and Accountability*. Available at: https://secure.edps.europa.eu/EDPSWEB/webdav/site/mySite/shared/Documents/Consultation/Opinions/2015/15-11-19_Big_Data_EN.pdf.

‡ Kubler, Kyle. 2016. The Black Box Society: The Secret Algorithms That Control Money and Information. *Information, Communication & Society*, 1–2. doi: 10.1080/1369118x.2016.1160142.

§ European Data Protection Supervisor. 2015. *Opinion 7/2015—Meeting the Challenges of Big Data: A Call for Transparency, User Control, Data Protection by Design and Accountability*. Available at: https://secure.edps.europa.eu/EDPSWEB/webdav/site/mySite/shared/Documents/Consultation/Opinions/2015/15-11-19_Big_Data_EN.pdf.

the concerned individual—data can be "volunteered, observed or inferred, or collected from public sources."* Apart from disclosing the logic involved in decision making based on big data analytics and ensuring that data subjects have access to their own data, as well as to information as to how it is processed, companies should also develop policies for the regular verification of data accuracy, data quality, and compliance with the relevant legislation. As the EDPS points out, "accountability is not a one-off exercise."† It needs to be undertaken continually, for as long as data are being processed by the company. The principle of data accountability is closely connected to privacy by design and by default—which, taken together, represent another modern data protection principle.

1.3.2.2 Privacy by Design and by Default

It is not enough anymore for data controllers to regard data privacy as an afterthought. Instead, data controllers should incorporate data protection into the design and architecture of communication systems that are meant for the collection or processing of personal data. Recitals 78 and 108 of the Regulation (EU) 679/2016 foreshadow the increasing importance of data privacy by design and by default, principles that are also explicitly addressed in Article 25 of the same legislation.‡ In particular, the first comma of Article 25 states that: "the controller shall, both at the time of the determination of the means for processing and at the time of the processing itself, implement appropriate technical and organisational measures, such as pseudonymisation, which are designed to implement data-protection principles, such as data minimisation, in an effective manner and to integrate the necessary safeguards into the processing in order to meet the requirements of this Regulation and protect the rights of data subjects," whereas comma 2 of the same article requires that "by default, only personal data which are necessary for each specific purpose of the processing are processed."§

When dealing with big datasets of personal data, taking into account privacy requirements right from the beginning ensures that only the data that is strictly necessary for the processing is being collected and, subsequently, that the data used in the relevant decision making is accurate. Moreover, as mentioned previously in this chapter (under Section 1.2.2), there is a direct connection between how much data subjects trust a data controller and the accuracy of data they choose to share with it. If privacy is embedded right from the very beginning in the collection and processing of personal data, data subjects are more likely to trust the data controller, thereby providing higher-quality data.

On the same note, as already mentioned above, the EDPS underlined in its Opinion 7/2015, the concept of "functional separation."¶ Functional separation requires data controllers to distinguish between personal data used for a specific purpose, such as "to detect trends or correlations in the information," from personal data used for another purpose, such as to make decisions based on the trends detected by means of processing the same information. This would allow data controllers to detect and analyze trends based on the collected data, without negatively affecting the data subjects from whom the data were collected in the first place. Such functional separation would ensure that the traditional data protection principle of purpose limitation is respected and that personal data are not processed for a purpose that is not compatible with the purposes for which it was collected, unless specific and informed consent of data subjects has been given *a priori*.

---

* European Data Protection Supervisor. 2015. *Opinion 7/2015—Meeting the Challenges of Big Data: A Call for Transparency, User Control, Data Protection by Design and Accountability*. Available at: https://secure.edps.europa.eu/EDPSWEB/webdav/site/mySite/shared/Documents/Consultation/Opinions/2015/15-11-19_Big_Data_EN.pdf.

† Idem.

‡ Regulation (EU) 2016/679 of the European Parliament and of the Council of 27 April 2016 on the protection of natural persons with regard to the processing of personal data and on the free movement of such data, and repealing Directive 95/46/EC (General Data Protection Regulation) (Text with EEA relevance).

§ Idem.

¶ European Data Protection Supervisor. 2015. *Opinion 7/2015—Meeting the Challenges of Big Data: A Call for Transparency, User Control, Data Protection by Design and Accountability*. Available at: https://secure.edps.europa.eu/EDPSWEB/webdav/site/mySite/shared/Documents/Consultation/Opinions/2015/15-11-19_Big_Data_EN.pdf.

1.3.2.3 Users' Control of Their Own Data

Finally, the principle of users' control of their own data is gaining importance. Traditionally, it was considered enough if users had access to their own data, along with a series of rights such as rectification, deletion, or objection to processing. The newly developed principle is recalled by Recital 7 of Regulation (EU) 679/2016, which states that "[Rapid technological developments and globalisation] require a strong and more coherent data protection framework in the Union, backed by strong enforcement, given the importance of creating the trust that will allow the digital economy to develop across the internal market. Natural persons should have control of their own personal data."* The right of access to data may be one of the fundamental principles of data protection, but the right to control the own personal information is quickly gaining importance, at the same pace with the rapid developments of the technological developments.

The EDPS speaks of the "featurisation" of personal data in its recent Opinion 7/2015 on big data, arguing that the degree of control over one's data can be construed as a feature of the service provided to the user.† Data controllers, argues the EDPS, should "share the wealth" created by the processing of the personal data with those persons whose data are being processed.

At the moment, users do not have easy access to the type of data stored about them by a specific company; most data controllers give users the possibility to contact them via email or telephone in order to enquire about their own data. Giving users easy access to their data, for example, by logging in to a control panel section on a website, along with the possibility of modifying it or changing the permissions to process it, data quality would likely increase. Users who have control of their data are likely to trust the data controller more and, potentially, to collaborate for various projects by volunteering their data or agreeing to participate in case studies—the EDPS speaks of "personal data spaces" ("data stores" or "data vaults") as "user-centric, safe and secure places to store and possibly trade personal data."‡

As a (highly positive) side effect, giving users more control of their data would contribute to increasing data quality, which, as explained previously, bears high significance on the relevance of the processing and of the decisions made as a result of it. According to a research conducted by the consultancy firm Deloitte, "given the time and expense involved in gathering and using big data, it pays to ask when, why, and how big data yields commensurately big value. [. . .] In reality, data volume, variety, and velocity is but one of many considerations. The paramount issue is gathering the right data that carries the most useful information for the problem at hand."§ Therefore, creating a fair "market" for data, in which users have not only access, but also control over their personal information, would help ensure that the data gathered are more accurate, useful, and updated.

Another aspect of user control of data is to be found in the principle of data portability, which is enshrined in Article 20 of the Regulation (EU) 679/2016: "[t]he data subject shall have the right to have the personal data transmitted directly from one controller to another, where technically feasible." This right clearly signifies a departure from the mere traditional access rights, in favor of the stronger right for users to control their own personal data, by moving it from one provider to another where they so wish. In the future, this will enable users to choose the service provider that best suits their needs, not only from the point of view of the services offered but also from the perspective of the privacy and data protection offered. Along with contributing to a more competitive market,

---

* Regulation (EU) 2016/679 of the European Parliament and of the Council of 27 April 2016 on the protection of natural persons with regard to the processing of personal data and on the free movement of such data, and repealing Directive 95/46/EC (General Data Protection Regulation) (Text with EEA relevance).

† European Data Protection Supervisor. 2015. *Opinion 7/2015—Meeting the Challenges of Big Data: A Call for Transparency, User Control, Data Protection by Design and Accountability*. Available at: https://secure.edps.europa.eu/EDPSWEB/webdav/site/mySite/shared/Documents/Consultation/Opinions/2015/15-11-19_Big_Data_EN.pdf.

‡ Idem.

§ Guszcza, James and Bryan, Richardson. 2014. Two Dogmas of Big Data: Understanding the Power of Analytics for Predicting Human Behavior. *Deloitte Review*, 15. http://dupress.com/articles/behavioral-data-driven-decision-making/#end-notes.

data portability will potentially allow users to draw a direct benefit from the value created by the processing of their data.

1.4 CONCLUSIONS AND RECOMMENDATIONS

This chapter has addressed the connections between personal data protection and big data, taking into consideration the recent legislative modifications at the EU level (in particular, the entry into force of Regulation (EU) 679/2016—"General Data Protection Regulation") as well as relevant opinions and recommendations by the Article 29 Data Protection Working Party and the EDPS.

The chapter began with a quick description of the topic, approach, and methodology (Section 1.1.1), after which it continued with an overview of the structure (Section 1.1.2). Sections 1.2 and 1.3 were dedicated to the main analysis. The authors discussed the personal data protection aspects of big data from a business perspective (Section 1.2), touching on topics related to the impact of data protection on competition between service providers. The analysis of Section 1.3 focused on the importance of data quality, as a prerequisite for a correct, useful, and accurate data processing; the analysis was structured in two sections, with the authors distinguishing between "traditional" and "modern" data protection principles. Throughout the chapter, a series of recommendations were made, where the case called for it. For convenience, the authors summarize these recommendations below, per section. However, they point out that the full understanding of the topic can only be gained by reading the specific section.

It was first concluded by the authors, in Section 1.2 of this chapter, that a connection between big data and personal data is increasingly easy to establish, since the cross-referencing of the various sources of information available on the Internet can lead to the identification of an individual, even when it is not personal data in the first place. Therefore, big data should be processed with the utmost attention, in order to ensure that either (a) no personal data are processed or (b) where personal data are processed, that the processing is done in full respect of the applicable legislation. Privacy and personal data protection compliance also gives a competitive advantage to companies in order for them to harness the full value of the data. In fact, it was shown that big data means big business only if personal data are lawfully collected and further processed. Only in this case it is possible to make the connection between the gathering and processing of big datasets and the monetization of the same by extracting value from them, thus enabling the ROI. Finally, data quality is extremely important in order to ensure that the results of the data analytics are relevant, accurate, and up to date. Enhancing the users' trust in the company by giving more information and designing easy-to-understand privacy policies can lead to an increase in the users' willingness to provide accurate data about themselves.

Section 1.3 dealt with the traditional and modern personal data protection principles. Of the traditional principles, transparency remains paramount for the correct processing of personal data in the context of big data. It was suggested by the authors that visually enhancing privacy policies, by using different color codes to show the level of privacy compliance, would contribute to increasing the transparency and therefore the users' trust in the data controller. As regards the modern data protection principles, they have been developed in response to the technological progress and the evolution of data analytics: accountability of the data controller, incorporating privacy by design and by default, and giving users more control over their own data are essential principles as far as the processing of big personal data is concerned. In particular, the authors agree with the suggestion of the EDPS, that "featurisation" of the personal data and the creation of "personal data stores" would enable data subjects to have more control over their data and would contribute to establishing a fairer balance between them and the data controllers.

In conclusion, personal data protection compliance and quality management play an extremely important role in the era of big data and the relevant safeguards must be taken by data controllers if they want to harness the full value of the data they own. If the reader takes away one lesson from this chapter, it should be the following: *it is not about the quantity of the data, but about the quality of it!* The authors have aimed at showing that privacy compliance is not merely a formal procedure, but can also help enhance the quality of data, by establishing a higher level of trust from the users and therefore determining them to provide more accurate data. Since one of the biggest problems with big data is the tendency for errors to snowball, ensuring the quality of data is of the utmost importance for the accuracy of the outcome of the analysis. All mechanisms or procedures, whether internal or external, that contribute to the quality of data are to be considered highly valuable and the authors strongly suggest that they be implemented.

2 Energy Management for Green Big Data Centers

Chonglin Gu, Hejiao Huang, and Xiaohua Jia

CONTENTS

ABSTRACT

With the increase of computing capacity of big data centers (or we say cloud), energy management is becoming more and more important. In this chapter, we will introduce the latest development of research on the energy management of green cloud data centers. First, we will introduce power metering methods for data centers, including both server power metering and virtual machine (VM) power metering. For physical server, its energy can be measured using power distribution unit, so we mainly focus on VM power metering. Second, we will discuss how to leverage the intermittent renewable energy to reduce total carbon emissions for the geographically distributed data centers. We consider using energy storage devices (ESDs) to store renewable energy and the brown energy when its price is low, so as to reduce carbon emissions within the budget of energy cost. We also discuss how to deploy ESDs, wind turbines, and solar panels for each data center to take the advantages of energy sources in different locations. Finally, we consider selling energy back to the power grid, so that the energy cost can be greatly reduced while retaining a lower level of carbon emissions.

2.1 POWER METERING FOR VIRTUAL MACHINES

The virtual machine (VM) is the most basic unit for virtualization and resource allocation. It is important to study power consumption and power metering of VMs. First, the study of the power consumption of VM would lead us to a better understanding about energy consumption in data centers, such that better energy-efficient algorithm or VM consolidation algorithm can be developed. Second, the study energy consumption of VMs can lead to more accurate power metering of VMs, such that a more reasonable pricing scheme can be employed for the charge of VMs. The current data center systems, such as EC2, charge users according to configuration types and rental time of VMs [1,2]. But VMs with the same configuration and rental time may have totally different amounts of energy consumption due to the running of different tasks. The amount of energy consumption should be considered in the charge of VMs. However, it is a difficult task to measure the energy consumption accurately for each VM. On the one hand, power models for the server cannot be directly applied in VM power metering. On the other hand, it is difficult to accurately measure the resources used by each VM. The latest cloud monitoring systems such as GreenCloud [3] and HP-iLO [4] can only measure the power consumption in the granularity of server and resource. There is no system so far that can measure power in the granularity of VM.

2.1.1 System Model and Architecture for VM Power Metering

2.1.1.1 System Model of VM Power Metering

For ease of understanding, the system model of VM power metering is illustrated in Figure 2.1 [5].

The total power consumption of a physical server consists of two parts, P_{Static} and $P_{Dynamic}$. P_{Static} is the fixed power of a server regardless of running VMs or not, and $P_{Dynamic}$ is the dynamic power that is consumed by VMs running on it. Suppose there are n VMs and each of them is denoted by VM_i, $1 \le i \le n$. Let P_{VM_i} denote the energy consumed by VM_i. Thus, we have

$$P_{Total} = P_{Static} + \sum P_{Dynamic} \tag{2.1}$$

$$= P_{Static} + \sum_{i=1}^{n} P_{VM_i} \tag{2.2}$$

P_{VM_i} can be further decomposed into the power consumption of components such as CPU, memory, and IO, denoted by $P_{VM_i}^{CPU}$, $P_{VM_i}^{Mem}$, and $P_{VM_i}^{IO}$, respectively. $P_{VM_i}^{IO}$ includes general energy cost of all devices that involve IO operations such as disk and network data transfer. Thus, the power

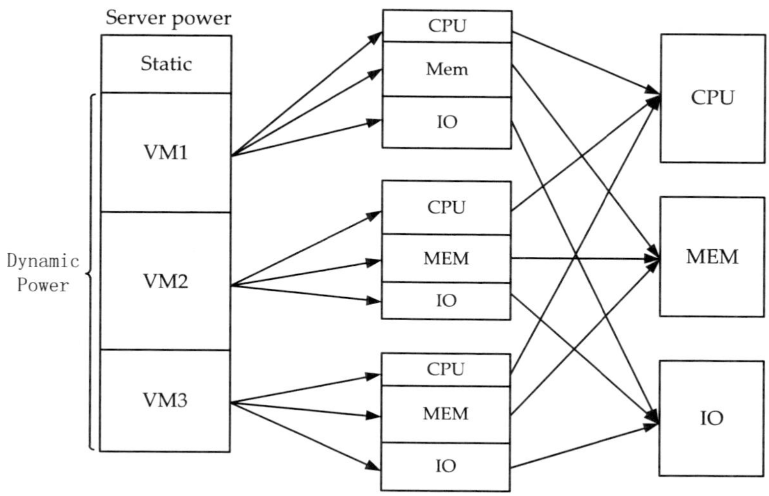

FIGURE 2.1 The system model of VM power metering.

consumption of VM_i is

$$P_{VM_i} = P_{VM_i}^{CPU} + P_{VM_i}^{Mem} + P_{VM_i}^{IO} \tag{2.3}$$

When using performance monitor counters (PMCs) for modeling, P_{VM_i} can be decomposed into the power consumption of PMCs of the system. Suppose there are m PMCs used for modeling with each denoted by e_j, $1 \leq j \leq m$. Let $P_{VM_i}^{e_j}$ denote the energy of e_j consumed by VM_i. Thus, we have

$$P_{VM_i} = P_{VM_i}^{e_1} + P_{VM_i}^{e_2} + \cdots + P_{VM_i}^{e_m} \tag{2.4}$$

2.1.1.2 Architecture of VM Power Metering

There are basically four steps for VM power metering: information collection, modeling, evaluation, and adjusting. The architectures for VM power metering can be classified into two categories: white-box and black-box architecture. For white-box architecture, a pitching-in or proxy program is inserted into each VM to collect resources utilization or PMC events of the VM for power modeling, as done in Reference 6. White-box architecture is simple in implementation, but it can be used only in private cloud where proxy programs are allowed to be inserted into VMs. For public cloud such as Amazon EC2, white-box method is almost infeasible due to the security and integrity worries from users. Besides, the resource usage information collected inside each VM cannot objectively reflect the usage of hardware resources by the VM. In contrast, black-box architecture is more practical, which collects modeling information such as PMCs of each VM at hypervisor level. A typical example of black-box architecture is Xen virtualization platform using Xenoprofile as tool to collect events of each VM on it, as shown in Figure 2.2 [7].

In this architecture, several VMs are running on the host, each with several applications running inside. The first step for VM power metering is information collection, and we use tools to collect modeling information such as physical server power, profiling resource features of host and each VM running on it. A separate server is running for gathering the modeling information of the host server and the information from power distribution unit (PDU). It is worth emphasizing that the information collecting server runs an Network Time Protocol (NTP) service for synchronizing the timestamps of resource information and power information. The second step is modeling, and there is a modeling module specifically responsible for training parameters based on collected samples. The last step is to evaluate the accuracy by calculating the error between estimated and measured

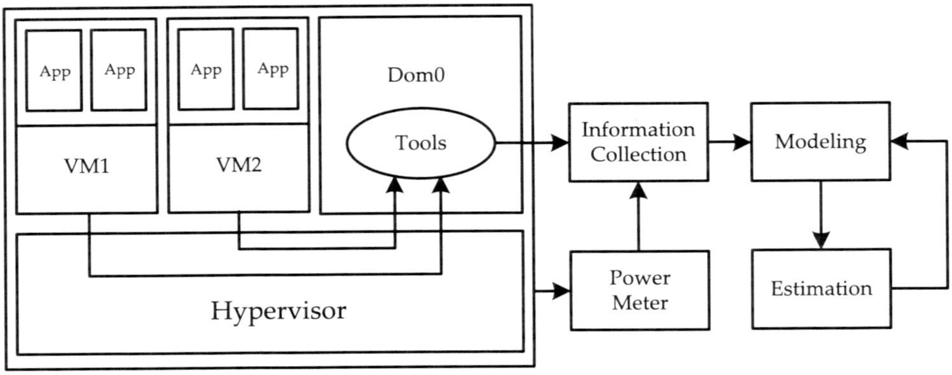

FIGURE 2.2 Black-box architecture of VM power metering.

server power. The estimation module is also responsible for updating parameters when errors exceed a certain threshold. With all these modules, this system can provide high-quality service for VM power metering in a real application.

2.1.2 Information Collection for Modeling

VM power is closely related to the usage of hardware resources, PMCs, and the power consumption of server. The modeling information to be collected includes two parts: physical server power and profiling features of the resources.

To collect server power, there are two methods: one is to use externally attached PDU like WattsUp series [8] and Scheleifenbauer power meter [9]. The data can be logged inside the PDU or can be accessed through local area network. The other is to use the Application Programming Interfaces (APIs) provided by the server with built-in power meter. For instance, Dell Power Series provide comprehensive power information for each component inside the server through Dell Open Management Suite [10]. PDU is convenient to be attached to and detached from servers, but infeasible in large scale. In contrast, a server with inner power meter is preferred for the power management of future data centers, though it may bring performance degradation when sampling too frequently. Still, others use wires to connect their self-developed power meter with each component in the server to measure the components' power [11–13]. But this method is too complex to be used widely, and Dell Series has already been able to provide power information of major components.

The profiling resources for modeling mainly include CPU, memory, and IO. To account the portion of CPU usage by each VM, Kansal et al. [14] propose to transform the tracked performance counters of each VM into the utilization of physical processor. Stoess et al. [15] directly use PMCs for each VM. Chen et al. [16] use time slices of processors to account the portion of CPU usage by each VM. For memory, Y. Bao et al. [17] believe the throughput of memory can well reflect the variation of memory power, while Kansal and Krishnan [14,18] profile their memory utilization using LLC missed. Still, Kim et al. [19] estimate the power consumption of memory using the number of memory accesses. For IO, Kansal proposes to use disk throughput to estimate disk power, while Stoess uses the finishing time of an IO request. Besides, IBM has implemented monitoring of IO throughput for each VM at the hypervisor level of Xen. In spite of this, it is not an easy thing to implement the above-mentioned methods for modeling information collection. Fortunately, there have been some tools for collecting profiling features of resources at the system level, and some are designed specifically for profiling VM. Table 2.1 summarizes the most commonly used tools for profiling in virtualization platform.

In information collection, the rate of sampling should also be taken into account. Sampling too frequently will incur degradation of performance; otherwise, the modeling accuracy will decline.

TABLE 2.1
Tools for Profiling in Virtualization Platform

Virtualization	Tools	
Xen	XenOprof	Xenperf
	Xentrace	Xentop
	Xenanalyze	Xenstat
	XenMon	
KVM	Perf Suite	Oprofile
	Perfmon2	
VMWare	ReTrace	vmkperf

An empirically setting for sampling rate is 1~2 seconds [20]. In fact, the sampling rate should be adjusted according to the variation of running applications, as is mentioned in Reference 21. In our system, we choose 2 seconds as our sampling rate.

2.1.3 Modeling Methods for VM Power Metering

VM power is usually calculated by fairly dividing the power consumption of server, which should be modeled first using the collected dataset composed of server power with resource features. This is a regression problem, and it can be formulated as follows: suppose there are n observations in the training dataset. Each observation has a vector of predictor variables R and a response variable $P_{Measured}$. $R = \{R_{CPU}, R_{memory}, R_{IO}\}$, where R_{CPU}, R_{memory}, and R_{IO} denote CPU utilization, last level cache missing (LLCM), and IO throughput, respectively. $P_{Measured}$ is the real server power measured using PDU. Thus, the training samples can be denoted as $D = \{(R_1, P_1), \ldots, (R_n, P_n)\}$. Our goal is to find a proper model to estimate server power $P_{Estimated}$ for any new predictor vector R. There are usually two types of models for estimating server power: linear and nonlinear.

For linear model, Kansal et al. [14] use CPU utilization, LLCM, and transfer time of IO for modeling. Krishnan et al. [18] only use instructions retired and last level cache (LLC) hits for his linear model. Kim et al. [19] consider the number of active cores, retired instructions, and number of memory accesses in his linear model. Similarly, Bertran et al. [22,23] also consider the number of active cores for his linear model. Chen et al. [21] propose a modified model using CPU and hard disk. Bohra et al. [24] use PMCs to represent the component states of CPU, memory, and caches for modeling. The only difference among those linear models is the component selection for modeling. In linear models, least squares is often used for multivariable linear regression.

For nonlinear models, Versick et al. [25,26] propose a polynomial formula, and it is the most accurate when the polynomial order is six. Xiao et al. [27] build their polynomial model using PMCs. Wen et al. [28] build a lookup table called LUT to store the CPU and LLC; the table is filled with collected data and interpolated data by the designed rule. But the table is too large to be retrieved when more features are considered. Yang et al. [29] adopts a machine learning method called ε-SVR (support vector regression) model for VM power metering.

Linear model is the most commonly used method in VM power metering for its simplicity in implementation, with low overhead when running. However, it assumes that all the input variables are independent of each other [20]. Besides, the parameters should be trained frequently when the behaviors of applications always vary, causing high overhead. Nonlinear model may improve the accuracy to a certain extent, but too complex especially in updating parameters. In view of this, we propose a tree regression-based method for VM power metering in Reference 7. The advantage of this method is that the collected dataset can be partitioned into easy-modeling pieces by a best

Algorithm 2.1 CreateTree

Require:

The training dataset D;

Ensure:

A tree T;

$(feature, value) = BestSplitSelection(D, s, t)$;
if $feature = null$ **then**
  return $value$;
else
  $T.feature = feature$;
  $T.value = value$;
  $(D_1, D_2) = SplitData(D, feature, value)$;
  $T.left = CreateTree(D_1)$;
  $T.right = CreateTree(D_2)$;
end if

selected resource feature with proper value. Regression tree is a binary tree, created by recursively partitioning data into subsets by a best selected feature-value pair, denoted as *(feature, value)*, until violating one of the constraints: the minimum size of node and the threshold of error reduction, as can be seen in Algorithm 2.1.

The partitions of regression tree rely on the characteristics of dataset rather than artificially setting. The dataset is added to the tree as a leaf node when there is no proper partitioning feature to be selected any more for this dataset. In our implementation, each leaf node only stores the parameters of a linear model fitted on the dataset of this leaf. Function *SplitData* in this algorithm is to partition the training dataset into two parts by the *value* of resource *feature*. Function *BestSplitSelection* returns the best selected *(feature, value)* pair for partition. If the dataset is not suitable for further partition, the returned *feature* is null.

The main idea of *BestSplitSelection* is to find the best *(feature, value)* pair from the training data for splitting, so that the accuracy can be enhanced after partitioning, as shown in Algorithm 2.2. There are two stopping conditions for partitioning. One is the minimum size of partitioned subset s, which ensures that the leaf is modeled with enough data. The other is the threshold of error reduction t, which means partition happens only when error reduction is obvious and exceeds a certain threshold. The feature will be returned as null when any stopping condition is satisfied, or the accuracy cannot be further improved by partitioning.

In this algorithm, the *Error* function is calculated like this:

$$Error(D) = \sum (P_{Estimated} - P_{Measured})^2 \tag{2.5}$$

$Error(D)$ is the quadratic sum of the error between real server power and estimated power for each observation in the training data. $MakeLeaf(D)$ returns the parameters of linear model fitted on D. Thus, each leaf node stores modeling parameters. For any new observation, a leaf node can be searched by repeatedly comparing feature values of the tree. Thus, $P_{Estimated}$ of this observation can be calculated using the linear model obtained by fitting the dataset of this leaf. Since the minimum size of each node is s, the complexity of *CreateTree* can be obtained easily, which is $O(3nlog_2^{n/s})$.

In our work, the resource features for modeling are CPU utilization, LLCM, and IO throughput, denoted as R_{CPU}, R_{LLCM}, and R_{IO}, respectively. Thus, the power consumption of a server is

Algorithm 2.2 BestSplitSelection

Require:
The training dataset D;
The minimum size of node s;
Threshold of error reduction t;

Ensure:
$(bestfeature, bestvalue)$;

```
olderr = Error(D);
newerr = 0;
besterr = Infinite;
bestfeature = nulls;
bestvalue = nulls;
for all d ∈ D do
   for all feature ∈ {CPU, memory, IO} do
      (D_1, D_2) = SplitData(D, feature, d.R_feature);
      if size(D_1) < s or size(D_2) < s then
         continue;
      end if
      newerr = Error(D_1) + Error(D_2);
      if newerr < besterr then
         besterr = newerr;
         bestfeature = feature;
         bestvalue = d.R_feature;
      end if
   end for
end for
if 0 < olderr − besterr < t then
   return (null, MakeLeaf(D));
end if
if size(D_1) < s or size(D_2) < s then
   return (null, MakeLeaf(D));
end if
return (bestfeature, bestvalue) ;
```

denoted as

$$P_{Server} = P_{Static} + P_{Dynamic} = P_{Static} + \alpha R_{CPU} + \beta R_{LLCM} + \gamma R_{IO} + e \quad (2.6)$$

where e is the adjusting bias in model and α, β, and γ are the parameters of the searched leaf node in the built regression tree for inputting the predictor vector $\{R_{CPU}, R_{LLCM}, R_{IO}\}$ of the server. P_{Static} can be obtained when there is no VM or application running on the server. Based on the parameters of the server power model, we calculate the power consumption of each VM like this:

$$P_{VM_i} = \alpha R_{VM_i}^{CPU} + \beta R_{VM_i}^{LLCM} + \gamma R_{VM_i}^{IO} + e_i \quad (2.7)$$

where $R_{VM_i}^{CPU}$, $R_{VM_i}^{LLCM}$, and $R_{VM_i}^{IO}$ denote CPU, LLCM, and IO throughput used by VM_i, respectively; n is the number of VMs on the server; and e_i is the bias of each VM i, which can be calculated as follows:

$$e_i = e * \left(\alpha R_{VM_i}^{CPU} + \beta R_{VM_i}^{LLCM} + \gamma R_{VM_i}^{IO}\right) / \sum_{j=1}^{n} \left(\alpha R_{VM_j}^{CPU} + \beta R_{VM_j}^{LLCM} + \gamma R_{VM_j}^{IO}\right) \tag{2.8}$$

2.1.4 Evaluation Methods

Since VM power is calculated by fairly dividing the server power, the commonly used evaluation method for VM power metering is to directly evaluate the accuracy of the server power model. Most of the work, in the literature use real error divided by the server power measured using PDU for evaluation. Thus, this evaluation method can be represented as follows:

$$Accuracy\ 1 = 1 - \frac{1}{n} \sum \frac{|P_{Estimated} - P_{Measured}|}{P_{Measured}} \tag{2.9}$$

When P_{Static} accounts for a large part of server power, the relative error will be very small. For instance, suppose the measured server power is 200 W, in which static power accounts for 160 W. If the error between estimated and real server power is 10 W, then we will get a relative error about 5%. This is in fact not as accurate as it seems. The real error shrinks after dividing it by such a big denominator in formula (2.9). Meanwhile, other papers give real error within 1~2 W to show the goodness of their result. However, it is indeed a very big error if $P_{Dynamic}$ is just 3~4 W. Therefore, we propose a novel but simple evaluation method as follows:

$$Accuracy\ 2 = 1 - \frac{1}{n} \sum \frac{|P_{Estimated} - P_{Measured}|}{P_{Dynamic}} \tag{2.10}$$

The advantage of our evaluation is that it reflects the modeling errors against dynamic power, not using a big denominator. Therefore, our evaluation method is more objective in real use.

We also use stability to make evaluation; it reflects the fluctuation of errors. The lower, the better. In fact, users always hope our regression tree can behave stably, and the errors do not always change suddenly. Therefore, we define stability using standard deviation of real errors, denoted as *Err*. So we have

$$E_{Stability} = \delta(Err) \tag{2.11}$$

For evaluation, various benchmarks are used to verify the effectiveness of the methods. Table 2.2 lists the most commonly used benchmarks as follows.

2.1.5 A Case Study of VM Power Metering

Figure 2.3 is an example showing the power consumption of server and three VMs running on it during 60 samplings.

The whole server power is composed of static power and dynamic power that are consumed by the three VMs running on this server, so we have

$$P_{Server} = P_{Static} + P_{VM1} + P_{VM2} + P_{VM3} \tag{2.12}$$

Based on the regression tree method, we can calculate the energy consumed by the server and each VM on it using the formula as follows:

$$W = \sum_{i=1}^{n} (P_i * \Delta(t_i)) \tag{2.13}$$

where W denotes the total energy consumed during n samplings, and its unit is Wh (watt hour), and $\Delta(t_i)$ denotes the sampling interval. P_i is the power consumption for the ith sampling interval.

TABLE 2.2
Benchmarks and Descriptions

Category	Benchmark	Function Description
Processor	SPEC CPU2006 [30]	A tool suite to test CPU performance through a wide range of CPU-intensive workload from real user applications
	Dhrystones [31]	A benchmark from Unix Benchmark suite for testing the performance of the processor
	BYTEmark [32]	Providing integer or floating points tests for CPU, memory, and cache
Memory	SPEC OMP2001 [33]	Benchmarks for measuring shared-memory parallel processing and metrics for energy consumption
	Cachebench [34]	A program testing memory hierarchy performance
Disk	Bonnie++ [35]	A tool for testing disk and file system IO performance
	IOzone [36]	A benchmark for testing the reading and writing performance for file system
	IOmeter [37]	Measuring the IO subcomponents performance for single server and clusters
Network	Netperf [38] and iPerf	Benchmark for testing network performance
Parallel	NAS-NPB [39]	A benchmark developed by NASA for parallel computing evaluation
System performance	Linpack [40]	Benchmarks to evaluate the system performance using scientific computation
	StressAppTest [41]	A high load benchmark to test hardware devices performance

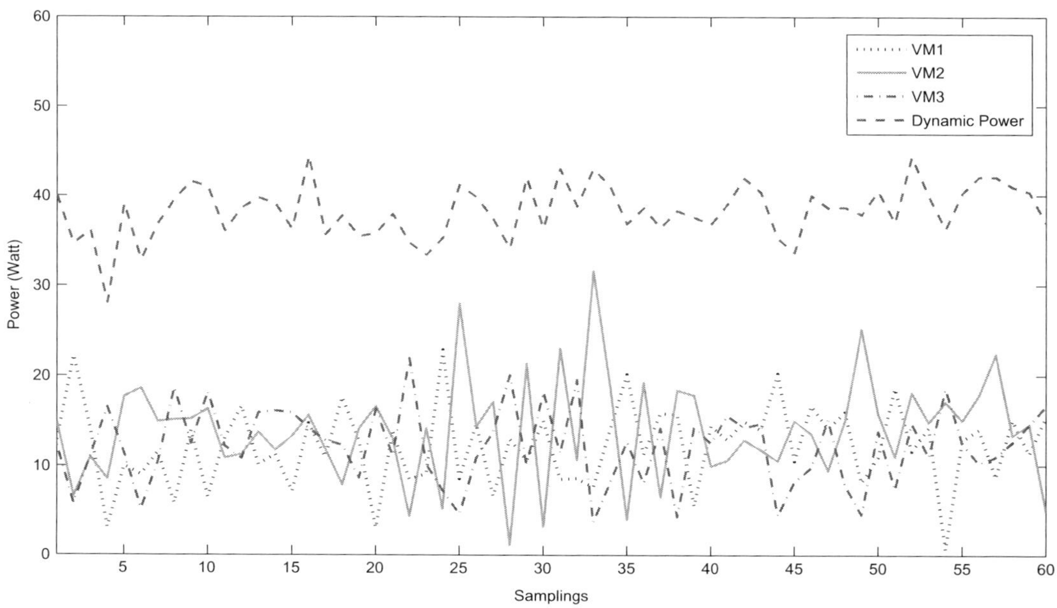

FIGURE 2.3 Power consumption of VMs and server.

Similarly, we can calculate the electricity cost, denoted as *Cost*, for each VM and server as follows:

$$Cost = \sum_{i=1}^{n} (P_i * \Delta(t_i) * Pr_i) \tag{2.14}$$

where Pr_i is the electricity price during the ith sampling interval.

Suppose the electricity price is 20 $/MWh during our 60 samplings; for each, the interval is 2 seconds. Based on the estimated power using the regression tree method during the period of 2 minutes, the energy consumption are 0.40 Wh, 0.46 Wh, and 0.41 Wh for each VM, and the server power is 6.8097 Wh, in which static power accounts for a large part. To estimate the total energy cost, we suppose all the VMs run in this pattern for an hour. Thus, the electricity expenditure for the server is 0.41 cents, and the cost for the three VMs are 0.024, 0.028, and 0.025 cents, respectively. The cheapest price for one EC2 VM with low configuration will cost 1.3 cents per hour, much more expensive than that of our server, because other operation cost such as management, and cooling expenditure is taken into account. Through our analysis, we hope future IaaS providers will charge users in a more fair way based on the power consumption or energy cost in the granularity of VM.

2.1.6 Open Research Issues

VM power metering is an important and emerging research topic. There are many research issues yet to be investigated. Here are some typical issues, including VM service billing, power budgeting, and energy-saving scheduling.

2.1.6.1 VM Service Billing

VM power is the basic unit for virtualized data centers, so future data centers will improve the monitoring system with the visibility of VM power. On the one hand, this will be helpful for us to understand the power consumption of data centers in a finer granularity; on the other hand, reasonable billing for VM services can be made. The traditional billing is based on the configuration and running time of VMs, but the resources usage can be different for VMs with the same configuration and running time. Therefore, future data centers will make full use of VM power metering technology to improve billing schemes in VM services, especially for services like Amazon EC2.

2.1.6.2 Power Budgeting

Power budgeting is playing an important role in modern data centers. To support more servers running in the data center without breaking the upper bound power, power capping technology is introduced. The problem is that too many CPU-intensive VMs consolidated to the same server may intrigue dynamic voltage and frequency scaling (DVFS) of the server so that all the VMs will suffer the degradation of the performance of the server. This breaks the isolation of each VM indirectly, and prolongs running time of tasks, even reduces energy efficiency. Therefore, VM consolidation cannot always save energy without budgeting VM power. For modern data centers with power capping servers, there is a need to budget power in different granularities. In VM granularity, the users can decide how much energy their VMs will use. They can budget the cost of applications running inside their VMs. In server granularity, VM consolidation will be reasonably designed so that the resources usage and the power efficiency can be enhanced without breaking the service-level agreement (SLA) or quality of service (QoS) of the servers. From data center level, more servers can be running at the same time without exceeding the peak power of the data center.

2.1.6.3 Power-Saving Scheduling

Future green data centers cannot go without good power-saving mechanisms. Many scheduling policies are studied in VM migration and consolidation with idle servers powered off. Those scheduling methods only consider the constraints of resources in deployment. In fact, the energy of each VM should also be considered so as to design power-saving scheduling for data centers. VM power metering provides an opportunity to optimize the already power-aware algorithms to save more energy cost in virtualized cloud data centers. Therefore, VM power metering is of great significance and it provides us opportunities to study new techniques for the future green cloud data centers.

2.2 GREEN BIG DATA CENTERS USING RENEWABLE ENERGY

In recent years, a large number of big data centers have been built to meet the ever-increasing demand for computing resources. However, it is the high power consumption of the powerful servers of the data centers that deteriorates the already serious global warming. According to a recent report, the power consumption of Google is over 1120 GWh with 67 million dollars per year, and Microsoft consumes 600 GWh with 36 million dollars [42] annually. The power consumption of data centers accounts for 1.3% currently, and it is estimated to reach 8% in 2020. Thus, cloud data centers contribute greatly to global warming, since 2/3 of the electricity of the world is generated by burning fossil fuels [43]. Some Internet service providers have already taken steps to promote the usage of renewable energy for data centers. For example, Google and Yahoo have already powered their own data centers using clean energy, which account for 39.4% and 56.4%, respectively. Therefore, it is significant for cloud data centers to make green scheduling using renewable energy. However, it is hard to design such a scheduler considering the intermittent supply of renewable energy that changes with time, and the fluctuating electricity prices. In this section, we will discuss how to green big data centers by using intermittent renewable sources while considering energy cost.

2.2.1 Literature Review

There are usually two categories of study on greening cloud data centers: enhancing energy efficiency and utilizing renewable energy.

2.2.1.1 Enhancing Energy Efficiency

Xie et al. [44] try to consolidate VMs onto fewer servers with idle servers in sleeping state. Srikantaiah et al. [45] try to consolidate heterogeneous workload onto fewer servers to minimize energy consumption. Elnozahy et al. [13] combine both DVFS and power on/off techniques to reduce total carbon emissions of data centers. Johan et al. [46] reduce the power consumption of server processors using an energy priority scheduling policy on a variable-voltage platform. Gandhi et al. [47] try to optimize the power allocation of the server farms through DVFS. Lin et al. [48] propose a dynamic power management (DPM) scheme called dynamic right-sizing method to reduce the number of active servers, such that the power consumption of data center can be reduced as much as possible. For green data center, however, enhancing energy efficiency can only slow down the growth of the carbon footprint of IT.

2.2.1.2 Utilizing Renewable Energy

In fact, using renewable energy sources is the radical way to reduce carbon emissions for cloud data centers. Zhang et al. [49] propose a scheduler called GreenWare trying to maximize the usage of renewable energy under a certain budget. Liu et al. [50] try to lower down the price of brown energy by using renewable resources in a specific market. Brown et al. [51] propose a simulation infrastructure called Rerack, which can be used to evaluate the cost of data centers using renewable energy. Li et al. [52] try to coordinate the workload power with the supply of the renewable energy to reduce the carbon footprint. The authors in References 53 and 54 built a demo system with solar panels to power a rack of servers. Based on this system, they designed two schedulers (Green Hadoop and Green Slot) to maximize the usage of renewable energy within deadlines of the tasks. In fact, carbon emissions should be regarded as a metric for the greenness of big data centers.

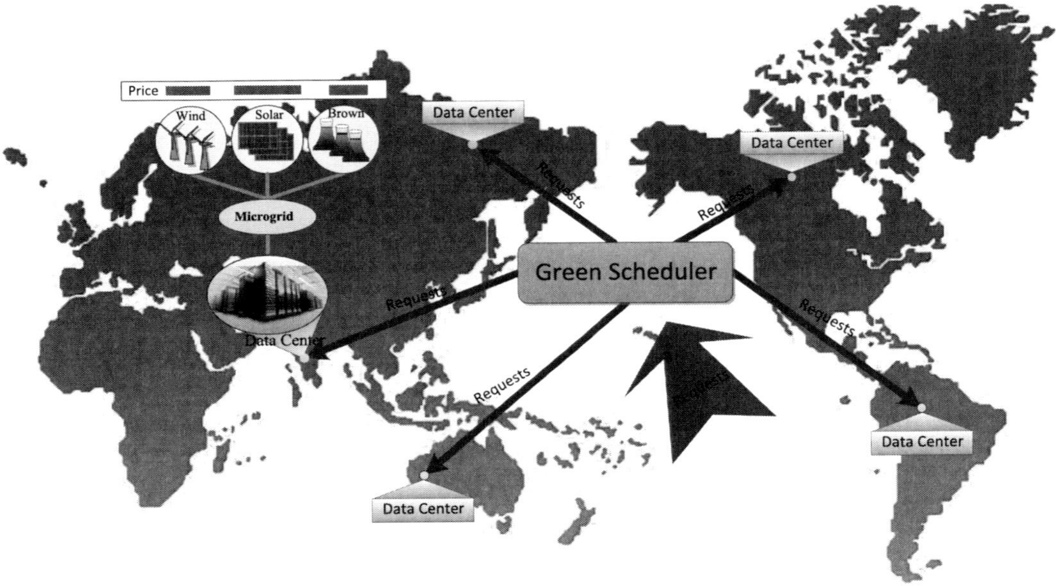

FIGURE 2.4 Architecture of a green scheduler.

In the following, the architecture of a green scheduler will be introduced. It will make a schedule of incoming requests, servers, and the usage of different types of energy, such that the total carbon emissions can be minimized under the budget of energy cost.

2.2.2 Architecture of Green Scheduler

Internet service operators like Google always build their data centers in geographically distributed locations to provide high-quality and reliable services. Wind and solar energy are the dominant renewable sources, which account for 62% and 13% nonhydro renewable sources, respectively. Therefore, we assume that all the data centers in our model are powered by solar, wind, as well as traditional brown energy. The architecture of our scheduling system is shown in Figure 2.4 [55].

As can be seen, there is a green scheduler responsible for dispatching the incoming requests to the data centers that are powered by intermittent renewable energy with fluctuating prices. The scheduler itself is a high-performance server or a cluster of servers. There are transmission delays from scheduler to each data center, which are different for data centers in different locations. The input for each scheduling includes: (1) weather conditions (including temperature, solar illumination, and wind speed), which are used for calculating the power supply of wind and solar in this time slot; (2) total budget of energy cost; (3) QoS, the maximum response time of the requests; (4) electricity prices in each time slot; and (5) the number of servers in each data center. The optimization goal is to minimize total carbon emissions under the budget of energy cost while satisfying constraints like QoS requirement within budget of energy cost.

2.2.3 Usage of Energy Storage Devices

To further reduce carbon emissions, energy storage devices (ESDs) should be taken into account. In the past, ESD is commonly used as uninterrupted power supply (UPS) to keep the normal operation of data centers when electricity failure happens, before any diesel generation can start to supply power. This transition may take only 10~20 seconds, while the energy stored in UPSs can sustain

5~30 minutes for data centers [56]. The excess storage capacity of those UPSs can be used to store renewable energy, or the energy from the power grid when its price is low, such that both carbon emissions and total energy cost can be further reduced by using ESDs as part of the normal energy supply. Therefore, we assume each data center is equipped with some ESDs to store energy and discharge it whenever necessary. By using ESDs in data centers, it brings some challenging issues for the scheduling of user requests and energy supply. First, since ESDs can store energy when the price is low, the scheduling of user requests needs to consider not only the current electricity price, but also the price of stored energy by ESDs. Second, since ESDs have energy loss during the process of charging/discharging and self-discharging as time goes, the decision making of when to charge and when to discharge becomes a time-dependent process. That is, any decision of charging and discharging will affect the decisions in the subsequent time slots. We mainly focus on minimizing carbon emissions under budget of energy cost, which can be modeled as follows.

2.2.3.1 Workload Model

Since the servers in each data center have a capacity, one constraint of scheduling is to make sure the requests assigned to a data center shall not exceed its capacity. Let N denote the number of geographically located data centers. The running period of our scheduler is T time slots, and for each slot t, $t \in \{1, 2, \ldots, T\}$. Let λ^t denote the number of incoming requests in time slot t, λ_i^t denote the number of requests dispatched to data center i in time slot t, and $\mathbb{N}$ denote natural numbers, then we have

$$\lambda^t = \sum_{i=1}^{N} \lambda_i^t$$

$$\lambda_i^t \in \mathbb{N}, \quad \forall i \in \{1, \ldots, N\}$$

We assume the servers in a data center are homogeneous (note that our solution can be easily changed to adapt for the case of heterogeneous servers). Let x_i^t denote the number of active servers with service rate μ_i (requests per second) in data center i during time slot t. The capacity constraint requires that the number of incoming requests should be within the service capacity of active servers. It can be expressed as

$$0 \leq \lambda_i^t \leq x_i^t \cdot \mu_i \tag{2.15}$$

$$0 \leq x_i^t \leq M_i \tag{2.16}$$

where M_i denotes the maximum number of servers in data center i.

2.2.3.2 Response Time Model

The QoS in our formulation is defined as the average response time of requests, denoted as R_i. It consists of transmission delay from scheduler to data center, waiting time, and processing time of the requests. Let $R_{i,max}$ denote the worst-case response time of data center i. It is a performance indicator, prespecified by the data center. To analyze the average waiting time, we adopt the M/M/n queuing model, as is done in Reference 56. We assume all active servers are busy with probability 1, such that the average waiting time and processing time can be represented as $1/(\mu_i x_i^t - \lambda_i^t)$ and $1/\mu_i$, respectively. Let d_i denote the transmission time from scheduler to data center i. The QoS requirement of a data center can be expressed by

$$R_i = \frac{1}{\mu_i \cdot x_i^t - \lambda_i^t} + \frac{1}{\mu_i} + d_i < R_{i,max} \tag{2.17}$$

2.2.3.3 Power Consumption of Data Centers

Let P_{idle} denote the idle power of a server, and P_{peak} denote the peak power when a server is busy processing requests with maximum power. We adopt the commonly used power consumption model in Reference 57, so we have

$$P_{server} = P_{idle} + u \times (P_{peak} - P_{idle})$$

where u is the utilization of this server.

The total power consumption of data centers can be estimated if we know the power consumption of the IT infrastructure and the power usage effectiveness (PUE) of this data center. The power consumption of the IT infrastructure is mainly consumed by servers in data centers. Thus, the total power consumption of data center i in time slot t, denoted as P_i^t, can be calculated as

$$P_i^t = x_i^t \cdot [P_{idle} + (P_{peak} - P_{idle}) \cdot u_i^t] \cdot \rho_i$$

where ρ_i denotes the PUE of data center i, u_i^t denotes the average server utilization at time slot t, and

$$u_i^t = \lambda_i^t / (x_i^t \cdot \mu_i)$$

2.2.3.4 Power Supply and Demand

In data centers, there are three types of energy supply: wind, solar, and brown energy. The issue is complicated by the introduction of ESDs. We need to determine how much energy of each type should be charged into ESDs, and how much to discharge from ESDs to power data centers in each time slot. We also consider electricity losses during charging, discharging, and that caused by self-discharging as time goes. Thus, the power supply and demand model can be formulated as follows.

Let wind, solar, and brown energy to be drawn from microgrid by data center i in time slot t be represented as Sw_i^t, Ss_i^t, and Sb_i^t, respectively. The upper bound of the supply for each type of energy can be denoted as $Sw_{i,max}^t$, $Ss_{i,max}^t$, and $Sb_{i,max}^t$, respectively. We have

$$0 \leq Sw_i^t \leq Sw_{i,max}^t \tag{2.18}$$

$$0 \leq Ss_i^t \leq Ss_{i,max}^t \tag{2.19}$$

$$0 \leq Sb_i^t \leq Sb_{i,max}^t \tag{2.20}$$

Let Rw_i^t, Rs_i^t, and Rb_i^t denote the three types of energy that should be charged into battery for data center i in time slot t, and Pw_i^t, Ps_i^t, and Pb_i^t denote the energy used to directly power data centers, respectively. We have

$$Sw_i^t = Rw_i^t + Pw_i^t$$

$$Ss_i^t = Rs_i^t + Ps_i^t$$

$$Sb_i^t = Rb_i^t + Pb_i^t$$

Usually, there are losses during charging and discharging for battery ESDs. Let α and β denote charging ratio and discharging ratio, respectively, whose values are usually between 85% and 95%, so that the losses are between 5% and 15%. Besides, electricity in the battery will dissipate with time due to self-discharging, which is usually 0.1~0.3% per day [58]. In our model, we also consider self-discharging with losses rate, which is denoted as θ.

Let D_i^t denote the energy that should be discharged to power data center i in time slot t, and E_i^t denote the amount of energy stored in the battery. We have

$$E_i^{t+1} = (1 - \theta)[E_i^t - D_i^t + \alpha(Rw_i^t + Rs_i^t + Rb_i^t)]$$

For the first time slot, we suppose there is no energy stored in advance, so that $E_i^1 = 0$ and $D_i^1 = 0$.

The energy stored in each battery should always be nonnegative, and should be bounded in its capacity, so we have

$$0 \leq E_i^t \leq E_{i,max} \tag{2.21}$$

where $E_{i,max}$ denotes the maximum capacity of the ESD in data center i.

The energy to be discharged in time slot t should be constraint by its energy stored inside, so we have

$$0 \leq D_i^t \leq E_i^t \tag{2.22}$$

The energy to be charged should not exceed the remaining capacity of this battery in this time slot, so we have

$$0 \leq Rw_i^t + Rs_i^t + Rb_i^t \leq E_{i,max} - E_i^t \tag{2.23}$$

The total energy consumed by data center i in time slot t should be equal to the sum of the three types of energy that directly power this data center and the energy discharged from ESDs. Note that there is electricity losses during discharging, so we have

$$Pw_i^t + Ps_i^t + Pb_i^t + \beta D_i^t = P_i^t$$

2.2.3.5 Total Cost

Let Qw_i^t, Qs_i^t, and Qb_i^t denote the price of wind, solar, and brown energy for data center i in time slot t, respectively. The total cost should be within budget constraint B during the whole period of time, so we have

$$C_i^t = [Sw_i^t \cdot Qw_i^t + Ss_i^t \cdot Qs_i^t + Sb_i^t \cdot Qb_i^t]$$

$$\sum_{t=1}^{T} \sum_{i=1}^{N} C_i^t \leq B \tag{2.24}$$

where C_i^t denotes the total cost of data center i in time slot t.

2.2.3.6 Total Carbon Emission

Carbon emission rate (CER) represents the amount of carbon emissions in unit energy (kWh), as can be seen in Table 2.3. Based on this, we can estimate how much carbon will be emitted when using each type of energy. Let Ew, Es, and Eb denote the CER of wind, solar, and brown energy, respectively. The carbon emissions for data center i in time slot t can be denoted as

$$Em_i^t = Ew \cdot Sw_i^t + Es \cdot Ss_i^t + Eb \cdot Sb_i^t$$

TABLE 2.3
CER of the Energy Sources

Energy Source	Coal	Wind	Solar
CER (gCO_2e/kWh)	968	22.5	53

2.2.3.7 Problem Formulation

Problem. Minimizing emissions using ESDs *(ME-ESD)*
Given the budget of energy cost, the number of requests in each time slot, the capacity of servers in each data center, and energy supplies from three types of energy sources, we design a schedule to minimize total carbon emissions under the budget of energy cost. Thus, the problem is formulated as the following:

$$\textbf{Minimize}: \sum_{t=1}^{T}\sum_{i=1}^{N} Em_i^t$$

$$\textbf{Subject to}: (2.15) \sim (2.24)$$

Renewable energy is usually more expensive than brown energy due to its intermittent nature and high generating cost. Therefore, we take budget constraint into account in this problem. In these two problems, the constraints are for each time slot t, and data center $i = 1, \ldots, N$. The decision variables include x_i^t, λ_i^t, Sw_i^t, Ss_i^t, Sb_i^t, Rw_i^t, Rs_i^t, Rb_i^t, and D_i^t. Thus, there are $9 \times N$ decision variables for each time slot, and $9 \times N \times T$ decision variables during the whole period of time.

2.2.3.8 Solution

From the above modelings, we found that each of the two problems can be well formulated as a mixed integer linear programming (MILP) problem during the whole period of time. We solve this problem using *Cplex* solver in MATLAB®. In particular, *Cplex* can solve the MILP problem using a simplex method with high efficiency, and it is feasible to run the experiments with reasonable size like that in our simulation. Thus, we can obtain decisions for each data center in each time slot, including the number of requests dispatched to each data center, the number of active servers, energy of different types that are drawn from microgrid, and energy of different types that are charged into or discharged from ESDs.

2.2.4 Planning for Green Data Centers

In fact, cloud data centers should be carefully planned so as to make the best use of the energy sources in different locations. For example, the data centers in locations with abundant wind sources should be deployed with more wind turbines, while data centers with abundant solar energy should be deployed with more PV panels. Besides, larger ESDs should be equipped to the data centers with abundant renewable energy. Note that, here we assume that each data center has its own wind turbines or solar panels to generate renewable energy. In this section, we study the issue of planning for green cloud data centers based on the optimized scheduling framework as mentioned above. Our plan includes: (1) How many servers each data center should have. (2) How many wind turbines and solar panels should be used to power each data center. (3) What capacity of ESD should be equipped for each data center. Thus, additional models are formulated as follows.

In our planning, the capacity of ESDs in different data centers should be different, so as to make the best use of the fluctuating electricity prices and the energy supply in different locations to reduce energy cost and carbon emissions. Considering the capital investment, we suppose the total capacity of ESDs of all data centers is $E0$, and we make planning about what capacity of the ESDs should be equipped for each data center, so we have

$$E0 = \sum_{i=1}^{N} E_{i,max} \tag{2.25}$$

In our model, the data centers can be powered directly by the power grid, or the renewable energy generated by wind turbines or solar panels. The number of wind turbines or solar panels of those data centers should be different due to the different climate conditions in those locations. Considering the capital investment, we assume there are totally Kw wind turbines and Ks solar panels. We plan how many of the wind turbines and solar panels should be deployed in each data center i, denoted as kw_i and ks_i, respectively. So we have

$$Kw = \sum_{i=1}^{N} kw_i \tag{2.26}$$

$$Ks = \sum_{i=1}^{N} ks_i \tag{2.27}$$

Let pw_i^t denote the generated energy of each wind turbine in data center i during time slot t, which can be calculated using the model proposed in Reference 59 when wind speed is given. Similarly, let ps_i^t denote the generated energy of each solar panel, which can be calculated using the PV model in References 60 and 61 when solar irradiation and temperature are given. Thus, the maximum energy supply of wind and solar, denoted as $Sw_{i,max}^t$, $Ss_{i,max}^t$, can be calculated as follows:

$$Sw_{i,max}^t = kw_i \times pw_i^t \tag{2.28}$$

$$Ss_{i,max}^t = ks_i \times ps_i^t \tag{2.29}$$

Our goal is to minimize carbon emissions when planning for green cloud data centers. Thus, the problem can be formulated as follows:

$$\textbf{Minimize}: \sum_{t=1}^{T}\sum_{i=1}^{N} Em_i^t$$

$$\textbf{Subject to}: (2.15) \sim (2.23), (2.25) \sim (2.29)$$

The decision variables of this problems include $x_i^t, \lambda_i^t, Pw_i^t, Ps_i^t, Pg_i^t, Rw_i^t, Rs_i^t, Rg_i^t, D_i^t, M_i, kw_i, ks_i$, and $E_{i,max}$. Thus, there are $9 \times N \times T + 4 \times N$ decision variables during the whole period of time. This formulated problem is also an MILP problem during the whole period of time, which can be solved using *Cplex* solver in MATLAB. In each time slot, the solutions of the formulated optimization problems determine: (1) how many requests should be dispatched into each data center; (2) how many servers should be running in each time slot; (3) how much energy of each type should be used to directly power each data center; (4) how much energy of each type should be stored into the ESDs of each data center; and (5) how much energy should be discharged from the ESDs to power the data centers. We also make planning during the whole period of time, and we determine (6) how many servers each data center should have; (7) how many wind turbines and solar panels should be deployed for each data center; and (8) what capacity of the ESDs should be equipped for each data center.

2.2.5 Reducing Energy Cost for Green Data Centers through Energy Trading

Cloud data centers consume a large amount of energy, which leads to high energy cost and carbon emissions. To reduce both energy cost and emissions, there have been endeavors trying to conserve energy consumption or to enhance energy efficiency using technologies such as workload consolidation or VM consolidation onto fewer servers, or using DVFS to adjust power to save energy. However, reducing energy consumption can only slow down the growth of carbon emissions [62]. Therefore, others are trying to power data centers using renewable energy to green cloud data centers. However, it is the high prices of renewable energy that hinder the extensive usage of renewable energy. In this section, we propose an improved scheduling architecture to reduce energy cost for green cloud data centers by using ESDs and energy trading with the power grid, as can be seen in Figure 2.5. Different from existing work, we consider lowering down total energy cost when greening data centers from the following three aspects:

1. Using cheap but green energy that are generated by the wind turbines and solar panels of each data center
2. Using ESDs to store renewable energy when its supply is abundant, or store the brown energy when its price is low and discharge when the energy price is high
3. Making profit by selling the energy (including the self-generated renewable energy and the energy stored inside the ESDs) back to the power grid, so as to further reduce total energy cost

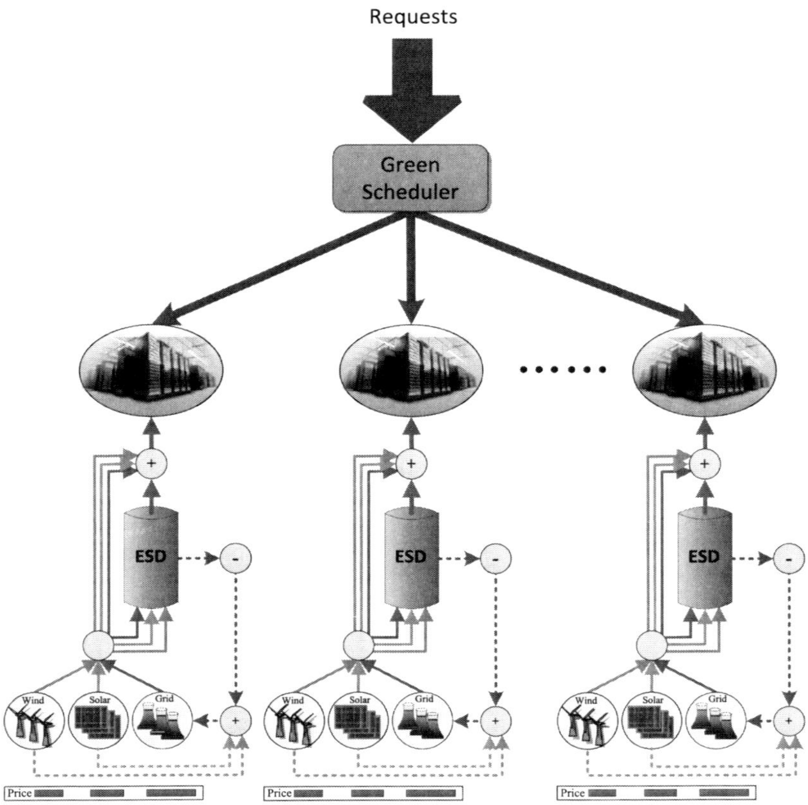

FIGURE 2.5 Architecture of a green scheduler. Solid arrows show the direction of energy to be bought by data centers; dashed arrows show the direction of energy to be sold back to the power grid.

Our goal is to minimize total energy cost under a certain level of carbon emissions. The constraints include the computing capacity of each data center, the QoS requirement of the requests, the capacity of ESDs, and the supply of renewable energy. Our scheduling decides:

1. The number of requests that should be dispatched to each data center in each time slot
2. The number of servers that should be switched into sleeping states or active states in each time slot
3. The usage of each type of energy, including powering the data centers, charging/discharging of the ESDs, and that should be sold back to the power grid in each time slot

Based on this architecture, additional formulations are added as follows. For each type of energy drawn, it will be used in three ways: (1) the energy to power data centers directly, denoted as Pw_i^t, Ps_i^t, and Pb_i^t, respectively; (2) the energy to be stored into ESDs, denoted as Rw_i^t, Rs_i^t, and Rb_i^t, respectively; and (3) the renewable energy to be sold back to the power grid, denoted as Gw_i^t, Gs_i^t, respectively. So we have

$$Sw_i^t = Rw_i^t + Pw_i^t + Gw_i^t$$
$$Ss_i^t = Rs_i^t + Ps_i^t + Gs_i^t$$
$$Sb_i^t = Rb_i^t + Pb_i^t$$

The energy discharged from ESD, denoted as D_i^t, is usually used in two ways: (1) to power data centers directly, denoted as $P_{(ESD)}{}_i^t$ and (2) to be sold back to the power grid, denoted as $G_{(ESD)}{}_i^t$. Thus, we have

$$D_i^t = P_{(ESD)}{}_i^t + G_{(ESD)}{}_i^t$$

The total energy used by data center i in time slot t, denoted as P_i^t, is

$$Pw_i^t + Ps_i^t + Pg_i^t + \beta P_{(ESD)}{}_i^t = P_i^t$$

The problem of minimizing total energy cost within the carbon emission level can be formulated as follows:

$$\textbf{Minimize: } C = \sum_{t=1}^{T}\sum_{i=1}^{N}[Sw_i^t \cdot Qw_i^t + Ss_i^t \cdot Qs_i^t + Sb_i^t \cdot Qb_i^t$$
$$- (Gw_i^t + Gs_i^t + \beta \cdot G_{(ESD)}{}_i^t) \cdot Qg_i^t]$$

Subject to: (2.15) $\sim$ (2.23), (2.25) $\sim$ (2.29)

$$\sum_{t=1}^{T}\sum_{i=1}^{N}[Sw_i^t \cdot Ew_i^t + Ss_i^t \cdot Es_i^t + Sb_i^t \cdot Eb_i^t] \le E$$

Thus, the problem is formulated as a typical MILP problem during the whole period of time that can be solved using Cplex. Thus, there are $12 \times N \times T$ decision variables in total during the whole period of time. In each time slot, the solutions of the formulated problems determine: (1) the number of requests that should be dispatched to each data center, (2) the number of active servers, (3) how much energy of each type (including that discharged from ESD) should be used to power data centers directly, (4) how much energy of each type (including renewable energy and brown energy) should be charged into ESDs, and (5) how much of the self-generated wind and solar energy, and the energy stored in ESDs should be sold back to the power grid.

TABLE 2.4
Parameters of Internet Data Centers

i	μ_i	M_i	d_i	P^i_{peak}	P^i_{idle}	ρ_i
1	1.75	4500	0.20	140	84	1.3
2	1.50	5000	0.25	90	54	1.5
3	1.25	6000	0.10	34	20	1.7
4	2.00	4000	0.15	150	90	1.3

2.2.6 Simulations and Analysis

Simulations are based on traces from real world, including the statistical request traces, electricity prices in different locations, and the power supply with respect to the weather conditions. All those data are collected hourly from June 1 to June 30, 2014, so there are 720 scheduling slots in total. We assume there are four data centers belonging to the same cloud operator. We use similar configuration parameters in Reference 63, as shown in Table 2.4.

For the traces of the incoming requests, we use the Wiki dump [64], which are varying with time periodically. For the electricity prices of brown energy from the power grid, we use the traces of four locations (including CAPITL, CENTRL, DUNWOD, and GENESE) from New York Independent System Operator (NYISO). For the supply of wind and solar energy, we use the power models proposed in Reference 49 to calculate the energy supply of wind and solar, with history weather conditions from MIDC of National Renewable Energy Laboratory [65]. We use the traces from four stations, including Loyola Marymount University, University of Arizona, Solar Technology Acceleration Center, and National Energy Laboratory Hawaii Authority. We suppose each data center has 50K BP-MSX-120 solar panels and 1000 NE-3000 wind turbines for each data center. The supply constraint of brown energy for each data center is five times of the maximum power of this data center. Let *Uhour* denote unit capacity of ESD, which equals to the total energy of the data center running in peak power for 1 hour. We suppose each data center has an ESD with a capacity of 1 *Uhour*. The parameters of electricity losses for α, β, and θ are 95%, 95% (per hour), and 0.3% (per day), respectively. The maximum response time of QoS is set to be 1 second for all data centers.

2.2.6.1 Usage of ESDs

For the renewable energy bought from a power plant, its price is usually more expensive than brown energy. Let the price of brown energy be denoted as Pb_i, and the prices of wind and solar energy be denoted as $Pb_i + 1.5$ cents and $Pb_i + 18$ cents per kWh, respectively [49]. Other parameters can be obtained from the literature [66]. To make comparison, we denote minimum cost with no ESD and that with ESD as *ME* and *ME-ESD*, respectively.

Figure 2.6 shows the trend of carbon emissions with budget. When the budget increases, the total carbon emission decreases. The upper bound of the budget is the maximum cost when carbon emission is minimized, so that any extra investment afterward will not bring reduction in carbon emissions anymore. When budget is fixed, we found that using ESDs can further reduce carbon emissions compared with that using no ESDs. There are two reasons. First, much more renewable energy will be used by storing it into ESDs when its price is low. Second, the total cost can be saved by storing brown energy into ESDs, and the saved money can be used to buy more renewable energy. Therefore, using larger ESDs can further reduce total carbon emissions.

Figure 2.7 shows the trend of minimum emissions with different ESD capacities. In this figure, *ME-N* denotes the minimum emissions with no budget constrain, and *ME-ESD-N* and *ME-ESD-B* denote minimum emissions using ESDs without budget constrain, and that within budget constraint of 60,000$, respectively. *ME-N* and *ME-ESD-N* use ESDs with a capacity of 0.5 *Uhour*; we use

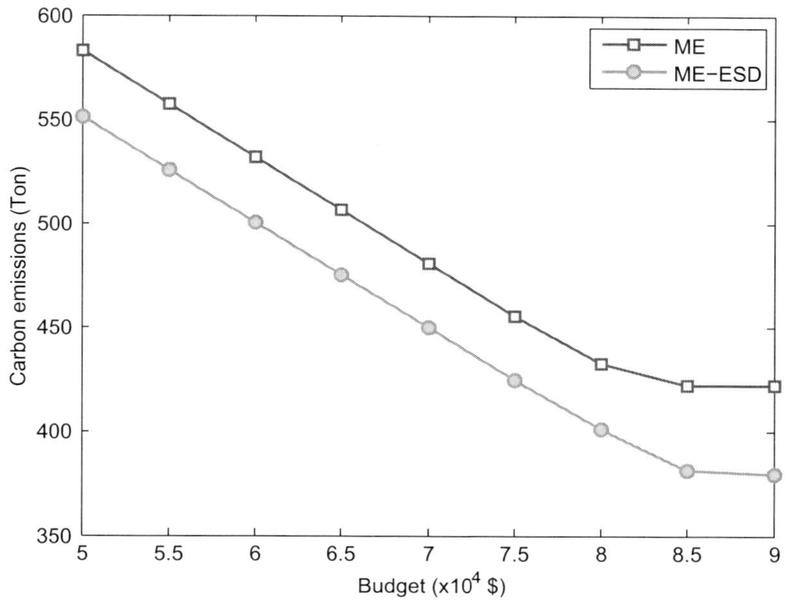

FIGURE 2.6 Carbon emissions with budget.

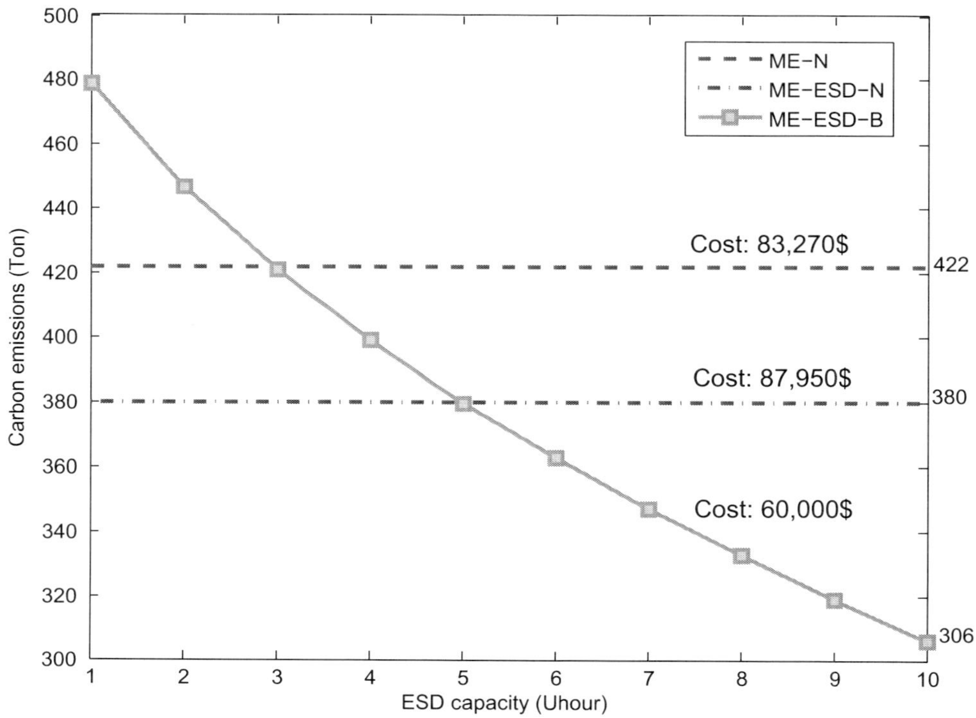

FIGURE 2.7 ME-ESD-B with ESD capacity.

them as our baselines. As can be seen in Figure 2.7, the total carbon emissions can be reduced with the increase of ESD capacity. Besides, when ESD is large enough (like 8 *Uhours*), using only 60,000$ can achieve much lower carbon emissions than that of using 80,000$ more dollars when ESD capacity is only 0.5 *Uhour*. Therefore, the capacity of ESD really matters when minimizing carbon emissions. With larger ESDs, we can achieve lower carbon emissions within a lower budget of energy cost, and the reduction can reach more than 25% when ESD capacity is 10 *Uhours*.

2.2.6.2 Planning for Green Data Centers

To make planning for green data centers, we assume that each data center has its own wind turbines and solar panels, so as to achieve low cost when using renewable energy. We suppose the operation and management cost for the self-generated renewable energy is 10 $/MWh for all data centers, as done in Reference 67. There are totally 40K BP-MSX-120 solar panels and 10K NE-3000 wind turbines to power each data center. We suppose there are 15,000 servers in total, and each data center has at least 2500 servers. Each server has the capacity of 7200 requests per hour with peak power 150 watt and idle power 90 watt. We assume the PUE of all those data centers can reach as low as 1.2 by using the state-of-the-art infrastructure. Let *Uhour* denote unit capacity of ESD, which equals to the total energy of all servers running in peak power for 1 hour. We assume the total capacity of the ESDs is 4 *Uhours*, and the upper bound of brown energy from the power grid for each data center is 2 *Uhours*.

Table 2.5 shows the deployment of servers, wind turbines, solar panels, and ESD capacities for the data centers under the planning goal of minimizing carbon emissions. The renewable energy produced by the data centers is usually much cheaper than that bought from the power grid while with low carbon emissions. Therefore, data centers with abundant renewable energy will be deployed with more servers, as well as wind turbines and solar panels. It can be inferred that Data Center 1 (DC1) is abundant in renewable energy of both wind and solar, so that most of the servers, wind turbines, and solar panels are deployed in this data center, as can be seen in Table 2.5. The data centers with more wind turbines and solar panels are always equipped with larger ESDs. With larger ESDs, more green but cheap energy can be utilized to reduce carbon emissions. Besides, the energy cost can be further reduced using ESDs. In the following, we will discuss how to reduce energy cost by using ESDs and energy trading.

2.2.6.3 Usage of ESDs and Energy Trading in Reducing Energy Cost

In the United States, the smart grid usually allows end-users to sell the self-generated solar energy back to the power grid, as studied in References 68 and 69. The selling-back price is lower than that from the power grid, due to the energy losses during AC/DC conversion, transmission losses, and profit consideration of the utility company. Let the selling price be denoted as Qg_i^t; it can be represented as $Qg_i^t = \gamma \cdot Qb_i^t$, where γ is between 0 and 1.

Figure 2.8 shows the trend of energy cost with the increase of parameter γ. As can be seen, the overall trend of the energy cost is decreasing with the increase of γ. There is no reduction in energy

TABLE 2.5
Deployment for the Four Data Centers

	DC1	DC2	DC3	DC4	Total
Servers	7500	2500	2500	2500	15,000
Wind turbines	10,000	0	0	0	10,000
Solar panels	31,650	0	8350	0	40,000
ESD (*Uhours*)	3.86	0	0.14	0	4

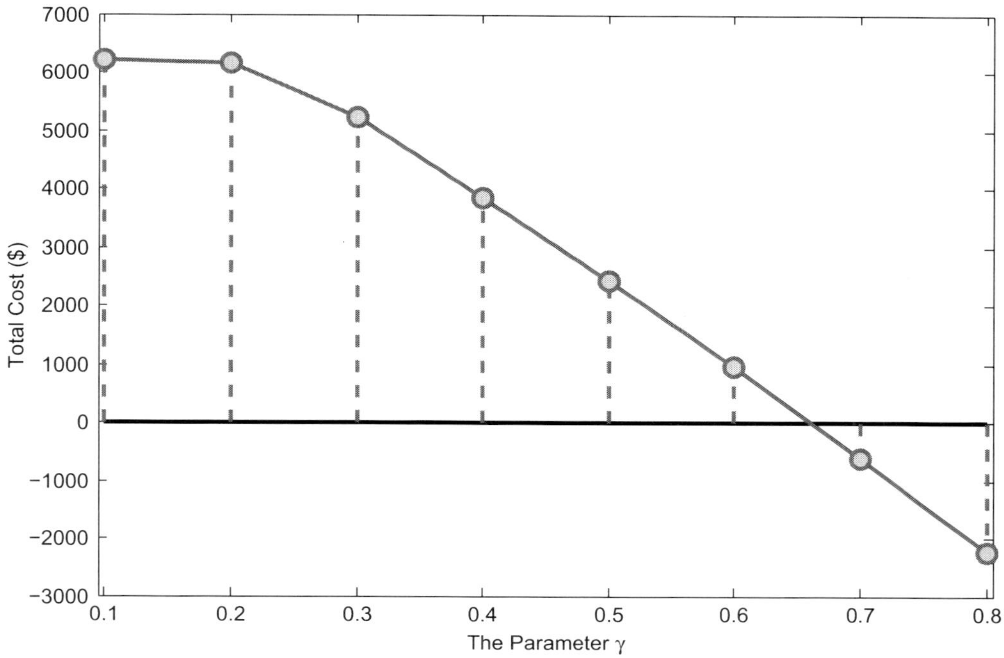

FIGURE 2.8 Trend of energy cost with different parameters of γ.

cost when γ is set to be 0.1 or 0.2. In this case, there is almost no energy sold back to the power grid, because it will not make any profit with such low selling-back prices, even incurring economic losses for the data centers. Interestingly, the data centers can make great profit by energy trading with the power grid when the parameter γ is above 0.3. When γ reaches 0.7, there even appears surplus profit for cloud operators after covering all the energy cost of the data centers. Therefore, the parameter for the selling-back prices affects the total energy cost greatly.

Figure 2.9 shows comparisons of our modeling method with different benchmarks. We have three benchmarks:

1. *MinCost-NoTrading-NoESD*: Minimizing total cost with no energy trading and no ESDs to store energy [63]
2. *MinCost-NoTrading-ESD*: Minimizing total cost with no energy trading, but uses ESDs to store energy [70]
3. *MinCost-Trading-NoESD*: Minimizing total cost with energy trading, but uses no ESDs

Our scheduling method is denoted as *MinCost-Trading-ESD*: minimizing total cost by using both energy trading and ESDs. As can be seen, our scheduling of *MinCost-Trading-ESD* can always achieve the lowest energy cost under different carbon emission levels. Without energy trading or ESDs, the energy cost of *MinCost-NoTrading-NoESD* is the highest among the four schedulings. It can be found that the energy cost can be reduced no matter using only energy trading or ESDs, and more energy cost can be reduced using energy trading than using only ESDs, as can be seen in *MinCost-Trading-NoESD* and *MinCost-NoTrading-ESD*. Energy trading is playing an important part in reducing total energy cost under different carbon emission levels. As can be seen, for *MinCost-NoTrading-NoESD* and *MinCost-NoTrading-ESD* with no trading, there is almost no change in energy cost under different emission levels. In contrast, the cost of *MinCost-Trading-NoESD* and *MinCost-Trading-ESD* change greatly under different emission levels. ESD is significant for the

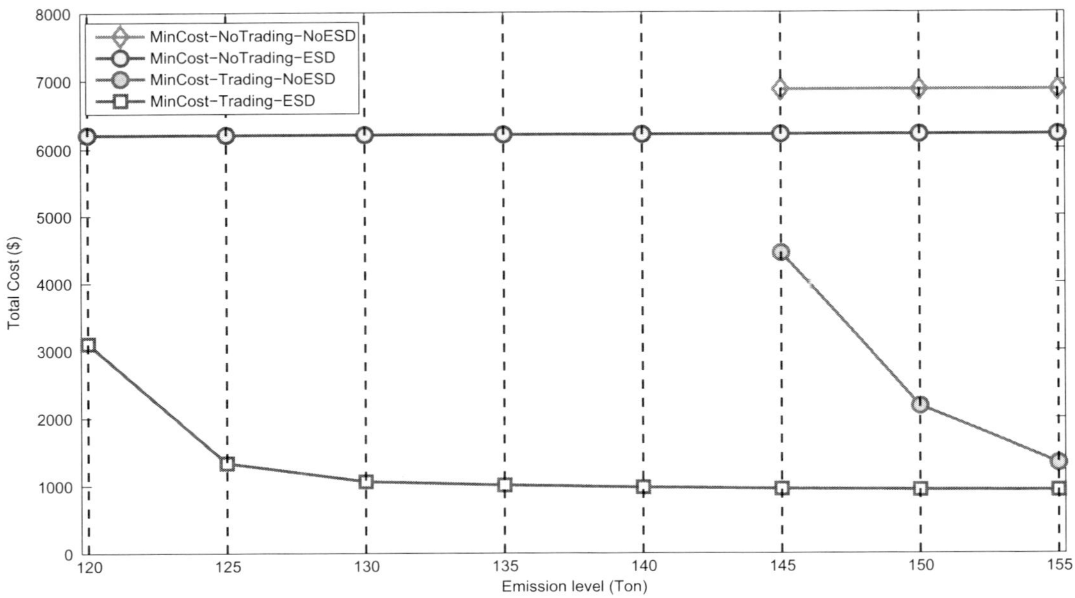

FIGURE 2.9 Comparisons of minimum cost with benchmarks.

lowest emission level that can be achieved in scheduling. For example, the lowest emission level for *MinCost-NoTrading-NoESD* and *MinCost-Trading-NoESD* is 145 tons, much more higher than that using ESDs. It can be concluded that our scheduling of *MinCost-Trading-ESD* can greatly reduce total cost with less carbon emissions by using both ESDs and energy trading.

2.3 CONCLUSION

In this chapter, we studied two most important issues for the energy management of big data centers: VM power metering and greening data centers using renewable sources.

VM power metering is very important for the power management of data centers. In this section, we introduced regression tree method to estimate the power consumption of each VM. It recursively partitions the dataset by a best selected feature with proper value using binary tree structure. It proved to be a well-designed solution in piecewise linear models, more relying on the characteristics of dataset, rather than artificial setting. In addition, a new evaluation method is proposed, which reflects the extent of error in a more objective way. We use standard deviation of errors to evaluate the stability of our method. Experiments show that our regression tree method can measure the power consumption of both VM and server with high accuracy and stability.

Greening cloud data center using renewable energy is the radical way to reduce carbon emissions. We first introduced a green scheduling framework, based on which we study three key issues:

1. Minimizing carbon emissions under budget of energy cost. We consider using ESDs to store three types of energy, wind, solar, and brown energy. By leveraging larger ESDs, the carbon emissions can be significantly reduced with a lower budget of energy cost.
2. Planning for green data center, which tries to optimally take the advantages of renewable energy in different locations by deploying proper number of server, wind turbines, solar panels, and ESD capacities for each data center. The data centers deployed with larger number of servers will always be correspondingly deployed with more wind turbines or solar panels, as well as larger ESDs.

3. Lowering energy cost through energy trading with the power grid. Simulation results show that our scheduler using both energy trading and ESDs can significantly reduce total cost within lower carbon emission levels. Besides, higher selling-back prices will incur more energy sold back to the power grid, reducing more cost as a result.

REFERENCES

1. Michael Armbrust, Armando Fox, Rean Griffith, Anthony D. Joseph, Randy Katz, Andy Konwinski, Gunho Lee, David Patterson, Ariel Rabkin, Ion Stoica et al. A view of cloud computing. *Communications of the ACM*, 53(4):50–58, 2010.
2. Erik Elmroth, Fermin Galan Marquez, Daniel Henriksson, and David Perales Ferrera. Accounting and billing for federated cloud infrastructures. In *Proceedings of IEEE GCC*, Lanzhou, Gansu, China, 2009.
3. Liang Liu, Hao Wang, Xue Liu, Xing Jin, Wen Bo He, Qing Bo Wang, and Ying Chen. Green cloud: A new architecture for green data center. In *Proceedings of ACM Conference Industry Session on Autonomic Computing and Communications Industry Session*, Barcelona, Spain, 2009.
4. HPiLO. http://h17007.www1.hp.com/us/en/enterprise/servers/management/ilo/#.U4Wk4uM_jKc. [Online; accessed May 29, 2014].
5. Chonglin Gu, Hejiao Huang, and Xiaohua Jia. Power metering for virtual machine in cloud computing-challenges and opportunities. *Access, IEEE*, 2:1106–1116, 2014.
6. Yanfei Li, Ying Wang, Bo Yin, and Lu Guan. An online power metering model for cloud environment. In *Proceedings of IEEE NCA*, Cambridge, MA, 2012.
7. Chonglin Gu, Pengzhou Shi, Shuai Shi, Hejiao Huang, and Xiaohua Jia. A tree regression-based approach for vm power metering. *Access, IEEE*, 3:610–621, 2015.
8. WattsUp Meter. https://www.wattsupmeters.com/secure/index.php. [Online; accessed May 29, 2014].
9. Public APIs of Schleifenbauer PDU. http://sdc.sourceforge.net/index.htm. [Online; accessed May 29, 2014].
10. John Jenne, Vijay Nijhawan, and Robert Hormuth. Architecture (desa) for 11g rack and tower servers, 2009. http://www.dell.com/downloads/global/products/pedge/en/poweredge-11g-desa-white-paper.pdf [Online; accessed Feb 23, 2017].
11. Waltenegus Dargie and Alexander Schill. Analysis of the power and hardware resource consumption of servers under different load balancing policies. In *Proceedings of IEEE CLOUD*, Honolulu, HI, 2012.
12. Dimitris Economou, Suzanne Rivoire, Christos Kozyrakis, and Partha Ranganathan. Full-system power analysis and modeling for server environments. In *Proceedings of IEEE ISCA*, Boston, MA, 2006.
13. Elnozahy, EN Mootaz, Michael Kistler, and Ramakrishnan Rajamony. Energy-efficient server clusters. In Proceedings of PACS, Cambridge, MA, 2002.
14. Aman Kansal, Feng Zhao, Jie Liu, Nupur Kothari, and Arka A. Bhattacharya. Virtual machine power metering and provisioning. In *Proceedings of ACM Cloud Computing*, Indianapolis, IN, 2010.
15. Jan Stoess, Christian Lang, and Frank Bellosa. Energy management for hypervisor-based virtual machines. In *USENIX Annual Technical Conference*, Santa Clara, CA, pages 1–14, 2007.
16. Ying Chen, Li Li, Liang Liu, Hao Wang, and Ying Zhou. Method and apparatus for estimating virtual machine energy consumption, August 28, 2012. US Patent App. 13/596,612.
17. Yungang Bao, Mingyu Chen, Yuan Ruan, Li Liu, Jianping Fan, Qingbo Yuan, Bo Song, and Jianwei Xu. HMTT: A platform independent full-system memory trace monitoring system. *ACM SIGMETRICS Performance Evaluation Review*, 36(1):229–240, 2008.
18. Bhavani Krishnan, Hrishikesh Amur, Ada Gavrilovska, and Karsten Schwan. VM power metering: Feasibility and challenges. *ACM SIGMETRICS Performance Evaluation Review*, 38(3):56–60, 2011.
19. Nakku Kim, Jungwook Cho, and Euiseong Seo. Energy-based accounting and scheduling of virtual machines in a cloud system. In *Proceedings of IEEE GreenCom*, Chengdu, China, 2011.
20. John C. McCullough, Yuvraj Agarwal, Jaideep Chandrashekar, Sathyanarayan Kuppuswamy, Alex C. Snoeren, and Rajesh K. Gupta. Evaluating the effectiveness of model-based power characterization. In *USENIX Annual Technical Conference*, Portland, OR, 2011.
21. Qingwen Chen, Paola Grosso, Karel van der Veldt, Cees de Laat, Rutger Hofman, and Henri Bal. Profiling energy consumption of VMs for green cloud computing. In *Proceedings of IEEE DASC*, Sydney, Australia, 2011.

22. Ramon Bertran, Yolanda Becerra, David Carrera, Vicenc Beltran, Marc Gonzalez, Xavier Martorell, Nacho Navarro, Jordi Torres, and Eduard Ayguade. Energy accounting for shared virtualized environments under DVFs using PMC-based power models. *Future Generation Computer Systems*, 28(2): 457–468, 2012.
23. Ramon Bertran, Yolanda Becerra, David Carrera, Vicenc Beltran, M. Gonzalez Tallada, Xavier Martorell, Jordi Torres, and Eduard Ayguade. Accurate energy accounting for shared virtualized environments using PMC-based power modeling techniques. In *Proceedings of IEEE CCGrid*, Melbourne, Victoria, Australia, 2010.
24. Ata E.H. Bohra and Vipin Chaudhary. Vmeter: Power modelling for virtualized clouds. In *Proceedings of IEEE IPDPSW*, Atlanta, GA, 2010.
25. Daniel Versick, Ingolf Waßmann, and Djamshid Tavangarian. Power consumption estimation of CPU and peripheral components in virtual machines. *ACM SIGAPP Applied Computing Review*, 13(3):17–25, 2013.
26. Ingolf Waßmann, Daniel Versick, and Djamshid Tavangarian. Energy consumption estimation of virtual machines. In *Proceedings of ACM SIGAPP*, Coimbra, Portugal, 2013.
27. Peng Xiao, Zhigang Hu, Dongbo Liu, Guofeng Yan, and Xilong Qu. Virtual machine power measuring technique with bounded error in cloud environments. *Journal of Network and Computer Applications*, 36(2):818–828, 2013.
28. Zhixiong Jiang, Chunyang Lu, Yushan Cai, Zhiying Jiang, and Chongya Ma. Vpower: Metering power consumption of VM. In *Proceedings of IEEE ICSESS*, Beijing, China, 2013.
29. Hailong Yang, Qi Zhao, Zhongzhi Luan, and Depei Qian. Imeter: An integrated VM power model based on performance profiling. *Future Generation Computer Systems*, 36:267–286, 2014.
30. John L. Henning. Spec cpu2006 benchmark descriptions. *ACM SIGARCH Computer Architecture News*, 34(4):1–17, 2006.
31. Unixbench project homepage. http://code.google.com/p/byte-unixbench/. [Online; accessed May 29, 2014].
32. Cho S, Kim Y. Linux BYTEmark Benchmarks: A Performance Comparison of Embedded Mobile Processors[C]. In The 9th International Conference on Advanced Communication Technology. IEEE, Phoenix Park, Korea, 2007.
33. Vishal Aslot and Rudolf Eigenmann. Performance characteristics of the Spec CPU2006 benchmarks. *ACM SIGARCH Computer Architecture News*, 29(5):31–40, 2001.
34. Cachebench: Benchmark for memory sub-system. http://asc.llnl.gov/computing_resources/purple/archive/benchmarks/memory/membench_bm_readme.html. [Online; accessed May 29, 2014].
35. Bonnie++: Filesystem performance benchmark. http://www.coker.com.au/bonnie++/. [Online; accessed May 29, 2014].
36. Don Capps and William Norcott. Iozone filesystem benchmark. http://www.iozone.org. [Online; accessed May 29, 2014].
37. Iometer. http://www.iometer.org. [Online; accessed May 29, 2014].
38. Rick Jones et al. Netperf: A network performance benchmark. Information Networks Division, Hewlett-Packard Company, 1996.
39. NAS parallel benchmark. http://www.nas.nasa.gov. [Online; accessed May 29, 2014].
40. Jack Dongarra and Piotr Luszczek. Linpack benchmark. *Encyclopedia of Parallel Computing*, 1033–1036, 2011.
41. Stressapptest. https://github.com/stressapptest/stressapptest. [Online; accessed May 29, 2014].
42. Asfandyar Qureshi. Power-demand routing in massive geo-distributed systems. PhD thesis, Massachusetts Institute of Technology, 2010.
43. Peter Xiang Gao, Andrew R. Curtis, Bernard Wong, and Srinivasan Keshav. It's not easy being green. *ACM SIGCOMM Computer Communication Review*, 42(4):211–222, 2012.
44. Ruitao Xie, Xiaohua Jia, Kan Yang, and Bo Zhang. Energy saving virtual machine allocation in cloud computing. In *Proceedings of IEEE ICDCSW*. IEEE, Philadelphia, PA, 2013.
45. Shekhar Srikantaiah, Aman Kansal, and Feng Zhao. Energy aware consolidation for cloud computing. In *Proceedings of the Conference on Power Aware Computing and Systems*, San Diego, CA, 2008.
46. Johan Pouwelse, Koen Langendoen, and Henk Sips. Energy priority scheduling for variable voltage processors. In *Proceedings of IEEE ISLPED*, Huntington Beach, CA, 2001.

47. Anshul Gandhi, Mor Harchol-Balter, Rajarshi Das, and Charles Lefurgy. Optimal power allocation in server farms. In *Proceedings of ACM SIGMETRICS*, Seattle, WA, 2009.
48. Minghong Lin, Adam Wierman, Lachlan L.H. Andrew, and Eno Thereska. Dynamic right-sizing for power-proportional data centers. *IEEE/ACM Transactions on Networking (TON)*, 21(5):1378–1391, 2013.
49. Yanwei Zhang, Yefu Wang, and Xiaorui Wang. Greenware: Greening cloud-scale data centers to maximize the use of renewable energy. In *Middleware 2011*. Springer, Lisbon, Portugal, 2011.
50. Zhenhua Liu, Minghong Lin, Adam Wierman, Steven H. Low, and Lachlan L.H. Andrew. Greening geographical load balancing. In *Proceedings of ACM SIGMETRICS Joint International Conference on Measurement and Modeling of Computer Systems*, San Jose, CA, 2011.
51. Michael Brown and Jose Renau. Rerack: Power simulation for data centers with renewable energy generation. *ACM SIGMETRICS Performance Evaluation Review*, 39(3):77–81, 2011.
52. Chao Li, Amer Qouneh, and Tao Li. Characterizing and analyzing renewable energy driven data centers. *ACM SIGMETRICS Performance Evaluation Review*, 39(1):323–324, 2011.
53. Íñigo Goiri, Ryan Beauchea, Kien Le, Thu D. Nguyen, Md E. Haque, Jordi Guitart, Jordi Torres, and Ricardo Bianchini. Greenslot: Scheduling energy consumption in green datacenters. In *Proceedings of ACM SC*, Seattle, WA, 2011.
54. Ínigo Goiri, Kien Le, Thu D. Nguyen, Jordi Guitart, Jordi Torres, and Ricardo Bianchini. Green-Hadoop: Leveraging green energy in data-processing frameworks. In *Proceedings of ACM Eurosys*, Bern, Switzerland, 2012.
55. Gu Chonglin, Liu Chunyan, Zhang Jiangtao, Huang Hejiao, and Xiaohua Jia. Green scheduling for cloud data centers using renewable resources. In *Proceedings of IEEE INFOCOM WKSHPS*, Hong Kong, China, 2015.
56. Yuanxiong Guo, Zongrui Ding, Yuguang Fang, and Dapeng Wu. Cutting down electricity cost in internet data centers by using energy storage. In *Proceedings of IEEE GLOBECOM*, Houston, TX, 2011.
57. Xiaobo Fan, Wolf-Dietrich Weber, and Luiz Andre Barroso. Power provisioning for a warehouse-sized computer. In *ACM SIGARCH Computer Architecture News*, volume 35, pages 13–23. ACM, 2007.
58. Di Wang, Chuangang Ren, Anand Sivasubramaniam, Bhuvan Urgaonkar, and Hosam Fathy. Energy storage in datacenters: What, where, and how much? In *ACM SIGMETRICS Performance Evaluation Review*, volume 40, pages 187–198. ACM, 2012.
59. Windpower program. http://www.wind-power-program.com/index.htm. [Online; accessed July 29, 2014].
60. Jinlei Ding and Rakesh Radhakrishnan. A new method to determine the optimum load of a real solar cell using the Lambert w-function. *Solar Energy Materials and Solar Cells*, 92(12):1566–1569, 2008.
61. Dezso Sera, Remus Teodorescu, and Pedro Rodriguez. PV panel model based on datasheet values. In *Proceedings of IEEE ISIE*, Vigo, Spain, 2007.
62. Wei Deng, Fangming Liu, Hai Jin, Bo Li, and Dan Li. Harnessing renewable energy in cloud datacenters: Opportunities and challenges. *IEEE Network*, 28(1):48–55, 2014.
63. Lei Rao, Xue Liu, Le Xie, and Wenyu Liu. Minimizing electricity cost: Optimization of distributed Internet data centers in a multi-electricity-market environment. In *Proceedings of IEEE INFOCOM*, San Diego, CA, 2010.
64. Wiki dump data. http://dumps.wikimedia.org/other/pagecounts-raw/. [Online; accessed 2014].
65. Measurement and instrumentation data center. http://www.nrel.gov/midc. [Online; accessed 2014].
66. Chonglin Gu, Hejiao Huang and Xiaohua Jia. Green scheduling for cloud data centers using ESDs to store renewable energy. In *Proceedings of IEEE ICC*, Kuala Lumpur, Malaysia, 2016.
67. Chuangang Ren, Di Wang, Bhuvan Urgaonkar, and Anand Sivasubramaniam. Carbon-aware energy capacity planning for datacenters. In *Proceedings of IEEE MASCOTS*, Washington, DC, 2012.
68. Shengbo Chen, Ness B. Shroff, and Pradeep Sinha. Energy trading in the smart grid: From end-user's perspective. In *Proceedings of IEEE Asilomar Conference on Signals, Systems and Computers*, Pacific Grove, CA, 2013.
69. Naouar Yaagoubi and Hussein T. Mouftah. Energy trading in the smart grid: A game theoretic approach. In *Proceedings of IEEE SEGE*, UOIT, Oshawa, Canada, 2015.
70. Chonglin Gu, Lingmin Zhang, Zhixiang He, Hejiao Huang, and Xiaohua Jia. Minimizing energy cost for green cloud data centers by using ESDs. In *Proceedings of IEEE IPCCC*, Nanjing, China, 2015.

3 The Art of In-Memory Computing for Big Data Processing

Mihaela-Andreea Vasile and Florin Pop

CONTENTS

ABSTRACT

Multiple applications from various domains, scientific or enterprise applications, generate huge amounts of data that have to be processed at real-time speed or acquired, cleaned, stored, and ready to be used. Examples of such big data sources could be airplane sensor monitoring to predict future engine crashes and avoid disaster (big data analytics) or a big data platform for modern healthcare. In the context of big data processing challenges, the in-memory computing paradigm has emerged and it is currently used by several big data platforms for data storage/query (in-memory data grids or databases) and for data processing (in-memory computing grids).

3.1 INTRODUCTION

Big data refers to data sets that cannot be managed, processed, or stored by traditional hardware/software solutions within a tolerable time interval due to various characteristics: very large dimensions of the set, the speed of producing the data, and the data may be structured or unstructured. We can find multiple examples of applications that generate such large data sets. The Montage general engine that computes the mosaic of input images and displays the northern part of the Milky Way in visible light has a database that contains more than 2 million images with a size of around 2 TB. When using Facebook, users may upload photos, share pages, or post comments. In a smart city, the real-time processing becomes the main issue for big data analytics [1].

Multiple solutions for processing big-data-scale data sets have been developed. The MapReduce framework introduces a programming model that is implemented and used successfully in different systems. We can identify some shortcomings for the MapReduce model like the overhead when starting a job and that it is not suited for real-time or interactive jobs. Therefore, solutions that add real-time capabilities or stream processing of big data appeared: in-memory computing (IMC), real-time queries for big data, or stream processing frameworks. The main idea for IMC is that the data is kept in a distributed main memory ready to be processed.

The chapter is organized as follows. Section 3.2 aims to provide a general context for IMC, including the motivation, general patterns, and evolution of this paradigm, together with its applicability for real-time big data processing. Section 3.3 analyzes the existing solutions for batch/streaming real-time processing considering also hybrid solutions. It describes traditional programming models and architectures and hybrid approaches suited for big data applications. Section 3.4 focuses on existing models and solutions of IMC. We also identify real applications of this paradigm and possible improvements in the context of big data processing. Section 3.5 focuses on technology survey and considers existing platforms and tools such as Spark, Spark Streaming, Main Memory MapReduce (M3R), Amazon Kinesis, Flink, etc. We compare the capabilities of these technologies and applicability in real-life use cases. Finally, Section 3.6 describes the main big data platforms, focusing on HPC, Cloud, and Datacenters from real-time processing perspective. The platforms may be open source or proprietary, and custom made for certain applications or general-use platforms.

3.2 GENERAL CONTEXT

3.2.1 Big Data

The big data concept has emerged rapidly in the last years and has been defined or characterized in different ways. We can state that big data refers to data sets that cannot be managed, processed, or stored by traditional hardware/software solutions. Some of the challenges in managing the data are the very large dimensions of the set and the fact that data is produced continuously or that the data should be cleaned before use to remove noise or outliers for the analysis [2]. Another characterization of big data is done using a multiple V's model [3]; some of these V's are as follows:

- *Volume*: The dimension of the data.
- *Variety*: Structured (well-defined data model)/unstructured (data model not defined)/semi-structured (not strict data model) or mixed (various types) data depending on the source that generates it: sensors gathering surrounding conditions, retailers that store all transactions for advanced analysis, genome analysis, and so on.
- *Velocity*: Data is generated and processed at different speeds: near-real-time manner (at small time intervals), real-time (continuous data), or streams of data.
- *Veracity*: "Clean" the data to remove noise or abnormality.
- *Value*: Big data can be used for multiple goals: reporting of business processes or transactions, churn analysis (why does user engagement drop?), diagnosing system failures, and also making different decisions.

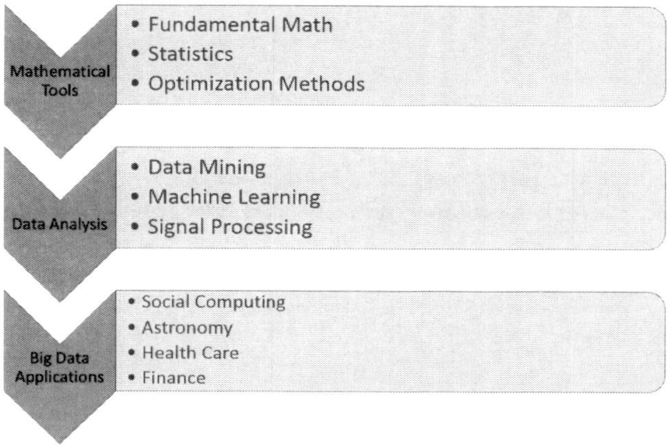

FIGURE 3.1 Big data analytics process.

- *Volatility*: The data should be stored for different amounts of time depending on its validity or importance.

As the big data sources increase and big data analysis is required in multiple domains, it is required intensive research to build solutions for efficiently acquiring data (this includes some preprocessing and data cleaning), storing it or processing it for big data analytics applications (Figure 3.1) to extract valuable information.

Big data analytics examples may be found in multiple domains. In e-commerce or retail industries, sentiment analysis, segmentation, or clustering techniques are frequently used based on user logs/searches and recent user transactions, so that the customers receive targeted and personalized recommendations and increase customer satisfaction [4]. Improved healthcare quality may be obtained using genomics and sequence analysis where the big data processing and analysis in a timely manner has a huge impact [5,6]. The Montage general engine [7] computes the mosaic of astronomical input images generated by projects such as IPHAS (INT Photometric Hα Survey of the Northern Galactic Plane) [8] that displays the northern part of the Milky Way in visible light. In this case, the database contains more than 2 million images with a size of around 2 TB.

The concept of many-task computing (MTC) has been introduced in [9] and was subject to extensive research. It has been defined as a combination of high-performance computing (HPC) and high-throughput computing (HTC) and it refers to applications that require the interaction with large data sets and generate a very large number of various tasks: independent/flows, small/large, and computational/data intensive. MTC may be classified using the number of tasks and the data sets size: big data (very large data sets and very high number of tasks), MapReduce (very large data sets and relatively reduced number of tasks), or HTC (smaller data sets and very high number of tasks). So, the big data may be considered as a data-intensive subset of MTC.

3.2.2 Big Data Management

The major challenges when thinking at the big data concept are acquiring, storing, processing, and querying the data. Multiple paradigms and solutions have been developed for efficiently processing big data that have to take into account the different characteristics of the data sets for which they are being used, like the data variety or the speed of producing data [10].

The Lambda architecture [11] proposes the decomposition of the big data processing problem into three layers: batch, serving, and speed layers.

- *Batch layer*: Stores the master data and computes primitive functions on any subset of the data. A representative example for the batch layer is the Hadoop stack.
- *Serving layer*: Randomly accesses the batch views/results of the batch layer, indexes the views, loads them, and performs queries on the data in the batch views.
- *Speed layer*: Reduces the latency of the previous two layers, by accessing the most recent data and updates the real-time view based on the new data, it does not recompute on the entire data set. Real-time/streaming systems implement the speed layer.

The MapReduce framework is an important solution for big data management, built for processing very large data sets in a distributed environment using commodity hardware. It uses a map function on the input and combines the intermediate results using a reduce function. The Apache implementation of the MapReduce framework relies on the Hadoop Distributed File System (HDFS) and a distributed database, HTable. Although it is highly used, MapReduce requires jobs that have all the data available at once so that it may not be used for applications that require real-time processing or streaming-like applications. Multiple extensions have been developed to add capabilities to this framework [3]: Twister/HaLoop/Tez allow iterative, recursive, and batch jobs. On the other hand, totally different paradigms and solutions have emerged to provide support for real-time big data processing or for handling stream processing.

Real-time processing solutions try to reduce the MapReduce overhead—IMC—or optimize real-time queries over a variety of big data types [12]. A cloud-based real-time system is AWS Kinesis, a system for real-time processing of streaming data that can acquire data from multiple sources. The processing of big data streams is also important, as the stream data pattern is very common. Spark (IMC framework implementation) may be used to process streams by converting the data streams into multiple batch jobs, but it is not suited for a real stream application. Storm is an example of actual streaming solution.

3.2.2.1 In-Memory Computing

The main idea for IMC is to keep data in a distributed main memory near to the application code, ready to be processed. This approach appeared over 20 years ago, but the main memory was very expensive, and also there was no motivation to implement an IMC framework. The drop in RAM costs and increasing need for real-time processing of big-data represented an incentive for this model to be developed [13]. In [6], the authors describe an in-memory cloud-based platform for real-time genome analysis. The data is stored in an in-memory database (IMDB), and the processing is performed in the platform layer, a distributed IMDB system.

In-memory storage and query solutions are IMDBs and in-memory data grids (IMDGs). IMDBs move the data to be queried in the main memory. There are native IMDBs (HANA or Altibase) or traditional databases with in-memory extensions (Oracle). For IMDGs, the data may be processed in a distributed system of commodity servers, using the MapReduce framework. An important point is the difference between IMC and IMDBs and IMDGs. IMC is a paradigm that deals with computing too and takes into account scheduling tasks and deciding whether to move the data near the code or the code near the data, in contrast to the data solutions that deal only with data. In-memory data solutions can be used as building blocks for an IMC solution.

3.3 BATCH/STREAMING REAL-TIME PROCESSING

3.3.1 Batch Processing for Big Data

Batch processing of big data assumes handling large volumes of data in batches, at regular intervals [14]. The most important generic implementation for batch-processing is Apache Hadoop and MapReduce. A number of other solutions have been built on top of Hadoop for specialized purposes: data mining or machine learning. Though batch solutions are widely used, they are not suited for real-time processing (Figure 3.2).

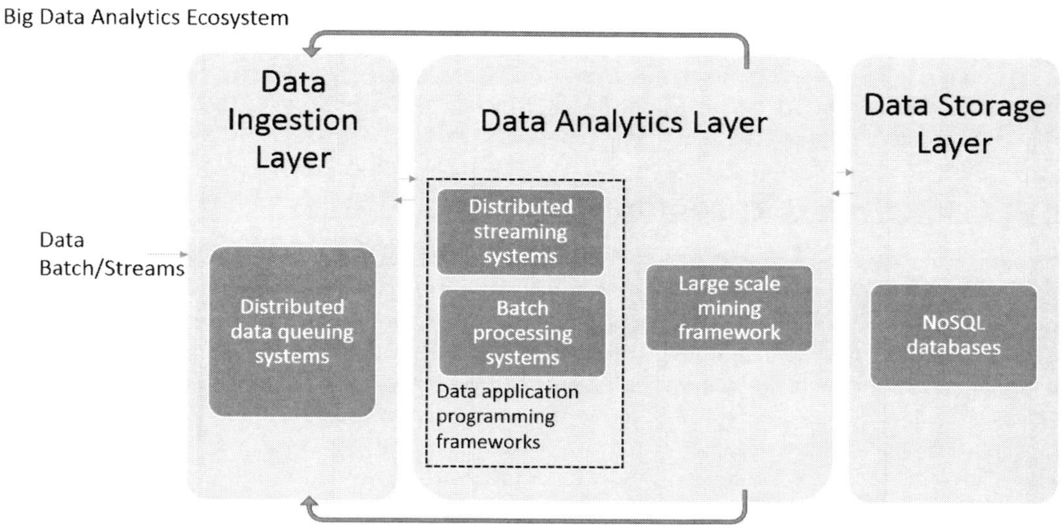

FIGURE 3.2 Big data task types.

3.3.1.1 Apache Hadoop and MapReduce

The Apache Hadoop [15] platform is the most important solution for big data batch processing using a cluster of commodity machines. It relies on HDFS as a distributed file system and MapReduce as a parallel programming model and a number of additional projects, available as services that may be installed in a Hadoop cluster (Hive, Pig, Mahout). Hadoop represents a reliable framework and it is a complete ecosystem (a wide range of services available for building a landscape).

The MapReduce [16] model may be formally described as follows: the input is split into small tasks of type (key, value) and is distributed along the system to the workers, and a mathematical function is used to process the input (map stage). The result of the map stage is shuffled across the system using the key, and a reduce function is used to combine the intermediate results. This model might be used for extracting data and producing reports or extracting properties of Web pages for localized search. In the case of large machine-learning problems, with iterative and recursive processes, MapReduce is not efficient, due to the overhead for starting a MapReduce job.

3.3.1.2 Apache Mahout

Apache Mahout is a library for building scalable data mining and machine-learning applications. Mahout provides multiple machine-learning algorithms implementations. It runs over Hadoop using MapReduce. Its main design goals are the efficient processing, the ease of use, or the fact that it might be easily integrated with different data stores and extended. It has been used in multiple applications requiring machine-learning implementations such as clustering Wikipedia's articles [17], collaborative filtering [18], or in bioinformatics (also the clustering algorithms are used in this case).

3.3.1.3 Dryad

The Dryad parallel computing model [19] allows building applications that scale well in clusters of different sizes. The framework is based on dataflow graph execution, where the vertices are the computational elements and the edges are the communication channels. One of the main purposes was the ease of writing programs using this framework. The developer does not take care of concurrency issues in parallel programming, but instead, he or she has to write several sequential programs (the "vertices") and connect them using one-way edges (the dataflow graph is a directed acyclic graph).

A Dryad job is coordinated by a job manager (JM). The JM is responsible to generate the job's communication graph for each application, so it contains application-specific code. It also takes care of scheduling the work across the available resources. The data is sent directly between nodes and does not get through the JM, which is just a decision maker and does not mediate the communication. The graph is built using a simple language composed of procedure calls, as a C++ library.

3.3.2 Big Data Streaming Processing

The stream processing pattern refers to processing input data without storing it completely: online machine learning, real-time analytics, process logs streams, or streams of different events [20]. The traditional batching systems could be enhanced toward a microbenchmarking-like processing, but there is a need for native stream processing systems. MapReduce might be enhanced to group the incoming stream into small batches. The authors of [21] proposed a prototype for online Hadoop suited for online/pipeline aggregations. For computations that require a single MapReduce job, the map and reduce phases are completely decoupled; the reduce step does not pull the map result any more, but rather the map worker will push its output into the reduce phase. For multijob online computations, storing the intermediate reduce results in HDFS will be skipped; instead, the result will be pushed into the next map phase.

A streaming processing solution based on Spark is Spark Streaming and it implements the D-Streams [22] processing model (discretized streams). The streaming computation consists in a series of deterministic batch computations for small time intervals without the need of synchronization. To address the latency challenge, the data structure of resilient distributed data sets (RDDs) is used for keeping the data in memory. Based on the determinism of the state of each batch computation, the fact that no replication or synchronization is used, a parallel recovery mechanism is triggered when a node is lost and its RDDs are recomputed by each node in the cluster [23].

3.3.2.1 Apache Storm

Storm is a reliable, fault-tolerant computation system for processing real-time data streams. It is highly used, thanks to the performances of the system (good scaling, work balancing, reliability) and the multilang feature that allows the use of multiple programming languages such as Java, Scala, or Python. Storm is used for stream aggregation and processing at Yahoo, Twitter, or Spotify [24]. Streamparse [25] is a Python library that provides an integration of Python and Storm and might be used as a starting point for Python projects that require the Storm processing model.

Storm uses a simple abstraction of the stream computing problem (Figure 3.3). The concepts that are used are *Tuples*—the data "unit," the basic component of a *Stream*. A *Spout* generates raw streams of data and sends them to *Bolts* based on different criteria such as grouping using a hash function. Bolts apply different functions such as aggregation, filtering, or custom functions on the input streams and might have as output other streams that are sent to other components. A *Topology* wires the spouts and bolts together.

The Storm architecture [20] is quite similar to Hadoop's and consists of one Nimbus master node and multiple worker nodes (a few ZooKeeper nodes and multiple Supervisor nodes). The Storm topology (an executable program) is deployed on the master node. The Nimbus node deals with the control, runs the scheduling, and sends the workers assignment to the ZooKeeper nodes. The latest ones contact the Supervisors to send the assignment information. Finally, the Supervisors launch the Workers that download the topology from the Nimbus, based on the assignment information. The workers implement the actual Storm topology.

3.3.2.2 Apache S4

Apache S4 (Simple Scalable Streaming System) [26] is a general distributed engine for processing streams. It relies on a decentralized cluster of commodity hardware: all the nodes are processing elements (PEs) that perform computations, and the interaction between PEs consists in input/output

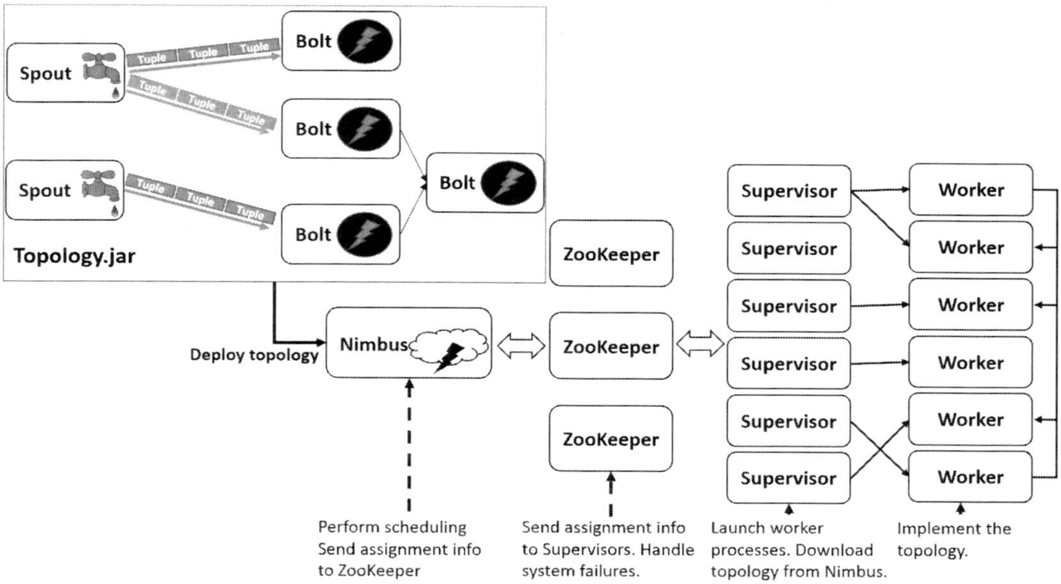

FIGURE 3.3 Storm basic concepts.

data streams that are consumed/emitted. The cluster management is handled using the ZooKeeper service, the data events can be routed to the appropriate PE, and PE instances may be created/removed when needed.

S4 provides a simple programming interface. The core code is written in Java and it was designed as a modular, pluggable, generic architecture that allows customizations as new modules, so developers may easily write and deploy applications as S4 jobs modules. It was initially released by Yahoo! before becoming an Apache project, so it has been tested in real-life systems for processing search queries, and has proven good performances.

3.3.2.3 Apache Flink

Apache Flink [27,28] is an open-source big data platform for distributed environments, developed since 2009 (in a research group) and became part of the Apache incubator in 2014. It provides a streaming dataflow engine that handles data distribution and communication in the cluster, fault tolerance, and scalability. It includes APIs and components for both streaming and batch processing and libraries for machine learning or complex events processing.

Flink uses the same runtime for batch and streaming applications and it manages the JVM memory itself avoiding expensive garbage collector operations. Flink optimizes iterative jobs (like machine-learning applications) and batch programs (it caches intermediary data to avoid expensive operations like shuffle or sort). Flink may be integrated with a wide range of other projects: HDFS, Kafka, or Yarn.

3.3.2.4 Splunk

Splunk [29] is a real-time, scalable, and versatile platform for IoT big data. It gathers the data streams from different sources such as sensors, network, applications, or end users and allows users to search, monitor, and analyze it via a Web interface. Splunk offers a large number of products suited for different users: Splunk Enterprise, Splunk Cloud (Splunk Storm is a cloud version), a lightweight service, or a platform for a Hadoop cluster, HUNK. A stand-alone application is Splunk App for Stream: it collects streaming application performance data from the network and makes it available for analysis in the Splunk platform.

Data processing in Splunk has some major phases. The data is acquired in the input segment as a stream from the source; some metadata is added without analyzing the data. Next, it goes in the parsing segment, when the stream is divided into events based on the contents and some more information is added to the metadata. The data is then indexed, so the data from diverse sources is combined into centralized indexes and may be searched quickly.

3.4 IN-MEMORY COMPUTING

IMC may be defined as a solution that stores data in RAM, across a distributed system (cluster, cloud), and processes it in parallel [30]. The key idea for IMC systems is that the RAM should be the primary storage for the code and the data the code works with. At some point, the data might not fit into the RAM anymore. In this case, the IMC systems should handle the mechanisms to place the data in a second storage.

In the traditional computing paradigm, the application code resides in the main memory and the required application data is brought from the hard disk into the main memory. If we keep the data in a distributed main memory ready to be processed, we avoid the latency introduced by the communication with the hard disk. So far, the main memory was very expensive, so the amount of data kept in the RAM was limited. Also, before the big data notion, there was no motivation to implement an IMC framework. The drop in RAM costs and increasing need for real-time processing of big data represented an incentive for this model to be developed. Some of the use cases for IMC are the same as the applications that generate big data sets: medical imaging processing, natural language processing, real-time sentiment analysis, or real-time machine learning. There is a demand for computation nodes with a very large main memory. Amazon has announced new X1 virtual machines of physical servers carrying up to 2 TB of RAM [31] for demanding applications or IMDBs.

IMC is a complex paradigm and it does not refer to only IMDB systems. The remaining of this section will cover IMC notions: in-memory cache systems, IMDGs, IMDBs, and in-memory processing systems or computing grids [13].

Caching has an important role for I/O optimizations because frequently accessed data is kept in the process memory (hence, *in-memory caching*) and it also optimizes the CPU workload by keeping intermediate results without recomputing. The cache systems are generally distributed in-memory key–value stores with put/get operations and may access the second storage via read/write functionality. Other features depend on the actual implementation like policies to evict the data or ACID transactions. Lately, the distributed caching has been disappearing, as the IMDGs or IMDBs have taken over the caching challenges.

The basic idea for *IMDBs* is that the data is kept in the main memory and the disk is used for backups, logs, and "cold" data that does not fit in the RAM. Relational databases have been developed and enhanced since 1970s, the data is organized into tables and relations, and ACID properties are guaranteed. In-memory relational databases have been studied since the 1980s, but they have appeared in the last decade, thanks to hardware advances. Some examples of relational IMDBs are SAP HANA or H-Store. Relational IMDBs pay attention also to how tables are stored in the memory (in the case of SAP HANA, the data in tables may be stored column-wise) and data partitioning. In NoSQL databases, the data may be stored as key–values, trees, or graphs. Several NoSQL IMDBs have appeared: MongoDB (document store), RAMCloud (in-memory key–value store), or Trinity (in-memory distributed graph database).

The *IMDGs* (Figure 3.4a) are also key–value stores distributed in a cluster, which have to take care of data high availability (they relay on a caching mechanism and take over the responsibility of in-memory caching systems). Data grids have additional features compared to the cache systems. The basic features of IMDGs include data partitioning across the nodes and transactional ACID support. Then, we can refer to a support for co-location of computations and data in IMDGs, meaning that the computation code should be moved near the data that is stored in the main memory of the nodes in the cluster. Data is moved only when nodes appear/are lost and the data has to be repartitioned.

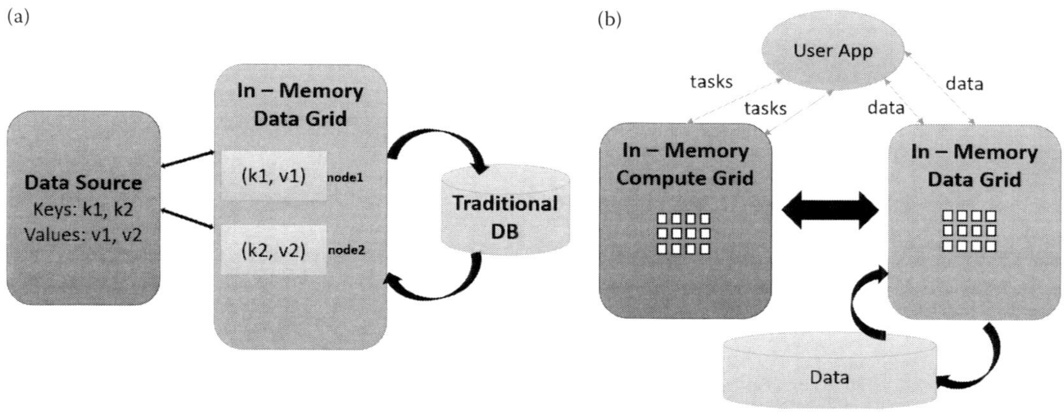

FIGURE 3.4 (a) In-memory data grid; (b) Ignite IMDG and IMC.

Massively parallel processing (MPP) is another important characteristic of IMDGs with support for SQL and/or MapReduce, which optimizes data computations across the cluster and may respond to complex data processing. The design of IMDGs allows them to scale up really well with the cluster size because they are native scalable as opposite to IMDBs.

If a user wants to upgrade the infrastructure to use the speed of IMC, there would be two options. A first possibility would be to use an IMDG that relies on an existing database (IMDGs are highly integrated with database systems) and make some changes to the application to take advantage of the new MPP, MapReduce, or other IMDG features. The other option to use an IMDB would require replacing the existing database (unless it already has an in-memory option), but the application code will not demand significant changes.

In-memory processing systems are focused on efficiently executing algorithms/code on the same set of computers in the grid, meaning that it has a main target to schedule the computations across the data stored in the cluster. IMC systems have to take care of other additional aspects: deployment of the code, resource management, distributed execution model (MapReduce, MPI, Stream Processing), or distributed execution services (taking care of reliability, load balancing fault recovery). We can distinguish between two types of in-memory processing systems: for data analytics (mainly batch systems), Spark or Grid-Gain; and solutions for real-time processing (stream processing), Storm, Yahoo! S4, Spark-Streaming, or XAP.

3.5 TECHNOLOGY SURVEY

In this section, we will take a closer look at two important IMC systems: Spark and M3R. The traditional solutions for big data management were described in Section 3.2.

3.5.1 Spark

Spark system [32] uses a data abstraction for big data called RDD. RDDs are deterministic, read-only (immutable) partitioned set of records. Every action or transformation on an RDD creates a new RDD, so an RDD can be created only via a deterministic sequence of transformations. RDDs have the following properties: an user can explicitly cache working sets for speedups, locality-aware scheduling, and fault tolerance.

Spark uses a persistence model that decides whether to persist the RDD in memory, on disk, or both. When persisting the RDD in memory, other subsequent applications that need to read the RDD

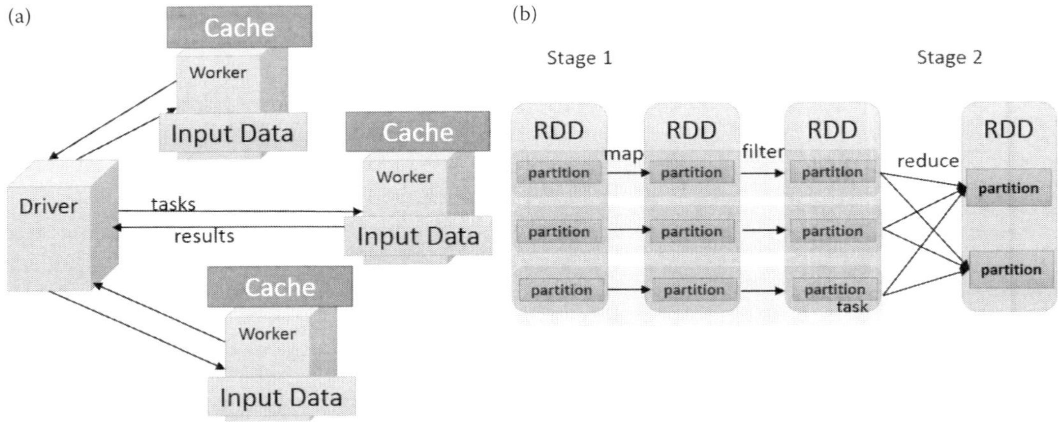

FIGURE 3.5 (a) Spark runtime; (b) Spark scheduler.

have it available in the main memory. The lightweight fault recovery mechanism relies on the fact that an RDD has the information on how it was derived from other RDDs (lineage).

In Figure 3.5a [13,32], the main runtime flow of a Spark job is described. A driver is launched to start the job. It starts multiple workers, defines one or more RDDs, and invokes the required actions on them. The workers can read the RDD from a distributed file system and can cache the RDD partitions.

3.5.2 Main Memory MapReduce

M3R [33] is a new implementation of the MapReduce framework and uses the IMC paradigm. The M3R engine follows the traditional MapReduce batch-processing model and implements the MapReduce API, so it has backwards compatibility and it can run existing Hadoop jobs or jobs generated by higher level services from the Hadoop Stack (Pig or SystemML).

M3R implements in-memory execution and stores key–value sequences in the heap. There is no resilience assured; if a node fails, then no recovery is possible. The improvements compared to the traditional MapReduce engine are as follows:

- The input/output is cached in the in-memory key–value store so that the output is not persisted and subsequent jobs will get their input directly from the main memory.
- The shuffle phase overhead is reduced by the following features: *co-location*—the M3R engine takes care of the case when a mapper has to send data to a reducer in the same JVM and avoid network or I/O involvement; *partition stability*—the partitioning of keys across the reducers is deterministic, and in the case of an iterative job, the mapper associated with a certain key will be assigned to the same place so that the key will be locally shuffled; *de-duplication*—do not send a copy of the map output to each reducer but to each reducer location.

3.6 BIG DATA PLATFORMS: HPC, CLOUD, AND DATACENTERS

3.6.1 Apache Ignite

Apache Ignite [34] is an in-memory data fabric that combines different components such as IMDG, IMC grid, and in-memory streaming into the same unique solution. Ignite is a general purpose platform for IMC that applies to a broad range of use cases, thanks to its multiple components: HPC,

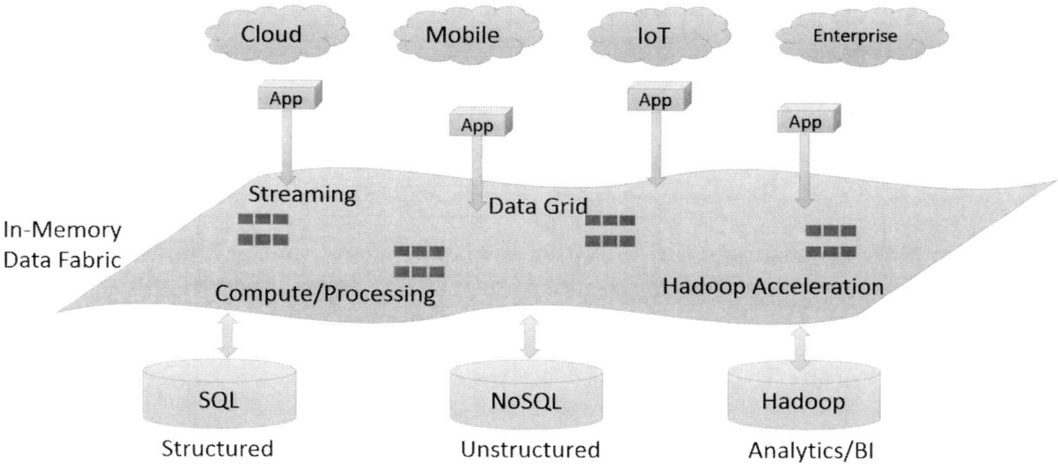

FIGURE 3.6 Apache Ignite overview.

data grid, service grid, or streaming applications. Apache Ignite works with multiple underlying data stores for structured (SQL), unstructured (NoSQL), or semistructured (Hadoop), and it offers real-time, interactive queries over the data layer. It also provides a unified API that allows integration with cloud IoT or enterprise applications.

From an architectural point of view, Apache Ignite is a middle ware software based on JVM for a decentralized homogeneous cluster (Figure 3.6). It relies on a service provider interface (SPI) design: each component is modular and pluggable so that the system is highly configurable and can be adapted for different infrastructures.

The Ignite *IMDG* uses the main memory as primary storage and offers distributed cache as a key–value store. Compared to Spark, Ignite provides SQL in-memory indexing, which speeds up the SQL queries 100 times faster than in the case of native Spark RDDs. Another important feature consists in the distributed SQL joins or cross-cache joins.

The Ignite *in-memory compute grid* provides a simple API for writing distributed computations or data processing in the cluster such as CPU-intensive applications or resource-intensive tasks (HPC or MPP). The important features of the in-memory compute grid that are implemented include different parallel processing paradigms such as in-memory fork-join or in-memory map-reduce engine implementation or fault tolerance. It also allows the collocation of code with data either automatically or manually (configured by the user/developer) as needed. The scheduler balances load distribution of the jobs and a default scheduling policy is applied, but the scheduling may be customized in the code [34]. Check-pointing allows saving the state of a job suited for long-running jobs.

Another important component is the *Hadoop Accelerator*, a module that allows in-memory Hadoop jobs execution and file system operations. The accelerator contains an implementation of an in-memory file system (IGFS), compatible with HDFS, which stores file system data in the main memory and optimizes I/O latency. It provides an in-memory MapReduce implementation that reduces some overhead from the traditional Hadoop architecture (name node, task trackers) and offers performance boosts for CPU-intensive tasks with only small changes in the application due to faster scheduling process and data-locality-aware nodes (the name node was the only responsible for the data location).

In-memory streaming support addresses a broad variety of big data applications that cannot be efficiently executed by traditional systems. It allows to process infinite streams of data that may arrive at different rates (even millions of events per second) in scalable and fault-tolerant fashion. It relies on the data grid for data locality. The streams are partitioned between the nodes and processed in sliding windows. Continuous queries may be registered for the changing data. It integrates with multiple solutions that acquire streams of data and consumes the streams into the Ignite cache: Apache Flume Sink, Apache Kafka, or Apache Camel Streamer.

3.6.2 SAP HANA

In the case of SAP, the IMC paradigm has a long history, and SAP technologies have evolved in the process of adopting the in-memory approach [35]. SAP TREX is a search engine for structured data (search and aggregate business data) or unstructured data (search and classify a large number of documents). TREX loads indexes into working memories because data compression is used, so large volumes of data may be processed entirely in memory. Next, SAP live Cache technology is a hybrid database: it is based on SAP MaxDB, a traditional relational database and combines in-memory data storage and object-oriented database technologies. SAP NetWeaver Business Warehouse Accelerator specializes on speeding reporting queries and SAP BusinessObjects Explorer Accelerated extends BW Accelerator, with a front end to navigate through the data in the BW Accelerator. SAP HANA is an IMDB that combined features from the previous in-memory solutions with research results from Hasso Plattner Institute (HPI) [36].

So, SAP HANA is the central element in SAP data management platform: an IMDB with the purpose of providing a generic and powerful system for large data analysis and aggregation [37]. It uses very large amounts of main memory, multicore CPUs on multiple nodes in a cluster, and SDD storage, to improve the performance. The main characteristics of SAP HANA that contribute to its goal are the following:

- Multiquery engine processing environment: offers support for structured, unstructured, or semistructured data. It allows joins on semistructured data. It uses a graph engine to run different algorithms (planning, supply chain), a text engine for unstructured data and a relational engine for structured data.
- Register semantic data structures and also business logic in the data management system (not the application layer).
- Use hardware advances: storage devices, large number of nodes and many cores per node, cluster configuration.
- Communicate with the application layer in an efficient way, when talking about SAP proprietary applications (using shared memory).

The SAP HANA application is suitable for multiple use cases. In [38], we can find the major areas for SAP HANA: real-time replication of data for BI analytics, using table replication for improving the speed of programs and reports from the SAP ERP system, as a replacement for BW, as a substitute for SAP ERP.

Some applications of HANA in big data, optimizing business operations, or real-time operational intelligence use cases are presented in [39]. HANA is suited for big data use cases for the following reasons: it may acquire data using real-time gathering systems (like event stream processing), use predictive analytics or data science to get data insights, and develop applications using integrated platform tools. An example of use case is managing energy resources: monitor loads (find peak loads) or guide the wise use of energy.

3.6.3 XAP

GigaSpaces eXtreme Application Platform (XAP) [40] is a platform built to scale applications in high-performance low-latency landscape, while the data volume, number of transactions, or number of user connections increase. The use cases for XAP include extreme transactional applications, such as trading or market data, and real-time analytics applications, such as air travel management (customer case—XAP for stream processing and real-time analytics).

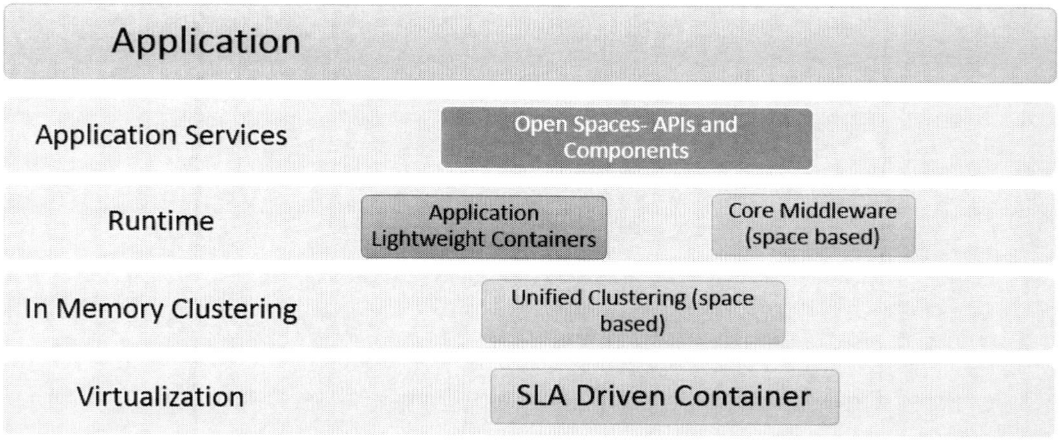

FIGURE 3.7 XAP components.

The main components of GigaSpaces XAP are represented in Figure 3.7:

- *OpenSpaces* is a Spring-based framework used to develop applications in GigaSpaces, and XAP uses a Space-Based Architecture (SBA) as a main design pattern. The *Space* is an in-memory service that contains entries of information and might be accessed using four operations: write, read, take, and notify. Space is a logical concept/interface that defines a memory location and represents the basic building block for XAP. An abstraction at the OpenSpaces layer is the Processing Unit; it encapsulates the middleware and the business logic in a single unit.
- Core Middleware uses the same space-based model that exposes both JavaSpaces API and other standard APIs such as JCache or JDBC. At this layer, the IMDG provides data caching and distributed state sharing.
- SLA-Driven Containers, lightweight containers—Java processes, are used to deploy Processing Units in a dynamic environment and they rely on SLA definitions. The main purpose of the container is to virtualize the underlying compute resources. These containers may be used to deploy also IMDGs within a Processing Unit and might relocate IMDGs instances depending on memory utilization and SLA.

As a short summary, the main features of XAP include that a single platform is able to run various applications and all tiers are included in a single container. Next, the data access is fast because all data is stored in-memory. Also, XAP provides high availability using in-memory backup for each container. The scaling for the applications may be automatically or on demand.

3.7 CONCLUSIONS

The big-data-scale data sets rise new challenges in terms of data management: acquiring, validation, storing, and processing to obtain meaningful results. The hardware evolution allowed the old IMC idea to be implemented as a paradigm in current systems and it is successfully used in big data platforms. In this chapter, we analyzed the evolution of the in-memory paradigm, emergence of IMC frameworks and platforms for big data scenarios, and the benefits of using IMC-based systems for real big data problems.

REFERENCES

1. Ciprian Barbieru and Florin Pop. Soft real-time Hadoop scheduler for big data processing in smart cities. In *2016 IEEE 30th International Conference on Advanced Information Networking and Applications (AINA)*, pp. 863–870. IEEE, 2016.
2. Min Chen, Shiwen Mao, and Yunhao Liu. Big data: A survey. *Mobile Networks and Applications*, 19(2):171–209, 2014.
3. Marcos D Assunção, Rodrigo N Calheiros, Silvia Bianchi, Marco AS Netto, and Rajkumar Buyya. Big data computing and clouds: Trends and future directions. *Journal of Parallel and Distributed Computing*, 79:3–15, 2015.
4. Hsinchun Chen, Roger HL Chiang, and Veda C Storey. Business intelligence and analytics: From big data to big impact. *MIS Quarterly*, 36(4):1165–1188, 2012.
5. Aisling ODriscoll, Jurate Daugelaite, and Roy D Sleator. Big data, Hadoop and cloud computing in genomics. *Journal of Biomedical Informatics*, 46(5):774–781, 2013.
6. Matthieu-P. Schapranow, Franziska Häger, and Hasso Plattner. High-performance in-memory genome project: A platform for integrated real-time genome data analysis. In *Proceedings of the 2nd International Conference on Global Health Challenges*, pp. 5–10, 2013.
7. Ewa Deelman, Gurmeet Singh, Miron Livny, Bruce Berriman, and John Good. The cost of doing science on the cloud: The montage example. In *Proceedings of the 2008 ACM/IEEE Conference on Supercomputing*, p. 50. IEEE Press, 2008.
8. Janet E Drew et al. The INT Photometric Hα Survey of the Northern Galactic Plane (IPHAS). *Monthly Notices of the Royal Astronomical Society*, 362(3):753–776, 2005.
9. Ioan Raicu, Ian T Foster, and Yong Zhao. Many-task computing for grids and supercomputers. In *Workshop on Many-Task Computing on Grids and Supercomputers, 2008 (MTAGS 2008)*, pp. 1–11. IEEE, 2008.
10. Florin Stancu, Dan Popa, Loredana-Marsilia Groza, and Florin Pop. Queuing-based processing platform for service delivery in big data environments. In *International Conference on Exploring Services Science*, pp. 497–508. Springer, 2016.
11. Nathan Marz and James Warren. *Big Data: Principles and Best Practices of Scalable Realtime Data Systems*. Manning Publications Co., 2015.
12. Saeed Shahrivari. Beyond batch processing: Towards real-time and streaming big data. *Computers*, 3(4):117–129, 2014.
13. Hao Zhang, Gang Chen, Beng Chin Ooi, Kian-Lee Tan, and Meihui Zhang. In-memory big data management and processing: A survey. *IEEE Transactions on Knowledge and Data Engineering*, 27(7):1920–1948, 2015.
14. CL Philip Chen and Chun-Yang Zhang. Data-intensive applications, challenges, techniques and technologies: A survey on big data. *Information Sciences*, 275:314–347, 2014.
15. Milind Bhandarkar. MapReduce programming with Apache Hadoop. In *2010 IEEE International Symposium on Parallel & Distributed Processing (IPDPS)*, pp. 1–10. IEEE, 2010.
16. Caesar Wu, Rajkumar Buyya, and Kotagiri Ramamohanarao. Big data analytics = machine learning + cloud computing. *arXiv preprint arXiv:1601.03115*, 2016.
17. Chunming Rong et al. Using Mahout for clustering Wikipedia's latest articles: A comparison between k-means and fuzzy c-means in the cloud. In *2011 IEEE Third International Conference on Cloud Computing Technology and Science (CloudCom)*, pp. 565–569. IEEE, 2011.
18. Sebastian Schelter and Sean Owen. Collaborative filtering with Apache Mahout. *Proceedings of ACM RecSys Challenge*, Dublin, Ireland, 2012.
19. Michael Isard, Mihai Budiu, Yuan Yu, Andrew Birrell, and Dennis Fetterly. Dryad: Distributed data-parallel programs from sequential building blocks. In *ACM SIGOPS Operating Systems Review*, Vol. 41, pp. 59–72. ACM, 2007.
20. Rajiv Ranjan. Streaming big data processing in datacenter clouds. *IEEE Cloud Computing*, 1(1):78–83, 2014.
21. Tyson Condie, Neil Conway, Peter Alvaro, Joseph M Hellerstein, Khaled Elmeleegy, and Russell Sears. MapReduce online. In *NSDI*, Vol. 10, p. 20, Berkeley, USA, 2010.
22. Matei Zaharia, Tathagata Das, Haoyuan Li, Timothy Hunter, Scott Shenker, and Ion Stoica. Discretized streams: Fault-tolerant streaming computation at scale. In *Proceedings of the Twenty-Fourth ACM Symposium on Operating Systems Principles*, pp. 423–438. ACM, 2013.

23. Mihaela-Andreea Vasile, Florin Pop, Radu-Ioan Tutueanu, Valentin Cristea, and Joanna KoϒodziejResource-aware hybrid scheduling algorithm in heterogeneous distributed computing. *Future Generation Computer Systems*, 51:61–71, 2015.
24. Apache storm: Talks and slideshows. `http://storm.apache.org/talksAndVideos.html`. Accessed: June 2, 2016.
25. Rosa Filguiera, Amrey Krause, Malcolm Atkinson, Iraklis Klampanos, and Alexander Moreno. dispel4py: A python framework for data-intensive scientific computing. *International Journal of High Performance Computing Applications*, 2016. http://journals.sagepub.com/doi/abs/10.1177/1094342016649766.
26. Leonardo Neumeyer, Bruce Robbins, Anish Nair, and Anand Kesari. S4: Distributed stream computing platform. In *2010 IEEE International Conference on Data Mining Workshops*, pp. 170–177. IEEE, 2010.
27. The Flink big data platform. `http://www.slideshare.net/GyulaFra/flink-apachecon`. Accessed: June 29, 2016.
28. Kevin Jacobs and Kacper Surdy. Apache Flink: Distributed stream data processing. Technical Report, 2016.
29. David Carasso. *Exploring Splunk*. CITO Research, New York, NY, John Wiley & Sons, Inc, Indianapolis, IN, USA, 2012.
30. Benoy Anthony, Konstantin Boudnik, Cheryl Adams, Branky Shao, Cazen Lee, and Kai Sasaki. In-memory computing in Hadoop stack. In *Professional Hadoop®*, pp. 161–182, 2016.
31. Siamack Haghighi. Systems and methods for memory management, January 19, 2016. US Patent 9,239,784.
32. Matei Zaharia, Mosharaf Chowdhury, Tathagata Das, Ankur Dave, Justin Ma, Murphy McCauley, Michael J Franklin, Scott Shenker, and Ion Stoica. Resilient distributed datasets: A fault-tolerant abstraction for in-memory cluster computing. In *Proceedings of the 9th USENIX Conference on Networked Systems Design and Implementation*, p. 2-2. USENIX Association, 2012.
33. Avraham Shinnar, David Cunningham, Vijay Saraswat, and Benjamin Herta. M3r: Increased performance for in-memory Hadoop jobs. *Proceedings of the VLDB Endowment*, 5(12):1736–1747, 2012.
34. Apache ignite features. `https://ignite.apache.org/features.html`. Accessed: June 25, 2016.
35. Gereon Vey, Martin Bachmaier, and Ilya Krutov. *In-Memory Computing with SAP HANA on IBM eX5 Systems*. IBM Corporation, International Technical Support Organization, 2013.
36. Hasso Plattner and Alexander Zeier. *In-Memory Data Management: Technology and Applications*. Springer, Science & Business Media, 2012.
37. Vishal Sikka, Franz Färber, Wolfgang Lehner, Sang Kyun Cha, Thomas Peh, and Christof Bornhövd. Efficient transaction processing in SAP HANA database: The end of a column store myth. In *Proceedings of the 2012 ACM SIGMOD International Conference on Management of Data*, pp. 731–742. ACM, 2012.
38. Timur Mirzoev and Craig Brockman. SAP HANA and its performance benefits. *arXiv preprint arXiv:1404.2160*, 2014.
39. Franz Färber, Sang Kyun Cha, Jürgen Primsch, Christof Bornhövd, Stefan Sigg, and Wolfgang Lehner. SAP HANA database: Data management for modern business applications. *ACM Sigmod Record*, 40(4):45–51, 2012.
40. GigaSpaces XAP. `http://docs.gigaspaces.com/product_overview/`. Accessed: July 19, 2016.

4 Scheduling Nested Transactions on In-Memory Data Grids

Junwhan Kim, Roberto Palmieri, and Binoy Ravindran

CONTENTS

ABSTRACT

Distributed software transactional memory (DTM) is an emerging, alternative concurrency control model for distributed systems that promises to alleviate the difficulties of lock-based distributed synchronization—for example, distributed deadlocks, livelocks, and lock convoying. A complementary approach for handling conflicts is through a transactional scheduler, which orders transactional requests to avoid or minimize conflicts. This chapter focuses on the *closed and open nesting* models of managing inner (distributed) transactions to improve throughput on in-memory data grids and presents three transactional schedulers, called *reactive transactional scheduler* (RTS), *dependency-aware transactional scheduler* (DATS), and *scheduling-based parallel-nested* (SPN) transactional scheduler to support closed-, open-, and parallel-nested transactions, respectively.

4.1 INTRODUCTION

The explosion of big data management and processing for data-intensive analytics has prompted much research to develop in-memory data grids. Processing data on in-memory has fueled dynamic scalability and high performance of applications for distributed processing over big data. Such an application requires more stringent atomicity to access shared and distributed data, and the code blocks in the application are accordingly synchronized [1]. Traditionally, lock-based synchronization has been exploited for processing the atomic code blocks, but it is inherently error-prone [2].

For example, coarse-grained locking, in which a large data structure is protected using a single lock, is simple and easy to use, but permits little concurrency. In contrast, with fine-grained locking, in which each component of a data structure (e.g., a hash table bucket) is protected by a lock, programmers must acquire only necessary and sufficient locks to obtain maximum concurrency without compromising safety, and must avoid deadlocks when acquiring multiple locks. Both these situations are highly prone to programmer errors. The most serious problem with locks is that they are not easily *composable*—that is, combining existing pieces of software to produce different functionality is not easy. This is because, lock-based concurrency control is highly dependent on the order in which locks are acquired and released. Thus, it would be necessary to expose the internal implementation of existing methods, while combining them, in order to prevent possible deadlocks. This breaks encapsulation, and makes it difficult to reuse software, a condition that has motivated transactional memory (TM) [2].

TM is an alternative synchronization model for shared memory data objects that promises to alleviate the difficulties of lock-based synchronization (i.e., scalability, programmability, and composability issues). As TM code is composed of read/write operations on shared objects, it is organized as memory transactions, which optimistically execute, while logging any changes made to accessed objects. Two transactions conflict if they access the same object and one access is a write. When that happens, a contention manager resolves the conflict by aborting one and allowing the other to commit, yielding (the illusion of) atomicity. Aborted transactions are restarted, often immediately, after rolling-back the changes. Sometimes, a transactional scheduler is also used, which determines an ordering of concurrent transactions so that conflicts are either avoided altogether or minimized.

Many libraries or third-party softwares contain atomic code, and application developers often desire to group such code, with user, other library, or third-party (atomic) code into larger atomic code blocks. This can be accomplished by nesting all atomic code within their enclosing code, as permitted by the inherent composability of TM. But doing so—that is, flat nesting—results in large monolithic transactions, which limits concurrency: when a large monolithic transaction is aborted, all nested transactions are also aborted and rolled back, even if they do not conflict with the outer transaction.

Further, in many nested settings, programmers desire to respond to the failure of each nested action with an action-specific response. This is particularly the case in distributed systems—for example, if a remote device is unreachable or unavailable, one would want to try an alternate remote device, all as part of a top-level atomic action. Furthermore, inadequate performance of a nested third-party or library code must often be circumvented (e.g., by trying another nested code block) to boost overall application performance. In these cases, one would want to abort a nested action and try an alternative, without aborting the work accomplished so far (i.e., aborting the top-level action).

Three types of nesting have been studied in TM: flat, closed, and open [3]. If an inner transaction I is flat-nested inside its outer transaction A, A executes as if the code for I is inlined inside A. Thus, if I aborts, it causes A to abort. If I is closed-nested inside A, the operations of I only become part of A when I commits. Thus, an abort of I does not abort A, but I aborts when A aborts. Finally, if I is open-nested inside A, then the operations of I are not considered as part of A. Thus, an abort of I does not abort A, and vice versa. We will discuss these types in Section 4.2.

If I aborts, A must abort because there may be dependency between I and A. However, if there is no dependency between both, aborting A leads to degraded performance. Even though all the inner transactions commit, A aborts. In this case, two actions can be considered as the following: (1) In closed nesting, all the inner transactions abort since they have committed internally. (2) In open nesting, the compensation actions corresponding to the inner transactions are executed. Also, both actions degrade performance. To cope with such a difficulty, this chapter will cover three transactional schedulers, called *reactive transactional scheduler* (RTS), *dependency-aware transactional scheduler* (DATS), and *scheduling-based parallel-nested* (SPN) transactional scheduler to support closed, open, and parallel-nested transactions, respectively.

RTS, DATS, and SPN have been implemented over a popular open-source transactional in-memory data store (i.e., Red Hat's Infinispan [4,5]). This chapter will provide how RTS, DATS, and SPN work in detail and their experimental evaluations on Infinispan.

4.2 PRELIMINARIES AND SYSTEM MODEL

We consider a distributed system that consists of a set of nodes $N = \{n_1, n_2, \ldots\}$ that communicate with each other by message-passing links over a communication network. Similar to Reference 6, we assume that the nodes are scattered in a metric space. The metric $d(n_i, n_j)$ is the distance between nodes n_i and n_j, which determines the communication cost of sending a message from n_i to n_j.

4.2.1 Distributed Transactions

A *distributed transaction* performs operations on a set of *shared objects* in a distributed system, where nodes communicate by message-passing links. Let $O = \{o_1, o_2, \ldots\}$ denote the set of shared objects. A transaction T_i is in one of three possible statuses: *live*, *aborted*, or *committed*. If an aborted transaction retries, it preserves the original starting timestamp as its starting time.

We consider Herlihy and Sun's dataflow distributed STM model [6], where transactions are immobile, and objects move from node to node. In this model, each node has a TM proxy that provides interfaces to its application and to proxies at other nodes. When a transaction T_i at node n_i requests object o_j, the TM proxy of n_i first checks whether o_j is in its local cache. If the object is not present, the proxy invokes a distributed cache coherence (cc) protocol to fetch o_j in the network. Node n_k holding object o_j checks whether the object is in use by a local transaction T_k when it receives the request for o_j from n_i. If so, the proxy invokes a contention manager to mediate the conflict between T_i and T_k for o_j.

When a transaction T_i invokes an operation on object o_j, the cc protocol is invoked by the local TM proxy to locate the current cached copy of o_j. We consider two properties of the cc. First, when the TM proxy of T_i requests o_j, the cc is invoked to send T_i's read/write request to a node holding a valid copy of o_j in a finite time period. A read (write) request indicates the request for T_i to conduct a read (write) operation on o_j. A valid object copy is defined as a valid version. Thus, a node holding versions of o_j replies with the version corresponding to T_i's request. Second, at any given time, the cc must locate only one copy of o_j in the network and only one transaction is allowed to eventually write to o_j.

4.2.2 Nested Transactions

The differences between the nesting models are shown in Figure 4.1, in which there are two transactions containing a nested transaction. With flat nesting illustrated in Figure 4.1a, transaction T_2 cannot execute until transaction T_1 commits. T_2 incurs full aborts, and thus has to restart from the beginning. Under closed nesting presented in Figure 4.1b, only T_2's inner transaction needs to abort and be restarted while T_1 is still executing. The portion of work T_2 executes before the data structure access does not need to be retried, and T_2 can thus finish earlier. Under open nesting in Figure 4.1c, T_1's inner transaction commits independently of its outer, releasing memory isolation over the shared

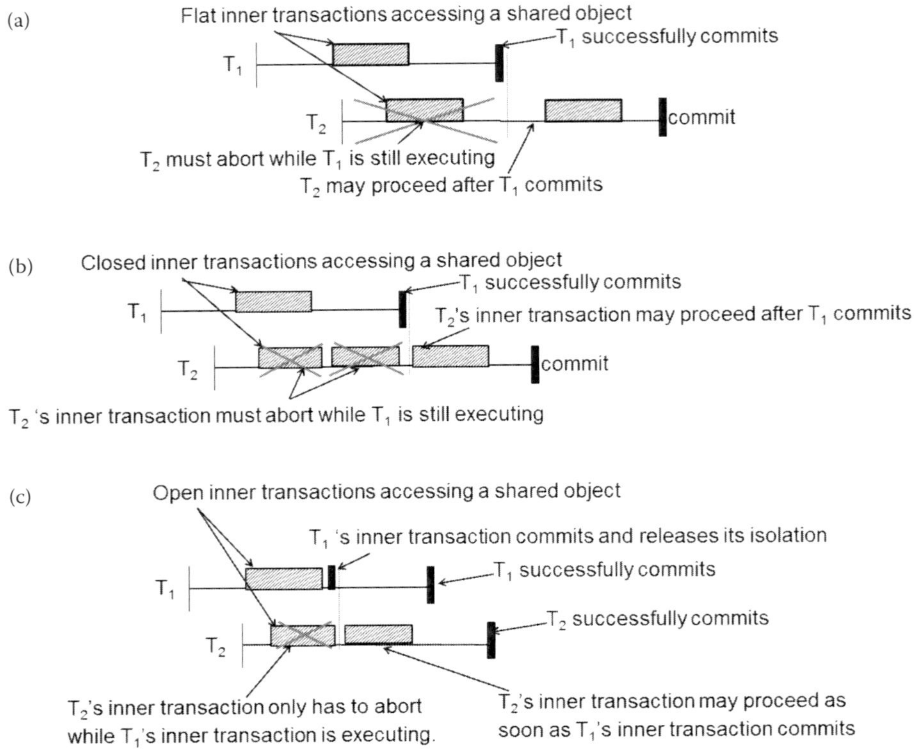

FIGURE 4.1 Two transactions under flat, closed, and open nesting. (a) Flat nesting. (b) Closed nesting. (c) Open nesting.

data structure. T_2's inner transaction can therefore proceed immediately, thus enabling T_2 to commit earlier than in both closed and flat nesting.

The flat- and closed-nested models have a clear negative impact on large monolithic transactions in terms of concurrency. In fact, when a large transaction is aborted, all its flat/closed-nested transactions are also aborted and rolled back, even if they do not conflict with any other transaction. Closed nesting potentially offers better performance than flat nesting because the aborts of closed-nested inner transactions do not affect their outer transactions. However, the open-nesting approach outperforms both in terms of concurrency allowed. When an open-nested transaction commits, its modifications on objects become immediately visible to other transactions, allowing those transactions to start using those objects without a conflict, increasing concurrency [7]. In contrast, if the inner transactions are closed- or flat-nested, then those object changes are not made visible until the outer transaction commits, potentially causing conflicts with other transactions that may want to use those objects.

To achieve high concurrency in open nesting, inner transactions have to implement *abstract serializability* [8]. If concurrent executions of transactions result in the consistency of shared objects at an "abstract level," then the executions are said to be abstractly serializable. If an inner transaction I commits, I's modifications are immediately committed in memory and I's read and write sets are discarded. At this time, I's outer transaction A does not have any conflict with I due to memory accessed by I. Thus, programmers consider the internal memory operations of I to be at a "lower level" than A. A does not consider the memory accessed by I when it checks for conflicts, but I must acquire an *abstract lock* and propagates this lock for A. When two operations try to acquire the same abstract lock, the open nesting concurrency control is responsible for managing this conflict (so this is defined "abstract level").

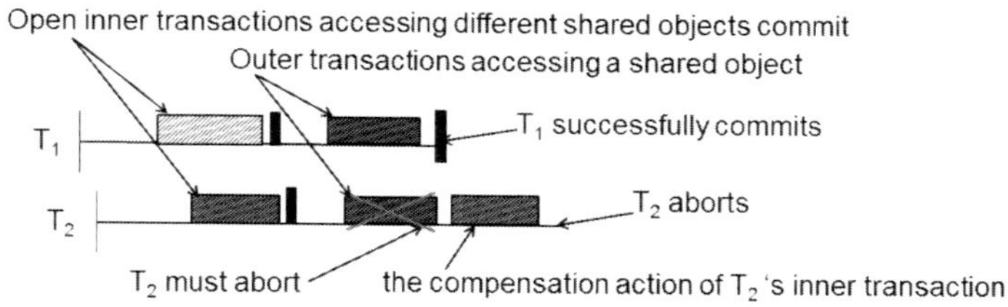

FIGURE 4.2 Aborting a transaction under open nesting.

Figure 4.2 shows that transaction T_2 aborts due to a conflict and the compensation action of its inner transaction is executed. Let us assume that T_1 and T_2's inner transactions access the different object and commit successfully. However, their outer transactions access the same object and T_2 aborts. The compensating action of T_2's inner transaction must be executed because the inner transaction's modification has become visible to other transactions. Even if open-nested transactions provide high concurrency of inner transactions, the open-nested model does not always perform better than flat- and closed-nested models due to a large number of abstract locks and compensation actions [9].

4.2.3 Atomicity, Consistency, and Isolation

We use the *transactional forwarding algorithm* (TFA) [10] to provide *early validation* of remote objects, guarantee a consistent view of shared objects between distributed transactions, and ensure atomicity for object operations in the presence of asynchronous clocks. TFA is responsible for caching local copies of remote objects and changing object ownership. Without loss of generality, objects export only read and write methods (or operations).

For completeness, we illustrate TFA with an example. In Figure 4.3, a transaction updates object o_1 at time t_1 (i.e., local clock [LC] is 14) and four transactions (i.e., T_1, T_2, T_3, and T_4) request o_1 from the object holder. Assume that T_2 validates o_1 at time t_2 and updates o_1 with LC = 30 at time t_3. A validation in distributed systems includes global registration of object ownership. Any read or write transaction (e.g., T_4) which has requested o_1 between t_2 and t_3 aborts. When write transactions T_1 and T_3 validate at times t_1 and t_2, respectively, transactions T_1 and T_3 that have acquired o_1 with LC = 14 before t_2 will abort, because LC is updated to 30.

RTS and SPN are associated with nested TFA (N-TFA) [11], which is an extension of TFA to implement closed nesting in distributed software transactional memory (DTM). DATS is associated with TFA with open nesting (TFA-ON) [9], which extends the TFA algorithm [10], to manage open-nested transactions. N-TFA [11] and TFA-ON [9] change the scope of object validations.

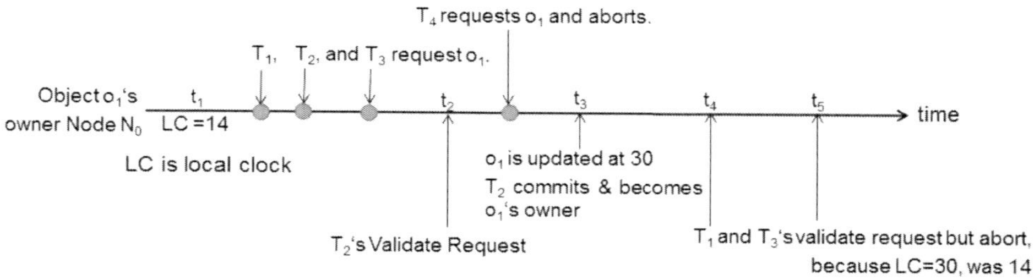

FIGURE 4.3 An example of TFA.

4.3 REACTIVE TRANSACTIONAL SCHEDULER

4.3.1 Motivation

Past transactional scheduler often causes only a small number of aborts and reduces the total communication delay in DTM [1]. However, aborts may increase when scheduling nested transactions. In the flat and closed nesting models, if an outer transaction, which has multiple nested transactions, aborts due to a conflict, the outer and inner transactions will restart and request all objects regardless of which object caused the conflict. Even though the aborted transactions are enqueued to avoid conflicts, the scheduler serializes the aborted transactions to reduce the contention on only the object that caused the conflict. With nested transactions, this may lead to heavy contention because all objects have to be retrieved again.

Proactive schedulers abort the losing transaction with a backoff time, which determines how long the transaction is stalled before it is restarted [12,13]. Determining backoff times for aborted transactions is generally difficult in DTM. For example, the winning transaction may commit before the aborted transaction is restarted due to communication delays. This can cause the aborted transaction to conflict with another transaction. If the aborted transaction is a nested transaction, this will increase the total execution time of its parent transaction. Thus, the backoff strategy may not avoid or reduce aborts in DTM.

Motivated by this, we propose the RTS scheduler for closed-nested DTM. RTS reduces the number of parent transactions' aborts to prevent their committed nested transactions from the aborts. RTS checks the length of the parent transaction's execution time and determines whether losing transaction is aborted or enqueued. If the parent transaction has a short execution time, it aborts. Otherwise, it is enqueued to preserve its nested transactions. A backoff time used for the enqueued parent transaction indicate, when the transaction is likely to receive an object.

4.3.2 Scheduler Design

We consider two kinds of aborts that can occur in closed-nested transactions when a conflict occurs: aborts of nested transactions and aborts of parent transactions. Closed nesting allows a nested transaction to abort without aborting its parent transaction. If a parent transaction aborts, however, all of its closed-nested transactions are aborted. Thus, RTS performs two actions for a losing parent transaction. First, determining whether losing transaction is aborted or enqueued by the length of its execution time. Second, the losing transaction is aborted if it is a parent transaction with a "high" contention level. A parent transaction with a "low" contention level is enqueued with a backoff time.

The contention level (CL) of an object o_j can be determined in either a local or distributed manner. A simple local detection scheme determines the local CL of o_j by how many transactions have requested o_j during a given time period. A distributed detection scheme determines the remote CL of o_j by how many transactions have requested other objects before o_j is requested. For example, assume that a transaction T_i is validating o_j, and T_k requests o_j from the object owner of o_j. The local CL of o_j is 1 because only T_k has requested o_j. The remote CL of o_j is the local CL of objects that T_k have requested if any. T_i's commit influences the remote CL because those other transactions will wait until T_k completes validation of o_j. If T_k aborts, the objects that T_k is using will be released, and the other transactions will obtain the objects. We define the CL of an object as the sum of its local and remote CLs. Thus, the CL indicates how many transactions want the objects that a transaction is using.

If a parent transaction with a short execution time is enqueued instead of aborted, the queuing delay may exceed its execution time. Thus, RTS aborts a parent transaction with a short execution time. If a parent transaction with a high CL aborts, all closed-nested transactions will abort even if they have committed with their parent and will have to request the objects again. This may waste more time than a queuing delay. As long as their waiting time elapses, their CL may increase. Thus,

RTS enqueues a parent transaction with a low CL. We discuss how to determine backoff times and CLs in Section 4.3.3.

4.3.3 Illustrative Example

RTS assigns different backoff times for each enqueued transaction. A backoff time is computed as a percentage of estimated execution time. Figure 4.4 shows an example of RTS. Three write transactions T_1, T_2, and T_3 request o_1 from the owner of o_1, and T_2 validates o_1 first at t_3. T_1 and T_3 abort due to the early validation of T_2. We consider two types of conflicts in RTS while T_2 validates o_1. First, a conflict between two write transactions can occur. Let us assume that write transactions T_4, T_5, and T_6 request o_1 at t_4, t_5, and t_6, respectively. T_4 is enqueued because the execution time $| t_4 - t_1 |$ of T_4 exceeds $| t_7 - t_4 |$ of T_2—the expected commit time t_7 of T_2. At this time, the local CL of o_1 is 1 and the CL will be 2 (i.e., the CLs of $o_3 + o_2 + o_1$), which is a low CL. Thus, $| t_7 - t_4 |$ is assigned to T_4 as a backoff time. When T_5 requests o_1 at t_5, even if $| t_5 - t_2 |$ exceeds $| t_5 -$ expected commit time of $T_4 |$, T_5 is not enqueued because the CL is 4 (i.e., the local CL of o_1 is 2 and the CL of o_4 is 2), which is a high CL. Owing to the short execution time of T_6, T_6 aborts. Second, a conflict between read and write transactions can occur. Let us assume that read transactions T_4, T_5, and T_6 request o_1. As backoff times, $| t_7 - t_4 |$, $| t_7 - t_5 |$, and $| t_7 - t_6 |$ will be assigned to T_4, T_5, and T_6, respectively. o_1 updated by T_2 will simultaneously be sent to T_4, T_5, and T_6, increasing the concurrency of the read transactions.

Given a fixed number of transactions and nodes, object contention will increase if these transactions simultaneously try to access a small number of objects. The threshold of a low or high CL relies on the number of nodes, transactions, and shared objects. Thus, the CL's threshold is adaptively determined. Assume that the CL's threshold in Figure 4.4 is decided as 3. When T_4 requests o_1, the CL for objects o_1, o_2, and o_3 is 2, meaning that two transactions want the objects that T_4 has requested, so T_4 is enqueued. On the other hand, when T_5 requests o_1, the CL of objects o_1 and o_4 is 4, representing that four transactions (i.e., more than the CL's threshold) want o_1 or o_4 that T_5 has requested, so T_5 aborts. As long as the waiting time elapses, their CL may increase. Thus, RTS enqueues a parent transaction with a low CL, which is defined as less than the CL's threshold.

To compute a backoff time, we use a transaction stats table that stores the average historical validation time of a transaction through a hash function. The table indicates the most current successful commit times of write transactions with a different number of nested transactions. Whenever

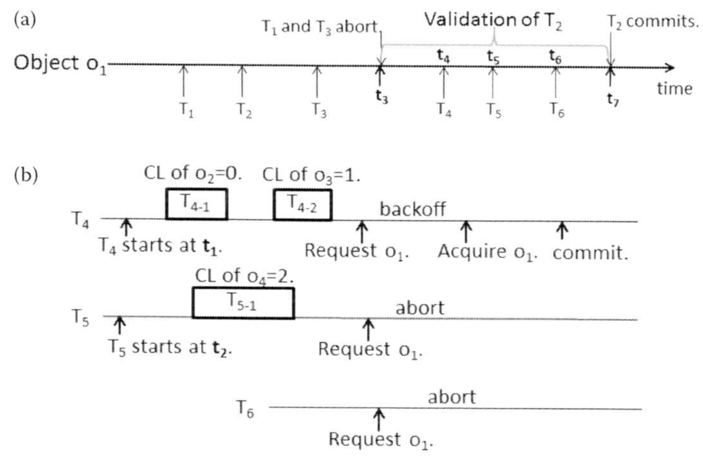

FIGURE 4.4 A reactive transactional scheduling scenario. (a) Object-based scenario. (b) Transaction-based scenario.

a transaction starts, an expected commit time is picked up from the table. The requesting message for each transaction includes three timestamps: the starting, requesting, and expected commit time of a transaction. In Figure 4.4, if T_5 is enqueued, its backoff time will be $| t_7 - t_5 |$ + the expected execution time (i.e., the expected commit – requesting time) of T_4.

If the backoff time expires before an object is received, the corresponding transaction will abort. Two possible cases exist in this situation. First, the transaction requests the object and is enqueued again as a new transaction. The duplicated transaction (i.e., the previously enqueued transaction) will be removed from a queue. Second, the object may be received before the transaction restarts. In this case, the object will be sent to the next enqueued transaction.

4.4 DEPENDENCY-AWARE TRANSACTIONAL SCHEDULER

4.4.1 Motivation

Figure 4.5 shows an example of open-nested transactions with compensating actions and abstract locks. Listings 4.1 and 4.2 in Figure 4.5 illustrate two outer transactions, T_1 and T_2, and an inner transaction in Listing 4.3. The inner transaction INSERT includes an *insert* operation in a Linked List. T_1 has a *delete* operation with a value. If the operation of T_1 executes successfully, its inner transaction INSERT executes. Conversely, regardless of the success of T_2's *delete* operation, its inner transaction INSERT will execute. *OnCommit* and *OnAbort*, which include a compensating action, are registered when the inner transaction commits. If the outer transaction (i.e., T_1 or T_2) commits, *OnCommit* executes. When the inner transaction commits, its modification becomes immediately visible for other transactions. Thus, if the inner transaction commits, and its outer transaction T_1 or T_2 aborts, a *delete* operation as a compensating action (described in *OnAbort*) executes. Let us assume that T_2 aborts, and *OnAbort* executes. Even though T_2's inner transaction (INSERT) does not depend on its *delete* operation, unlike T_1, *OnAbort* will execute. Thus, the conflict of object "tree-2" in T_2 causes the execution of compensating action on object "tree-1" in INSERT. The INSERT operation acquires the abstract lock again when it restarts. Finally, whenever an outer transaction aborts, its inner transaction must execute a compensating action, regardless of the operation's dependencies.

This drawback is particularly evident in distributed settings. In fact, distributed transactions typically have an execution time several orders of magnitude bigger than in a centralized STM, due to communication delays that are incurred in requesting and acquiring objects. If an outer transaction aborts, clearly the impact of the time needed for running compensating actions and for acquiring abstract locks for distributed open-nested transactions is exacerbated due to the communication overhead. Moreover it increases the likelihood of conflicts, drastically reducing concurrency and degrading performance.

Motivated by these observations, we propose the DATS scheduler for open-nested DTM. DATS, for each outer transaction T_a, identifies the number of inner transactions depending from T_a and schedules the outer transactions with the greatest number of dependencies to validate first and (hopefully) commit. This behavior permits the transactions with high compensation overhead to commit; the remaining few outer transactions that are invalidated will be restarted excluding their independent inner transactions to avoid useless compensating actions and acquisition of abstract locks. In the next subsection, the meaning of dependent transactions for DATS will be described.

4.4.2 Abstract- and Object-Level Dependencies

Abstract-level dependency indicates the dependency between an outer transaction and its inner transactions at an abstract level. We define the *dependency level* (*DL*) as the number of inner transactions that will execute *OnAbort* when the outer transactions abort. For example, T_1 illustrated in Figure 4.5 depends on its INSERT due to the *deleted* variable. Thus, DATS detects a dependency between T_1 and its INSERT (its inner transaction) because the *delete* operations in T_1 shares the variable *deleted*

Listing 4.1 Transaction T_1

```
new Atomic<Boolean >(){
 @Override boolean atomically(Txn t){
  List ll = (List)t.open(tree -2);
  deleted = ll.delete(7,t);
  if(deleted) INSERT(t,10); //inner transaction
   return deleted;
 }
}
```

Listing 4.2 Transaction T_2

```
new Atomic<Boolean >(){
 @Override boolean atomically(Txn t){
  List ll = (List)t.open(tree -2);
  deleted = ll.delete(9,t);
  INSERT(t,10); //inner transaction
  return deleted;
 }
}
```

Listing 4.3 Inner Transaction INSERT

```
public boolean INSERT(Txn t, int value){
 private boolean inserted = false;
 @Override boolean atomically(t){
  List ll = (List)t.open(tree -1);
  inserted = ll.insert(value,t);
  t.acquireAbstractLock (ll,value);
  return inserted;
 }
 @Override onAbort(t){
  List ll = (List)t.open(tree -1); //compensation action
  if(inserted)ll.delete(value,t);
  t.releaseAbstractLock(ll,7);
 }
 @Override onCommit(t){
  List ll = (List)t.open(tree -1);
  t.releaseAbsractLock(ll,value);
 }
}
```

FIGURE 4.5 Two open-nested transactions with abstract locks and compensating actions.

with the conditional *if* statement declared for executing INSERT. In this case, the $DL = 1$ for T_1. Conversely, T_2 executes INSERT without checking any precondition, so its $DL = 0$ because T_2 does not have dependencies with its inner transactions. The purpose of the abstract-level dependency is to avoid unnecessary compensating actions and abstract locks. Even though T_2 aborts, *OnAbort* in INSERT will not be executed because its $DL = 0$, and the compensating action will not be processed. Meanwhile, executing *OnAbort* implies running INSERT and acquiring the abstract lock again when T_2 restarts.

Summarizing, aborting outer transactions with smaller *DL*s leads to a reduced number of compensating actions and abstract lock acquisitions. Such identification can be done automatically at run-time by DATS using byte-code analysis or relying on explicit indication by the programmer. The first scenario is completely transparent from the application point of view but in some cases could add additional overhead. The second approach, although it requires the collaboration of the developer, is more flexible because it allows the programmer to bias the behavior of the scheduler. In fact, even though the logic of an outer transaction reveals a certain number of dependencies, the programmer may want to force running compensations in case of an abort. This can be done by simply changing the value of *DL* associated to the outer transaction.

Object-level dependency indicates the dependency among two or more concurrent transactions accessing the same shared object. For example, in Figure 4.5, T_1 depends on T_2 because they share the same object "tree-2." If T_1 and T_2 work concurrently, a conflict between them occurs. However, *delete*(7) of T_1 and *delete*(9) of T_2 commute because they are two operations executing on the same object ("tree-2") but accessing different items (or fields when applicable) of the object (item "7" and item "9"). We recall that two operations commute if applying them in either order, they leave the object in the same state and return the same responses [14]. DATS detects object-level dependency at the transaction commit phase, splitting the validation phase into two. Say, T_a is the transaction that is validating. In the first phase, T_a checks the consistency of the objects requested during the execution. If a concurrent transaction T_b has requested and already committed a new version of some object requested by T_a, then T_a aborts in order to avoid isolation corruption. After the successful completion of the first phase of T_a's validation, DATS detects the object-level dependencies among concurrent transactions that are validating with T_a in the second phase. To do that, DATS relies on the notion of commutativity: Two transactions are defined as commutable if they conflict and they leave the state of the shared data set consistent even if validated and committed concurrently.

A very intuitive example of commutativity is when two operations, *call*1(X) and *call*2(X), both access the same object X but different fields of X. Suppose T_a and T_b are conflicting transactions but simultaneously validating. If all of T_a's operations commute with all of T_b's operations, they can proceed to commit together avoiding a useless abort. Otherwise, one of T_a or T_b must be aborted. This scheduler is in charge of the decision (see next subsection).

In order to compute commutativity, DATS joins two supports. In the first, the programmer annotates each transaction class with the fields accessed. The second is a field-based timestamping mechanism, used for checking the field-level invalidation. The goal is to reduce the granularity of the timestamp from object to field. With a single object timestamp, it is impossible to detect commutativity because of field's modifications. In fact, writes to different fields of the same object are all reflected with the increment of the same object timestamp. In order to do that efficiently, DATS exploits the annotations provided by the developer on the fields accessed by the transaction to directly point only to the interested fields (instead of iterating on all the object fields, looking for the ones modified). On such fields, it uses field-based timestamping to detect object invalidation.

The purpose of the object-level dependency is to enhance concurrency of outer transactions. Even though inner transactions terminate successfully, aborting their outer transactions affects these inner transactions (due to compensation). Thus, DATS checks for the commutativity of conflicting transactions and permits them to be validated, reducing the aborts.

4.4.3 Scheduler Design

We designed DATS using abstract-level dependencies and object-level dependencies. When outer transactions are invoked, the *DL* with their inner transactions is checked. When the outer transactions request an object from its owner, the requests with their *DL*s will be sent to the owner and moved into its scheduling queue. The object owner maintains the scheduling queue holding all the ongoing transactions that have requested the object with their *DL*s. When T_1 (one of the outer transactions) validates an object, we consider two possible scenarios. First, if another transaction T_2 tries to validate the same object, a conflict between T_1 and T_2 is detected on the object. Thus, DATS checks for the object-level dependency. If T_1 and T_2 are independent (according to the object-level dependency rules), DATS allows T_1 and T_2 to proceed with the validation. Otherwise, the transaction

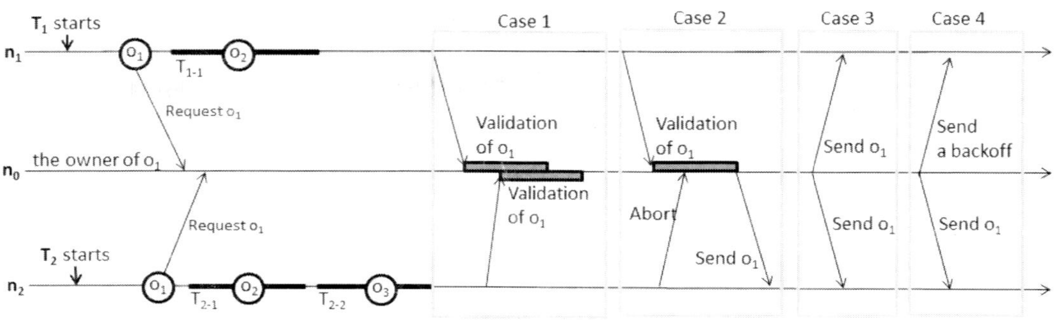

FIGURE 4.6 Four different cases for two transactions T_1 and T_2 in DATS.

with lower *DL* will be aborted. In this way, dependent transactions with the minimal cost of abort and compensating actions are aborted and restarted, permitting transactions with a costly abort operation to commit.

Figure 4.6 illustrates an example of DATS with two transactions T_1 and T_2 invoked on nodes n_1 and n_2, respectively. The transaction T_1 has a single inner transaction and T_2 has two nested transactions. Let us assume that T_1's $DL = 1$ and T_2's $DL = 2$. The circles indicate written objects. The horizontal line corresponds to the status of each transaction described in the time domain. Figure 4.6 shows four different cases when T_1 and T_2 terminate. When T_1 and T_2 are invoked, DATS analyzes their *DL*s, operations, and values. When T_1 requests o_1 from n_0, the metadata for *DL*s, operations, and values of o_1 will be sent to n_0. These are moved to the scheduling queue of n_0. We consider four different cases regarding the termination of T_1 and T_2.

- *Case 1.* T_1 and T_2 validate concurrently o_1. DATS checks for the object-level dependency. If T_1 and T_2 are not dependent at the object level (i.e., the operations of T_1 and T_2 over o_1 commute), T_1 and T_2 commit concurrently.
- *Case 2.* T_1 starts to validate and detects it is dependent with T_2 (that is still executing) at the object level on the object o_1. In this case T_2 will abort due to early validation. When T_1 commits, the updated o_1 is sent to n_2.
- *Case 3.* Another transaction committed o_1 before T_1 and T_2 validate. If T_1 and T_2 are not dependent at the object level, o_1 is sent to n_1 and n_2 simultaneously as soon as the transaction commits.
- *Case 4.* Another transaction committed o_1 before T_1 and T_2 validate. If T_1 and T_2 are dependent at the object level, DATS checks for the abstract-level dependency, and o_1 is sent to n_2 because T_2's *DL* is larger than that of T_1. Aborting T_1, the scheduler is forced to run a single compensation (for T_{1-1}) instead of two compensations (T_{2-1} and T_{2-2}) in case of T_2's abort. Further, considering the case in which the *DL* of T_1 is 0, the abort of T_1 does not affect T_{1-1}. In fact, its execution will be preserved and only the operations of T_1 will be re-executed.

4.5 SCHEDULING-BASED PARALLEL NESTING

4.5.1 MOTIVATION

The execution of nested inner transactions in the context of a parent transaction can be conceptually represented by a dynamic tree, called transaction tree, in which transactions represent the vertex of the tree and edges are used for defining the conflict relation between transactions. The topology of the tree is not defined *a priori*. Originally, all the inner transactions belong to the same level of the tree and their parent represents the parent transaction. Sibling transactions (belonging to the same level of the transaction tree) are executed in parallel, assuming their conflict independence. The approach does not assume previous knowledge on transaction conflicts; therefore, some (or all) of the sibling transactions cannot execute in parallel due to transaction dependencies. When a conflict happens, the aborted transactions are moved on a lower level with an edge representing the just detected dependency. In case all the inner transactions are not conflicting with the others, the parallel process allows to execute only the inner conflicting transaction on the critical path and the others in parallel.

In closed nesting, all the inner transactions must commit successfully for triggering the parent's commit. In case they are independent, they can be executed and committed in parallel allowing the parent transaction to commit just after the longest inner transaction completes its execution. However, if there is dependency among them, conflicts occur, so their parallel activation may not be effective. Figure 4.7 shows new order transaction T_1 [15], including multiple inner transactions. T_1 opens warehouse and district to extract a tax and stock to get a price, the first two inner transactions, respectively. These two inner transactions do not have dependency. Executing two transactions in parallel may lead to high performance.

Closed nesting performs better than flat nesting and the program model of closed nesting differs from that of open nesting. Even though open nesting yields high concurrency, it has inherent

Listing 4.4 Transaction T_1

```
Atomic{
  // innerTxs: a number of inner transactions
  String w_id = rand(WAREHOUSES) + 1;
  String d_id = rand(DISTRICT) + 1;
  String c_id = rand(CUSTOMER) + 1;
  Atomic{
   // In the warehouse table: retrieve an object
   Object warehouse = (warehouse)open(w_id);
   W_TAX = warehouse.W_TAX
   // In the district table: retrieve D_TAX, get and inc D_NEXT_O_ID
   Object district = (district)open(w_id, d_id);
   D_TAX = district.D_TAX;
   // In the customer table: retrieve an object
  }
  for(i=0; i< GetItemList(); i++){
   Atomic{
    Object stock = (Stock)open(w_id, d_id, c_id, i);
    stock.quantity = getQuantity();
    stock.order_cnt++;
    Price = stock.price;
   }
   Atomic{
    Object customer = (customer)open(w_id, d_id, c_id);
    Discount = customer.Discount;
    // Create entries in ORDER
    Object order = new TpccOrder(w_id, d_id, o_id, i)
    order.Supply_W_ID = w_id;
    order.delivery = null;
    order.totalAmount = Price*(1-Discount)*(1+W_TAX+D_TAX);
   }
  }
 }
}
```

FIGURE 4.7 New order transaction with multiple inner transactions in TPC-C.

overheads such as commit overheads or abstract locking overheads [9]. Thus, open nesting does not always perform better than closed nesting.

Motivated by this, we propose an SPN transactional memory model focusing on how to identify whether or not inner transactions should be executed in parallel and how to enhance the performance of parallel inner transactions in DTM.

4.5.2 Scheduler Design

SPN consists of two steps: (1) converting the sequence of inner transactions to parallel inner transactions and running them simultaneously, and (2) maintaining a "transaction table" of ongoing parallel inner transactions. In the first step, nodes invoking transactions execute all inner transactions simultaneously and request their objects from object owners simultaneously. Each object request is composed of four elements—the order number of the inner transaction (*NiTx*), object id (*oID*), type of the transaction (*Type*), and outer transaction id (*TxID*). An order number is assigned from 1 to the total number of parallel inner transactions of the same parent transaction. Different inner transactions may request the same object. Thus, in the second step, the owner moves these elements (i.e., *NiTx*, *oID*, *Type*) to the transaction table and identifies which inner transactions can be executed in parallel. The transaction table is updated when requesting and validating objects. At both times, object owners maintain the transaction table after storing the elements as follows:

- *Requesting*: If *NiTx* is 1, the object owner sends the object of *oID* to the requester on TFA policy and updates its status as *Responded*. If *NiTx* is not 1, the object owner checks whether the prior *NiTx*s of current requesters have requested the same *oID*. The prior *NiTx*s indicates lower numbers than *NiTx* with the same *TxID*. If *NiTx* is not 1 and no prior *NiTx*s have requested the same *oID*, the owner sends the object to the requester because of no conflict. If any prior *NiTx*s have requested the same *oID*, the owner updates its status as *Wait* and sends a backoff time to the requester.
- *Validating*: When one requesting transaction validates before others, allow the requested validation and remove corresponding *TxID*s from the transactional table. Other transactions that requested the same objects are aborted. Without requesting the object again, the aborted transactions will receive the updated objects.

A requester may receive multiple backoff times from an owner. Receiving a backoff time means that an inner transaction is using the same object. Different backoff times are assigned to different inner transactions accessing the same object. Thus, we represent how the owner decides a backoff time and the requester maintains the backoff time. When parallel inner transactions with different *NiTx*s request objects, backoff times are calculated using a number of *Wait* statuses. Even if a prior status is not updated (or is delayed) for some reason, an owner checks whether to reply with an object or a backoff time using existing statuses. If a conflict is detected after updating prior statuses, conflicting ongoing inner transactions receive backoff times and abort. In order to compute a backoff time, we use the number of *Wait* statuses in the transaction table. If the *NiTx*'s status is *Wait*, its backoff time will be the execution time $\times$ the number of *Wait* statuses. When the inner transaction commits internally, another inner transaction with the smallest backoff time is woken up and starts using the updated object.

Transactions' backoff time is stored in an hash table. The backoff time of a transaction corresponds to the average execution time of that transaction. The key of the table is the name of the transaction. If a *new order* transaction in TPC-C requests an object, for example, its owner creates a bucket with key "new_order." When the transaction commits, the execution time is computed as its commit time—its starting time. Later, if SPN detects a conflict with another new order transaction, the execution time is assigned to the new order as a backoff time. As soon as an object is updated, a

	NiTx	oID	Type	Status
T1	T_{1-1}	o_1	w	Responded
	T_{1-2}	o_1	w	Wait
	T_{1-3}	o_2	w	Responded
T2	T_{2-1}	o_1	r	Responded
	T_{2-1}	o_1	w	Responded
T3	T_{3-1}	o_2	w	Responded
	T_{3-2}	o_2	r	Wait

FIGURE 4.8 An example for maintaining a transactional table.

transaction receiving a backoff time is woken up to access the object. Thus, SPN does not need an exact backoff time, so SPN uses an approximated execution time.

SPN also identifies conflicts between write and read transactions. If write and write or write and read transactions access an object, the first write transactions' status will be *Responded* and the second write or read transactions' status will be *Wait*. Read and write or read and read transactions accessing an object simultaneously receive the object.

Figure 4.8 illustrates an example for a transaction table containing three outer transactions. T_1 contains three write inner transactions. T_2's inner transactions access object o_1, and T_3's inner transactions access object o_2. If the owner receives the requests from the node invoking T_{1-1}, T_{1-2}, and T_{1-3}, o_1, a backoff time, and o_2 are sent to T_{1-1}, T_{1-2}, and T_{1-3}, respectively. T_{1-2} waits for the backoff time. As soon as T_{1-1} commits, T_{1-2} that waits for o_1 is woken up and use o_1 updated by T_{1-1}. T_{2-1} and T_{2-2} receive o_2 because of no conflict. If T_1 commits first, T_2 and T_3 will be aborted. If T_2 commits first, T_1 will be aborted.

As executing inner transactions in parallel, the purpose of SPN is to maximize their parallelism in DTM. SPN keeps track of the access pattern of inner transactions and uses it for resolving conflicts. Nonconflicting inner transactions are executed in parallel. Conversely, conflicting inner transactions accessing the same objects are serialized.

4.6 IMPLEMENTATION AND EVALUATION

4.6.1 Implementation

We implemented Infinispan-based Hyflow [5] DTM framework, called iHyflow for experimental studies. Figure 4.9 shows an architecture of iHyflow. The dark box indicates the object access module, including the CC protocol and cache management implemented on Infinispan for iHyflow.

A CC protocol keeps track of objects' location to retrieve objects from their owner nodes over the network. It requires the identifier of the requested object and it generally caches a copy of the requested object on the local node. Thus, the cache management is tightly related with the CC protocol to access objects, so that we modified the object access module using Infinispan to evaluate RTS, DATS, and SPN. Infinispan is a JAVA-based open-source NoSQL data platform developed by Red Hat [5]. iHyflow differs from Hyflow on the CC protocol and cache management developed with Infinispan core library.

Infinispan includes a key-value store interface targeting scalability by natively replying on weak data consistency models [5]. Unlike Infinispan, Hyflow ensures strong consistency through early validation. To implement the early validation in iHyflow, setting a flag to an object in the cache has been used when a transaction starts validation remotely or locally. If a transaction requests an object

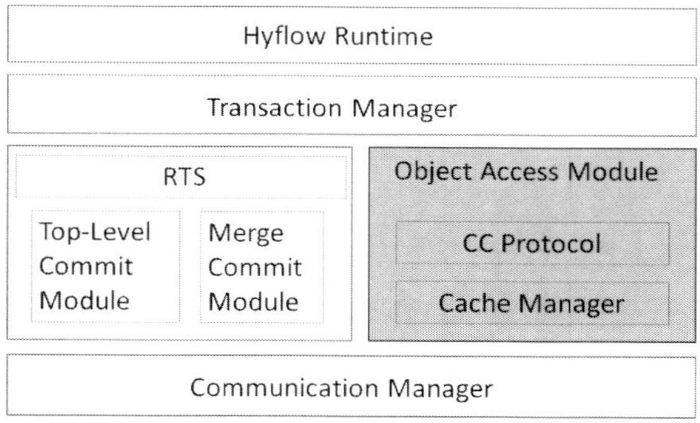

FIGURE 4.9 Architecture of Hyflow.

from its owner, the owner checks whether the object is set to a flag. A flag indicates that a transaction is validating the object. Inherently, Infinispan supports a control-flow model. To implement dataflow, iHyflow uses the *find_owner*(*oid*) function to find a real object owner. *oid* implies the address of the original owner. If *oid* is 21 in 10 nodes, for example, n1 is an original owner. A transaction picks the address of n1 and finds the address of *oid*'s real owner in n1. An original owner maintains a hashmap consisting of the *oid*s of objects and the addresses of real owners. The original owner returns the address of *oid*'s real owner. For RTS, the real owner maintains CLs for each object. The transaction requests the object from the real owner, the real owner sends the object and CL corresponding to *oid*.

There are two kinds of commit models in Hyflow. First, the commit of parent transactions—*top-level commit model* is used when a top-level transaction commits the changes from its log to the globally committed memory after the successful validation of all objects in its read-set. Second, the *merge commit model* is used when a nested transaction commits the changes from its log to the log of its parent. The parent transaction identifies the changes from its nested transactions or itself and maintains a CL. RTS is integrated with these commit models. The top-level commit and merge commit models implemented in Hyflow have been used for iHyflow to maintain the commits of nested transactions. In the top-level commit model in iHyflow, however, the committed objects must be updated in the Infinispan cache. This operation happens in a validation.

4.6.2 Experimental Evaluation

For the effectiveness of the transactional schedulers described in this chapter, we cannot compare our results with any competitor DTM based on transactional data grids, as none of the DTMs that we are aware of support closed- and open-nested transactions. Thus, we measured the throughput (i.e., the number of committed transactions per second) of RTS, DATS, SPN, N-TFA (closed nesting without a transactional scheduler), and TFA-OPEN (open nesting without a transactional scheduler) and compared the speedup of RTS over N-TFA, DATS over TFA-OPEN, and SPN over N-TFA. RTS and SPN represent N-TFA with RTS and SPN in iHyflow, respectively. RTS assumes that an outer transaction includes operations defined as external codes of its inner transactions, but an outer transaction does not have any operations for SPN because no dependency between the outer and inner transactions is assumed. Thus, although RTS and SPN are designed on closed nesting, the comparison between both is not appropriate. Also, two versions of N-TFA are implemented with and without operations in an outer transaction, respectively. DATS represents TFA-OPEN with DATS in iHyflow. The speedups were obtained with 2, 4, 8, 12, and 24 threads on a distributed system consisting of 80 nodes, called PRObE [16]. Each node is an Opteron 6272, 64 bit, 16 MB L2, 8-core 2.1 GHz CPU.

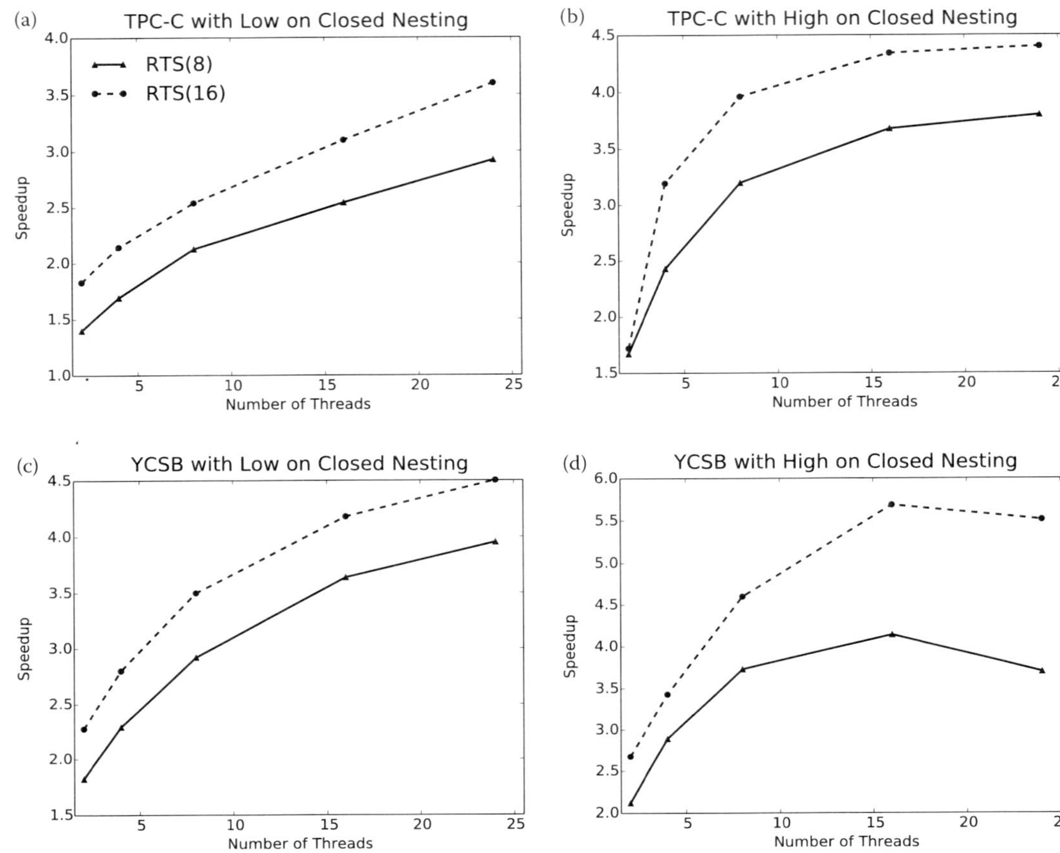

FIGURE 4.10 Performance speedup of RTS over N-TFA on TPC-C and YCSB. (a) TPC-C with low on RTS. (b) TPC-C with high on RTS. (c) YCSB with low on RTS. (d) YCSB with high on RTS.

The Yahoo Cloud Servicing Benchmark (YCSB) [17] is the most well-known benchmark implemented in Infinispan for NoSQL database. TPC-C [15] is the most used benchmark for DTM evaluation. According to the standard of the benchmarks, 50% write transactions of 10,000 active concurrent transactions per node have been configured. The high and low contention is configured with 5 and 10 warehouses, respectively. In the benchmarks, keys (i.e., object id) used to identify the object are generated using uniform probability. Each transaction includes 8 or 16 inner transactions, which are defined as a length of a transaction. For example, RTS(8) indicates that a transaction including 8 inner transactions is used to evaluate RTS, and TPC-C with low on closed nesting means the TPC-C benchmark defined with closed nesting and 10 warehouses.

Figure 4.10 shows the speedup of RTS over N-TFA with 8 and 16 inner transactions per transaction. We observe that RTS outperforms N-TFA up to 6× speedup. If an outer transaction including multiple inner transactions aborts, it requests all the objects from their object owners again and restarts the inner transactions, resulting in the degraded performance in N-TFA.

Figure 4.11 shows the speedup of DATS over TFA-OPEN. DATS performs better than TFA-OPEN because a number of requested abstract locks is minimized.

Figure 4.12 shows that SPN outperforms N-TFA up to 12× speedup due to the penalization of inner transactions. The overhead to create and maintain a transaction table is involved to SPN, so that SPN(16) performs worth than SPN(8) with 2 and 4 threads. However, as long as the contention increases, the performance gain of SPN(16) is higher than that of SPN(8).

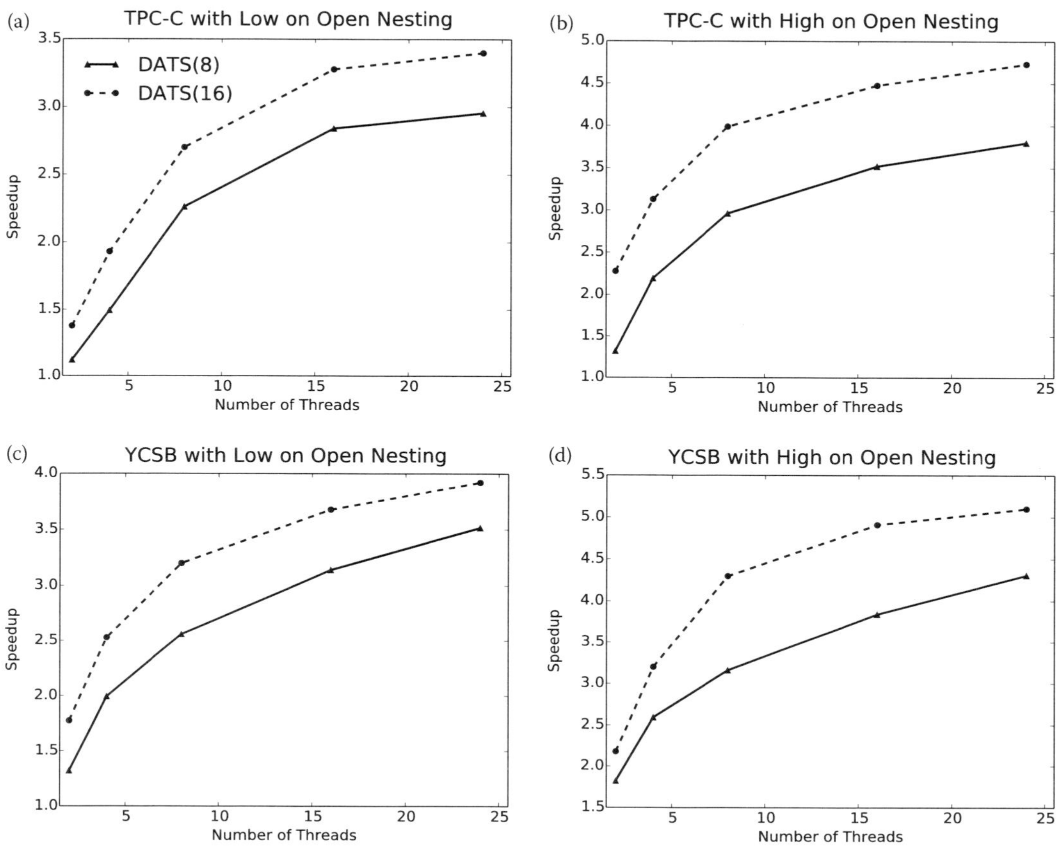

FIGURE 4.11 Performance speedup of DATS over TFA-OPEN on TPC-C and YCSB. (a) TPC-C with low on RTS. (b) TPC-C with high on RTS. (c) YCSB with low on RTS. (d) YCSB with high on RTS.

Additional experimental results for RTS, DATS, and SPN are described in Reference 1. Given these results, a long running transaction including a large number of inner transactions suffers from degraded performance regardless of the type of nested transactions. The results show that the proposed transactional schedulers, identifying such underlying causes, and eliminating them can yield significant throughput improvement.

4.7 SUMMARY

In this chapter, we studied three different schedulers to improve throughput in dataflow DTM on in-memory transactional data grids. First, RTS focuses on scheduling closed-nested transactions. The scheduler heuristically determines transactional contention level to determine whether a live parent transaction aborts or enqueues. RTS is shown to enhance throughput at high and low contention, by as much as 4.5× and 5.6× speedup, respectively.

Second, DATS schedules open-nested transactions. The key idea behind DATS is to avoid compensating actions regardless of conflicted objects and minimize the number of requesting abstract locks, improving performance. Our implementation and experimental evaluation shows that DATS enhances throughput for open-nested transactions by as much as 3.7× and 5× under low and high contention, respectively.

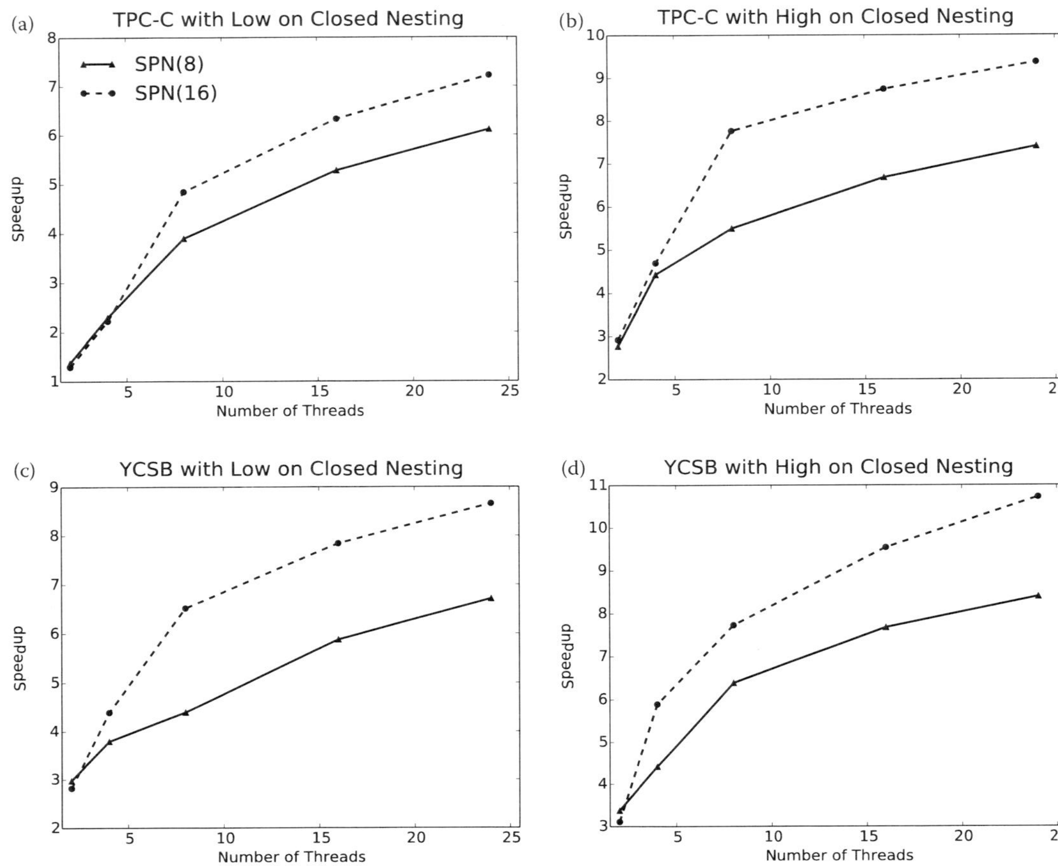

FIGURE 4.12 Performance speedup of SPN over N-TFA on TPC-C and YCSB. (a) TPC-C with low on RTS. (b) TPC-C with high on RTS. (c) YCSB with low on RTS. (d) YCSB with high on RTS.

Third, SPN considers parallel closed-nested transactions in DTM. Object owners maintain a transactional table containing ongoing inner transactions to identify which inner transactions can be executed in parallel. SPN exploits the parallelism of executing inner transactions and requesting objects in DTM. SPN reveals that throughput is improved by up to 8.5× and 10.5× under low and high contention, respectively.

REFERENCES

1. Junwhan Kim. Scheduling Memory Transactions in Distributed Systems. PhD thesis, Virginia Tech, 2013.
2. Nir Shavit and Dan Touitou. Software transactional memory. In Proceedings of the Fourteenth Annual ACM Symposium on Principles of Distributed Computing (PODC), pages 204–213, ACM, Ottowa, Ontario, Canada, 1995.
3. J. Eliot B. Moss. Open nested transactions: Semantics and support. In *Workshop on Memory Performance Issues*, 2005.
4. Junwhan Kim. Partial rollback-based scheduling on in-memory transactional data grids. In *Big Data (Big Data), 2014 IEEE International Conference on*, pages 80–89, IEEE, Washington, DC, October 2014.
5. Francesco Marchioni and Manik Surtani. *Infinispan Data Grid Platform*. PACKT Publishing, Birmingham, UK, August 2012.

6. Maurice Herlihy and Ye Sun. Distributed transactional memory for metric-space networks. In *Proceedings of the 19th International Conference on Distributed Computing, DISC'05*, pages 324–338, Springer-Verlag, Berlin, Heidelberg, 2005.
7. J. Eliot B. Moss and Antony L. Hosking. Nested transactional memory: Model and architecture sketches. *Science of Computer Programming*, 63:186–201, December 2006, Elsevier.
8. Yang Ni, Vijay S. Menon, Ali-Reza Adl-Tabatabai, Antony L. Hosking, Richard L. Hudson, J. Eliot B. Moss, Bratin Saha, and Tatiana Shpeisman. Open nesting in software transactional memory. In *Proceedings of the 12th ACM SIGPLAN Symposium on Principles and Practice of Parallel Programming, PPoPP'07*, pages 68–78, ACM, New York, NY, USA, 2007.
9. Alex Turcu and Binoy Ravindran. On open nesting in distributed transactional memory. In *Proceedings of the 5th Annual International Systems and Storage Conference, SYSTOR'12*, pages 12:1–12:12, ACM, New York, NY, USA, 2012.
10. Mohamed M. Saad and Binoy Ravindran. Supporting STM in distributed systems: Mechanisms and a Java framework. In *Sixth ACM SIGPLAN Workshop on Transactional Computing*, ACM, San Jose, CA, USA, June 2011.
11. Alexandru Turcu and Biony Ravindran. On closed nesting in distributed transactional memory. In *Seventh ACM SIGPLAN Workshop on Transactional Computing*, ACM, New Orleans, LA, USA, February 2012.
12. Geoffrey Blake, Ronald G. Dreslinski, and Trevor Mudge. Proactive transaction scheduling for contention management. In *Proceedings of the 42nd Annual IEEE/ACM International Symposium on Microarchitecture, MICRO 42*, pages 156–167, ACM, New York, NY, USA, 2009.
13. Richard M. Yoo and Hsien-Hsin S. Lee. Adaptive transaction scheduling for transactional memory systems. In *Proceedings of the Twentieth Annual Symposium on Parallelism in Algorithms and Architectures, SPAA'08*, pages 169–178, ACM, New York, NY, USA, 2008.
14. Maurice Herlihy and Eric Koskinen. Transactional boosting: A methodology for highly-concurrent transactional objects. In *Proceedings of the 13th ACM SIGPLAN Symposium on Principles and Practice of Parallel Programming, PPoPP '08*, pages 207–216, ACM, New York, NY, USA, 2008.
15. TPC Council. TPC-C Benchmark, revision 5.11. February 2010.
16. Garth Gibson, Gary Grider, Andree Jacobson, and Wyatt Lloyd. Probe: A thousand-node experimental cluster for computer systems research, *The USENIX Magazine*, 38(3), June 2013.
17. Brian F. Cooper, Adam Silberstein, Erwin Tam, Raghu Ramakrishnan, and Russell Sears. Benchmarking cloud serving systems with YCSB. In *Proceedings of the 1st ACM Symposium on Cloud Computing, SoCC'10*, pages 143–154, ACM, New York, NY, USA, 2010.

5 Co-Scheduling High-Performance Computing Applications

Guillaume Aupy, Anne Benoit, Loic Pottier, Padma Raghavan, Yves Robert, and Manu Shantharam

CONTENTS

ABSTRACT

Big data applications play an increasing role in high-performance computing. They are perfect candidates for co-scheduling, as they obey flexible speedup models, alternating I/O operations and intensive computation phases. In this chapter, we discuss co-scheduling on failure-prone platforms. Checkpointing helps to mitigate the impact of a failure on a given application, but it must be complemented by redistributions to rebalance the load among all applications. Co-scheduling usually involves partitioning the applications into *packs*, and then scheduling each pack in sequence, as efficiently as possible. The objective is therefore to determine a partition into packs, and an assignment of processors to applications, that minimize the sum of the execution times of the packs. On the theoretical side, we assess the problem complexity. On the practical side, we design several polynomial-time heuristics to deal with the general problem with failures and redistribution costs. The proposed heuristics show very good performance while executing in very short time, hence validating the approach.

5.1 INTRODUCTION

With the advent of multicore platforms, high-performance computing (HPC) applications can be efficiently parallelized on a flexible number of processors. Usually, a speedup profile determines the performance of the application for a given number of processors. For instance, the applications in Reference 1 were executed on a platform with up to 256 cores, and the corresponding execution times were reported. A perfectly parallel application has an execution time t_{seq}/p, where t_{seq} is the sequential execution time, and p is the number of processors. In practice, because of the overhead due to communications and due to the inherently sequential fraction of the application, the parallel execution time is larger than t_{seq}/p. The speedup profile of the application is assumed to be known (or estimated) before execution, through benchmarking campaigns.

Big data applications play an increasing role in HPC. They are perfect candidates for co-scheduling, as they obey flexible speedup models a la BSP, alternating I/O operations and intensive computation phases. A simple scheduling strategy on HPC platforms is to execute each application in dedicated mode, assigning all resources to each application throughout its execution. However, it was shown recently that rather than using the whole platform to run one single application, both the platform and the users may benefit from *co-scheduling* several applications, thereby minimizing the loss due to the fact that applications are not perfectly parallel. Sharing the platform between two applications already leads to significant performance and energy savings [2], which become even more important when the number of co-scheduled applications increases [3].

Furthermore, large-scale platforms are prone to failures. Indeed, for a platform with p processors, even if each node has an individual MTBF (mean time between failures) of 120 years [4], we expect a failure to strike every $120/p$ years, for instance, every hour for a platform with $p = 10^6$ nodes. Failures are likely to destroy the load-balancing achieved by co-scheduling algorithms: if all applications were assigned resources by the co-scheduler so as to complete their execution approximately at the same time, the occurrence of a failure will significantly delay the completion time of the corresponding application. In turn, several failures may well create severe imbalance among the applications, thereby significantly degrading performance. To cope with failures, the *de facto* general-purpose error recovery technique in HPC is checkpoint and rollback recovery [5]. The idea consists of periodically saving the state of the application, so that, when an error strikes, the application can be restored into one of its former states. The most widely used protocol is coordinated checkpointing, where all processes periodically stop computing and synchronize to write critical application data onto stable storage. The frequency at which checkpoints are taken should be carefully tuned, so that the overhead in a fault-free execution is not too important, but also so that the price to pay in case of failure remains reasonable. The Young and Daly formulas [6,7] provide good approximations of the optimal checkpointing interval.

In this chapter, we discuss co-scheduling on failure-prone platforms. Checkpointing helps to mitigate the impact of a failure on a given application, but it must be complemented by redistributions to rebalance the load among applications. Co-scheduling usually involves partitioning the applications into *packs*, and then scheduling each pack in sequence, as efficiently as possible. The objective is therefore to determine a partition into packs, and an assignment of processors to applications, that minimize the sum of the execution times of the packs. Given a pack, that is, a set of parallel tasks that start execution simultaneously, there are two main opportunities for redistributing processors. First, when a task completes, the applications that are still running can claim its processors. Second, when a failure strikes a task, that task is delayed. By adding more resources to it, we can reduce its final completion time. However, we have to be careful, because each redistribution has a cost, which depends on the volume of data that is exchanged, and on the number of processors involved in redistribution. In addition, adding processors to a task increases its probability to fail, so there is a trade-off to achieve in order to minimize the expected completion time of the pack.

The major contributions of this work are the following:

1. The NP-completeness proof for the general partitioning problem with $k \geq 3$ tasks per pack in a fault-free context, and an approximation algorithm.
2. The design of a detailed and comprehensive model for scheduling a given pack of tasks on a failure-prone platform.
3. An optimal algorithm to assign processors to applications when the tasks that form a pack are given and when no redistributions can be done.
4. The NP-completeness proof for the problem with redistributions.
5. The design and assessment of several polynomial-time heuristics to deal with the general problem with failures and redistribution costs. These heuristics show very good performance while executing in very short time, hence validating the approach.

The chapter is organized as follows. We discuss related work in Section 5.2. The problem is then formally defined in Section 5.3. Theoretical results are presented in Section 5.4, exhibiting the problem complexity, discussing subproblems and optimal solutions, and providing an approximation algorithm. Building upon these results, several polynomial-time heuristics are described and thoroughly evaluated in Section 5.5. Finally, we conclude and discuss future work in Section 5.6.

5.2 RELATED WORK

In this chapter, we deal with pack scheduling for parallel tasks, aiming at makespan minimization (recall that the makespan is the total execution time). The corresponding problem with sequential tasks (tasks that execute on a single processor) is easy to solve for the makespan minimization objective: simply make a pack out of the largest p tasks, and proceed likewise while there remain tasks. Note that the pack scheduling problem with sequential tasks has been widely studied for other objective functions, see Reference 8 for various job cost functions, and Reference 9 for a survey. Back to the problem with sequential tasks and the makespan objective, Koole and Righter in Reference 10 deal with the case where the execution time of each task is unknown but defined by a probabilistic distribution. They improve the result of Deb and Serfozo [11], who considered the stochastic problem with identical jobs. Ikura et al. [12] solve the makespan minimization problem where tasks have identical execution times, but different release times and deadlines; they assume agreeable deadlines, meaning that if a task has an earlier release time than another, it also has an earlier deadline. Koehler et al. [13] propose a linear time solution to this last problem, and further give a $O(n^3)$ solution to the problem of minimizing the number of packs while achieving optimal makespan.

We focus next on the problem of co-scheduling parallel tasks in Section 5.2.1, and then we discuss related work on resilience in Section 5.2.2.

5.2.1 Parallel Tasks

To the best of our knowledge, the problem with parallel tasks has not been studied as such. However, it was introduced by Dutot et al. [14] as a moldable-by-phase model to approximate the moldable problem. The moldable task model is similar to the pack scheduling model, but without the additional constraint (pack constraint) that the execution of new tasks cannot start before all tasks in the current pack are completed. Dutot et al. [14] provide an optimal polynomial-time solution for the problem of pack scheduling identical independent tasks, using a dynamic programming algorithm. This is the only instance of pack scheduling with parallel tasks that we found in the literature.

In practice, pack scheduling is really useful as shown by recent results. Li et al. [15] propose a framework to predict the energy and performance impacts of power-aware message passing interface (MPI) task aggregation. Frachtenberg et al. [16] show that system utilization can be improved through their schemes to co-schedule jobs based on their load-balancing requirements and interprocessor communication patterns. Shantharam et al. [2] study co-scheduling based on speedup profiles, similar to our work, but packs can have only one or two tasks; still, they report faster workload completion and corresponding savings in system energy.

Several publications [17–19] consider co-scheduling at a single multicore node, when contention for resources by co-scheduled tasks leads to complex trade-offs between energy and performance measures. Chandra et al. [18] predict and utilize interthread cache contention at a multicore in order to improve performance. Hankendi and Coskun [19] show that there can be measurable gains in energy per unit of work through the application of their multilevel co-scheduling technique at runtime, which is based on classifying tasks according to specific performance measures. Bhaduria and McKee [17] consider local search heuristics to co-schedule tasks in a resource-aware manner at a multicore node to achieve significant gains in thread throughput per watt.

These publications demonstrate that complex trade-offs cannot be captured through the use of the speedup measure alone, without significant additional measurements to capture performance variations from cross-application interference at a multicore node. Additionally, and following Reference 2 where packs have one or two tasks only, we expect significant benefits even when we aggregate only across multicore nodes because speedups suffer due to the longer latencies of data transfer across nodes. We can therefore project savings in energy as being commensurate with the savings in the time to complete a workload through co-scheduling. Hence, we only test configurations where no more than a single application can be scheduled on a multicore node.

One could ask, given a set of n tasks to schedule, why schedule them in packs rather than globally? A global schedule would avoid the gaps incurred by some processors between the end of a pack and the beginning of the next pack, thereby potentially decreasing the makespan. However, there are several reasons to prefer pack scheduling. First, a global schedule is very hard to construct. Best-known heuristics greedily assign a new task to a set of processors as soon as this set terminates execution, thereby constraining the number of resources to be the same for the new task as for the last task. Our co-schedule does not suffer from this rigidity in processor assignment decisions. Second, the cost of scheduling itself is greatly reduced with pack scheduling. The scheduler launches a set of tasks and transfers corresponding input data only at the beginning of a pack. No overhead is paid until all tasks in the pack return, and a new pack is executed.

5.2.2 Resilience

One of the most used technique to handle fail-stop errors in HPC is checkpoint and rollback recovery [5]. The idea is to periodically save the system state, or the application memory footprint onto a stable storage. Then, after a downtime and a recovery time, the system can be restored into a former valid state (rollback step). Another technique to dealing with fail-stop errors is process replication, which consists of replicating a process and even replicate communications. For instance, the project RedMPI [20] implements a process replication mechanism and quadruplicates each communication.

In this chapter, we use a lightweight checkpointing protocol called the *double checkpointing algorithm* [21,22]. This is an in-memory checkpointing protocol, which avoids the high overhead of disk checkpoints. Processors are paired: each processor has an associated processor called its *buddy processor*. When a processor stores its checkpoint file in its own memory, it also sends this file to its buddy, and the buddy does the same. Therefore, each processor stores two checkpoints, its own and that of its buddy. When a failure occurs, the faulty processor loses these two checkpoint files, and the buddy must resend both checkpoints to the faulty node. If a second failure hits the buddy during this recovery period (which happens with very low probability), we have a fatal failure and the system cannot be recovered.

To the best of our knowledge, this is the first work to consider co-schedules and failures, and hence to use malleable applications [23,24] to allow redistributions of processors between applications. More related work on models for parallel applications and resilience are discussed in Reference 25.

We point out that co-scheduling with packs can be seen as the static counterpart of batch scheduling techniques, where jobs are dynamically partitioned into batches as they are submitted to the system (see Reference 26 and the references therein). Batch scheduling is a complex online problem, where jobs have release times and deadlines, and where only partial information on the whole workload is known when taking scheduling decisions. On the contrary, co-scheduling applies to a set of applications that are all ready for execution. When considering failures, we restrict to a single pack, because scheduling already becomes difficult for a single pack with failures and redistributions.

5.3 PROBLEM DEFINITION

The application consists of n independent tasks $T_1, \ldots, T_n$. The target execution platform consists of p identical processors, and each task T_i can be assigned an arbitrary number $\sigma(i)$ of processors, where $1 \leq \sigma(i) \leq p$. The objective is to minimize the total execution time by co-scheduling several tasks onto the p resources. Note that the approach is agnostic of the granularity of each processor, which can be either a single CPU or a multicore node.

5.3.1 SPEEDUP PROFILES

Let $t_{i,j}$ be the execution time of task T_i with j processors, and $work(i,j) = j \times t_{i,j}$ be the corresponding work. We assume the following for $1 \leq i \leq n$ and $1 \leq j < p$:

$$\text{Weakly decreasing execution time: } t_{i,j+1} \leq t_{i,j}. \tag{5.1}$$

$$\text{Weakly increasing work: } work(i,j+1) \geq work(i,j). \tag{5.2}$$

Equation 5.1 implies that execution time is a nonincreasing function of the number of processors. Equation 5.2 states that efficiency decreases with the number of enrolled processors: in other words, parallelization has a cost! As a side note, we observe that these requirements make good sense in practice: many scientific tasks T_i are such that $t_{i,j}$ first decreases (due to load-balancing) and then increases (due to communication overhead), reaching a minimum for $j = j_0$; we can always let $t_{i,j} = t_{i,j_0}$ for $j \geq j_0$ by never actually using more than j_0 processors for T_i.

Remarks

Determining j_0 for a given application is a challenge by itself. In most cases, it is obtained by profiling and interpolation. Also, in case of an imperfect knowledge of execution-time profiles, it is possible to use curve-fitting techniques to construct near complete knowledge, and then use this constructed knowledge. We treat the same application with two different problem sizes as two different applications (their execution-time profiles could potentially be different). Thus, sensitivity of runtime to different parameters that could change runtime profiles is inherently taken care of.

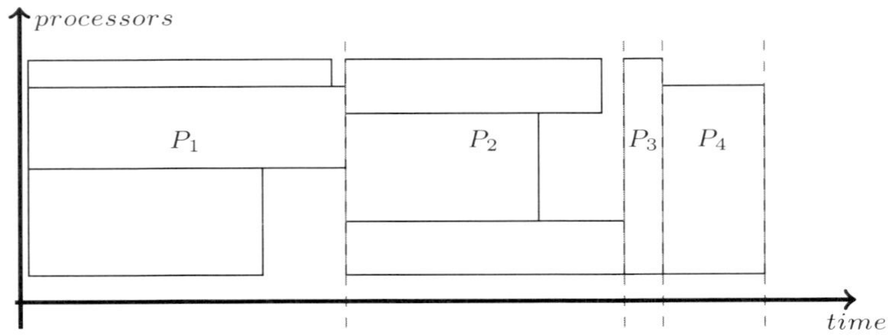

FIGURE 5.1 A co-schedule with four packs P_1 to P_4.

5.3.2 Co-Schedules

A co-schedule partitions the n tasks into groups (called *packs*), so that (i) all tasks from a given pack start their execution at the same time; and (ii) two tasks from different packs have disjoint execution intervals. For instance, in the example of Figure 5.1, the two first packs have three tasks, the third pack has only one task, and the last pack has two tasks. The execution time, or *cost*, of a pack is the maximal execution time of a task within that pack, and the cost of a co-schedule is the sum of the costs of all packs.

5.3.3 Fault Model

We consider fail-stop errors, which are detected instantaneously. To model the rate at which faults occur on one processor, we use an exponential probability law of parameter λ. The mean (or MTBF) of this law is $\mu = 1/\lambda$. The MTBF of an application depends upon the number of processors it is using, and hence changes whenever a redistribution occurs. Specifically, if application T_i is (currently) executed on j processors, its MTBF is $\mu_{i,j} = \mu/j$ (see Proposition 1.2 in Reference 4 for a proof).

To recover from fail-stop errors, we use a lightweight checkpointing protocol called the *double checkpointing algorithm*, or *buddy algorithm* [21,22]. This is an in-memory checkpointing protocol, which avoids the high overhead of disk checkpoints. Processors are paired: each processor has an associated processor called its *buddy processor*. When a processor stores its checkpoint file in its own memory, it also sends this file to its buddy, and the buddy does the same. Therefore, each processor stores two checkpoints, its own and that of its buddy. When a failure occurs, the faulty processor loses these two checkpoint files, and the buddy must resend both checkpoints to the faulty node. If a second failure hits the buddy during this recovery period (which happens with very low probability), we have a fatal failure and the system cannot be recovered. Note that the number of processors assigned to each application must be even.

We enforce periodic checkpointing for each application. Formally, if application T_i is executed on j processors, there is a checkpoint every period of length $\tau_{i,j}$, with a cost $C_{i,j}$. We now explain how to compute the cost $C_{i,j}$ of a checkpoint when application T_i executes with j processors. Let m_i be the memory footprint (total data size) of application T_i. Each of the j processors holds m_i/j data, which it must send to its buddy processor. The time to communicate a message of size s is $\beta + s/\tau$, where β is a start-up latency and τ the link bandwidth. We derive that $C_{i,j} = (m_i/j\tau) + \beta$.

As for the checkpointing period $\tau_{i,j}$, we use Young's formula [7] and let

$$\tau_{i,j} = \sqrt{2\mu_{i,j}C_{i,j}} + C_{i,j}. \tag{5.3}$$

Because $\tau_{i,j}$ is a first-order approximation, the formula is valid only if $C_{i,j} \ll \mu_{i,j}$. When a fault strikes, there is first a downtime of duration D, and then a recovery period of duration $R_{i,j}$. We assume that $R_{i,j} = C_{i,j}$, while the downtime value D is platform-dependent and not application-dependent.

5.3.4 Execution Time without Redistribution

To compute the expected execution time of a schedule, we first have to compute the expected execution time of an application T_i executed on j processors subject to failures. We first consider the case without redistribution (but taking failures into account). Recall that $t_{i,j}$ is the execution time of application T_i on j processors in a fault-free scenario. Let $t^R_{i,j}(\alpha)$ be the expected time required to compute a fraction α of the total work for application T_i on j processors, with $0 \leq \alpha \leq 1$. We need to consider such a partial execution of T_i on j processors to prepare for the case with redistributions.

Recall that the execution of application T_i is periodic, and that the period $\tau_{i,j}$ depends only on the number of processors, but not on the remaining execution time (see Equation 5.3). After a work of duration $\tau_{i,j} - C_{i,j}$, there is a checkpoint of duration $C_{i,j}$. In a fault-free execution, the time required to execute the fraction of work α is $\alpha t_{i,j}$, hence a total number of checkpoints of

$$N^{\mathrm{ff}}_{i,j}(\alpha) = \left\lfloor \frac{\alpha t_{i,j}}{\tau_{i,j} - C_{i,j}} \right\rfloor. \tag{5.4}$$

Next, we have to estimate the expected execution time for each period of work between checkpoints. We are able to calculate the expectation of one period of work according to an MTBF value and a number of processors. The expected time to execute successfully during T units of time with j processors (there are $T - C$ units of work and C units of checkpoint, where T is the period) is equal to $((1/\lambda j) + D)\,(e^{\lambda j T} - 1)$ [4]. Therefore, in order to compute $t^R_{i,j}(\alpha)$, we compute the sum of the expected time for each period, plus the expected time for the last (possibly incomplete) period. This last period is denoted as τ_{last} and defined as

$$\tau_{last} = \alpha t_{i,j} - N^{\mathrm{ff}}_{i,j}(\alpha)(\tau_{i,j} - C_{i,j}). \tag{5.5}$$

Note that τ_{last} depends on α because τ_{last} represents the incomplete fraction of $\tau_{i,j} - C_{i,j}$ at the end of the application. The first $N^{\mathrm{ff}}_{i,j}(\alpha)$ periods are equal (of length $\tau_{i,j}$), and hence have the same expected time. Finally, we obtain:

$$t^R_{i,j}(\alpha) = e^{\lambda j R_{i,j}} \left(\frac{1}{\lambda j} + D\right) \left(N^{\mathrm{ff}}_{i,j}(\alpha)(e^{\lambda j \tau_{i,j}} - 1) + (e^{\lambda j \tau_{last}} - 1)\right). \tag{5.6}$$

In a fault-free environment, it is natural to assume that the execution time is nonincreasing with the number of processors. Here, this assumption would translate into the condition:

$$t^R_{i,j+1}(\alpha) \leq t^R_{i,j}(\alpha) \quad \text{for } 1 \leq i \leq n, \quad 1 \leq j < p, \quad 0 \leq \alpha \leq 1. \tag{5.7}$$

However, when we allocate more processors to an application, even though the work is further parallelized, the probability of failures increases, and the corresponding waste increases as well. Therefore, adding resources to an application is useful up to a threshold. After this threshold, we have $t^R_{i,j+1} \geq t^R_{i,j}$. In order to satisfy Equation 5.7, we restrict the number of processors assigned to each application, and never assign more processors than the previous threshold. In other words, if T_i is already assigned j processors, we consider assigning more processors to it only if $t^R_{i,j+1} \leq t^R_{i,j}$. Formally, this defines a maximum number of processors, $j_{\max}(i)$, for each application T_i:

$$j_{\max}(i) = \min_{1 \leq j \leq p} \{j \text{ such that } t^R_{i,k} \geq t^R_{i,j} \text{ for all } k > j\}, \tag{5.8}$$

and we assume that $t^R_{i,j+1} \leq t^R_{i,j}$ for all $j < j_{\max}(i)$.

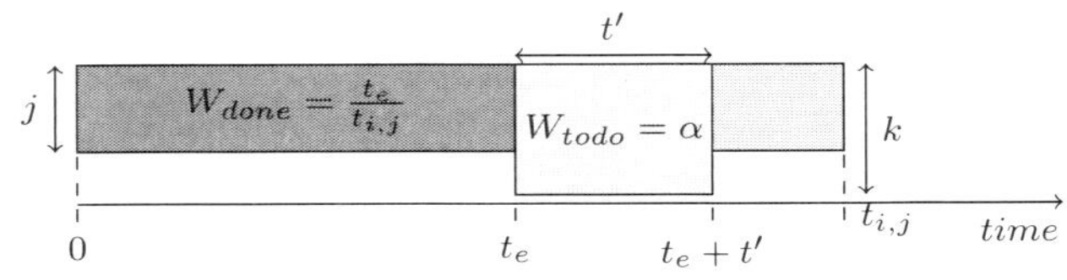

FIGURE 5.2 Work representation for application T_i at time t_e.

Another common assumption for malleable applications is that the work is nondecreasing when the number of processors increases [23]: this amounts to say that no super-linear speedup is possible, as stated earlier for the fault-free scenario. Hence, we assume here that for $1 \leq i \leq n$, $1 \leq j < p$ and $0 \leq \alpha \leq 1$, $(j+1) \times t^R_{i,j+1}(\alpha) \geq j \times t^R_{i,j}(\alpha)$.

For convenience, we denote by t^U_i the current expected finish time of application T_i at any point of the execution. Initially, if application T_i is allocated to j processors, we have $t^U_i = t^R_{i,j}(1)$.

5.3.5 Redistributing Processors

There are two major cases for which it may be useful to redistribute processors: (1) in a fault-free scenario, when an application ends, it releases processors that can be used to accelerate other applications, and (2) when an error strikes, we may want to force the release of processors, so that we can assign more processors to the application that has been slowed down by the error.

5.3.5.1 Fault-Free Scenario

We first consider a simplified scenario without checkpoint (nor failure), in order to explain how redistribution works. Consider for instance that q processors are released when application T_2 ends. We can allocate q_1 new processors to application T_1, and q_3 new processors to application T_3, where $q_1 + q_3 = q$. This redistribution will take some time (redistribution cost RC_i, detailed below), after which T_1 and T_3 will resume execution, and we first need to compute the new expected completion time for their remaining fraction of work.

Consider that a redistribution is conducted at time t_e (the end time of an application), and that application T_i, initially with j processors, now has $k = j + q > j$ processors. What will be the new finish time of T_i? The fraction of work already executed for T_i is $t_e/t_{i,j}$, because the application was supposed to finish at time $t_{i,j}$ (see Figure 5.2). The remaining fraction of work is $\alpha = 1 - (t_e/t_{i,j})$, and the time required to complete this work with k processors is t', where $t'/t_{i,k} = \alpha$; hence

$$t' = \alpha t_{i,k} = \left(1 - \frac{t_e}{t_{i,j}}\right) t_{i,k}.$$

Furthermore, we need to add a redistribution cost: when moving from j to $k = j + q$ processors, the application T_i must redistribute its m_i data across the processors. The application keeps its initial j processors, which now hold too much data, and enrolls $q = k - j$ new processors, which have no data yet. Each of the original j processors initially holds m_i/j data and will keep only m_i/k after the redistribution; it sends m_i/jk data to each of the newly enrolled q processors, thereby keeping $(m_i/j) - (k - j)(m_i/jk) = (m_i/k)$ data. In turn, each new processor receives m_i/jk data from j processors and duly gets m_i/k data in the end.

What is the best schedule for such a redistribution, and what time does it require? We first account for a constant start-up overhead S, paid for initiating the redistribution call. Then we adopt a realistic one-port communication model [27] where a processor can send and receive at most one message at any time-step. Independent communications, involving distinct sender/receiver pairs, can take place in parallel; however, two messages sent by the same processor will be serialized. Recall that the time to communicate a message of size s is $\beta + (s/\tau)$. To schedule the redistribution, we build a bipartite graph G with j nodes on the left and q nodes on the right, and we count the number of rounds required to schedule the redistribution. Thanks to Konig's theorem [28], we obtain a number of rounds equal to $\max(j, k-j)$ (see Reference 25 for details), and the redistribution cost is

$$RC_i^{j\to k} = S + \max(j, k-j) \times \left(\frac{m_i}{jk\tau} + \beta\right). \tag{5.9}$$

Needless to say, we would perform a redistribution if the cost of redistribution is lower than the benefit of allocating new processors to the application, that is, if

$$t_{i,j} - \left(t_e + t'\right) > RC_i^{j\to k}.$$

5.3.5.2 Accounting for Failures

When struck by a fault, an application needs to recover from the failure and to re-execute some work. While the application loads were well balanced initially in order to minimize total execution time, now the faulty application is likely to exceed its expected execution time. If it becomes the longest application of the schedule, we try to assign it more processors so as to reduce its completion time, hence redistributing processors.

Because we use the double checkpointing algorithm as the resilience model, we consider processors by pairs. We aim at redistributing pairs of processors either when an application is finished, at time t_e (as in the fault-free scenario discussed above), or when a failure occurs, say at time t_f. In each case, we need to compute the remaining work, and the new expected completion time of the applications that have been affected by the event. Given an application T_i, we keep track of the time when the last redistribution or failure occurred for this application, denoted as t_{lastR_i}. At time t (corresponding to the end of an application or to a failure), we know exactly how many checkpoints have been taken by application T_i executed on j processors since t_{lastR_i}, and we let this number be $N_{i,j}$:

$$N_{i,j} = \left\lfloor \frac{t - t_{lastR_i}}{\tau_{i,j}} \right\rfloor. \tag{5.10}$$

We begin with the case of an application completion: consider that an application finishes its execution at time t_e, hence releasing some processors. We consider assigning some of these processors to an application T_i currently running on j processors. The fraction of work executed by T_i since the last redistribution is $(t_e - t_{lastR_i} - N_{i,j}C_{i,j})/t_{i,j}$, because we have to remove the cost of the checkpoints, during which the application did not execute useful work.

We apply the same reasoning for the second case, when a fault occurs. In this case, we need to consider the application T_i where the failure stroke, and other applications $T_{i'}$ from which we would remove some processors (in order to give them to T_i).

1. Consider that application T_i is running on j processors and subject to a failure at time t_f. Therefore, T_i needs to recover from its last valid checkpoint, and the fraction of work executed by T_i corresponds to the number of entire periods completed since the last failure or redistribution t_{lastR_i}, each followed by a checkpoint. We can express it as $(N_{i,j} \times (\tau_{i,j} - C_{i,j}))/t_{i,j}$.
2. At time t_f, consider application $T_{i'}$, on which we perform a redistribution, moving from j' to $j' - q$ processors, with $q > 0$. The fraction of work executed by $T_{i'}$ can be computed as in the application ending case scenario: it is $(t_f - t_{lastR_{i'}} - N_{i',j'}C_{i',j'})/t_{i',j'}$.

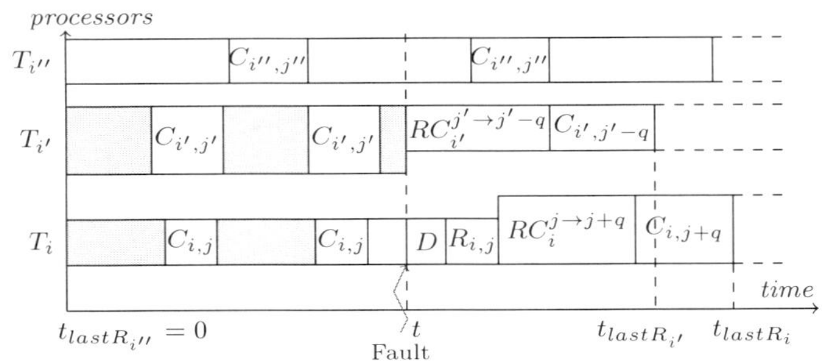

FIGURE 5.3 Example of redistribution when a fault strikes application T_i. The shaded rectangles correspond to useful work done by T_i and $T_{i'}$ before the failure. $T_{i''}$ is not affected by the failure, since it does not perform a redistribution.

Finally, for any application subject to a redistribution or a failure, let α_i be the remaining fraction of work to be executed by T_i, that is, 1 minus the sum of the fraction of work executed before t_{lastR_i} and the fraction of work expressed above (computed between t_{lastR_i} and t).

Similarly to the fault-free scenario, $RC_i^{j\to k}$ denotes the redistribution cost for application T_i when moving from j to k processors. Redistribution can now add ($k > j$) or remove ($k < j$) processors to application T_i, and the cost is expressed as

$$RC_i^{j\to k} = S + \max(\min(j,k), |k-j|) \times \left(\frac{m_i}{kj\tau} + \beta\right). \tag{5.11}$$

We are now ready to compute the new values of t_{lastR_i} for all applications subject to a failure or a redistribution, and we illustrate the different scenarios in Figure 5.3. Let t be the time of the event (end of application $t = t_e$, or failure $t = t_f$), and consider that a redistribution is done either for a faulty application T_i or for another application $T_{i'}$. After a redistribution, we always start by taking a checkpoint before computing with the new period. Therefore, if a fault occurs, we do not have to redistribute again.

For the faulty application T_i, the new value of t_{lastR_i} hence becomes $t_{lastR_i} = t + D + R_{i,j} + RC_i^{j\to k} + C_{i,k}$ (we need to account for the downtime and recovery). However, if $T_{i'}$ is performing a redistribution but it was not struck by a failure, it can start the redistribution at time t: either it is getting new processors that are available following the end of an application, or is using less processors and can perform its redistribution. In all cases, we have $t_{lastR_{i'}} = t + RC_{i'}^{j'\to k'} + C_{i',k'}$. Note that we can have processors involved simultaneously in two redistributions, as they will only receive data from the other processors of the faulty application T_i, and send data to the other processors of the nonfaulty application $T_{i'}$. We assume that sends and receives can be done in parallel without slowdown.

Finally, the expected finish time of an application T_i for which we have updated t_{lastR_i} becomes $t_i^U = t_{lastR_i} + t_{i,k}^R(\alpha_i)$, where k is the new number of processors on which T_i is executed, and α_i the remaining fraction of work. Similarly to the fault-free scenario, we give extra processors to an application only if the new expected finish time t_i^U is lower than the one with no redistribution.

Note that we consider that we cannot enroll processors that have not yet finished the current redistribution, that is, if an event happens between t and $t_{lastR_{i'}}$ in Figure 5.3, the processors involved in T_i and $T_{i'}$ cannot be considered for a new redistribution.

5.3.6 Optimization Problems

We consider two optimization problems.

The general one is studied in a fault-free context with no redistribution, and builds packs with at most k tasks. The most general problem is when $k = p$, but, in some frameworks, we may have an upper bound $k < p$ on the maximum number of tasks within each pack.

Definition 5.1 (k-IN-p-COSCHEDULE)

Given a fixed constant $k \leq p$, find a co-schedule with at most k tasks per pack that minimizes the execution time.

When considering failures and redistributions, we focus on a single pack made of n applications.

Definition 5.2 (RESILIENT-COSCHED-1PACK)

Given n malleable applications $\{T_1, \ldots, T_n\}$, their speedup profiles, and an execution platform with p identical processors subject to failures with individual rate λ, minimize the maximum of the expected completion times of the applications. Redistributions are allowed only when an application completes execution or is struck by a failure (with a cost specified in Section 5.3.5).

5.4 THEORETICAL ANALYSIS

In this section, we first focus on the problem in a failure-free scenario, where no checkpoints are taken. We discuss the complexity of the problem in Section 5.4.1, by exhibiting polynomial and NP-complete instances. Next we discuss how to optimally schedule a set of k tasks in a single pack (Section 5.4.2), both in the failure-free scenario and when accounting for failures but not doing any redistributions. Then, focusing again on the failure-free scenario, we explain how to compute the optimal solution of k-IN-p-COSCHEDULE (in expected exponential cost) in Section 5.4.3, and we provide an approximation algorithm in Section 5.4.4. Finally, we prove the NP-completeness of the problem RESILIENT-COSCHED-1PACK when considering failures and performing redistributions in Section 5.4.5.

5.4.1 COMPLEXITY

Theorem 5.1

The 1-IN-p-COSCHEDULE and 2-IN-p-COSCHEDULE problems can both be solved in polynomial time.

Proof. This result is obvious for 1-IN-p-COSCHEDULE: Each task is assigned exactly p processors (see Equation 5.1) and the minimum execution time is $\sum_{i=1}^{n} t_{i,p}$.

The proof is more involved for 2-IN-p-COSCHEDULE, and we start with the 2-IN-2-COSCHEDULE problem to get an intuition. Consider the weighted undirected graph $G = (V, E)$, where $|V| = n$, each vertex $v_i \in V$ corresponding to a task T_i. The edge set E is the following: (i) for all i, there is a loop on v_i of weight $t_{i,2}$; (ii) for all $i < i'$, there is an edge between v_i and $v_{i'}$ of weight $\max(t_{i,1}, t_{i',1})$. Finding a perfect matching of minimal weight in G leads to the optimal solution to 2-IN-2-COSCHEDULE, which can thus be solved in polynomial time.

For the 2-IN-p-COSCHEDULE problem, the proof is similar, the only difference lies in the construction of the edge set E: (i) for all i, there is a loop on v_i of weight $t_{i,p}$; (ii) for all $i < i'$, there is an edge between v_i and $v_{i'}$ of weight $\min_{j=1..p}\left(\max(t_{i,p-j}, t_{i',j})\right)$. Again, a perfect matching of minimal weight in G gives the optimal solution to 2-IN-p-COSCHEDULE. We conclude that the 2-IN-p-COSCHEDULE problem can be solved in polynomial time. ■

Theorem 5.2

When $k \geq 3$, the k-IN-p-COSCHEDULE problem is strongly NP-complete.

Algorithm 5.1: Finding the Optimal 1-Pack-Schedule σ of k Tasks in the Same Pack

```
Procedure Optimal-1-pack-schedule(T_1, ..., T_k)
begin
    for i = 1 to k do
    |   σ(i) ← 1;
    end
    Let L be the list of tasks sorted in nonincreasing values of ≼_σ;
    p_available := p − k;
    while p_available ≠ 0 do
    |   T_{i*} := head(L);
    |   L := tail(L);
    |   σ(i*) ← σ(i*) + 1;
    |   p_available := p_available − 1;
    |   L := Insert T_{i*} in L according to its ≼_σ value;
    end
    return σ;
end
```

The proof can be found in Reference 3. It is based on a reduction from 3-PARTITION. Note that the 3-IN-p-COSCHEDULE problem is NP-complete, and the 2-IN-p-COSCHEDULE problem can be solved in polynomial time; hence, 3-IN-3-COSCHEDULE is the simplest problem whose complexity remains open.

5.4.2 SCHEDULING A PACK OF TASKS

In this section, we discuss how to optimally schedule a set of k tasks in a single pack: the k tasks $T_1, \ldots, T_k$ are given, and we search for an assignment function $\sigma : \{1, \ldots, k\} \rightarrow \{1, \ldots, p\}$ such that $\sum_{i=1}^{k} \sigma(i) \leq p$, where $\sigma(i)$ is the number of processors assigned to task T_i. Such a schedule is called a 1-pack-schedule, and its *cost* is $\max_{1 \leq i \leq k} t_{i,\sigma(i)}$. In Algorithm 5.1, we use the notation $T_i \preccurlyeq_\sigma T_j$ if $t_{i,\sigma(i)} \leq t_{j,\sigma(j)}$:

Theorem 5.3

Given k tasks to be scheduled on p processors in a single pack, Algorithm 5.1 finds a 1-pack-schedule of minimum cost in time $O(p \log(k))$.

In this greedy algorithm, we first assign one processor to each task, and while there are processors that are not processing any task, we select the task with the longest execution time and assign an extra processor to this task. Algorithm 5.1 performs $p - k$ iterations to assign the extra processors. We denote by $\sigma^{(\ell)}$ the current value of the function σ at the end of iteration ℓ. For convenience, we let $t_{i,0} = +\infty$ for $1 \leq i \leq k$. We start with the following lemma:

Lemma 5.1

At the end of iteration ℓ of Algorithm 5.1, let $T_{i^\star}$ be the first task of the sorted list, that is, the task with longest execution time. Then, for all i, $t_{i^\star,\sigma^{(\ell)}(i^\star)} \leq t_{i,\sigma^{(\ell)}(i)-1}$.

Proof. Let $T_{i^\star}$ be the task with longest execution time at the end of iteration ℓ. For tasks such that $\sigma^{(\ell)}(i) = 1$, the result is obvious since $t_{i,0} = +\infty$. Let us consider any task T_i such that $\sigma^{(\ell)}(i) > 1$. Let $\ell' + 1$ be the last iteration when a new processor was assigned to task T_i: $\sigma^{(\ell')}(i) = \sigma^{(\ell)}(i) - 1$

and $\ell' < \ell$. By definition of iteration $\ell' + 1$, task T_i was chosen because $t_{i,\sigma^{(\ell')}(i)}$ was greater than any other task, in particular, $t_{i,\sigma^{(\ell')}(i)} \geq t_{i^\star,\sigma^{(\ell')}(i^\star)}$. Also, since we never remove processors from tasks, we have $\sigma^{(\ell')}(i) \leq \sigma^{(\ell)}(i)$ and $\sigma^{(\ell')}(i^\star) \leq \sigma^{(\ell)}(i^\star)$. Finally, $t_{i^\star,\sigma^{(\ell)}(i^\star)} \leq t_{i^\star,\sigma^{(\ell')}(i^\star)} \leq t_{i,\sigma^{(\ell')}(i)} = t_{i,\sigma^{(\ell)}(i)-1}$. ■

Proof of Theorem 5.3. Let σ be the 1-pack-schedule returned by Algorithm 5.1 of cost $c(\sigma)$, and let $T_{i^\star}$ be a task such that $c(\sigma) = t_{i^\star,\sigma(i^\star)}$. Let σ' be a 1-pack-schedule of cost $c(\sigma')$. We prove below that $c(\sigma') \geq c(\sigma)$; hence, σ is a 1-pack-schedule of minimum cost:

1. If $\sigma'(i^\star) \leq \sigma(i^\star)$, then $T_{i^\star}$ has fewer processors in σ' than in σ; hence, its execution time is larger, and $c(\sigma') \geq c(\sigma)$.
2. If $\sigma'(i^\star) > \sigma(i^\star)$, then there exists i such that $\sigma'(i) < \sigma(i)$ (since the total number of processors is p in both σ and σ'). We can apply the previous lemma at the end of the last iteration, where $T_{i^\star}$ is the task of maximum execution time: $t_{i^\star,\sigma(i^\star)} \leq t_{i,\sigma(i)-1} \leq t_{i,\sigma'(i)}$, and therefore $c(\sigma') \geq c(\sigma)$.

Finally, the time complexity is obtained as follows: first, we sort k elements, in time $O(k \log k)$. Then there are $p - k$ iterations, and at each iteration, we insert an element in a sorted list of $k - 1$ elements, which takes $O(\log k)$ operations (use a heap for the data structure of L). ■

Note that it is easy to compute an optimal 1-pack-schedule using a dynamic-programming algorithm: the optimal cost is $c(k,p)$, which we compute using the recurrence formula

$$c(i,q) = \min_{1 \leq q' \leq q} \{\max(c(i-1, q-q'), t_{i,q'})\}$$

for $2 \leq i \leq k$ and $1 \leq q \leq p$, initialized by $c(1,q) = t_{1,q}$, and $c(i,0) = +\infty$. The complexity of this algorithm is $O(kp^2)$. However, we can significantly reduce the complexity of this algorithm by using Algorithm 5.1.

With failures. It is not difficult to extend this algorithm to solve the problem with failures, but still without redistributions:

Theorem 5.4

The RESILIENT-COSCHED-1PACK problem without redistributions can be solved in polynomial time $O(n)$, where n is the number of applications.

We replace $t_{i,j}$ by $t^R_{i,j}(1)$, and instead of adding processors one-by-one, we add them two-by-two.

5.4.3 OPTIMAL SOLUTION OF *k*-IN-*p*-COSCHEDULE

In this section, we sketch two methods to find the optimal solution to the general k-IN-p-COSCHEDULE problem. This can be useful to solve some small-size instances, albeit at the price of a cost exponential in the number of tasks n.

The first method is to generate all possible partitions of the tasks into packs. This amounts to computing all partitions of n elements into subsets of cardinality at most k. For a given partition of tasks into packs, we use Algorithm 5.1 to find the optimal processor assignment for each pack, and we can compute the optimal cost for the partition. We still have to calculate the minimum of these costs among all partitions.

The second method is to cast the problem in terms of an integer linear program:

Theorem 5.5

The following integer linear program characterizes the k-IN-p-COSCHEDULE problem, where the unknown variables are the $x_{i,j,b}$'s (Boolean variables) and the y_b's (rational variables), for $1 \leq i, b \leq n$ and $1 \leq j \leq p$:

$$\begin{array}{ll} \text{Minimize } \sum_{b=1}^{n} y_b & \text{subject to} \\ \text{(i) } \sum_{j,b} x_{i,j,b} = 1, & 1 \leq i \leq n \\ \text{(ii) } \sum_{i,j} x_{i,j,b} \leq k, & 1 \leq b \leq n \\ \text{(iii) } \sum_{i,j} j \times x_{i,j,b} \leq p, & 1 \leq b \leq n \\ \text{(iv) } x_{i,j,b} \times t_{i,j} \leq y_b, & 1 \leq i, b \leq n, 1 \leq j \leq p. \end{array} \quad (5.12)$$

Proof. The $x_{i,j,b}$'s are such that $x_{i,j,b} = 1$ if and only if task T_i is in the pack b and it is executed on j processors; y_b is the execution time of pack b. Since there are no more than n packs (one task per pack), $b \leq n$. The sum $\sum_{b=1}^{n} y_b$ is therefore the total execution time ($y_b = 0$ if there are no tasks in pack b). Constraint (i) states that each task is assigned to exactly one pack b, and with one number of processors j. Constraint (ii) ensures that there are not more than k tasks in a pack. Constraint (iii) adds up the number of processors in pack b, which should not exceed p. Finally, constraint (iv) computes the cost of each pack. ■

5.4.4 Approximation Algorithm

In this section, we introduce PACK-APPROX, a 3-approximation algorithm for the p-IN-p-COSCHEDULE problem: if COST_{OPT} is the optimal solution, and $\text{COST}_{\text{algo}}$ is the output of the algorithm, we guarantee that $\text{COST}_{\text{algo}} \leq 3\text{COST}_{\text{OPT}}$. The design principle of PACK-APPROX is the following: we start from the assignment where each task is executed on one processor, and use Algorithm 5.2 to build a first solution. Algorithm 5.2 is a greedy heuristic that builds a co-schedule when each task is preassigned a number of processors for execution. Then, we iteratively refine the solution, adding a processor to the task with longest execution time, and re-executing Algorithm 5.2. Here are the details on both algorithms:

Algorithm 5.2. The k-IN-p-COSCHEDULE problem with processor preassignments remains strongly NP-complete (use a similar reduction as in the proof of Theorem 5.2). We propose a greedy procedure in Algorithm 5.2 that is similar to the First Fit Decreasing Height algorithm for strip packing [29]. The output is a co-schedule with at most k tasks per pack, and the complexity is $O(n \log(n))$ (dominated by sorting).

Algorithm 5.3. We iterate the calls to Algorithm 5.2, adding a processor to the task with longest execution time, until (i) either the task of longest execution time is already assigned p processors, or (ii) the sum of the work of all tasks is greater than p times the longest execution time. The algorithm returns the minimum cost found during execution. The complexity of this algorithm is $O(n^2 p)$ in the simplest version presented here: in the $O(np)$ calls to Algorithm 5.2, we do not need to re-sort the list but we maintain it sorted instead, thus each call except the first one has linear cost. The complexity can be reduced to $O(n \log(n) + np)$ using standard algorithmic techniques [30].

Theorem 5.6

PACK-APPROX is a 3-approximation algorithm for the p-IN-p-COSCHEDULE problem.

The involved proof can be found in Reference 3.

Algorithm 5.2: Creating Packs of Size at Most k, When the Number $\sigma(i)$ of Processors per Task T_i Is Fixed

```
Procedure MAKE-PACK (n, p, k, σ)
begin
    Let L be the list of tasks sorted in non-increasing values of execution times t_{i,σ(i)};
    while L ≠ ∅ do
        Schedule the current task on the first pack with enough available processors and fewer
        than k tasks. Create a new pack if no existing pack fits;
        Remove the current task from L;
    end
    return the set of packs
end
```

Algorithm 5.3: PACK-APPROX

```
Procedure PACK-APPROX(T_1, ..., T_n)
begin
    COST = +∞;
    for j = 1 to n do σ(j) ← 1;
    for i = 0 to n(p − 1) − 1 do
        Let A_tot(i) = Σ_{j=1}^{n} t_{j,σ(j)} σ(j);
        Let T_{j*} be one task that maximizes t_{j,σ(j)};
        Call MAKE-PACK (n, p, p, σ);
        Let COST_i be the cost of the co-schedule;
        if COST_i < COST then COST ← COST_i;
        if (A_tot(i)/p > t_{j*,σ(j*)}) or (σ(j*) = p) then
        return COST ;                                        /* Exit loop */
        else σ(j*) ← σ(j*) + 1;                   /* Add a processor to T_{j*} */
    end
    return COST;
end
```

Minimum resource requirement. We conclude this section on theoretical analysis in a fault-free scenario by the following remark. We point out that all results can be extended to deal with the variant of the problem where each task T_i has a minimum compute node requirement m_i. Such a requirement is typically provided by the user. In that variant, Equation 5.2 is defined only for j greater than m_i. For all previous algorithms, the difference lies in the preliminary step where one assigns one processor to each task: one would now assign m_i processors to task i, for all i. The number of total steps in the algorithms becomes smaller (because there are fewer processors available). One should note that with this constraint, all results (Theorems 5.1 through 5.6) are still valid, and proofs are quite similar.

5.4.5 With Redistributions

We can easily build examples to show the difficulty of RESILIENT-COSCHED-1PACK when redistributions are allowed, even when there are no failures: (i) Algorithm 5.1 is no longer optimal because it may give processors to an application with a poor speedup profile (i.e., it does not gain much from the additional processors); and (ii) the greedy variant where remaining processors are allocated to the application with the best speedup profile can also lead to nonoptimal schedules (see Reference

25 for details). Intuitively, these little examples show that RESILIENT-COSCHED-1PACK seems to be of combinatorial nature when redistributions are taken into account, even with zero cost.

To establish the complexity of the problem with redistributions, we consider the simple case with no failures. Therefore, redistributions occur only at the end of an application, and any application changes at most n times its number of processors, where n is the total number of applications. We further consider that the redistribution cost is a constant equal to S, that is, we let $\beta = 0$ and $\tau = +\infty$ in Equation 5.11. Even in this simplified scenario, the problem is NP-complete:

Theorem 5.7

With constant redistribution costs and without failures, RESILIENT-COSCHED-1PACK is NP-complete (in the strong sense).

The involved reduction comes from 3-PARTITION, and can be found in Reference 25.

Remarks

We conjecture that RESILIENT-COSCHED-1PACK remains NP-complete with zero redistribution cost. This is because of the combinatorial exploration suggested by the examples. But this remains an open problem!

5.5 HEURISTICS AND SIMULATIONS

In this section, we introduce and evaluate polynomial-time heuristics to solve the general RESILIENT-COSCHED-1PACK problem with both failures and redistributions. Before performing any redistribution, we need to choose an initial allocation of the p processors to the n applications. We use the optimal algorithm without redistribution, Algorithm 5.1. Note that heuristics for the k-IN-p-COSCHEDULE general problem can be found in Reference 3, together with their evaluation.

We first discuss the general structure of the heuristics in Section 5.5.1. Then, we explain how to redistribute available processors in Section 5.5.2, and the two strategies to redistribute when failures occur in Section 5.5.3. The pseudo-codes for all algorithms are available in Reference 25. The simulation settings are discussed in Section 5.5.4, and results are presented in Section 5.5.5.

5.5.1 GENERAL STRUCTURE

All heuristics share the same skeleton: we iterate over each event (either a failure or an application termination) until total remaining work is equal to zero. If some applications are still working for a previous redistribution (i.e., the current time t is smaller than t_{lastR_i} for these applications), then we exclude them for the next redistribution, and add them back into the list of applications after the current redistribution is completed. If an application ends, we redistribute available processors as will be discussed in Section 5.5.2. Then, if there is a failure, we calculate the new expected execution time of the faulty application. Also, we remove from the list the applications that end before t_{lastR_f}, and we release their processors.

Afterward, we have to choose between trying to redistribute or do nothing. If the faulty application is not the longest application, the total execution time has not changed since the last redistribution. Therefore, because it is the best execution time that we could reach, there is no need to try to improve it. However, if the faulty application is the longest application, we apply a heuristic to redistribute processors (see Section 5.5.3).

5.5.2 Redistribution When an Application Ends

When an application ends, the idea is to redistribute the processors that it releases in order to decrease the expected execution time. The easiest way to proceed consists of adding processors greedily to the application with the longest execution time, as was done in Algorithm 5.1 to compute an optimal schedule. This time, we further account for the redistribution cost, and update the values of α_i, t_{lastR_i}, and t_i^U for each application i that encountered a redistribution. Therefore, this heuristic, called EndLocal, returns a new distribution of processors.

Rather than using only local decisions to redistribute available processors at time t, it is possible to recompute an entirely new schedule, using the greedy algorithm Algorithm 5.1 again, but further accounting for the cost of redistributions. This heuristic is called EndGreedy. Now, we need to compute the remaining fraction of work for each application, and we obtain an estimation of the expected finish time when each application is mapped on two processors. Similarly to Algorithm 5.1, we then add two processors to the longest application while we can improve it, accounting for redistribution costs.

Note that we effectively update the values of α_i and t_{lastR_i} for application T_i only if a redistribution was conducted for this application. It may happen that the algorithm assigns the same number of processors as was used before. Therefore, we keep the updated value of the fraction of work in a temporary variable α_i^t and update it whenever needed at the end of the procedure.

5.5.3 Redistribution When There Is a Failure

Similarly to the case of an application ending, we propose two heuristics to redistribute in case of failures. The first one, ShortestApplicationsFirst, takes only local decisions. First, we allocate the k available processors (if any) to the faulty application if that application is improvable. Then, if the faulty application is still improvable, we try to take processors from shortest applications (denoted T_s) in the schedule, and give these processors to the faulty application, until the faulty application is no longer improvable, or there are no more processors to take from other applications. We take processors from an application only if its new execution time is smaller than the execution time of the faulty application.

The second heuristic, IteratedGreedy, uses a modified version of the greedy algorithm that initializes the schedule (Algorithm 5.1) each time there is a failure, while accounting for the cost of redistributions. This is done similarly to the redistribution of EndGreedy explained in Section 5.5.2, except that we need to handle the faulty application differently to update the values of α_f and t_{lastR_f}.

5.5.4 Simulation Settings

To assess the efficiency of the heuristics, we have performed extensive simulations. Note that the code is publicly available at http://graal.ens-lyon.fr/~abenoit/code/redistrib, so that interested readers can experiment with their own parameters.

To evaluate the quality of the heuristics, we conduct several simulations, using realistic parameters. The first step is to generate a fault distribution: we use an existing fault simulator developed in References 31 and 32. In our case, we use this simulator with an exponential law of parameter λ. The second step is to generate a fault-free execution time for each application (the $t_{i,j}$ value). We use a *synthetic* model to generate the execution profiles in order to represent a large set of scientific applications. The application model that we use is a classical one, similar to the one used in Reference 3. For a problem of size m, we define the sequential time: $t(m, 1) = 2 \times m \times \log_2(m)$. Then we can define the parallel execution time on q processors:

$$t(m, q) = f \times t(m, 1) + (1 - f)\frac{t(m, 1)}{q} + \frac{m}{q}\log_2(m). \quad (5.13)$$

The parameter f is the sequential fraction of time, we fix it to $f = 0.08$. So 92% of time is considered as parallel. The factor $(m/q)\log_2(m)$ represents the overhead due to communications and synchronizations. Finally, we have $t_{i,j}(m_i) = t(m_i, j)$, where $t_{i,j}(m_i)$ is the execution time for application T_i with a problem of size m_i on j identical processors.

Finally, we assign to each application T_i a random value for the number of data m_i such that: $m_{inf} \leq m_i \leq m_{sup}$. We set $m_{inf} = 1,500,000$ and $m_{sup} = 2,500,000$ to have execution times long enough so that several failures are likely to strike during execution. With such a value for m_{sup}, the longest execution time in a fault-free execution is around 100 days. We also consider two different data distribution cases: (i) very heterogeneous with $m_{inf} = 1,500$, and (ii) homogeneous with $m_{inf} = 2,499,000$, and detailed results for these distributions are available in Reference 25.

The cost of checkpoints for an application T_i with j processors is $C_{i,j} = C_i/j$, where C_i is proportional to the memory footprint of the application. We have $C_i = m_i \times c$, where c is the time needed to checkpoint one data unit of m_i. The default value is $c = 1$, unless stated otherwise. The synchronization cost value S is fixed to $S = 0$ for all following experiments. Finally, the MTBF of a single processor is fixed to 100 years, unless stated otherwise.

Note that we assume that a failure can strike during checkpoints but not during downtime, during recovery, and while the processor is performing some redistribution.

5.5.5 Results

To evaluate the heuristics, we execute each heuristic 50 times and we compute the average *makespan*, that is, the longest execution time in the pack. We compare the makespan obtained by the heuristics to the makespan (i) in a faulty context without any redistribution (worst case) and (ii) in a fault-free context with redistributions (best case). We normalize the results by the makespan obtained in a faulty context without any redistribution, which is expected to be the worst case. The execution in a fault-free setting provides us an optimistic value of the execution of the application in the ideal case where no failures occur. We consider all four possible combinations of EndLocal or EndGreedy with ShortestApplicationsFirst or IteratedGreedy.

5.5.5.1 Performance in a Fault-Free Context

Figure 5.4 shows the impact of redistribution in a fault-free context with 1000 applications, where we vary the number of processors from 2000 to 10,000. In this case, we compare EndLocal with EndGreedy (see Section 5.5.2). The two heuristics have a very similar behavior, leading to a gain of more than 20% with less than 4000 processors, and a slightly better gain for the EndGreedy global heuristic. When the number of processors increases, the efficiency of both heuristics decreases to converge to the performance without redistribution. Indeed, there are then enough processors so that each application does not make use of the extra processors released by ending applications. In the heterogeneous context (with $m_{inf} = 1500$), the gain due to redistribution is even larger (see Reference 25).

5.5.5.2 Impact of *n*

Figure 5.5 shows the impact of the number of applications n when the number of processors is fixed to 5000. The results show that having more applications increases the efficiency of both heuristics. With $n = 1000$, we obtain a gain of more than 40% due to redistributions. The reason is that when n increases, the number of processors assigned to each application decreases, then heuristics have more flexibility to redistribute.

Note that, as expected, IteratedGreedy is better than ShortestApplicationsFirst, because it recomputes a complete new schedule at each fault, instead of just allocating available processors from shortest applications to the faulty application. Using EndGreedy with IteratedGreedy does not improve the performance, while EndGreedy is useful with ShortestApplicationsFirst, hence

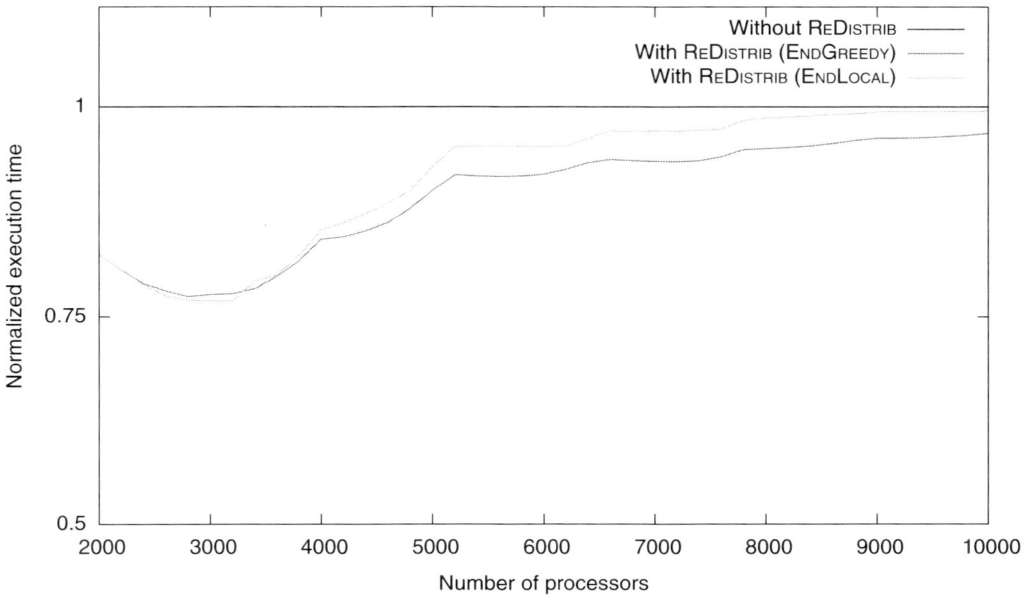

FIGURE 5.4 Redistribution in a fault-free context.

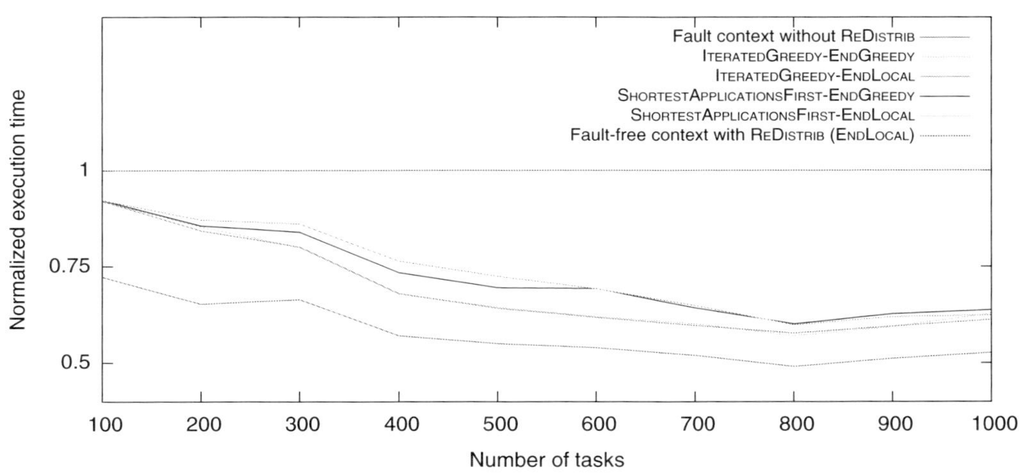

FIGURE 5.5 Impact of n with $p = 5000$ processors.

showing that complete redistributions are useful, even when only performed at the end of an application. Similar results can be observed in the homogeneous and heterogeneous cases, and similar conclusions are drawn when varying p for a fixed value of n (see Reference 25).

5.5.5.3 Impact of MTBF

Figure 5.6 shows the impact of the MTBF on the performance of redistributions. We vary the MTBF of a single processor between 5 and 125 years. When the MTBF decreases, the number of failures increases; consequently, the performance of both heuristics decreases. The performance of ITERATEDGREEDY is closely linked to the MTBF value. Indeed, it tends to favor a heterogeneous distribution of processors (i.e., applications with many processors and applications with few processors). If an

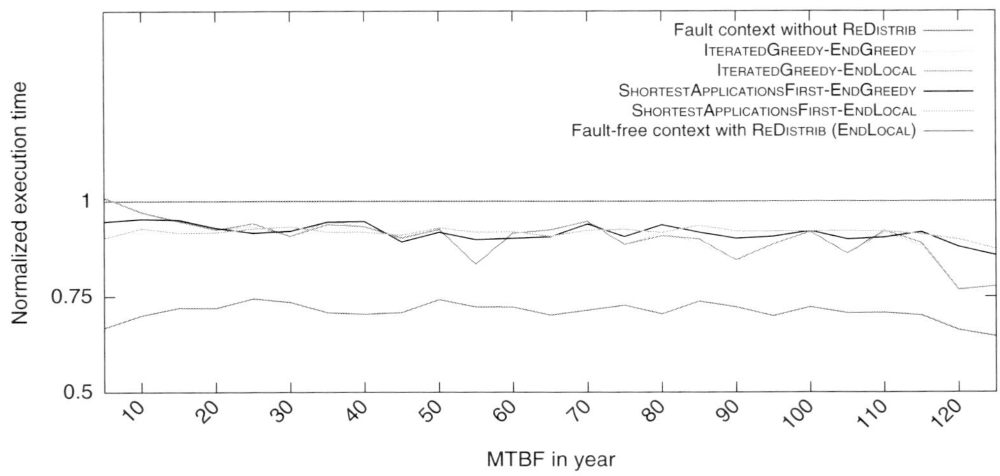

FIGURE 5.6 Impact of MTBF with $n = 100$ and $p = 5000$.

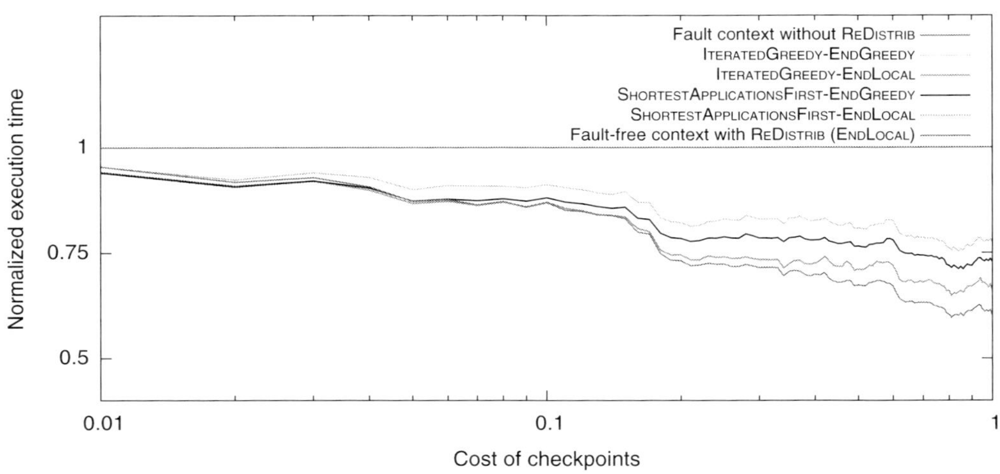

FIGURE 5.7 Impact of checkpointing cost.

application is executed on many processors, its MTBF becomes very small and this application will be hit by more failures; hence, it becomes even worse than without redistribution!

5.5.5.4 Impact of Checkpointing Cost

Figure 5.7 shows the impact of the checkpointing cost on a platform with 100 applications and 1000 processors. To do so, we multiply the checkpointing cost by c in Figure 5.7 (recall that c is the time needed to checkpoint one data unit). When c decreases, the performance of the heuristics increases and the gap between the execution time in a fault-free context and a fault context becomes small. Indeed, if checkpoints are cheap, a lot of checkpoints can be taken, and the average time lost due to failures decreases.

Additionally, we show in Reference 25 that the sequential fraction of time f of the applications also has an impact on performance: as expected, when applications are more parallel, the redistribution is more efficient.

5.5.5.5 Summary

Altogether, we observe that IteratedGreedy achieves better performance than ShortestApplicationsFirst, mainly because it rebuilds a complete schedule at each fault, which is very efficient but also costly. Nevertheless, when the MTBF is low (around 10 years or less), ShortestApplicationsFirst becomes better than IteratedGreedy. In a faulty context, we gain flexibility from the failures and we can achieve a better load balance. We observe that the ratio between the number of applications and the number of processors plays an important role, because having too many processors for few applications leads to a deterioration of performance. We also show that the cost of checkpointing and the fraction of sequential time have a significant impact on performance.

Finally, we point out that all four heuristics run within a few seconds, while the total execution time of the application takes several days; hence, even the more costly combination IteratedGreedy-EndGreedy incurs a negligible overhead.

5.6 CONCLUSION

In this chapter, we have provided theoretical results to assess the complexity of the general partitioning problem in a fault-free scenario; the problem is NP-complete when a pack can contain at least three tasks, and we have provided an approximation algorithm. When accounting for failures, we have designed a detailed and comprehensive model for scheduling a single pack of applications on a failure-prone platform, with processor redistributions. We have introduced a greedy polynomial-time algorithm that returns the optimal solution (for a single pack) when there are failures but no processor redistribution is allowed, or in a fault-free scenario. We have shown that the problem of finding a schedule that minimizes the execution time when accounting for redistributions is NP-complete in the strong sense, even with constant redistribution costs and no failures. Finally, we have provided several polynomial-time heuristics to redistribute efficiently processors at each failure or when an application ends its execution and releases processors. The heuristics are tested through extensive simulations, and the results demonstrate their usefulness: a significant improvement of the execution time can be achieved thanks to the redistributions.

Further work will consider partitioning the applications into several consecutive packs (rather than one) and conduct additional simulations in this context. We also plan to investigate the complexity of the online redistribution algorithms in terms of competitiveness. It would also be interesting to deal not only with fail-stop errors, but also with silent errors. This would require adding verification mechanisms to detect such errors.

REFERENCES

1. M. A. Heroux, D. W. Doerfler, P. S. Crozier, J. M. Willenbring, H. C. Edwards, A. Williams, M. Rajan, E. R. Keiter, H. K. Thornquist, and R. W. Numrich. Improving Performance via Mini-applications. Research Report 5574, Sandia National Laboratories, USA, September 2009.
2. M. Shantharam, Y. Youn, and P. Raghavan. Speedup-aware co-schedules for efficient workload management. *Parallel Processing Letters*, 23(2):1340001, 2013.
3. G. Aupy, M. Shantharam, A. Benoit, Y. Robert, and P. Raghavan. Co-scheduling algorithms for high-throughput workload execution. *Journal of Scheduling*, 19(6):627–640, 2016.
4. T. Herault and Y. Robert. *Fault-Tolerance Techniques for High-Performance Computing*. Heidelberg, Germany, Springer International Publishing, 2015.
5. E. N. M. Elnozahy, L. Alvisi, Y.-M. Wang, and D. B. Johnson. A survey of rollback-recovery protocols in message-passing systems. *ACM Computing Surveys*, 34(3):375–408, 2002.
6. J. T. Daly. A higher order estimate of the optimum checkpoint interval for restart dumps. *FGCS*, 22(3):303–312, 2004.
7. J. W. Young. A first order approximation to the optimum checkpoint interval. *Communications of the ACM*, 17(9):530–531, 1974.

8. P. Brucker, A. Gladky, H. Hoogeveen, M. Y. Kovalyov, C. Potts, T. Tautenhahn, and S. Van De Velde. Scheduling a batching machine. *Journal of Scheduling*, 1:31–54, 1998.
9. C. N. Potts and M. Y. Kovalyov. Scheduling with batching: A review. *European Journal of Operational Research*, 120(2):228–249, 2000.
10. G. Koole and R. Righter. A stochastic batching and scheduling problem. *Probability in the Engineering and Informational Sciences*, 15(04):465–479, 2001.
11. R. K. Deb and R. F. Serfozo. Optimal control of batch service queues. *Advances in Applied Probability*, 5(2):340–361, 1973.
12. Y. Ikura and M. Gimple. Efficient scheduling algorithms for a single batch processing machine. *Operations Research Letters*, 5(2):61–65, 1986.
13. F. Koehler and S. Khuller. Optimal batch schedules for parallel machines. In *Proceedings of the 13th Annual Algorithms and Data Structures Symposium, AA-DSA'2013*, 2013, London, Canada.
14. P.-F. Dutot, G. Mounié, D. Trystram. Scheduling parallel tasks: Approximation algorithms. In Joseph T. Leung (ed.). Handbook of Scheduling: Algorithms, Models, and Performance Analysis, CRC Press, Boca Raton, USA, 2004, chapter 26.
15. D. Li, D. S. Nikolopoulos, K. Cameron, B. R. de Supinski, and M. Schulz. Power-aware MPI task aggregation prediction for high-end computing systems. In *IPDPS 10*, pages 1–12, 2010, Atlanta, USA.
16. E. Frachtenberg, D. Feitelson, F. Petrini, and J. Fernandez. Adaptive parallel job scheduling with flexible coscheduling. *IEEE Transactions on Parallel and Distributed Systems*, 16(11):1066–1077, 2005.
17. M. Bhadauria and S. A. McKee. An approach to resource-aware co-scheduling for CMPs. In *Proceedings of the 24th ACM International Conference on Supercomputing ICS'10*. ACM, 2010, Tsukuba, Ibaraki, Japan.
18. D. Chandra, F. Guo, S. Kim, and Y. Solihin. Predicting inter-thread cache contention on a chip multi-processor architecture. In *Proceedings of the 11th International Symposium on High-Performance Computer Architecture HPCA'05*, pages 340–351. IEEE, 2005, San Francisco, CA, USA.
19. C. Hankendi and A. Coskun. Reducing the energy cost of computing through efficient co-scheduling of parallel workloads. In *Design, Automation Test in Europe Conference Exhibition DATE'12*, pages 994–999, 2012, Dresden, Germany.
20. D. Fiala, F. Mueller, C. Engelmann, R. Riesen, K. Ferreira, and R. Brightwell. Detection and correction of silent data corruption for large-scale high-performance computing. In *Proceedings of the International Conference on High Performance Computing, Networking, Storage and Analysis, SC'12*, pages 78:1–78:12, Los Alamitos, CA, USA, 2012. IEEE Computer Society Press.
21. J. Dongarra, T. Hérault, and Y. Robert. Performance and reliability trade-offs for the double checkpointing algorithm. *International Journal of Networking and Computing*, 4(1):23–41, 2014.
22. X. Ni, E. Meneses, and L. Kale. Hiding checkpoint overhead in HPC applications with a semi-blocking algorithm. In *2012 IEEE International Conference on Cluster Computing Cluster'12*, pages 364–372, September 2012, Beijing, China.
23. J. Blazewicz, M. Machowiak, G. Mounié, and D. Trystram. Approximation algorithms for scheduling independent malleable tasks. In R. Sakellariou, J. Gurd, L. Freeman, and J. Keane, editors, *Euro-Par 2001 Parallel Processing*, volume 2150 of *Lecture Notes in Computer Science, EuroPar'2001*, pages 191–197. Springer, Manchester, UK, 2001.
24. M. Frigo, C. E. Leiserson, and K. H. Randall. The implementation of the Cilk-5 multithreaded language. In *Proceedings of the ACM SIGPLAN 1998 Conference on Programming Language Design and Implementation, PLDI'98*, pages 212–223, ACM, 1998, Montreal, Canada.
25. A. Benoit, L. Pottier, and Y. Robert. Resilient application co-scheduling with processor redistribution. Research Report RR-8795, INRIA, 2015. Available: graal.ens-lyon.fr/~abenoit.
26. N. Muthuvelu, I. Chai, E. Chikkannan, and R. Buyya. Batch resizing policies and techniques for fine-grain grid tasks: The nuts and bolts. *Journal of Information Processing Systems*, 7(2):299–320, 2011.
27. P. B. Bhat, C. S. Raghavendra, and V. K. Prasanna. Efficient collective communication in distributed heterogeneous systems. *Journal of Parallel and Distributed Computing*, 63(3):251–263, 2003.
28. J. A. Bondy and U. S. R. Murty. *Graph Theory with Applications*. Amsterdam, Netherlands, North Holland, 1976.
29. E. G. Coffman Jr, M. R. Garey, D. S. Johnson, and R. E. Tarjan. Performance bounds for level-oriented two-dimensional packing algorithms. *SIAM Journal on Computing*, 9(4):808–826, 1980.

30. T. H. Cormen, C. E. Leiserson, R. L. Rivest, and C. Stein. *Introduction to Algorithms*. Boston, USA, The MIT Press, 2009.
31. G. Bosilca, A. Bouteiller, E. Brunet, F. Cappello, J. Dongarra, A. Guermouche, T. Herault, Y. Robert, F. Vivien, and D. Zaidouni. Unified model for assessing checkpointing protocols at extreme-scale. *Concurrency and Computation: Practice and Experience*, 26(17):2772–2791, 2014.
32. M. Bougeret, H. Casanova, M. Rabie, Y. Robert, and F. Vivien. Checkpointing strategies for parallel jobs. In *2011 International Conference for High Performance Computing, Networking, Storage and Analysis SC'2011*, pages 1–11, November 2011, Seattle, USA.

6 Resource Management for MapReduce Jobs Performing Big Data Analytics

Norman Lim and Shikharesh Majumdar

CONTENTS

ABSTRACT

For various types of enterprise and scientific applications as well as cyber-physical systems (such as sensor-equipped bridges, smart buildings, and industrial machinery), processing and analyzing data is important for gaining insights and making meaningful decisions. The amount of data analyzed, however, is sometimes very large, and conventional processing tools and techniques cannot be used for analyzing such *Big Data*. A programming model, called *MapReduce*, is proposed by Google to simplify performing massively distributed parallel processing so that very large and complex datasets can be processed and analyzed efficiently. A popular implementation of the MapReduce programming model, called *Hadoop*, is used by many companies and institutions, typically in conjunction with cloud computing, for executing various Big Data applications, including web analytics applications, scientific applications, data mining applications, and enterprise data-processing applications. The focus of this chapter is on describing effective resource management algorithms and techniques for processing MapReduce jobs, including MapReduce jobs with an associated completion deadline. Effective resource management strategies are crucial for processing the MapReduce jobs submitted to the system and to achieve user satisfaction and high system performance that includes a high quality of service as reflected in a low ratio of jobs with missed deadlines, low job response times, high job throughput, and high resource utilization.

6.1 INTRODUCTION

Modern large-scale processing systems have to be capable of processing large volumes of data (often referred to as *Big Data*) that are prevalent in today's world. For example, businesses as well as academic and research institutions can generate terabytes (TB) of data each day [1] and store petabytes (PB, 2^{50} bytes) of data on their systems [2]. The prevalence of data in today's world is a result of the numerous sources of data available from various industries and institutions, including:

- *Scientific* data (e.g., health-related data, weather data, satellite data)
- *Industrial/organizational* data (e.g., financial data, manufacturing data, retail data)
- *Business intelligence* data (e.g., sales data, customer behavior data, product data)
- *System* data (e.g., system logs, network logs, status files)

In addition, with the advent of the Internet of Things (IoT) paradigm leading to a popularity of smart facilities and cyber-physical systems, such as sensor-equipped bridges, smart buildings, and industrial machinery, a new source of Big Data (from sensors, for example) has emerged. Analyzing this Big Data for making meaningful decisions and obtaining knowledge and insights is important in various types of environments, including enterprise and scientific applications as well as cyber-physical systems. However, the volume of data analyzed is too *large* for conventional processing tools and techniques to handle efficiently. One of the main problems of processing Big Data is that the rate at which data can be read from hard drives (*access speed*) is a bottleneck. The capacity of hard drives has increased exponentially over the years. In comparison, the access speeds of hard drives have increased at a slower rate. For example, it is common for hard drives to have capacities of over 1 TB, but the access speed is typically only 100 MB/s [2]. This means that it can take over 2.5 hours to read 1 TB of data from the hard drive. One solution to solve this problem and improve performance is to use *parallelism*. Instead of reading the 1 TB data from a single hard drive, 1 GB partitions of the data can be read from 1000 hard drives in parallel. By using the parallelism of 1000 hard drives, reading 1 TB of data can be accomplished at a much faster time: 100 s instead of 2.5 hours. However, there are a number of challenges with using parallelism, including how to perform communication and coordination among the different machines, and how to handle and recover from machine failures. In addition, developing and debugging/testing a distributed (parallel) application is more difficult than developing an application that runs on a single machine.

MapReduce [1], originally proposed by Google, is a programming model whose purpose is to simplify performing massively distributed parallel processing so that very large and complex datasets can be processed and analyzed efficiently (discussed in detail in Section 6.2.1). When dealing with a large volume of data, it is necessary to distribute the computation among multiple machines to enable parallel processing and reduce the overall processing time. MapReduce is a popular parallel processing model that is often used in conjunction with cloud computing to facilitate Big Data analytics [3–5], which can include processing web analytics applications, scientific applications, social networks, and enterprise data. Many companies and institutions also use MapReduce for a variety of other applications, including large-scale data processing (e.g., sorting, indexing, and grouping), data mining (e.g., web crawling), artificial intelligence (e.g., machine learning), and scientific research (e.g., bioinformatics) [5]. For example, Google has previously used MapReduce applications to analyze web documents to generate search indices for its web search engine, whereas Facebook uses MapReduce to analyze its users' activities and the success of advertisements on its website [6]. More recently, MapReduce jobs with an associated completion deadline have become important for latency-sensitive applications, such as those used in the context of live business intelligence, personalized advertising, spam/fraud detection, real-time analysis of event logs, and various additional real-time data analytics applications [7]. Business intelligence refers to analyzing the raw data of a business or corporation so that smart and effective business strategies can be developed. Event log analysis involves processing event logs to find particular patterns, filter event occurrences, and group similar event occurrences together. Such event log analysis can be used for various types of computing systems that have event monitors to collect and signal event occurrences, including operating systems, database management systems, and cyber-physical systems. More generally, allowing users to specify job deadlines permits the resource manager to prioritize jobs and ensure that time-critical jobs are completed on time. In some situations, it is ideal to analyze the most up-to-date data and receive the results in a timely manner (e.g., in real-time) so that the best decisions can be made. Thus, it is common for various companies and institutions to submit MapReduce jobs to a cluster or a cloud for processing. In both scenarios, a resource management middleware is required to efficiently and intelligently execute the submitted MapReduce jobs.

The focus of this chapter is on describing effective algorithms and techniques for resource management for MapReduce jobs, including jobs characterized by service level agreements (SLAs). An SLA defines a contract between the service requester and the service provider regarding the level of quality of service (QoS) associated with a request [8]. The SLA may vary from application to application, but handling of requests with an SLA often leads to an advance reservation request [9] that is characterized by an *earliest start time*, a required *execution time*, and end-to-end *deadline* for completion. Public cloud service providers such as Amazon and Microsoft deploy data centers that comprise a large pool of resources. In addition, many enterprises and institutions have their own private clouds for IT management, performing data-processing operations, and facilitating research. Irrespective of the type of cloud deployed, effective and intelligent resource management is necessary for harnessing the power of the underlying distributed hardware and achieving high system performance [10], including high job throughput, low job response times, efficient use of resources, and a high QoS as reflected in a low ratio of jobs with missed deadlines, for example.

Resource management for an open stream of MapReduce jobs, which comprises of multiple phases of execution with multiple tasks in each phase, is a complex problem with a number of challenging issues that include how to devise effective techniques to perform *matchmaking* and *scheduling* such that the submitted jobs meet their SLA requirements. Matchmaking and scheduling (collectively referred to as *mapping*) are two key operations performed by a resource manager deployed in the resource management middleware of a cloud. When an incoming request (or job) arrives from the user, the resource manager invokes a *matchmaking* algorithm that selects the resource (or resources) from a given pool of resources to be allocated to the request. Once a number of requests are allocated to a specific resource, a *scheduling* algorithm is used to determine the order in which the requests assigned to the resource are to be executed. Matchmaking and scheduling is a well-known computationally hard (NP-hard) problem, and the problem becomes more difficult to solve when having to satisfy a user's QoS requirements that is often captured in an SLA, while also achieving the desired system objectives of the service providers, such as generating high revenue and maintaining high resource utilization. Furthermore, when considering an open stream of requests with SLAs and requests requiring processing from multiple system resources, the complexity of the resource management problem increases significantly. Effective management of the resources that are used for executing the MapReduce applications is crucial for achieving the satisfaction of users as well as high system utilization and is the focus of attention for this chapter.

The rest of the chapter is organized as follows. In Section 6.2, background information on MapReduce and Hadoop, which is a popular implementation of the MapReduce programming model, is provided. Section 6.3 describes resource management techniques that focus on various aspects of processing MapReduce jobs, including reducing job completion times and reducing the energy consumption of resources executing the jobs. Next, in Section 6.4, resource management techniques for MapReduce jobs with deadlines are presented. Lastly, Section 6.5 concludes the chapter and provides directions for future work.

6.2 BACKGROUND

This section presents background information on the concepts and technologies relevant to this chapter.

6.2.1 MapReduce

A MapReduce application (or job) is characterized by multiple phases of execution and each phase has multiple tasks [1] as illustrated by Figure 6.1. Many computations can be expressed using the MapReduce programming model. A classic example is the *URL access frequency* application that processes the logs of web servers to count the number of distinct URL accesses [1]. This application is a variation of the well-known *WordCount* MapReduce application. The input that needs to be processed is the logs of the web server. The first step is to split the input data into blocks with a default size of 64 MB, which are called *splits* (refer to Figure 6.1). Next, in the *map* phase, map tasks, which execute a user-defined mapper function, are created to process each of the partitions of the input data (i.e., the splits). Note that the map tasks are independent from one another and can be executed in parallel, possibly on different resources. In the URL access frequency application, the mapper function reads each URL in the logs and generates a set of intermediate key/value pairs of the form: `{URL, 1}`. This key/value pair specifies that one instance of a particular URL is found. The intermediate dataset generated by the map phase can contain multiple duplicate key/value pairs. For example, the key/value pair `{www.carleton.ca, 1}` can appear multiple times in the intermediate dataset. Next, in the *shuffle* phase, the intermediary key/value pairs with the same key are grouped together as shown in Figure 6.1. The sorted intermediary key/value pairs are then passed onto the *reduce* phase. During the reduce phase, reduce tasks that execute a user-defined reducer function process the intermediate key/value pairs to produce the final output, which is typically an aggregate or summary of the original input data and is smaller and more meaningful than the original input data. Similar to the map phase, the reduce tasks are independent from one another and can be executed in parallel, possibly on different resources. Note that reduce tasks cannot complete their execution until all the map tasks have finished executing. In the URL access frequency application, the reducer function sums all the values with the same key to emit the output dataset: `{URL, total count}`. Therefore, the final output will be a list of URLs and total number of times each URL is accessed.

6.2.2 Apache Hadoop

Apache Hadoop [11] is an open-source software framework (written in Java) that implements the MapReduce programming model (discussed in Section 6.2.1). Hadoop is designed for executing data-intensive distributed computing applications (i.e., Big Data applications), such as web analytics applications, scientific applications, and applications processing the data from social networks or enterprises [3,12]. Hadoop comprises three main subframeworks: Hadoop Common, Hadoop Distributed File System (HDFS), and Hadoop MapReduce. *Hadoop Common* provides the utility functions, including remote procedure call (RPC) facilities and object serialization libraries, that are leveraged by the HDFS and MapReduce frameworks. *HDFS* is an implementation of a distributed

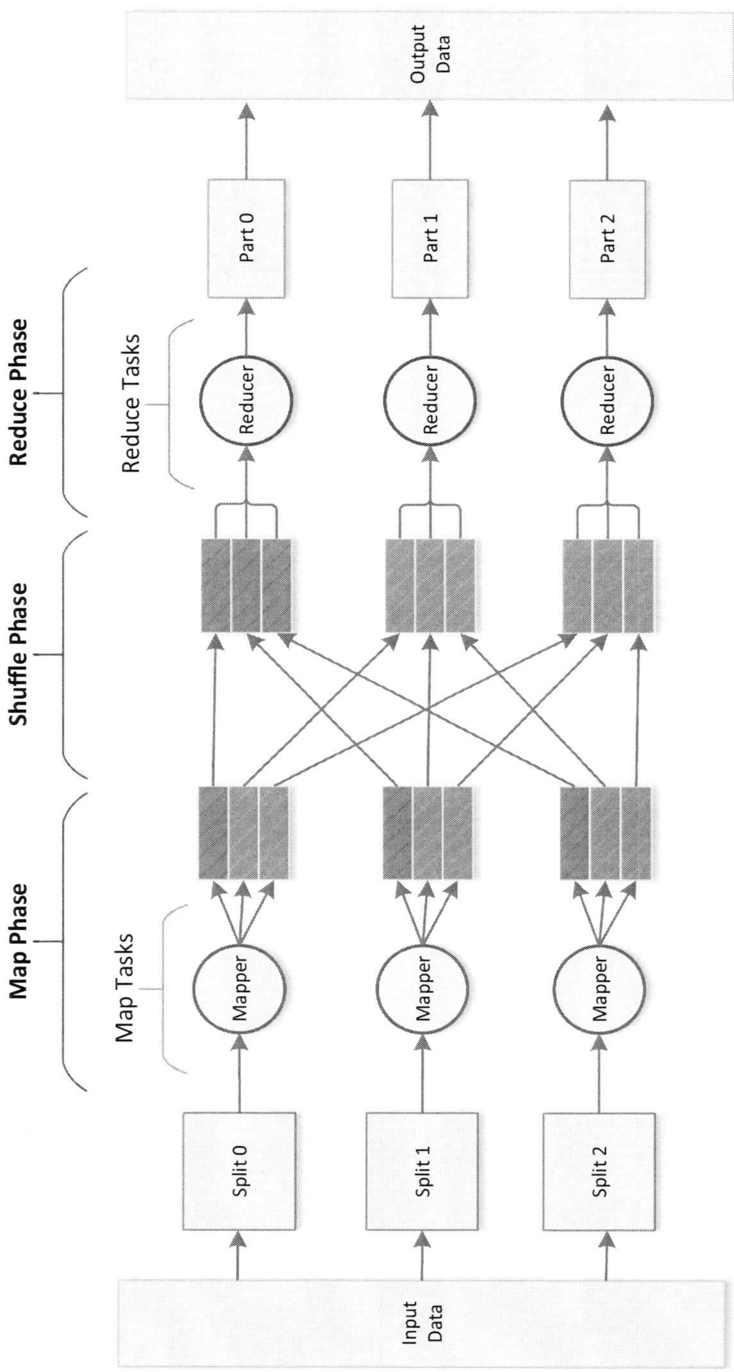

FIGURE 6.1 Example of a MapReduce job.

file system that is based on Google's distributed file system, named GFS (Google File System) [13]. HDFS provides redundant storage for the input data required by Hadoop jobs, and it also stores the intermediary data and output data generated by Hadoop jobs.

A set of machines (where each machine is called a *node*) that runs Hadoop is referred to as a *Hadoop cluster* (see Figure 6.2). A typical Hadoop cluster comprises a single *master* node and one or more *slave* nodes. The master node is responsible for maintaining HDFS and assigning MapReduce tasks to slave nodes for execution. The slave nodes perform work (e.g., read/write to HDFS or execute MapReduce tasks) that the master node assigns to them. In the original Hadoop MapReduce architecture (MRv1), the master node runs two Hadoop components (which are often called *Hadoop daemons*): *NameNode* and *JobTracker*. Each slave node in the Hadoop cluster also runs two Hadoop daemons: *DataNode* and *TaskTracker*.

The NameNode and DataNodes are the Hadoop daemons in charge of managing HDFS. Each file that is written to HDFS is split into blocks of 64 MB (default value) and each block is stored on the storage device of the node where DataNode is running. In addition, each block is replicated three times (default value) and stored on different DataNodes to provide data redundancy and availability. It is the job of NameNode to keep track of which DataNode stores the blocks of a particular file (which is referred to as the *metadata* of HDFS). Another important function of NameNode (master) is to direct DataNodes (slaves) to perform HDFS block operations (creation, deletion, and replication). DataNodes keep in constant contact with NameNode to receive instructions and also have to handle read and write requests from HDFS clients. An example illustrating HDFS is presented in Figure 6.3. Note that in this example, the block replication factor is two. As shown in this illustration, the NameNode maintains the metadata of HDFS, and the file named "file.txt" is composed of two blocks: Block 1A is replicated twice and stored on DataNode 1 and DataNode 2, and Block 1B is also replicated twice and stored on DataNode 1 and DataNode 3.

JobTracker provides the connection between user applications and the Hadoop cluster, and it has the following main responsibilities: initialize jobs and prepare them for execution, perform the matchmaking and scheduling of MapReduce jobs, and monitor the status of the jobs that are currently running. JobTracker is also responsible for managing TaskTrackers, which operate as the JobTracker's slaves and their primary purpose is to execute the map tasks or reduce tasks that the JobTracker assigns to them. Each TaskTracker periodically sends polling/update messages (called *heartbeats*) to JobTracker to receive new tasks and to update its progress on the tasks that it is currently executing (if any). If JobTracker does not receive a heartbeat message from a TaskTracker

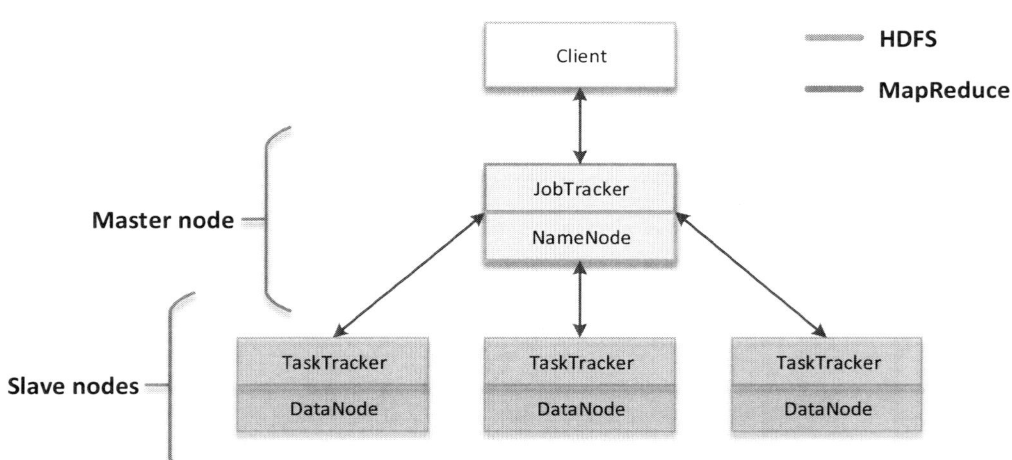

FIGURE 6.2 Example of a Hadoop cluster using Hadoop MapReduce Architecture v1 (MRv1).

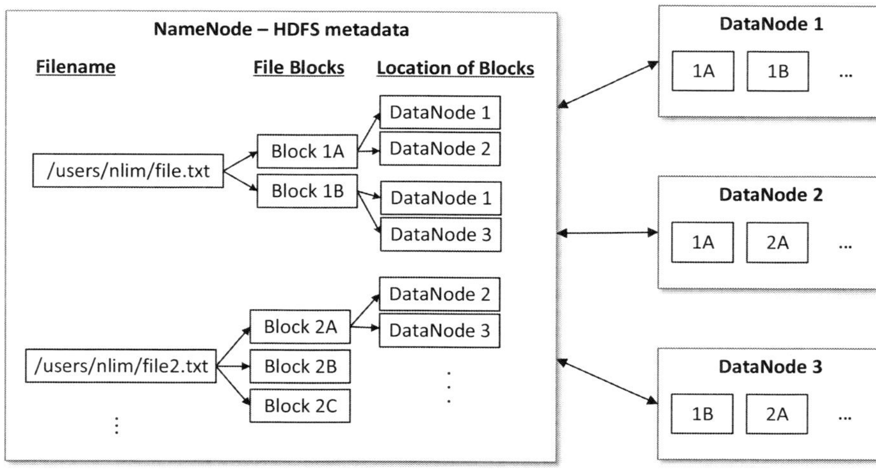

FIGURE 6.3 Example of HDFS.

within a specified time period (by default 1 minute), JobTracker assumes that the TaskTracker is lost and remaps all the tasks that are assigned to the lost TaskTracker to other available TaskTrackers. Each TaskTracker in the Hadoop cluster has a *map task capacity* (or number of *map slots*) and a *reduce task capacity* (or number of *reduce slots*), which specify the maximum number of map tasks and maximum number of reduce tasks, respectively, that the TaskTracker can execute in parallel at any point in time. An overview of Hadoop MapReduce is presented in Figure 6.4. As shown in the illustration, JobTracker maintains a list of active jobs and a list of completed jobs. There are two active jobs in the example system, and JobTracker has assigned TaskTracker 1 two map tasks to execute: Map Task 1 from Job B (Map B1) and Map Task 2 from Job C (Map C2).

6.2.2.1 Hadoop MapReduce v2 Architecture (MRv2)

The Hadoop MapReduce v1 architecture (MRv1) described earlier was found to have two main inadequacies when used in very large clusters comprising more than 4000 nodes [14]. The first

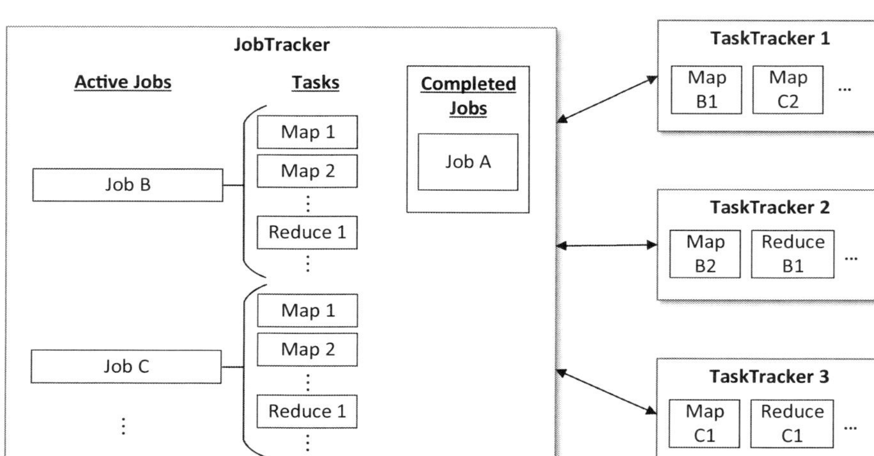

FIGURE 6.4 Example of Hadoop MapReduce (MRv1).

deficiency is *limited scalability*. On very large clusters (more than 4000 nodes, for example), it was reported that system performance deteriorates because there is a single entity, JobTracker, managing all the slave nodes. For example, after a failure of a slave node, attempts to re-replicate the data could cause network flooding. The second deficiency is the lack of support for *multitenancy* and lack of support for running alternative frameworks and paradigms other than MapReduce. As the cluster size increases, it becomes more desirable to share the cluster's resources by partitioning the available resources among multiple independent organizations such that different programs and applications, other than MapReduce, can be run on the cluster. Lack of support for multitenancy can also result in inefficient use of resources (e.g., low resource utilization) because there can be times when the processing of only MapReduce jobs cannot utilize all the resources in a cluster with thousands of nodes.

To solve the inadequacies of MRv1, a new Hadoop MapReduce architecture (*MRv2*) named *Yet Another Resource Negotiator* (*YARN*) [15] was devised. The major change in MRv2 from MRv1 is the introduction of a new hierarchical approach that replaces JobTracker and divides its functionality into two main responsibilities: allocation of system resources and job scheduling/monitoring. More specifically, JobTracker and TaskTracker from MRv1 are replaced by three new components (or Hadoop daemons) in MRv2: *ResourceManager*, *NodeManager*, and *ApplicationMaster*. Thus, a Hadoop cluster based on MRv2 has a single ResourceManager daemon running on the master node, a NodeManager daemon executing on each slave node in the cluster, and an ApplicationMaster daemon for each application running on the cluster (refer to Figure 6.5). As illustrated in Figure 6.5, there are two applications submitted to the ResourceManager: Client 1 submits a MapReduce job for processing whereas Client 2 submits a non-MapReduce job for processing. As a result, there are two ApplicationMasters running on the Hadoop cluster: one ApplicationMaster running on Slave Node 3 for the MapReduce job submitted by Client 1 and another ApplicationMaster running on Slave Node 1 for the non-MapReduce job submitted by Client 2.

The functionality of the ResourceManager is divided into two main components: *Scheduler* and *ApplicationManager*. The main purpose of the Scheduler is to allocate resources (e.g., compute, memory, and bandwidth) to each of the applications running on the cluster. In MRv2, the resource(s) that an application requires to execute is defined based on the abstract notion of a *resource container*. A resource container defines an application's resource requirements that can include the following: number of CPU cores, memory size, disk size, and network bandwidth. For instance, in Figure 6.5, each application executing on the cluster has two resource containers, where each container resides on a different slave node. This means that the MapReduce job submitted by Client 1 can execute on Slave Node 2 and Slave Node 3, but not on Slave Node 1 since there is no resource container for Client 1's MapReduce job on the first slave node. Moreover, it can be observed that the resources of Slave Node 2 are divided among two containers, which permits the execution of both jobs on that node. The ApplicationManager is responsible for accepting job submissions from users, obtaining the resource container for starting the ApplicationMaster, and restarting the execution of ApplicationMasters due to application or hardware failures. The ApplicationMaster is the Hadoop daemon responsible for negotiating resource containers from the Scheduler for executing the client's application. In addition, ApplicationMasters also work in conjunction with the NodeManagers (of the slave nodes) to execute and monitor the status/progress of the applications as well as to track and monitor the status and usage of the resource containers. The NodeManager reports this status and usage information of the resource containers to the ResourceManager. Overall, the changes made in MRv2 improve Hadoop by improving reliability and scalability, and enable greater resource sharing through multitenancy.

6.3 RESOURCE MANAGEMENT FOR MAPREDUCE JOBS

This section describes resource management techniques for MapReduce jobs that focus on different aspects of processing MapReduce jobs and have a variety of different objectives, including reducing

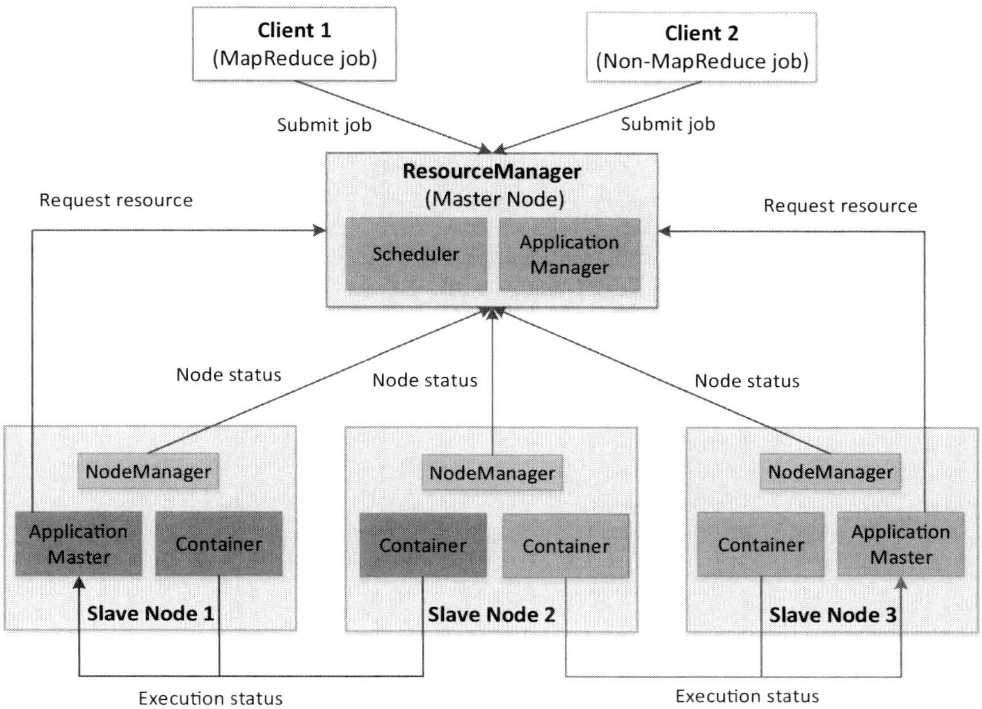

FIGURE 6.5 Example of a Hadoop cluster using Hadoop MapReduce Architecture v2 (MRv2).

job completion times, reducing data transmission between resources to minimize network traffic, handling of heterogeneous resources, sharing of resources, and managing the energy consumption of resources.

6.3.1 Techniques to Reduce Job Completion Times

In Reference 16, the authors present an abstraction of the MapReduce matchmaking and scheduling problem by formulating it as an optimization problem using mixed integer linear programming (MILP) where the objective is to find a schedule that minimizes the overall completion time of the jobs in the cluster. Since using MILP to solve such a problem is NP-hard [17], optimal solutions are difficult and time-consuming to compute even for offline versions where job arrivals are predetermined. As such, the authors propose algorithms with heuristics to approximate the optimal solutions within a factor of three of the optimal value. Using simulation, the authors compare their algorithm with other well-known scheduling algorithms such as first-in-first-out (FIFO), shortest job first (SJF), and shortest task first (STF). The results show that while FIFO, SJF, and STF only work well for specific workloads, their proposed algorithm consistently performs better.

The authors of Reference 18 also model the MapReduce scheduling problem as a linear program where the objective is to minimize the overall completion time of the jobs in the cluster. Two types of jobs are considered. The first type is *data-intensive* jobs which require performing data mining and analysis of very large datasets, including system logs and historical data. The second type of job is *computationally-intensive* jobs, that involve running algorithms or operations with high-processing complexity, such as floating point operations. The modeling of the linear program is based on the traditional job shop scheduling theory. A dispatch-rule-based online scheduling policy called LPT-θ that is based on existing algorithms is proposed to approximate the optimal solution.

Similar to Reference 18, in Reference 19, the authors present a resource management technique to handle heterogeneous MapReduce workloads, comprising CPU-bound computationally-intensive jobs and I/O-bound data-intensive jobs. The authors present a Triple-Queue Scheduler (TQS) that includes a mechanism called MR-Predict to predict the type of workload that needs to be executed. As the name suggests, TQS uses three queues: a CPU-bound job queue, an I/O-bound job queue, and a wait queue. Through experimentation, the authors show that TQS can effectively schedule CPU-bound and I/O-bound jobs such that the throughput of map tasks can increase by 30% compared to the throughput achieved with the default Hadoop FIFO scheduler.

The authors of Reference 20 present a MapReduce framework called Dynamically ELastic MApReduce (DELMA) that is capable of dynamically adjusting the cluster size (i.e., adding and removing nodes from the processing of a job) on the fly while a job is being processed. The main features of DELMA include the following: (1) ability to adjust the cluster size dynamically without having to restart jobs already executing; (2) ability to lower completion time of jobs by adding voluntary or unutilized nodes to the cluster; and (3) ability to replace slow or faulty nodes while a job is being processed. The authors evaluate DELMA under various processing and workload scenarios, including adding nodes to the cluster at various times during job execution. The experimental results showed that compared to Hadoop, DELMA can lower average job completion times by up to 50% in the best-case scenario and up to 10% in the worst-case scenario.

In Reference 21, a cloud service model for MapReduce named Cura is presented. The objective of Cura is to provide cost-effective MapReduce services in the cloud by implementing an efficient resource allocation scheme that reduces the monetary cost of provisioning resources from the cloud. The core resource management schemes that Cura provides include cost-aware resource provisioning, VM-aware scheduling, and online virtual machine reconfiguration. Experimental results show that Cura provides an 80% reduction in the cost of provisioning resources from the cloud and reduces job response times by up to 65%.

6.3.2 Data Locality-Aware Techniques

MapReduce applications typically have to process very large datasets and frequent transmission of data from one machine in the cluster to another machine in the cluster over the network can severely reduce system performance due to limited network bandwidth in the cluster. Therefore, it is beneficial to use a *data locality-aware system* to limit the data transfer between nodes as much as possible. A data locality-aware system assigns tasks to execute on nodes that contain (or are close to) the input data of the task in order to eliminate (or minimize) data transmission over the network.

In Reference 22, the authors propose a scheduling algorithm for workflows comprising multiple MapReduce jobs with precedence relationships. The workflow is represented by a directed acyclic graph (DAG). The proposed scheduling algorithm uses a predata placement strategy that reduces data transmission over the network, and it also adopts the list scheduling algorithm, which is a priority-based scheduling algorithm. The basic idea of the list scheduling algorithm is to assign each job in the workflow a priority and schedule the job with the highest priority first. In the context of the predata placement strategy, it is important to determine how to group datasets, where to place them, and how many times to replicate the datasets. The authors propose using a *data cohesion* score, which is used to represent the number of common datasets that there is between the datasets used by task t and the datasets residing in each group of nodes. Preferably, task t will be assigned to the group of nodes with the highest data cohesion score.

The authors of Reference 23 propose a scheduling technique that takes advantage of data locality when scheduling map tasks. As discussed, the data locality-based technique advocates assigning tasks to nodes that also contain the input data in order to prevent unnecessary data transmission over the network. The proposed scheduling technique attempts to assign map tasks to a node that already contains the input data (referred to as *local map tasks*). More specifically, the technique gives each node in the cluster a chance to take any local map task in the queue before any nonlocal map tasks are assigned. The authors compared a prototype of their scheduler with the default Hadoop FIFO scheduler and another algorithm called *delay scheduling*. The basic idea of the delay scheduling algorithm is to improve data locality when scheduling map tasks by delaying the execution of a task if it cannot be executed on a node where its input data is stored. A maximum delay, D, is used to prevent a task from being starved. The experimental results show that, for the workloads experimented with, the authors' proposed technique achieves a lower average job response time in comparison to that achieved by both FIFO and delay scheduling.

A Locality-Aware Reduce Task Scheduler (LARTS) is presented in Reference 24, which considers data locality when scheduling reduce tasks. LARTS considers the size and the location of the input data for reduce tasks when making scheduling decisions with the goal of minimizing network traffic, which can in turn improve system performance. Through experimentation, the authors showed that using LARTS over the traditional Hadoop FIFO scheduler can lead to a 7% reduction in job execution times.

The authors of Reference 25 propose a technique to improve the effectiveness of Hadoop's Fair Scheduler (described in more detail in Section 6.3.4). The *Fair Scheduler* [26] assigns each job a pool of resources to use. When a job does not use all the resources in their pool, the Fair Scheduler may assign the unused resources to the other jobs executing on the cluster. Furthermore, the Fair Scheduler can also kill low-priority jobs to free up resources for higher-priority jobs. The problem with the Fair Scheduler is that it does not consider data locality and other job properties when removing resources from one job and reassigning them to other jobs. The technique proposed in Reference 25 aims to fix these problems. For example, for I/O-bound jobs, the improved Fair Scheduler starts killing tasks that are running on hosts that are furthest away from where the task's input data is located in order to reduce network traffic. Through experimentation, the authors show that the improved Fair Scheduler can reduce network bandwidth usage, which in turn speeds up the execution time of jobs by approximately 7% on average.

6.3.3 Techniques for Handling Heterogeneous Computing Environments

This section describes resource management techniques for environments where the resources may have different processing, memory, and network capacity (i.e., heterogeneous resources).

In Reference 27, the authors propose a new approach to solving the MapReduce resource management problem on the cloud where the system is characterized by heterogeneous resources. The objective of the proposed approach is to minimize the total monetary cost of executing MapReduce jobs on the cloud. The authors model the resource management problem as a constrained combinatorial optimization problem and solve the problem using an innovative constructive algorithm. The results of the experiments showed a 2.8%–23.3% reduction in monetary cost compared to using other resource management algorithms that consider heterogeneous resources in the cloud.

The authors of Reference 28 also focus on resource management for MapReduce workloads in a heterogeneous computing environment. More specifically, a load-balancing algorithm whose purpose is to evenly distribute the workload among nodes with different processing speeds is presented. The algorithm is based on genetic algorithm theory, which is an artificial intelligence-based search heuristic that solves optimization problems by simulating how natural evolution works. Simulation results show that the proposed algorithm is effective in balancing the workload among heterogeneous nodes, leading to a reduction in job completion times.

A MapReduce framework called MApReduce with adaptive Load balancing for heterogeneous and Load imbalAnced clusters (MARLA), which is aimed at working efficiently in heterogeneous and load-imbalanced computing environments, is presented in Reference 29. The problem with the traditional approach is that, in heterogeneous clusters, nodes that have a lower performance profile are assigned a similar workload (i.e., equal-sized data partition to process) to those nodes that exhibit higher performance. MARLA alleviates this problem by using a dynamic task-scheduling mechanism that allows each node in the cluster to request tasks at its own pace.

6.3.4 Resource Sharing Techniques

Resource management techniques that focus on fairly sharing the resources of a cluster among multiple users as well as techniques that borrow unused resources from other clusters are described in this section.

Two of Hadoop's default schedulers, the *Fair Scheduler* and *Capacity Scheduler*, focus on fairly sharing the resources of the cluster among multiple users. The Fair Scheduler [26] is developed by Facebook, and its objective is to ensure that each job (on average) gets an equal share of the available resources in the cluster. The idea is to prevent many small jobs from starving the execution of a long job and vice versa. The Fair Scheduler groups jobs into pools and each pool is assigned a minimum share of the cluster's resources (e.g., a minimum number of map slots and reduce slots). A separate pool can also be assigned for each user so that all users get an equal share of the cluster's resources. The Capacity Scheduler [30] is developed by Yahoo and its objective is similar to the Fair Scheduler: share a large cluster among many different independent users (or organizations). Jobs are placed in queues and each queue is allocated a guaranteed capacity, which is a proportion of the total resource slots of the cluster. Note that the unused capacity of a queue can be temporarily allocated to other queues when needed. Furthermore, the jobs within a queue can be prioritized and the jobs with a higher priority gain access to the queue's resources first. The queues also support access control mechanisms for restricting which users can submit jobs to a particular queue.

A technique called *resource stealing*, which allows currently running tasks to use the unutilized task slots of a node (which the authors call *residual* resources), is presented in Reference 31. The idea is that when there are available task slots on a node, the system splits the input data of a task into two or more smaller blocks of data and creates an additional subtask to process each block of data in order to make use of the unutilized task slots. In MapReduce, a fault-tolerance mechanism called *speculative execution* is used. When a job is close to completion, but its completion is being slowed down by a few straggling tasks that include slowly executing tasks and tasks that have crashed, redundant tasks (called *speculative tasks*) are created and assigned to nodes that currently do not have other tasks to execute. The idea is that one of the speculative tasks can finish executing earlier than the original tasks, and thus the completion time of the job can be reduced. The authors of Reference 31 introduce an improvement to MapReduce's default speculative execution mechanism called Benefit Aware Speculative Execution. The new mechanism predicts if it is beneficial to launch a speculative task, and only starts a speculative task if it is expected to finish earlier than the original task.

In Reference 32, the authors introduce a hierarchical MapReduce framework (HMR), which supports executing MapReduce jobs on multiple clusters, such as clusters with unused resources. A hierarchical MapReduce programming model is proposed where computations are expressed with three functions: *Map*, *Reduce*, and *GlobalReduce*. The input to the GlobalReduce comprises the output from all the reduce tasks of a job and is executed on only one node in the cluster. By supporting the execution of MapReduce jobs in multiple clusters, a more effective resource sharing can be achieved.

6.3.5 Techniques for Energy Management of Resources

This section presents resource management techniques that focus on green computing issues in the context of MapReduce jobs: minimizing the energy consumed by a distributed system, such as a cloud or cluster, when executing MapReduce jobs.

The authors of Reference 33 investigate techniques to improve the energy efficiency of running MapReduce jobs in data centers and computational grids without severely affecting performance. The authors study the performance and energy efficiency trade-offs of Hadoop using various workloads. The system activity traces that were recorded during experiments show that MapReduce computations involve a large number of I/O operations (e.g., reading/writing a large volume of data from/to disks) as well as network I/O operations, leading to low CPU utilization at some points in time. Through their study, the authors have found that careful resource allocation to match an application's degree of parallelism and using the well-known dynamic voltage and frequency scaling (DVFS) technique can improve energy efficiency without a large performance cost.

The focus of Reference 34 is also on the challenge of making the execution of MapReduce jobs more energy efficient. The paper considers a very bursty MapReduce workload with distinct CPU, memory, and network requirements that is executed on a heterogeneous data center. An online energy minimization path algorithm is presented and implemented in a new scheduler called the Green MapReduce Scheduler (GEMS). GEMS reduces energy consumption while maintaining a low task response time by using effective sleeping policies on the compute servers and the network switches. More specifically, GEMS puts the compute servers and network switches to sleep when the load on the system is low to save energy. Simulation experiments showed that GEMS produces up to 35% energy saving and improves job response times by 35% on heterogeneous data centers compared to techniques that do not use sleeping policies on the compute and network devices and only focus on the minimization of energy consumption on compute servers (without considering network switches). The policies that only focus on the minimization of energy consumption typically use a strategy where jobs are tightly packed on to a small number of servers, which leads to an increase in response times and the servers running for a longer period of time. On the other hand, GEMS keeps a larger number of servers active, allowing for a looser packing of jobs, which in turn reduces the response times of the jobs. Energy savings are gained by putting servers and network switches to sleep whenever possible.

6.4 RESOURCE MANAGEMENT FOR MAPREDUCE JOBS WITH DEADLINES

This section presents resource management techniques for MapReduce jobs with deadlines. Recall from Section 6.1 that MapReduce jobs with deadlines have become increasingly important for latency-sensitive applications such as those used in the context of live business intelligence and real-time analysis of event logs [7].

6.4.1 MapReduce Budget-Based Resource Management Technique

In Reference 35, a MapReduce budget-based resource management algorithm (MRBB-RM) is presented. MRBB-RM is devised to intelligently perform matchmaking and scheduling (collectively called *mapping*) for an open stream of MapReduce jobs with SLAs, where each SLA is characterized by an earliest start time, a required execution time, and an end-to-end deadline, on a distributed environment such as a cloud or a cluster. MRBB-RM uses a deadline budgeting algorithm to decompose the end-to-end deadline of a job into components (subdeadlines), each of which is associated with a specific task in the job. The individual tasks of the job are then mapped on to the resources using a matchmaking and scheduling algorithm where the objective is to minimize the number of jobs that miss their deadlines.

Figure 6.6 presents an overview of MRBB-RM's *Algorithm 1*: *Job and Task Mapping Algorithm*. A more detailed and complete description of MRBB-RM and its associated algorithms can be found in Reference 35. When MRBB-RM is available (i.e., not busy scheduling another job), it retrieves the first job from its *job queue* and invokes Algorithm 1. The job queue stores the jobs that users submit to the system and the jobs in the queue are sorted in nondecreasing order of their deadlines. The input required by Algorithm 1 is a job *j* to map. As shown in Figure 6.6, the first step of Algorithm 1 is to invoke *Algorithm 2*: *Deadline Budgeting Algorithm* to decompose job *j*'s end-to-end deadline into components to give each of *j*'s tasks a *subdeadline* (step 1). More specifically, a separate subdeadline is calculated for the map phase of the job and the reduce phase of the job. Each map task of the job then has its subdeadline set to the subdeadline of the map phase, and similarly each reduce task of the job has its subdeadline set to the subdeadline of the reduce phase. The subdeadlines of the map phase and reduce phase are calculated by distributing the job's *laxity*, where the amount of laxity that

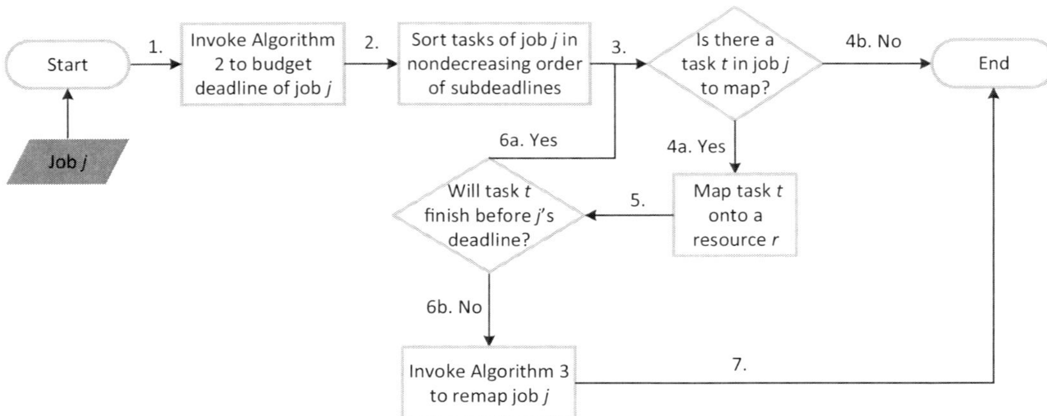

FIGURE 6.6 Overview of MRBB-RM's Job and Task Mapping algorithm.

is assigned to the map phase and reduce phase is proportional to the execution time of the respective phases. The laxity of a job (also called *slack time*) is the extra time that a job has to complete its execution before its deadline and is calculated as follows: $d_j - (E_j + s_j)$ where d_j is the deadline of job j, E_j is the execution time of job j, and s_j is the earliest start time of job j.

After assigning a subdeadline to each task, Algorithm 1 then sorts the tasks of job j in nondecreasing order of their subdeadlines with ties broken in favor of the task that has a higher execution time (i.e., the task with less slack time) (step 2). Next, Algorithm 1 maps each of j's tasks (in the specified order) by finding a resource r in the system that can execute a task t at its earliest possible start time (steps 3 and 4a). Note that Algorithm 1 schedules each task of job j such that the task can complete executing before job j's deadline and also before its subdeadline if possible. However, if the task is a map task and it misses its subdeadline, the algorithm uses some of the laxity from the next phase of execution (i.e., reduce phase) to schedule the map task as long as job j's deadline is not violated. In the case of reduce tasks, the subdeadlines of the tasks cannot be violated because the reduce phase is the final phase of execution and the subdeadline of the reduce tasks is equal to job j's deadline. After the task is mapped, Algorithm 1 checks if the task is scheduled to complete at or before job j's deadline (step 5). If the task is scheduled to complete before j's deadline (step 6a), then Algorithm 1 continues by mapping the next task of the job. This sequence of operations is performed until all the tasks of the job are mapped, in which case the algorithm ends (step 4b). If the task cannot be scheduled to finish executing before j's deadline, *Algorithm 3*: *Job Remapping Algorithm* is invoked (step 6b). Algorithm 3 remaps j and a set of jobs S that may have caused j to miss its deadline. This includes jobs that are scheduled to start at or complete executing within the interval: [start time of job j, deadline of job j]. Note that only tasks in jobs that have previously been scheduled, but have not started executing, are remapped. If all the jobs in S are able to be remapped and meet their deadlines, job j is said to be successfully mapped; otherwise, mapping job j is said to have failed (i.e., one of the jobs cannot meet its deadlines). Depending on the scheduling policy, job j can either be mapped ignoring its deadline (default behavior) or the job can be rejected. The implementation of the algorithm supports both policies, but in the experiments described in Section 6.4.1.1, the former approach is chosen: jobs are mapped even if they miss their deadlines. After Algorithm 3 completes and returns control, Algorithm 1 ends (step 7).

6.4.1.1 Performance Evaluation of MRBB-RM

A simulation-based performance evaluation of MRBB-RM is conducted. The following metrics are used to evaluate system performance: (1) proportion of late jobs (P), which is equal to the ratio between the number of late jobs and the number of jobs executed in an experiment, (2) average job turnaround time (T), and (3) average job matchmaking and scheduling time (O).

First, MRBB-RM is compared with the Minimum Resource Quota Earliest Deadline First with Work-Conserving Scheduling (MinEDF-WC) technique [7], which has objectives that are similar to that of MRBB-RM. MinEDF-WC is a resource allocation and scheduling technique for processing MapReduce jobs with deadlines that is based on the well-known earliest deadline first scheduling policy. MinEDF-WC allocates the minimum number of resources required for completing a job before its deadline and also has the ability to dynamically allocate and deallocate resources from active jobs when required. This ability to dynamically allocate and deallocate resources allows a machine with spare resources to share its unused resources with other jobs that need them. A comparison between the performance of MRBB-RM with that of MinEDF-WC is presented next. The workload used is a synthetic workload generated from workload traces of a Hadoop cluster used at Facebook in October 2009 that is described in Reference 7.

Figure 6.7 presents a comparison of T between MRBB-RM and MinEDF-WC (presented in Reference 7). As shown in Figure 6.7, MRBB-RM achieves a comparable or lower T compared to MinEDF-WC. With regards to P, it is observed that when λ is less than 1/5000 jobs per second, MRBB-RM and MinEDF-WC perform comparably. However, at higher values of λ, a trade-off between T and P is observed. When λ is greater than 1/5000 jobs per second, MinEDF-WC exhibits a smaller P, whereas MRBB-RM achieves a lower T. This is attributed to MRBB-RM's Job and Task Mapping Algorithm attempting to schedule tasks to start executing at their earliest possible time, which in turn reduces the job's turnaround time. However, scheduling tasks to start at their earliest possible times may not always achieve a mapping that minimizes the number of jobs that miss their deadlines. For example, in certain situations delaying some jobs for a longer period of time can prevent other jobs from missing their deadlines, but this in turn leads to an increase in the job's turnaround time.

Furthermore, experiments are also conducted with MRBB-RM to investigate how changing various system and workload parameters, including the job arrival rate (λ), the task execution times, the earliest start time of jobs, the deadline of jobs, and the number of resources, can affect system performance [35]. From the results of these experiments P, T, and O are observed to increase with an increase in λ or an increase in the task execution times. This can be attributed to MRBB-RM being subjected to a higher system load when λ or the task execution times are increased, which in turn generates a high contention for resources. Conversely, it is observed that P, T, and O tend to

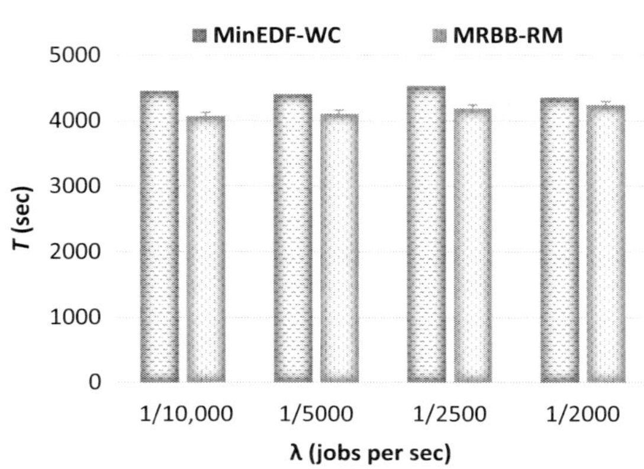

FIGURE 6.7 MRBB-RM versus MinEDF-WC: average job turnaround time when average job arrival rate is varied. (Adapted from N. Lim et al., Resource management techniques for handling requests with service level agreements, *International Symposium on Performance Evaluation of Computer and Telecommunication Systems (SPECTS)*, Monterey, CA, USA, 6–10 July 2014, pp. 618–625.)

decrease, as the number of resources increases or as the deadlines of the jobs increase (i.e., jobs have more slack time). Overall, MRBB-RM is observed to be able to effectively match-make and schedule an open stream of MapReduce jobs with deadlines while incurring a very small O (on average 42 ms). The O/T ratio, which is an indicator of the processing overhead of the algorithm, is observed to be less than 0.02% in all experiments conducted, demonstrating the efficiency of MRBB-RM. A more detailed discussion of the results of these experiments can be found in Reference 35.

6.4.2 Resource Management for MapReduce Jobs with SLAs Using Optimization Methods

Resource management techniques that model and solve the problem of matchmaking and scheduling MapReduce jobs with SLAs, where each SLA comprises an earliest start time, a required execution time, and an end-to-end deadline, using various optimization methods are presented in Reference 36. More specifically, the resource management problem for MapReduce jobs with SLAs is formulated using MILP [37] and constraint programming (CP) [38] (refer to Figure 6.8). The resource management model that is formulated using CP is called the *CP Model* and similarly, the resource management model that is formulated using MILP is referred to as the *MILP Model*. The use of MILP and CP in the proposed resource management techniques leads to an optimal solution in the sense that the schedule that is generated results in the number of jobs that miss their deadlines being minimized. The input required by the resource management model consists of a set of jobs, J, and a set of resources, R, on which to execute J. The *objective* is to minimize the number of jobs that miss their deadlines. Both the CP Model and the MILP Model have the same general structure: decision variables, objective function, and constraints. The *decision variables* are the variables that are initially unknown and are assigned values once the problem is solved (i.e., they represent the output of the model). The *objective function* is a mathematical function that generates the value that needs to be optimized (minimized or maximized). Lastly, the *constraints* are a set of mathematical formulas that restrict the values that the decision variables can be assigned. Solving the optimization model involves assigning values to the *decision variables* to optimize the value generated by the *objective function*, while also ensuring that none of the *constraints* are violated. Three implementations of the MILP Model and CP Model using different software packages are considered:

- *Approach 1*: The MILP Model is implemented and solved using LINGO [39] (commercial software).
- *Approach 2*: The CP Model is implemented using MiniZinc/FlatZinc [40] and solved using Gecode [41] (both open-source software).
- *Approach 3*: The CP Model is implemented and solved using IBM ILOG CPLEX Optimization Studio (CPLEX) [42] (commercial software).

The *output* produced after solving the resource management model includes the following: (1) the assigned resource and scheduled start time for the tasks of each job, (2) the completion time of the batch of jobs, and (3) the number of jobs that miss their deadlines. The *measurements* that are made on the system to evaluate the performance of the different approaches include the processing time required by the solver to produce the output.

6.4.2.1 Performance Evaluation of MILP Model-Based and CP Model-Based Resource Management Techniques

To compare the effectiveness and performance of the three approaches, simulation experiments are performed using various batch workloads, where each batch comprises multiple jobs to execute. Each experiment concluded after successfully matchmaking and scheduling all the jobs in the batch and a schedule and completion time for the batch of jobs is determined. The performances of the three approaches are compared using the following metrics: *completion time of the workload* (C),

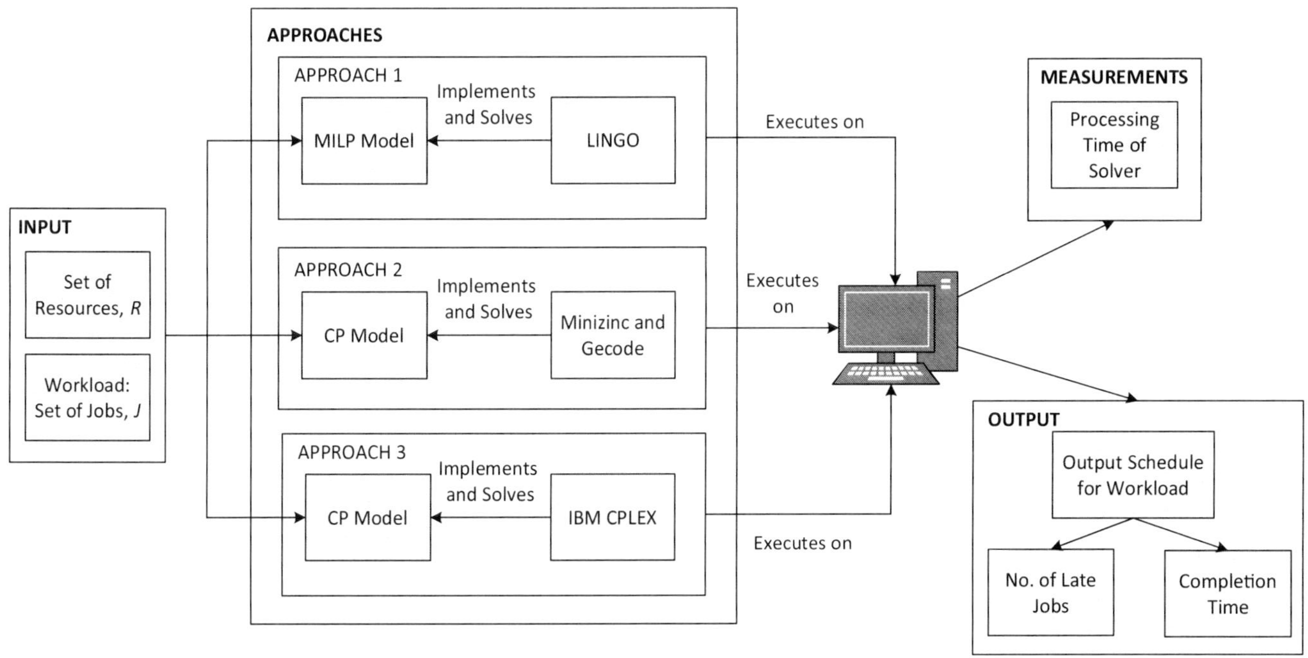

FIGURE 6.8 Approach to solving the resource management problem using optimization methods. (Adapted from N. Lim et al., Engineering resource management middleware for optimizing the performance of clouds processing MapReduce jobs with deadlines, *International Conference on Performance Engineering (ICPE)*, Dublin, Ireland, 24–26 March 2014, pp. 161–172.)

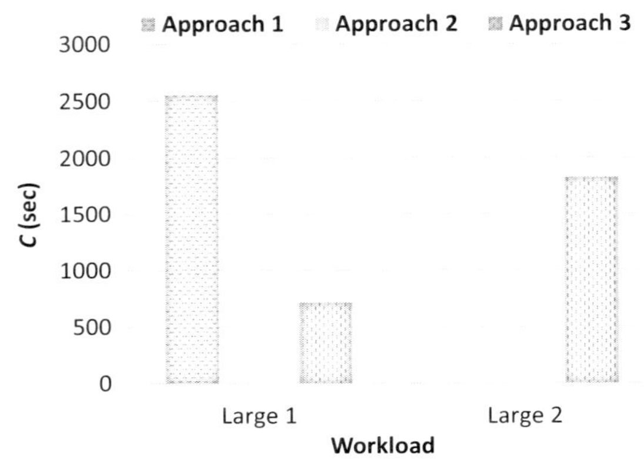

FIGURE 6.9 Comparison of workload completion time for the large workloads. (Adapted from N. Lim et al., Engineering resource management middleware for optimizing the performance of clouds processing MapReduce jobs with deadlines, *International Conference on Performance Engineering (ICPE)*, Dublin, Ireland, 24–26 March 2014, pp. 161–172.)

processing time overhead (*PO*), and the *size of workload* (number of tasks) that the approach can successfully process. Since all three approaches perform matchmaking and scheduling by solving an optimization problem, each approach is able to generate a schedule where the number of late jobs is minimized. In the set of experiments conducted to evaluate the three approaches, each approach generates a schedule where none of the jobs missed their deadlines. A representative set of results from the performance evaluation of the MILP Model and CP Model are discussed next. A full discussion of the performance evaluation and the results is provided in Reference 36.

The values of *C* and *PO* for the three approaches when executing the large workloads are shown in Figures 6.9 and 6.10, respectively. The Large 1 workload has 2 jobs with each job having 100 map tasks and 30 reduce tasks. On the other hand, the Large 2 workload comprises 50 jobs with each job having a varying number of map tasks from 1 to 100 and a varying number of reduce tasks ranging from 1 to the number of map tasks. Therefore, on an average, the Large 2 workload has approximately 3750 tasks. A more detailed description of the workloads can be found in Reference 36. From Figures 6.9 and 6.10, it is observed that Approach 2 is not able to process these larger

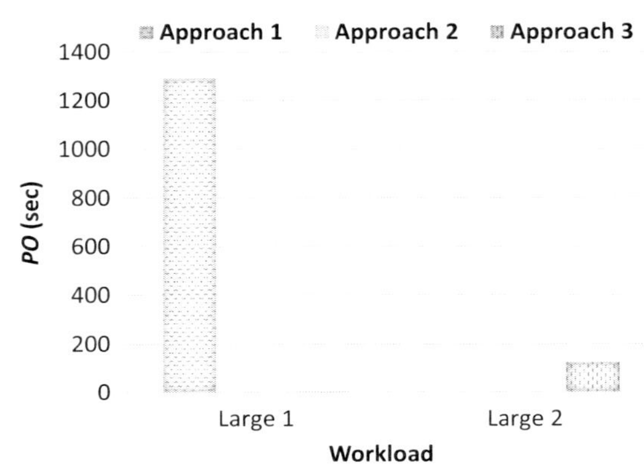

FIGURE 6.10 Comparison of processing time overhead for the large workloads. (Adapted from N. Lim et al., Engineering resource management middleware for optimizing the performance of clouds processing MapReduce jobs with deadlines, *International Conference on Performance Engineering (ICPE)*, Dublin, Ireland, 24–26 March 2014, pp. 161–172.)

workloads and Approach 1 is only able to generate a schedule for the Large 1 workload (as indicated by the missing bars in the graphs). When attempting to generate solutions for the larger workloads with Approaches 1 and 2, the experimental system eventually ran out of memory and the solver crashed. This means that the solvers of Approach 1 and 2 could not handle such a large number of decision variables on the system that was used to conduct the experiments. On the other hand, the results show that Approach 3 is capable of processing both the large workloads and performed well in terms of *PO* and *C*. Note that Approach 3 achieves a very small *PO* (1.08 s) for the Large 1 workload, and thus, the bar is not clearly visible in Figure 6.10.

6.4.3 MapReduce Constraint Programming-Based Resource Management Technique

The results of the experiments discussed in Reference 36 and summarized in Section 6.4.2.1 demonstrate the superiority of Approach 3: the CP Model implemented using IBM CPLEX, including its more intuitive and simple formulation of constraints, lower processing overhead, and its ability to handle larger workloads. This motivated the investigation of a novel MapReduce Constraint Programming-based Resource Management algorithm (MRCP-RM) [43] that can effectively perform matchmaking and scheduling for an open stream of MapReduce jobs with SLAs, where each SLA is characterized by an earliest start time, a required execution time, and an end-to-end deadline. The objective of MRCP-RM is to minimize the number of jobs that miss their deadlines. The key difference between MRCP-RM and the techniques described in Reference 36 is that MRCP-RM can handle an open stream of job arrivals whereas the techniques described in Reference 36 only support a batch workload with a fixed number of jobs (i.e., a closed system).

Figure 6.11 presents a diagram showing an environment using MRCP-RM. Users submit MapReduce jobs to the system, which are placed in a *job queue*. If the resource manager is available (i.e., not busy mapping the previous set of jobs), it invokes MRCP-RM to map the set of jobs in the job queue. MRCP-RM uses IBM CPLEX [42] to generate an OPL Model, which is an implementation of the CP Model using IBM's Optimization Programming Language (OPL). More specifically, an

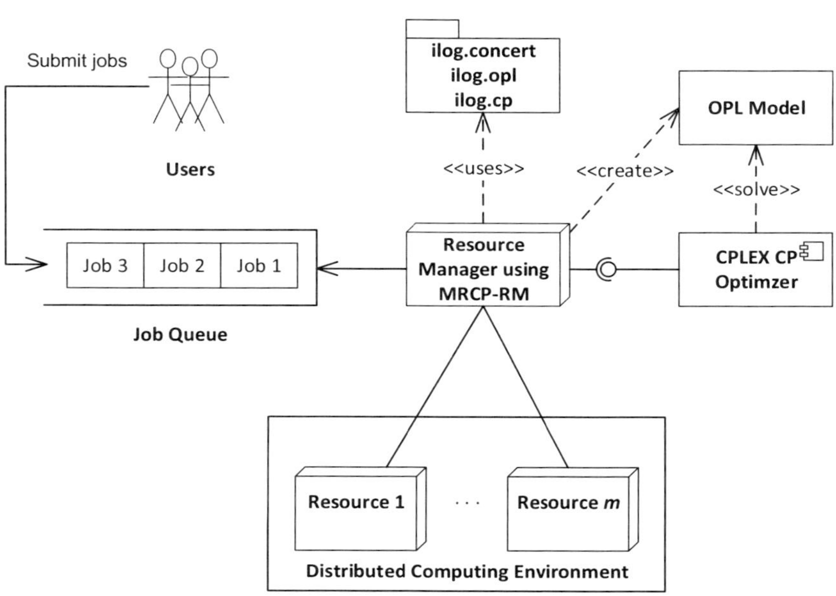

FIGURE 6.11 Overview of MRCP-RM. (Adapted from N. Lim et al., A constraint programming-based resource management technique for processing MapReduce jobs with SLAs on clouds, *International Conference on Parallel Processing (ICPP)*, Minneapolis, MN, USA, 9–12 September 2014, pp. 411–421.)

OPL Model that has new constraints added for each of the tasks that have started but not completed executing is created. To solve the OPL Model, MRCP-RM invokes IBM CPLEX's CP Optimizer solving engine. Note that if this is not the first time that MRCP-RM is invoked, the set of jobs to process includes the new jobs retrieved from the job queue as well as the jobs that are scheduled or currently executing, but have not completed yet. MRCP-RM schedules all the newly submitted jobs (i.e., jobs in the job queue), but also remaps the tasks of jobs that have not started executing to provide the most flexibility in scheduling in order to minimize the number of late jobs. For example, the tasks of a new job with an earlier deadline may need to be mapped in the place of the tasks of a previously scheduled job that has a later deadline. Once a solution to the OPL Model is found, the resource manager is able to determine the tasks to assign to a particular resource (matchmaking) and when the tasks assigned to a particular resource should start to execute (scheduling).

6.4.3.1 Performance Evaluation of MRCP-RM

To investigate the effectiveness of MRCP-RM, a simulation-based performance evaluation is conducted. Three performance metrics are used to evaluate the performance of MRCP-RM: proportion of late jobs (P), average job turnaround time (T), and average job matchmaking and scheduling time (O) (recall Section 6.4.1.1). First, experiments are performed to investigate the effect of various system and workload parameters on the performance of MRCP-RM. For example, Figure 6.12 shows the effect of the job arrival rate (λ) on T and O of MRCP-RM. The values of P achieved by MRCP-RM for each value of λ experimented with are as follows: 0.04%, 0.55%, 1.03%, and 1.70% when λ (in jobs per second) is 0.001, 0.01, 0.015, and 0.02, respectively. The results show that P, T, and O increase with λ because of the increased contention for resources. In particular, one of the main reasons for O increasing with λ is the existence of multiple scheduled tasks that have not started executing at a given point in time, as well as multiple executing tasks that have not completed yet. This large number of tasks to process leads to MRCP-RM requiring more time to generate and solve the OPL Model, which in turn increases O. However, O/T, which is an indicator of the processing overhead, is still observed to be small (less than 0.04%) in the experiments conducted.

A brief discussion of the results of the other experiments performed to investigate the effect of changing various system and workload parameters on the performance of MRCP-RM is provided next. A more detailed discussion can be found in Reference 43. It is observed that P, T, and O tend to decrease with an increase in one of the following parameters: the number of resources in the system, the earliest start times of the jobs, and the deadlines of the jobs. This can be attributed to an increase

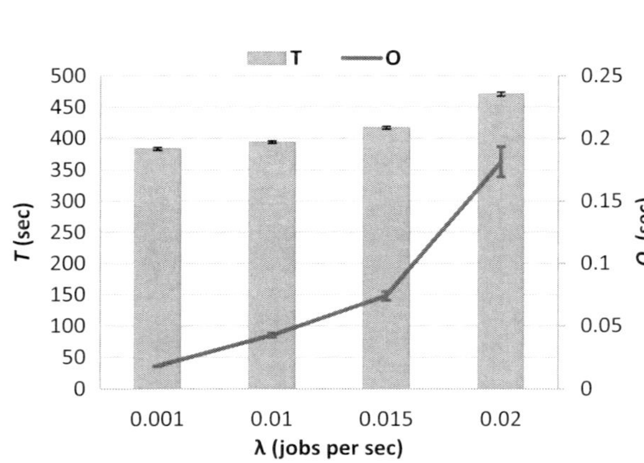

FIGURE 6.12 Effect of job arrival rate on the average job turnaround time and average job matchmaking and scheduling time of MRCP-RM. (Adapted from N. Lim et al., A constraint programming-based resource management technique for processing MapReduce jobs with SLAs on clouds, *International Conference on Parallel Processing (ICPP)*, Minneapolis, MN, USA, 9–12 September 2014, pp. 411–421.)

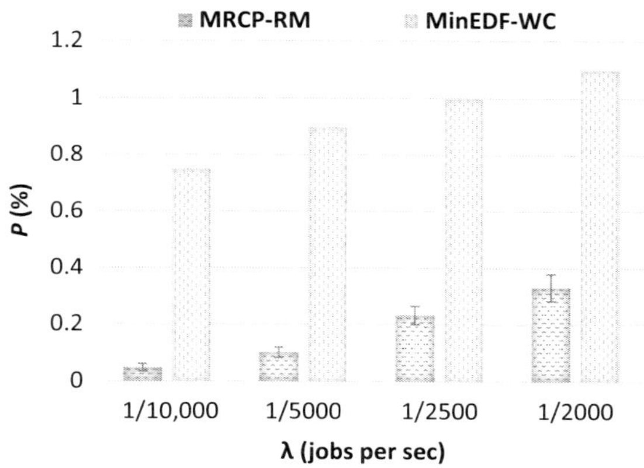

FIGURE 6.13 MRCP-RM versus MinEDF-WC: proportion of late jobs when average job arrival rate is varied. (Adapted from N. Lim et al., A constraint programming-based resource management technique for processing MapReduce jobs with SLAs on clouds, *International Conference on Parallel Processing (ICPP)*, Minneapolis, MN, USA, 9–12 September 2014, pp. 411–421.)

in these parameters generating a situation where there is less contention for resources. Overall, from the experiments conducted, it is observed that MRCP-RM is able to generate a schedule that leads to a small P (less than 3.46%) with a small matchmaking and scheduling overhead as indicated by the O/T ratio (less than 0.09%).

In addition, a performance comparison between MRCP-RM and the MinEDF-WC [7] technique from the literature (recall Section 6.4.1.1), which has similar objectives to MRCP-RM, is also conducted. A synthetic MapReduce workload from Facebook that is described in Reference 7 is used in these experiments. Figure 6.13 presents a comparison of P between MRCP-RM and MinEDF-WC (presented in Reference 7). As shown in Figure 6.13, MRCP-RM achieves a significantly lower P (up to 93% lower) in comparison to MinEDF-WC. With respect to T (see Reference 43 for more details), MRCP-RM is observed to have a comparable or lower T (up to 7% lower) in comparison to MinEDF-WC. Note that the jobs in this workload have small slack times, leading to the jobs having more stringent deadlines. This means that jobs need to be executed as close as possible to their earliest start times (i.e., have a small turnaround time) in order to meet their deadlines. The improved performance of MRCP-RM compared to MinEDF-WC when using the synthetic Facebook workload can be attributed to the use of the optimization technique, constraint programming, to perform matchmaking and scheduling.

6.4.4 Constraint Programming-Based Scheduler for Hadoop

The strong performance of MRCP-RM, observed from the simulation experiments, motivated the research presented in Reference 44, which focuses on devising a *revised* version of MRCP-RM and implementing it on a real system that implements the MapReduce programming model: Hadoop [11]. The new technique is referred to as the *Constraint Programming-based Scheduler* for Hadoop (abbreviated *CP-Scheduler*). The CP-Scheduler can perform matchmaking and scheduling for an open stream of Hadoop jobs with deadlines. Figure 6.14 illustrates a Hadoop cluster deploying the CP-Scheduler. The Hadoop cluster comprises a single master node (NameNode and JobTracker) and m slave nodes (DataNodes and TaskTrackers). Recall the discussion of Hadoop provided in Section 6.2.2. Users submit Hadoop jobs to the JobTracker, which uses the CP-Scheduler to matchmake and schedule the map and reduce tasks of the jobs onto the TaskTrackers. More specifically, the CP-Scheduler uses IBM CPLEX's Java APIs to create and solve the CP Model that formulates the matchmaking and scheduling problem as an optimization problem (recall Section 6.4.2).

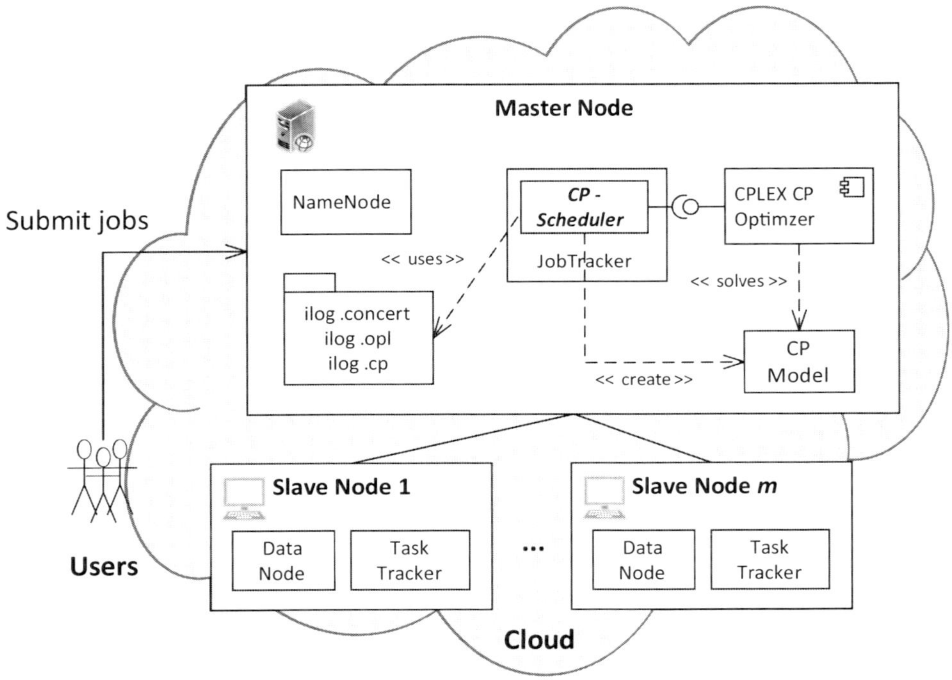

FIGURE 6.14 Hadoop cluster deploying the CP-Scheduler. (Adapted from N. Lim et al., A constraint programming based Hadoop scheduler for handling MapReduce jobs with deadlines on clouds, *International Conference on Performance Engineering (ICPE)*, Austin, TX, USA, 31 January–4 February 2015, pp. 111–122.)

An overview of the CP-Scheduler algorithm is presented in Figure 6.15 as a flowchart. A more detailed and complete description of the CP-Scheduler algorithm can be found in Reference 44. The CP-Scheduler is invoked by the JobTracker each time it receives a heartbeat message from a TaskTracker (recall Section 6.2.2) to perform matchmaking and scheduling. The input required by the CP-Scheduler algorithm is a TaskTracker to assign tasks too. The first step is to create the input data required by the CP Model, which includes a set of jobs to schedule, J, and a set of resources, R (step 1). The set of jobs (J) includes newly arriving jobs that have not been scheduled and jobs that have been previously scheduled, but not finished executing. Next, the CP-Scheduler checks if

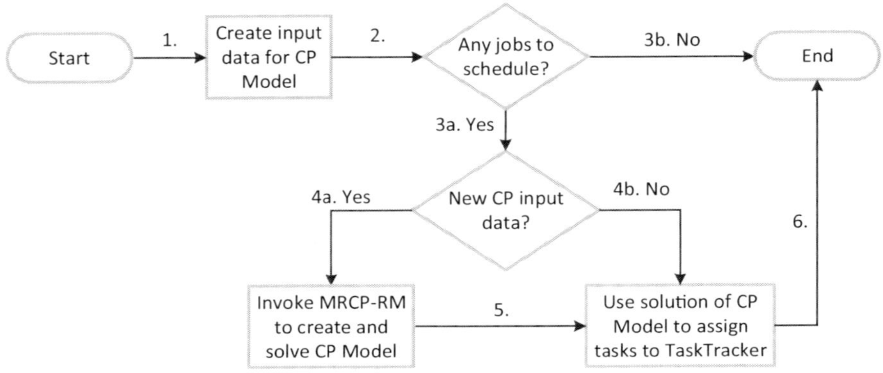

FIGURE 6.15 Overview of CP-Scheduler algorithm.

there are any jobs in J (step 2). If J is empty, meaning there are no new jobs to schedule and no jobs currently scheduled or executing on the system, the algorithm ends (step 3b). Otherwise, the CP-Scheduler checks to see if there are any new jobs to schedule in J or any new resources in R (step 3a). Note that the resources in R can change in two cases: (1) resources are added to R if there are new TaskTrackers added to the Hadoop cluster, or (2) resources are removed from R if TaskTrackers that are part of the Hadoop cluster fail or crash. If there is new input data, the CP-Scheduler creates and solves a new CP Model to perform matchmaking and scheduling (step 4a). Checking for new input data in J and R is performed to prevent unnecessarily creating and solving a CP Model (which is a source of overhead) when a solution for the same input has already been found previously. In step 5, the CP-Scheduler extracts the solution from the solved CP Model to assign tasks to the supplied TaskTracker for execution.

6.4.4.1 Performance Evaluation of the CP-Scheduler

A performance evaluation of the CP-Scheduler is conducted on a Hadoop cluster deployed on Amazon EC2 to determine the effectiveness of MRCP-RM on a real system and to obtain insights into system behavior and performance. The CP-Scheduler's performance is compared with the performance achieved by an earliest deadline first (EDF) Hadoop scheduler (called the *EDF-Scheduler*), which is implemented by extending Hadoop's default FIFO scheduler. The comparison with the EDF-Scheduler is made to investigate if the CP-Scheduler is more effective than a scheduler using the well-known EDF scheduling policy when matchmaking and scheduling an open stream of MapReduce jobs with deadlines. The workload used in these experiments is an open stream of Hadoop WordCount jobs (recall Section 6.2.1) processing various input data sizes. More specifically, three job types are used in the experiments: *small* containing 3 files (~3 MB in total), *medium* containing 10 files (~5 MB in total), and *large* containing 20 files (~10 MB in total). The input files are e-books (in plain text format) that are obtained from Project Gutenberg (www.gutenberg.org). A detailed discussion of the performance evaluation of the CP-Scheduler and EDF-Scheduler can be found in Reference 44. A representative set of the experimental results is presented next.

Experiments are performed for systems subjected to a *mixed workload* as well as a *single class workload*. The mixed workload comprises jobs from each of the three job types: small, medium, and large. The single class workload is characterized by jobs of any one type: small or medium or large. Figures 6.16 and 6.17 show the results of the experiments conducted using the *mixed workload*, which is the workload where the three job types defined earlier have an equal probability of being

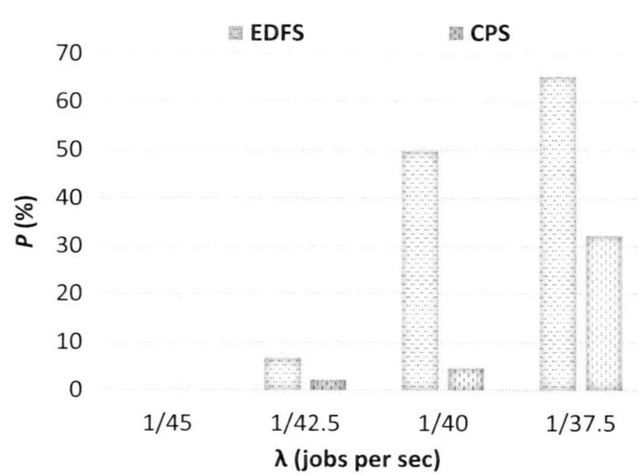

FIGURE 6.16 CP-Scheduler (CPS) versus EDF-Scheduler (EDFS): proportion of late jobs when using the mixed workload and the average job arrival rate is varied. (Adapted from N. Lim et al., A constraint programming based Hadoop scheduler for handling MapReduce jobs with deadlines on clouds, *International Conference on Performance Engineering (ICPE)*, Austin, TX, USA, 31 January–4 February 2015, pp. 111–122.)

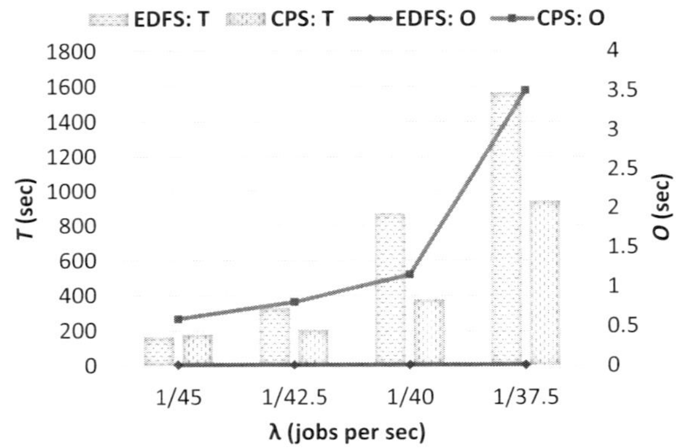

FIGURE 6.17 CP-Scheduler (CPS) versus EDF-Scheduler (EDFS): average job turnaround time and average job matchmaking and scheduling time when using the mixed workload and the average job arrival rate is varied. (Adapted from N. Lim et al., A constraint programming based Hadoop scheduler for handling MapReduce jobs with deadlines on clouds, *International Conference on Performance Engineering (ICPE)*, Austin, TX, USA, 31 January–4 February 2015, pp. 111–122.)

submitted to the system. It is observed that the CP-Scheduler (abbreviated CPS) outperforms the EDF-Scheduler (abbreviated EDFS) by a large margin in terms of *P* (up to 91%) and *T* (up to 57%). CPS is able to efficiently interleave the execution of multiple jobs and make more efficient use of the system's resources such that the number of jobs that miss their deadlines is minimized. Conversely, EDFS simply selects the first job in its ordered job queue (i.e., the job with the earliest deadline) to execute, which in turn results in inferior performance in terms of *P* and *T*. However, as shown in Figure 6.17, EDFS achieves a much lower *O* (on average 0.012 s) compared to CPS (on average 1.51 s). CPS has a higher *O* because it uses a more complex matchmaking and scheduling algorithm that requires generating and solving a constraint program (recall Section 6.4.4). Although the *O* of CPS is higher compared to the *O* of EDFS, the *O*/*T* ratio, which is an indication of the processing overhead in relation to the average job turnaround time, is still very low (less than 0.4%). The *O*/*T* ratio is an appropriate indication of the processing overhead because it puts the measured values of the algorithm runtimes into context by considering the algorithm run time (*O*) relative to the average job turnaround time (*T*).

Figures 6.18 and 6.19 show the results of the experiments conducted with the single class workload comprising only of large jobs. As shown in Figure 6.18, CPS achieves a *P* equal to 0 for all λ experimented with (as indicated by the nonvisible bars), while the *P* of EDFS increases from 0% to 49% as λ increases from 1/77.5 to 1/70 jobs per second. Furthermore, the performance improvement of CPS over EDFS in terms of *T* is observed to increase from 32% to 62% as λ increases from 1/77.5 to 1/70 jobs per second. All the jobs in this workload have a large number of input files to process, resulting in longer job execution times. Since EDFS does not efficiently interleave the execution of multiple jobs, scheduling jobs that have long execution times tends to lead to more late jobs because it is possible for jobs with tight deadlines to arrive on the system during the execution of another job. On the other hand, CPS effectively interleaves the execution of multiple jobs on the system and also reschedules the tasks of jobs that have not started executing when a job with an earlier deadline arrives on the system. As a result, using CPS gives rise to a smaller *P* and *T* in comparison to using EDFS. The trend for *O* (refer to Figure 6.19) is similar to that observed when using the mixed workload: CPS has a higher *O* compared to EDFS, but the processing overhead, as indicated by *O*/*T*, is still small. Note that the performance trends that are observed when using the workload comprising only small jobs and the workload comprising only medium jobs are similar to that achieved with the workload comprising only large jobs. That is, in general it is observed that CPS achieves a lower *P*,

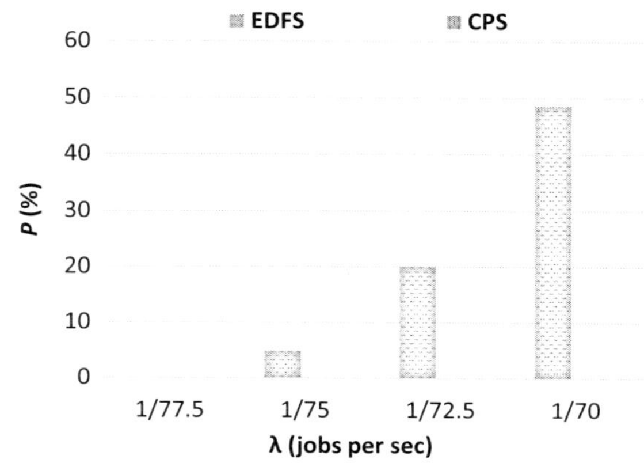

FIGURE 6.18 CP-Scheduler (CPS) versus EDF-Scheduler (EDFS): proportion of late jobs when using the large workload and the average job arrival rate is varied. (Adapted from N. Lim et al., A constraint programming based Hadoop scheduler for handling MapReduce jobs with deadlines on clouds, *International Conference on Performance Engineering (ICPE)*, Austin, TX, USA, 31 January–4 February 2015, pp. 111–122.)

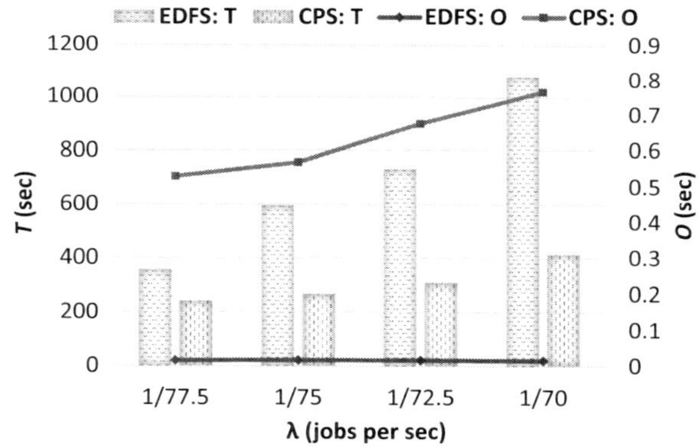

FIGURE 6.19 CP-Scheduler (CPS) versus EDF-Scheduler (EDFS): average job turnaround time and average job matchmaking and scheduling time when using the large workload and the average job arrival rate is varied. (Adapted from N. Lim et al., A constraint programming based Hadoop scheduler for handling MapReduce jobs with deadlines on clouds, *International Conference on Performance Engineering (ICPE)*, Austin, TX, USA, 31 January–4 February 2015, pp. 111–122.)

a lower T, and a higher O compared to EDFS; however, O/T remains small (less than 0.7%). A more in-depth discussion of the experimental results can be found in Reference 44.

6.4.5 Other Techniques

The authors of Reference 45 propose a Deadline Constraint Scheduler for Hadoop. The authors develop a *job execution cost model* that considers parameters such as the execution time of map tasks, the execution of reduce tasks, and the size of the input data. This model is used for a schedulability test that is performed to determine if the job can be completed before its deadline given the current available resources in the cluster. In Reference 46, the authors investigate the problem of scheduling MapReduce workloads comprising jobs without deadlines and jobs with deadlines. The authors present a scheduler that adopts a sampling-based technique called *Tasks Forward Scheduling* (TFS) to predict the execution time of map tasks and reduce tasks. TFS predicts task execution times by initially executing a few tasks and then using the execution times of these initial tasks to predict the execution times of future tasks. In addition, the proposed scheduler also leverages a resource allocation model named *Approximately Uniform Minimum Degree of Parallelism* (AUMD) to dynamically control the execution of jobs such that each job executes at its minimum degree of task parallelism to meet its deadline. The idea is to prevent a single job from monopolizing all the resources in the cluster and to allow more jobs to be executed on the cluster simultaneously.

In Reference 47, the authors describe a policy for dynamic provisioning of public cloud resources to schedule MapReduce jobs with deadlines. Initially, jobs are executed on a local cluster, and if required, resources from the cloud are dynamically provisioned to meet the application's deadline. Moreover, the authors of Reference 48 investigate resource management algorithms for minimizing the cost of allocating virtual machines to execute MapReduce jobs with deadlines. Two VM provisioning strategies are proposed: (1) List and First-Fit (LFF) and (2) Deadline-aware Tasks Packing (DTP). The LFF approach sorts the pricing policies of VMs according to either increasing order of unit cost or decreasing order of VM performance. Each map task is assigned to its own VM and reduce tasks are assigned to one of the VMs already provisioned for map tasks. In the DTP approach, the idea is to assign the map tasks and reduce tasks of jobs to execute on existing VMs as much as possible until a job cannot meet its deadline, in which case a new VM needs to be provisioned.

The authors of Reference 49 focus on the joint considerations of workload balancing and meeting deadlines for MapReduce jobs. Scheduling algorithms are proposed that are based on integer linear programming and solved with a linear programming solver using a rounding approach. The proposed scheduling algorithms are implemented and evaluated in Hadoop 1.1.2. The experimental results using a workload with a fixed number of jobs show that the proposed technique can balance workloads and achieve a higher deadline satisfaction ratio compared to existing Hadoop schedulers.

In Reference 50, the authors propose a scheduler for MapReduce jobs with deadlines based on bipartite graph modeling called the Bipartite Graph Modeling MapReduce Scheduler (BGMRS). BGMRS focuses on scheduling MapReduce jobs with deadlines on a heterogeneous cloud computing environment (i.e., on an environment where nodes exhibit different performance). BGMRS is able to obtain the optimal solution to the scheduling problem by transforming the problem into a well-known graph problem: minimum weighted bipartite matching. The authors conducted simulation and testbed-based experiments using a workload with a fixed number of jobs to demonstrate the effectiveness of the technique.

6.5 CONCLUSIONS AND FUTURE WORK

Analyzing data for making meaningful decisions is important in various types of environments, including enterprise and scientific applications as well as cyber-physical systems, such as sensor-equipped bridges, smart buildings, and industrial machinery. However, the volume of data analyzed is sometimes very large and conventional processing tools and techniques cannot be used for analyzing such Big Data. MapReduce/Hadoop has emerged as a popular technique and tool for processing Big Data applications. MapReduce is a programming model proposed by Google that simplifies performing massively distributed parallel processing, whereas Hadoop is an open-source software framework (written in Java) that implements MapReduce. Hadoop is used by many companies and institutions, typically in conjunction with cloud computing, for processing and analyzing large datasets (i.e., performing Big Data analytics). The focus of this chapter was on describing resource management algorithms and techniques for processing MapReduce jobs, including MapReduce jobs with SLAs, on a distributed system such as a cloud or cluster. The SLA may vary from application to application and often includes an earliest start time, a required execution time, and an end-to-end deadline. Intelligent and efficient resource management techniques are necessary for harnessing the power of the underlying distributed hardware and for achieving a high system performance that includes a high QoS as reflected in a low ratio of jobs missing their deadlines. A number of resource management techniques for processing MapReduce jobs with different goals, including reducing job completion times, reducing data transmission between resources to minimize network traffic, handling of heterogeneous resources, sharing of resources, and managing the energy consumption of resources, were discussed in this chapter. Furthermore, a number of techniques for processing an open stream of MapReduce jobs with deadlines were also described in this chapter, including:

- A MapReduce Budget-based Resource Management algorithm (MRBB-RM) that decomposes the end-to-end deadline for a job into components (i.e., subdeadlines), each of which is associated with a specific task in the job
- A MapReduce Constraint Programming-based Resource Management algorithm (MRCP-RM) that performs matchmaking and scheduling by solving a constraint programming model
- A Hadoop Constraint Programming-based Scheduler (CP-Scheduler), which is designed and devised to implement MRCP-RM on Hadoop—a real MapReduce system

The results from a rigorous performance evaluation of the resource management techniques demonstrate that these techniques are effective in processing an open stream of MapReduce jobs with deadlines. More specifically, the techniques are capable of generating a schedule leading to a low number of jobs missing their deadlines with an acceptable processing overhead, as indicated by the low values of O/T (less than 0.7% in all experiments conducted). The O/T ratio places the processing time required by a matchmaking and scheduling algorithm (O) into context by considering the value of O in relation to the mean job turnaround time (T). In addition, the techniques were also observed to outperform techniques from the literature such as MinEDF-WC. A direction for future research includes the extension of the deadline budgeting algorithms to support general workflows with different kinds of precedence relationships (not just MapReduce jobs with two phases of execution), such as scientific workflows in the field of physics and biology. Moreover, investigating how the error/inaccuracies in user-estimated execution times can affect system performance and how to handle these errors/inaccuracies forms an interesting direction for future work. Constraint programming-based energy-aware algorithms for handling workflows with deadlines also warrant investigation.

ACKNOWLEDGMENTS

We are grateful to Huawei Technologies Canada and the Natural Science and Engineering Research Council of Canada for supporting some of the research, the results of which are included in this book chapter. The authors would like to thank Adam Gregory for his comments on the manuscript.

REFERENCES

1. J. Dean and S. Ghemawat, MapReduce: Simplified data processing on large clusters, International Symposium on Operating System Design and Implementation (OSDI), San Francisco, CA, USA, December 6–8, 2004, pp. 137–150.
2. T. White, *Hadoop: The Definitive Guide*, 2nd Edition, O'Reilly Media, Inc., Sebastopol, CA, USA, 2011.
3. J. Dittrich and J.-A. Quiane-Ruiz, Efficient big data processing in Hadoop MapReduce, Proceedings of VLDB 2012/PVLDB, vol. 5, no. 12, 2012, pp. 2014–2015 (Tutorial).
4. M. Collins, Hadoop and MapReduce: Big data analytics, *Gartner*, 14 January 2011.
5. N. Gift, Solve cloud-related big data problems with MapReduce, IBM, 8 November 2010. [Online]. Available: http://www.ibm.com/developerworks/cloud/library/cl-bigdata/ [Accessed April 1, 2016].
6. S. Baker, The two flavors of Google, *Bloomberg Businessweek Magazine*, 12 December 2007.
7. A. Verma, L. Cherkasova, V. S. Kumar, and R. H. Campbell, Deadline-based workload management for MapReduce environments: Pieces of the performance puzzle, Network Operations and Management Symposium, Maui, Hawaii, USA, 16–20 April 2012, pp. 900–905.

8. R. Buyya, S. K. Garg, and R. N. Calheiros, SLA-oriented resource provisioning for cloud computing: Challenges, architecture, and solutions, International Conference on Cloud and Service Computing (CSC), Hong Kong, China, 12–14 December 2011, pp. 1–10.
9. I. Foster, C. Kesselman, C. Lee, B. Lindell, K. Nahrstedt, and A. Roy, A Distributed Resource Management Architecture that Supports Advance Reservations and Co-Allocation, International Workshop on Quality of Service, London, England, UK, 1–4 June 1999, pp. 27–36.
10. S. S. Manvi and G. K. Shyam, Resource management for Infrastructure as a Service (IaaS) in cloud computing: A survey, *Journal of Network and Computing Applications*, vol. 41, 2013, pp. 424–440.
11. The Apache Software Foundation, Hadoop. [Online]. Available: http://hadoop.apache.org [Accessed: April 1, 2016].
12. The Apache Software Foundation, Hadoop Wiki. [Online]. Available: http://wiki.apache.org/hadoop/PoweredBy [Accessed: April 1, 2016].
13. S. Ghemawat, H. Gobioff, and S.-T. Leung, The Google File System, *ACM SIGOPS Operating Systems Review*, vol. 37, no. 5, 2003, pp. 29–43.
14. M. Jones and M. Nelson, Moving ahead with Hadoop YARN, IBM developerWorks, 2013. [Online]. Available: http://www.ibm.com/developerworks/library/bd-hadoopyarn/ [Accessed: April 5, 2016].
15. The Apache Software Foundation, Apache Hadoop YARN. [Online]. Available: http://hadoop.apache.org/docs/r2.7.2/hadoop-yarn/hadoop-yarn-site/YARN.html [Accessed: April 5, 2016].
16. H. Chang, M. Kodialam, R. R. Kompella, T. V. Lakshman, M. Lee, and S. Mukherjee, Scheduling in MapReduce-like systems for fast completion time, *IEEE INFOCOM 2011*, Shanghai, China, 10–15 April 2011, pp. 3074–3082.
17. A. S. Schulz, Scheduling to minimize total weighted completion time: Performance guarantees of LP-based heuristics and lower bounds, International Conference on Integer Programming and Combinatorial Optimization (IPCO), Vancouver, BC, Canada, 3–5 June 1996, pp. 301–315.
18. X. Gao, Q. Chen, Y. Chen, Q. Sun, Y. Liu, and M. Li, A dispatching-rule-based task scheduling policy for MapReduce with multi-type jobs in heterogeneous environments, ChinaGrid Annual Conference, Beijing, China, 20–23 September 2012, pp. 17–24.
19. C. Tian, H. Zhou, Y. He, and Li. Zha, A dynamic MapReduce scheduler for heterogeneous workloads, International Conference on Grid and Cooperative Computing (GCC), Lanzhou, China, 27–29 August 2009, pp. 218–224.
20. Z. Fadika and M. Govindaraju, DELMA: Dynamically ELastic MapReduce Framework for CPU-intensive applications, IEEE/ACM International Symposium on Cluster, Cloud and Grid Computing (CCGrid), Newport Beach, CA, USA, 23–26 May 2011, pp. 454–463.
21. B. Palanisamy, A. Singh, and L. Liu, Cost-effective resource provisioning for MapReduce in a cloud, *IEEE Transactions on in Parallel and Distributed Systems*, vol. 26, no. 5, 2015, pp. 1265–1279.
22. D. Yoo and K. M. Sim, A scheduling mechanism for multiple MapReduce jobs in a workflow application (position paper), Computing, Communications and Applications Conference (ComComAp), Hong Kong, China, 11–13 January 2012, pp. 405–410.
23. C. He, Y. Lu, and D. Swanson, Matchmaking: A new MapReduce scheduling technique, International Conference on Cloud Computing Technology and Science (CloudCom), Athens, Greece, 29 November–1 December 2011, pp. 40–47.
24. M. Hammoud and M. F. Sakr, Locality-aware reduce task scheduling for MapReduce, International Conference on Cloud Computing Technology and Science (CloudCom), Athens, Greece, 29 November–1 December 2011, pp. 570–576.
25. Y. Tao, Q. Zhang, L. Shi, and P. Chen, Job scheduling optimization for multi-user MapReduce clusters, International Symposium on Parallel Architectures, Algorithms and Programming (PAAP), Tianjin, China, 9–11 December 2011, pp. 213–217.
26. The Apache Software Foundation, Hadoop 1.2.1 Documentation: Fair Scheduler. [Online]. Available: http://hadoop.apache.org/docs/r1.2.1/fair_scheduler.html [Accessed: April 10, 2016].
27. X. Xu and M. Tang, A new approach to the cloud-based heterogeneous MapReduce placement problem, *IEEE Transactions on in Services Computing*, vol. PP, no. 99, 2015, pp. 1–12.
28. Y. Liu, M. Li, N. K. Alham, S. Hammoud, and M. Ponraj, Load balancing in MapReduce environments for data intensive applications, International Conference on Fuzzy Systems and Knowledge Discovery (FSKD), Shanghai, China, 26–28 July 2011, pp. 2675–2678.

29. Z. Fadika, E. Dede, J. Hartog, and M. Govindaraju, MARLA: MapReduce for Heterogeneous Clusters, IEEE/ACM International Symposium on Cluster, Cloud and Grid Computing (CCGrid), Ottawa, ON, Canada, 13–16 May 2012, pp. 49–56.
30. The Apache Software Foundation, Hadoop 1.2.1 Documentation: Capacity Scheduler. [Online]. Available: http://hadoop.apache.org/docs/r1.2.1/capacity_scheduler.html [Accessed: April 10, 2016].
31. Z. Guo and G. Fox, Improving MapReduce performance in heterogeneous network environments and resource utilization, IEEE/ACM International Symposium on Cluster, Cloud and Grid Computing (CCGrid), Ottawa, ON, Canada, 13–16 May 2012, pp. 714–716.
32. Y. Luo and B. Plale, Hierarchical MapReduce programming model and scheduling algorithms, IEEE/ACM International Symposium on Cluster, Cloud and Grid Computing (CCGrid), Ottawa, ON, Canada, 13–16 May 2012, pp. 769–774.
33. T. Wirtz and R. Ge, Improving MapReduce energy efficiency for computation intensive workloads, International Conference on Green Computing Conference and Workshops (IGCC), Orlando, FL, USA, July 2011, pp. 1–8, 25–28.
34. D. Cavdar, L. Y. Chen, and F. Alagoz, Green MapReduce for heterogeneous data centers, IEEE Global Communications Conference (GLOBECOM), Austin, TX, USA, 8–12 December 2014, pp. 1120–1126.
35. N. Lim, S. Majumdar, and P. Ashwood-Smith, Resource management techniques for handling requests with service level agreements, International Symposium on Performance Evaluation of Computer and Telecommunication Systems (SPECTS), Monterey, CA, USA, 6–10 July 2014, pp. 618–625.
36. N. Lim, S. Majumdar, and P. Ashwood-Smith, Engineering resource management middleware for optimizing the performance of clouds processing MapReduce jobs with deadlines, International Conference on Performance Engineering (ICPE), Dublin, Ireland, 24–26 March 2014, pp. 161–172.
37. R. Bosch and M. Trick, Integer programming, in: *Search Methodologies: Introductory Tutorials in Optimization and Decision Support Techniques*, E.K. Burke and G. Kendall, Eds. Boston, MA: Springer US, 2005, pp. 69–95.
38. F. Rossi, P. Beek, and T. Walsh, Chapter 4: Constraint programming, in: *Handbook of Knowledge Representation*, F. van Harmelen, V. Lifschitz, and B. Porter, Eds. San Diego, CA: Elsevier, 2008, pp. 181–211.
39. Lindo Systems Inc., Lindo Systems—Optimization Software, [Online]. Available: http://www.lindo.com/ [Accessed: April 12, 2016].
40. NICTA, MiniZinc and FlatZinc, [Online]. Available: http://www.MiniZinc.org/ [Accessed: April 12, 2016].
41. Gecode, Generic Constraint Development Environment, [Online]. Available: http://www.gecode.org/ [Accessed: April 12, 2016].
42. IBM, IBM ILOG CPLEX Optimization Studio, [Online]. Available: http://pic.dhe.ibm.com/ infocenter/cosinfoc/v12r5/index.jsp [Accessed: April 12, 2016].
43. N. Lim, S. Majumdar, and P. Ashwood-Smith, A constraint programming-based resource management technique for processing MapReduce jobs with SLAs on clouds, International Conference on Parallel Processing (ICPP), Minneapolis, MN, USA, 9–12 September 2014, pp. 411–421.
44. N. Lim, S. Majumdar, and P. Ashwood-Smith, A constraint programming based Hadoop scheduler for handling MapReduce jobs with deadlines on clouds, International Conference on Performance Engineering (ICPE), Austin, TX, USA, 31 January–4 February 2015, pp. 111–122.
45. K. Kc and K. Anyanwu, Scheduling Hadoop jobs to meet deadlines, International Conference on Cloud Computing Technology and Science (CloudCom), Indianapolis, IN, USA, 30 November–3 December 2010, pp. 388–392.
46. X. Dong, Y. Wang, and H. Liao, Scheduling mixed real-time and non-real-time applications in MapReduce environment, International Conference on Parallel and Distributed Systems (ICPADS), Tainan, Taiwan, 7–9 December 2011, pp. 9–16.
47. M. Mattess, R. N. Calheiros, and R. Buyya, Scaling MapReduce applications across hybrid clouds to meet soft deadlines, International Conference on Advanced Information Networking and Applications (AINA), Barcelona, Spain, 25–28 March 2013, pp. 629–636.
48. E. Hwang and K. H. Kim, Minimizing cost of virtual machines for deadline-constrained MapReduce applications in the cloud, International Conference on Grid Computing (GRID), Beijing, China, 20–23 September 2012, pp. 130–138.

49. Z.-R. Lai, C.-W. Chang, X. Liu, T.-W. Kuo, and P.-C. Hsiu, Deadline-aware load balancing for MapReduce, International Conference on Embedded and Real-Time Computing Systems and Applications (RTCSA), Chongqing, China, 20–22 August 2014, pp. 1–10.
50. C. Chen, J. Lin, and S. Kuo, MapReduce scheduling for deadline-constrained jobs in heterogeneous cloud computing systems, *IEEE Transactions on Cloud Computing*, vol. PP, 2015, pp. 1–14.

7 Tyche
An Efficient Ethernet-Based Protocol for Converged Networked Storage

Pilar González-Férez and Angelos Bilas

CONTENTS

ABSTRACT

Tyche is a network storage protocol directly on top of raw Ethernet, which does not require any hardware support from the network interface. It provides high I/O throughput and low I/O latency via a copy-reduction technique, preallocation of memory, custom network queues and structures, using remote direct memory access-like operations without hardware assistance, and storage-specific packet processing. Tyche transparently bundles multiple network interface cards (NICs) and offers scaling with the number of links and cores via reduced synchronization, proper packet queue design, and nonuniform memory access affinity management.

7.1 INTRODUCTION

Storage in datacenters is typically a separate tier from application servers and access happens mostly via a storage area network (SAN). Current efforts to improve efficiency of datacenters in terms of capital expenses and operational expenses, such as reduced energy consumption or less expensive storage, dictate bringing storage closer to applications and computation by converging the two tiers. *Converged storage* advocates placing storage devices, most likely performance-oriented devices, such as solid-state disks (SSD) or nonvolatile memory (NVM)-based cards, in all servers where computation occurs and adapting the current I/O stack to the new model. Therefore, compute servers are used as a single distributed storage system as well, in a departure from traditional SAN and network attached storage (NAS) approaches. In this model, where computation and storage are co-located, the role of the network becomes more important for achieving high storage I/O throughput.

Although there has been a lot of research on high-speed interconnects, such as Infiniband, Ethernet-based networks today dominate the datacenter due to management reasons, cost-efficiency, and the software stack that is already in use. There are many advantages to using Ethernet-based networks for storage as well. Ethernet has caught up with other technologies, especially in terms of throughput. However, an area where Ethernet still lacks significantly is protocol overhead, as exhibited in terms of CPU cycles. Technologies such as Infiniband are able to support more lightweight protocols than IP-based protocols used over Ethernet. As Ethernet is starting to be used for accessing storage in the datacenter, protocol overheads are becoming a main concern. Therefore, the network protocol used on top of Ethernet plays a significant role in achieving high efficiency for storage access.

Table 7.1 provides a summary of storage-specific and general-purpose network protocols based on Ethernet. We classify these protocols into two categories, whether they need hardware support or not. Software-only protocols typically exhibit relatively low throughput for small requests and incur high overheads. A main reason is that either they mostly use TCP/IP or they are not optimized for storage. TCP/IP inherently incurs high overheads due to its streaming semantics. On the other hand, hardware-assisted protocols usually obtain maximum link throughput at lower CPU overheads, but they require custom NICs or other extensions to the underlying interconnect, which is a significant impediment for deployment and adoption.

In this chapter, we examine the issues associated with networked storage access over raw Ethernet, and we describe the design of Tyche, a network storage protocol that achieves high efficiency, without requiring any hardware assistance. Tyche delivers high I/O throughput and low I/O latency by employing numerous techniques: copy-reduction, storage-specific packet processing, preallocation of memory, nonuniform memory access (NUMA) affinity management, remote direct memory access (RDMA) like operations, bundling multiple NICs transparently, avoiding context switches (when possible), and adaptive batching mechanism. Tyche can be deployed in existing infrastructures and to co-exist with other Ethernet-based protocols. To the best of our knowledge, our approach

TABLE 7.1
Network Storage Protocol and Generic Network Protocol Based on Ethernet

	Software	Hardware
Storage	NBD, iSCSI, AoE, FCoE	iSER [1], SRP [2], gmblock [3]
Generic	PortLand [4]	iWARP, RoCE, JNIC [5]

is the first to achieve 90% of link efficiency for 16 kB request sizes without any specialized hardware support.

Our results show that Tyche achieves scalable throughput, up to 6.4 GB/s for reads and 6.7 GB/s for writes on 6 × 10 Gbits/s network links without requiring any hardware support. This is 89% and 93%, respectively, of the peek throughput available with six NICs. In addition, our optimized protocol that reduces context switching is particularly effective for low degrees of I/O concurrency and reduces host CPU overhead by 31% per 4 kB-I/O request. For high degrees of I/O concurrency, an adaptive batching significantly improves link utilization for small I/Os, and allows Tyche to achieve up to 88% of the theoretical link utilization for 4 kB requests.

Our analysis shows that network storage protocols for modern servers with multiple resources need to be designed for NUMA affinity and synchronization to achieve high network throughput. Otherwise, performance degrades significantly. For small I/Os, two aspects are particularly effective for improving link utilization: reducing overhead for low degrees of I/O concurrency and batching several requests in a single message for high degrees of I/O concurrency.

The rest of this chapter is organized as follows. Sections 7.2 and 7.3 present Tyche and the main decisions taken during its design to achieve high throughput and low latency. Section 7.4 discusses performance results. Section 7.5 describes related work and Section 7.6 concludes our work.

7.2 SYSTEM DESIGN

Tyche [6–8] is a network storage protocol on top of raw Ethernet that achieves high I/O throughput and low latency without any hardware support. Tyche presents the remote storage device locally by creating at the client (initiator) a block device that can be used as a regular block device. Tyche is independent of the storage device, and supports any existing file system.

Figure 7.1 depicts the overall design of Tyche that is composed of two layers. The block layer is in charge of managing I/O requests and I/O completions. The network layer is in charge of network messages and packets.

7.2.1 Communication Channels

Tyche uses the concept of communication channel to establish a connection between the initiator and the target. Each channel allows a host to send/receive data to/from a remote host. Thus, Tyche is a connection-oriented protocol that creates channels to perform the communication between both nodes.

A channel is directly associated to the NIC that it uses for sending/receiving data. Although a channel is mapped to a single NIC, several channels can be mapped to the same NIC. When there are

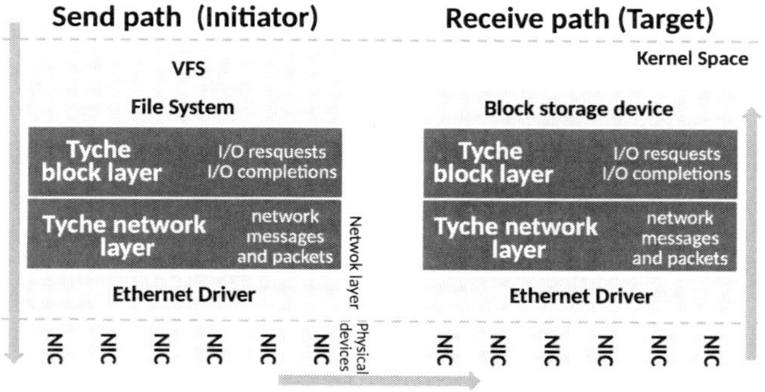

FIGURE 7.1 Overview of the send and receive path from the initiator to the target.

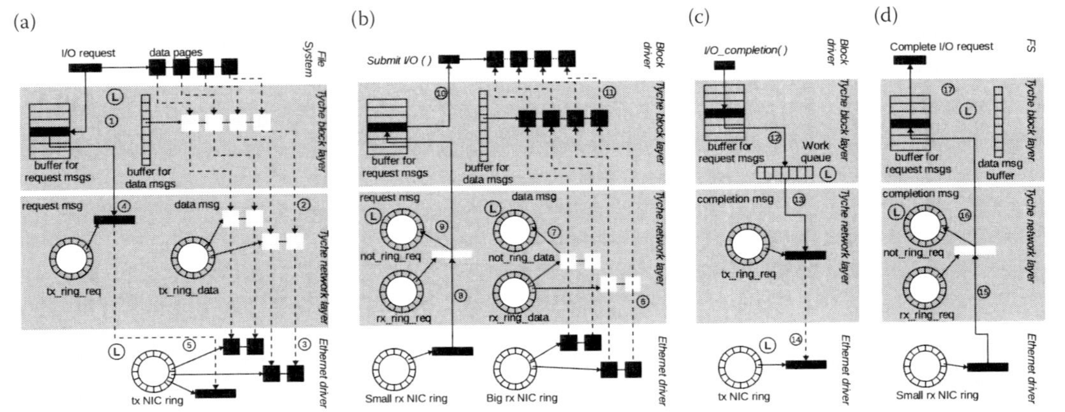

FIGURE 7.2 End-to-end I/O path through a channel for a write request of 16 kB when Tyche works in the inline mode. Lines and numbers indicate the execution order. Solid lines indicate that there is a copy of data. Dashed ones indicate that there is no copy of data. “L” means the action requires a lock. (a) Initiator send path. (b) Target receive path. (c) Target send path. (d) Initiator receive path.

several NICs available, Tyche creates a channel per NIC, allowing the creation of multiple channels between initiator and target. Therefore, Tyche is able to simultaneously and transparently manage several channels/NICs.

To initialize the network stack, Tyche opens a channel per available NIC between initiator and target. During the handshake phase, for each channel, the initiator and target exchange information about resources. Then the initiator creates a local device for the remote device, and it is ready to receive I/O requests for this new device.

Whether there are several channels open for the same remote device, Tyche uses a dynamic scheduler to select the channels (see Section 7.3.2).

Figure 7.2 depicts the end-to-end I/O path of a write request through a channel. A read follows the same path, except that the data message is sent from the target to the initiator. We use a 16 kB request for clarifying purpose. The following sections explain in detail this end-to-end I/O path.

7.2.2 Network Messages

As shown in Figure 7.2a, Tyche receives regular I/O requests from the above layer (normally the file system) to be issued to the remote device. An I/O request is composed of its parameters (request type, LBA sector, size, and flags) and the pages with the data to be written or where to place the data to be read. For this reason, Tyche supports two different types of messages: request messages and data messages.

Request messages are used for transferring request parameters and for sending I/O completions back from the target to the initiator. Data messages are used for sending data pages. For writes, data messages are sent from the initiator to the target, whereas for reads, data messages are sent from the target to the initiator. An I/O request corresponds to three network messages: two request messages (the request itself and its completion) and a data message. Tyche always sends these three messages through the same channel.

A request message corresponds to a single request packet, that is small (less than 100 bytes in size), and is transferred using an Ethernet frame. Data messages are sent via RDMA-type messages by using scatter-gather lists of memory pages (I/O buffers). The corresponding (data) packets are transferred in separate Jumbo Ethernet frames of 4 or 8 kB. A data packet can carry at most two 4 kB pages, so, a data message for an I/O request of N pages corresponds to $N/2$ data packets.

7.2.3 Main Data Structures

In order to reduce the overhead that implies the memory management, to minimize synchronization for shared structures, and to allow scaling with the number of NICs and cores, Tyche allocates all the resources per channel. Therefore, each channel has and manages its own private resources: two buffers for messages at the block layer and several rings at the network layer.

At the block layer, each channel has two separate and preallocated buffers (see Figure 7.2), one for request messages and one for data messages. Messages are sent and received by using these buffers. I/O completions, which are handled as request messages, are prepared in the same buffer where the corresponding request message was received.

At the target, the buffer for data messages contains lists of preallocated pages. The target uses these pages not only for sending and receiving data messages but also for issuing regular I/O requests to the local device. On the contrary, the initiator has no preallocated pages. For sending or receiving data messages, the initiator uses the pages already provided by the regular I/O requests, avoiding, in this way, any extra copy of data.

Although both, initiator and target, have allocated these buffers, the initiator handles the buffers from both sides. During the connection handshake phase, the buffer information is exchanged, so the initiator knows all necessary identification handlers of the target buffers. For each message, the initiator specifies, in the packet header, its positions on the corresponding buffer. On its reception, the network layer directly places a message in its buffer's position. For instance, the initiator specifies on behalf of the target the position (pages) where data packets have to be placed when they arrive (for writes), and the target uses these pages for submitting the regular I/O write requests.

At the network layer, each channel uses three rings (see Figure 7.2), one for transmitting, `TX_ring`, one for receiving, `RX_ring`, and one for notifications, `Not_ring`. Since Tyche handles two kinds of packets (request and data packets), each channel also has two instances for each ring. A request packet is sent using `TX_ring_req`, received in `RX_ring_req`, and its notification is placed in `Not_ring_req`. In the same way, a data packet uses `TX_ring_data`, `RX_ring_data`, and `Not_ring_data`.

7.2.4 Storage-Specific Network Protocol

The header of our packets includes information to facilitate communication between the network and block layers, to allow several channels per NIC, and to provide end-to-end flow control.

For each packet, the header includes the identifier of the channel, the local position in the transmission ring that also denotes the position on the remote receive ring, the position of its message on the corresponding message buffer, and positive and negative acknowledgments.

For data packets, the header also includes the number of pages that composes the data packet, the position of these pages on the data message, and the total number of pages of the data message.

By using the same position on the transmission and receive rings, we reduce packet processing overhead in the receive path. By including for each message its position in the buffer, upon its arrival, a message is placed in its final position and we avoid the copy from the network layer to the block layer.

Thanks to these fields, Tyche also allows out-of-order transfer, and delivery of packets over multiple links in case a channel is mapped to several NICs.

7.2.5 Networked I/O Path

Figure 7.2 depicts the end-to-end I/O path of a 16 kB write request. In addition, Figures 7.3 through 7.6 describe this flow path providing more detail. On these figures, the numbers on the arrows denote the execution order when several actions are run after a previous one. Figures 7.2 through 7.4 mark with the label "L" some actions that require synchronization. For simplicity, figures do not include error handling and retransmission paths.

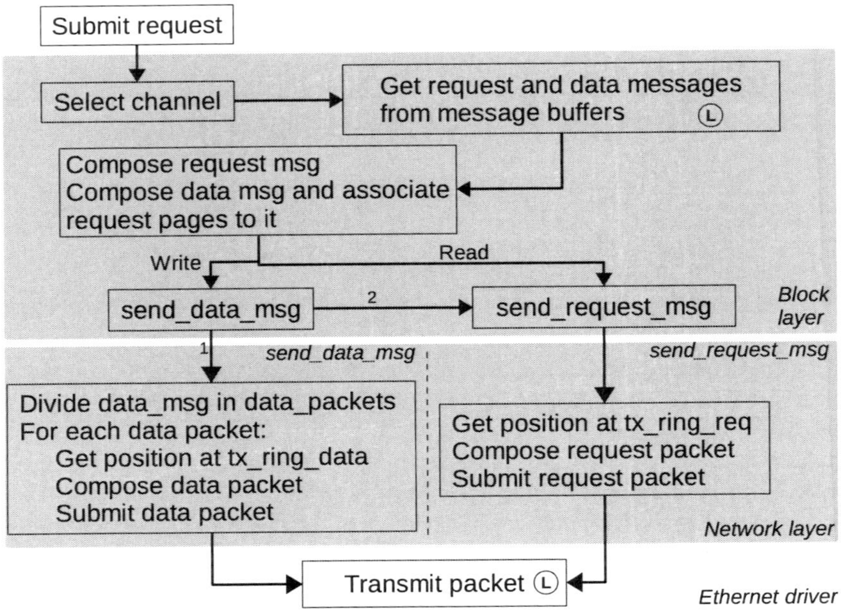

FIGURE 7.3 Overview of the send path at the initiator.

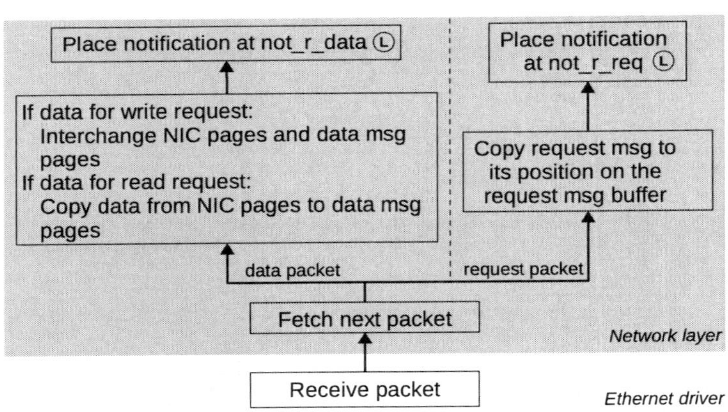

FIGURE 7.4 Overview of the receive path at the network layer.

For each I/O request, the initiator selects one channel, and from the buffers of this channel, it gets one request message and one data message. Then it composes the messages, and transmits them. Figure 7.3 shows this send path.

At the target, dedicated network threads, one per NIC, process incoming packets, compose messages, and generate notifications to the block layer. Block layer threads, several per channel, process request messages and, for each request, construct a proper Linux kernel I/O request and issue it to the local block device. Figures 7.4 and 7.5a summarize these receive paths for the network and block layers, respectively.

The target uses a work queue to send completions back to the initiator. Local I/O completions run in an interrupt context, which is not able to perform actions that can block such as sending/receiving

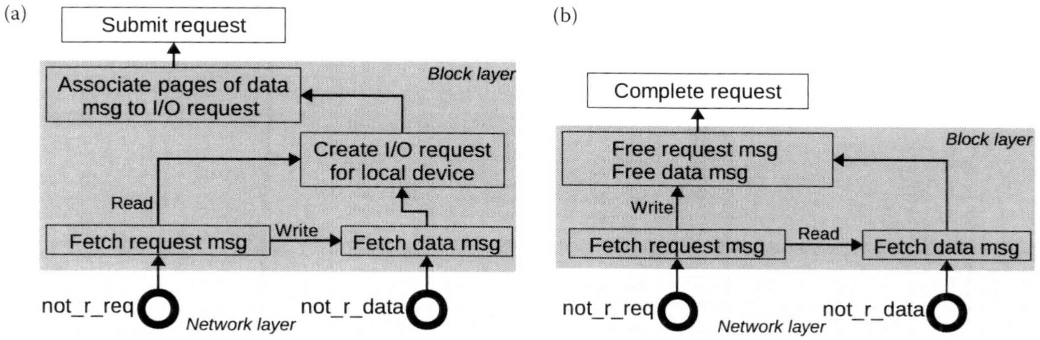

FIGURE 7.5 Overview of the receive path at the block layer. (a) At the target. (b) At the initiator.

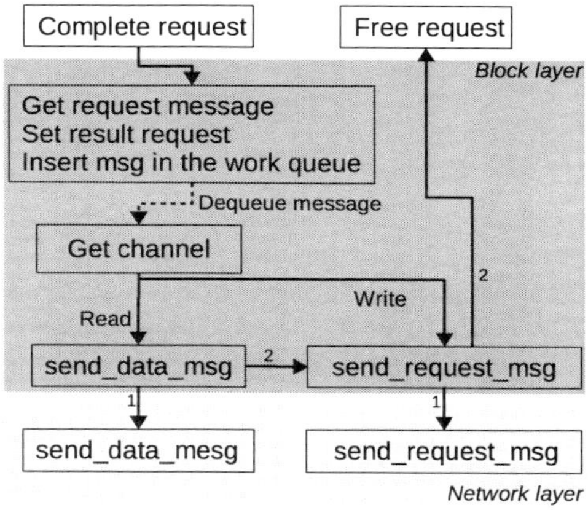

FIGURE 7.6 Overview of the completion path at the target.

network messages. For this reason, the local I/O completion schedules a work queue task that executes the required operations. Figure 7.6 depicts this completion path, and the network send path is shown in Figure 7.3.

When a completion arrives, the initiator runs the receiving tasks to complete the corresponding I/O request. Figure 7.5b depicts the receive path of the block layer at the initiator, and Figure 7.4 the network receive path.

Tyche can operate in two different modes. In the "inline" mode (Figures 7.1 through 7.3), the application context issues I/O requests to the target, without requiring any context switch in the issue path. In the "queue" mode, regular I/O requests are inserted in a queue, and several threads dequeue these I/O requests and issue them to the target. With the queue mode, the issuing context blocks just after enqueuing the request.

7.3 MAIN CHALLENGES

In our design, we deal with the following main challenges: (i) memory management overhead; (ii) NUMA affinity; (iii) synchronization; (iv) many cores accessing a single NIC; (v) latency; (vi) batching; and (vii) elasticity. Next, we discuss how Tyche addresses these challenges.

7.3.1 Memory Management

Each channel has preallocated buffers to reduce memory management overhead when receiving/sending messages. At the target, each channel also has preallocated pages that are used for sending and receiving data messages as well as for issuing regular I/O requests to the local storage device.

Network protocols over Ethernet involve a copy of data in the receive path from NIC buffers to the actual data location. The reason is that arriving data is placed in the physical pages belonging to the NIC's receive ring; however, these data should be placed eventually in the pages of the corresponding request. The copy of data should occur in the target for write requests and in the initiator for reads.

For write requests, Tyche avoids the overhead of the memory copy from NIC buffers to Tyche pages by interchanging the pages. On the arrival of a data packet, the target interchanges pages between the NIC receive ring and the data buffers. This interchange of pages is possible because the initiator specifies at the header of the data packet the position (pages) for these data at the target side.

For reads, Tyche cannot apply this interchange technique, and performs a single copy at the initiator. When a read is sent over the network, the layer that initially issued the request expects specific nonsequential *physical* pages (`struct page` objects in the Linux kernel) to be filled with the received data. Therefore, exchanging pages does not work, and a memory copy is required.

7.3.2 NUMA Affinity

For efficiency and scalability purposes, modern servers employ NUMA architectures, such as the one depicted in Figure 7.7 that corresponds to the servers used in our work. These servers use multiple processor sockets with memory attached to each socket, resulting in nonuniform latencies from processor to different memories. Each I/O device is placed to a specific NUMA node via an I/O hub (Figure 7.7). Processors, memories, and I/O hubs are connected through high-speed interconnects, for example, QPI (QuickPath Interconnect) [9]. Accessing remote memory (in a different NUMA node) incurs significantly higher latency than accessing local memory [10,11], up to a factor of 2×.

In the I/O path, the elements related to NUMA affinity are application buffers, protocol data structures, kernel (I/O and NIC) data buffers, placement of NICs on server sockets, application threads, protocol threads, work queues, and interrupt handlers.

Tyche orchestrates affinity of memory and threads by considering the system topology and the location of NICs. It creates a communication channel per NIC, and associates resources exclusively with a single channel.

Each channel allocates memory for all purposes in the same NUMA node where its NIC is attached, and it also pins its threads to the same NUMA node. For instance, in the architecture of Figure 7.7, a channel mapped to NIC-0 allocates resources in Memory-0 and runs its threads in cores within Processor-0, a channel mapped to NIC-3 uses Memory-1 and Processor-1.

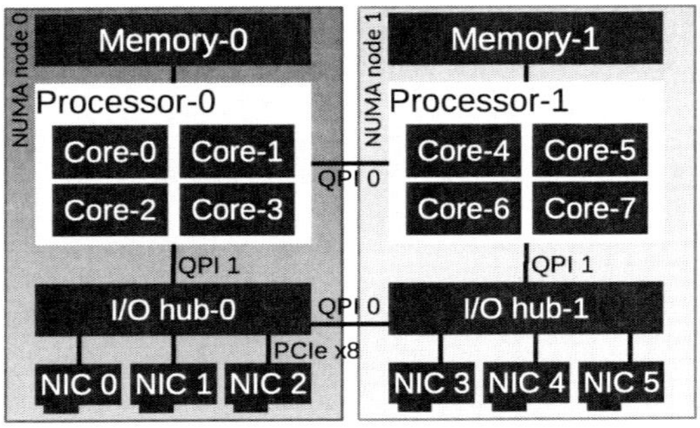

FIGURE 7.7 Internal data paths in our NUMA servers.

The NIC driver has, per NIC, transmission and receive rings. We also force the allocation of these resources in the same node where the NIC is attached, making them part of the NIC channel.

We implement a NUMA-awareness work queue as well, because in the Linux kernel used it is not possible to apply affinity on the assignment of tasks to work queues. Our work queue launches a thread per core, and each thread is pinned in its corresponding core. The target submits completion messages to the work queue by using its NUMA information.

There are still points uncovered, such as, in the Linux kernel, it is not possible to force placement of I/O completions, or to control placement of buffer cache pages; and controlling application thread placement can have adverse effects on application performance.

In addition, we implement a channel scheduler [8] that is able to dynamically select the scheduling policy depending on the throughput achieved by each NUMA node and the current load in terms of requests. The goal is to deal with load imbalance among nodes. Our channel scheduler uses by default the affinity-based policy. It switches to a round-robin policy when it detects that better balancing of requests across NUMA nodes may lead to higher throughput. It then switches back to affinity scheduling when it finds that balancing requests across NUMA nodes creates unnecessary cross-NUMA traffic.

7.3.3 Synchronization

Using private resources per channel allows Tyche to minimize synchronization. However, Tyche still has to grant exclusive access to each channel, because several threads can simultaneously use the same channel. For the same reason, the NIC driver has to grant exclusive access to its rings as well.

Figures 7.2 through 7.4 mark with "L" the locks of the end-to-end I/O path in the inline mode. Table 7.2, for each lock, gives its name, the layer, path, and host in which the lock is used, the data structure or task protected, and the steps in Figure 7.2 in which it is held. All the locks are spin-locks.

In addition, Tyche uses atomic operations to control access to other data structures such as its transmission rings. An atomic operation per-buffer also avoids the (uncommon) case of concurrently processing overlapped messages.

For packets and messages, Tyche assigns in advance its position on the receive rings and buffers; consequently, the receive path does not require locks. Sending completions neither requires locks, since the target sends a completion message by using the corresponding request message.

The initiator path can operate in two different modes. In the inline mode, application threads simultaneously submit their requests without performing a context switch. The queue mode uses a context switch to avoid having many threads accessing the send path and incurring a significant

TABLE 7.2
Locks on the Tyche End-to-End I/O Path for the Inline and Queue Modes

Lock	Layer	Path	Data Structure/Task	Steps in Figure 7.2
Mes	Block	IS, IR	Message buffers	1, 17
NIC	Network driver	IS, TS	NIC transmission ring	3, 5, 14
Not	Network	IR, TR	One per notification rings	7, 9, 10, 11, 16, 17
Work	Block	TS	Work queue	12, 13
Pos	Network	IS, TS	To send positive ack	Not included
Neg	Network	IS, TS	To send negative ack	Not included
Que	Block	IS	Request queue (queue mode)	Not included

Note: S, R, I, and T stand for send, receive, initiator, and target, respectively.

synchronization overhead. The queue mode introduces a new queue at the initiator block layer, and therefore a lock is required.

Our previous results [8] show that the inline approach where application threads issue requests with no context switch is preferable to using a queuing approach that trades locks for context switches, when NUMA affinity is enabled end-to-end. Indeed, in these cases, the inline approach outperforms by up to 24% the queuing approach.

7.3.4 Many Cores Accessing a Single Network Link

The increasing number of cores in modern servers also increases the contention when threads from multiple cores access a single network link. In the send path, the initiator uses the queue mode to limit the number of threads that can access each link. At the target, work queues send completions back, limiting the number of contexts (one per core) that interact with each NIC. In the receive path, Tyche uses one thread per NIC to process incoming data. Our analysis [6] shows that one core can sustain higher network throughput than a single 10 GigE NIC, and therefore it does not limit the maximum throughput.

7.3.5 Reducing Latency for Small I/O Requests

Our analysis of the host CPU overheads in the networked I/O path (see Section 7.4.3) finds out that there are two fundamental limitations to achieve high input/output operations per second (IOPS) for small requests: Context switches impose significant CPU overhead whereas network packet processing dominates over link throughput. Tyche significantly reduces network packet processing, and here we propose an optimization for context switches.

Figure 7.8 marks with green circles the context switches done; in addition, Table 7.5 describes them. Serving a 4 kB request involves, at least, six context switches. For larger requests, more contest switches are expected because the number of data packets sent/received depends on the request size.

We propose Tyche-NoCS, a variant of our protocol that avoids the context switches on the receive path and on the target send path. Section 7.4.3 shows that this design is particularly effective for low degrees of I/O concurrency.

Tyche-NoCS avoids CS-Rec, that is, the context switch done between the network and block threads, by using a single thread to run the whole receive path. The network thread processes a packet, composes the message, and checks whether any data message related to the request message just composed has arrived. When all the messages (request message and data message if any) have been received, the network thread runs the block layer tasks through a callback function. To avoid blocking this thread, we also use callback functions to check whether all the messages that compose an I/O request have been received. In addition, the notification rings that communicate both threads are not used, and we reduce overhead by avoiding them and, for instance, the lock to ensure exclusive access to them as well.

Tyche-NoCS also eliminates CS-WQ, that is, the context switch done in the target send path due to the work queue, by attempting to send the response to the initiator from the completion context of the local I/O. If it succeeds, there will be no context switch. But, if the operation needs to block, which is not allowed in the completion context, it will fall back to the work queue of the base version. Note that the completion context will block if, for instance, there is no room in the transmission ring. Avoiding the work queue results in avoiding the management associated, for instance, the lock that is required to insert/dequeue tasks into/from the work queue.

It is worth emphasizing that Tyche cannot avoid CS-IRQ, the context switch done when the NIC interrupt is raised in the receive path, because interrupt handler functions cannot do anything that could sleep. Previous works [12,13] have examined how to avoid this context switch by using polling instead of interrupts. However, we have not considered this option because the spinning time could be significant larger, especially for large requests. In our case, the NIC interrupt handler just wakes up our network thread.

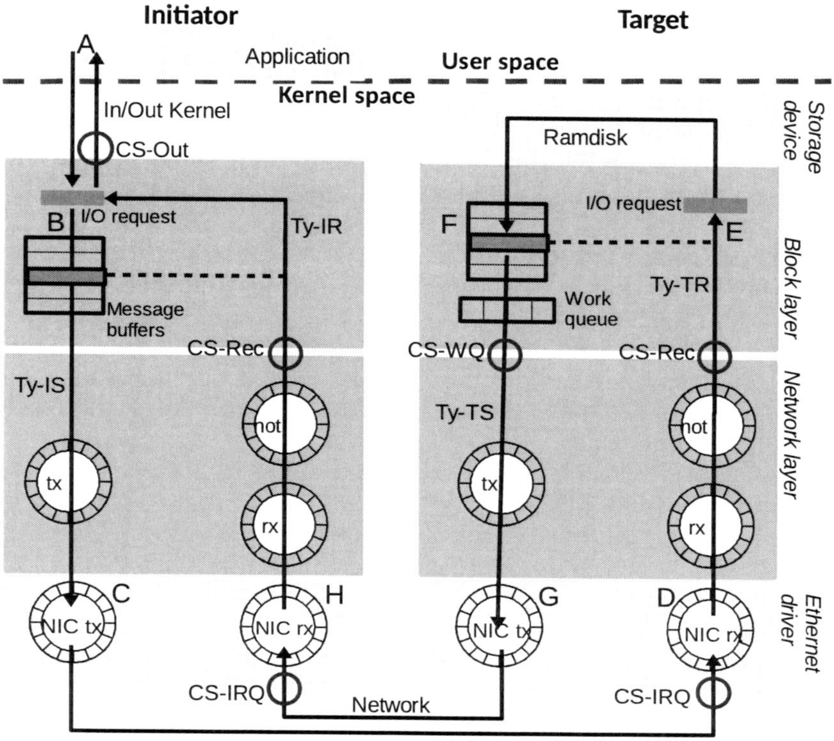

FIGURE 7.8 End-to-end I/O path showing the components we measure, and the associated context switches that are marked with a small circle. Labels A, B, C, etc., describe the computed values. We show the path for a request message. Data messages follow a similar path, using different rings.

To avoid CS-Out, done to complete the request, layers above Tyche should be modified. But, this is beyond our scope, since this context switch is out of the control of Tyche. One option could be that the application thread waits for the completion spinning [12,14]. But, when there are a large number of threads concurrently issuing I/O requests, the spinning option is not viable.

7.3.6 Adaptive Batching

At high concurrency when there is a large number of outstanding small requests, the previous design cannot achieve high link utilization and consequently high IOPS. For this reason, we propose an adaptive batching that can improve significantly link utilization for small requests. The novelty of our proposal is a dynamic technique that varies the degree of batching without increasing I/O overhead and response time.

We introduce a new request message, called batch request message or batch message. A batch message is a single network message that includes several I/O requests, reads, or writes, issued by the same or different threads. When a batch message is received, the target issues to the local device a regular I/O request per request included in the batch message. Completions are sent as batch messages as well. The target sends the completion message when all the requests within the batch message are completed. Batch messages significantly reduce the number of messages and the associated message processing.

We also introduce batch data messages that transmit the data of two 4 kB requests by batching them in a single data packet of 8 kB. This method may be applied to larger requests as well, but the main benefit occurs when 4 kB requests are batched and sent in 8 kB packets.

There are two general remarks about batching. First, batching makes sense up to some request size. Large I/O requests already make efficient use of the network, and batching offers no benefit. Given the low overhead of Tyche, this size is 8 kB, so our proposal only batches 4 kB requests. Other systems, with higher overheads, will benefit from batching larger requests as well. Second, static batching does not work in practice, as our results show. Thus, we employ an adaptive technique that constantly adjusts the number of requests batched. When our technique chooses a batch degree of one, it incurs no additional overhead compared to the optimized inline mode.

Our batching mechanism is built around a batch queue introduced in the send path of the inline mode. Now, at the initiator, each I/O request is inserted into the batch queue. Then, a single (batch) thread dequeues requests and includes them in a batch request message.

A key aspect of our batching approach is to decide when to wait for new requests or when to send the batch message immediately. We use a parameter, the current batch level (`current_batch_level`), to determine the number of requests to include in a batch message. We send a batch message when it has `current_batch_level` requests. We dynamically calculate `current_batch_level` based on the link throughput achieved. If by increasing or decreasing the batch level compared to the current value results in increased throughput, we will keep moving in the same direction.

The value of `current_batch_level` varies between 1 and `max_batch_level`, where `max_batch_level` corresponds to the maximum number of requests that a batch message can carry.

To compute the value of `current_batch_level`, our batch mechanism calculates two values: (1) the throughput achieved (`Xput` and `Xput_p`) in the last and previous intervals; and (2) the average number of outstanding I/O requests (`a_out_r`) in the batch queue during the last interval.

We then calculate the improvement in the throughput of the last interval over the previous interval, and we set `current_batch_level` as:

If the improvement is larger than 3%, the new value of `current_batch_level` will be increased to: $\frac{\texttt{current\_batch\_level}+\mathit{min}(\texttt{a\_out\_r},\texttt{max\_batch\_level})}{2}$.

If the improvement is smaller than −3%, the value of `current_batch_level` will be reduced to: $\frac{1+\mathit{min}(\texttt{a\_out\_r},\texttt{current\_batch\_level})}{2}$.

Otherwise, no change is made to the batch level.

To avoid delaying requests too long, we use a maximum amount of time (`max_delay`) that the first request batched may be delayed. A batch message will be sent if `current_batch_level` is reached or `max_delay` expires.

Finally, we avoid the case where the batch level remains unmodified because throughput is stable, although there is potential for better link utilization. For this reason, if after 10 consecutive intervals there are no changes, we compare the throughput of `current_batch_level` to the throughput of `current_batch_level` − 1 and `current_batch_level` + 1. If, for one of these new values, there is an improvement of at least 3%, we start adjusting `current_batch_level` again.

7.3.7 Elasticity

Elasticity refers to the ability to automatically remove or add resources according to the current workload with the aim of efficiently using resources. For instance, a typical server today has a few 10s of cores and a few 10 GigE links. Tyche uses a two-phase process to deal with elasticity on such systems. The first phase allows to dynamically add or remove NICs to the system without rebooting the system. We use ioctl commands to invoke this process from user space. When adding a new NIC, new channels could be opened for it. Whereas, when removing an NIC, channels opened and mapped to this NIC will be closed and this resources will be released.

The second phase is applied by the initiator, and implies to use or not NICs already connected to the system depending on the throughput achieved for the current workload. The issue is to ensure proper utilization of network throughput from multiple and diverse application workloads running. The NICs that Tyche is not using could be used by other protocols.

Let us suppose that the servers have two NUMA nodes, and that each NUMA node has attached n NICs. If each NIC provides a maximum throughput of T MB/s, therefore, the maximum throughput achieved per NUMA node could be $n \times T$. Tyche opens a channel per NIC, and initially all the channels are active and in use. Every 5 seconds, Tyche applies the following policy to decide whether a channel should be kept active or not:

If, for a NUMA node with n channels active, the throughput achieved is less than 75% of the maximum throughput that $n - 1$ channels could provide, one channel is turned off, and the corresponding NIC is not used.

If, for a NUMA node with p channels active, the throughput achieved is more than 75% of the maximum throughput that these NICs could provide, a new channel is turned on.

If the NUMA node does not have more channels available (all the channels mapped to NICs on this NUMA node are already active), and other NUMA node has channels available (because they are inactive), the NUMA node achieving the maximum throughput will borrow one of these channels, and it will use $n + 1$ channels.

7.4 EXPERIMENTAL EVALUATION

This section evaluates our proposals with an implementation of Tyche in Linux kernel 2.6.32. We use as baseline NBD (Network Block Device), which is a popular, software-only solution for accessing remote storage. NBD can only use one NIC per remote storage device. We tested iSCSI as well, but NBD outperforms iSCSI, so we only include NBD in our graphs. For evaluation purposes, and as an intermediate design point, we also implement a version of Tyche, called TSockets, that uses TCP/IP. TSockets uses sockets to perform the communication, and uses all available NICs by creating a connection per NIC. Here, we provide a baseline analysis, and then we analyze the impact of NUMA, our proposals to increase performance for small requests, and our approach for elasticity. Analysis for other aspects can be found in References 6–8 and 15.

Our experimental platform consists of two systems (initiator and target) connected back-to-back with multiple NICs. Both nodes have two, quad core, Intel(R) Xeon(R) E5520 CPUs running at 2.7 GHz. The operating system is the 64-bit version of CentOS 6.3 testing with Linux kernel version 2.6.32. Each node has six Myricom 10G-PCIE-8A-C cards. Each card is capable of about 10 Gbits/s throughput in each direction for a full-duplex throughput of about 20 Gbits/s. The target node is equipped with 48 GB DDR-III DRAM and the initiator with 12 GB. The target uses 12 GB as RAM and 36 GB as ramdisk. Note that we use ramdisk only to avoid the overhead of the storage devices, since we are interested in focusing on the network path.

We evaluate the main features of our approach with two microbenchmarks zmIO and FIO. zmIO is an in-house microbenchmark that uses the asynchronous I/O API of the Linux kernel to issue concurrent I/Os at low CPU utilization [16]. FIO is a flexible workload generator [17].

7.4.1 Baseline Performance

First, we analyze the baseline performance with zmIO. We run zmIO with sequential reads and writes, synchronous operations, direct I/O, 32 threads submitting requests and two outstanding requests per thread, a request size of 1 MB, and a run time of 60 s. The remote storage device is accessed in a raw manner (there is no file system). The test is run for one to six NICs, with one channel per NIC. Tyche applies NUMA affinity.

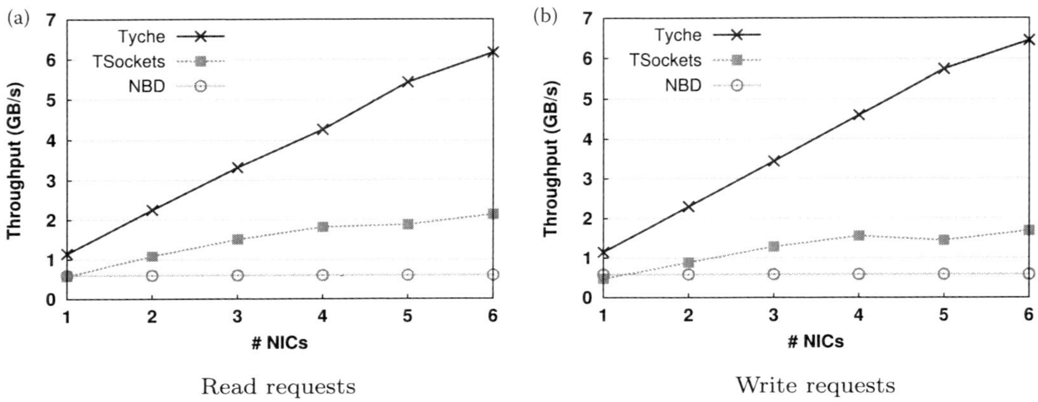

FIGURE 7.9 Throughput (in GB/s) achieved by Tyche, TSockets and NBD with zmIO, sequential reads and writes, and 1 MB requests. (a) Read requests. (b) Write requests.

Figure 7.9 depicts results for Tyche, TSockets, and NBD. For reads, with up to three NICs, Tyche achieves the maximum throughput of the NICs. With four or more NICs, Tyche provides a bit lower throughput, 4.3, 5.4, and 6.2 GB/s, respectively. This is due to the overhead of copying pages in the initiator that becomes noticeable at high rates. For writes, Tyche achieves the maximum throughput provided by the NICs except for six NICs, that it obtains 6.5 GB/s. With six NICs, when running this benchmark, the initiator is almost a 100% CPU utilization. TSockets achieves a throughput of 2.1 and 1.7 GB/s for reads and writes, respectively. NBD obtains a throughput of 609 MB/s because it is only able to use a single NIC. Therefore, Tyche outperforms up to 10× the throughput of NBD and more than 3× the throughput of TSockets. We also see that TSockets is more than 3× better than NBD, which shows that TCP/IP is responsible only for part of the overheads when accessing remote storage.

Tyche throughput scales with the number of NICs, and our proposal achieves between 82% and 92% of NIC throughput. NBD is only able to use a single link. TSockets does not scale with the number of NICs, and by using six NICs, it is able to saturate at most two NICs.

7.4.2 Dealing with NUMA

Our analysis [6,8,15] shows that NUMA affinity is an important issue that spans the whole I/O path and has a significant performance impact. Indeed, Tyche achieves the maximum throughput only when the right placement of memory and threads is done by improving performance by up to 97% [6].

We now analyze the impact of NUMA effects depending on the placement applied by Tyche and the application. Table 7.3 summarizes the configurations evaluated: Ideal, TyNuma, and Worst. With Ideal, we manually configure the NUMA placement of the application. With TyNuma and Worst, we run the application without any affinity hint. We use six NICs, three on each NUMA node, and one channel per NIC. Further analysis can be found in References 6, 8, and 15.

We analyze the QPI traffic with the open-source Intel Performance Counter Monitor (PCM) [18] that provides estimations of traffic transferred through QPI links. Table 7.4 describes the estimations analyzed.

We use zmIO, because when zmIO is run without affinity hint, it allocates 99% of writes and around 75% of reads on a single NUMA node (node 0). Therefore, almost all writes issued to channels allocated in node 1 have their resources allocated in node 0, and for reads, this rate is only 50%. Consequently, with zmIO, the performance also depends on the request type.

TABLE 7.3
Configuration of the Tests Run for the NUMA Study

Test	NUMA Affinity: Tyche	NUMA Affinity: Application	Channel Scheduler
Ideal	Yes	Yes	Affinity-aware
TyNuma	Yes	No	RR
Worst	No	No	RR

Note: RR stands for round-robin scheduling.

TABLE 7.4
Estimations of Data Traffic through the QPI Links Given by PCM Excluding the QPI Traffic between I/O Hubs

Name	Node	Traffic	Direction
Q1-N0	0	Local	I/O-Hub-0 ⇔ Processor-0
Q1-N1	1	Local	I/O-Hub-1 ⇔ Processor-1
Q0-N0	1	Remote	Processor-0 ⇒ Processor-1
Q0-N1	0	Remote	Processor-1 ⇒ Processor-0

We run zmIO with random reads and writes, direct I/O, 128 kB requests, and a runtime of 60 s. The remote storage device is accessed as a raw device. We run 4, 8, 16, and 32 application threads. Figure 7.10 provides throughput, in GB/s, achieved by Tyche as a function of the number of application threads, and the percentage of the total traffic through each QPI-node link at the initiator as a function of the application threads and configuration.

For writes, only Ideal configuration achieves its maximum throughput, being 6.25 GB/s. Almost all the data traffic comes through the QPI-1 link, having a similar amount of traffic at both nodes. Worst only obtains up to 3.73 GB/s, and Ideal outperforms Worst by up to 86%. Now, data traffic is only through the QPI-1 link on node 0, since almost all the requests are allocated in this node. There is no data traffic through QPI-1 on node 1, and there is a significant amount of traffic through QPI-0. TyNuma only achieves up to 4.92 GB/s, and Ideal improves this throughput by up to 27%. Regarding QPI traffic, TyNuma behaves like Worst.

Owing to the QPI data traffic, Worst and TyNuma are not able to provide better performance. TyNuma outperforms Worst because, at the Target, TyNuma is applying NUMA affinity, whereas Worst is not.

For reads, Ideal and TyNuma achieve up to 6.85 and 6.64 GB/s, respectively, whereas Worst only up to 4.17 GB/s. Ideal improves throughput by up to 73% comparing with Worst.

This difference in performance between Ideal and Worst is again due to the QPI traffic. Ideal has all the data traffic through the QPI-1 links, both nodes having the same amount of traffic. However, Worst has up to 33% of the total traffic coming through QPI-0.

When comparing Ideal and TyNuma, there is only a small difference in throughput; however, regarding QPI traffic, TyNuma behaves more similar to Worst. With TyNuma, at the initiator, the QPI traffic is quite similar to that with Worst, since application buffers are allocated there, and the application is not applying NUMA affinity. At the target, the QPI traffic is the same as with Ideal. At

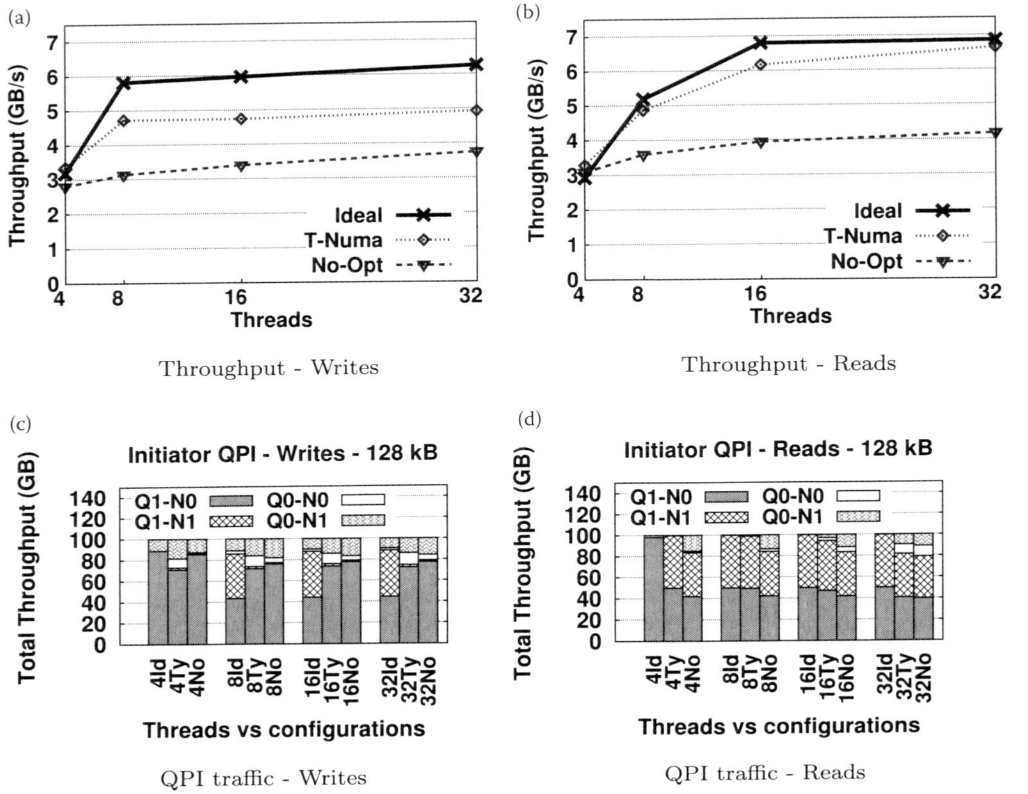

FIGURE 7.10 Throughput (in GB/s) and percentage of QPI for Tyche with varying affinity, zmIO, 128 kB requests, and random reads and writes. (a) Throughput—writes. (b) Throughput—reads. (c) QPI traffic—writes. (d) QPI traffic—reads.

the target, Ideal and TyNuma apply NUMA placement, but Worst does not. So Worst has a significant amount of traffic through QPI-0 links.

With four threads, threads and resources are allocated in NUMA node 0; for this reason, with Ideal, data traffic is only through the QPI-1 link of node 0.

7.4.3 Latency Evaluation

Now we analyze the cost of the I/O path for a request. Table 7.5 summarizes the individual and cumulative overheads computed. Figure 7.8 marks with arrows and labels the parts of the I/O path that we measure in our study.

In spite of the improvements implemented, Tyche exhibits high host CPU overhead and low network link utilization for small I/Os. Figure 7.11 that depicts the theoretical link utilization achieved by Tyche when FIO is run with direct I/O, and random reads. For a baseline comparison, we include the link utilization achieved by NBD. Tyche provides up to 5× the link utilization of NBD. But Tyche is able to achieve only up to 56% of the maximum link utilization for 4 kB requests, whereas, for 8 kB requests, the link efficiency is 90%.

Table 7.6 presents overheads, in μs, and throughput, in MB/s, obtained by Tyche, for requests of 4 and 128 kB. We use a single NIC connected to NUMA node 0, and we open a single channel on this NIC. We run FIO during 60 s with direct I/O, and random requests. The storage device is accessed

TABLE 7.5
Overhead Breakdown for the End-to-End Path of Tyche, as Shown in Figure 7.8

Name	Path	Description
Total	A - B - E - B - A	Overhead, reported by the application, of serving the request measured as the time delay between the application issues the request until it is completed.
Tyche	B - E - B	Overhead measured by Tyche as the time between the arrival of the request to its block layer until its completion. Effectively, this is the overhead of our protocol excluding the above layers.
Ty-IS	B - C	
Ty-TR	D - E	Overhead of the Tyche (Ty): send path at the initiator (IS) and target (TS) and
Ty-TS	F - G	receive path at the initiator (IR) and target (TR).
Ty-IR	H - B	
CS-WQ		Cost of the context switch due to the work queue.
CS-Rec		Cost of the context switches between the network layer and block layer threads.
CS-IRQ		Cost of the context switches done when an NIC's IRQ is raised. Measured as the time spent since the IRQ handler function executes the wake up function until the network thread starts its execution.
Ramdisk	E - F	Overhead of the ramdisk from issuing a request until receiving its completion. Ramdisk is synchronous, so IO happens inline without context switches.
I/O kernel	A - B and B - A	Time needed by a request to arrive from the application to Tyche and to be completed from Tyche. It is calculated (not measured) as the difference between total and Tyche overheads.
Network	C - D and G - H	Overhead of the network interface and network link(s). It is calculated (not measured) as the difference between Tyche overhead and the sum of Ty-IS, Ty-TR, Ty-TS, Ty-IR, CS-WQ, CS-Rec, CS-IRQ, and Ramdisk. It includes the overhead of the corresponding driver at the host, which, however, is low compared to the rest of the host overheads.

in a raw manner. There is one application thread issuing I/O requests, and one outstanding request. Tyche applies NUMA affinity.

For small requests, message processing is the most important source of per-I/O request overhead and the main bottleneck when using fast storage devices, being up to 65% of the total overhead. For 4 kB requests, Tyche overheads (Ty-IS, Ty-TR, Ty-TS, Ty-IR, CS-WQ, CS-Rec, and CS-IRQ) are 47% of the total, and only 20% without taking into account the context switches done along the Tyche path. Similar percentages are true for other request sizes.

The I/O kernel overhead is high, and depends on the request type and its size. A significant component of this overhead is the overhead due to the context switch done to complete the request (CS-Out), as we prove in Reference 7.

Each context switch costs around 4 μs. At Tyche level, the contest switches represent 27.5% and 20.0% of the total overhead for 4 and 128 kB requests, respectively.

Now we evaluate Tyche-NoCS, our proposal to reduce context switches. Table 7.7 provides the overhead breakdown, in μs, and throughput, in MB/s, for the same test under the same configuration.

Total overhead is reduced by up to 27.6% for 4 kB reads, and throughput is improved by up to 39.1%. For 128 kB reads, overhead is reduced by up to 8.1%, and throughput is improved by up to 8.8%. For writes, this reduction is 30.8% and 5.2% for 4 and 128 kB requests, respectively, and throughput is improved by up to 44.8% and 5.5%, respectively.

CS-Rec is reduced to zero, since no context switch is done on the receive path. Ty-TR and Ty-IR are significantly reduced as well. There are two reasons: (i) the notification rings are not used

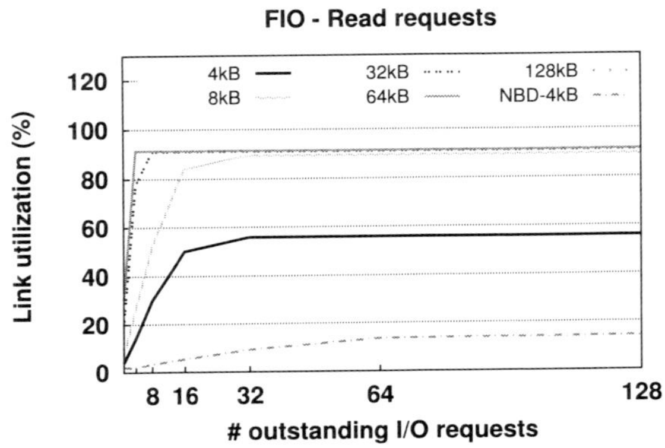

FIGURE 7.11 Link utilization achieved by Tyche and NBD with varying number of outstanding I/O requests, FIO, direct I/O, and random reads.

TABLE 7.6
Overhead (in μs) and Throughput (in MB/s) Measured for Tyche, by Running FIO with a Single Thread and a Single Outstanding I/O, Direct I/O, and Random Reads and Writes

		Read Requests		Write Requests	
Overhead (μs)		**4 kB**	**128 kB**	**4 kB**	**128 kB**
Software	I/O kernel	13.19	15.33	12.80	40.96
	Ty-IS	2.75	2.00	4.75	26.25
	Ty-TR	3.00	4.25	5.00	24.25
	Ty-TS	4.00	22.00	3.00	3.00
	Ty-IR	5.00	45.00	2.25	2.00
	CS-WQ	4.00	4.00	4.00	3.00
	CS-Rec	8.00	7.00	8.00	7.00
	CS-IRQ	8.15	30.54	8.13	37.90
Hardware	Ramdisk	1.00	30.75	1.00	31.00
	Network	24.60	60.21	24.87	63.35
Total		73.69	221.08	73.80	238.71
Throughput (MB/s)		52.50	565.00	52.50	523.25

because a single thread runs the whole receive path; and (ii) the locks to protect these rings are not required.

CS-WQ is reduced to zero, since the context switch due to the work queues is not done. Ty-TS is also reduced because the management of the work queue is avoided, for instance, we avoid the lock to add a job to the work queue.

The I/O kernel overhead is also slightly reduced. We believe that the reduction is due to the system caches as Li et al. [19] point out, since there are fewer threads running and fewer context switches.

7.4.4 Evaluation of Adaptive Batching

To study the effects of batching, we modify the implementation done of Tyche that now batches requests and data messages and applies the dynamic algorithm to choose the batch level. The new version is called Tyche-Batch. In addition, we have implemented a static version with a fixed batch level during the whole execution.

TABLE 7.7
Overhead (in μs) and Throughput (in MB/s) Measured for Tyche-NoCS, by Running FIO with a Single Thread and a Single Outstanding I/O, Direct I/O, and Random Reads and Writes

		Read Requests		Write Requests	
Overhead (μs)		**4 kB**	**128 kB**	**4 kB**	**128 kB**
Software	I/O Kernel	11.38	14.77	12.11	42.36
	Ty-IS	2.00	2.00	3.00	23.75
	Ty-TR	1.00	2.50	2.00	20.25
	Ty-TS	3.00	20.00	1.00	2.00
	Ty-IR	1.00	40.00	0.00	0.25
	CS-WQ	0.00	0.00	0.00	0.00
	CS-Rec	0.00	0.00	0.00	0.00
	CS-IRQ	8.09	30.71	8.01	38.92
Hardware	Ramdisk	1.00	30.50	1.00	31.00
	Network	25.91	62.79	23.99	67.83
Total		53.38	203.27	51.11	226.36
Throughput (MB/s)		73.00	614.75	76.00	552.00

We run FIO during 60 s with direct I/O, random reads and writes, 4 kB request size, 1, 2, 4, 8, 16, 32, 64, and 128 threads issuing requests, and four outstanding requests per thread. The remote storage device is accessed in a raw manner. We have also tested that our batch technique provides no benefit for larger sizes, but it does not hurt. Tyche applies NUMA affinity.

The dynamic version is configured with 1 s as check interval, 64 requests as `max_level_batch`, and 5 ms as `max_delay`. We run the static version with 2, 4, 8, 16, 32, and 64 requests as `max_batch_level`. However, we only present results for 2, 8, and 64 requests, since all of them have similar behavior.

Figure 7.12 depicts the theoretical link utilization, depending on the number of outstanding requests, achieved by the dynamic Tyche-Batch version (DyB in the figure), and the static version with 2, 8, and 64 requests as batch level (B-2, B-8, and B-64), and Tyche with no batching (NoB).

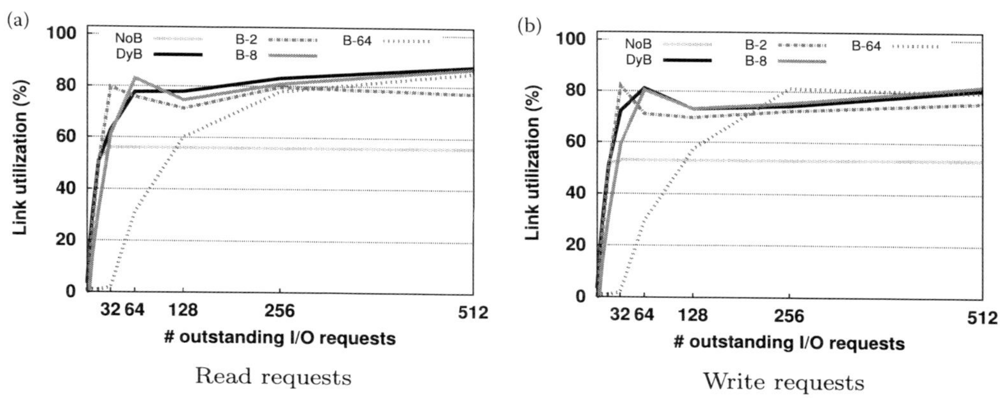

FIGURE 7.12 Link utilization achieved by the dynamic and static Tyche-Batch versions and Tyche with no batching, when data messages are also batched, with FIO, direct I/O, and random reads and writes of 4 kB. (a) Read requests. (b) Write requests.

Dynamic Tyche-Batch outperforms the no batch version up to 57% and 53% for reads and writes, respectively. For reads, our proposal achieves up to 88% of link utilization, and for writes up to 81%.

Comparing the dynamic version to the static versions, we see that the dynamic version achieves the best performance and follows the static version providing the best behavior. Sometimes, a static version outperforms the dynamic version, but the larger difference between them is quite small. In these cases, the algorithm took a conservative decision when, by batching a large number of requests, it could achieve a higher throughput.

The static versions achieve poor performance and link utilization at low concurrency. The reason is that batch messages are sent to the target because `max_delay` expires and not because the batch level is reached.

7.4.5 Elasticity Evaluation

We analyze now the elasticity process proposed with zmIO and different workloads. The test is run with direct I/O, asynchronous operations, sequential reads and writes, 32 threads submitting requests, two outstanding requests, and using a raw device. To change the workload, we run the test six times in a row with different request sizes, each one during 30 s. The request sizes tested are 4 kB, 16 kB, 64 kB, and 1 MB, and the order of the tests is 4 kB, 16 kB, 1 MB, 64 kB, 4 kB, and 1 MB.

Initially, six channels, one per NIC, are active, and Tyche checks the throughput every 5 s. Tyche applies affinity optimizations, and the minimum number of channels active will be two, one per each node.

Figure 7.13 depicts the throughput in MB/s achieved by Tyche (solid curve plotted left axis), and the number of channels-NICs on during the execution of the tests (dashed curve right axis).

With 4 kB requests, Tyche turns off four channels, two per each NUMA node, since two channels are enough to provide the maximum throughput for this size. When the request size changes to 16 kB, Tyche turns on one channel on each node, the steps around the 35 second shows this behavior. When the request size is 1 MB, Tyche turns on a third channel per node, being all the NICs working. The channels will be on until the request size changes to 4 kB at the second 125. At this point, Tyche turns off four channels, two per node, and keeps active only two channels. Finally, when the size changes to 1 MB, all the channels are turned on again, and the maximum throughput is reached.

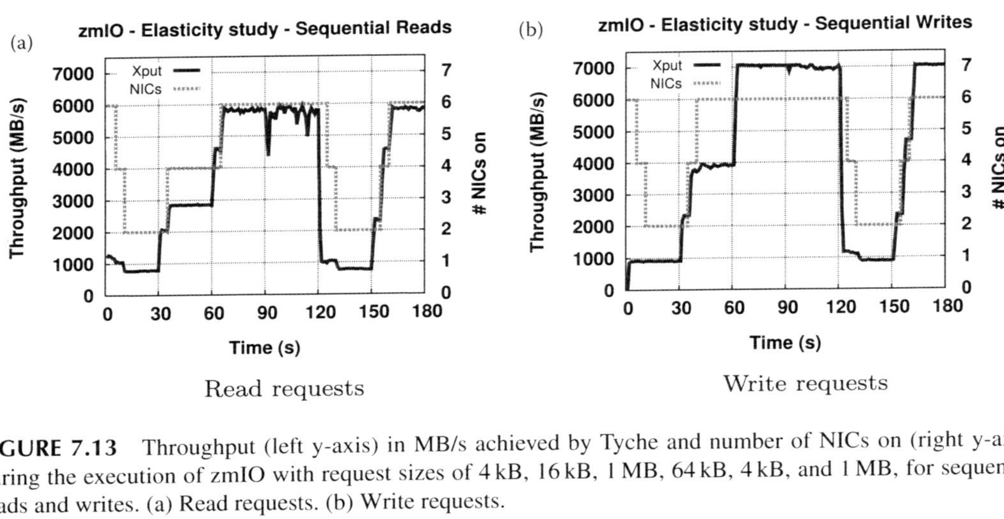

Read requests

Write requests

FIGURE 7.13 Throughput (left y-axis) in MB/s achieved by Tyche and number of NICs on (right y-axis) during the execution of zmIO with request sizes of 4 kB, 16 kB, 1 MB, 64 kB, 4 kB, and 1 MB, for sequential reads and writes. (a) Read requests. (b) Write requests.

When increasing the request size, Figure 7.13 depicts steps on the curves that show how Tyche is turning on channels. However, when channels are turned off, the throughput curve does not have these steps, since the throughput just drops, although the steps appear on the curve for the NIC number.

7.5 RELATED WORK

Regarding network storage protocols, iSCSI and NBD are built over TCP/IP and are widely used in Linux. In contrast, Tyche uses its own Ethernet-based transport, which incurs less overhead. HyperSCSI [20] modifies iSCSI to use raw Ethernet instead of TCP/IP. It turns Ethernet into a usable storage infrastructure by adding missing components such as flow control, segmentation, and reassembly. Compared to HyperSCSI, Tyche transparently uses multiple NICs, it deals with NUMA and synchronization issues, and it uses RDMA-like operations and a copy-reduction technique. All the techniques used in Tyche can eventually be incorporated in HyperSCSI as well.

RDMA has been used extensively by protocols such as iSER (iSCSI Extension for RDMA) [1], SCSI RDMA Protocol (SRP), and RDMA-assisted iSCSI [2], which improve the performance of iSCSI by taking advantage of RDMA-operations. Two commonly known protocols are Internet Wide Area RDMA Protocol (iWARP) and RDMA over Converged Ethernet (RoCE). iWARP performs RDMA over TCP, and RoCE over Ethernet. However, all these protocols focus on providing RDMA capabilities by using hardware support. Tyche focuses on using existing Ethernet and exploring issues at the software interface between the host and the NIC.

Regarding the copy-reduction technique, several authors proposed similar techniques [21–23] typically to avoid the copy between the kernel and user space. Rizzo proposes to remove data-copy costs by granting applications direct access to the packet buffers [23]. Our approach avoids the copy at kernel space by ensuring that Ethernet frames are prepared properly and then interchanging pages between the Ethernet ring and the Tyche queues.

Recently, there has been a lot of work on for NUMA-aware process scheduling and memory management in the context of many-core and systems [24–27]. Moreaud et al. [28] study NUMA effects on high-speed networking in multicore systems, and show that placing a task on a node far from the NIC leads to a performance drop. Their results show that NUMA effects on throughput are asymmetric since only the target destination buffer appears to need placement on a node close to the interface. In our case, NUMA affects both sides, target and initiator.

Community has long recognized lock contention as a key impediment to achieve high performance for shared-memory parallel programs [12,27,29,30]. Today, the potential for performance losses in parallel systems due to synchronizations is well understood. Bjørling et al. [29] demonstrate that, in the Linux block layer, the single lock used for protecting the I/O request queue can become a bottleneck for SSDs. They propose to use a queue per core to solve it. In our case, we use a queue approach to avoid the lock contention that happens for the NIC lock when there is a high concurrency of large write requests and the application has not applied memory placement.

Lately, there have been renewed interest in latency and overhead for storage access due to SSDs and emerging storage devices [31–34]. Rumble et al. [34] analyze the latency problem of network protocols, and they claim that operating systems should implement a new networking architecture and new protocols to solve the latency problem end-to-end. Recently, several works have proposed to bypass the kernel and to run in user-space I/O stacks to reduce latency by eliminating kernel crossing overheads [12,14,35]. However, our proposal is to reduce latency by redesigning the network I/O path and without modifying the operating system.

Gim et al. [13] show that the overhead of a context switch mostly comes from the pollution of the data cache. They propose a mechanism that performs or not a context switch base on several features such as CPU utilization, I/O latency, and request size. Our approach, however, is to eliminate context switches for 4 kB requests by using a single thread that runs the whole path.

Currently, many network storage protocols are using batch messages or batch operations [12,36]. IX [12] batches network requests in the presence of network congestion and allows application threads to issue batched system calls. Similarly, we batch I/O requests based on the observed I/O concurrency by examining the queues in the I/O path and additionally we use a performance feedback mechanism (achieved throughput) to adapt batching, regardless of the network conditions.

Lately, there have been a significant interest in elasticity with many works in this field [37–40]. However, to the best of our knowledge, elasticity has not been proposed for network storage protocols as we do here.

7.6 CONCLUSIONS

In this chapter, we present the design of Tyche, a networked storage protocol that is deployed directly on top of Ethernet. Tyche provides RDMA-like operations without requiring hardware support from the network interface. Tyche provides reliable delivery, framing, and transparent bundling of multiple NICs. It is an end-to-end protocol that does not require any hardware support. Tyche uses a copy-reduction technique based on virtual memory page remapping to reduce processing cost. The target avoids all copies for writes by interchanging pages between the NIC receive ring and Tyche. The initiator requires a single copy for reads, due to OS-kernel semantics for buffer allocation. Tyche reduces overheads for small I/O requests by avoiding context switches for low degrees of I/O concurrency, or by dynamically batching messages for high degrees of I/O concurrency. We would like to remark that Tyche does not use RDMA in Ethernet, instead our protocol uses a similar, memory-oriented abstraction that allows us to perform RDMA-like operations.

Our results show that network storage protocols for modern servers with multiple resources need to consider NUMA affinity and synchronization to achieve high throughput. Indeed, our protocol is able to achieve up to 6.7 GB/s when using 6×10 Gbits/s network links. For small requests and low degrees of I/O concurrency, avoiding context switches significantly reduces CPU overhead (by 31% per 4 kB-I/O request), whereas with high degrees of I/O concurrency, an adaptative batching is needed to achieve high link utilization (by up to 88% of the theoretical link utilization for 4 kB requests). Therefore, network protocols for converged storage over raw Ethernet without hardware support are a viable approach.

ACKNOWLEDGMENTS

We thankfully acknowledge the support of the European Commission under the 7th Framework Programs through the NanoStreams (FP7-ICT-610509) project, the HiPEAC3 (FP7-ICT-287759) Network of Excellence, and the COST programme Action IC1305, "Network for Sustainable Ultrascale Computing (NESUS)."

REFERENCES

1. Mike Ko, John Hufferd, Mallikarjun Chadalapaka, Uri Elzur, Hemal Shah, and Patricia Thaler. iSCSI Extensions for RDMA Specification (Version 1.0). http://www.rdmaconsortium.org/home/draft-ko-iwarp-iser-v1.PDF. Last accessed: July 11, 2016.
2. Jiuxing Liu, Dhabaleswar K. Panda, and Mohammad Banikazemi. Evaluating the impact of RDMA on storage I/O over InfiniBand. In *Proceedings of the SAN Workshop*, 2004, Madrid, Spain.
3. Evangelos Koukis, Anastassios Nanos, and Nectarios Koziris. GMBlock: Optimizing data movement in a block-level storage sharing system over Myrinet. *Cluster Computing*, 13(4):349–372, December 2010.
4. Radhika Niranjan Mysore, Andreas Pamboris, Nathan Farrington, Nelson Huang, Pardis Miri, Sivasankar Radhakrishnan, Vikram Subramanya, and Amin Vahdat. PortLand: A scalable fault-tolerant layer 2 data center network fabric. *SIGCOMM Computer Communication Review*, 39(4):39–50, August 2009.

5. Michael Schlansker, Nagabhushan Chitlur, Erwin Oertli, Paul M. Stillwell, Jr, Linda Rankin, Dennis Bradford, Richard J. Carter, Jayaram Mudigonda, Nathan Binkert, and Norman P. Jouppi. High-performance Ethernet-based communications for future multi-core processors. In *Proceedings of the Conference on Supercomputing*, 2007, Reno, Nevada, USA.
6. Pilar González-Férez and Angelos Bilas. Tyche: An efficient Ethernet-based protocol for converged networked storage. In *Proceedings of the IEEE Conference on MSST*, 2014, Santa Clara, California, USA.
7. Pilar González-Férez and Angelos Bilas. Reducing CPU and network overhead for small I/O requests in network storage protocols over raw Ethernet. In *Proceedings of the IEEE Conference on MSST*, 2015, Santa Clara, California, USA.
8. Pilar González-Férez and Angelos Bilas. Mitigation of NUMA and synchronization effects in high-speed network storage over raw Ethernet. *The Journal of Supercomputing*, DOI: 10.1007/s11227-016-1726-7, 2016.
9. Intel. An Introduction to the Intel® QuickPath Interconnect. http://www.intel.com/content/www/us/en/io/quickpath-technology/quick-path-interconnect-introduction-paper.html, 2009. Last accessed: July 11, 2016.
10. Matthew Dobson, Patricia Gaughen, Michael Hohnbaum, and Erich Focht. Linux support for NUMA hardware. In *Ottawa Linux Symposium*, 2003, Ottawa, Canada.
11. Christoph Lameter. Local and remote memory: Memory in a Linux/NUMA system. In *Ottawa Linux Symposium*, 2006, Ottawa, Canada.
12. Adam Belay, George Prekas, Ana Klimovic, Samuel Grossman, Christos Kozyrakis, and Edouard Bugnion. IX: A protected dataplane operating system for high throughput and low latency. In *Proceedings of the 11th USENIX Symposium on Operating Systems Design and Implementation (OSDI 14)*, 2014, Broomfield, Colorado, USA.
13. Jongmin Gim, Taeho Hwang, Youjip Won, and Krishna Kant. SmartCon: Smart context switching for fast storage devices. *Transactions on Storage*, 11(2):5:1–5:25, March 2015.
14. Steven Swanson and Adrian M. Caulfield. Refactor, reduce, recycle: Restructuring the I/O stack for the future of storage. *Computer*, 46(8):52–59, 2013.
15. Pilar González-Férez and Angelos Bilas. NUMA impact on network storage throughput over high-speed raw Ethernet. In *Proceedings of the International Workshop of Sustainable Ultrascale Network*, 2015, Krakow, Poland.
16. zmIO Benchmark. http://www.ics.forth.gr/carv/downloads.html. Last accessed: July 11, 2016.
17. Jens Axboe. FIO Benchmark. http://freecode.com/projects/fio. Last accessed: July 11, 2016.
18. Thomas Willhalm (Intel). Intel® Performance Counter Monitor—A better way to measure CPU utilization. https://software.intel.com/en-us/articles/intel-performance-counter-monitor, 2012. Last accessed: July 11, 2016.
19. Chuanpeng Li, Chen Ding, and Kai Shen. Quantifying the cost of context switch. In *Proceedings of the 2007 Workshop on Experimental Computer Science*, 2007, San Diego, California, USA.
20. Wilson Yong Hong Wang, Heng Ngi Yeo, Yao Long Zhu, Tow Chong Chong, Teck Yoong Chai, Luying Zhou, and Jit Bitwas. Design and development of Ethernet-based storage area network protocol. *Computer Communications*, 29(9):1271–1283, 2006.
21. Hai Jin, Minghu Zhang, and Pengliu Tan. Lightweight messages: True zero-copy communication for commodity gigabit ethernet. In *Proceedings of the International Conference on Emerging Directions in Embedded and Ubiquitous Computing*, 2006, Seoul, Korea.
22. Dong-Jae Kang, Young-Ho Kim, Gyu-Il Cha, Sung-In Jung, Myung-Joon Kim, and Hae-Young Bae. Design and implementation of zero-copy data path for efficient file transmission. In *Proceedings of the International Conference on High Performance Computing and Communications*, 2006, Munich, Germany.
23. Luigi Rizzo. Netmap: A novel framework for fast packet I/O. In *Proceedings of the USENIX Annual Technical Conference*, 2012, Boston, Massachusetts, USA.
24. Mohammad Dashti, Alexandra Fedorova, Justin Funston, Fabien Gaud, Renaud Lachaize, Baptiste Lepers, Vivien Quema, and Mark Roth. Traffic management: A holistic approach to memory placement on NUMA systems. In *Proceedings of the Eighteenth International Conference on Architectural Support for Programming Languages and Operating Systems*, 2013, Houston, Texas, USA.

25. Baptiste Lepers, Vivien Quema, and Alexandra Fedorova. Thread and memory placement on NUMA systems: Asymmetry matters. In *2015 USENIX Annual Technical Conference (USENIX ATC 15)*, pages 277–289, Santa Clara, CA, 2015. USENIX Association.
26. Stelios Mavridis, Yannis Sfakianakis, Anastasios Papagiannis, Manolis Marazakis, and Angelos Bilas. Jericho: Achieving scalability through optimal data placement on multicore systems. In *Proceedings of the IEEE Conference on MSST*, 2014, Santa Clara, California, USA.
27. Da Zheng, Randal Burns, and Alexander S. Szalay. Toward millions of file system IOPS on low-cost, commodity hardware. In *Proceedings of the International Conference on High Performance Computing, Networking, Storage and Analysis*, 2013, Denver, Colorado, USA.
28. Stéphanie Moreaud and Brice Goglin. Impact of NUMA effects on high-speed networking with multi-opteron machines. In *Proceedings of the International Conference on Parallel and Distributed Computing and Systems*, 2007, Cambridge, Massachusetts, USA.
29. Matias Bjørling, Jens Axboe, David Nellans, and Philippe Bonnet. Linux block IO: Introducing multi-queue SSD access on multi-core systems. In *Proceedings of the 6th International Systems and Storage Conference*, 2013, Haifa, Israel.
30. Nathan R. Tallent, John M. Mellor-Crummey, and Allan Porterfield. Analyzing lock contention in multithreaded applications. *SIGPLAN Notices*, 45(5):269–280, January 2010.
31. Mario Flasjslik and Mendel Rosenblum. Network interface design for low latency request-response protocols. In *Proceedings of the USENIX Annual Technical Conference*, 2013, San Jose, California, USA.
32. Anuj Kalia, Michael Kaminsky, and David G. Andersen. Using RDMA efficiently for key-value services. In *Proceedings of the 2014 ACM Conference on SIGCOMM*, 2014, Hong Kong, China.
33. Christopher Mitchell, Yifeng Geng, and Jinyang Li. Using one-sided RDMA reads to build a fast, CPU-efficient key-value store. In *Proceedings of the 2013 USENIX Conference on Annual Technical Conference*, 2013, San Jose, California, USA.
34. Stephen M. Rumble, Diego Ongaro, Ryan Stutsman, Mendel Rosenblum, and John K. Ousterhout. It's time for low latency. In *Proceedings of the 13th USENIX Conference on HotOS*, 2011, Napa, California, USA.
35. Simon Peter, Jialin Li, Irene Zhang, Dan R. K. Ports, Doug Woos, Arvind Krishnamurthy, Thomas Anderson, and Timothy Roscoe. Arrakis: The operating system is the control plane. In *11th USENIX Symposium on Operating Systems Design and Implementation (OSDI 14)*, 2014, Broomfield, Colorado, USA.
36. Ana Aviles-González, Juan Piernas, and Pilar González-Férez. Batching operations to improve the performance of a distributed metadata service. *The Journal of Supercomputing*, 72(2):654–687, 2016.
37. Artur Baruchi and Edson Toshimi Midorikawa. A survey analysis of memory elasticity techniques. In *Proceedings of the 2010 Conference on Parallel Processing*, 2011, Ischia, Italy.
38. Guilherme Galante and Luis Carlos E. de Bona. A survey on cloud computing elasticity. In *Proceedings of the 2012 IEEE/ACM Fifth International Conference on Utility and Cloud Computing*, 2012, Chicago, Illinois, USA.
39. Vincenzo Gulisano, Ricardo Jimenez-Peris, Marta Patino-Martinez, Claudio Soriente, and Patrick Valduriez. Streamcloud: An elastic and scalable data streaming system. *IEEE Transactions on Parallel and Distributed Systems*, 23(12):2351–2365, December 2012.
40. Sebastian Lehrig and Steffen Becker. The cloudscale method for software scalability, elasticity, and efficiency engineering: A tutorial. In *Proceedings of the 6th ACM/SPEC International Conference on Performance Engineering*, 2015, Austin, Texas, USA.

8 Parallel Backpropagation Neural Network for Big Data Processing on Many-Core Platform

Boyang Li and Chen Liu

CONTENTS

ABSTRACT

With the rapid data scale growth, machine-learning algorithms are widely adopted to deal with big data. It naturally becomes the focus of researchers and software developers how to run such algorithms efficiently on modern many-core platforms. In this chapter, two unique hardware platforms, Intel® Single-Chip Cloud Computer (SCC) and Intel® Xeon® Phi™ coprocessor, are employed to accelerate the backpropagation (BP) neural network and lead to a better performance for data processing. Furthermore, we also explored dynamic voltage and frequency scaling (DVFS) on the many-core platform in searching of the suitable configuration to aid the processing of big data when the power/energy savings need to be taken into consideration.

8.1 INTRODUCTION

Over the past 20 years, data have increased in large scale in various fields. According to a report published by International Data Corporation (IDC) (one of the most influential leaders in big data

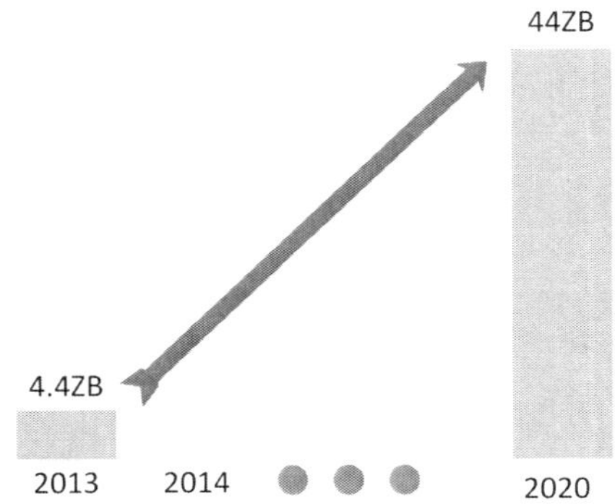

FIGURE 8.1 Data big bang.

and its research fields) in 2013, the overall created and copied data volume in the world was 4.4 zettabytes (ZB). It is doubling in size every 2 years, and by 2020, the digital universe—the data we create and copy annually—will reach 44 ZB or 44 trillion gigabytes (IDC 2014), as shown in Figure 8.1.

Under the explosive increase of global data, the term of "big data" is mainly used to describe enormous data sets. Compared with traditional data sets, big data typically includes masses of unstructured data that need more real-time analysis (Chen et al. 2014). While the term "big data" itself is relatively new, the act of gathering and storing large amounts of information for analysis is ages old. The concept gained momentum in the early 2000s when industry analyst Doug Laney articulated the now-mainstream definition of big data as the three Vs (Laney 2001). In the "3V" model, *volume* means, with the generation and collection of masses of data, data scale becomes increasingly big; *velocity* means the timeliness of big data, specifically, data collection and analysis must be rapidly and timely conducted, so as to maximally utilize the commercial value of big data; *variety* indicates the various types of data, which include semistructured and unstructured data such as audio, video, Web page, and text, as well as traditional structured data.

In 2011, IDC added another V (*value*) to this definition to form the "4V" model. It was expressed as "big data technologies describe a new generation of technologies and architectures, designed to economically extract value from very large volumes of a wide variety of data, by enabling the high-velocity capture, discovery, and/or analysis" (Gantz and Reinsel 2011).

8.2 BACKPROPAGATION NEURAL NETWORK

In terms of big data processing, people want to find out the meaningful relationship among the data. Traditional analytics methods struggle to discover the underlying structure of the big data because it would not be feasible to implement a comprehensive analysis due to the "4V" model of the data. In addition the huge range of potential correlations and relationships between disparate data sources make it impossible for any analyst to test all hypotheses and search out all the opportunities hidden in the data (Skytree 2015). Thus, machine learning becomes a research focus in dealing with big data.

Machine learning evolves from pattern recognition and computation learning theory in artificial intelligence. Compared to traditional methods, it focuses on the study and construction of algorithms that can learn from and make predictions on data (Kohavi and Provost 1998; Werbos 1994). Machine learning is data driven and relies little on human direction. Furthermore, unlike traditional methods, machine learning thrives on increasing data set (Skytree 2015). All these make it an ideal tool to analyze the big data.

Backpropagation (BP) neural network is a widely used machine-learning method. It is usually regarded as a supervised learning method that can be employed in both classification and regression problems. BP neural network can learn their weights and biases using the gradient descent algorithm.

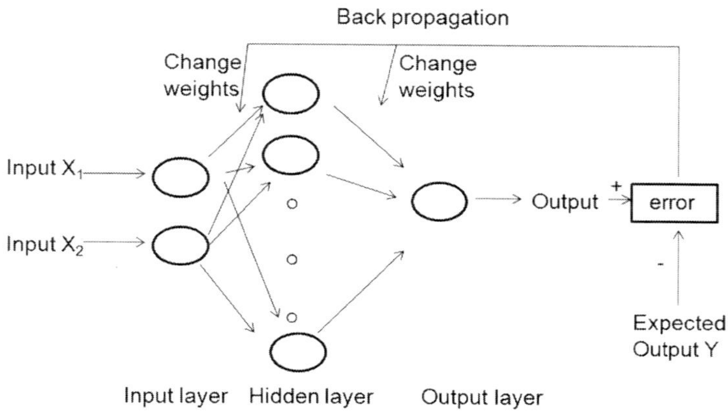

FIGURE 8.2 Typical BP neural network architecture with two inputs, one output, and one hidden layer.

For each sample, BP neural network requires a desired output in order to calculate the loss function gradient.

BP neural network needs to calculate the loss function gradient (we call it "error"). As shown in Figure 8.2, the error propagates backwards from the output node(s) to the input node(s). That is where the name "backpropagation" derives from. Then the gradient error of the network based on the network's modifiable weights is calculated (Werbos 1994). Finally, the stochastic gradient descent algorithm uses this gradient to find weights that will finally minimize the error. If the weight is updated every time after one input sample, the performance of the network would depend on the input sequence of the samples to a large degree. To eliminate the impact of the input sequence of the samples, batch learning is a good choice in which the training phase and testing phase are separate. Hence, batch learning is employed in this work.

Although BP neural network is a relatively simple neural network, it is the foundation of many advanced machine-learning methods. It is still widely used in many applications. For example, scientists have used large amount of hydrological data set to train the BP neural network to get a real-time robust hydrological prediction (Wan et al. 2015) In addition, researchers presented the cable joint conductor based on the PSO algorithms of BP neural network (Zhou et al. 2015). BP neural network is also used in emerging areas such as smart grid (Rui et al. 2014).

8.3 HIGH-PERFORMANCE COMPUTING

Due to the "4V" model of big data, the computation incurred from machine-learning method can be intensive. Thus, the execution speed to deal with big data could easily become a bottleneck. High-performance computing would be an effective way to overcome this obstacle. High-performance computing refers to the use of parallel processing for running programs efficiently, reliably and accurately. In addition, in certain scenarios reduced power/energy consumption is desired, especially when we want to deal with big data with highperformance computing. Luckily, modern microprocessors are generally equipped with dynamic voltage and frequency scaling (DVFS) capability. DVFS allows microprocessors to complete necessary tasks with reduced power/energy consumption by varying the voltage and frequency of the computing elements.

Since the training process of BP neural network would be very time consuming and computation intensive, in this work, we implemented the training process of BP neural network on advanced parallel computing platforms, Intel® Single-Chip Cloud Computer (SCC) and Intel® Xeon® Phi™ coprocessors. Our research focus is how to use the many-core platform to speed up the computation of BP neural network for data processing. We also studied how to use DVFS for power-/energy-aware computing of BP neural network on many-core platform.

8.4 TEST CONFIGURATION

As an exemplary study, in our experiment, we try to train the BP neural network to learn the operation of addition on SCC and Intel® Xeon® Phi™ platforms. We also train the BP neural network to learn the operation of multiplication on Intel® Xeon® Phi™ platform. We try to train the BP neural network to learn the addition and multiplication operations solely based on the data provided. BP neural network built for this purpose has two input variables, one hidden layer, one output layer, and one output variable. The number of training samples is set to 9600. Since there are two input variables, from our observation too many neurons (nodes) in the hidden layer can lead to overfitting. Hence, the numbers of nodes that we use in the hidden layer are 5, 10, and 20, respectively, for Intel® SCC. For Intel® Xeon® Phi™, we choose to employ 10 nodes in the hidden layer. We set the training iteration's upper limit to 20,000. We assume that the performance of neural network is satisfactory when the average error is less than 0.001. Thus, either on the condition that the iterations of training reach 20,000 or on the condition that the average error is less than 0.001, training is stopped. There are two widely used parallel approaches: task parallelism and data parallelism. In task parallelism, various tasks are partitioned among the cores to carry out the computation in solving the problem. In data parallelism, the data used in solving the problem are partitioned among the cores and each core carries out more or less similar operations on its part of the data (Pacheco 2011). In our experiment, data parallelism is employed.

8.5 PARALLEL BP NEURAL NETWORK ON SCC

The SCC experimental processor is a 48-core concept vehicle created by Intel Labs as a platform for many-core software research (Intel 2010). The SCC contains 48 Pentium™ class IA-32 cores on a 6 × 4 2D-mesh network of tiled core clusters with high-speed I/Os on the periphery (Howard et al. 2010). Every tile consists of two cores and a router shared by the two cores. The 48 cores are divided into 6 voltage domains and 24 frequency domains on the SCC chip, where the routers and other peripherals are on separate voltage and frequency domains. As shown in Figure 8.3, every four tiles share a power domain, and the programmer can change the voltage for all the cores in a voltage domain. Every two cores on the same tile can also have their own frequency within the frequency domain. The SCC also provides the capability of manipulating the voltage and frequency directly at the application level, which supports the research on power-/energy-aware computing applications.

Since the SCC comes equipped with the DVFS capability, besides execution time, several power-/energy-related metrics can also be measured or calculated, including power consumption, power per speedup (PPS), energy consumption, and energy-delay product (EDP). The execution time includes the communication time among cores, since the SCC follows a message-passing programming model. Power consumption is obtained by measuring the voltage and current of the SCC chip only. The overhead time that it takes to measure the power consumption has been deducted in our experiment. The power reading does not include DDR DIMMs, which are off-chip. PPS is calculated by dividing power consumption by the speedup achieved with increasing the number of cores. What is more, energy and EDP are calculated based on the power and execution time readings we get. On SCC, the number of cores in use is 1, 2, 4, 8, 16, 32, and 48, separately. We implemented three voltage and frequency settings, being High (1.2 V/800 MHz), Medium (0.9 V/533 MHz), and Low (0.8 V/400 MHz).

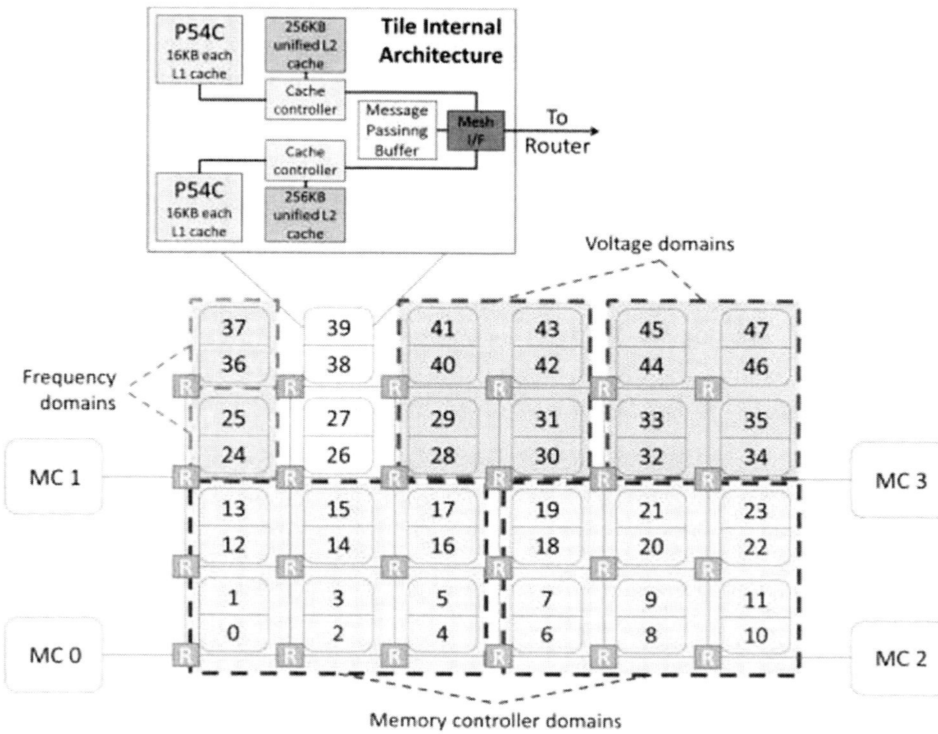

FIGURE 8.3 SCC architecture and tile internal structure. (From Torres et al. 2015. An auto-tuning assisted power-aware study of iris matching algorithm on Intel's SCC. *Journal of Signal Processing Systems*, 80(3): 261–276.)

8.5.1 Execution Time

Figure 8.4 reflects the relationship between the execution time (in seconds) and the number of cores in a log–log scale, while we vary the number of nodes in the hidden layer of the BP neural network. The results show that for a fixed number of nodes in the hidden layer, first, with the number of cores used for computation increasing from 1 to 32, the execution time decreases correspondingly; second, when the number of cores is fixed, the higher the frequency is, the less time it takes to execute the program. Overall, the high voltage and frequency setting (1.2 V/800 MHz) gives the best performance for our computation-intensive benchmark.

Another interesting observation is that with the number of nodes in the hidden layer decreasing, the decreasing rate of execution time becomes slow when the number of cores increases from 32 to 48. When the number of nodes in the hidden layer is five, the execution time even increases with the number of cores increasing from 32 to 48. In this case, the time saved by distributing the workload in a parallel fashion cannot make up the communication overhead caused by message passing among the cores.

8.5.2 Power Consumption

The experiment results show that no matter the number of nodes in the hidden layer is 5, 10, or 20, the power consumption (in watts) is identical, which means that the number of nodes in the hidden layer has no effect on the power assumption. Thus, only the data of five nodes in the hidden layer are presented here. Figure 8.5 reflects the relationship between the power consumption (in watts)

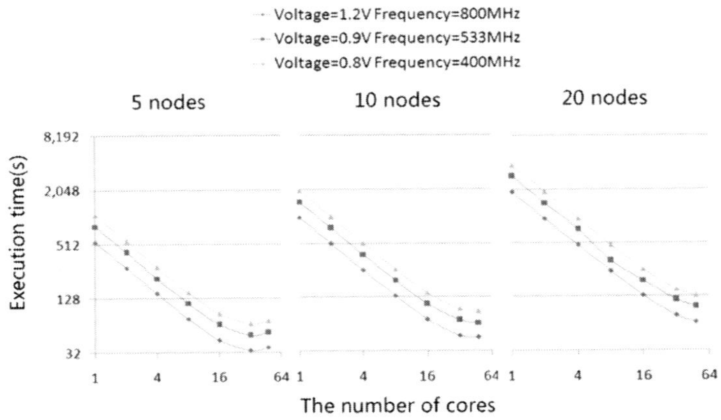

FIGURE 8.4 Relationship between execution time and the number of cores.

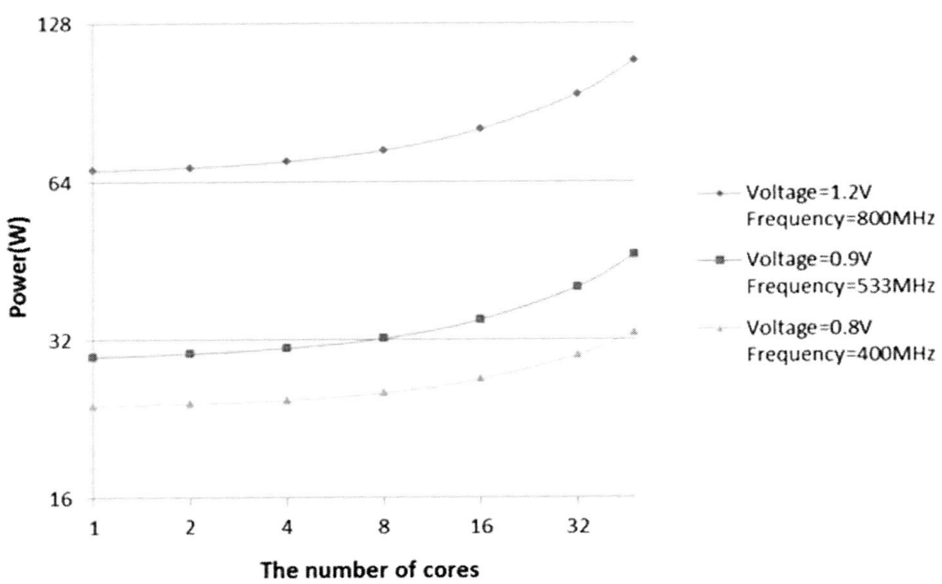

FIGURE 8.5 Relationship between power consumption and the number of cores.

and the number of cores in a log–log scale. With the number of cores increasing, the increasing rate of power consumption becomes faster, as more power domains are involved in the computation. Overall, the low voltage and frequency setting (0.8 V/400 MHz) gives the best power reading for our benchmark, with a sacrifice on the performance.

8.5.3 Power per Speedup

PPS was proposed as an indicator to measure energy efficiency (Mair et al. 2010). This metric gives the power required for a given level of speedup through parallelism. Therefore, a small PPS value is desired. Figure 8.6 reflects the relationship between the PPS (in watts) and the number of cores in a log–log scale. When the number of nodes in the hidden layer is fixed, configuration (0.8 V/400 MHz) provides the best PPS results for all core counts. So it is more power efficient to use the low

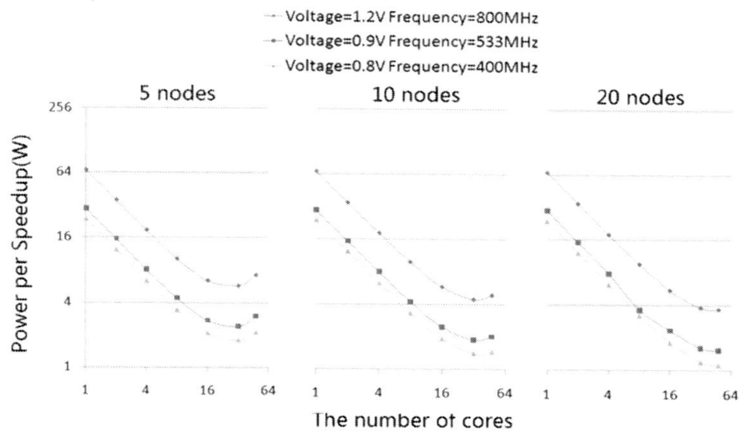

FIGURE 8.6 Relationship between PPS and the number of cores.

voltage and frequency setting to achieve a given speedup when we increase the number of cores for our benchmark.

8.5.4 Energy Consumption

Figure 8.7 reflects the relationship between the energy consumption (in joules) and the number of cores in a log–log scale, while varying the number of nodes in the hidden layer. It can be seen that with the number of nodes in the hidden layer increasing, the minimum energy consumption will move in the direction where the number of cores increases. As discussed above, the number of nodes in the hidden layer of the neural network has no effect on the power assumption. Thus, for BP neural network, energy is more affected by execution time. The similarity between the energy consumption curve and the execution time curve under each configuration also supports this point of view.

8.5.5 Energy-Delay Product

Figure 8.8 reflects the relationship between the EDP (in joules-seconds) and the number of cores in a log–log scale, while varying the number of nodes in the hidden layer. The experiment results show

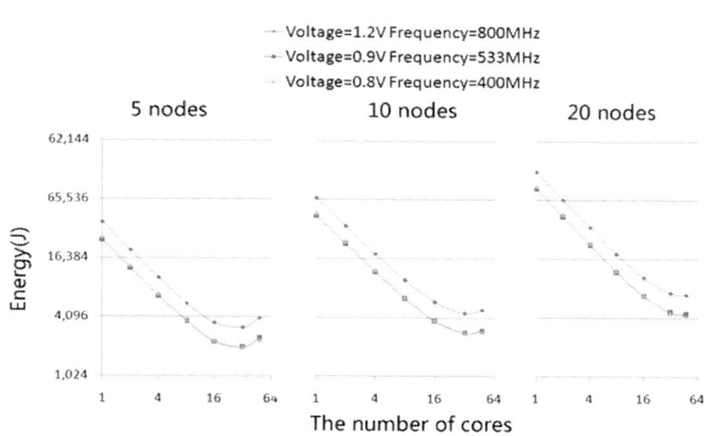

FIGURE 8.7 Relationship between energy and the number of cores.

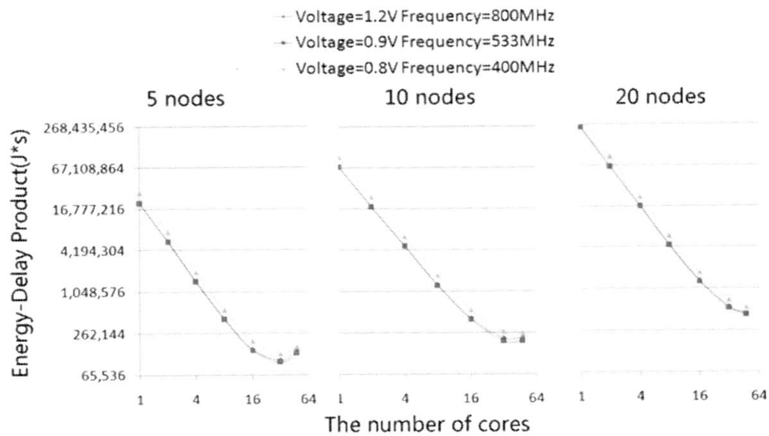

FIGURE 8.8 Relationship between EDP and the number of cores.

TABLE 8.1
Best Configuration for Each Metric

		Energy-Related Metrics			
Number of Nodes	**Execution Time**	**Power**	**PPS**	**Energy**	**EDP**
5	32 cores 1.2 V/800 MHz	1 cores 0.8 V/400 MHz	32 cores 0.8 V/400 MHz	32 cores 0.8 V/400 MHz	32 cores 0.9 V/533 MHz
10	48 cores 1.2 V/800 MHz	1 cores 0.8 V/400 MHz	32 cores 0.8 V/400 MHz	32 cores 0.8 V/400 MHz	32 cores 0.9 V/533 MHz
20	48 cores 1.2 V/800 MHz	1 cores 0.8 V/400 MHz	48 cores 0.8 V/400 MHz	48 cores 0.8 V/400 MHz	48 cores 0.9 V/533 MHz

that the shape of the EDP curve for different number of nodes in the hidden layer is very similar to the energy curve shape. The minimum point of EDP will move in the same direction as the minimum point of energy moves. The difference is that when the number of nodes and the number of cores are constant, EDP under configuration 0.9 V/533 Hz is the smallest, and EDP under configuration 0.8 V/400 MHz is the largest, though the EDP difference between configurations 0.9 V/533 Hz and 1.2 V/800 MHz is very small. Overall, the medium voltage and frequency configuration gives us the best of both worlds when we take both energy and user experience (in terms of system response time to finish the job) into consideration.

8.5.6 Best Configuration for Each Metric

Table 8.1 summarizes the best configuration (number of cores and voltage/frequency) for each metric. Depending on specific user's requirement, suitable configuration can be employed.

8.6 PARALLEL BP NEURAL NETWORK ON INTEL® XEON® PHI™

8.6.1 Introduction about Intel® Xeon® Phi™

Intel® Many Integrated Core (Intel® MIC) architecture integrates many Intel CPU cores onto a single chip for a high parallelism (Chrysos 2014). In our research, we implement the BP neural

TABLE 8.2
Specs of Intel® Xeon® Phi™ 5110P and Intel® Xeon® Phi™ 7120P

	Intel® Xeon® Phi™ 7120P	Intel® Xeon® Phi™ 5110P
Number of cores	61	60
Processor turbo frequency	1.238 GHz	1.053 GHz
Max turbo frequency	1.333 GHz	N/A
TDP	300 W	225 W

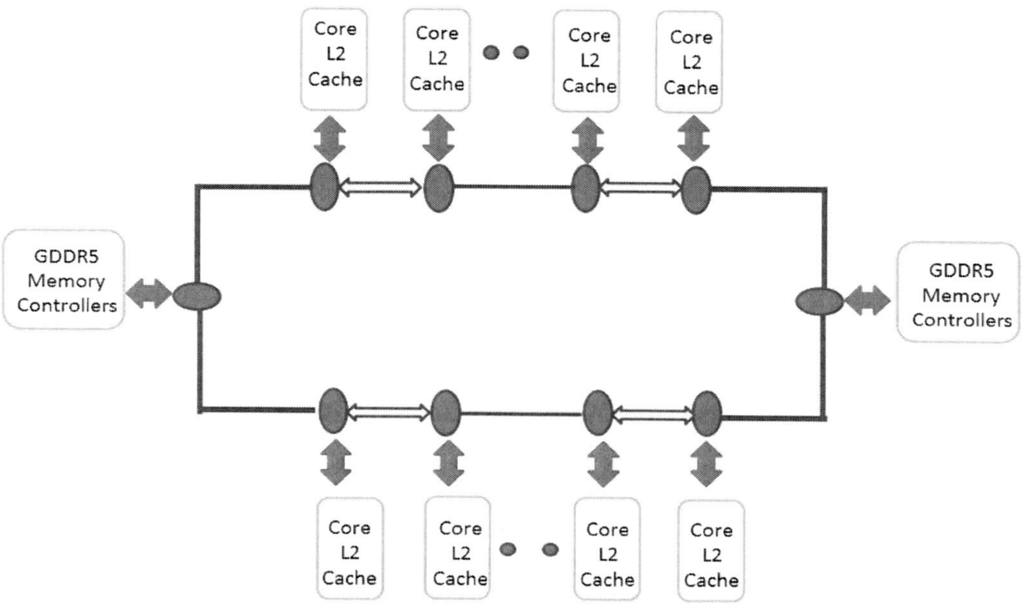

FIGURE 8.9 Architecture of Intel® Xeon® Phi™ coprocessor.

network on both the Intel® Xeon® Phi™ 5110P and Intel® Xeon® Phi™ 7120P coprocessors. Table 8.2 summarizes the specifications of these two coprocessors.

Figure 8.9 shows the architecture of the Intel® Xeon® Phi™ coprocessor. The coprocessor is mainly composed of processing cores, caches, memory controllers, and PCIe client logic (Chrysos 2014). All the cores are interconnected in a ring topology. Each core supports up to four hardware threads. There are two common programming models for the Intel® MIC architecture, the native programming model, and the heterogeneous offload model.

- *Offload Mode:* It refers to writing a program from the point of view of running on the main processor and offloading part of the work from the main processor to one or more Intel® Xeon® Phi™ coprocessors. The program initially starts on the host processor, which is commonly a Xeon processor. Then based on user's definition in the code (directive-based), part of the code is allocated to the coprocessor for execution. The key feature is that the compiled binary runs whether there is a coprocessor or not (Jeffers and Reinders 2013).
- *Native Mode:* Since Intel® Xeon® Phi™ hosts a Linux micro OS in it and can appear as another machine connected to the host like another node in a cluster, the user can take the

coprocessor as another computer node. An application has to be cross-compiled for Xeon® Phi™ operating environment if it needs to be run natively.

Compared to offload mode, native mode is more appropriate for programs that are largely performing operations that map to parallelism either in threads or vectors, and are not performing significant amounts of I/O or serial execution. Usually, if we want to use native mode, we need to use the compiler flag "-mmic" when compiling the program.

Since Intel® Xeon® Phi™ cannot easily measure energy-related metrics, we mainly focus on the performance of paralleling BP neural network on different modes.

8.6.2 Test Results

In this experiment, the training ending condition for both multiplication and addition is that the training iterations reach the limit. Furthermore, there are two input variables and one output variable for both multiplication and addition. The structure of BP neural network is the same as we used in the SCC case. For addition operation, the results implemented on Xeon® Phi™ 5110P and Xeon® Phi™ 7210P are represented. For multiplication operation, we present the result on Xeon® Phi™ 5110P as a representative. The number of threads in use is 1, 2, 4, 8, 16, 32, 64, 128, and 240, respectively, and the thread affinity type in use is compact. Both native mode and offload mode are tested.

Figure 8.10 presents the relationship between the execution time and the number of threads for the test case of addition on the Xeon® Phi™ 7120P platform. The performance under native mode and offload mode is very similar. Under each mode, the execution time decreases significantly when the number of threads increases from 1 to 128. However, with the number of threads increasing from 128 to 240, the execution time decrease is not that obvious. Figure 8.11 presents the relationship between the speedup and the number of threads for the test case of addition on Xeon® Phi™ 7120P. The speedup reaches maximum when the number of threads is 240 although the speedup increases little when the number of threads varies from 128 to 240.

Figure 8.12 presents the relationship between execution time and the number of threads for the test case of addition on the Xeon® Phi™ 5110P platform while Figure 8.13 presents the relationship between speedup and the number of threads for the test case of addition on the Xeon® Phi™ 5110P

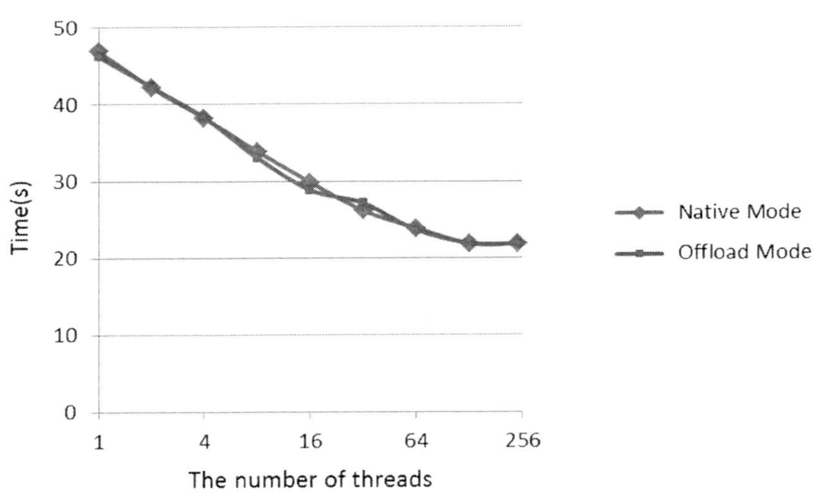

FIGURE 8.10 Relationship between the execution time and the number of the threads for addition on Xeon® Phi™ 7120P.

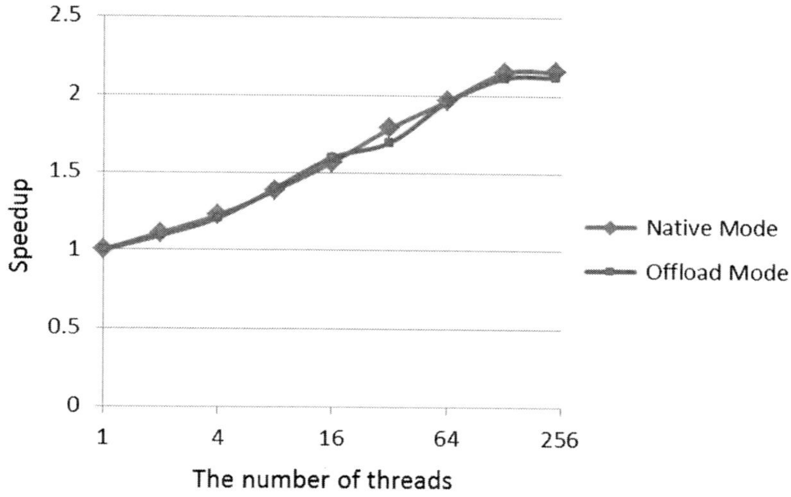

FIGURE 8.11 Relationship between the speedup and the number of the threads for addition on Xeon® Phi™ 7120P.

platform. Overall, the performance on Xeon® Phi™ 5110P is very similar to the performance on Xeon® Phi™ 7120P. Compared to the Xeon® Phi™ 7210P platform, the speedup is a little smaller, which can be indicated by Table 8.2. We can observe that the processor turbo frequency is 1.238 GHz for Xeon® Phi™ 7210P while Intel® Xeon® Phi™ 5110P possesses the processor turbo frequency of 1.053 GHz.

Figures 8.14 and 8.15 show the execution time and speedup change when varying the number of threads on the Xeon® Phi™ 5110P platform for the test case of multiplication. Due to the same neural network architecture and the same training ending condition, the performance for multiplication is almost the same as the performance for addition. The speedup reaches the largest when the number of threads is 240. Correspondingly, the execution time is smallest when there are 240 threads. Hence, the results on the 7120P platform are omitted.

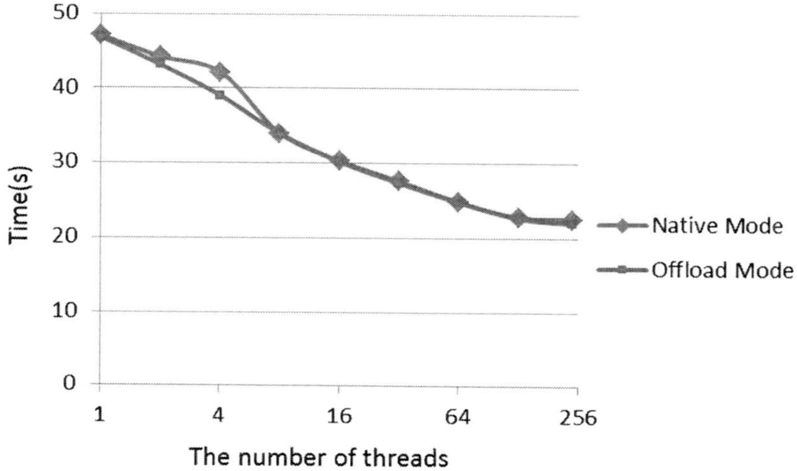

FIGURE 8.12 Relationship between the execution time and the number of the threads for addition on Xeon® Phi™ 5110P.

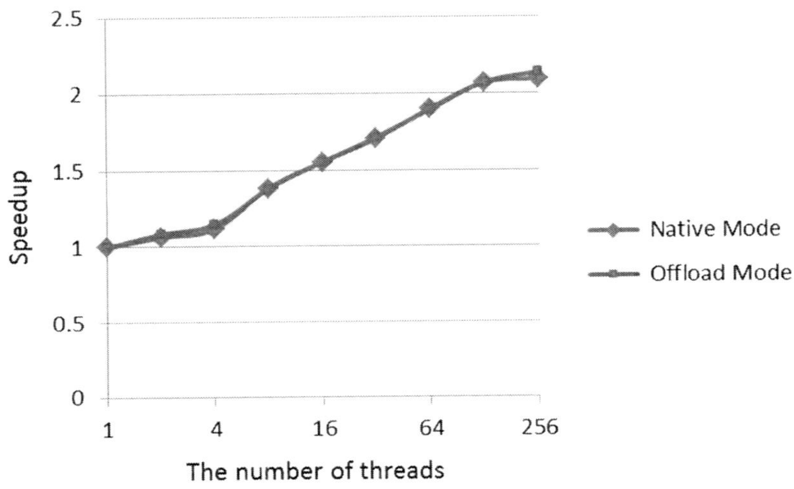

FIGURE 8.13 Relationship between the speedup and the number of the threads for addition on Xeon® Phi™ 5110P.

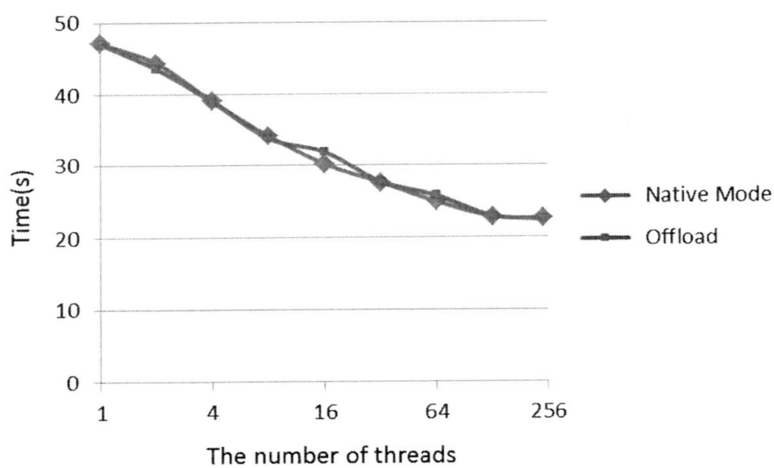

FIGURE 8.14 Relationship between the execution time and the number of the threads for multiplication on Xeon® Phi™ 5110P.

8.7 CONCLUSIONS

With machine-learning technique widely adopted to deal with the processing of big data, how to efficiently running this algorithm on emerging many-core platform has been of the interest for researchers and software developers. In this work, we studied the performance of BP neural network on innovative Intel® SCC and Intel® Xeon® Phi™ platforms. We can conclude that paralleling BP neural network on SCC and Intel MIC contributes to a better performance for data processing. Researchers can implement their machine-learning algorithms dealing with big data on many-core platforms to get a speedup. In addition, if power/energy saving is a crucial factor when processing big data, DVFS can be employed on the many-core platform to search out the suitable configuration to meet the power/energy requirement.

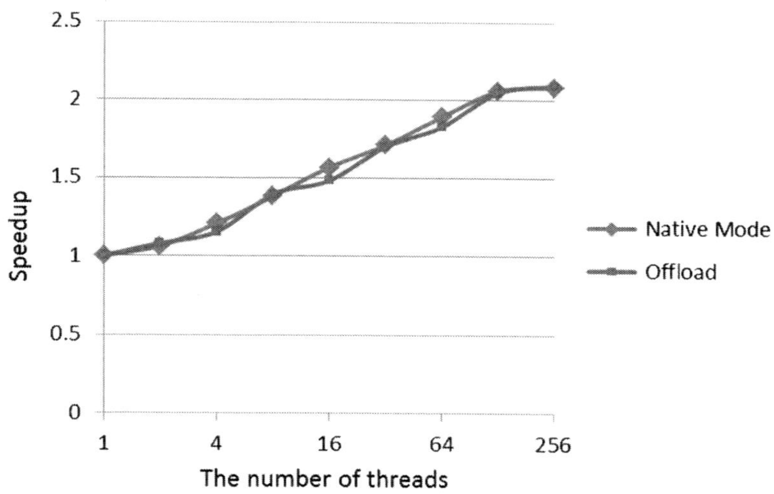

FIGURE 8.15 Relationship between the speedup and the number of the threads for multiplication on Xeon® Phi™ 5110P.

ACKNOWLEDGMENTS

We would like to thank Intel Labs for providing the SCC, as well as the National Institute for Computational Sciences for providing access to Beacon cluster, to conduct this research. We would like to thank Gildo Torres for his technical knowledge of the SCC platform. This work is supported by the National Science Foundation under Grant Number ECCS-1301953. Any opinions, findings, and conclusions or recommendations expressed in this material are those of the authors and do not necessarily reflect the views of the National Science Foundation.

REFERENCES

Chen, M., S. Mao, and Y. Liu. 2014. Big data: A survey. *Mobile Networks and Applications* 19(2):171–209. (Intel 2012).

Chrysos, G. 2014. Intel® Xeon Phi™ coprocessor—The architecture. *Intel Whitepaper*.

Gantz, J. and D. Reinsel. 2011. Extracting value from chaos. *IDC iView* 1142:1–12.

Howard, J., S. Dighe, Y. Hoskote, S. Vangal, D. Finan, G. Ruhl, D. Jenkins, H. Wilson, N. Borkar, and G. Schrom. 2010. A 48-core IA-32 message-passing processor with DVFS in 45 nm CMOS. In *2010 IEEE International Solid-State Circuits Conference (ISSCC)*, San Francisco, CA, 2010, pp. 108–109. doi: 10.1109/ISSCC.2010.5434077.

The IDC study. 2014. The digital universe of opportunities: Rich data and the increasing value of the Internet of things. http://www.emc.com/leadership/digital-universe/2014iview/index.htm (access date 28/05/2016).

Intel Lab. 2010. The SCC platform overview. Revision 0.7. pp. 1–23. http://www.intel.com/content/dam/www/public/us/en/documents/technology-briefs/intel-labs-single-chip-platform-overview-paper.pdf.

Jeffers, J. and J. Reinders. 2013. *Intel Xeon Phi Coprocessor High-Performance Programming*. Morgan Kaufmann, Boston.

Kohavi, R. and F. Provost. 1998. Glossary of terms. *Machine Learning* 30(2–3):271–274.

Laney. 2001. 3-D data management: Controlling data volume, velocity and variety. *META Group Research Note*. https://blogs.gartner.com/doug-laney/files/2012/01/ad949-3D-Data-Management-Controlling-Data-Volume-Velocity-and-Variety.pdf.

Mair, J., K. Leung, and Z. Huang. 2010. Metrics and task scheduling policies for energy saving in multicore computers. In *2010 11th IEEE/ACM International Conference on Grid Computing*, Brussels, 2010, pp. 266–273. doi: 10.1109/GRID.2010.5697984.

Pacheco, P. S. 2011. *An Introduction to Parallel Programming*. Morgan Kaufmann, Boston.

Rui, L., Y. Xiong, K. Xiao, and X. Qiu. 2014. BP neural network-based web service selection algorithm in the smart distribution grid. In *The 16th Asia-Pacific Network Operations and Management Symposium*, Hsinchu, 2014, pp. 1–4. doi: 10.1109/APNOMS.2014.6996111.

Skytree. 2015. Why do machine learning on big data. http://www.skytree.net/machine-learning/why-do-machine-learning-big-data/.

Torres, G., C. Liu, J. K.-T. Chang, F. Hua, and S. Schuckers. 2015. An auto-tuning assisted power-aware study of iris matching algorithm on Intel's SCC. *Journal of Signal Processing Systems* 80(3):261–276.

Wan, D., Y. Xiao, P. Zhang, and H. Leung. 2015. Hydrological big data prediction based on similarity search and improved BP neural network. In *2015 IEEE International Congress on Big Data*, New York, NY, 2015, pp. 343–350. doi: 10.1109/BigDataCongress.2015.58.

Werbos, P. J. 1994. *The Roots of Backpropagation: From Ordered Derivatives to Neural Networks and Political Forecasting*. Wiley-Interscience, New York, NY.

Zhou, H., J. Wang, K. Liu, and L. Wang. 2015. Temperature prediction study of cable joint conductor based on the PSO algorithms of BP neural network. In *2015 IEEE Magnetics Conference (INTERMAG)*. Beijing, 2015, pp. 1–1. doi: 10.1109/INTMAG.2015.7157609.

9 SQL-on-Hadoop Systems

State-of-the-Art Exploration, Models, Performances, Issues, and Recommendations

Alfredo Cuzzocrea, Rim Moussa, and Soror Sahri

CONTENTS

ABSTRACT

Analytics of tremendous big data generated from natural systems (e.g., tectonic plates' movement, atmospheric data), engineered systems (e.g., servers, electronic devices), and human activities (e.g., trajectories, Web click-streams, health records, customers' transactions, user interactions in social networks) require highly scalable data management systems with new capabilities in both algorithms and architectures. SQL-on-Hadoop bridging Relational Database Management technologies and Hadoop Ecosystem technologies are becoming mainstream for big data analytics.

9.1 INTRODUCTION

Big data features characteristics, which traditional systems cannot handle, such as (i) *high volume*—volume refers to the amount of data, which henceforth increased to the range of tera- and petabyte scale; (ii) *high velocity*—velocity refers to the speed at which new data is generated and processed, henceforth the challenge is to analyze data while it is being generated; and (iii) *high variety*—variety refers to different types of data, for example, structured (relational data), semistructured (XML, JSON), and unstructured (text and multimedia contents). Recently, additional features were added, namely, (iv) *veracity*—veracity refers to the messiness or trustworthiness of the data, which usually lacks quality and accuracy and (v) *value*—value refers to getting value out of the data.

The relational database management systems (RDBMSs) are de facto the solution for data storage. However, the volume, the type, and the velocity of business data have changed. To address *high volume*, RDBMS technologies are scaled-up vertically through hardware upgrade with more central processing units and memory. Vertical scale-up turns out to be expensive. Also, RDBMSs are designed to accommodate structured data, while the majority of the data comes in a semistructured or unstructured format. Finally, RDBMS technologies lack in high velocity because they are designed for steady data retention. Indeed, data warehousing technologies are designed as batch systems refreshed periodically. Nevertheless, stream-based applications require eager increments' management. As a result, relational databases fail to handle big data, and new technologies are emerging. The past decade had witnessed a growing number of new big data management technologies, which are becoming mainstream for big data analytics.

Along Ralph Kimball, *Big data is a paradigm shift in how we think about data assets, where do we collect them, how do we analyze them, and how do we monetize the insights from the analysis*. Therefore, the *big data* has several impacts on data management technologies and requires rethinking every aspect of data processing. First, big data management systems are deployed on top of clusters of commodity hardware, which aggregate I/O bandwidth and flops/s, and which should be elastic, such that storage and computing resources are added and released as needed. Second, *big data* implies collecting, cleansing, and analyzing data at scale.

Apache Hadoop ecosystem is one of the most widely open-source heralded new platforms for managing big data. Hadoop comes with a distributed file system (*HDFS*) and a framework for processing large data sets on computer clusters (*MapReduce framework*). New Hadoop-based technologies foster a programming interface with high-level and declarative language. Thus, *SQL-on-Hadoop data management systems* enable the use of SQL-like languages on top of MapReduce-based systems (e.g., HiveQL/Apache Hive, Spark SQL, and Cloudera Impala). Early published comparisons of Hadoop technologies to RDBMSs demonstrated that RDBMSs outperform Hadoop for structured data analytics. These comparisons do not hold for big data management and processing challenges.

This chapter looks into requirements to assess *SQL-on-Hadoop big data management systems*. The outline of the chapter is as follows: Section 9.2 reviews advances in history in data management systems. First, we depict advanced hardware architectures and query processing techniques implemented in *RDBMSs*. Second, we present the *Apache Hadoop Ecosystem*. Section 9.3 describes SQL-on-Hadoop technologies and more precisely open-source projects such as Hive, Spark, and Impala. Section 9.4 outlines requirements for SQL-on-Hadoop technologies assessment. Finally, Section 9.5 concludes the chapter.

9.2 BIG DATA MANAGEMENT SYSTEMS

Dealing with huge data sets, most online analytical processing (OLAP) systems are I/O-bound and CPU-bound. First, this is due to hard drives' I/O performances, which do not evolve as fast as storage, computing hardware (*Moore Law*), and network hardware (*Gilder Law*). Second, OLAP systems require high computing capacities. Since the 1980s with RAID (Redundant Arrays of Inexpensive Disk) systems [1] and seminal research on distributed data structures [2,3], both practitioners and experts admitted that dividing disk I/O across disk drives allows to aggregate drives' I/O throughputs and prevents *I/O bottleneck*. In order to achieve high performance and large capacity, database systems and distributed file systems rely upon data partitioning, parallel processing, and parallel I/Os.

In this section, we overview big data management systems dealing with both OLAP and online transaction processing (OLTP) workloads. First, we depict advanced hardware architectures and query processing techniques implemented by *RDBMSs*. Second, we present the *Apache Hadoop Ecosystem*. Third, we overview *New SQL Systems*.

9.2.1 Relational Database Management Systems

RDBMSs are based on the relational model invented by E. F. Codd [4]. In this section, we overview (i) hardware architectures, (ii) storage layouts, and (iii) data-processing techniques of RDBMSs for processing OLAP workloads.

9.2.1.1 Parallel Computer Architectures

There are two different types of database hardware architectures for big data management: (1) *symmetric multiprocessing* (SMP) and (2) *massively parallel processing* (MPP). The second is more cost-effective as the system growth is practically unlimited.

The SMP environment is a tightly coupled multiprocessor system where processors, the same memory, disk space, and I/O devices use a single operating system and are connected using a common bus. Communication between nodes occurs via shared memory. The workload is distributed across the processors in the system. The actual speed at which the job completes is limited by the shared resources in the system. Note that performance is limited by the bandwidth of the memory bus. The system might be upgraded vertically, that is, *vertical scale-up*.

The MPP environment is a loosely coupled or a shared-nothing multiprocessor system. Each node has its own computing units, operating system, and memory. Nodes are connected through a high speed network and communicate with each other through message sending. MPP can be setup with a shared-nothing or shared-disk architecture. To scale the MPP system, compute nodes and associated memory and disk resources are added (i.e., *horizontal scale-up*).

9.2.1.2 Data Fragmentation

Data fragmentation (a.k.a. sharding, or partitioning) involves splitting a data set into smaller fragments and distributing them across a large number of machines. It aims at minimizing (i) query running times through enabling *intraquery parallelism* and *interquery parallelism*, (ii) the cost of maintenance of the data warehouse through targeted and parallel refresh operations, and (iii) the cost of ownership of a data warehouse through the use of commodity hardware with a shared-nothing architecture rather than expensive server architectures.

9.2.1.3 Storage Layouts

In terms of storage layouts, there are two different types of storage layouts for big data management, namely (i) *row-oriented stores* and (ii) *column-oriented stores*. A column-oriented DBMS stores data tables as columns of data. The main difference between a columnar database and a traditional row-oriented database is centered around performance, efficient memory management through loading only useful attributes, storage necessities which are reduced through compression of repeating values, and schema modifying techniques. Recent years have seen the introduction of a number of *column-oriented database systems*, including *MonetDB* [5], *C-Store* [6], and *VectorWise* [7]. Column-oriented storage layouts are well-suited for OLAP-like workloads, while row-oriented storage layouts are well-suited for OLTP workloads.

9.2.1.4 Data-Processing Techniques

Recent years have seen the investigation of efficient data-processing techniques for OLAP-like workloads such as (1) *parallel query processing*, (2) *materialized views and calculated attributes*, (3) *vectorized query processing*, (4) *materialization strategies*, (5) *index-only plans*, and (6) *invisible joins*.

- *Parallel query processing*: Parallel query processing of database clusters is based on two nonexclusive techniques known as *intraquery parallelism* and *interquery parallelism*. In *intraquery parallelism*, a query divides into multiple subqueries. Each subquery processes a different subset of data. Subqueries run in parallel. In *interquery parallelism*, queries execute concurrently in order to improve the system throughput.
- *Aggregate tables and calculated attributes*: An *aggregate table* (a.k.a. materialized view) summarizes large number of detail rows into information that has a coarser granularity, and so fewer rows. As the data is precomputed, an aggregate table allows faster OLAP cube processing. *Derived attributes* are calculated from other attributes. In [8,9], authors propose sound recommendations for usage of aggregate tables and calculated attributes for OLAP workloads.
- *Vectorized query processing*: A standard query execution system processes one row at a time. Vectorized query execution streamlines operations by processing a block of rows at a time. Within the block, each column is stored as a vector. Simple operations like arithmetic and comparisons are done by quickly iterating through the vectors in a loop, with no or very few function calls or conditional branches [7].
- *Materialization strategies*: In row-oriented stores, nonselected columns are removed from the result set as soon as they are unnecessary. In column-oriented stores, it is necessary to decide when to materialize the columns together. There are two choices: *early materialization* and *late materialization*. *Early materialization* retrieves all the columns necessary and materializes them together upfront. *Late materialization* combines columns together at the very end of the processing, just before presentation. In [10], authors report their experiences with late and early materialization and highlight their strengths and weaknesses.
- *Index-only plans*: This technique consists in creating indices for all needed columns so that the database system would not need to do any table scans during query execution. Thus, base relations are stored row-oriented, and an additional unclustered B+ Tree index is added on every column of every table [11].
- *Invisible joins*: This technique aims at speeding up star joins in a column store. The *invisible join* performs joins in three phases. First, each predicate is applied to the appropriate dimension table to extract a list of dimension table keys that satisfy the predicate. These keys are used to build an in-memory hash table. In the second phase, each hash table is used to extract the positions of records in the fact table that satisfy the corresponding predicate. Then, the position lists from all of the predicates are intersected to generate a list of satisfying positions in the fact table. The third phase of the join uses the list of satisfying positions in the fact table. For each column in the fact table containing a foreign key reference to a dimension table that is needed to answer the query, foreign key values are extracted using satisfying positions list and are looked up in the corresponding dimension table [11].

9.2.1.5 Benchmarking RDBMS

There are few RDBMS benchmarks out of the TPC benchmarks [12]. The Transaction Processing Council proposes a set of benchmarks for assessing (i) OLTP systems, such as TPC-C and TPC-E; (ii) OLAP, such as TPC-H and TPC-DS; (iii) virtualization systems, such as TPC-VMS and TPCx-V; and (iv) green systems, such as TPC-Energy.

9.2.2 Apache Hadoop Ecosystem

Apache Hadoop [13] allows distributed processing of large data sets across clusters of computers using a simple programming model. It is designed to scale up from single servers to thousands of machines, each offering local computation and storage. Rather than rely on hardware to deliver high-availability, Hadoop is designed to detect and handle failures at the application layer, so delivering a highly-available service on top of a cluster of computers, each of which may be prone to failures. Hadoop clusters grow very large up to thousands of nodes.

Hadoop YARN (Yet Another Resource Negotiator or MRv2) provides several advantages over the previous version of Hadoop (MRv1) [14]. It enables dynamic resource configurations on individual nodes and a flexible resource model. Indeed, it advocates support for programming model diversity, and provides a generic resource management framework for implementing distributed applications. A basic Apache Hadoop system has two core components:

- *Hadoop Distributed File System*: HDFS is designed to manage large amounts of data. It stores files as big *data blocks*. HDFS block sizes are in megabytes (typical values are 128 MB, 256 MB, etc.), which are significantly larger than the block sizes used in traditional file systems (4 or 8 KB). HDFS distributes data blocks across the entire cluster. For fault tolerance, blocks are replicated a number of times to ensure high data availability. HDFS provides a high aggregate I/O bandwidth across a large cluster of servers.
- *MapReduce Framework* [15]: It serves for implementing applications to process data. The MapReduce processing model consists of multiple stages: the first is a parallel Map phase, in which input data is split into discrete chunks that can be processed independently. Each Map task output is partitioned and sorted in memory and Combiner functions run on it. This output is written to local disk called as Intermediate Data. The Map phase is followed by a shuffle and a sort proper to the Hadoop MR framework. In the reduce phase, the output of the Map phase is aggregated in order to produce the desired result.

9.2.2.1 Tuning a MapReduce Job

In order to maximize MapReduce job performance, it is important (i) to balance the load equally across nodes in the cluster, (ii) to set appropriate memory settings, (iii) to set containers: mappers and reducers, (iv) to select appropriate codecs, and (v) to adjust the replication factor according to input data and processing complexity. Hereafter, we enumerate the most important parameters to adjust for tuning a MapReduce job.

- *Memory and computing resources*: Hadoop uses environment variables that determine the heap sizes and the number of computing units allocated for each Hadoop process such as Mappers and Reducers (YARN children) during the execution of a MapReduce job.
- *Data block size*: The block size setting is used by HDFS to divide files into blocks and then distribute those blocks across the cluster. The block size might be set different for each HDFS file. Indeed, in order to gain maximum parallelism within each MapReduce job, it is recommended to have large blocks for big files and small blocks for small files.
- *Input split size*: By default, the *input split size* is equal to the *block size*. MapReduce data processing is driven by the input splits. Indeed, in order to gain maximum parallelism, that is, increasing the number of Mappers, each HDFS block is logically divided into *input splits* and each *input split* is assigned to a Mapper for processing.
- *Reducers*: The optimal number of Reducers depends on the cluster computing capacities as well as the input data volume for Reducers.
- *Combiners*: Combiners are local Reducers, which are set in order to lessen the number of intermediate keys that are being passed to the Reducers. Each combiner processes the output of a Mapper and performs aggregation like a reducer.

- *Data compression and decompression*: Compression enables to shift the computation load from IO to CPU. During the shuffle phase, the intermediate key–value pairs are shuffled over the network to Reducers, and all of intermediate data and output data are flushed on the hard drives. These I/O operations are expensive. Intermediate data compression saves storage space requirements and speeds up the transfer of data throughout the network. Note also that Hadoop can process compressed files, but some formats are not splittable, such as Gzip and Snappy. Consequently, each non-splittable file is entirely processed by a Mapper. The reduction of the number of Mappers, despite the availability of hardware resources, lead to poor parallel processing performance and under-utilization of hardware resources. Apache Hadoop supports most known compressing formats such as Gzip, Snappy, Bzip2, and LZO. Commonly codecs are compared through the degree of compression and compression/decompression speed. In [16], authors investigate green MapReduce computing, sketching tradeoffs of energy efficiency, and Hadoop codecs usage.
- *Replication factor*: The replication factor is a property that can be set and updated for each HDFS file. File replication operates through declustering data blocks and their replicas throughout the Hadoop cluster.

9.2.2.2 Apache Pig Latin

Apache Hadoop is an ecosystem of related projects. It includes a high-level script language *Apache Pig Latin* [17]. The latter organizes a workflow of MapReduce jobs in a directed-acyclic graph (DAG) of computations.

Hereafter, we show translation and processing of TPC-H business question Q5 (Figure 9.1) in pig latin script (respectively, Figures 9.2 and 9.3). Q5 lists for each *nation* in a *region* the revenue volume that resulted from *lineitem* transactions in which the customer ordering parts and the supplier filling them were both within that nation. Q5 has two parameters, namely, a year (for instance, 1994) and a region name (for instance, ASIA).

9.2.2.3 Benchmarking Hadoop Ecosystem Projects

Releases of Apache Hadoop include benchmarks such as (i) *TeraSort—Teragen* generates 100 B-records in which *TeraSort* performs the sort and (ii) *TestDFSIO*—it is a MapReduce implementation of distributed IO benchmark. A number of benchmarking projects investigated Hadoop clusters performances with well-known TPC decision-support systems benchmarks. In [19], *TPC-H* benchmark is translated into *HiveQL* for assessing the performance of *Apache Hive*. In [8,18,20], *TPC-H*

```
SELECT n_name, sum(l_extendedprice*(1-l_discount)) as rev
FROM customer,orders,lineitem,supplier,nation,region
WHERE c_custkey = o_custkey
AND l_orderkey = o_orderkey
AND l_suppkey = s_suppkey
AND c_nationkey = s_nationkey
AND s_nationkey = n_nationkey
AND n_regionkey = r_regionkey
AND r_name = '[REGION]'
AND o_orderdate >= date '[DATE]'
AND o_orderdate < date '[DATE]' + interval '1' year
GROUP BY n_name
ORDER BY revenue desc;
```

FIGURE 9.1 SQL statement of TPC-H business question Q5.

```
---- orders of 1994
Orders = LOAD '/home/TPCH/orders.tbl' USING Pig-Storage('|')
       AS (o_orderkey:int, ..., o_comment:chararray);
orders_94 = FILTER orders BY o_orderdate MATCHES '1994.*';
orders_1994 = FOREACH orders_94 GENERATE o_orderkey,o_custkey;
---- lineitems of 1994
lineitem = LOAD '/home/TPCH/lineitem.tbl' USING PigStorage('|')
         AS (l_orderkey:int, ..., l_comment:chararray);
lineitems_94 = JOIN lineitem BY l_orderkey, orders_1994 BY o_orderkey;
lineitems_1994 = FOREACH lineitems_94 GENERATE
      l_orderkey, o_custkey,l_extprice, l_discount,l_suppkey;
---- Region ASIA
region = LOAD '/home/TPCH/region.tbl' USING Pig-Storage('|')
 AS (r_regionkey:int, r_name:chararray, r_comment:chararray);
asia = FILTER region BY r_name MATCHES 'ASIA';
----- Suppliers of ASIA
supplier = LOAD '/home/TPCH/supplier.tbl' USING PigStorage('|')
     AS (s_suppkey:int, ..., s_comment:chararray);
nation = LOAD '/home/TPCH/nation.tbl' USING Pig-Storage('|')
       AS (n_natkey:int, ..., n_comment:chararray);
join_supp_asia = JOIN asia BY r_regionkey, nation BY n_regionkey;
supp_asia = JOIN join_supp_asia BY n_natkey, supplier BY s_natkey;
supp_nations_asia = FOREACH supp_asia GENERATE s_suppkey,s_natkey,n_name;
----- join all, customers of nations of ASIA
customer = load '/home/TPCH/customer.tbl' USING PigStorage('|')
        AS (c_custkey:int,..., c_comment:chararray);
join_customer_orders = JOIN lineitems_1994 BY o_custkey,
                            customer BY c_custkey;
join_line_supp = JOIN join_customer_orders BY l_suppkey,
                      supp_nations_asia BY s_suppkey;
same_nation = FILTER join_line_supp BY s_natkey == c_natkey;
selected = FOREACH same_nation
    GENERATE n_name,(l_extprice*(1-l_discount)) AS rev:float;
group_nation = GROUP selected BY n_name;
sum_group = FOREACH group_nation
  GENERATE flatten(group), SUM(selected.rev) AS sum_rev;
result = ORDER sum_group BY sum_rev DESC;
STORE result INTO 'OUTPUT_PATH/tpch_query5';
```

FIGURE 9.2 Pig script of TPC-H business question Q5. (Adapted from Moussa, R.: TPC-H benchmarking of Apache Pig Latin on Hadoop Cluster. https://sites.google.com/site/rimmoussa/CC_pig_tpch.tar, 2011.)

benchmark is translated into *Pig Latin Scripts* for assessing the performance of *Apache Pig Latin*. A comparison of *Hive* and *Pig Latin* is reported in [21].

While MapReduce supports a wide range of use cases, it is not the ideal model for all large-scale computations, namely, iterative jobs and join operations.

9.2.3 NewSQL Systems

The *NewSQL* was coined by the 451 Group [22] as a class of *ScalableSQL* RDBMSs that provide scalable performance for OLTP read–write workloads with the ACID guarantees [23–27]. *VoltDB* and *Clustrix data store* use a traditional approach in which each table is partitioned using a single key and rows are distributed among servers using a consistent hashing algorithm. *Googles Spanner* uses

JobId	Maps	Reduces	AvgMapTime	AvgReduceTime	Alias	Feature
job_0278	15	1	10	72	join_customer_orders, lineitem, lineitems_1994, lineitems_94, orders, orders_1994, orders_94	HASH_JOIN
job_0279	2	1	3	12	asia, join_supp_asia, nation, region, supp_asia	HASH_JOIN
job_0280	2	1	9	27	customer, join_customer_orders, join_line_supp	HASH_JOIN
job_0281	2	1	3	12	join_line_supp, supp_asia, supp_nations_asia, supplier	HASH_JOIN
job_0282	2	1	7	21	join_line_supp, same_nation, selected	HASH_JOIN
job_0283	1	1	3	12	group_nation, sum_group	GROUP_BY, COMBINER
job_0284	1	1	3	12	result	SAMPLER
job_0285	1	1	3	12	result	OROER_BY

Outputs hdfs://borderline-3.bordeaux.grid5000.fr:54310/user/rmoussa/OUTPUT_PATH/tpch_query5,

FIGURE 9.3 DAG and statistics of Q5 processing.

a different partitioning model. A spanner deployment contains a set of servers known as *spanservers*, which are the nodes responsible for serving data to clients. A *spanserver* manages hundreds to thousands of tablets, each of which contains a set of *directories*. *NuoDB* is another NewSQL solution that uses a completely different approach for data partitioning. A *NuoDB* deployment is made up of a number of *Storage Managers* (SMs) and *Transaction Managers* (TMs). The SMs are the nodes responsible for maintaining the data, while the TMs are the nodes that process the queries. Each SM has a complete copy of the entire data, which basically means that no partitioning takes place within the SM [28].

Almost all of the NewSQL systems eschew the 2PL (phase locking) because of the complexity in dealing with deadlocks. Some of the NewSQL solutions implement innovative approaches to concurrency control. For example, *Googles Spanner* uses a hybrid approach in which read–write transactions are implemented through read–write locks, but read-only transactions are lock-free. *VoltDB* assumes that the total available memory is large enough to store the entire data store and transactions are short-lived. Based on these assumptions, all transactions are then executed sequentially in a single-threaded and lock-free environment [28].

NewSQL systems are benchmarked with *Yahoo Cloud Serving Benchmark* (YCSB) and *TPC-C* [24].

9.3 SQL-ON-HADOOP SYSTEMS

New *SQL-on-Hadoop systems* such as *Apache Shark*, *Apache Spark*, and *Cloudera Impala* target (i) high performance through implementing traditional RDBMS optimizations and (ii) interoperability through support of different source formats. Next, we overview open-source projects such as *Apache Hive*, *Apache Spark*, and *Cloudera Impala*.

9.3.1 Apache Hive

Apache Hive [29] is an open-source data warehousing solution built on top of Hadoop and released by Facebook. Hive supports queries expressed in *HiveQL*, an SQL-like declarative language, which are compiled into MapReduce jobs. Figure 9.4 illustrates HiveQL code for TPC-H business question Q5. Similar to traditional databases, Hive stores data in tables, where each table consists of a number of rows, and each row consists of a specified number of columns. Each column has an associated type. The latter is either primitive type (integer, float, etc.) or complex type (map, list, struct). *HiveQL* supports analysis expressed as MapReduce programs by users and in the programming language of their choice.

9.3.2 Apache Spark

The framework MapReduce might be cumbersome. The underlying file system incurs overheads due to data replication, disk I/O, and serialization. For applications that require data reuse, *Pregel* [30] is a system for iterative graph computations that keeps intermediate data in memory, while *HaLoop* [31]

```
-- create tables and load data
CREATE EXTERNAL TABLE customer (c_custkey int,..., c_comment string)
       ROW FORMAT DELIMITED FIELDS TERMINATED BY '|'
       STORED AS TEXTFILE LOCATION '/tpch/customer';
CREATE EXTERNAL TABLE lineitem (l_orderkey int,..., l_comment string)
       ROW FORMAT DELIMITED FIELDS TERMINATED BY '|'
       STORED AS TEXTFILE LOCATION '/tpch/lineitem';
CREATE EXTERNAL TABLE orders (o_orderkey int,..., o_comment string)
       ROW FORMAT DELIMITED FIELDS TERMINATED BY '|'
       STORED AS TEXTFILE LOCATION '/tpch/orders';
CREATE EXTERNAL TABLE supplier (s_suppkey int,..., s_comment string)
       ROW FORMAT DELIMITED FIELDS TERMINATED BY '|'
       STORED AS TEXTFILE LOCATION '/tpch/supplier';
CREATE EXTERNAL TABLE nation (n_nationkey int,...,n_comment string)
       ROW FORMAT DELIMITED FIELDS TERMINATED BY '|'
       STORED AS TEXTFILE LOCATION '/tpch/nation';
CREATE EXTERNAL TABLE region (r_regionkey int,..., r_comment string)
       ROW FORMAT DELIMITED FIELDS TERMINATED BY '|'
       STORED AS TEXTFILE LOCATION '/tpch/region';
-- create the target table
CREATE EXTERNAL q5_local_supplier_volume (N_NAME STRING, REVENUE DOUBLE);
-- the query
INSERT OVERWRITE TABLE q5_local_supplier_volume
SELECT n_name, sum(l_extendedprice*(1-l_discount)) AS revenue
FROM customer c JOIN
 (SELECT n_name, l_extendedprice, l_discount, s_nationkey, o_custkey
  FROM orders o JOIN
   (SELECT n_name, l_extendedprice, l_discount, l_orderkey, s_nationkey
    FROM lineitem l JOIN
     (SELECT n_name, s_suppkey, s_nationkey FROM supplier s JOIN
       (SELECT n_name, n_nationkey
        FROM nation n JOIN region r
        ON n.n_regionkey = r.r_regionkey AND r.r_name = 'ASIA'
       ) n1 ON s.s_nationkey = n1.n_nationkey
     ) s1 ON l.l_suppkey = s1.s_suppkey
   ) l1 ON l1.l_orderkey = o.o_orderkey and o.o_orderdate >= '1994-01-01'
  AND o.o_orderdate < '1995-01-01') o1
ON c.c_nationkey = o1.s_nationkey AND c.c_custkey = o1.o_custkey
GROUP BY n_name
ORDER BY revenue DESC;
```

FIGURE 9.4 HiveQL code for TPC-H business question Q5. (Adapted from Yuntao, J.: Running the TPC-H benchmark on Hive. https://github.com/rxin/TPC-H-Hive, 2009.)

offers an iterative MapReduce interface. Nevertheless, these frameworks do not provide abstractions for more general reuse, for example, to let a user load several data sets into memory and run ad hoc queries across them. Inspired by *distributed shared memory*, in [32], authors propose *resilient distributed data sets* (RDDs). *RDDs* implement distributed memory abstraction that allows programmers perform in-memory computations on large clusters in a fault-tolerant manner. They target applications that MapReduce framework handles inefficiently, such as iterative algorithms and interactive data-mining tools.

Spark SQL is open source [33]. It provides a *DataFrame API* that performs relational operations on both external data sources and Sparks built-in distributed collections. A *DataFrame* is equivalent to a table in a relational database and can also be manipulated in similar ways to RDDs. Unlike RDDs, *DataFrames* keep track of their schema and support various relational operations that lead to more optimized execution (see translation of Q5 TPC-H into Spark SQL in Figure 9.5).

9.3.3 Cloudera Impala

Cloudera Impala [35] is an open-source, MPP SQL query engine designed specifically to leverage the flexibility and scalability of Hadoop as well as decades of research in parallel databases (semijoin, vectorized processing, run time code generation [36]).

Custom application logic can be incorporated through user-defined functions (UDFs) in Java and C++, and user-defined aggregate functions (UDAs) in C++. Due to the limitations of HDFS as a storage manager, Impala does not support UPDATE or DELETE. Impala supports bulk data deletion

```
import org.apache.spark.sql.functions.sum
import org.apache.spark.sql.functions.udf

class Q05 extends TpchQuery {
  import sqlContext.implicits._
  override def execute(): Unit = {
    val decrease = udf { (x: Double, y: Double) => x * (1 - y) }
    val forders = order.filter($"o_orderdate" < "1995-01-01"
    && $"o_orderdate" >= "1994-01-01")
    val res = region.filter($"r_name" === "ASIA")
      .join(nation, $"r_regionkey" === nation("n_regionkey"))
      .join(supplier, $"n_nationkey" === supplier("s_nationkey"))
      .join(lineitem, $"s_suppkey" === lineitem("l_suppkey"))
      .select($"n_name", $"l_extendedprice", $"l_discount",
              $"l_orderkey", $"s_nationkey")
      .join(forders, $"l_orderkey" === forders("o_orderkey"))
      .join(customer, $"o_custkey" === customer("c_custkey")
            && $"s_nationkey" === customer("c_nationkey"))
      .select($"n_name",
              decrease($"l_extendedprice", $"l_discount").as("value"))
      .groupBy($"n_name")
      .agg(sum($"value").as("revenue"))
      .sort($"revenue".desc)
    outputDF(res)
  }
}
```

FIGURE 9.5 Spark code for TPC-H business question Q5. (Adapted from Savvides, S.: TPC-H queries implemented in Spark using the DataFrames API. https://github.com/ssavvides/tpch-spark, 2015.)

by dropping a table partition. Typically, the user recomputes parts of the data set to incorporate updates and then replaces the corresponding data files, often by dropping and re-adding the partition as demonstrated in [8] for handling TPC-H refresh functions in a Hadoop cluster.

9.3.4 TPC Benchmarking Experiences of SQL-on-Hadoop Systems

SQL-on-Hadoop systems are benchmarked using the most prominent decision support systems benchmarks, namely, TPC-H and TPC-DS. Hereafter, we overview relevant benchmarking studies of SQL-on-Hadoop systems. In [19], *TPC-H* benchmark is translated into *HiveQL* for assessing the performance of *Apache Hive*. Performance studies show that *Hive+Tez* outperforms *Hive+Oozie*. The workflow orchestrator *Apache Oozie* bad performs parallelism and performs expensive I/O operations. It was replaced with *Tez* [37], which enhances tasks scheduling and avoids materialization overheads of Hadoop.

In [34], *TPC-H* benchmark is translated into *Spark* for assessing the performance of *Apache Spark*. In [38], authors compare *MapReduce* to *Spark* using the *TeraSort* benchmark. In [39], Floratou et al. compare *Hive-MR*, *Hive-Tez*, and *Impala* for different file formats (*ORC*, *Parquet*) and compression types (no compression, *Snappy*) using TPC-H benchmark (SF=1000, i.e., 1 TB) and a microworkload of TPC-DS showing out-performance of Impala. In [35], authors compare different storage options for TPC-H benchmark data with SF=1000 (1 TB of raw data), where the combination of *Parquet* columnar file format and *Snappy* compression algorithm outperforms all other combinations of storage options and compression algorithms. Authors report also performance measurements for a subset of TPC-DS benchmark (namely, Q27, Q34, Q42, Q43, Q46, Q52, Q55, Q59, Q65, Q73, Q79, Q96), which demonstrate that *Parquet* consistently outperforms by up to five times all the other formats. Compared to *Hive*, *SparkSQL*, and *Presto*, *Impala* is the highest performing SQL-on-Hadoop system, for both single-user and multiuser workloads composed of 10 users.

Floratou et al. [40] demonstrate that TPC-H and TPC-DS rules for benchmarking are not followed. Indeed, (i) the performance measurements are limited to a subset of TPC-DS benchmark workload, that is, a single datamart and a dozen of queries among 99 TPC-DS queries, and (ii) the workload is rewritten either because *Impala* does not support windowing functions and rollup or for optimizing expensive operations and introducing hints for the optimizer.

9.4 ASSESSING SQL-ON-HADOOP SYSTEMS

Hadoop vendors have added functionalities to the open-source edition of Hadoop, which focus on client support, graphical user interfaces for cluster management, and query optimization techniques for high performance. Henceforth, multiple distributions of Hadoop exist and include *Amazon Web Services Elastic MapReduce Hadoop Distribution* by *Amazon*, *Hortonworks Hadoop Distribution* by *Hortonworks*, *Cloudera Hadoop Distribution* by *Cloudera*, *IBM Infosphere BigInsights Hadoop Distribution* by *IBM*, etc. As the number of SQL-on-Hadoop systems is increasing, it becomes necessary to be able to assess offers. Reviewed research papers [19,34,35,38,40] use TPC benchmarks, namely, TPC-H and TPC-DS benchmarks, which are not representatives of *Big data*. Next, we argue that TPC-H and TPC-DS mismatch *big data rationale* and are insufficient for comparing SQL-on-Hadoop systems. Then, we propose new requirements to consider for assessing big data management systems in general.

9.4.1 TPC Benchmarks Shortcomings

The use of TPC benchmarks mismatches *big data rationale*. It reveals the following shortcomings for assessing big data management systems:

- First, TPC-H and TPC-DS benchmarks implement limited refresh functions, while *big data velocity* deals with the pace at which massive data flows in continuously from sources.

- Second, TPC-H and TPC-DS benchmarks data fall in the structured data model, while *big data* incorporates all the varieties of data, including structured, semistructured, and unstructured data.
- Third, TPC-H and TPC-DS include solely OLAP workload, while *big data* is subject to different *workload types*, including OLTP, Create–Read–Update–Delete (CRUD), OLAP, Sort, IO operations, Information Retrieval, Machine Learning, and Multimedia Analytics Workloads.
- Fourth, big data management systems are deployed on top of clusters of commodity hardware, and each node may be prone to failures. It is very important to report system performances, that is, query response times under failure scenarios as well as time to recover lost data.
- Fifth, TPC benchmarks are synthetic benchmarks, while *big data veracity* refers to the biases, noise, and abnormality in data sets.

In order to overcome TPC-H and TPC-DS shortcomings, new benchmarks are proposed, namely,

- *BigBench Benchmark*: The *BigBench* [41] data model is adopted from the TPC-DS data model. Its schema uses the data of the store and Web sales distribution channel and augments it with semistructured and unstructured data.
- *TPC-DI Benchmark*: TPC-DI [42] fosters manipulation and loading of large volumes of data having different formats (multirow formats and XML), complex transformations, historical loading, and incremental updates, as well as consistency requirements ensuring that the integration process results in reliable and accurate data.

9.4.2 Key Requirements and Constraints for SQL-on-Hadoop Systems Assessment

In this section, we propose key requirements and constraints to consider for assessing big data management systems.

9.4.2.1 Quality of Service Requirements

- *Service-Level Agreement (SLA)*: SLAs capture the agreed-upon guarantees between a service provider and a customer. They define the characteristics of the provided service including service-level objectives, as maximum response times, minimum throughput rates, and data consistency, and define penalties if these objectives are not met by the service provider.
- *Client Support*: Ideally, every customer receives 24 × 7 × 365 support.

9.4.2.2 Capacity Requirements

SQL-on-Hadoop systems rely on Hadoop capacities plus their SQL engines.

- *Data Models*: SQL-on-Hadoop systems should be designed to deal with the variety of big data. They should support all types of data, that is, (1) *structured*, (2) *semistructured*, and (3) *unstructured* data. *Structured data* refers to any data that resides in fields that have predefined lengths and formats (e.g., relational databases). *Semistructured data* are schemaless data that have an hierarchical structure (e.g., XML, JSON, or BSON). Semistructured data often consists of complex, nested elements having schema-less fields that differ typewise from row to row. The data can constantly evolve. *Unstructured data* represent around 80% of data. It includes text and multimedia content (e.g., text documents, videos, photos, audio files).
- *Storage Formats*: SQL-on-Hadoop systems should implement effective data formats and support efficiently existing formats. Hadoop file formats include (1) *SequenceFiles*, (2)

serialization formats, and (3) *columnar formats*. *SequenceFiles* store data as binary key–value pairs. There are three formats available for records stored within SequenceFiles, which are (i) uncompressed, (ii) record-compressed, and (iii) block-compressed. Uncompressed SequenceFiles are not efficient for input/output (I/O) since they occupy more space on disks, and block-based compression provides better compression ratios compared to record-compressed SequenceFiles.

Compression codecs commonly used with Hadoop have different characteristics (compress/uncompress speed and rate). The ability to split compressed files is also a very important consideration. Splittable formats enable Hadoop to split files into chunks for parallel processing.

Serialization refers to the process of turning data structures into byte streams either for storage or transmission over a network. Conversely, *deserialization* is the process of converting a byte stream back into data structures. There are serialization frameworks within the Hadoop ecosystem, including *Facebook Thrift*, *Google Protocol Buffers*, and *Apache Avro* [43] (a binary row format).

Columnar file formats supported on Hadoop include the *RCFile format*, the *Optimized Row Columnar* (ORC), and *Apache Parquet* [44]. *Parquet* is a customizable PAX-like format optimized for large data blocks (tens, hundreds, thousands of megabytes) with built-in support for nested data. The most recent version (Parquet 2.0) also implements embedded statistics: inlined column statistics for further optimization of scan efficiency, for example, min/max indexes.

- *Consistency Model*: It is well admitted that no single consistency model is appropriate for all uses. SQL-on-Hadoop systems focus on scalability and availability; for these purposes, they replicate data asynchronously. Guaranteeing ACID properties (*Atomicity*, *Consistency*, *Isolation*, *Durability*) [45] in a distributed transaction across a distributed data management system is complex. Network connections might fail, or one node might successfully complete its part of the transaction and then be required to roll back its changes because of a failure on another node. Moreover, the CAP theorem [46] asserts that any networked shared-data system can have only two of three properties: *consistency*, *availability*, and *partition tolerance*. *Consistency* ensures that all the servers in the system will have the same data, so anyone using the system will get the same query answer regardless of which server answers their request. *Availability* ensures that the system will always respond to a request. *Partition Tolerance* ensures that the system continues to operate as a whole even if individual servers fail or can't be reached.

  Systems are Basically Available, in Soft state, and Eventually consistent (i.e., BASE). Therefore, (i) the system does guarantee the availability of the data as well as a response to any request, (ii) the state of the system could change over time, so even during times without input there may be changes going on due to *eventual consistency*, thus the state of the system is always *soft*. The system will eventually become consistent once it stops receiving input. The data will propagate to everywhere it should sooner or later, but the system will continue to receive input and is not checking the consistency of every transaction before it moves onto the next one. Consistency guarantees affect latency and system response to concurrent read and write requests. One of the biggest challenges with HDFS is that it is not designed for incremental updates. *VectorH* is the only system that addresses this challenge and supports updates efficiently [47]. *VectorH* implements a fully ACID compliant transactional database with multiversion read consistency. Any new transaction will see all previously committed transactions, both small incremental transactions and large bulk data loads. Changes are always written persistently to a transaction log before a commit completes to always ensure full recoverability.
- *Security Policies*: It is important that an SQL-on-Hadoop system implements a security policy which allows (i) to secure data sets right accesses, so that only authorized users can

view and update particular data sets, (ii) to audit each user actions, (iii) to encrypt the data at-rest as well as on-the-wire, and (iv) to enable fine-grained access control, which restricts users to accessing only certain columns in a table. The most recent version of Cloudera Hadoop (CDH) implements Access Control Lists (ACLs) for HDFS. ACLs allow to define an arbitrary number of user groups and then assign each of them specific permissions on directories and files.

Apache Sentry is an open-source project that enables role-based access control for Hive and Impala tables. Sentry allows to implement a database-like security policy, through the grant of SELECT, INSERT, or ALL privileges to a group on a particular Hive or Impala table, rather than on the underlying HDFS directories and files.

- *High Availability*: Data distribution among multiple disks increases the distributed storage system failure likelihood. Many approaches to build highly available distributed data storage systems have been proposed. They generally use either (i) replication or (ii) parity calculus. The latter approach uses systematic erasure codes (e.g., Reed Solomon [RS] codes, Low-Density Parity-Check codes, Tornado code). With replication, data management is straightforward. However, the storage overhead with replication is always higher than it is with systematic erasure codes. When a certain level of availability is targeted, the erasure codes are able to provide service with a lower storage overhead than replication techniques. For data warehousing, high availability through erasure codes saves storage costs, particularly for big data of type *write-once* (i.e., not subject to delete refreshes). Nevertheless, data recovery is more complicated than replication. Indeed, *first* data recovery is not a simple *copy to operation* as for replication, it performs complex decoding calculus, and *second* data recovery involves different servers, which send their contents to a recovery manager and consequently it implies a high communication overhead. Erasure codes were investigated and proved efficient for highly available distributed storage systems [48,49]. The *Quantcast File System* (QFS) [50] is a free, high-performance, fault-tolerant, distributed file system developed to support MapReduce processing, or other applications reading and writing large files sequentially, which uses erasure codes to ensure high availability of data files.
- *Streams Data Integration and Processing*: Data warehouse systems are deployed as part of an OLAP system separated from the OLTP system. Data propagates down to the OLAP system, but typically after some lag. This system architecture is sufficient for *retrospective analytics*, but does not suffice in situations that require real-time analytics. The *Lambda Architecture* coined by Natan Marz [51,52] defines a robust framework for ingesting streams of fast data while providing efficient real-time and historical analytics. The *Lambda architecture* requires revision of software layers. Hence, to deal with the velocity of big data, SQL-on-Hadoop systems should process data streams in real-time to keep up with their arriving speed. The open-source *Apache Storm* and *Apache Flink* process data streams as true streams, that is, data streams are immediately pipelined as soon as they arrived, while *SparkStreaming* processes data streams on microbatching basis.

9.4.2.3 System Constraints

System constraints are related to first *setup constraints* such as specific operating system (e.g., Red Hat Enterprise Linux for IBM BigInsights) and hardware specifications such as minimum number of nodes (e.g., 3 nodes), CPU type (e.g., 64-bit systems), minimum RAM capacities (e.g., 16 GB), and number and capacities of hard drives for management and compute nodes; and second *operation constraints* such as the maximum number of concurrent users.

9.4.2.4 Cost Constraints

There are two types of SQL-on-Hadoop solutions' deployment methods, which lead to a different cost model. The first is an on-premises deployment, while the second is a cloud-based deployment.

With an on-premises deployment, the company is responsible for setting up the appropriate hardware and software, the acquisition of software licenses, and hiring qualified staff for system functioning and maintenance. With a cloud-based deployment, the client accesses the system off-premises via the Internet and cloud providers deliver and shrink IT resources on-demand and align costs to actual usage.

Apache Hive, Apache Spark, and Cloudera Impala are free and open source. Nevertheless, the deployment of free software on HPC platforms is costly, taking into account human expertise as well as the HPC platform cost. A closer look at commercial offers such as IBM BigInsights available on IBM bluemix cloud portal gives ideas on nonfree software costs. IBM proposes three modules to install on a cluster: (i) *IBM Open Platform*—a distribution that is based on open-source Apache Hadoop Ecosystem, (ii) *BigInsights Data Analyst*—which provides specific tools for data analysis as well as *Big SQL* and *BigSheets*, and (iii) *BigInsights Data Scientist*—which offers in-Hadoop analytics and predictive modeling for data science teams with *Big R*, *Text Analytics*, and *SystemML* included. Costs vary along *cluster size*, *module*, and *number of nodes*. For a small cluster of three nodes (16 TB), *IBM Open Platform* costs US$ 12,510/month, *BigInsights Data Analyst* US$ 17,807/month, and *BigInsights Data Scientist* US$ 20,145/month. For a small cluster of 10 nodes (53 TB), *IBM Open Platform* costs US$ 28,680/month, *BigInsights Data Analyst* US$ 37,414//month, and *BigInsights Data Scientist* US$ 42,090/month.

9.5 CONCLUSIONS

In this chapter, we studied big data management systems, in particular *SQL-on-Hadoop systems*. Specifically, we have reviewed SQL-on-Hadoop open-source projects and we identified requirements and constraints for assessing SQL-on-Hadoop systems. The focus in big data management systems is on (1) horizontal scalability and high performance, (2) continuous availability, (3) un-structured data processing, and (4) real-time processing. The proposed requirements and constraints aim at allowing a fair comparison of different offerings.

REFERENCES

1. Patterson, D.A., Gibson, G.A., Katz, R.H.: A case for redundant arrays of inexpensive disks (RAID). In: *Proceedings of the 1988 ACM SIGMOD International Conference on Management of Data*, Chicago, Illinois, USA, June 1–3, 1988, pp. 109–116.
2. Devine, R.: Design and implementation of DDH: A distributed dynamic hashing algorithm. In: *Foundations of Data Organization and Algorithms, 4th International Conference*, Chicago, Illinois, USA, October 13–15, 1993, pp. 101–114.
3. Litwin, W., Neimat, M., Schneider, D.A.: LH*—A scalable, distributed data structure. *ACM Trans. Database Syst.* **21**, 1996, 480–525.
4. Codd, E.F.: A relational model of data for large shared data banks. *Commun. ACM* **13**, 1970, 377–387.
5. Héman, S., Zukowski, M., de Vries, A.P., Boncz, P.A.: Efficient and flexible information retrieval using MonetDB/X100. In: *CIDR 2007, Third Biennial Conference on Innovative Data Systems Research*, Asilomar, CA, USA, January 7–10, 2007, pp. 96–101.
6. Stonebraker, M., Abadi, D.J., Batkin, A., Chen, X., Cherniack, M., Ferreira, M., Lau, E. et al.: C-store: A column-oriented DBMS. In: *Proceedings of the 31st International Conference on Very Large Data Bases*, Trondheim, Norway, August 30–September 2, 2005, pp. 553–564.
7. Zukowski, M., van de Wiel, M., Boncz, P.A.: Vectorwise: A vectorized analytical DBMS. In: *IEEE 28th International Conference on Data Engineering ICDE*, Washington, DC, USA, April 1–5, 2012, pp. 1349–1350.
8. Moussa, R.: Massive data analytics in the cloud: TPC-H experience on Hadoop clusters. *IJWA* **4**, 2012, 113–133.

9. Cuzzocrea, A., Moussa, R.: Multidimensional database design via schema transformation: Turning TPC-H into the TPC-H*d multidimensional benchmark. In: *19th International Conference on Management of Data COMAD*, Ahmedabad, India, December 19–21, 2013, pp. 56–67.
10. Shrinivas, L., Bodagala, S., Varadarajan, R., Cary, A., Bharathan, V., Bear, C.: Materialization strategies in the Vertica analytic database: Lessons learned. In: *29th IEEE International Conference on Data Engineering ICDE*, Brisbane, Australia, April 8–12, 2013, pp. 1196–1207.
11. Abadi, D.J., Madden, S., Hachem, N.: Column-stores vs. row-stores: How different are they really? In: *Proceedings of the ACM SIGMOD International Conference on Management of Data SIGMOD*, Vancouver, BC, Canada, June 10–12, 2008, pp. 967–980.
12. Transaction Processing Council: TPC benchmarks. http://www.tpc.org/, 2016.
13. White, T.: *Hadoop—The Definitive Guide: MapReduce for the Cloud*. O'Reilly Media/Yahoo Press, Sebastopol California. 2009.
14. Vavilapalli, V.K., Murthy, A.C., Douglas, C., Agarwal, S., Konar, M., Evans, R., Graves, T. et al.: Apache Hadoop YARN: Yet another resource negotiator. In: *ACM Symposium on Cloud Computing, SOCC*, Santa Clara, CA, USA, October 1–3, 2013, pp. 5:1–5:16.
15. Dean, J., Ghemawat, S.: MapReduce: Simplified data processing on large clusters. In: *6th Symposium on Operating System Design and Implementation (OSDI)*, San Francisco, California, USA, December 6–8, 2004, pp. 137–150.
16. Chen, Y., Ganapathi, A., Katz, R.H.: To compress or not to compress—Compute vs. IO tradeoffs for MapReduce energy efficiency. In: *Proc. of the 1st ACM SIGCOMM Workshop on Green Networking, ACM*, New Delhi, India, August 30, 2010, pp. 23–28.
17. Olston, C., Reed, B., Srivastava, U., Kumar, R., Tomkins, A.: Pig latin: A not-so-foreign language for data processing. In: *Proceedings of the ACM SIGMOD International Conference on Management of Data, SIGMOD*, Vancouver, BC, Canada, June 10–12, 2008, pp. 1099–1110.
18. Moussa, R.: TPC-H benchmarking of Apache Pig Latin on Hadoop Cluster. https://sites.google.com/site/rimmoussa/CC_pig_tpch.tar, 2011.
19. Yuntao, J.: Running the TPC-H benchmark on Hive. https://github.com/rxin/TPC-H-Hive, 2009.
20. Moussa, R.: TPC-H benchmarking of pig latin on a Hadoop cluster. In: *International Conference on Communications and Information Technology (ICCIT)*, Hammamet, Tunisia, June 26–28, 2012, pp. 85–90.
21. Jakobus, B., McBrien, P.: Pig vs Hive: Benchmarking high level query languages. http://www.ibm.com/developerworks/library/ba-pigvhive/ba-pigvhive-pdf.pdf, 2013.
22. Aslett, M.: 451 group blog. https://blogs.the451group.com/information_manage ment/2011/04/06/what-we-talk-about-when-we-talk-about-newsql/, 2011.
23. Moniruzzaman, A.B.M.: NewSQL: Towards next-generation scalable RDBMS for online transaction processing (OLTP) for big data management. *CoRR*. arXiv:1411.7343, 2014.
24. Yuan, L., Wu, L., You, J., Chi, Y.: Rubato DB: A highly scalable staged grid database system for OLTP and big data applications. In: *Proceedings of the 23rd ACM International Conference on Conference on Information and Knowledge Management (CIKM)*, Shanghai, China, November 3–7, 2014, pp. 1–10.
25. Yuan, L., Wu, L., You, J., Chi, Y.: A demonstration of Rubato DB: A highly scalable newSQL database system for OLTP and big data applications. In: *Proceedings of the 2015 ACM SIGMOD International Conference on Management of Data, Melbourne*, Melbourne, Victoria, Australia, May 31–June 4, 2015, pp. 907–912.
26. Kallman, R., Kimura, H., Natkins, J., Pavlo, A., Rasin, A., Zdonik, S., Jones, E.P.C. et al.: H-store: A high-performance, distributed main memory transaction processing system. *PVLDB* **1**, 2008, 1496–1499.
27. Stonebraker, M., Weisberg, A.: The VoltDB main memory DBMS. *IEEE Data Eng. Bull.* **36**, 2013, 21–27.
28. Grolinger, K., Higashino, W.A., Tiwari, A., Capretz, M.A.: Data management in cloud environments: NosSQL and newSQL data stores. *Journal of Cloud Computing: Advances, Systems and Applications* **2**, 2013, 22.
29. Thusoo, A., Sarma, J.S., Jain, N., Shao, Z., Chakka, P., Zhang, N., Anthony, S., Liu, H., Murthy, R.: Hive—A petabyte scale data warehouse using Hadoop. In: *Proceedings of the 26th International Conference on Data Engineering, ICDE*, Long Beach, California, USA, March 1–6, 2010, pp. 996–1005.
30. Malewicz, G., Austern, M.H., Bik, A.J.C., Dehnert, J.C., Horn, I., Leiser, N., Czajkowski, G.: Pregel: A system for large-scale graph processing. In: *Proceedings of the ACM SIGMOD*, Indianapolis, Indiana, USA, June 6–10, 2010, pp. 135–146.

31. Bu, Y., Howe, B., Balazinska, M., Ernst, M.D.: The HaLoop approach to large-scale iterative data analysis. *VLDB J.* **21**, 2012, 169–190.
32. Zaharia, M., Chowdhury, M., Das, T., Dave, A., Ma, J., McCauly, M., Franklin, M.J., Shenker, S., Stoica, I.: Resilient distributed datasets: A fault-tolerant abstraction for in-memory cluster computing. In: *Proceedings of the 9th USENIX Symposium on Networked Systems Design and Implementation (NSDI)*, San Jose, CA, USA, April 25–27, 2012, pp. 15–28.
33. Armbrust, M., Xin, R.S., Lian, C., Huai, Y., Liu, D., Bradley, J.K., Meng, X. et al.: Spark SQL: Relational data processing in spark. In: *Proceedings of the 2015 ACM SIGMOD International Conference on Management of Data. SIGMOD'15*, Melbourne, Victoria, Australia, May 31–June 4, 2015, pp. 1383–1394.
34. Savvides, S.: TPC-H queries implemented in Spark using the DataFrames API. https://github.com/ssavvides/tpch-spark, 2015.
35. Kornacker, M., Behm, A., Bittorf, V., Bobrovytsky, T., Ching, C., Choi, A., Erickson, J. et al.: Impala: A modern, open-source SQL engine for Hadoop. In: *CIDR 2015, Seventh Biennial Conference on Innovative Data Systems Research*, Asilomar, CA, USA, January 4–7, 2015.
36. Li, N.: Inside Cloudera Impala: Runtime code generation. http://blog.cloudera.com/blog/ 2013/02/inside-cloudera-impala-runtime-code-generation/, 2016.
37. Saha, B., Shah, H., Seth, S., Vijayaraghavan, G., Murthy, A., Curino, C.: Apache Tez: A unifying framework for modeling and building data processing applications. In: *Proceedings of ACM SIGMOD International Conference on Management of Data. SIGMOD'15*, Melbourne, Victoria, Australia, May 31–June 4, 2015, pp. 1357–1369.
38. Shi, J., Qiu, Y., Minhas, U.F., Jiao, L., Wang, C., Reinwald, B., Özcan, F.: Clash of the Titans: MapReduce vs. Spark for large scale data analytics. *PVLDB* **8**, 2015, 2110–2121.
39. Floratou, A., Minhas, U.F., Özcan, F.: SQL-on-Hadoop: Full circle back to shared-nothing database architectures. *PVLDB* **7**, 2014, 1295–1306.
40. Floratou, A., Özcan, F., Schiefer, B.: Benchmarking SQL-on-Hadoop systems: TPC or not TPC? In: *Big Data Benchmarking WBDB*, Potsdam, Germany, August 5–6, 2014, pp. 63–72.
41. Ghazal, A., Rabl, T., Hu, M., Raab, F., Poess, M., Crolotte, A., Jacobsen, H.: BigBench: Towards an industry standard benchmark for big data analytics. In: *ACM SIGMOD*, New York, NY, USA, June 22–27, 2013, pp. 1197–1208.
42. Poess, M., Rabl, T., Caufield, B.: TPC-DI: The first industry benchmark for data integration. *PVLDB* **7**, 2014, 1367–1378.
43. Apache: Avro. https://avro.apache.org/, 2016.
44. Apache: Parquet. https://parquet.apache.org/, 2016.
45. Härder, T., Reuter, A.: Principles of transaction-oriented database recovery. *ACM Comput. Surv.* **15**, 1983, 287–317.
46. Brewer, E.A.: A certain freedom: Thoughts on the CAP theorem. In: *Proceedings of the 29th Annual ACM Symposium on Principles of Distributed Computing (PODC)*, Zurich, Switzerland, July 25–28, 2010, p. 335.
47. Costea, A., Ionescu, A., Raducanu, B., Switakowski, M., Barca, C., Sompolski, J., Luszczak, A., Szafraski, M., de Nijs, G., Boncz, P.: VectorH: Taking SQL-on-Hadoop to the next level. In: *Proceedings of the 2016 ACM SIGMOD International Conference on Management of Data*, San Francisco, CA, USA, June 26–July 01, 2016.
48. Litwin, W., Moussa, R., Schwarz, T.J.E.: LH*RS—A highly-available scalable distributed data structure. *ACM Trans. Database Syst.* **30**, 2005, 769–811.
49. Pitkänen, M., Moussa, R., Swany, D.M., Niemi, T.: Erasure codes for increasing the availability of grid data storage. In: *AICT/ICIW 2006*, Guadeloupe, French Caribbean, February 19–25, 2006, p. 185.
50. Ovsiannikov, M., Rus, S., Reeves, D., Sutter, P., Rao, S., Kelly, J.: The Quantcast File System. *PVLDB* **6**, 2013, 1092–1101.
51. Marz, N., Warren, J.: *Big Data: Principles and Best Practices of Scalable Realtime Data Systems.* 1st edn. Manning, Shelter Island, New York, 2015.
52. Kiran, M., Murphy, P., Monga, I., Dugan, J., Baveja, S.S.: Lambda architecture for cost-effective batch and speed big data processing. In: *IEEE International Conference on Big Data*, Santa Clara, CA, USA, October 29–November 1, 2015, pp. 2785–2792.

10 One Platform Rules All
From Hadoop 1.0 to Hadoop 2.0 and Spark

Xiongpai Qin and Keqin Li

CONTENTS

ABSTRACT

In the big data era, traditional relational database systems cannot effectively handle the big volume of data due to their limited scalability. People are seeking new ways to tackle the problem of big data. After Google published its work of MapReduce, Hadoop (an open-source implementation of

MapReduce) has risen to be the de facto standard tool for big data processing. People have applied Hadoop to various big data application scenarios, which show the power of Hadoop. However, the 1.0 version of Hadoop supports only one computing model of MapReduce, which is not efficient enough to provide higher performance.

Now Hadoop has evolved into Hadoop 2.0 (YARN). Hadoop 2.0 has a newly designed architecture, which separates resource management and job scheduling. Hadoop 2.0 supports other computing models besides MapReduce, including complex computing work expressed in a DAG (directed acyclic graph). People also try to improve the execution layer of Hadoop, such as the work of Tez from Hortonworks, to provide lower latency.

In the meantime, AMP lab of California University at Berkeley brought out Spark, which now draws more and more attention from academia and industry. The Spark ecosystem includes the core and four major components surrounding it, including Spark SQL for structured data processing, Spark Streaming for stream data processing, MLLib for machine learning, and GraphX for graph data processing. In essence, Spark and Hadoop provide similar functionalities; however, in some application scenarios, Spark outperforms Hadoop by many times.

Hadoop and Spark are two ecosystems. Both of them can play the central role in future big data warehouses. On one hand, they are replacement to each other; on the other hand, they can be used together to get work done. For example, people can use Spark in exploratory analysis and get instant feedback, and use Hadoop to consolidate all data in one place, and conduct a thorough analysis on the whole data set.

In this chapter, we analyze limitations of different technologies and the business requirements behind the continuous innovations. We also try to point out some lessons that the database research community and the database industry should have learned.

10.1 ONE SIZE CANNOT FIT ALL

10.1.1 A Brief Introduction to Relational Database Management Systems

In early 1970s, IBM scientist E. F. Codd, who later won Turing Award, published the famous paper of "A Relational Model of Data for Large Shared Data Banks." The paper laid down the theoretic foundation of modern relational database management systems (RDBMSs). The relational model is as simple as some tables with rows and columns. The rows correspond to entities and the columns correspond to attributes of entities. Upon the data model, some basic operations are defined, including selection (filtering), projection, and join. The selection operation is to select a subset of rows of the table, the projection operation is to select a subset of columns of the table, and the join operation is to create new rows by combining rows from two or more tables, which have some semantic relationship. For example, each row of the department table corresponds to some rows of the employee table, which means that these employees are working in the department. On the basis of the basic operations, complex queries could be composed to fetch desired results.

Many researchers put their efforts into developing working database management systems, which are completely based on the new relational model. Two of the works are prominent: one is Ingres from University of Californian at Berkeley and the other is System R from IBM. In 1974, IBM engineers invented a query language named SEQUEL (structured English query language) for System R, which was predecessor of the SQL language. Besides that, researchers have developed storage methods, indexing techniques, query optimization techniques, transaction-processing methods, and database recovery techniques for RDBMS. These methods made RDBMS an efficient and reliable data engine for various online transaction-processing (OLTP) applications.

From 1970s till now, RDBMS has become the dominant data management technology in the market. RDBMSs have been applied to industries such as banking, aviation, and government agencies. Critical data is stored in RDBMSs and various applications are run over RDBMSs to support business activities pertaining to our daily life.

After more and more data are collected, people are increasingly interested in analyzing the data to find some valuable information concerning what has happened and what will happen, for decision making. RDBMSs are also the underlying engine of such decision support systems, running online analytic processing (OLAP) and data-mining applications.

10.1.2 The Big Data Era

Now comes the big data era. According to Wikipedia [1], big data is defined as "a collection of data sets so large and complex that it becomes difficult to process using on-hand database management tools or traditional data-processing applications." Big data comes from various sources including e-commerce Web sites, sensors in internet of thing (IOT), observations of scientific experiments, and user-generated contents on the Web. For example, the volume of data generated by LHC (Large Hadron Collider) of CERN in one experiment can easily reach PB (petabyte) level. Several forces drive the arise of big data; one of them is that the price of storage is getting lower and lower, giving people the possibility to collect more and more data at very low cost. In the above scientific scenario, people need to collect data in a finer granularity to find out some interesting patterns inside it.

Big data have several characteristics; the "three Vs" that most people agreed on are *volume*, *velocity*, and *variety*. Volume is the primary characteristic of a big data set. The volume is so big that the data set could not be efficiently handled by traditional database techniques. Velocity refers to some scenarios that the data is generated in a high pace; we need some efficient tools to handle the data timely, otherwise the data will be lost. Variety means various types of data, including structured data such as relational tables, unstructured data such as text, audio and video, and semistructured data such as XML files.

10.1.3 Limitations of RDBMS to Handle Big Data

RDBMS is not ready for handling of big data. It is designed to run on reliable hardware, which usually takes the form of proprietary high-end servers. To process big data, we can scale up such high-end servers by adding more CPUs, memories, storage devices, and network bandwidth. However, there is an upper limit and the cost is prohibitive.

The alternative method is to scale out the system by distributing data and processing onto a cluster, which is composed of hundreds to thousands of not-so-expensive commodity servers. We can add more nodes to the cluster to achieve satisfactory performance when the load becomes heavier. Big data needs thousands and even ten thousands of nodes to process it. No RDBMS has run on a cluster of up to more than 1000 nodes till now. Due to the limited scalability of RDBMS, people are seeking new ways.

10.2 THE HADOOP 1.0 ECOSYSTEM

10.2.1 Introduction to the Hadoop 1.0 Ecosystem

Search is Google's main business in its early days. The search engine scrawls the World Wide Web to grab Web pages and indexes the pages to serve later user search requests. The data set of Web pages is really big. It is uneasy to store and process the data set on several big servers, such as mainframes. Google used a cluster of commodity servers to do the job and designed GFS (Google File System) and MapReduce to index the Web pages.

GFS is a distributed file system running on a large cluster. Data is organized into blocks of large sizes (64 or 128 MB). Each block has three replicas, which are stored on different nodes to provide fault tolerance. MapReduce is a computing model running over GFS.

The MapReduce runtime takes care of job scheduling, task assignment, recovery from failures, etc. Users only need to provide two functions, that is, the *Map* function and the *Reduce* function. The input of MapReduce is a list of <key1, value1> pairs and the Map function is applied to each

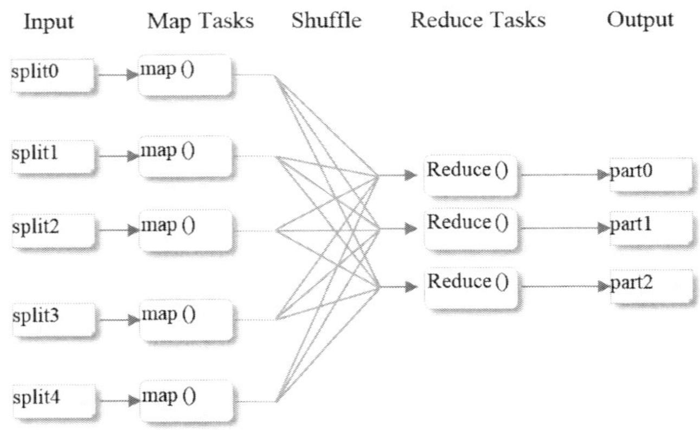

FIGURE 10.1 MapReduce computing model.

key–value pair to compute intermediate key–value pairs <key2, value2>. The intermediate key–value pairs are grouped together on the basis of key equality, that is, <key2, list<value2>>. For each key2, the Reduce function is applied to the list of value2, and aggregated results are generated. Users write MapReduce programs to perform various data-processing works by designing different Map function and Reduce functions. The general MapReduce computing model is depicted in Figure 10.1.

Hadoop is an Apache project founded by Doug Cutting. The Hadoop software stack is an open-source implementation of the MapReduce technology. In the following text, we will use MapReduce to refer to the MapReduce computing model, not specifically referring to Google's proprietary technology.

In Hadoop, HDFS (Hadoop distributed file system) is the counterpart of GFS. HDFS has a master/slave style of architecture. NameNode acts as master and DataNodes are workers. The NameNode is responsible for the management of metadata, such as the locations of data blocks, and DataNodes are responsible for the storage of data blocks.

The MapReduce runtime runs over HDFS, which includes two major components, that is, a JobTracker and TaskTrackers, which are running on the NameNode and the DataNodes, respectively. Users write MapReduce programs and submit to JobTracker as MapReduce Jobs.

The JobTracker coordinates the execution of a MapReduce Job by assigning Map and Reduce tasks to TaskTrackers on workers in the cluster. It is intelligent enough to assign tasks to TaskTrackers who are near to the data. A TaskTracker executes Map tasks or Reduce tasks assigned by the JobTracker. Figure 10.2 shows the components of MapReduce runtime and their relationships. The JobTracker (and the node it runs on) is also called the master node. The TaskTrackers (and the nodes they run on) are also called worker nodes.

A MapReduce job is executed in two phases: Map stage and Reduce stage. The detailed execution flow of a MapReduce job is as follows:

1. The data set to be processed (i.e., the input file) is loaded to the distributed file system. At loading, the file is split into multiple data blocks, which have the typical size of 64 or 128 MB. Each block is replicated three times onto different nodes by the underlying distributed file system.
2. The JobTracker receives a MapReduce job from some client, executes the job by assigning map tasks and reduce tasks onto TaskTrackers, and monitors the status of TaskTrackers. Suppose that there are M map tasks and R reduce tasks to assign.
3. Each block is then assigned to a mapper, that is, a worker which is assigned a map task. Each worker processes the contents of the input split and generates key–value pairs from the input data and passes the pairs to the user-defined Map function one by one. The generated

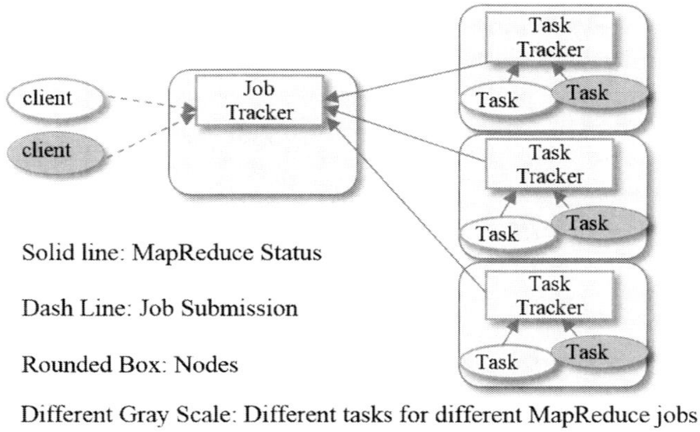

FIGURE 10.2 Execution runtime of MapReduce.

intermediate key–value pairs are buffered in memory, and it is periodically written to local disk. Persistence of intermediate results provides the nice property of fault tolerance.

The intermediate outputs produced by the mappers are sorted locally to group key–value pairs having the same key, and the file in local disk is organized into *R* regions, each region corresponding to one key. The locations of the *R* regions are sent to the master for later forwarding to the reduce workers.

4. When all Map tasks are finished, the JobTracker assigns Reduce tasks to workers. The intermediate data is shuffled to reducers. As described before, Map function outputs are already partitioned and stored in local disks; reducers simply pull specific partitions of the Map function outputs from different nodes, using the locations notified by the master. The reducers merge intermediate results by the intermediate keys (key2), and all values of the same key are grouped together. Then each reducer applies Reduce function to the values of key2 to generate some aggregation results. The output of reducers is stored into the distributed file system.
5. When all map tasks and reduce tasks have been completed, the JobTracker returns control to the user program, which can access the final result in the distributed file system.

To describe the MapReduce computing model more clearly, the frequently used example of word count is shown below. The word count program is to count occurrence of each distinct word in a big file loaded into the distributed file system.

The Map function of the job is to generate <word,1> for each word it encounters, as shown in Figure 10.3. The Reduce function is to compute the occurrence of each word according to the output of Mappers, as illustrated in Figure 10.4.

Execution flow of the word count program is illustrated in Figure 10.5. After the MapReduce runtime receives the word count program, it launches mappers on workers for the file splits. The map function scans its corresponding data block and generates <word,1> for each word in the block, and the intermediate results are stored in local disks of worker nodes. After that, MapReduce runtime launches Reducers, which pulls data from intermediate results. Reducers count occurrences of each word by sorting and counting the <word,1> list.

10.2.2 The Ecosystem of Hadoop 1.0

On the basis of HDFS and the MapReduce computing model, several tools together form the whole Hadoop ecosystem (Figure 10.6). These tools are briefly introduced as follows.

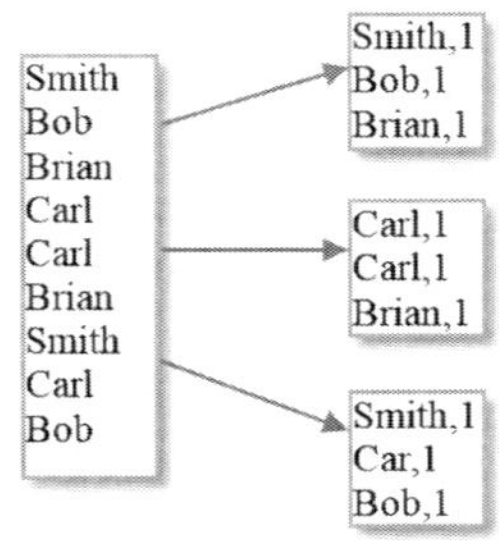

FIGURE 10.3 Map function for word count.

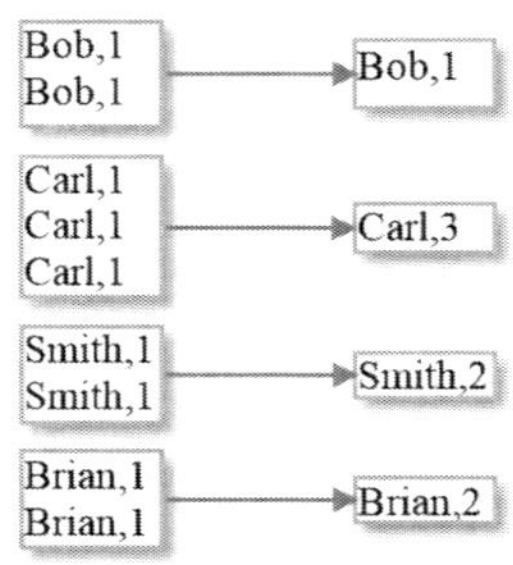

FIGURE 10.4 Reduce function for word count.

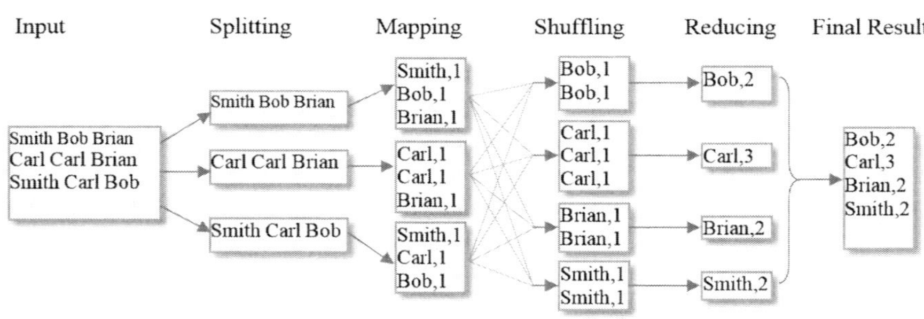

FIGURE 10.5 Execution flow of the word count program.

Hive is a data warehouse upon Hadoop. It provides SQL like query language HQL (Hive query language) for users to query the data. The queries are translated into MapReduce jobs and run on the Hadoop cluster.

HBase is the counterpart of Google *Big Table* on the Hadoop Platform. It is a scalable, highly reliable, and highly performant distributed database for structured data processing. It uses the column family data model, which is similar to the one that *Big Table* uses. HBase supports updating one row of data in the table, and it is used in data-serving applications.

Pig implements the procedural script language of Pig Latin. Programs written in Pig Latin are translated into MapReduce jobs and run upon the Hadoop platform. Some data-processing work, such as the join operation, is not straightforward to write in the form of MapReduce jobs. Pig Latin provides primitives such as join to facilitate writing of complex data-processing programs. Just like Hive, Pig is used to do offline data analysis. The difference between the two is that Hive uses a declarative language of HQL and Pig uses a procedural language of Pig Latin.

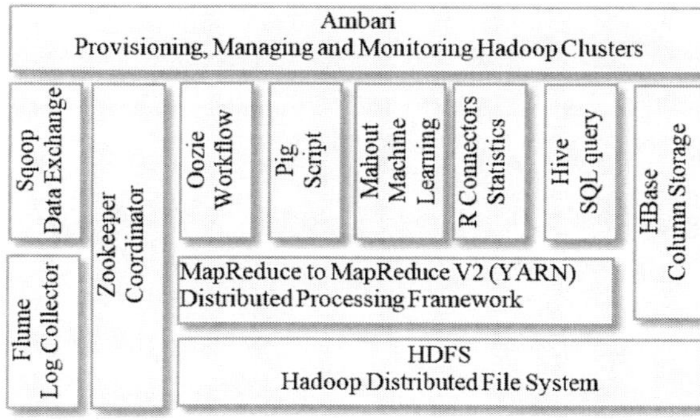

FIGURE 10.6 Apache Hadoop ecosystem.

Flume is a highly scalable, highly reliable, and highly fault-tolerant distributed log data collecting system. It is used to aggregate mass of log data from numerous servers into one big data platform. Flume provides some simple functionalities for log data processing, such as filtering and format conversion. Flume can be configured to write log data to various data sinks (destination).

Sqoop is an abbreviation for "SQL to Hadoop." It is a tool to move data from relational databases or other structured data sources to Hadoop. For example, Sqoop can import data in a MySQL database into Hadoop platform; the data can be imported into raw HDFS files, Hive tables, or HBase tables. On the other hand, Sqoop can also export Hadoop data into a MySQL database. The import/export program is written as a MapReduce program, which can fully leverage the parallel processing capability and high-fault tolerance of the MapReduce computing model.

Mahout is a machine-learning software package on the Hadoop platform. It aims to provide scalable machine-learning algorithms to run on a large cluster to analyze very big data sets. Classical data-mining and machine-learning algorithms such as clustering, classification, collaborative filtering (used in recommendation), and frequent item set mining are implemented.

Oozie is a workflow scheduler system to manage Apache Hadoop jobs. Oozie supports several types of Hadoop jobs such as MapReduce jobs, pig scripts, Hive queries, and Sqoop data import and export jobs. Oozie workflows are triggered by time (frequency) and/or data availability.

Zookeeper is open-source implementation of Google's *Chubby*. Chubby is a distributed lock service. Most distributed applications need common services such as a unified naming service, status synchronization service, central management of configuration data, and cluster management (including management of node's status and notification of data changes on nodes). These services are hard to implement and debug. By using zookeeper, people do not need to reinvent the wheel again and again. By handing such functionalities over to Zookeeper, the complexity of the whole distributed system is reduced. In a distributed system that is composed of a master node and a number of slave nodes, the master node could be the single point of failure. By replacing the master node with a small number of nodes managed by Zookeeper, we can reduce such failures.

10.2.3 Application of Hadoop 1.0 to Various Scenarios

It seems that the MapReduce computing model is too simple; however, it is not that simple. Various data-processing and analytic algorithms have been translated into MapReduce jobs to run on Hadoop to analyze big data sets.

Besides simple SQL summarization, researchers have migrated many complex algorithms onto the Hadoop/MapReduce platform including OLAP, data mining, machine learning, information retrieval, multimedia data processing, science data processing, and graph processing [2]. MapReduce is not only a tool for unstructured data processing, but it can also handle structured data efficiently [3] when the data is organized properly.

10.2.4 Continuous Improvement of Hadoop 1.0

From the advent of Hadoop/MapReduce, researchers from industry and academia have improved Hadoop/MapReduce from many aspects [4–6], including (1) storage layout and data placement optimization, handling of data skew, index support, and data variety support; (2) extension of MapReduce for stream processing, incremental processing, and iterative processing; (3) two-way join, multi-way join, theta join optimization, and parallelization of data-mining/machine-learning algorithms; (4) scheduling strategies for multicore CPU, GPGPU, heterogeneous environment, and cloud; (5) easy-to-use interfaces for SQL query, statistical, data-mining, and machine-learning algorithms, such as Hive, Pig, System ML, and Mahout; and (6) energy saving techniques and privacy and security guarantee techniques.

For example, some researchers of Saarland University believe that by carefully choosing of implementation techniques in Hadoop, they can solve the performance of Hadoop/MapReduce to some extent. They brought forth Hadoop++ [7] and HAIL [8]. Hadoop++ employed the following techniques. (1) *The Hadoop plan*: The team make Hadoop's hard-coded query processing pipeline explicit and represent it as a DB-style physical query plan to reason on it and optimize it. (2) *Trojan index*: At data load time, a read optimized index is created for each split; it is called a Trojan index. The indexes can improve later query performance. Since Trojan indexes are created at data load time, they have no penalty at query time. (3) *Trojan join*: Trojan join co-partitions the data at data load time for later high performance of joining operation. Preliminary results show an improvement of Hadoop++ over Hadoop by up to a factor of 20. HAIL (Hadoop Aggressive Indexing Library) changes the upload pipeline of HDFS in order to create different clustered index for each block replica. HAIL improves both data uploading to HDFS (up to 60% with the replication factor of 3) and the runtime of MapReduce jobs (up to 68× faster than Hadoop).

10.2.5 Merits and Limitations of Hadoop 1.0

The most important merit of Hadoop 1.0 is its scalability. Hadoop has been deployed to large cluster of thousands of nodes in real-life production environment, which cannot be imaged by RDBMS before. Why we need a scalability like this; the reasons include cost and I/O bandwidth.

The first reason is the cost to scale. Hadoop can run on large clusters of commodity hardware to support big data processing. SQL on Hadoop systems are more cost efficient than MPP databases such as Teradata, Vertica, and Netezza, which need to run on expensive high-end servers and do not scale out to thousands of nodes.

The second reason is the I/O bottlenecks. When the volume of data is really big, only some portion of data can be loaded into main memory and the remaining data has to be stored on disks. By spreading I/O onto a large number of nodes, we can speed up data loading and subsequent data processing with a big aggregated I/O bandwidth, which is tens to hundreds times of the I/O bandwidth that only one high-end server can provide.

In 2008, one of Yahoo's Hadoop clusters, which is composed of 910 nodes, sorted 1 terabytes of data in 209 s, setting the new record for the terabyte sort benchmark. The previous record is 297 s. The significance lies in that it is the first time an open-source Java program won the sort benchmark [9].

In March 2011 [10], the Apache Hadoop project was awarded the top prize of MediaGuardian Innovation Awards of the year. The judging panel described the Hadoop project as a "Swiss army knife of the twenty-first century," and it has the potential to change the face of media innovations. The Hadoop platform has become the de facto standard tool for big data processing, and the important role it plays has been recognized by more and more people.

Although Hadoop has achieved a great success in handling big data, it has some major limitations, which hinder it from being a tool for diverse applications. For Hadoop 1.0, there are two major limitations. (1) It only supports one computing model, that is, MapReduce. The MapReduce computing model has limited expressive capability. It is not straightforward to express a complex data-processing work in a single MapReduce job; such work has to be translated into a series of MapReduce jobs, which are run one after another. (2) The fact that the intermediate results are persisted to disks has a big negative impact on system performance; it is hard to further cut down the response time of queries.

10.3 HADOOP 2.0 AND SPARK

10.3.1 Business Requirements

Because Hadoop has shown its potential of processing very big data sets, people hope that all data, whether it is structured or unstructured, or wherever it comes from, could be consolidated in one place. After various types of data are in one place, one needs various data-processing methods to analyze these data of different types.

Hadoop is a tool for batch processing of big volume of data. It is designed to process the data with an as high as possible throughput. However, there is an emerging need for interactive query, which Hadoop 1.0 could not support. The MapReduce computing model of Hadoop 1.0 is also not well suited for iterative processing of data, which is required in machine learning. The reasons have been mentioned in the above section, that is, the overhead of launching multiple jobs and materializing intermediate results to the file system.

10.3.2 Introduction to the Hadoop 2.0 Ecosystem

Since there is a need that Hadoop could support different processing models on one platform, developers of the Hadoop project introduced Hadoop 2.0 (or Yet Another Resource Negotiator, YARN in short) [11,12], which won best paper award on Symposium of Cloud Computing in 2013. YARN separates the MapReduce computing model from resource management functionality, which are tied together in Hadoop 1.0.

Now several data-processing models can work side by side on top of YARN, including traditional MapReduce job for batch processing, Tez for interactive processing, Spark for in-memory iterative processing, Storm for real-time stream processing, and GraphLab/Giraph for graph processing, as shown in Figure 10.7. In all, YARN has taken Hadoop from a batch-processing tool to a tool for more diverse data-processing applications, including interactive queries.

Figure 10.8 shows major components of Hadoop 2.0 runtime and the workflow of job scheduling. The ResourceManager and NodeManagers form the data-processing framework. The ResourceManager running on the Master node, together with NodeManagers running on Slave nodes, takes charge of running distributed applications. On the Hadoop 2.0 platform, an application can be a MapReduce job, a Hive query, a Pig script, or a Giraph query.

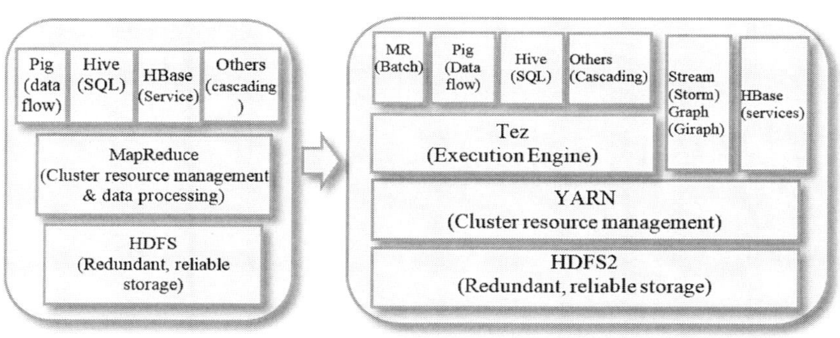

FIGURE 10.7 From Hadoop 1.0 to Hadoop 2.0.

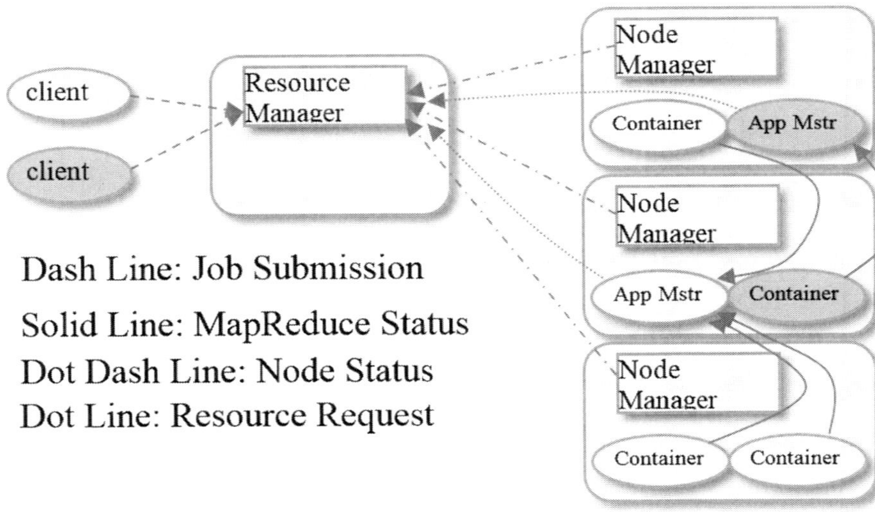

FIGURE 10.8 Components of Hadoop 2.0 runtime and job scheduling.

ResourceManager is the highest authority to allocate resources for all applications. It is composed of two main components, that is, a Scheduler and an ApplicationsManager. The Scheduler is responsible for allocating resources to various running applications subject to constraints of capacities, queues, etc. It performs the scheduling function based on resource requirements of the applications and constraints. Hadoop uses resource containers to organize necessary resources (CPU, memory, etc.) to run tasks of applications.

The ApplicationsManager accepts job submissions, negotiates the first container for executing the per-application specific ApplicationMaster, and provides the service for restarting the ApplicationMaster container on failures. The per-application ApplicationMaster negotiates resource containers for the application from the Scheduler of the ResourceManager and works with the NodeManagers to execute applications and track their status and monitor their progress.

A NodeManager running on a slave node launches containers for applications, monitors its resource usage (including CPU, Memory, disks, network bandwidth usages), and reports the information to ResourceManager.

Compared with Hadoop 1.0, Hadoop 2.0 has several advantages, including the following aspects. (1) *Higher scalability*: The ResourceManager focuses on scheduling of resources, and it can easily manage a very larger cluster up to tens of thousands of nodes, thus Hadoop 2.0 could achieve higher scalability than Hadoop 1.0. (2) *Resource use efficiency*: The ResourceManager could optimize resource usage according to per-application resource requirements, fairness, service level agreements, etc., thus improving resource use efficiency. (3) *Diverse workloads*: Besides MapReduce jobs (primary for batch processing), YARN supports more programming models, including graph data processing, iterative processing, real-time stream data processing, and interactive query. Machine-learning algorithms usually need several iteration of processing over the data to get the final results. (4) *Flexibility*: Hadoop 2.0 provides backward compatibility; MapReduce programs written for Hadoop 1.0 could directly run on YARN without any modifications. Programming models such as MapReduce can evolve independently.

10.3.2.1 Tez

To address the shortcoming of high latency of Hadoop/MapReduce, Hortonworks has proposed Tez as an Apache Incubator project. Tez is a highly efficient and scalable execution engine that can be easily leveraged by existing tools such as Hive, Pig, or Cascading to run faster (Figure 10.7). Tez runs on Hadoop 2.0 YARN [13–16].

The Tez project is aimed at building a framework, which supports processing the data with a complex directed acyclic graph (DAG) of tasks. A DAG defines the data flow of an application. Vertices represent data-processing tasks and reflect some of the business logic that transforms and/or analyzes the data. Edges represent movement of data.

Tez models each vertex as a composition of *Input*, *Processor*, and *Output* modules. Input and Output determine the data format and how and where it is read from/written to. An input represents a pipe through which a processor can accept input data from a data source such as HDFS or the output generated by another vertex, while an output represents a pipe through which a Processor can generate output data for another vertex to consume or to a data sink such as HDFS. Processor holds the data transformation logic, which consumes one or more Inputs and produces one or more Outputs. Users can plug in input, processing, and output logic into vertexes and then build a DAG to perform arbitrary data-processing works.

Tez runtime automatically maps a DAG onto physical resources, parallelizes the logic, and executes it in Hadoop. Tez expands the logical graph into a physical graph by adding parallelism at the vertices; that is, multiple tasks are created per logical vertex to perform the computation in parallel. A logical edge in a DAG is also materialized as a number of physical connections between the tasks of two connected vertices.

With the expressive capability of DAG, some works took multiple MapReduce jobs, now can be a single job. An example is given as follows. The following Hive statement joins three tables and computes some aggregations.

```
SELECT a.state, COUNT (*), AVERAGE(c.price)
FROM a
JOIN b ON (a.id = b.id)
JOIN c ON (a.itemId = c.itemId)
GROUP BY a.state
```

In Hive, the statement is translated into several MapReduce jobs, which run one after another; Figure 10.9a depicts the execution flow of the MapReduce jobs. In Tez, the statement is translated into only one job expressed in a DAG as depicted in Figure 10.9b. We can see from the figure that, to run the statement above, Tez requires fewer jobs (1 vs. 3) and no IO synchronization barriers (provided via HDFS for the MR jobs) are required.

By executing series of MR tasks in a single job, and by eliminating unnecessary tasks, synchronization barriers, and reads from and writes to HDFS, Tez speeds up data processing across both small-scale and low-latency, and large-scale and high-throughput workloads. Tez can speed up Pig and Hive workloads by an order of magnitude. It is the basis for Hive 1.3 (Stinger).

One of the unique features of Tez is the ability to dynamically optimize the DAG execution. Tez allows users to plug in vertex management modules to collect runtime information and change the dataflow graph dynamically to optimize performance and resource utilization.

The vertex state machine invokes the user module at significant transition points such as vertex start, source task completion, etc. At these points, the user logic can examine the runtime state and provide hints to the main Tez execution engine to decide runtime attributes such as task parallelism of vertex.

10.3.3 Introduction to the Spark Ecosystem

Apache Spark is a powerful big data-processing tool, with rich functionalities such as machine learning, real-time stream processing, and graph computations. Since first introduced in 2010 by University of California at Berkeley, Spark and its ecosystem [17] have grown to be an alternative

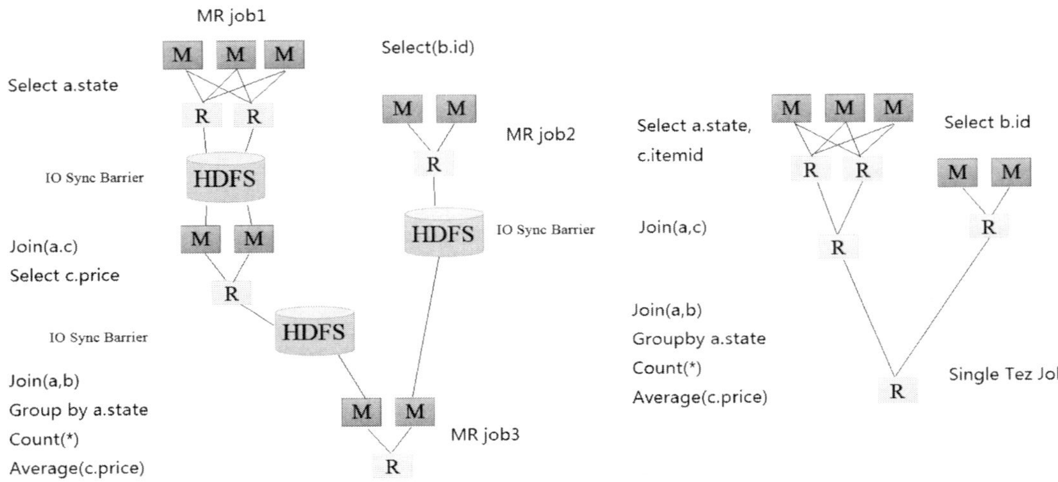

FIGURE 10.9 (a) MapReduce jobs. (b) Tez job.

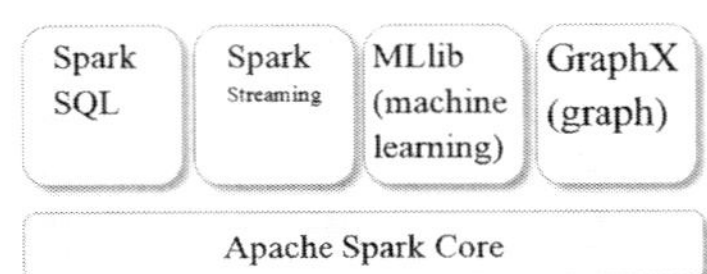

FIGURE 10.10 Spark ecosystem and components.

of Hadoop ecosystem, not only as a component of the Hadoop platform. Now, the largest known cluster of Apache Spark has more than 8000 nodes.

The Spark ecosystem consists of several components, including Spark Core, Spark SQL, Spark Streaming, MLlib, and GraphX, as depicted in Figure 10.10.

The Spark Core component is the cornerstone for parallel and distributed processing of large data sets. Spark Core is responsible for all basic I/O functionalities, scheduling and monitoring the jobs on clusters, dispatching tasks, accessing to different storage systems, memory management, and fault recovery.

The Spark SQL component is a library riding on top of Apache Spark. Users and developers can leverage the power of declarative queries and optimized storage to run SQL queries on data, which is stored in RDDs (Resilient Distributed Datasets, will be introduced later) format. Data from various sources such as JSON, Parquet, or Hive can be extracted, transformed, and loaded into Spark as RDDs. After that, users can run ad hoc SQL queries to retrieve interesting results.

Spark Streaming is a light-weight API that allows developers to perform streaming analytics by ingesting data in mini-batches. Transformations are applied on mini-batches of data. Spark Streaming consumes data from various data sources and live streams such as Twitter, Apache Kafka, IOT sensors, and Apache Flume. The component has potential applications in log processing, intrusion detection, fraud detection, online advertisements and campaigns, supply chain management, etc.

To extract valuable information from big data sets, there is an increasing need for analyzing large data sets with complex machine-learning algorithms to extract deep insights. MLlib is a low-level machine-learning library on Spark platform. It can be called from Scala, Python, and Java programming languages. MLlib eases the development of scalable machine-learning pipelines. Commonly used machine learning and data-mining algorithms have been implemented in MLlib, including clustering, classification, decomposition, regression, and collaborative filtering.

GraphX is an API on top of Apache Spark for graph data processing. Spark GraphX introduces Resilient Distributed Graph (RDG, an abstraction of Spark RDDs), which associates records with the vertices and edges of a graph. RDG helps data analysts perform graph operations through various expressive primitives. Developers can use these primitives to implement graph data analysis algorithms such as *PageRank*, in a few lines of code. The GraphX component supports many use cases such as recommendation and fraud detection.

The Spark Core component makes use of a special data structure known as RDD. RDDs are immutable, partitioned collection of records that can be operated on in parallel. Since RDD is immutable, it has no overhead related to synchronization. Any kind of data can be put in RDDs. RDDs are usually created by either transforming existing RDDs or by loading an external data set from HDFS or HBase.

10.3.3.1 Resilient Distributed Dataset

RDD is designed to keep the whole data set in memory for faster computation (since the data can be accessed with lower latency), which is beneficial to data-processing work of iterative style, such as machine-learning algorithms. RDD uses a unique lineage-based technique to provide fault-tolerance guarantee. When some downstream RDD is lost due to failures, it can be re-constructed from upstream RDD by applying transformations between the two RDDs in the DAG, which described the logic of the data-processing flow. Basically, the re-construction of lost partition is exactly the same as the lazy evaluation of the DAG (will be introduced later).

By keeping the data in memory, Spark has avoided the overhead of I/O operations related to writing the intermediate results to disks and reading the data back from disks, which has been the pain point of Hadoop/MapReduce. When the memory is not sufficient to keep the whole RDD, Spark will perform the eviction based on an LRU (Least Recently Used) strategy.

Typically, an application logic expressed in a sequence of operations on RDDs includes *transformation* and *action*. Transformations are coarse-grained operations such as join, union, filter, or map on existing RDDs, which produce a new RDD. Actions are operations such as count, first, and reduce, which returns some values after being applied to existing RDDs.

All transformations are lazy, which means that Spark will not execute them immediately, but tracks all the transformations to be applied to upstream RDDs, tracing back the dependencies on what parent RDD is needed and then eventually track all the way to the source node of a DAG. Activation of actions, which starts from the leaf node of a DAG, will trigger downstream transformations first and upstream transformations later on RDDs.

Data processing works can be expressed in a series of transformations and actions on RDDs; the former tells how to generate a new RDD from an old RDD by some operations and the latter specifies how to generate the final result. RDD, transformations and actions together, constitutes a DAG.

A realistic DAG looks like the one shown in Figure 10.11. Some data files in HDFS are loaded into two RDDs. Then a series of transformations (map, flatMap, filter, groupBy, join, etc.) are run against the RDDs one by one. After one transformation is run against an RDD, a new RDD is generated. Then the next transformation will be run against the newly generated RDD to generate another new RDD, etc. Finally, an action (count, collect, save, take) is invoked on the last RDD, and the final result is generated and written to storage devices.

There are two forms of dependencies between partitions of a child RDD and a parent RDD (please refer to Figure 10.12). Narrow dependency means that each partition of the parent RDD is used by at most one partition of the child RDD. Wide dependency means that multiple child partitions may depend on one partition of the parent RDD. Operations such as group-by-keys, reduce-by-keys, and sort-by-keys need wide dependency to achieve correct results. The processing of narrow dependency (generating child RDD from parent RDD) can be done within a machine without data shuffling across network. However, wide dependencies involve data shuffling.

The DAGScheduler is the scheduling layer of Spark that implements stage-oriented scheduling. The basic concepts of the DAGScheduler are jobs and stages. A job is a top-level work item submitted

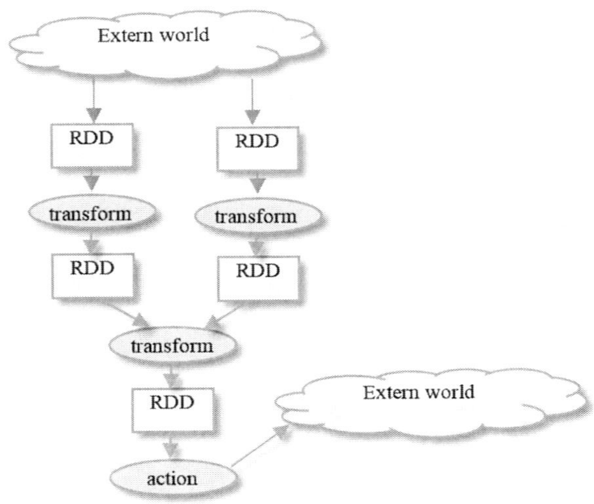

FIGURE 10.11 Typical DAG of RDDs.

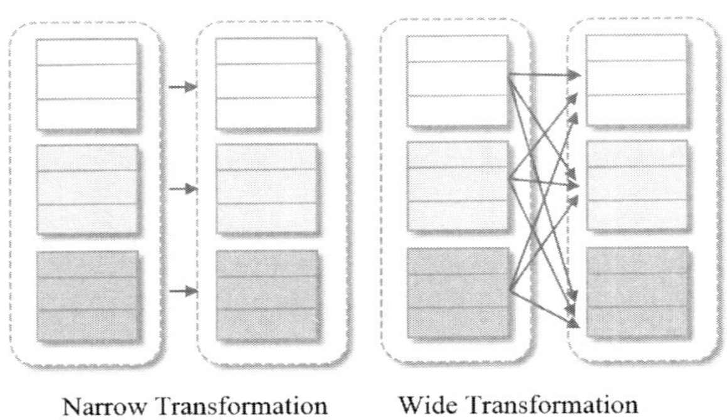

FIGURE 10.12 Narrow dependency and wide dependency.

to DAGScheduler to compute the result of an action. A job ends with a single final RDD. A stage is a set of parallel tasks, one per partition of an RDD, that compute partial results as part of a Spark job. It is a unit of data processing.

The DAGScheduler will examine the type of dependencies and group the narrow dependency RDDs into a stage. Wide dependencies will span across consecutive stages within the execution flow. Figure 10.13 shows a job and its corresponding stages that joins two tables and performs aggregation.

The DAGScheduler generates a DAG of stages for each job, keeps track of which RDDs and stage outputs are materialized, and finds a minimal schedule to run jobs. It then submits stages to TaskScheduler to run.

DAGScheduler also determines the preferred locations to run each task on, based on the current cache status (some partitions of an RDD are cached in memory), and hands over the information to TaskScheduler. Furthermore, DAGScheduler handles failures due to shuffle output files being lost, in which case old stages may need to be resubmitted. Failures within a stage that are not caused by shuffle file loss are handled by the TaskScheduler itself, which will retry each task a small number of times before cancelling the whole stage.

10.3.3.2 DataFrame

DataFrame adds an abstraction layer on RDD for Spark SQL. In the earlier versions of Spark SQL, DataFrame was named SchemaRDD. Basically, a SchemaRDD is an RDD with a layer of schema on

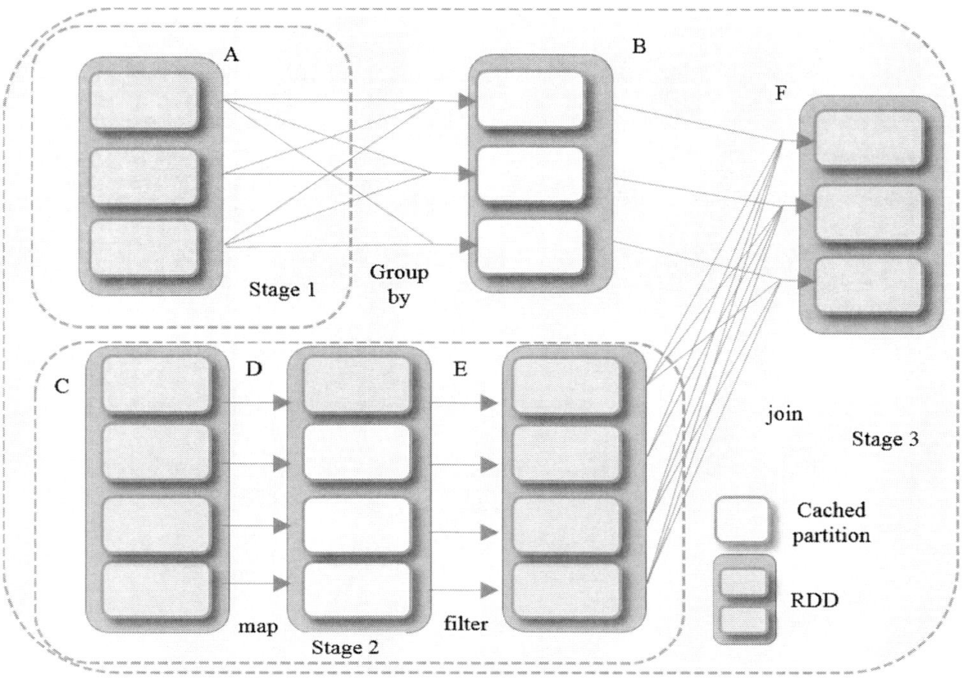

FIGURE 10.13 Job and corresponding stages.

top, which gives formal names and data types to different columns in the data set. The DataFrame API evaluates operations in a lazy manner to provide support for relational optimizations and optimization of the whole data-processing workflow. Programmers can integrate procedural and relational processing by calling DataFrame API in Scala or Java program.

10.3.4 Performance of Spark

10.3.4.1 Performance of Shark (Spark SQL) for SQL Queries

AMP Lab of University of California at Berkley has drawn workloads and queries from Reference 18 to provide quantitative and qualitative comparisons of five systems, including Redshift, Hive (v0.12), Shark, Impala (v1.2.3), and Stinger/Tez (v0.2.0).

Redshift is an MPP database offered by Amazon.com based on the ParAccel data warehouse. Shark is a predecessor of Spark SQL, a Hive-compatible SQL engine running on top of Spark Core. Impala from Cloudera is a Hive-compatible SQL engine with its own MPP-like execution engine.

The data set contains three tables. The *Ranking* table stores Web sites and their page ranks. The *UserVisits* table stores server logs for each Web page. And the *Documents* table stores unstructured HTML pages. There are four queries in the workload. Query 1 (a scan query) and Query 2 (an aggregation query) are exploratory SQL queries. Query 3 is a join query with a small result set. Query 4 is a bulk UDF query. It calculates a simplified version of PageRank using a sample of the Common Crawl (http://commoncrawl.org/) data set.

For Query 1 (scan query), when the data set can be kept in memory, Spark outperforms other systems for all selectivity. For Query 2 (aggregation query), Spark running on in-memory data set achieves higher performance than other systems except RedShift.

For Query 3 (join query), when the selectivity is low, Spark achieves similar response times to Redshift and Impala (in-memory means the data set is resident in memory), and outperforms

TABLE 10.1
Median Response Times of Query 3 for Different Systems (Settings)/Selectivity (Seconds)

System (Setting)	Version	Query 3A 485,312 Rows (Low Selectivity)	Query 3B 53,332,015 Rows (Median Selectivity)	Query 3C 533,287,121 Rows (High Selectivity)
Redshift (HDD)	Current	33.29	46.08	168.25
Impala—Disk	1.2.3	108.68	129.815	431.26
Impala—Mem	1.2.3	41.21	76.005	386.6
Shark—Disk	0.8.1	111.7	135.6	382.6
Shark—Mem	0.8.1	44.7	67.3	318
Hive—YARN	0.12	561.14	717.56	2374.17
Tez	0.2.0	323.06	402.33	1361.9

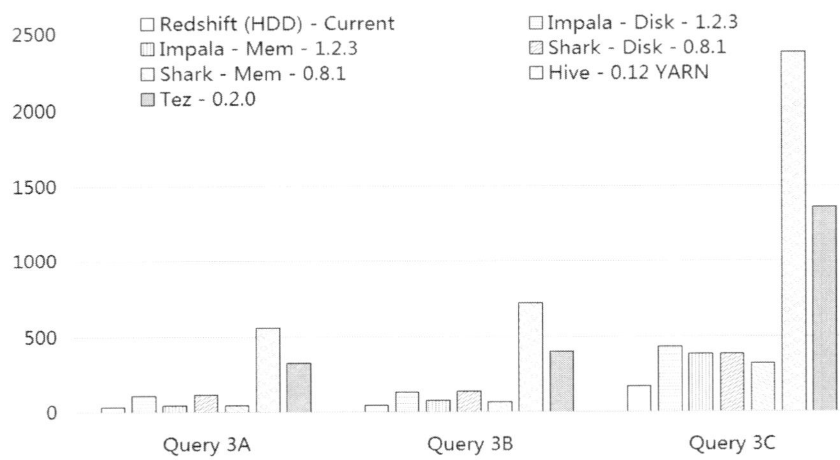

FIGURE 10.14 Median response times of Query 3 for different systems (settings)/selectivity.

other systems. When the selectivity is higher, Spark (in-memory) outperforms other systems or settings except Redshift, which always outperforms Spark. For Query 4 (query with UDFs), Spark (in-memory) outperforms Hive and Tez by a large margin. Table 10.1 and Figure 10.14 show the results of the join query (Query 3) on different systems. Readers can refer to Reference 19 for more benchmark results.

From the results above, we can see that Shark (now Spark SQL) is a very competitive one among currently available big data-processing systems for structured data.

10.3.4.2 Performance of Spark for Machine-Learning Algorithms

Designers of Spark [20] have also compared the performance of the logistic regression implementation on Spark platform to an implementation for Hadoop, using a 29-GB data set on 20 "m1. xlarge" EC2 (Amazon Elastic Compute Cloud) nodes with four cores each.

The results are shown in Figure 10.15. With Hadoop, each iteration takes 127 s, because it runs as an independent MapReduce job. With Spark, the first iteration takes 174 s, which they think the reason is due to using Scala instead of Java, but subsequent iterations take only 6 s, because the cached data can be reused. This allows the job to run up to 10× faster.

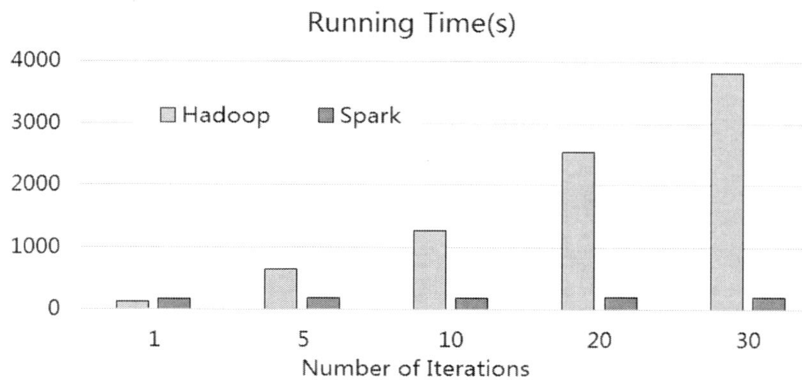

FIGURE 10.15 Logistic regression performance in Hadoop and Spark.

10.3.4.3 Awards That Spark Received

Spark has officially won the Daytona GraySort contest (http://sortbenchmark.org/) in 2014 [21]. People of Databricks sorted 100 TB of data on disk in 23 min, using Spark on 206 EC2 machines. The previous world record set by Hadoop/MapReduce used 2100 machines and took 72 min. The result showed that Spark could sort the same amount of data faster (3× faster) and use less hardware resources (10× fewer machines). All the sorting work took place on disk (HDFS), without using Spark's in-memory cache.

Winning the benchmark is a prominent milestone for Spark. The sorting results demonstrate that Spark can handle data set of very big size, from GBs to TBs. Databricks has enhanced the Spark platform with new techniques, including sort-based shuffle, a new Netty-based transport module, and external shuffle service, which make the winning of the benchmark possible.

Although no official PB sort competition exists, Databricks also sorted 1 PB (10 trillion records) of data on 190 machines and released the result; they took less than 4 h. The PB time is over 4× faster than previously reported result based on Hadoop/MapReduce, which took 16 h on 3800 machines.

People from Spark community and Databricks company continuously improve Spark from many aspects, including scalability, reliability, and performance. Now all Spark operators can do external (disk) operations when the whole data set cannot fit into memory, and the operators are a superset of map and reduce, which make writing complex data-processing program more convenient. The result of 1 PB sorting shows that Spark is able to process data sets bigger than the aggregate memory of the whole cluster.

Table 10.2 shows some settings in sorting and some performance metrics achieved. The results are compared with the results of earlier record Hadoop/MapReduce had made.

10.3.5 Hadoop and Spark: Coexist or Compete?

Both Hadoop and Spark can manage data sets of very big sizes and provide similar analytic functionalities over the data. Naturally, one question is coming into the minds of people. The two platforms will coexist or compete with each other, and finally who can win?

Spark has not implemented its own file systems and storage formats (RDD is a memory-oriented storage format). It relies on distributed file systems such as HDFS and storage formats such as parquet (a columnar file format for query-intensive data warehouse applications). Except that, Spark can run in a standalone mode without any more dependency on the Hadoop platform.

Spark aims to become a unified data hub, which not only processes native data sets (in-memory RDDs loaded from disk-resident parquet files), but also accepts data from any sources, including RDBMS such as MySQL, stream processing systems such as Storm, message queues such as Kafka,

TABLE 10.2
Comparison of Hadoop and Spark 100 TB Sorting Results

	Items	Hadoop MR Record	Spark Record	Spark 1 PB
Configuration	# Nodes	2100	206	190
	# Cores	50,400 physical nodes	6592 virtualized nodes	6080 virtualized nodes
	Cluster disk throughput	3150 GB/s (est.)	618 GB/s	570 GB/s
	Network	Dedicated data center, 10 Gbps	Virtualized (EC2) 10 Gbps network	Virtualized (EC2) 10 Gbps network
Results	Data size	102.5 TB	100 TB	1000 TB
	Elapsed time	72 min	23 min	234 min
	Sort rate	1.42 TB/min	4.27 TB/min	4.27 TB/min
	Sort rate/node	0.67 GB/min	20.7 GB/min	22.5 GB/min
	Sort Benchmark Daytona Rules	Yes	Yes	No

Source: From Reynold Xin. Spark the fastest open source engine for sorting a petabyte. https://databricks.com/blog/2014/11/05/spark-officially-sets-a-new-record-in-large-scale-sorting.html, 2014.

and other big data systems such as Hive and HBase. People can join data sets from various sources (e.g., joining Spark native RDD data sets loaded from HDFS files and data sets fetched from an RDBMS) and pump the data into a processing pipeline, which completely runs inside the Spark framework.

On the other hand, YARN takes Hadoop from a batch-processing tool to an interactive one. By separating the resource management functionality from programming models, the Hadoop 2.0 platform supports various applications, including batch MapReduce jobs, interactive queries, iterative machine-learning algorithms, stream data processing, and graph data processing. Spark can be embedded into Hadoop platform as an application to provide interactive query processing capabilities.

From above description, we can see that there is functionality overlapping and inter-dependency between the two platforms. The two platforms and their ecosystems will coexist and evolve forward to more advanced tools.

However, one thing could not be denied. The two platforms will compete with each other. Besides achieving higher performance than Hadoop in many application scenarios, Spark can now process very big data sets up to PBs, which is the strength of Hadoop traditionally.

Spark gains many attractions over Hadoop. For example, Mahout, a machine-learning library for Hadoop since 2009, has been moved on top of Spark for higher performance. In early version of Mahout, machine-learning algorithms are implemented as MapReduce programs, which run inefficiently due to the limitation of MapReduce computing model. In 2014, the Mahout community decided to move Mahout codebase onto other data-processing systems. It would no longer accept Hadoop MapReduce code and completely switched new development to Spark. However, MapReduce algorithms already in the codebase are kept there and maintained by the community. The reason to move Mahout to Spark is that Spark provides a more flexible program model and a more efficient execution engine.

The community of Mahout project reworks Mahout to leverage in-memory data-processing capability of Spark for higher performance. Now, Mahout is refactored to be a more general library, not only running on Spark, but also on other data-processing systems, such as H2O engine. H2O was developed separately by a startup called 0xdata. It is an in-memory data engine specifically designed for running various types of machine learning and statistical workloads on data stored in the HDFS at scale.

However, the Hadoop community also continuously improves Hadoop to support low-latency queries, which is the strength of Spark platform. The two platforms will compete and coexist for a long time. People will not abandon Hadoop entirely because it is still a great tool for storing lots and lots of data, and some people still use MapReduce for batch processing of data.

After adding the capability of interactive query to Hive by designing and implementing of Tez, Hortonworks unveiled a new strategy called Stinger. Next [22] will rework Hive to handle read/write transactions, support the full set of SQL, and provide sub second response times. They also try to integrate Hive and Apache Spark so that the former can handle machine-learning jobs. A more powerful Hive will be appealing to lots of users who have been using Hive for a long time and are not willing to transfer to a completely new technology such as Spark.

10.3.6 Hadoop/Spark's Role in Future Big Data Warehouses

Both Hadoop and Spark can place a central role in future generation of big data warehouses. Databases such as VoltDB/Sap HANA can manage data marts and support real-time queries over analytic results on the edge of a data center. There are three symbiosis scenarios, that is, *Hadoop dominant*, *Spark dominant*, and *Coexist* (please refer to Figure 10.16).

In a Hadoop dominant scenario, Hadoop is the final backend to consolidate all data in one place. The data can be structured, semistructured, or unstructured. Over the Hadoop platform, people can

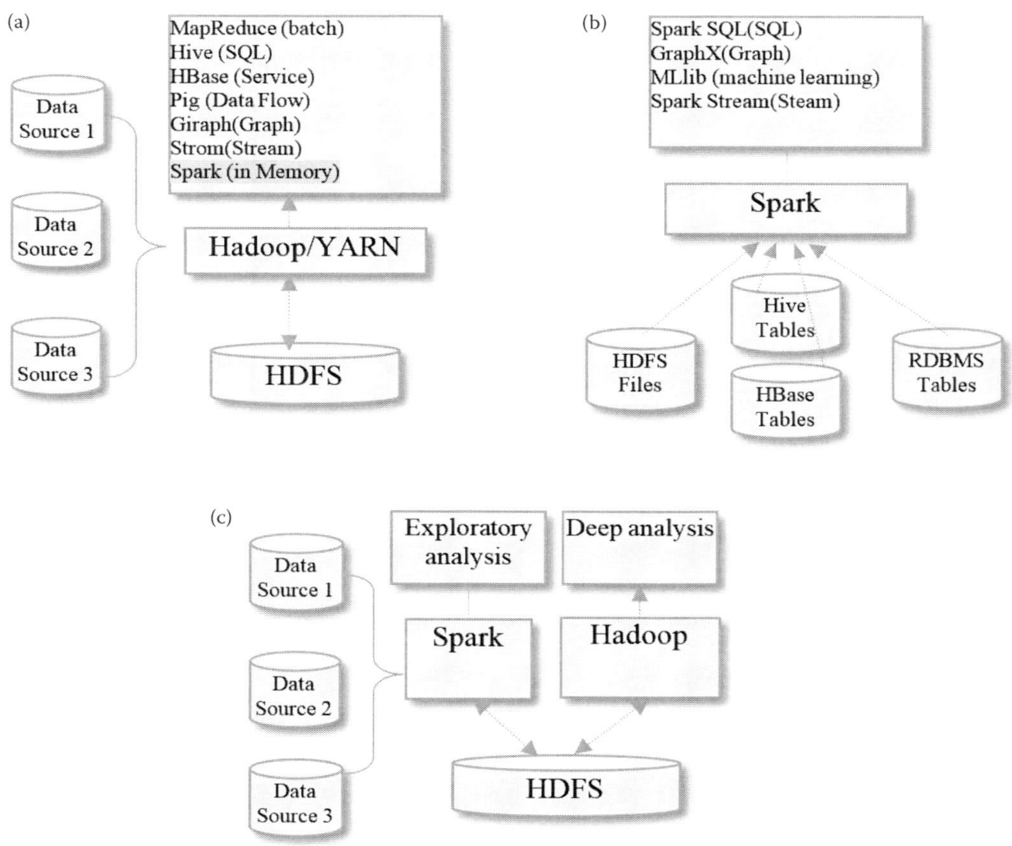

FIGURE 10.16 Role of Hadoop and Spark in future generation of data warehouses. (a) Hadoop dominant. (b) Spark dominant. (c) Coexist.

perform various analytics over different data sets, including simple statistics and complex machine-learning and data-mining algorithms. In this scenario, Spark can be a component of Hadoop platform to provide in-memory processing of moderate-sized data sets.

However, Spark does not want to be only a component of other frameworks. The community of Spark is trying to make Spark a fully functional framework. It can also play a dominant role in the next generation of data warehouses. Spark will act as a data hub, receives data from various sources, including streaming sources, files, and other RDBMS, and pumps the data through an analytic pipeline. It is the final place to gather all related data for people to derive insights. Spark can extract data from Hadoop, such as data in HDFS, Hive table, and HBase table. Although Spark can run over YARN of Hadoop 2.0, it is Spark that rules all, not Hadoop.

In the above two scenarios, Hadoop and Spark both try to embrace the other into its arms.

In the third scenario, data is sent to Spark first, and people do some exploratory analysis over subset of data on Spark. And then, all data is handed over to Hadoop for further deep analysis. Deep analysis needs data that spans a longer period of time, thus taking more time to finish. Spark and Hadoop are used together by leveraging their strengths for different stages of data processing.

10.4 CONCLUSIONS

10.4.1 Business Requirements Drive Innovations

The capacity of storage devices is increasing, while the price is going down, making collecting and saving data sets of very big sizes possible. In old days, when people have some data, they resort to database (specifically RDBMS). RDBMSs become a "one size fits all" tool. Now people have really big data sets in hand, but they lack proper tools to process the data. Traditional RDBMS could not handle data sets of very big sizes due its scalability limitation. The requirements of people to derive insights from big data sets give the birth to tools such as Hadoop and Spark.

Hadoop 1.0 is a tool that mimics MapReduce technology of Google. It is a batch-processing tool from the very beginning of design. However, people are eager to get the results earlier for fast decision making; there is a demand for lower latency for data-processing works including exploratory analysis and machine learning. Timeliness of analysis (latency) is becoming the pain point of Hadoop 1.0.

Spark was born to meet such requirements with its in-memory processing design principle. By keeping the data set in the aggregate memory of a cluster, Spark can process big data sets and achieve fast response times. In the new version of Spark, operators can also operate on disk-resident data too, which makes Spark a strong competitor of Hadoop.

However, Hadoop has evolved into Hadoop 2.0 with a cleaner architecture, which separates resource management and programming models. It has become a more powerful tool; it can process more data types and provide lower latency.

In all, the requirements of timely analysis of big data sets drive these innovations. We can see that the two camps inspire each other, limitations of Hadoop 1.0 spark the enthusiasm of some researchers to develop Spark, and higher performance of Spark spurs the evolution of Hadoop.

10.4.2 Lessons That Database Research Community and Database Industry Should Have Learned

In early days, some people have criticized the over-simplicity, programming at very low level, and low performance of Hadoop/MapReduce. However, for really big data sets, which could not be handled by traditional RDBMSs, people can only rely on Hadoop/MapReduce. More and more people use Hadoop, and it became more and more popular. Hadoop has become a standard tool for big data processing.

We can recall that in early days of RDBMS when relational systems were first introduced, hierarchical (IMS) and network (IDMS) database camps argued that relational systems were much inferior and could not provide good enough performance. Over time, these arguments turned out to be false (http://www.b-eye-network.com/view/10786). Researchers and developers of RDBMS have brought out optimization techniques for efficient execution of transactions, as well as other techniques to make RDBMS a reliable and high-performance database for vast number of operational and analytical applications.

RDBMS has become a big success, and it is the dominant technology in the database market and fosters several big companies such as Oracle and TeraData. History repeats itself again and again. In early days of Hadoop/MapReduce, there is a debate [23] around Hadoop/MapReduce whether it is an innovation or a major step backward. Time has passed, and the big success of Hadoop/MapReduce may have given an answer to the debate.

Hadoop is a tool, and so is Spark, just like RDBMS is a tool. RDBMSs are suitable for data management requirements of OLTP applications, while Hadoop or Spark is a proper tool for big data processing; it can process any type of data and it supports batch processing as well as interactive analysis. Different jobs need different tools. Hadoop (and the MapReduce programing model) has its merits, including lower cost than proprietary tools, highly scalability, and highly reliability. Hadoop/MapReduce is an innovative tool. When Spark breaks the establishment of Hadoop in big data-processing domain, people are more careful and no one denies advancement of Spark over Hadoop; we hear no criticism this time.

Hadoop and Spark were not born from traditional database research community or database companies. The first paper of MapReduce was not published on a database conference.

Some people from database research community overemphasized the limitations of Hadoop/MapReduce, and they are blind to its merits. They are unwilling to admit disruptiveness of the technology, even after they see the increasing popularity of Hadoop/MapReduce. Some companies have looked down on Hadoop/MapReduce or ignored it in early days. There are some lessons for the database research community and database companies to learn.

The penetration power of new data-processing technologies is so powerful that no vendors can resist the popularity of Hadoop and continue to reject it. EMC, formerly not as a database vendor, became a strong player in the market overnight through acquiring Greenplum, which has combined scalability of MapReduce and high performance of PostgreSQL (an open-source RDBMS). The coming of EMC into the database market, just like throwing a stone into the water, breaks the calmness and forces traditional database vendors to rethink their attitudes toward new technologies such as Hadoop and Spark. To maintain its leadership in the market, TeraData acquired AsterData company to obtain the AsterData database, which used MapReduce-style parallelization to enrich its product line. Oracle, a leader in traditional database market, looked down on and rejected Hadoop/MapReduce before 2011, finally published its *Big Plan*, which incorporated NoSQL and Hadoop into its software line in late 2011. Microsoft rejected Hadoop/MapReduce in 2009, and in 2012 due to more and more popularity and success of Hadoop, it closed its Dryad project and hugged Hadoop [24].

Popularity instead of dying out of Hadoop/MapReduce and 180° turning around of Oracle and Microsoft's attitude toward Hadoop/MapReduce can tell something.

Microsoft is an interesting company. When Netscape grabbed most of the market share of WWW browser, Microsoft provided Internet Explorer for free. When Real player began to gain attraction in the audio and video streaming market, Microsoft provided similar product of Media Tools almost for free. When Java became a popular programming language, Microsoft delivered C# language on the .Net platform, which is very similar to Java. When Apple Siri became a popular digital assistant on iPhone, Microsoft brought out Cortana on Windows. Microsoft succeeded to some extent in all above cases to compete with other products. When Hadoop became a standard tool for big data processing, Microsoft introduced Dryad, which is also a parallel computing framework to process big data. This time the outcome is somewhat different.

Dryad adopts the concept of DAG to express complex data-processing work. In a DAG, each vertex is a program and edges represent data channels, which can be files, TPC pipes, or shared memory FIFO queues. Due to the huge popularity of Hadoop/MapReduce, Microsoft discontinued the development of Dryad and shifted its focus to Hadoop framework in 2011 as mentioned above.

In our opinion, Dryad may have been an alternative to Hadoop/MapReduce. In recent several years after Microsoft abandoned Dryad, Apache Hadoop community picked up the basic idea of Dryad and developed Apache Tez, a new runtime framework on YARN to provide interactive query capability. DAG is also one of basic concepts and techniques on which Spark is based; other techniques include in-memory data sets, lineage-based fault-tolerance guarantee, etc. The Spark community has developed Spark into a reliable and high-performance big data platform, which not only challenges Hadoop, but also, together with Hadoop, challenges traditional databases; they are not friends but foes [25]. Who knows whether it is a wrong decision for Microsoft not to insist on developing Dryad to be a general and high-performance big data framework?

Basically, traditional databases such as Oracle, IBM DB2, Microsoft SQL Server, TeraData, MySQL, and PostgreSQL, and new tools such as Hadoop and Spark do the same thing, that is, data management and data analysis. New tools have begun to eat up some market shares of traditional databases, challenging heavy weight companies such as Oracle and TeraData, just as reported in *Wall Street Journal* [26]. Hadoop and Spark are disruptive innovations, and they are breaking the monopoly of traditional technologies, specifically RDBMS. It is one of the reasons that Hadoop received criticism, because Hadoop has become a stronger and stronger competitor and may one day come in the center of stages in many application scenarios.

10.4.2.1 Lesson 1: Standing Up to New Requirements

What lessons database vendors should have learned? One important lesson is that vendors should have really cared about customers and listened to them. Customers need some software that is scalable, they want to enjoy higher performance at lower cost, they have many types of data to process, and the data size is really big.

The basic requirement is that they want to run some low-cost software on low-cost clusters to get big data analysis work done. Traditional databases fall short of the expectation. Database vendors and the database research community enjoy the big success of traditional database technology and react somehow slowly to new requirements of people in the new era.

Though not all database vendors are slow, IBM moves fast in the big data era. When Hadoop began to attract huge attention, IBM has integrated Hadoop into its analytic software stack. IBM had done the right thing to meet customer's requirements.

Since RDBMS had become a dominant technology in database market, people from traditional database community and traditional database vendors naturally dislike something with a NoSQL label. Successes of new tools such as Hadoop and Spark have pushed them to become more acute, not to be indulged in old success any more. Hadoop and Spark do not mean to be a friend of traditional databases. They are alternatives; they are replacements; they are competitors; and they are game changers.

Hadoop is designed for management and processing of hundreds of TB or even tens of PB of data. When the volume of data is merely tens of TB, performance of the old version of Hive is much inferior to MPP database and people use a hybrid architecture to handle the big data. Some recent data is stored in an MPP database for higher performance of processing, and all data is consolidated in Hadoop for later batch processing. Now the situation is changing; new execution engine such as *Tez of Hadoop* or *Spark* can achieve much higher performance, and it is possible to build the whole data warehouse upon Hadoop or Spark with all data in one place. It is possible that traditional RDBMSs that stand in the center of the stage may be expelled to the edge of the stage.

10.4.2.2 Lesson 2: Being More Open Minded

Another lesson that people should have learned is that researchers and developers should be more open minded. RDBMS is a tool, so is Hadoop, and so is Spark, although the latter two have learned some ideas from RDBMS, there are also critical innovations in them. And both of them have some advantages over traditional RDBMSs such as much higher scalability. New techniques that can tackle challenges of big data processing should be respected, no matter what labels are attaching to them—NoSQL or SQL—and no matter what techniques they use.

Now more and more database researchers admit the importance of open-source big data platforms such as Hadoop and Spark. They have seen rapid adoption of such platforms for processing of big data even in traditional enterprise using RDBMS before [27]. From the author list of Reference 27, we can see that the author of the first MapReduce paper and the researcher who led the lab where Spark was born were invited to the meeting dominated by database researchers before.

They realize that diverse data sources require diverse programming abstractions to operate on data sets, besides SQL. Although SQL RDBMs are still widely used, key–value stores, data stream processors, Hadoop and Spark frameworks, etc. play more and more important roles in data management and analytic applications. It is the time to rethink what a database means and what a database curriculum looks like.

Big data has generated a growing demand for data scientists, who can extract actionable knowledge from large volumes of diverse data. The skill set of a data scientist includes not only traditional know-how of data management and business intelligence, but also mathematics, statistics, artificial intelligence, and machine learning, as well as new data-processing tools such as Hadoop and Spark.

REFERENCES

1. Wikipedia. Big data. https://en.wikipedia.org/wiki/Big_data, 2016.
2. Jimmy Lin, Michael Schatz. Design patterns for efficient graph algorithms in MapReduce. *8th Workshop on Mining and Learning with Graphs*, Washington, DC, USA, 2010, pp. 78–85.
3. Tim Kaldewey, Eugene J. Shekita, Sandeep Tata. Clydesdale: Structured data processing on MapReduce. *EDBT*, Berlin, Germany, 2012, pp. 15–25.
4. Sherif Sakr, Anna Liu, Ayman G. Fayoumi. The family of MapReduce and large scale data processing systems. http://arxiv.org/abs/1302.2966, 2013.
5. Kyong-Ha Lee, Yoon-Joon Lee, Hyunsik Choi, Yon Dohn Chung, Bongki Moon. Parallel data processing with MapReduce: A survey. *SIGMOD Record* 2011, 40(4): 11–20.
6. Xiongpai Qin, Huiju Wang, Furong Li, Baoyao Zhou, Yu Cao, Cuiping Li, Hong Chen, Xuan Zhou, Xiaoyong Du, Shan Wang. Beyond simple integration of RDBMS and MapReduce—Paving the way toward a unified system for big data analytics: Vision and progress. *GCC*, Xiangtan, China, 2012, pp. 716–725.
7. Jens Dittrich, Jorge-Arnulfo Quiane-Ruiz, Alekh Jindal, Yagiz Kargin, Vinay Setty, Jorg Schad. Hadoop++: Making a yellow elephant run like a cheetah. *PVLDB* 2010, 3(1–2): 515–529.
8. Stefan Richter, Jorge-Arnulfo Quiane-Ruiz, Stefan Schuh, Jens Dittrich. Towards zero-overhead adaptive indexing in Hadoop. Technical Report, Information Systems Group, Saarland University, 2012.
9. Aanand. Apache Hadoop wins Terabyte Sort Benchmark. https://developer.yahoo.com/blogs/hadoop/apache-hadoop-wins-terabyte-sort-benchmark-408.html, 2008.
10. Apache Hadoop takes top prize at Media Guardian Innovation Awards. http://www.theguardian.com/technology/2011/mar/25/media-guardian-innovation-awards-apache-hadoop, 2011.
11. Vinod Kumar Vavilapalli, Arun C. Murthy, Chris Douglas et al. Apache Hadoop YARN: Yet another resource negotiator. *SOCC*, Santa Clara, CA, USA, 2013, Article No. 5.
12. HortonWorks. Apache Hadoop YARN wins best paper award at SoCC 2013! http://zh.hortonworks.com/blog/apache-hadoop-yarn-wins-best-paper-award-at-socc-2013/, 2013.
13. HortonWorks. Apache Tez—A framework for YARN-based, data processing applications in Hadoop. http://zh.hortonworks.com/hadoop/tez/, 2015.
14. Apache Tez. http://incubator.apache.org/projects/tez.html, 2016.

15. Arun C. Murthy, Bikas Saha. Apache Tez: Accelerating Hadoop query processing. *Hadoop Summit*, San Jose, USA, 2013.
16. HortonWorks. Interactive query for Hadoop with Apache Hive on Apache Tez, benefits of the Stinger Initiative delivered. http://hortonworks.com/hadoop-tutorial/supercharging-interactive-queries-hive-tez/, 2015.
17. Apache Spark ecosystem and Spark components. https://www.dezyre.com/article/apache-spark-ecosystem-and-spark-components/219, 2016.
18. Andrew Pavlo, Erik Paulson, Alexander Rasin, Daniel J. Abadi, David J. DeWitt, Samuel Madden, Michael Stonebraker. A comparison of approaches to large-scale data analysis. *SIGMOD*, Providence, Rhode Island, USA, 2009, pp. 165–178.
19. Amp Lab. Big data benchmark. https://amplab.cs.berkeley.edu/benchmark/, 2016.
20. Matei Zaharia, Mosharaf Chowdhury, Michael J. Franklin, Scott Shenker, Ion Stoica. Spark: Cluster computing with working sets. *HotCloud*, Boston, MA, USA, 2010.
21. Reynold Xin. Spark the fastest open source engine for sorting a petabyte. https://databricks.com/blog/2014/11/05/spark-officially-sets-a-new-record-in-large-scale-sorting.html, 2014.
22. Gigaom. Hortonworks lays out a future for Hive that includes transactions, Spark and sub-second queries. https://gigaom.com/2014/09/03/hortonworks-lays-out-a-future-for-hive-that-includes-transactions-spark-and-sub-second-queries/, 2014.
23. David J. DeWitt, Michael Stonebraker. MapReduce: A major step backwards. http://homes.cs.washington.edu/~billhowe/mapreduce_a_major_step_backwards.html, 2008.
24. Mary Jo Foley. Microsoft drops Dryad; puts its big-data bets on Hadoop. http://www.zdnet.com/blog/microsoft/microsoft-drops-dryad-puts-its-big-data-bets-on-hadoop/11226, 2011.
25. Michael Stonebraker, Daniel Abadi, David J. DeWitt, Sam Madden, Erik Paulson, Andrew Pavlo, Alexander Rasin. MapReduce and parallel DBMSs: Friends or foes? *Communications of the ACM* 2010, 53(1): 64–71.
26. Wall Street Journal. Open-source projects like Hadoop affects growth for Oracle, Teradata. http://finance.yahoo.com/news/open-source-projects-hadoop-affects-100545583.html, 2013.
27. Daniel Abadi, Rakesh Agrawal, Anastasia Ailamaki et al. The Beckman report on database research. *Communications of the ACM* 2016, 59(2): 92–99.

11 Security, Privacy, and Trust for User-Generated Content

The Challenges and Solutions

Yuhong Liu, Yu Wang, and Nam Ling

CONTENTS

ABSTRACT

With the rapid development of ubiquitous computing, more individual users are getting used to generate, share, and exchange excessive amount of digital media content on the Internet. Such content, which is also called user-generated content (UGC), has become an essential source of today's big data. The anonymity and simplicity of generating such content, however, make it extremely difficult to guarantee the quality. Furthermore, the significant value of UGC also attracts malicious users' attention and leads to diverse profit-driven attacks, raising great concerns on its security, trustworthiness, and privacy.

This chapter starts with introducing the relationship between UGC and big data as well as UGC classification. A system model is then established to describe UGC-centric platforms, providing the foundation for the later understanding of the challenges and solutions in such platforms. The main theme of this chapter is to provide a comprehensive review on the emerging security, privacy, and trust challenges for UGC as well as the state-of-the-art defense solutions. The relationship among security, privacy, and trust in the big data context is also discussed in details.

11.1 INTRODUCTION

Recent years, big data has attracted increasing attention from both academia and industry. Although the definition of big data varies across different fields and is still evolving, it is commonly agreed that big data has five essential characteristics, which are often described as five Vs: volume, velocity, variety, value, and veracity [1,2]. Specifically, the meaning of these five Vs is listed below:

- Volume refers to the size of the data. The data generated and stored by today's cyber systems is huge, which may need to be measured by petabytes or even exabytes.
- Velocity refers to the high speed of data generation, which requires more powerful data-processing capability.
- Variety refers to various types of unstructured data, such as image, video, social networking conversations, geographic location information, etc., which is much more complex to process than the traditional structured data.
- Value refers to the meaningful information that can be extracted from the large amount of data.
- Veracity refers to the trustworthiness of the data. When the data is generated and accessed by diverse parties, it becomes extremely challenging to ensure the quality and truthfulness of the information.

Big data can be generated from diverse sources, such as health data from medical industry, sensor data from Internet of Things (IoT) applications, business transaction data from stock market, etc. Beyond these sources, big data is also generated by individual Internet users everyday, where it is called user-generated content (UGC).

As ubiquitous computing dramatically changes the way people think, work, and interact, it has become much easier and more convenient for individual users to proactively generate, share, and exchange diverse digital media content on the Internet, such as question–answer databases, digital video, blogging, forums, review sites, online social conversations, mobile phone photography, and wikis. Such UGC has experienced exponential increase recently and is recognized as an important component of big data.

11.1.1 UGC and Big Data

As one type of big data, UGC also shares the "five-V" characteristics.

The flexibility of generating UGC by anyone from any devices at anywhere has led to an exponential increase in its volume and velocity. For example, YouTube users were uploading 300 hours of new videos every minute in the year 2014, three times more than 1 year earlier [3]; 500 million tweets are generated on Twitter everyday, bringing around 30% growth in volume every year [4]; by the end of the first quarter 2016, cumulative reviews on Yelp have grown to approximately 102 million with a 32% growth compared to the same period last year [5].

Furthermore, due to individual users' subjective preferences, the format of UGC is quite diverse by nature. Images, videos, audios, social interactions, and conversations are frequently created, posted, and shared online by individual users.

The value of UGC is significant. UGC has been utilized in a number of research studies to predict events, such as movie box-office income [6], natural disasters such as earthquake [7] and typhoon [8], and even political elections [9,10]. In addition, more users are relying on UGC to make their online purchasing and downloading decisions. For example, in online review systems, for example, Amazon, Yelp, Reditt, and IMDB, users refer to ratings and reviews generated and shared by other users to evaluate the trustworthiness of online items.

The veracity of UGC, however, is difficult to control due to two reasons. On the one hand, the easiness of creating and sharing such contents allows unconscious mistakes from individual users. On the other hand, UGC's significant value has provided strong motivation for profit-driven manipulations, which aim to conduct unethical promotions, to spread rumors and to mislead public's decision makings. For example, more businesses aware of the influence of online ratings/reviews are developing their online marketing strategies accordingly or even trying to manipulate user ratings/reviews [11].

In this chapter, we mainly discuss the veracity of UGC, with specific focus on the security, trust, and privacy challenges and the corresponding defense solutions.

11.1.2 Classification of UGC

Among diverse channels allowing individual users to generate online content, three categories of emerging applications, which motivate individual users' contribution from different aspects, are gaining popularity and become major sources for UGC.

11.1.2.1 Online Social Network

Online social networks provide various ways to involve users in online social interactions and entertainments. For example, LinkedIn users are able to post their professional profiles, build up business connections, and search out job opportunities; Twitter users can explicitly express their opinions, comments, and sentiments through tweets and re-tweets; Facebook users can share their photos and status and comment on friends' walls to socialize with their family and friends; YouTubers are able to publish videos about their daily lives and interesting experiences to attract subscribers.

Online social network platforms rich in UGC have already become the most popular Internet destinations [12]. In the year 2009, the amount of time users spent on social networking and blogging sites tripled and accounted for 17% of their total time spent online [13].

11.1.2.2 Crowdsourcing

Crowdsourcing, emerging recently, is an online, distributed problem-solving and production model [14], in which problems can be published through open calls to an unknown group of solvers (i.e., crowd) [15]. Crowdsourcing can be in many forms and for different purposes, including fund raising (i.e., crowdfunding), knowledge gathering and sharing (e.g., Stackoverflow and Wikipedia), human intelligent tasks (e.g., Amazon Mechanical Turk), etc. Specifically, a typical crowdsourcing procedure involves breaking a huge task into micro ones by the requestor and then completing the micro tasks by the crowd.

By leveraging intelligence from diverse crowd, crowdsourcing is gaining popularity. On the one hand, more companies and institutions rely on crowdsourcing for finding solutions to different problems due to its low cost and high efficiency. One example is the Defense Advanced Research Projects Agency (DARPA) balloon experiment in 2009, where the crowd was asked to compete to first find and report the location of 10 balloon markers placed by DARPA across the United States. Another example is the Netflix prize in 2009, where the crowd was asked to design a recommendation algorithm as more accurate than Netflix's own algorithm. On the other hand, individual users are motivated to get involved as crowd workers for money, social recognition (i.e., social badges), or the common good. For example, individual users from all over the world spontaneously post and revise edits on Wikipedia and its sister projects, leading to over 10 edits per second, more than 800 new articles per day [16].

11.1.2.3 Online Word-of-Mouth Network

With the simplicity of generating and sharing personal experiences online, word-of-mouth (i.e., WoM), one of the most ancient mechanisms in the history of human society, is gaining new significance in the cyber world. The trustworthiness of the online contents/users can be evaluated based on feedback from large-scale, virtual WoM networks in which individuals share their own opinions and experiences. The aggregated results of such feedback are called online reputation. For example, viewers on YouTube may "like" or "dislike" a video clip; buyers on Amazon share their purchasing experiences; travelers evaluate hotels or restaurants on Yelp; readers can either "dig" or "bury" a piece of social news on Reddit; etc.

The Pew Internet & American Life Project has found that 26% of adult Internet users in the United States have provided reviews for at least one product, service, or person using online review systems. The online WoM network is playing an increasingly important role in influencing users' online decisions. For instance, eBay sellers with established reputation can expect about 8% more revenue than new sellers marketing the same goods [17]; a survey conducted by comScore Inc. and The Kelsey Group reveals that consumers are willing to pay at least 20% more for services receiving an "Excellent," or 5-star, rating than for the same services receiving a "Good," or 4-star, rating [18].

Different from online social networks and crowdsourcing, online WoM networks are originally designed to focus more on evaluating existing data instead of producing new data. Nevertheless, the excessive amount of evaluation data itself also forms an essential component of the UGC big data.

11.1.3 System Model

In this section, we would like to provide an abstract system model for network or platforms where the digital contents are mainly generated by users. Specifically, as shown in Figure 11.1, the system contains two layers: the user layer and the content layer.

On the user layer, there are two types of users: generators who create at least one piece of content and consumers who view the contents created by generators. For example, generators may be users uploading posts on social networks, workers committing crowdsourcing tasks, and reviewers in online WoM networks. Consumers may be users who retweet a post on Twitter or like a post on Facebook, requestors who collect submissions from the crowd, or online users who make their

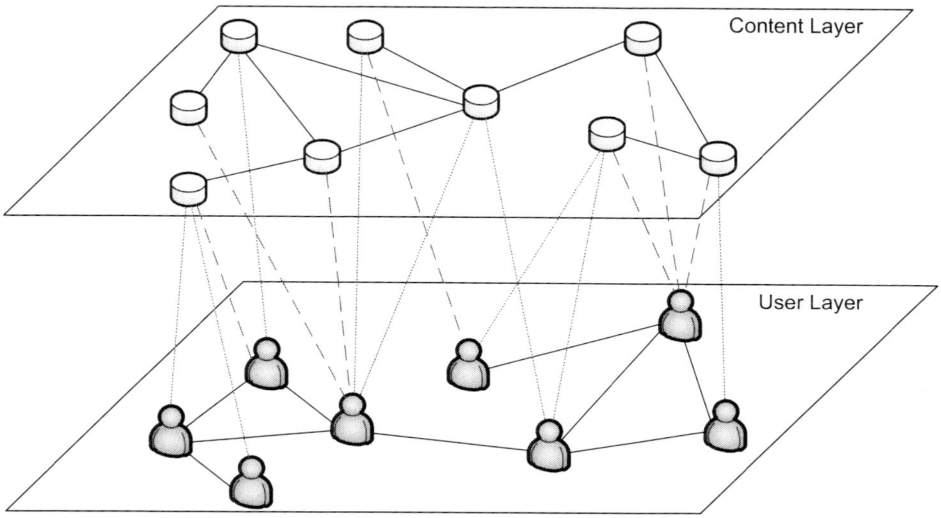

FIGURE 11.1 System model of UGC-centric platforms.

purchasing or downloading decisions based on others' reviews/ratings. It is possible for an individual user to be a pure generator, a pure consumer, or a mixture who both generates and consumes contents. In addition, a pair of connected users can represent people who (1) have social connections, either professional or personal, (2) co-workers who have been involved in the same crowdsourcing tasks, or (3) reviewers who have reviewed same online items.

On the content layer, we use a star to represent each piece of content generated by a user. The contents could be posts from social network users, submissions from crowdsourcing workers, or reviews/ratings from online WoM network reviewers. In addition, multiple-linked contents can represent (1) related social conversation topics; (2) submissions toward the same crowdsourcing task; or (3) ratings/reviews evaluating the same online item.

More important, two types of links are employed to connect the user layer and the content layer. A dotted link connecting a piece of content C and a user U_i represents that C is generated by U_i. Such links indicate many-to-one relationship, where one user can generate multiple contents while one piece of content can only be generated by one user. A dashed link connecting U_j and C represents that C is consumed by U_j. Such links indicate many-to-many relationship, where one user can consume multiple contents and one piece of content can be consumed by multiple users.

11.1.4 Emerging Security, Privacy, and Trust Challenges

As normal users are motivated in numerous ways to contribute to UGC, the incentive to manipulate such content is also increasing, raising great challenges for *data security, privacy*, and *trust*.

11.1.4.1 Relationship among Security, Privacy, and Trust

Recently, security, trust, and privacy are often mentioned together in discussions on attacks and protections of information systems or networks. Although these three terms are closely related with one another, each one of them has its own emphasis. Therefore, before discussing UGC-related security, trust, and privacy challenges, we would like to first clarify these three terms through their definitions.

Security is defined as preservation of information confidentiality, integrity, and availability. In addition, "other properties such as authenticity, accountability, nonrepudiation, and reliability can also be involved" [19]. In other words, the ultimate goal of security defenses is to deny illegitimate access to data.

Privacy is defined as "the ability of data owners to seclude themselves, or information about themselves, and thereby express themselves selectively" [20]. Different from confidentiality, which is considered as part of security, privacy is more subjective since data owners may determine if a piece of information is private in diverse ways according to their own background, interests, education, culture, etc.

Trust is defined as "how much confidence one party has about whether the other party will conduct a certain action or possess a certain property" [21]. Different from security and privacy, trust represents the relationship between two parties, with an expectation on the future activities.

Attacks launched against security, privacy, or trust often have different attack goals and need to be addressed through different solutions. In this chapter, we discuss typical attacks/defenses for security, privacy, and trust separately, with the purpose of comparing underlying similarities and differences among these attacks and defenses.

11.1.4.2 Security Challenges

Driven by the huge profits behind the big data economy, various security attacks against UGC are emerging rapidly.

Due to the simplicity of creating online accounts, Sybil attacks, where a single attacker creates a large amount of fake online accounts to dominate information propagated in UGC applications, are getting popular and may cause severe damage.

Moreover, security risks are raised due to the exposure of user data. Users generate contents online to share experiences and to build relationships in a much bigger cyber community. Such contents, however, may also expose users to a wide range of other users and groups, such as strangers, the hosting site, third parties connecting to the hosting site, hackers, etc. Such exposure may introduce diverse risks to individual users, such as identity theft, physical or cyber stalking, phishing attacks, social spams, etc.

11.1.4.3 Privacy Challenges

UGC may explicitly or implicitly contain personal information, which raises wide concerns on user privacy. People carelessly posting their personal information on social media can easily have their privacy breached. For example, a research conducted by Carnegie Mellon University has shown that it is possible to predict most and sometimes all of an individual's nine-digit Social Security Number using information gleaned from social networks and online databases [22]. A study [23] has shown that a large percentage of Facebook users investigated in the study disclose their personal information including real name, address, date of birth, hobbies and interests, etc., with or without awareness.

Moreover, even information that is supposed to be well protected may be breached by advanced privacy attacks. For example, a recent research shows that even users who carefully protect their own information may still have their personal attributes disclosed by hackers examining their friends' list [24]. Another example is the Netflix Prize 2006, an open contest for movie recommendation algorithm based on previous ratings from anonymous Netflix users. In this contest, Netflix has released a data set with 100,480,507 ratings provided by 480,189 anonymous Netflix subscribers to the public. Two researchers from the University of Texas at Austin developed a de-anonymization attack model and applied their model to the data set. They have demonstrated [25] that the identity of some subscribers can be easily unmasked by matching up their ratings at Netflix and at IMDB, another movie rating Web site. The authors also claim that sensitive information such as political preference can be inferred from this data set using their attack model.

In the context of crowdsourcing, privacy issues are raised from two perspectives. On the one hand, workers' personal data may be exposed to attackers while they are fulfilling tasks. For example, To et al. [26] claim that the location of a worker can be obtained by an adversary when the worker reports events (e.g., disaster) happening in his or her area to a Spatial Crowdsourcing (SC) server. On the other hand, the raw data provided by a task requestor may include sensitive information that should be protected from misappropriating by the workers. Varshney [27] points out that requestors also need to obscure raw data provided to workers for processing, correction, or evaluation in order to protect their intellectual capital and confidential information. In both cases, random noises may need to be added to data values for privacy preservation purposes. However, such noises have to be controlled to not significantly affect the result accuracy. The trade-off between privacy and result accuracy is challenging and needs to be carefully considered in the design of crowdsourcing tasks.

11.1.4.4 Trust Challenges

The simplicity of creating digital content online has also led to an increase of users' uncertainty in providing high-quality information, which makes the trustworthiness of such content questionable.

Data quality in the crowdsourcing scenario has been raised as a critical issue due to two reasons. First, participants with diverse background or sometimes even lack of knowledge may get involved and contribute a large number of unusable submissions. Second, ill-designed tasks by inexperienced requestors may also lead to poor quality of collected data [28]. As a consequence, crowdsourcing has rarely been used for mission critical systems, unless the trustworthy issues of crowd submissions could be resolved. A number of studies have been conducted to improve data quality [29] by using redundant nonexpert labels in image annotation [30], repeated labeling [31], setting qualification test [32], etc.

As discussed before, online WoM network is initially established to help individual users differentiate high-quality online items from low-quality ones by utilizing ratings/reviews from individual online users. Unfortunately, most, if not all, of the evaluation data on such platforms also has the same quality issue. For example, one category in the "Amazon window shop app" for iPad, called "peculiar products," contains a lot of kooky and fake products, such as uranium ore, or a $50 Tuscan whole milk [33]. Surprisingly, these products receive thousands of ratings/reviews, although Amazon does not really sell them. Users in this example are just providing those reviews for fun. But it also shows how easy it is to generate fake content (i.e., reviews) online.

In addition, many companies aggressively take advantage of online WoM marketing by manipulating online user discussions. Book authors and eBay users are shown to write or buy favorable reviews for their own products [34–36]. A recent study has identified that 10% online products have manipulated user reviews [11]. The boom of review companies, which provide sophisticated review manipulation packages at affordable prices, reinforces the prevalence of such manipulations. For just $9.99, a company named "IncreaseYouTubeViews.com" can provide 30 "I like" ratings or 30 real user comments to your video clips on YouTube. Taobao, which is the largest Internet retail platform in China, has identified these review boosting services as a severe threat. Such manipulations may significantly distort the review results, undermine users' confidence about online WoM systems, and may eventually make such systems lose their worthiness.

Diverse signal processing techniques and statistic analysis have been employed to detect dishonest ratings/reviews [37–39]. In addition, quantitative trust models are developed to dynamically evaluating reviewers' trustworthiness in providing honest ratings/reviews. On the other hand, advanced attacks that explore vulnerabilities of detection methods and trust models are also evolving rapidly. An "arm-race" between trust model defenses and attacks is taking place.

In the rest part of this chapter, we discuss specific attacks and defenses from security, privacy, and trust aspects, respectively.

11.2 SECURITY ATTACKS AND DEFENSES

11.2.1 Sybil Attack

Sybil attacks, initially proposed by Douceur [40], denote attacks where a single malicious entity (i.e., attacker) creates excessive pseudonymous online IDs to gain disproportionately large influence in the system [41]. By controlling these pseudo IDs to coordinately conduct malicious behavior, the attacker could obtain significant resources of the system and cause severe damage.

Carefully designed Sybil attacks can be launched in a wide range of applications, such as peer-to-peer (P2P) networks and wireless sensor networks. For example, to mitigate risks of data loss and leakage, large-scale P2P networks often make multiple nodes carry on replicated tasks to introduce redundancy. In Sybil attacks, however, the large amount of Sybil accounts can dramatically increase the chance of malicious attacker being repetitively selected to perform a task and thus defeats this redundancy [40].

In UGC-centric systems, information is usually aggregated based on "majority vote" or "majority opinion," with the assumption that majority of the user accounts are honest. In normal cases, each user account expresses its opinion by only one vote. Sybil attacker, however, can easily turn normal users into minority by taking up multiple votes through its fake accounts and thus significantly distort the general public's opinion. For example, in Google PageRank, malicious attacker may increase a Web page's rank by creating multiple other Web pages linking to it [42]. In online WoM systems, such as eBay or Amazon rating systems, Sybil accounts could spread rumors about honest vendors to downgrade their reputation or self-promote themselves to obtain financial profits [43].

Extensive studies have been conducted to detect and prevent Sybil attacks. For example, in [44], users and their trust relationships are modeled as a social graph, where vertexes represent users and links represent user relationship. The defense scheme, SybilGuard, is proposed to differentiate Sybil accounts from normal ones by identifying the disproportionately small "cut" in the social graph based on the assumption that malicious users can create many identities but few trust relationships. In their later study in [45], an improved protocol named SybilLimit has been proposed to optimize the approach by further minimizing the number of Sybil account in million-node synthetic social network. A Bayesian-based inference approach, SybilInfer, has been proposed in [46] that consists of a probabilistic model of honest social networks as well as an inference engine. Buchegger and Boudec [47] have proposed a solution to detect and eliminate Sybil accounts by periodically re-evaluating the behavior of accounts and discounting historical ratings. In [48], the authors have examined the graph of distributed hash tables (DHTs) (a graph showing a node is introduced by which node) to identify Sybil accounts, based on the assumption that a large number of malicious accounts are introduced by a small number of Sybil entities. In addition, Sybil attacks can also be prevented by utilizing a centralized authority, which issues trusted certifications to ensure that only one identity would be assigned to a given entity [49]. Other solutions may include checking resource owned by identities, increasing cost to create Sybil identities, using trusted devices, etc. [49].

In spite of the rapid development of diverse defenses, it is very challenging to completely eliminate Sybil attacks in practice. The research on defending against Sybil attacks is still very active today.

11.2.2 Security Attacks Based on Users' Sensitive Information

UGC-centric systems are now a prime target of diverse security attacks due to the rich information about personal details posted on these systems everyday, including but not limited to people's real full name and home address, date of birth, email address, user name and password, friendship, geographical locations, credit card details, etc. In this section, we discuss several typical security attacks such as identity theft, social spam, and phishing attacks, which have been developed long time ago even before the prosperity of UGC-centric systems. However, UGC-centric systems, especially social networking Web sites, provide a new venue for these old frauds.

11.2.2.1 Identity Theft

In identity theft attacks, attacker attempts to obtain users' personally identifiable information (PII) and deliberately uses such information to impersonate the victim for the purpose of fraud such as posting spam, sending out malware, stealing the private data of contacts, or even soliciting contacts to send money [50].

The reasons for the success of identity theft are multifaceted. Users' identity information may be disclosed due to the vulnerabilities of UGC-centric systems. For example, in [51], a friend-in-the-middle attack has been proposed to retrieve users' sensitive data from social networking sites by hijacking HTTP sessions on the network layer, which most social networking sites fail to secure. Furthermore, users' personal information may also be breached through third-party applications. Most social networking sites have apps that ask for permission to access their account information. Poorly secured or even already compromised third-party apps bring high risks of identity theft.

Identity theft attacks are prevalent in UGC-centric systems. For example, in 2013, a 18-year-old student of the Sullivan County School District in Sullivan County, Tennessee, opened a fake Twitter account under the name of the district superintendent, Dr. Yennie, and posted a number of inappropriate tweets through that account [52]. In recent years, a popular identity theft scam on Facebook is that a stolen user account sends out desperate messages to its friends asking for money. Such messages could be something like "I'm traveling abroad and lost my wallet. Please wire me $x so I can get home."

There are also research studies on the feasibility of large-scale identity theft. For example, the authors in [41] have proposed an automated way to launch identity theft attacks on social networks. Specifically, by forging an existing victim user's identity and sending out friend requests to the victim's friends, the attacker could connect to some of the victim's friends, access their sensitive personal information, and turn them into victims. With the retrieved sensitive information, the attacker is able to forge more existing users and further launch identity theft attacks against their friends.

11.2.2.2 Social Spam and Phishing Attack

As online social networks such as Facebook and Twitter are getting popularity, social spams are also emerging rapidly. According to [53], by exploiting target users' social relationship and connecting to them, social networking spammers can make up to 10 times more money than that made from their traditional way of spamming through emails. These spams may yield thousands of views since people are more likely to trust something sent from their social network "friends." A recent example is that, in the year 2015, 1.5 million Facebook accounts were stolen and sold to businesses who send out advertisements to friends through those compromised accounts [54].

Social phishing often goes hand in hand with social spams, in which attacker aims to fraudulently acquire sensitive information by impersonating a trustworthy party. Social phishing often contains malicious links to forgery Web sites or Web sites that are infected with malware. For example, an attack was launched against Facebook users in 2012, where malicious accounts impersonating Facebook security sent out fake messages and a forgery link to normal users asking their Facebook login info as well as credit card information [52]. Experiments conducted in [55] show that social phishing attacks can achieve 70% success rate on social networks.

11.2.2.3 Defense

Extensive studies have been conducted to prevent users from being attacked. Solutions are proposed from social, technical, and legal perspectives, for example, educating people to be aware of such attacks, enhancing monitoring of such attacks, blacklisting malicious Web sites and taking them down once they are detected, increasing security of Web browsers, filing lawsuits against suspected attackers, etc.

Among these solutions, the most essential one is to educate UGC-centric system users to be cautious about the contents that they are posting online everyday and to minimize the disclosure of their sensitive information. Technical solutions will never be sufficient without individual users being aware of the potential security risks.

11.3 PRIVACY ATTACKS AND DEFENSES

Thanks to the convenience of online communications, more people are getting used to move their social activities from offline to online, such as making friends, searching jobs, building relationships, exchanging knowledge and information, etc. The increase of online activities creates massive UGC when people exchange information through the Internet. However, when people generate and share these contents, they often do not expect such information to be later retrieved, mined, and even used to hurt themselves.

Privacy, a subjective concept, denotes the ability of an individual or a group to control the amount of personal information available to the public. In other words, data owners should have the privilege to control, according to their own preferences, what information to share and shared to whom.

11.3.1 Understanding Privacy Threats and Defenses

According to the privacy definition above, privacy threats and defenses can be analyzed from two perspectives: the information-type perspective and the adversary-type perspective.

11.3.1.1 Private Information Type

Different types of private information often face different privacy challenges and hence may require distinct privacy preserving solutions. In the context of UGC, we classify users' private information into two types: profile (i.e., *Type I*) information, which denotes a user's personal information, including but not limited to one's identity, age, gender, addresses, photos, location, religious beliefs, etc., and relationship (i.e., *Type II*) information, which includes the family, friend, colleague, and social relationship.

While profile information is usually generated and owned by one user, relationship information can be generated and shared by multiple users, which obscures the information ownership and often leads to complex privacy scenarios.

11.3.1.2 Privacy Adversary Type

While UGC may be easily accessed by different parties, the user who generates such data may not always be aware of all these parties. We summarize all the potential parties that may access users' data and violate their privacy as follows:

- *Other users in the system*. According to their relationship with the data owner, these users can be further divided into three categories as directly connected users, indirectly connected users, and general public [56]. Specifically, directly connected users denote friends, family members, or colleagues who are closely connected with the data owner; indirectly connected users denote friends of friends (FOF) who may connect to the data owner through one or two hops; and general public denotes users who have no relationship with the data owner at all.
- *Third parties, such as app developers and advertising agencies*. These third parties are often the consumers of user behavior data generated in UGC-centric systems and thus provide most of the revenue for UGC system providers. There is a strong motivation for UGC system providers to share their data with such parties. Nevertheless, due to the more-than-necessary data acquisition and imperfect anonymization, such data sharing often leads to user privacy violation by third parties.
- *UGC system providers*. From technical aspect, UGC system providers can arbitrarily access all the data generated and shared in their systems. Therefore, their inappropriate usage of users' data may cause more severe damage yet could hardly be detected by individual users.

11.3.2 Privacy-Related Threats

Various privacy threats against UGC are rapidly emerging and dynamically evolving in recent years. In this section, we classify typical privacy threats into two categories: profile privacy threats and relationship privacy threats.

11.3.2.1 Profile Privacy Threats

Users' sensitive profile (i.e., *Type I*) information may be breached due to (1) vulnerable privacy settings made by data owners, (2) information leakage through legitimate parties, or (3) information inference made by illegitimate parties. Note that whether a party is legitimate or not is determined by the data owners' own preferences. Here, illegitimate parties can refer to any parties who are not permitted by a user to access his or her private information.

Arbitrary disclosure of the private information can cause severe damage to individual users. For example, there is an emerging trend of users sharing their location information in online social networks, especially mobile-based networks. Although it allows users to benefit from more dynamic and personalized services, the exposure of their location information may also raise high risks of physical harm such as stalking. Appropriate privacy setting is the first step to protect user privacy. This first step, however, still requires a lot of effort. Currently, when users post contents online with no explicit privacy settings, such contents are often made open to public by default without users' awareness. Even though more users are aware of their privacy, the controls over their privacy settings are often too complex to follow.

In addition, even with perfect privacy settings, where only legitimate users are allowed to access the sensitive information, there is very limited control over the privacy leakage made by these legitimate users, no matter intentionally or incautiously. For example, a user obtaining others' sensitive information may simply spread it out over the network. Similar behavior often occurs in offline human society as "telling the secret" [56]. Furthermore, the study in [57] shows that users with insufficient privacy settings will increase the privacy vulnerability of their friends as well as that of the entire social community. Moreover, inappropriate data usage/sharing made by UGC platform providers forms another source of privacy leakage.

Finally, illegitimate users may exploit privacy vulnerabilities and infer users' sensitive profile information from anonymized data set. Specifically, attackers attempt to de-anonymize a user by linking anonymized demographic data sets publicly or semipublicly released [58]. A study [59,60] described another attack using photo tagged in other users' content to link user profile and reveal users' sensitive data, for example, current location. Other than location data, more sensitive data can be inferred from publicly released data, despite being anonymized. The attack described in [61] can even predict a user's social security number based on publicly available information.

11.3.2.2 Relationship Privacy Threats

Relationship (i.e., *Type II*) privacy can also be violated due to (1) vulnerable privacy settings made by data owners, (2) information leakage through legitimate parties, or (3) information inference from complex privacy scenarios caused by multiple data owners.

The first two threats are similar to that against profile privacy. The major difference is the third threat, which is challenging since multiple parties involved in one relationship often have their privacy requirements different from and even conflicting with one another. Intelligent illegitimate users taking advantage of such conflicts among different parties may infer individual users' sensitive relationship and even re-construct the social graph of the entire network.

A typical example is the exposure of users' friendship in online social networks. To encourage users' social connections and interactions, popular online social networks such as Facebook and Twitter have recently provided a friend search engine, which allows any individual users to query another user's friend list. Meanwhile, to address the increasing concerns about friendship privacy,

OSNs also allow individual users to set their entire friend list as "private," which is supposed to be unsearchable by any other users.

However, even if a user set his or her friend list as private, such information can still be easily breached by his or her friends if their friendship information is set as open to public. This problem is called "mutual effect" [62]. For example, Facebook actually releases "mutual friends" between two users as long as one of them sets his or her friend list as open to public. Wagner [63] has conducted an experiment on Mark Zuckerberg. Although Mark sets his friend list as "private," meaning that no other users except him can see his friendship, anyone, by searching the "mutual friends" between Mark and Chris Cox, the chief product officer of Facebook, can see a detailed list of their 621 mutual friends. Mark's friendship privacy is compromised. More important, if any of these 621 friends also sets his or her friend list as open, even more friends of Mark may be retrieved. After a few rounds of such friend search, the entire friend list of Mark might be disclosed, making the "private" setting meaningless.

Various attack strategies to discover private friendship by taking advantage of mutual effect are discussed in [64]. To resolve mutual effect, a privacy preserving friend search engine has been proposed in [62], where a piece of friendship will not be released unless both friends (i.e., the owners of this information) agree to disclose it. This defense scheme can effectively prevent privacy inference attacks launched by an individual attacker. Yet an advanced collusion attack has been recently proposed in [65], where a victim user's friendship privacy setting can still be compromised through a carefully designed query sequence coordinately launched by multiple malicious requestors. Active research studies on friendship privacy attacks and defenses are still rapidly evolving.

Beyond individual user's relationship privacy, social network topology, which contains all friendship connections among users, is also the target of privacy attacks. A study [66] claims that a complete social graph can be identified by randomly crawling data in the social graph and repetitively querying user data. To prevent such arbitrary crawling, Facebook has once limited the number of friends exposed in the public listings to a fixed number, eight [12]. Soon after that, some researchers have noticed that although the number of displayed friends is limited, showing eight friends is already enough for a third party to crawl data so as to estimate the network topology [12]. To effectively protect social network topology from advanced privacy attacks remains a challenging issue.

11.3.2.3 A Mixture

Note that although we differentiate privacy threats against user profile from that against relationship, privacy breach of one could lead to breach of the other. For example, a study [67] has introduced an attack to unmask anonymous users through their social relationship. In the study, an attacker, with some knowledge of a user's friendship pattern (i.e., relationship privacy), can re-identify the user (i.e., profile privacy) in a social graph by mapping the pattern on the graph.

11.3.3 Privacy Preserving Solutions for UGC

11.3.3.1 Enhancing User Privacy Settings

As mentioned above, enhancing user privacy settings provides the first step protection. A lot of efforts have been made to help individual users understand the meaning of their privacy settings. For example, in [68], the authors propose to help a user check his or her profile by demonstrating it from different people's view, including a friend, a friend of friend, and general public. Moreover, a "privacy wizard" has been developed in [69] to help users specify their privacy intentions easily.

Extensive efforts are also made to help users improve the granularity of their privacy settings. For instance, in [70], a privacy preserving architecture has been developed to disclose different levels of user private information to different groups of people at different time. In [69], the authors have proposed a personalized privacy setting approach, which first asks users to manually categorize their social relationship and corresponding privacy settings, and then automates such process through machine-learning mechanisms.

11.3.3.2 Data Encryption

To handle potential privacy leakage caused by untrustworthy UGC system providers, some research studies propose to encrypt users' sensitive data and only allow UGC system providers to access the cipher text. For example, a "flybynight" system has been implemented as a Facebook application, which helps users send encrypted messages to one another [71]. Instead of directly developing applications based on UGC-centric systems, authors in [72] implement a Web browser extension to enable user data encryption.

However, these encryption-based schemes often sacrifice the convenience of user operations and suffer from the high-computational costs introduced by the encryption process.

11.3.3.3 Defenses against Private Information Inference

Diverse privacy preserving approaches have been proposed to prevent illegitimate users from inferring user private information. We classify these studies into two categories according to the type of private information they aim to protect.

Privacy preserving approaches in the first category focus on anonymizing the profile data of individual user to prevent attackers from identifying targeted users or inferring their sensitive attributes (i.e., *Type I* information). Defense in this category is often performed proactively when data are created by the user online. Traditional privacy preserving technologies, such as clustering [73], k-anonymity [74], l-diversity [75], t-closeness [76], or differential privacy [77], are often adopted.

Approaches in the second category particularly address how to preserve sensitive relationship (i.e., *Type II* information), which engages multiple users [78]. Most efforts have been made to anonymize users' sensitive relationship when such data is released to third parties [79–88]. These defense schemes use either graph clustering-generalization techniques or graph manipulation-based solutions (i.e., inserting/deleting nodes/edges from original graphs) for anonymization.

Defense Solutions for Profile Privacy—Type I

k-Anonymity: As mentioned above, attackers can make inference on released anonymous data from multiple sources that have overlapping attributes. By doing so, they can re-identify a targeted user and acquire sensitive information. Sweeney [74] has developed a model named k-anonymity to protect anonymous data from being recognized. The study states that a data set satisfies k-anonymity if, for each individual record, the data set contains at least k records that cannot be distinguished from this record (these k records form an equivalent class). Altering data to satisfy k-anonymity can deter data holder from mapping/linking users with external information and acquiring sensitive data.

l-Diversity: Despite its simplicity and prominence, k-anonymity has its drawback and may be vulnerable under attacks when sensitive information is not diversified or attackers have better background information. Based on k-anonymity approach, Machanavajjhala et al. [89] have proposed an approach named l-diversity against attacks mentioned above, by maintaining at least l distinct values of a sensitive attribute for each equivalent class. This way, a data set can be anonymized by l-diversity even if attackers have background information about the user to be re-identified.

t-Closeness: A study [90] further improves l-diversity by introducing the t-closeness approach, which requires the value distribution of a sensitive attribute in one equivalent class to be close to that in the whole data set. The t-closeness approach prevents attackers from narrowing sensitive data down to a specific range so that they cannot easily identify users' private information.

Differential Privacy: Another approach to preserve privacy is named differential privacy proposed in [91]. Differential privacy is a statistic approach to encrypt data in a data set while maximally maintaining the query accuracy.

Defense Solutions for Relationship Privacy—Type II

Clustering-Based Approach: Clustering-based approach is to classify data into groups based on some attributes so that data within a cluster are more similar than data from different clusters [92]. A variety of algorithms have been developed and applied in defining clusters and classifying data. A clustering algorithm can be applied to anonymize user data to prevent attacks through friendship, communication, or shared activity [93], by generalizing either the nodes (i.e., individual users) or the edges (i.e., relationships) [94] in a relationship graph [93].

Graph Modification Approach: Graph modification approach is another important approach that adds noise to the graph, for example, inserting/deleting edges. After such modifications, a node will have a different pattern from the original one and thus is hard to be re-identified [95–98].

11.3.4 Summary

In summary, the development of both attack and defense on privacy of UGC is a dynamically evolving process. With the increase of computing power and massive data created online, data become more complicated and highly dimensional, which leads to more research challenges in the future.

11.4 TRUST MODELS, ATTACKS, AND DEFENSES

As mentioned before, a number of trust-related challenges have been raised in UGC-centric systems. As it is critical for such systems to ensure their trustworthiness and encourage user collaborations, establishing fair and accurate trust evaluation models is required. The development of such trust models, however, is challenging especially with the existence of dynamically evolving attacks. In this section, we discuss different trust evaluation models, attacks against such models, and their corresponding defense solutions.

11.4.1 Ensuring Trustworthiness of UGC

11.4.1.1 Web-of-Trust

In the context of "Web-of-Trust," graph-based models have been developed, where users are represented by vertexes and their trust relationship is represented by edges [99,100]. The basic assumption is that trust value can get propagated through either concatenation or multipath recommendations. Some simple mathematics approaches, such as minimum, maximum, weighted average, etc., have been involved to model the propagation of trust.

Web-of-Trust was initially developed for cryptography applications, such as PGP and GnuPG. The decentralized trust model provides an alternative to the public key infrastructure (PKI), which has a centralized structure. Nevertheless, the decentralized trust propagation idea provides the foundation for trust models developed later and has been widely utilized in different applications.

11.4.1.2 Direct/Indirect Trust Model

Direct/indirect trust model is a classic model that mimics the trust establishment process in human society. In particular, if a person A needs to determine whether to trust another person B or not, he or she may directly make the decision if he or she knows B well; or otherwise refer to another person C for recommendation. Similarly, in direct/indirect trust models, a trustee's trust value is calculated by integrating trustor's own observations (i.e., direct trust) as well as others' recommendations (i.e., indirect trust).

Direct/indirect trust models have been applied in peer-to-peer networks [101], ad hoc and sensor networks [102], and online WoM networks [39].

11.4.1.3 Bayesian-Based Trust Model

The Bayesian model, introduced by Thomas Bayes, is a well-known, widely applied statistic methodology of interpreting probability.

The Bayesian model well fits the trust establishment scenario by its nature. Different from frequency-based probability models, which interpret probability as the frequency of an event's occurrence in a certain number of experimental trials, the Bayesian model assigns a predetermined probability (i.e., prior) to a hypothesis based on past knowledge or experience. Each time when new data is obtained, it will be integrated with the prior probability to get an updated probability (i.e., posterior). The philosophy behind the Bayesian model, dynamically updating existing knowledge with new observations, matches the practical way of people recognizing the world and building up trust relationship.

In online WoM systems, the Bayesian-based model has been utilized to evaluate the trustworthiness of online items. In [103], a Bayesian model that takes binary user ratings as input has been developed to assess online items' posterior reputation score based on users' prior experiences. A Bayesian trust framework is proposed in [104,105] to dynamically evaluate online items' trustworthiness. In particular, user ratings have been considered to follow beta distribution, and the probability density function is updated each time when a new user rating comes in. Furthermore, the model is also extended in [106] to evaluate users' trustworthiness and based on that, to detect malicious users who provide unfair ratings.

11.4.1.4 Dempster–Shafer Theory

The Dempster–Shafer theory (DST), introduced by Arthur P. Dempster and Glenn Shafer, is a framework for combining evidence from independent sources to achieve a degree of belief [107]. By introducing the concept of "uncertainty" to represent ignorance, DST has been widely adopted for decision-making processes, especially when there is a lack of evidence. Specifically, the probability for any set of propositions is bounded by belief (the lower bound) and plausibility (the upper bound), where the difference between the lower and upper bounds represents "uncertainty." Furthermore, to achieve the overall degree of belief, the Dempster's rule of combination integrates evidence from independent sources by keeping commonly shared belief while ignoring conflicts.

DST has initially been applied in expert systems, computer systems that facilitate decision making for risk assessment and decision-making support. For example, belief function is adopted in [108] to model uncertainty in expert system. In [109], an improved DST framework for combining belief has been proposed. The introduction of uncertainty makes DST more flexible and easier to be applied in diverse research areas, such as neural networks [110], sensor fusion [111], etc.

In recent literature on UGC, how to handle large volume of low-quality or even conflict information provided by untrustworthy users has attracted increasing attention. In this context, DST plays an important role through explicitly reasoning process with uncertainty and incomplete information. Kim and Ahmad [112] have introduced the concepts of trust, distrust, and a lack of confidence when analyzing the trustworthiness of UGC. In their study, DST is adopted to measure the level of trust for a content provider by combining trust evidence, distrust evidence, and lack of evidence. In [113], the authors have developed a malicious agent detection model based on DST in distributed reputation systems. The model evaluates the trustworthiness of an agent by obtaining and combining testimonies from other agents (i.e., witnesses). A witness trustworthiness model based on DST is proposed in [114] to detect unfair ratings to e-commerce sellers. DST has been adopted in [115] to evaluate the trustworthiness of ratings provided by different reviewers in an online reputation system.

11.4.1.5 Fuzzy Logic

Both the Bayesian-based trust model and the DST, as discussed above, compute trust values by applying probability-based models on crisp input values. In real life, however, human users often recognize the world through some fuzzy values. For example, human's perception about the temperature is usually not some crisp values as 70° or 80°, but some fuzzy values as cold, normal, and hot. As a consequence, most of the time, their decision-making processes may rely on some simple fuzzy rules instead of precise mathematics equations. We use an online WoM system example to demonstrate such process. Assume a human user checks a product's rating value and volume to make his or her purchasing decision. The user may obtain the decision based on some simple fuzzy rules, such as "I will purchase it if the rating value is high and rating volume is large" or "I will not purchase it if the rating value is average and rating volume is too small." In such scenario, two rating values as 4.9 and 4.8 may both be considered as high value and are not explicitly differentiated during the decision-making process, which does not match the basic assumptions of Bayesian or DST.

A different model, fuzzy logic, introduced by Zadeh [116], has been applied to mimic such human users' fuzzy decision-making process. There are three steps involved in a typical fuzzy logic decision-making process. First, crisp input values are converted into fuzzy values. Second, some fuzzy rules, such as IF A and B then C, will be applied on the converted fuzzy inputs to derive fuzzy outputs. At the end, the fuzzy outputs will be converted back to crisp output values through a defuzzification process.

Fuzzy logic has been widely applied in trust evaluation and decision-making processes. For example, a fuzzy logic-based trust model [117], which considers the vagueness and ambiguity of customers' domain and specificity, has been proposed for customers to evaluate the trustworthiness of e-commerce platforms. Fuzzy logic has also been adopted in a recommender system, which recommends UGC based on users' social trust [118]. Such systems can effectively retrieve high-quality recommendations and significantly enhance the quality of UGC.

11.4.1.6 Entropy-Based Trust Model

Information entropy (or the Shannon entropy), originally proposed by Claude Shannon in information theory in [119], is used to describe how much uncertainty or randomness an event has. In general, higher entropy value represents more uncertainty and randomness, indicating that more questions or investigations are required to know the state of an event. In [102], an entropy-based trust model has been proposed, where trust is considered as a measure of uncertainty, quantified by entropy. The entropy-based model addresses trust concatenation and propagation problems by evaluating trustworthiness through recommendations from multiple sources. Wang and Gui [120] described a recommendation trust model, where the trust between recommendation nodes and subject (i.e., trustor) nodes is calculated based on information entropy algorithm. By evaluating the trust value, a node can identify malicious nodes in its neighbors and avoid interacting with them.

11.4.2 Trust-Related Attacks and Defenses

With the rapid development of trust models, profit-driven attacks that exploit vulnerabilities of trust evaluation schemes also gain popularity. Specifically, these attacks may set one or several attack goals as follows:

- To conduct bad behavior while maintaining high trust values to avoid punishment
- To downgrade trust values of honest users
- To undermine users' trust relationship

In this section, some typical trust-related attacks and their defenses are discussed in details. Some of the attacks can be conducted by a single malicious user, while others have to be launched by a group of malicious users. Note that, due to the limited influence of one individual user, most attacks in practice are performed by a group of malicious users, which are also called collusion attacks. In collusion attacks, multiple malicious IDs sharing the same attack goals are either controlled by one attacker (i.e., Sybil attacks) or actively collaborating with one another to coordinately conduct bad behavior.

11.4.2.1 New Comer Attack

A straightforward attack is the new comer attack, where a malicious user with low trust value simply drops its original ID and re-joins the system with a new user ID to refresh its trust value. New comer attacks are especially popular and efficient in systems where the cost of registering new user IDs is trivial.

To defend against such attacks, many UGC-centric systems restrict the number of online pseudonym that can be obtained by their users. They increase the cost of acquiring a new user ID by binding user identities with IP address [121] and requiring entry fees [122]. Furthermore, trust bootstrap studies suggest reasonably assigning trust for a newcomer, such as low initial trust [123] and initial trust based on majority behavior [124], so that new IDs have to conduct a number of good behavior to accumulate sufficient trust values.

11.4.2.2 Self-Boosting and Bad-Mouthing Attack

In self-boosting attacks, multiple colluded malicious users positively recommend each other to their peers, aiming to boost their own trust values. On the other hand, these malicious users may also conduct bad-mouthing attacks, where they spread bad comments on targeted honest users, aiming to downgrade their trust values. These attacks are especially effective against trust models where peer recommendation plays a critical role.

The defenses against self-boosting and bad-mouthing attacks require the separation of recommendation trust from behavior trust. In other words, each user should have two types of trust: behavior trust that evaluates how likely a user may conduct good behavior and recommendation trust that evaluates how likely a user may provide good recommendation. As a consequence, a user with a low recommendation trust value will have very limited influence on other users' decision making [21].

11.4.2.3 On–Off Attack

In *on–off attacks*, malicious users conduct good and bad behavior alternatively, aiming at damaging the system through bad behavior while maintaining their trust values above the threshold through good behavior to avoid being penalized.

To defend against such attacks, the dynamic properties of trust should be considered. In particular, a good user account may be compromised and starts to conduct bad behavior or an incompetent user account may turn into a competent one due to environment changes [21]. As a result, the trust value of a user should be dynamically changing according to the user's most recent behavior pattern. To implement such dynamics, many trust models control the influence of historical behavior through forgetting schemes. In [125], only the most recent behavior is considered in trust calculation. This scheme, however, raises wide concerns because both good and bad behavior is forgotten equally fast, which may help the attacker to re-gain reputation. Then, the fading factor [105] is introduced to gradually reduce the weights of behavior provided long time ago. Furthermore, the system can count users' good behavior and bad behavior asymmetrically. The adaptive forgetting scheme in [21] makes good reputation be built up through consistent good behavior but can be easily ruined by only a few bad behavior.

11.4.2.4 More Advanced Attack

In *conflicting behavior attacks*, a malicious user performs differently to different groups of honest peers to cause conflicts in their recommendations, aiming at undermining the recommendation trust among different groups of honest peers.

To strengthen attacks and to avoid being detected, a smart attacker makes malicious user IDs collaborate in more complicated ways. In the *oscillation attack* [125], malicious user IDs are divided into different groups and each group plays a dynamically different role. At a given time, some groups focus on bad-mouthing honest users while other groups focus on self-boosting attacks. The roles of those groups switch dynamically. In the RepTrap attack proposed in [126], malicious user IDs coordinately break the "majority rule"-based trust, by making the majority recommendations on some items be considered as dishonest recommendations. These items are referred to as traps. In this attack, malicious users take turns to make one trap after another. By doing so, they can increase their own recommendation trust as well as reduce honest users' recommendation trust.

To handle attacks with complicated collusion, defense schemes [38,127] have been proposed from two new angles: temporal analysis, which explores the rich user behavior information in time domain (e.g., time when different behavior is conducted, behavior changing trend, etc.), and user correlation analysis, which aims to identify close relationship among colluded malicious users. These advanced defense schemes are compatible with most of the earlier defense schemes and have shown promising results when tested against real user data.

There is a fierce competition between trust-related attacks and defenses. This competition will surely continue to evolve and lead to new research challenges and opportunities.

11.5 CONCLUSION

In conclusion, the flexibility and convenience of creating and sharing contents online have greatly encouraged individual users' contribution to today's digital information. As a consequence, UGC has become a major source of big data. Such data provides rich information for human user behavior-related studies across different disciplines, including but not limited to computer science, sociology, economics, marketing, etc.

In spite of the substantial value, its sheer volume, on the other hand, also raises great challenges. In this chapter, we analyze the "five-V" characteristics of UGC and mainly focus on the discussions about veracity—the trustworthiness of the data. In particular, we introduce three major platforms where UGC is generated and shared, describe an abstract system model for these UGC-centric platforms, and provide an overview of diverse security, privacy, and trust challenges against such platforms. In the rest part of the chapter, we discuss the state-of-the-art security, privacy, and trust attacks and defenses on UGC in details, including their definitions, impact, application scenarios, advantages and limitations, etc., with the purpose of providing the readers a comprehensive understanding of the challenges as well as opportunities in this newly emerging and rapidly evolving research field.

REFERENCES

1. Yuri Demchenko, Paola Grosso, Cees De Laat, and Peter Membrey. Addressing big data issues in scientific data infrastructure. In *2013 International Conference on Collaboration Technologies and Systems (CTS)*, pp. 48–55. IEEE, 2013.
2. Doug Laney. 3D data management: Controlling data volume, velocity and variety. *META Group Research Note*, 6:70, 2001.
3. Mark R. Robertson. *300+ Hours of Video Uploaded to YouTube Every Minute*. http://www.reelseo.com/youtube-300-hours/.
4. *Twitter Usage Statistics*. http://www.internetlivestats.com/twitter-statistics/.
5. *Yelp Announces First Quarter 2016 Financial Results*. http://www.businesswire.com/news/home/20160505006373/en/Yelp-Announces-Quarter-2016-Financial-Results.
6. Sitaram Asur and Bernardo A. Huberman. Predicting the future with social media. In *2010 IEEE/WIC/ACM International Conference on Web Intelligence and Intelligent Agent Technology (WI-IAT)*, Vol. 1, pp. 492–499. IEEE, Toronto, Canada, 2010.

7. Takeshi Sakaki, Makoto Okazaki, and Yutaka Matsuo. Earthquake shakes Twitter users: Real-time event detection by social sensors. In *Proceedings of the 19th International Conference on World Wide Web*, pp. 851–860. ACM, Raleigh, NC, 2010.
8. Cheng-Min Huang, Edward Chan, and Adnan A. Hyder. Web 2.0 and Internet social networking: A new tool for disaster management? Lessons from Taiwan. *BMC Medical Informatics and Decision Making*, 10(1):57, 2010.
9. Andranik Tumasjan, Timm Oliver Sprenger, Philipp G. Sandner, and Isabell M. Welpe. Predicting elections with Twitter: What 140 characters reveal about political sentiment. *ICWSM*, 10:178–185, 2010.
10. Christine Williams and Girish Gulati. *What Is a Social Network Worth? Facebook and Vote Share in the 2008 Presidential Primaries*. American Political Science Association, Washington, DC, 2008.
11. Nan Hu, Indranil Bose, Noi Sian Koh, and Ling Liu. Manipulation of online reviews: An analysis of ratings, readability, and sentiments. *Decision Support Systems*, 52(3):674–684, 2012.
12. Nielsen. *Net Ratings*. http://en-us.nielsen.com/rankings/insights/rankings/internet/, 2009.
13. Sarah Perez. *Social networking use triples from only a year ago*. http://www.nytimes.com/external/readwriteweb/2009/09/25/25readwriteweb-social-networking-use-triples-from-only-a-y-72670.html, 2009.
14. Daren C. Brabham. Crowdsourcing as a model for problem solving: An introduction and cases. *Convergence: The International Journal of Research into New Media Technologies*, 14(1):75–90, 2008.
15. Jeff Howe. The rise of crowdsourcing. *Wired Magazine*, 14(6): 1–4, 2006.
16. *Wikipedia:Statistics*. https://en.wikipedia.org/wiki/Wikipedia:Statistics.
17. Daniel Houser and John Wooders. Reputation in auctions: Theory and evidence from eBay. *Journal of Economics and Management Strategy*, 15:353–369, June 2006.
18. comScore Inc. and The Kelsey Group. *Press Release: Online Consumer-Generated Reviews Have Significant Impact on Offline Purchase Behavior*. http://www.comscore.com/press/release.asp?press=1928, November 2007.
19. British Standard. Information security management systems—Specification with guidance for use. *British Standards Institution, BS*, 7799(2), 2002.
20. *Privacy*. https://en.wikipedia.org/wiki/Privacy.
21. Yan Lindsay Sun, Zhu Han, Wei Yu, and KJ Ray Liu. Attacks on trust evaluation in distributed networks. In *2006 40th Annual Conference on Information Sciences and Systems*, pp. 1461–1466. IEEE, Princeton University Princeton, NJ, 2006.
22. Alessandro Acquisti and Ralph Gross. Predicting social security numbers from public data. *Proceedings of the National Academy of Sciences*, 106(27):10975–10980, 2009.
23. Ralph Gross and Alessandro Acquisti. Information revelation and privacy in online social networks. In *Proceedings of the 2005 ACM Workshop on Privacy in the Electronic Society*, pp. 71–80. ACM, Alexandria, VA, 2005.
24. Alan Mislove, Bimal Viswanath, Krishna P. Gummadi, and Peter Druschel. You are who you know: Inferring user profiles in online social networks. In *Proceedings of the Third ACM International Conference on Web Search and Data Mining*, pp. 251–260. ACM, New York City, 2010.
25. Arvind Narayanan and Vitaly Shmatikov. Robust de-anonymization of large sparse datasets. In *2008 IEEE Symposium on Security and Privacy (SP 2008)*, pp. 111–125. IEEE, Oakland, CA, 2008.
26. Hien To, Gabriel Ghinita, and Cyrus Shahabi. A framework for protecting worker location privacy in spatial crowdsourcing. *Proceedings of the VLDB Endowment*, 7(10):919–930, 2014.
27. Lav R. Varshney. Privacy and reliability in crowdsourcing service delivery. In *2012 Annual SRII Global Conference*, pp. 55–60. IEEE, San Jose, CA, 2012.
28. Gabriella Kazai. In search of quality in crowdsourcing for search engine evaluation. In *European Conference on Information Retrieval*, pp. 165–176. Springer, Dublin, Ireland, 2011.
29. Man-Ching Yuen, Irwin King, and Kwong-Sak Leung. A survey of crowdsourcing systems. In *2011 IEEE Third International Conference on Privacy, Security, Risk and Trust (PASSAT) and 2011 IEEE Third International Conference on Social Computing (SocialCom)*, pp. 766–773. IEEE, Boston, MA, 2011.
30. Rion Snow, Brendan O'Connor, Daniel Jurafsky, and Andrew Y. Ng. Cheap and fast—But is it good?: Evaluating non-expert annotations for natural language tasks. In *Proceedings of the Conference on Empirical Methods in Natural Language Processing*, pp. 254–263. Association for Computational Linguistics, Honolulu, Hawaii, 2008.

31. Victor S. Sheng, Foster Provost, and Panagiotis G. Ipeirotis. Get another label? Improving data quality and data mining using multiple, noisy labelers. In *Proceedings of the 14th ACM SIGKDD International Conference on Knowledge Discovery and Data Mining*, pp. 614–622. ACM, Las Vegas, NV, 2008.
32. Cyrus Rashtchian, Peter Young, Micah Hodosh, and Julia Hockenmaier. Collecting image annotations using Amazon's mechanical turk. In *Proceedings of the NAACL HLT 2010 Workshop on Creating Speech and Language Data with Amazon's Mechanical Turk*, pp. 139–147. Association for Computational Linguistics, 2010.
33. Riyad Kalla. *Apparently It Is Easy to Game Amazons Reviews*. http://www.thebuzzmedia.com/apparently-it-is-easy-to-gameamazons-reviews/.
34. Jennifer Brown and John Morgan. Reputation in online auctions: The market for trust. *California Management Review*, 49(1):61–81, 2006.
35. Suw Charmen-Anderson. *Fake Reviews: Amazon's Rotten Core*. Forbes, 2012, http://www.forbes.com/sites/suwcharmananderson/2012/08/28/fake-reviews-amazons-rotten-core/#623d6afd66d6.
36. Amy Harmon. Amazon glitch unmasks war of reviewers. *The New York Times*, 14(8), 2004. http://www.nytimes.com/2004/02/14/us/amazon-glitch-unmasks-war-of-reviewers.html.
37. Paulo Laureti, Lionel Moret, Y.-C. Zhang, and Y.-K. Yu. Information filtering via iterative refinement. *EPL (Europhysics Letters)*, 75(6):1006, 2006.
38. Yuhong Liu and Yan Sun. Anomaly detection in feedback-based reputation systems through temporal and correlation analysis. In *2010 IEEE Second International Conference on Social Computing (SocialCom)*, pp. 65–72. IEEE, Minneapolis, MN, 2010.
39. Jie Zhang and Robin Cohen. A personalized approach to address unfair ratings in multiagent reputation systems. In *Proceedings of the AAMAS Workshop on Trust in Agent Societies*. Citeseer, Hakodate, Japan, 2006.
40. John R. Douceur. The Sybil attack. In *International Workshop on Peer-to-Peer Systems*, pp. 251–260. Springer, Cambridge, MA, 2002.
41. Leyla Bilge, Thorsten Strufe, Davide Balzarotti, and Engin Kirda. All your contacts are belong to us: Automated identity theft attacks on social networks. In *Proceedings of the 18th International Conference on World Wide Web*, pp. 551–560. ACM, Madrid, Spain, 2009.
42. Alice Cheng and Eric Friedman. Manipulability of PageRank under Sybil strategies. In *First Workshop on the Economics of Networked Systems* (*NetEcon06*),2006.
43. Yafei Yang, Qinyuan Feng, Yan Lindsay Sun, and Yafei Dai. RepTrap: A novel attack on feedback-based reputation systems. In *Proceedings of the Fourth International Conference on Security and Privacy in Communication Networks*, p. 8. ACM, Istanbul, Turkey, 2008.
44. Haifeng Yu, Michael Kaminsky, Phillip B. Gibbons, and Abraham Flaxman. SybilGuard: Defending against Sybil attacks via social networks. *ACM SIGCOMM Computer Communication Review*, 36: 267–278, 2006.
45. Haifeng Yu, Phillip B. Gibbons, Michael Kaminsky, and Feng Xiao. SybilLimit: A near-optimal social network defense against Sybil attacks. In *2008 IEEE Symposium on Security and Privacy (SP 2008)*, pp. 3–17. IEEE, Oakland, California, 2008.
46. George Danezis and Prateek Mittal. SybilInfer: Detecting Sybil nodes using social networks. In *NDSS*, San Diego, CA, 2009.
47. Sonja Buchegger and Jean-Yves Le Boudec. A robust reputation system for mobile ad-hoc networks. *Technical Report*, 2003.
48. George Danezis, Chris Lesniewski-Laas, M. Frans Kaashoek, and Ross Anderson. Sybil-resistant DHT routing. In *European Symposium on Research in Computer Security*, pp. 305–318. Springer, 2005.
49. Brian Neil Levine, Clay Shields, and N. Boris Margolin. A survey of solutions to the Sybil attack. University of Massachusetts Amherst, Amherst, MA, 7, 2006.
50. Chris Joy Hoofnagle. Identity theft: Making the known unknowns known. *The Harvard Journal of Law and Technology*, 21:97, 2007.
51. Markus Huber, Martin Mulazzani, Edgar Weippl, Gerhard Kitzler, and Sigrun Goluch. Friend-in-the-middle attacks: Exploiting social networking sites for spam. *IEEE Internet Computing*, 15(3):28–34, 2011.
52. Jessica Velasco. *4 Case Studies in Fraud: Social Media and Identity Theft*. http://socialnomics.net/2016/01/13/4-case-studies-in-fraud-social-media-and-identity-theft/.

53. ITworld. *Social Spam Is Taking Over the Internet*. http://www.itworld.com/article/2832566/it-management/social-spam-is-taking-over-the-internet.html.
54. Vinh Nguyen. *More Facebook Accounts Got Hacked, 1.5 Million Credentials Were Stolen*. http://essayboard.com/2010/04/26/more-facebook-accounts-got-hacked-1-5-million-credentials-were-stolen/, April 26, 2010.
55. Tom N. Jagatic, Nathaniel A. Johnson, Markus Jakobsson, and Filippo Menczer. Social phishing. *Communications of the ACM*, 50(10):94–100, 2007.
56. Ed Novak and Qun Li. A survey of security and privacy in online social networks. *College of William and Mary Computer Science Technical Report*, 2012.
57. Pritam Gundecha, Geoffrey Barbier, and Huan Liu. Exploiting vulnerability to secure user privacy on a social networking site. In *Proceedings of the 17th ACM SIGKDD International Conference on Knowledge Discovery and Data Mining*, pp. 511–519. ACM, San Diego, CA, 2011.
58. Latanya Sweeney. Simple demographics often identify people uniquely. *Health (San Francisco)*, 671: 1–34, 2000.
59. João Paulo Pesce, Diego Las Casas, Gustavo Rauber, and Virgílio Almeida. Privacy attacks in social media using photo tagging networks: A case study with Facebook. In *Proceedings of the First Workshop on Privacy and Security in Online Social Media*, p. 4. ACM, Lyon, France, 2012.
60. Matthew Smith, Christian Szongott, Benjamin Henne, and Gabriele Von Voigt. Big data privacy issues in public social media. In *2012 Sixth IEEE International Conference on Digital Ecosystems Technologies (DEST)*, pp. 1–6. IEEE, Campione d'Italia, Italy, 2012.
61. Hal Berghel. Identity theft, social security numbers, and the web. *Communications of the ACM*, 43(2): 17–21, 2000.
62. Na Li. Privacy-aware display strategy in friend search. In *Proceedings of IEEE International Conference on Communications (ICC), Communication and Information Systems Security Symposium*, pp. 951–956. IEEE, Sydney, Australia, 2014.
63. Kurt Wagner. *Your Private Facebook Friends List Isn't Actually That Private*, 2014, http://mashable.com/2014/06/02/facebook-friends-list-privacy/#FFEz3NsU4gqN.
64. Akira Yamada, Tiffany Hyun-Jin Kim, and Adrian Perrig. Exploiting privacy policy conflicts in online social networks. *Technical Report*, 2012.
65. Yuhong Liu and Na Li. An advanced collusion attack against user friendship privacy in OSNs. In *The 40th IEEE Computer Society International Conference on Computers, Software & Applications*. IEEE, Atlanta, GA, 2016.
66. Joseph Bonneau, Jonathan Anderson, Ross Anderson, and Frank Stajano. Eight friends are enough: Social graph approximation via public listings. In *Proceedings of the Second ACM EuroSys Workshop on Social Network Systems*, pp. 13–18. ACM, Nuremberg, Germany, 2009.
67. Bin Zhou and Jian Pei. Preserving privacy in social networks against neighborhood attacks. In *IEEE 24th International Conference on Data Engineering, 2008 (ICDE 2008)*, pp. 506–515. IEEE, Cancun, Mexico, 2008.
68. Heather Richter Lipford, Andrew Besmer, and Jason Watson. Understanding privacy settings in Facebook with an audience view. *UPSEC*, 8:1–8, 2008.
69. Lujun Fang and Kristen LeFevre. Privacy wizards for social networking sites. In *Proceedings of the 19th International Conference on World Wide Web*, pp. 351–360. ACM, Raleigh, NC, 2010.
70. Farzana Rahman, Md Endadul Hoque, Ferdaus Ahmed Kawsar, and Sheikh Iqbal Ahamed. Preserve your privacy with PCO: A privacy sensitive architecture for context obfuscation for pervasive e-community based applications. In *2010 IEEE Second International Conference on Social Computing (SocialCom)*, pp. 41–48. IEEE, Minneapolis, MN, 2010.
71. Matthew M. Lucas and Nikita Borisov. FlyByNight: Mitigating the privacy risks of social networking. In *Proceedings of the Seventh ACM Workshop on Privacy in the Electronic Society*, pp. 1–8. ACM, Alexandria, VA, 2008.
72. Wanying Luo, Qi Xie, and Urs Hengartner. FaceCloak: An architecture for user privacy on social networking sites. In *International Conference on Computational Science and Engineering, 2009 (CSE'09)*, Vol. 3, pp. 26–33. IEEE, Vancouver, BC, 2009.
73. Alina Campan and Traian Marius Truta. A clustering approach for data and structural anonymity in social networks. In *PinKDD'08*, Las Vegas, NV, 2008.

74. Latanya Sweeney. k-Anonymity: A model for protecting privacy. *International Journal on Uncertainty, Fuzziness and Knowledge-Based Systems*, 10(5):557–570, December 2002.
75. Ashwin Machanavajjhala, Daniel Kifer, Johannes Gehrke, and Muthuramakrishnan Venkitasubramaniam. ℓ-Diversity: Privacy beyond *k*-anonymity. *ACM Transactions on Knowledge Discovery from Data (TKDD)*, 1(1):3, 2007.
76. Ninghui Li, Tiancheng Li, and Suresh Venkatasubramanian. t-Closeness: Privacy beyond k-anonymity and l-diversity. In *Proceedings of the 23rd International Conference on Data Engineering*, Istanbul, Turkey, 2007.
77. Cynthia Dwork. Differential privacy. In *Proceedings of the 33rd International Colloquium on Automata, Languages and Programming*, Venice, Italy, 2006.
78. Na Li, Nan Zhang, and Sajal K. Das. Preserving relation privacy in online social network data. *Internet Computing, IEEE*, 15(3):35–42, May–June 2011.
79. James Cheng, Ada Wai-Chee Fu, and Jia Liu. K-isomorphism: Privacy preservation in network publication against structural attack. In *SIGMOD'10*, Indianapolis, IN, 2010.
80. Sudipto Das, Ömer Egecioglu, and Amr El Abbadi. Anonymizing edge-weighted social network graphs. *Technical Report CS-2009-03*, Computer Science, The University of California, Santa Barbara, 2009.
81. Michael Hay, Gerome Miklau, David Jensen, Don Towsley, and Philipp Weis. Resisting structural reidentification in anonymized social networks. In *PVLDB'08*, 2008.
82. Na Li, Nan Zhang, and Sajal Das. Relationship privacy preservation in publishing online social networks. In *Proceedings of the Third IEEE International Conference on Social Computing (SocialCom'11)*. MIT, Boston, MA, 2011.
83. Kun Liu, Kamalika Das, Tyrone Grandison, and Hillol Kargupta. Privacy-preserving data analysis on graphs and social networks. In H. Kargupta, J. Han, P. Yu, R. Motwani, and V. Kumar, editors, *Next Generation Data Mining*. CRC Press, Boca Raton, 2008.
84. L. Liu, J. Wang, J. Liu, and J. Zhang. Privacy preserving in social networks against sensitive edge disclosure. *Technical Report CMIDA-HiPSCCS 006-08*, Department of Computer Science, University of Kentucky, KY, 2008.
85. E. Zheleva and L. Getoor. Preserving the privacy of sensitive relationships in graph data. In *Proceedings of the First ACM SIGKDD International Workshop on Privacy, Security, and Trust in KDD, PinKDD2007, in Conjunction with the 13th ACM SIGKDD International Conference in Knowledge Discovery and Data Mining, KDD, (PinKDD'07)*, San Jose, CA, 2007.
86. B. Zhou and J. Pei. Preserving privacy in social networks against neighborhood attacks. In *Proceedings of the 24th IEEE International Conference on Data Engineering (ICDE'08)*, Cancun, Mexico, pp. 506–515, 2008.
87. B. Zhou, J. Pei, and W. Luk. A brief survey on anonymization techniques for privacy preserving publishing of social network data. *SIGKDD Explorations*, 10(2):12–22, December 2008.
88. Lei Zou , Lei Chen, and M. Tamer Özsu. K-automorphism: A general framework for privacy preserving network publication. *Proceedings of the VLDB Endowment (PVLDB'09)*, 2(1):946–957, August 2009.
89. Ashwin Machanavajjhala, Daniel Kifer, Johannes Gehrke, and Muthuramakrishnan Venkitasubramaniam. l-Diversity: Privacy beyond k-anonymity. *ACM Transactions on Knowledge Discovery from Data (TKDD)*, 1(1):3, 2007.
90. Ninghui Li, Tiancheng Li, and Suresh Venkatasubramanian. t-Closeness: Privacy beyond k-anonymity and l-diversity. In *IEEE 23rd International Conference on Data Engineering, 2007 (ICDE 2007)*, pp. 106–115. IEEE, Istanbul, Turkey, 2007.
91. Cynthia Dwork. Differential privacy. In *Automata, Languages and Programming*, pp. 1–12. Springer, 2006.
92. Anil K. Jain, M. Narasimha Murty, and Patrick J. Flynn. Data clustering: A review. *ACM Computing Surveys (CSUR)*, 31(3):264–323, 1999.
93. Michael Hay, Gerome Miklau, David Jensen, Don Towsley, and Philipp Weis. Resisting structural reidentification in anonymized social networks. *Proceedings of the VLDB Endowment*, 1(1):102–114, 2008.
94. Alina Campan and Traian Marius Truta. A clustering approach for data and structural anonymity in social networks, Las Vegas, NV, 2008.
95. Sudipto Das, Omer Egecioglu, and Amr El Abbadi. Anonymizing weighted social network graphs. In *2010 IEEE 26th International Conference on Data Engineering (ICDE)*, pp. 904–907. IEEE, Long Beach, CA, 2010.

96. Lian Liu, Jie Wang, Jinze Liu, and Jun Zhang. Privacy preserving in social networks against sensitive edge disclosure. *Technical Report CMIDA-HiPSCCS 006-08*, Department of Computer Science, University of Kentucky, KY, 2008.
97. Xiaowei Ying and Xintao Wu. Randomizing social networks: A spectrum preserving approach. In *SDM*, Vol. 8, pp. 739–750. SIAM, 2008.
98. Bin Zhou, Jian Pei, and WoShun Luk. A brief survey on anonymization techniques for privacy preserving publishing of social network data. *ACM Sigkdd Explorations Newsletter*, 10(2):12–22, 2008.
99. Ueli Maurer. Modelling a public-key infrastructure. In *European Symposium on Research in Computer Security*, pp. 325–350. Springer, 1996.
100. Michael K. Reiter and Stuart G. Stubblebine. Resilient authentication using path independence. *IEEE Transactions on Computers*, 47(12):1351–1362, 1998.
101. Farag Azzedin and Muthucumaru Maheswaran. Trust modeling for peer-to-peer based computing systems. In *Proceedings of the International Parallel and Distributed Processing Symposium, 2003*, 10 pp. IEEE, Nice, France, 2003.
102. Yan Lindsay Sun, Wei Yu, Zhu Han, and KJ Ray Liu. Information theoretic framework of trust modeling and evaluation for ad hoc networks. *IEEE Journal on Selected Areas in Communications*, 24(2):305–317, 2006.
103. Lik Mui, Mojdeh Mohtashemi, Cheewee Ang, Peter Szolovits, and Ari Halberstadt. Ratings in distributed systems: A Bayesian approach. In *Proceedings of the Workshop on Information Technologies and Systems (WITS)*, pp. 1–7, New Orleans, LA, 2001.
104. Audun Jøsang and Jochen Haller. Dirichlet reputation systems. In *Proceedings of the Second International Conference on Availability, Reliability and Security, 2007, (ARES 2007)*, pp. 112–119. IEEE, Vienna, 2007.
105. Audun Jøsang and Roslan Ismail. The beta reputation system. In *Proceedings of the 15th Bled Electronic Commerce Conference*, Vol. 5, pp. 2502–2511, 2002.
106. Andrew Whitby, Audun Jøsang, and Jadwiga Indulska. Filtering out unfair ratings in Bayesian reputation systems. In *Proceedings of Seventh International Workshop on Trust in Agent Societies*, Vol. 6, pp. 106–117, 2004.
107. Glenn Shafer. The Dempster-Shafer theory. In *Encyclopedia of Artificial Intelligence*, pp. 330–331. 1992.
108. Peter Walley. Measures of uncertainty in expert systems. *Artificial Intelligence*, 83(1):1–58, 1996.
109. Ronald R. Yager. On the Dempster-Shafer framework and new combination rules. *Information Sciences*, 41(2):93–137, 1987.
110. Galina Rogova. Combining the results of several neural network classifiers. *Neural networks*, 7(5):777–781, 1994.
111. Huadong Wu, Mel Siegel, Rainer Stiefelhagen, and Jie Yang. Sensor fusion using Dempster-Shafer theory [for context-aware HCI]. In *Proceedings of the 19th IEEE Instrumentation and Measurement Technology Conference, 2002 (IMTC/2002)*, Vol. 1, pp. 7–12. IEEE, Anchorage, AK, 2002.
112. Young Ae Kim and Muhammad A. Ahmad. Trust, distrust and lack of confidence of users in online social media-sharing communities. *Knowledge-Based Systems*, 37:438–450, 2013.
113. Bin Yu and Munindar P. Singh. Detecting deception in reputation management. In *Proceedings of the Second International Joint Conference on Autonomous Agents and Multiagent Systems*, pp. 73–80. ACM, Melbourne, VIC, Australia, 2003.
114. Siyuan Liu, Alex C. Kot, Chunyan Miao, and Yin-Leng Theng. A Dempster-Shafer theory based witness trustworthiness model to cope with unfair ratings in e-marketplace. In *Proceedings of the 14th Annual International Conference on Electronic Commerce*, pp. 99–106. ACM, Singapore, 2012.
115. Yuhong Liu, Yan Lindsay Sun, Siyuan Liu, and Alex C. Kot. Securing online reputation systems through Dempster-Shafer theory based trust model. *IEEE Transactions on Information Forensics and Security*, 8(6), 2013.
116. Lotfi A. Zadeh. Toward a theory of fuzzy information granulation and its centrality in human reasoning and fuzzy logic. *Fuzzy Sets and Systems*, 90(2):111–127, 1997.
117. Samia Nefti, Farid Meziane, and Khairudin Kasiran. A fuzzy trust model for e-commerce. In *Seventh IEEE International Conference on E-Commerce Technology, 2005 (CEC 2005)*, pp. 401–404. IEEE, Munich, Germany, 2005.
118. Yung-Ming Li and Chien-Pang Kao. Trepps: A trust-based recommender system for peer production services. *Expert Systems with Applications*, 36(2):3263–3277, 2009.

119. Claude Elwood Shannon. A mathematical theory of communication. *ACM SIGMOBILE Mobile Computing and Communications Review*, 5(1):3–55, 2001.
120. Gang Wang and Xiaolin Gui. Dynamic recommendation trust model based on information entropy and heuristic rules in e-commerce environment. *Elektronika ir Elektrotechnika*, 19(4):71–76, 2013.
121. Martin Abadi, Michael Burrows, Butler Lampson, and Gordon Plotkin. A calculus for access control in distributed systems. *ACM Transactions on Programming Languages and Systems (TOPLAS)*, 15(4): 706–734, 1993.
122. Michal Feldman, Christos Papadimitriou, John Chuang, and Ion Stoica. Free-riding and whitewashing in peer-to-peer systems. In *Proceedings of the ACM SIGCOMM Workshop on Practice and Theory of Incentives in Networked Systems*, pp. 228–236. ACM, Portland, OR, 2004.
123. Giorgos Zacharia, Alexandros Moukas, and Pattie Maes. Collaborative reputation mechanisms for electronic marketplaces. *Decision Support Systems*, 29(4):371–388, 2000.
124. Zaki Malik and Athman Bouguettaya. Reputation bootstrapping for trust establishment among web services. *IEEE Internet Computing*, 13(1):40–47, 2009.
125. Mudhakar Srivatsa, Li Xiong, and Ling Liu. Trustguard: Countering vulnerabilities in reputation management for decentralized overlay networks. In *Proceedings of the 14th International Conference on World Wide Web*, pp. 422–431. ACM, Chiba, Japan, 2005.
126. Yafei Yang, Qinyuan Feng, Yan Sun, and Yafei Dai. Reputation trap: An powerful attack on reputation system of file sharing p2p environment. In *Proceedings of the Fourth International Conference on Security and Privacy in Communication Networks*. Istanbul, Turkey, 2008.
127. Yafei Yang, Yan Lindsay Sun, Steven Kay, and Qing Yang. Defending online reputation systems against collaborative unfair raters through signal modeling and trust. In *Proceedings of the 2009 ACM Symposium on Applied Computing*, pp. 1308–1315. ACM, Honolulu, HI, 2009.

12 Role of Real-Time Big Data Processing in the Internet of Things

Miyuru Dayarathna, Paul Fremantle, Srinath Perera, and Sriskandarajah Suhothayan

CONTENTS

ABSTRACT

Increasing deployments of the Internet of Things (IoT) applications have brought forward the requirement of processing massive volumes of streaming data generated by the IoT sensors. The general real-time big data processing has been confronted with multiple new challenges when addressing the data-processing requirements of the IoT applications. In this chapter, we describe the specifics of the challenges/issues faced by the IoT data-processing applications and how real-time big data processing and various related technological paradigms have been used to mitigate them. The chapter sheds light on key areas such as maintaining real-time responses, handling massive amounts of data, different flavors of data analytics, as well as information security aspects of real-time data processing in the context of the IoT. We observed that while multiple data-stream processing systems and architectures have been proposed and implemented, very few, if any, stream-processing systems specifically targeted for IoT use cases exist. Furthermore, we observed that detailed investigations need to be carried out in applying real-time big data-processing technologies in the context of IoT. We envision multiple works will appear in the near future that will fill the gaps of applying real-time big data-processing technologies for the IoT.

12.1 INTRODUCTION

Real-time and near-real-time processing of big data has gained significant attention in recent times due to the rise of the Internet of Things (IoT). Out of the 3Vs of big data—volume, velocity, and variety [1]—successful handling of the velocity and volume aspects has a major impact on what can be achieved with IoT. Real-time big data-processing technologies are the enablers for achieving this impact. However, conventional real-time data-processing technologies often have challenges in specific areas to make them scale and run efficiently when faced with IoT-scale data. The aim of this chapter is to evaluate the challenges arising in real-time processing of large amounts of data generated by the IoT, and to look at ways that technology is improving to meet these challenges.

IoT refers to connecting set of devices (their sensors and actuators) and systems with the Internet in order to create seamless interactions between the users of the system. IoT use cases come in all sizes and shapes. They can be part of our daily lives and have the potential to transform day-to-day lives. It is estimated that by 2020, more than 20 billion IoT-enabled devices will be used across a wide range of industries [2]. Cisco Consulting Services estimates that more than 8 trillion US dollars in value at stake for the private and public sectors will be generated by IoT between 2013 and 2022 [3]. Hence, IoT provides significant opportunities to create value in business processes such as automation of many manual processes, which enables the creation of entirely new products and services [4,5]. The following are some of the key IoT use cases:

1. Predictive maintenance
2. Tracking moving "things" and alerting
3. Improving logistic of thing networks
4. Smart health and in-home care
5. Personal tracking and health (e.g., Fitbit)
6. Sports analytics
7. Security and surveillance, for example, surveillance, security, asset tracking, wildlife tracking, forest tracking, safety and security via home surveillance, monitor health and kids, and perimeter checks for pets and kids
8. Calculating and acting on user context (targeted advertising)
9. Transport: trains, buses
10. Energy efficiency (load prediction, smart lighting, metering, heating)
11. Smart agriculture (watering based on moisture levels, pest control, livestock management) correlate with other data sources like weather and delivery of pesticides, etc. through drones
12. Smart retail and restaurants: monitoring stores, supply chain, logistics, customer tracking in store, etc.
13. Smart buildings (power, security, proactive maintenance, heating, ventilation, and air conditioning [HVAC], etc.)
14. Smart logistics, supply chain, and operations (e.g., airlines, hospitality)
15. Financial services, smart banking, usage-based insurance, better data for insurance, and fraud detection via better data

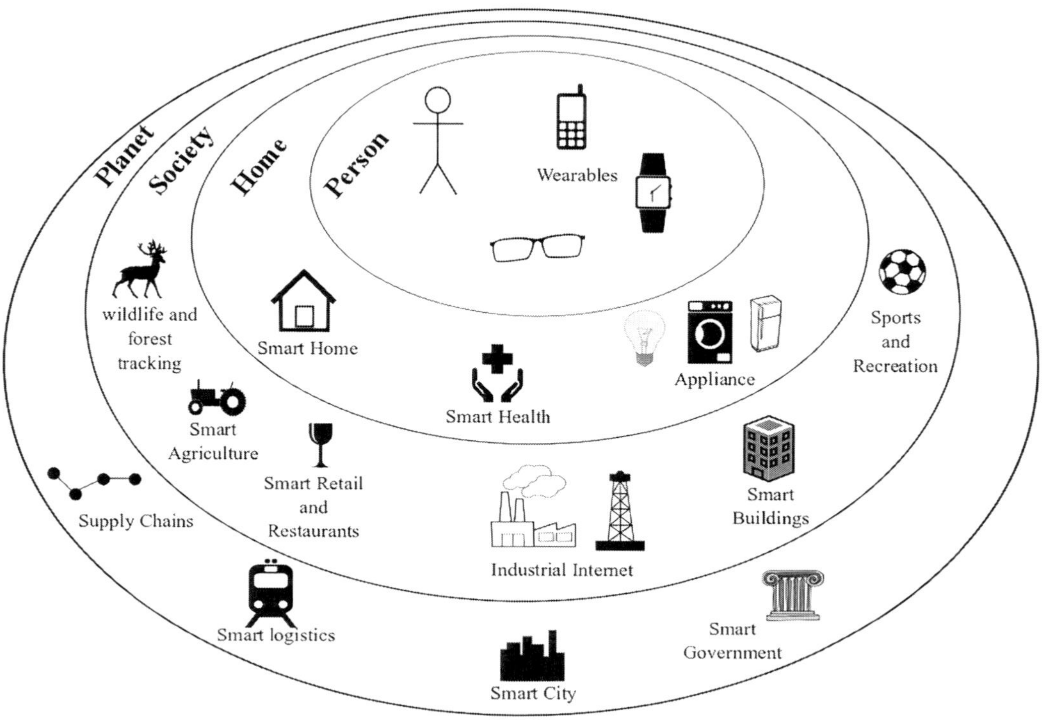

FIGURE 12.1 A taxonomy of IoT use cases.

16. Smart city (e.g., waste management, traffic, pollution monitoring, parking, urban planning, smart parking, road tax)

A classification of the IoT use cases is shown in Figure 12.1. The taxonomy is grouped into four areas as Person, Home, Society, and Planet. While they are grouped into four such categories, some use cases overlap with each other. For example, home refrigerator will be connected to a supply chain management system, which will automatically order consumables when they run out of stock.

Real-time analytics conducts data processing online with low latency values. Real-time analytics becomes important when the velocity and the volume of the data being received by the system are very large and when the type of data processing is mostly one-time operation. For example, filtering call detail records (CDR) based on the customer's status (e.g., blacklisted) [6], radio astronomy [7], road traffic management [8,9], etc. are examples for such applications. For example, LOFAR's 77 antenna stations distributed in a 10,000-square-km area may generate data around 37 Tbit/s [7]. In such situations, the data-processing system should be capable of handling such huge data rate, where real-time data processing has a significant role to play.

Real-time processing is critical for IoT due to several reasons. First, millions of sensors may get connected in a typical IoT installation, which produce immense amounts of data. Most of the data produced by such sensors may not necessarily be required to be stored. Hence, the use of real-time processing technologies fits well with such data-processing scenario since the data get processed as and when they arrive at the real-time data-processing system. Second, the devices in an IoT installation need to respond in a timely fashion. For example, the warning messages emitted by the pacemaker of a heart patient need to be reached by the paramedical team within seconds in order to provide fast emergency treatments. Many of the prominent IoT software platforms have been developed with the ability of conducting real-time data processing due to the significance of real-time data processing in IoT data analytics (see Table 12.1 for examples).

In this chapter, first, we will elaborate on specific challenges that need to be addressed in Section 12.2. Next, we move on to describing real-time IoT data-processing architectures in Section 12.3. We describe how to respond to events generated by IoT systems in a timely fashion in Section 12.4. Handling the data deluge is described in Section 12.5 while data analysis techniques are presented in Section 12.6. Information security aspects of real-time IoT data processing are described in Section 12.7. Finally, we summarize the findings made through this chapter and provide guidelines for further improvements in Section 12.8.

12.2 CHALLENGES AND TECHNOLOGIES

There have been multiple challenges for effective implementation of real-time big data processing in the IoT scenarios. In this section, first, we iterate these issues one by one. Next, we describe the technologies that have been developed to address these challenges.

The main challenge has been adaptation of conventional data-processing system architectures to the IoT scenarios. Because of the distributed nature of IoT applications, it becomes difficult to map centralized data-processing architectures such as Apache Spark, Apache Hadoop, Apache Flink, etc. to function effectively. Many of such big data-processing systems do batch processing, which requires the data to be in one single location (such as a flat file) in order to conduct processing. Even the conventional real-time data-processing systems such as Apache Storm, IBM Infosphere Streams, etc. have been conducting processing in centralized computer cluster. The process of getting the data to such centralized location and sending the processed results back to the devices has to confront large network latencies.

Most of the clocks used in IoT devices are susceptible for time drifts. Furthermore, network interruptions are typical in such systems. Owing to such reasons, disorders are prevalent in data streams generated by many IoT systems. Hence, the need of handling disordered streams has become a significant challenge than ever before. Furthermore, there can be missing values in such data streams, which makes it harder to conduct calculations exactly. Hence, disorder handling and approximation techniques are vital for handling such scenarios.

Data collection protocols also play a vital role on the types of analytics that could be conducted on IoT data streams. These protocols need to be lightweight. However, based on the circumstance, these protocols may have to communicate encrypted data and also may bear different levels of reliability requirements. Table 12.1 shows details of communication protocols used by some of the famous IoT platforms [10]. It can be observed that Message Queue Telemetry Transport (MQTT), which is a lightweight, open, simple client server publish/subscribe messaging transport protocol, has been mostly used by many IoT software platforms. Hence, real-time big data-processing systems that are intended for processing IoT data need to support widely used protocols such as MQTT.

Furthermore, IoT platforms require much higher information security measures compared to general software applications and services. Since the information flow happens across multiple devices, and tens of thousands or even millions of devices get connected to such IoT system, it means there is increased risk of information security violations happening in such an ecosystem. Therefore, the real-time data-processing system designer has to take into consideration the requirement for placing appropriate information security measures.

12.3 REAL-TIME IoT DATA-PROCESSING ARCHITECTURES

Real-time data processing plays a key role in IoT data processing. System architectures of real-time data processing have been shaped by different usage patterns of IoT data. The following are some usage patterns where real-time processing will be useful:

TABLE 12.1

Comparison of Types of Data Analytics Used as Well as Protocols Used for Data Collection by Different IoT Software Platforms

IoT Software Platform	Types of Analytics	Security	Protocols for Data Collection
21emetry—IoT Analytics Platform[a]	Real-time analytics (Apache Storm)	Link Encryption (SSL), Standards (ISO 27001, SAS70 Type II audit)	MQTT, CoAP, STOMP, M3DA
Appcelerator	Real-time analytics (Titanium [9])	Link Encryption (SSL, IPsec, AES-256)	MQTT, HTTP
AWS IoT platform	Real-time analytics (Rules Engine, Amazon Kinesis, AWS Lambda)	Link Encryption (TLS), Authentication (SigV4, X.509)	MQTT, HTTP1.1
Bosch IoT Suite—MDM IoT Platform	Unknown	Unknown	MQTT, CoAP, AMQP, STOMP
Ericsson Device Connection Platform (DCP)—MDM IoT Platform	Unknown	Link Encryption (SSLTSL), Authentication (SIM based)	CoAP
EVRYTHNG—IoT Smart Products Platform	Real-time analytics (Rules Engine)	Link Encryption (SSL)	MQTT, CoAP, WebSockets
IBM IoT Foundation Device Cloud	Real-time analytics (IBM IoT Real-Time Insights)	Link Encryption (TLS), Authentication (IBM Cloud SSO), Identity management (LDAP)	MQTT, HTTPS
ParStream—IoT Analytics Platform[b]	Real-time analytics, Batch analytics (ParStream DB)	Unknown	MQTT
PLAT.ONE—end-to-end IoT and M2M application platform	Unknown	Link Encryption (SSL), Identity Management (LDAP)	MQTT, SNMP
ThingWorx—MDM IoT Platform	Predictive analytics (ThingWorx Machine Learning), Real-time analytics (ParStream DB)	Standards (ISO 27001), Identity Management (LDAP)	MQTT, AMQP, XMPP, CoAP, DDS, WebSockets
Xively—PaaS enterprise IoT platform	Unknown	Link Encryption (SSL/TSL)	HTTP, HTTPS, Sockets/Websocket, MQTT

Source: Adapted from M. Dayarathna, 2016, Comparing 11 IoT Development Platforms, https://dzone.com/articles/iot-software-platform-comparison

Note: The cells marked with Unknown indicate that the relevant information could not be found from the available documentation.

[a] 2lemetry has been acquired by AWS IoT.

[b] ParStream has been acquired by Cisco.

1. Provide a real-time dashboard that shows the current status of the system in real-time. For example, the following dashboard shows a real-time view of the vehicles based on Transport for London (TFL) data feeds [11]. Similarly, some dashboards would update real-time, showing updates to the data in the chart itself.
2. Generate alerts based on simple or complex patterns. For example, the following SQL-like query will generate an event if the power consumption has increased by more than 30% within 10 min:

   from e1=PowerStream->PowerStream[power> 03 & (power-p.power)/p.power > 0.3]
   insert into PowerAlerts

3. Run a machine-learning model generated from batch processing against the incoming data in real-time. For example, learn a fraud detection model using batch processing and use that model against the incoming data in real-time fashion.
4. Tracking—tracking assets, vehicle, animal, or a human and alert if they deviate from the desired behavior.
5. Data correlation—correlating data coming through multiple data streams and taking decisions. Since data joins are complex, this processing is complicated with batch processing and it can be easily implemented using complex event-processing (CEP) windows.
6. Lambda architecture—combining data from batch and real-time processing.
7. Detecting and switching to detailed analysis—detecting a condition and switching to detailed analysis, for example, detect a suspicious user and analyze his actions in detail (with human in the loop and batch processing).

Implementing such use cases is very difficult using batch processing technologies such as Apache Hadoop or Apache Spark. Batch processing needs to write data to the disk, read it again, and process them in batch style. Often, with tuning, these processes take minutes. In contrast, real-time technologies such as event stream processing (ESP) and CEP are designed to produce results in seconds and milliseconds because they process the data in memory event by event or using small batches. The work conducted on the development of real-time big data-processing architectures in the context of IoT applications can be categorized as system architecture-level developments and protocol-level developments. Next, we will delve into the details of each of these two areas.

12.3.1 Data-Processing Architectures

In terms of system architecture-level developments, there are several novel real-time data-processing systems being developed recently targeting specifically the IoT runtime environments such as real-time data processing on in-vehicular networks, enterprise communication systems, smart cities, smart grids, etc.

Automotive Embedded Data Stream Management System (AEDSMS) is a platform for data integration and management of an automotive embedded system via a DSMS [12]. It is one of the unique examples for the application of real-time big data-processing technologies in the context of IoT. A significant feature of an AEDSMS is that hardware and software that run in a vehicle are determined during the design phase of the automotive. AEDSMS exposes high-level queries (HLQs) interface, which are less dependent on the physical structure. The HLQs are compiled into low-level queries (LLQs) that match the physical structure (Figure 12.2).

Ali et al. [13] described a solution that reduces the gap between IoT and online enterprise communication systems. Their approach had a stream processing and reasoning layer implemented using CQELS (Continuous Query Evaluation over Linked Streams) query engine, which is a resource description framework (RDF) stream-processing engine. CQELS supports reasoning through relating patterns of events to actions via event–condition–action (ECA) rules in AnsProlog.

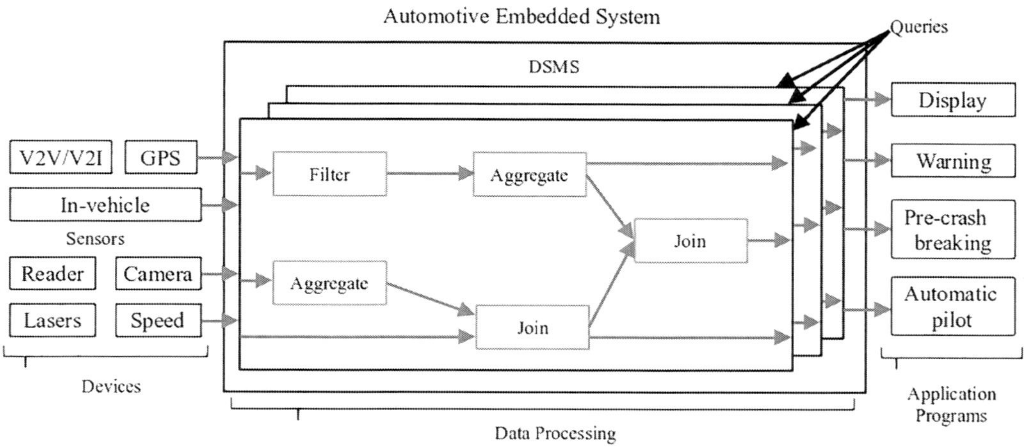

FIGURE 12.2 Automotive Embedded Data Stream Management System (AEDSMS) is an example of a real-time data-processing system developed for Internet of Things. (Adapted from A. Yamaguchi et al., 2015, AEDSMS: Automotive embedded data stream management system, In *2015 IEEE 31st International Conference on Data Engineering*. Seoul, pp. 1292–1303. doi: 10.1109/ICDE.2015.7113377.)

Similarly, the application of CQELS for IoT in smart cities has been developed. ACEIS is an integration and automated discovery system for urban data streams [14]. An important characteristic of their work is that they created a Complex Event Service Ontology, which is used to represent service requests and semantic event services. Through this ontology, ACEIS automatically produces CQELS queries and deploys the queries to a CQELS engine. The use of such semantic technologies is important for handling the issue of data deluge, which is described later in this chapter.

ParStream IoT Analytics Platform (shown in Figure 12.3) is one example for an industrial geo-distributed edge analytics platform [15]. SQL queries are received by ParStream from a variety of analytical applications, which get connected to it. ParStream query is broken down into a series of smaller SQL queries for each of the nodes. Each of these subqueries along with the central data (these are small tables) gets distributed to the federated nodes for executing joins. The partial answers are passed back to the geo-distributed analytics where they get aggregated. Event stream analytics can be performed on the data collected by *EdgeAnalyticsBoxes*, which are specifically designed to enable edge analytics or can be performed in any standard hardware with certain processing and storage capabilities.

12.3.2 Data Collection Protocols

Power efficiency, reliability, data footage, security, etc. are some of the key concerns of communication protocols developed for IoT applications. In terms of protocol-level development, there are initiatives taken to create standardized approaches by various standardization bodies such as World Wide Web Consortium (W3C), Institute of Electrical and Electronic Engineers (IEEE), Internet Engineering Task Force (IETF), EPCglobal, and the European Telecommunications Standards Institute (ETSI).

Out of the protocols described in Figure 12.4, application protocols such as Constrained Application Protocol (CoAP), MQTT, Advanced Message Queuing Protocol (AMQP), Extensible Messaging and Presence Protocol (XMPP), and Data Distribution Service (DDS) are of importance for real-time big data processing in the IoT.

CoAP is a web transfer protocol based on REpresentational State Transfer (REST) on top of HTTP [16]. CoAP is based on UDP by default, which makes CoAP more suitable for IoT applications.

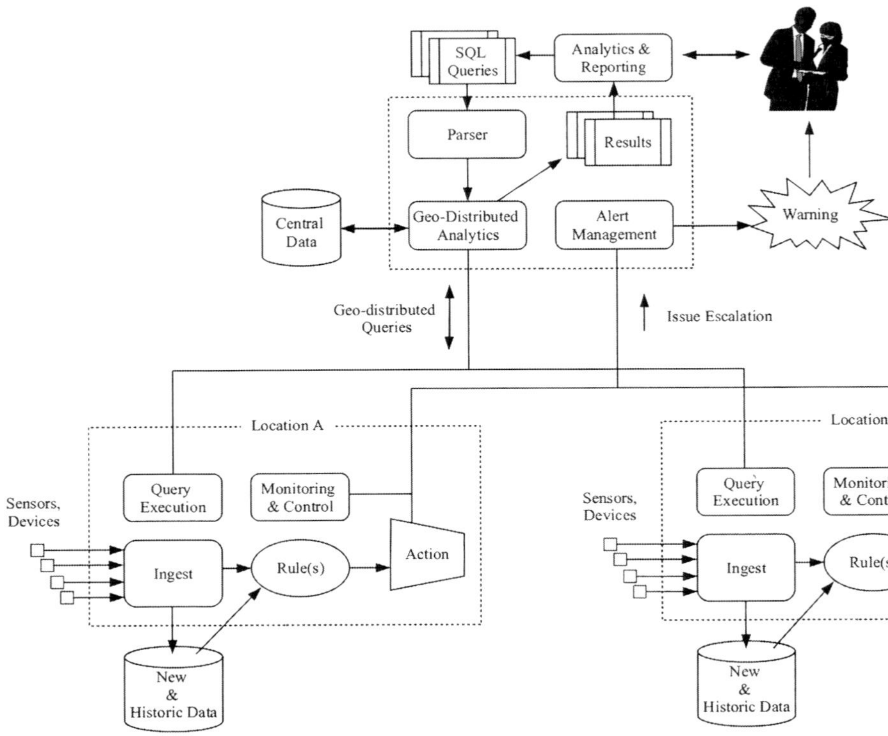

FIGURE 12.3 ParStream's Distributed Architecture for IoT. (Adapted from R. Bloor and R. Jozwiak, 2014, *A Database Platform for the Internet of Things*, The Bloor Group.)

Furthermore, some of the HTTP functionalities have been modified to meet the IoT requirements such as low power consumption and operation with noisy and lossy links. It is easy to convert between the two protocols in REST-CoAP proxies since CoAP has been designed based on REST.

The MQTT protocol has been developed based on publish/subscribe pattern through which message brokers operate. The message broker acts as a server as well as it relays messages between clients, which enables the messages to cross firewall boundaries. MQTT connects embedded devices and networks with applications and middleware. MQTT is aimed for resource-constrained devices that use unreliable, low-bandwidth links. MQTT is based on TCP protocol. MQTT has been used in multiple applications such as energy meters, Facebook notifications, healthcare, monitoring, etc. MQTT represents an ideal messaging protocol for the IoT and M2M communications and is able to create routing for small, low-cost, low-power, and low-memory devices in vulnerable and low-bandwidth networks.

AMQP [17] is an application layer protocol for the IoT focusing on the message-oriented environments. AMQP exchanges messages via a reliable transport protocol such as TCP. AMQP has been developed based on a layered architecture with the lowest level having an efficient, binary, peer-to-peer protocol for transporting messages between two processes over a network. A layer of messaging has been defined on top of AMQP's transport layer.

DDS is a middleware protocol and API standard for data-centric connectivity [18]. DDS architecture is designed to be scalable from small devices to the cloud. Different from MQTT or AMQP, DDS depends on a brokerless architecture and it uses multicasting to maintain excellent quality of service (QoS) and high reliability to its applications.

Several comparisons have been made on the characteristics of the above-mentioned protocols. Packet loss rate is an important measure when comparing MQTT and CoAP. If the communication

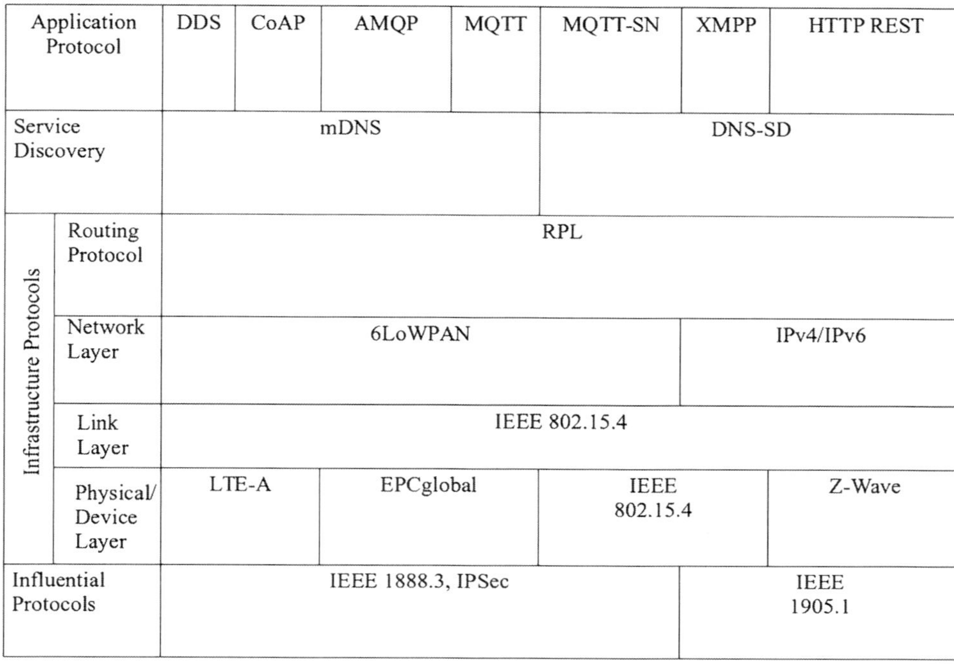

FIGURE 12.4 IoT network protocols and standardization efforts. (From A. Al-Fuqaha et al., 2015, Internet of things: A survey on enabling technologies, protocols, and applications. *IEEE Communications Surveys & Tutorials*, 17(4), 2347–2376, Fourth quarter 2015. doi: 10.1109/COMST.2015.2444095.)

involves small-sized messages with loss rate under 25%, CoAP outperforms MQTT by generating less extra traffic. A similar observation has been made by Caro et al. [19] where they found that in the case of smartphone application environment, CoAP's round trip time and bandwidth usage are smaller than those of MQTT. It has also been found that CoAP is more efficient than HTTP in transmission time and energy usage. With high volume of message exchanges, AMQP produced better results than RESTful web services. In real-time processing of IoT data, it is very important to have the IoT system to operate with lightweight protocols. However, different protocols will perform well in specific scenarios [16]. A comparison of the IoT data collection protocols is shown in Table 12.2.

12.4 RESPONDING IN A TIMELY FASHION

The most significant problem that needs to be addressed in real-time big data-processing of the IoT is responding to the events generated in a timely fashion. If we look at the IoT use cases listed in the introduction section, except for few use cases such as urban planning, the usefulness of those use cases requires us to react to the data immediately. For example, in use cases such as in-home care, logistic network, traffic, and surveillance, the value of the information reduces sharply with time. In such use cases, immediate intervention can save lives and money. For example, in the DEBS grand challenge 2014, four-node CEP cluster did smart meter forecasts, processing 0.8 million events per second with less than 100 ms latency [20]. These types of numbers are impossible to achieve with batch processing.

12.4.1 Batched Event Processing in IoT

Batched event processing (i.e., batched stream processing) is a distributed data-processing technique that models recurring batch computations as incrementally bulk-appended data streams. In

TABLE 12.2
Comparison between the IoT Application Protocols

Application Protocol	RESTful	Transport	Publish/ Subscribe	Request/ Response	Security	QoS	Header Size (byte)
CoAP	Yes	UDP	Yes	Yes	DTLS	Yes	4
MQTT	No	TCP	Yes	No	SSL	Yes	2
MQTT-SN	No	TCP	Yes	No	SSL	Yes	2
XMPP	No	TCP	Yes	Yes	SSL	No	–
AMQP	No	TCP	Yes	No	SSL	Yes	8
DDS	No	UDP	Yes	No	DTLS	Yes	–
HTTP	Yes	TCP	No	Yes	SSL	No	–

Source: Adapted from A. Al-Fuqaha et al., 2015, Internet of things: A survey on enabling technologies, protocols, and applications. *IEEE Communications Surveys & Tutorials*, 17(4), 2347–2376, Fourth quarter 2015. doi: 10.1109/COMST.2015.2444095.

this paradigm, either queries or data can be batched. In query batching, the queries from multiple query series operating on the same input data stream can be aligned to execute together when new bulk update happens [21]. In data batching, the stream computation is conducted as a series of deterministic batch computations that are conducted on small time intervals [22].

Query batching provides the ability of removing redundant computations or I/O across the queries, which arises from spatial correlations among the queries. Comet is a system that was developed on this concept. Users of Comet can submit a query series. Comet implements a set of global optimizations that takes the advantage of the notion of query series. When a new bulk update arrives, Comet's query execution gets triggered. In Comet, a query is decomposed into a number of subqueries. A single large query is formulated by comet by aligning subqueries from different query series into the large query. Optimizations are carried out on the large query to remove redundancies and improve performance (Figure 12.5).

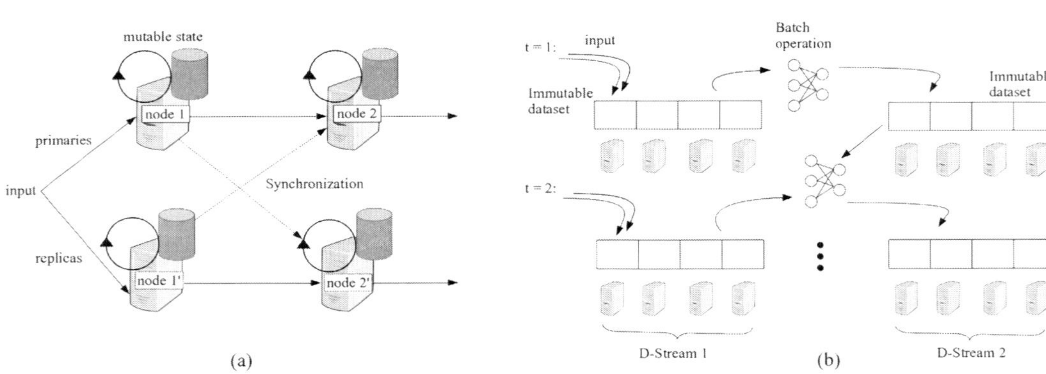

FIGURE 12.5 Continuous versus batched stream-processing paradigms. (a) In the continuous processing model, each and every record received by the nodes is continuously processed and new records are sent downstream. (b) In the D-Stream-processing model, in each time interval, each and every record that arrives is stored reliably across the cluster to form an immutable, partitioned dataset. This dataset is processed to compute other distributed datasets that represent program output or state to pass to the next interval. (Adapted from M. Zaharia, T. Das, H. Li, S. Shenker, and I. Stoica, 2012, Discretized streams: An efficient and faulttolerant model for stream processing on large clusters, In *Proceedings of the 4th USENIX Conference on Hot Topics in Cloud Computing (HotCloud'12)*. USENIX Association, Berkeley, CA, USA, pp. 10–10.)

In data-batching technique, which is also followed in the D-Streams model, the streaming computation is treated as a series of deterministic batch computations on discrete time intervals [22]. In each time interval, the data is stored reliably across the cluster, which creates an input dataset for that interval. The dataset is processed via deterministic parallel operations once the time interval is complete. Deterministic operations such as *map*, *reduce*, and *groupBy* are followed to create new datasets that resemble either program outputs or intermediate state. The results are stored in resilient distributed datasets (RDDs), which are a fast storage abstraction.

Latency is a critical parameter that determines the usefulness of most of the real-time IoT applications. In such applications, continuous processing needs to be given priority over data-batching techniques. This can be observed even from the data-processing architectures described in Section 3.1. Even if data-batching techniques are used in the higher levels of event-processing system hierarchy, the event batching interval needs to be chosen with low time intervals as much as possible to avoid long end-to-end event-processing latencies.

12.4.2 Power Consumption versus Response Time

There are challenges with battery-powered and distributed sensors, where there is a very high probability of devices losing network connections or even dying due to low power; further low quality sensors may also produce incorrect sensor reading. Data loss due to these scenarios should not be considered as special, but rather they should be considered as a norm and handled. Techniques such as using redundant sensors with overlapping coverage area and predictions based on the neighborhood can be used to provide timely response even during data losses.

IoT systems often face the scarcity of power. Power issues may arise in multiple levels such as at the sensor/device level, fog computing (intermediate computing) devices, data centers, etc. The typical energy-aware data stream scheduling can be classified into three groups: hardware-based techniques (dynamic power management and dynamic voltage frequency scaling), software-based stream scheduling techniques (e.g., virtual machine consolidation, elastic scaling), and application-based stream scheduling techniques (e.g., task duplication) [23]. In most of the scenarios, a trade-off exists between the power consumption and the response times in energy-aware data stream scheduling techniques. If the system can be operated with high power envelope, the response times can be kept at the minimum level. On the other hand, then the power availability reduces, and the system performance (and the response time) needs to be updated accordingly.

For example, Sun et al. [23] used an energy model to estimate the energy consumption of each computing node in a data stream environment. They have investigated the relationship between energy consumption, response time, and resource utilization in data stream computing to generate conditions to meet the high energy efficiency and low response time requirements. They use an energy-efficient consolidation of noncritical query operators on noncritical path to maximize the energy efficiency without distributing the response time of the data stream graph [23]. The critical path is a path having the longest latencies from source vertex *vs* to end vertex *ve* in the data stream graph. The proposed Re-Stream system implements two new models on Apache Storm: first, a critical vertex-based real-time scheduling model, and second, an energy-aware consolidation model. It is a typical observation that the response time of a stream-processing application increases with increasing amounts of input data rates. Similarly, the increase of input data rate results in increased energy consumption rate. However, in the proposed Re-Stream approach, there can exist a sweetspot input data rate where despite the relatively large input data rate, the energy consumption remains at a low value.

In performance-sensitive stream-processing applications that have the ability of elastic scaling, it is necessary to avoid unnecessary or very frequent reconfigurations by keeping the actual QoS close to the user's specifications [24]. Such technique allows the delivery of high performance in a cost-effective manner. Matteis et al. [24] modeled the cost of operating such elastic stream-processing system as L, where

$$L = \text{QoS cost} + \text{resource cost} + \text{switching cost} \tag{12.1}$$

$$\text{Resource cost} = \text{per core cost} + \text{power cost} \tag{12.2}$$

For different levels of power consumption, we could find the resource allocation that maximizes performance compared to historical workload so that one could identify whether significant reduction in power can be achieved with slight increase (e.g., 50 ms) in the desired response time [25]. We could also predict how much power would be needed to decrease the response time significantly in the context of real-time IoT data-processing applications.

12.5 HANDLING THE DATA DELUGE

The second most significant problem that needs to be addressed in real-time big data processing in IoT is how to handle the huge amounts of data produced by the IoT sensors. There are obviously two approaches for handling the surge of data generated by IoT sensors: either summarize the data to match with the current computing environment or provision the environment to meet the increasing demand. The former approach has been followed in most of the use cases since most of the time the value exists with timely processed information rather than on raw data.

12.5.1 Data Summarization

Various data summarization techniques can be employed with reduction in the size of the data, which will be handled by the system. Data summarization algorithms as well as techniques such as edge analytics, complementing sensor readings, etc. can be employed for constructing effective data summarization pipelines. Next, we will present the details of these techniques.

12.5.1.1 Edge Analytics

One of the solutions in the data summarization realm is edge analytics. In this technique, raw data generated from the sensors are partially processed to extract summarized information, which will then be transmitted higher up in the system hierarchy. An analysis by Cisco Consulting Services indicates that for a retail store with $20 million in annual sales and 100 security and video analytics cameras, edge computing/analytics can provide savings of 33,800 US dollars annually, and a 1.7% annual EBIT (earnings before interest and tax) increase [3]. According to International Data Corporation (IDC), by 2018, about 40% of the data created by IoT systems will be handled close to or at the edge of a network [26]. There are several variations of edge analytics and related system architectures present today. There are several notable IoT platforms built using edge analytics concepts. Among them, the ParStream IoT Analytics Platform (described in Section 3.1) is one of the notable systems that conducts edge analytics. Another example is the Dell Edge Gateway 5000 Series, which aggregates and relays data securely from a variety of sensors and equipment [27]. These gateways consist of Intel Atom processors that provide the ability of conducting local analytics at the gateway itself, which allows for sending only meaningful information to the next tier. The next tier can be another gateway, the data center, or the cloud.

The decision of how much data to send to the centralized event-processing cluster can be decided either by edge nodes or by the centralized server cluster, for example, if the rate of change on the measured values is high or if it fluctuates, the edge nodes might decide to send events in higher frequency under the assumption that there is some interesting thing happening at its end, or the centered processing node can ask a set of sensors to send events in higher frequency if it has predicted that there can be some abnormal conditions where the sensors are. The cost of edge computing

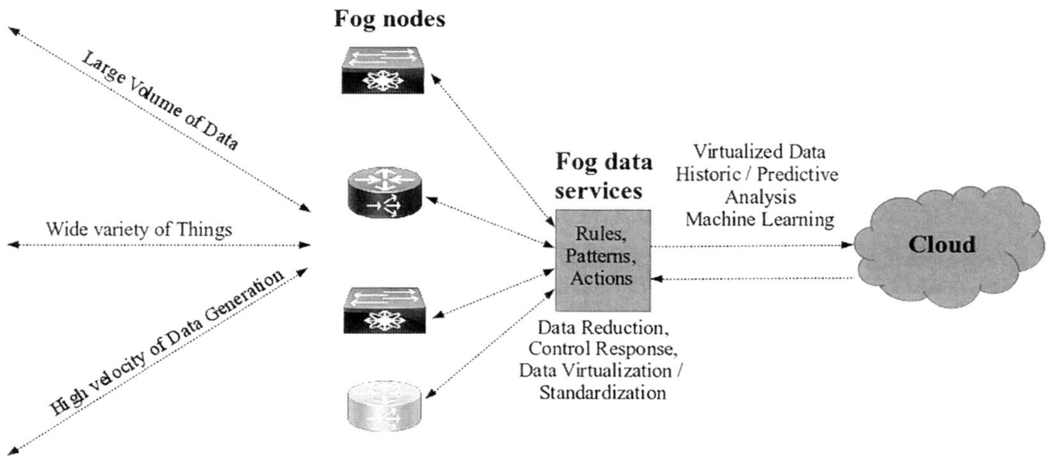

FIGURE 12.6 Data movement from fog to cloud. Fog data services act as the coordinator in between. (Adapted from Cisco, 2015, *Cisco Fog Computing Solutions: Unleash the Power of the Internet of Things*, Cisco Systems, Inc.)

infrastructure can be easily offset by the reduced bandwidth costs, storage, and processing costs enabled by processing the sensor data locally [3].

Fog computing is a variation of edge analytics where it extends the cloud computing paradigm toward the edge analytics. Fog computing in simple terms is a highly virtualized platform that provides compute, storage, and networking services between the end devices and traditional cloud computing data centers. Fog services can be hosted either in the network or in the end devices such as set-top boxes or access points. This provides the benefit of combining intelligence of the edge with the proximity to obtain predictable latency for streaming applications. Some of the key features of fog computing include the geographically distributed nature, very large number of nodes, support for mobility, real-time interactions, predominance of wireless access, heterogeneity, interoperability and federation, support for online analytics, and interplay with the cloud [28] (Figure 12.6).

12.5.1.2 Complementing Sensor Readings

Complementing sensor readings is one of the techniques used when sensors cannot send readings in a continuous manner, when certain readings of the sensor can be derived from other attributes, sending those values is unnecessary, and they can be calculated at the server side. In cases where there is no mathematical model, machine-learning techniques can also be used to estimate the sensor readings. In this case, to validate the correctness and to adjust the errors, the actual readings could be sent time to time in low frequencies. The use of such sensor reading complementing techniques is inevitable when the rate of sampling by the sensors is insufficient to capture the level of details of the real world, which needs to be captured. This is called misrepresentation of data [30]. Query execution costs can be significantly larger than what is a reasonably reliable answer.

The incorporation of statistical models of real-world processes into a sensornet query processing architecture can help to solve this issue. In such a technique, sensors need to be used for reading data only when the model itself is insufficient to answer the query with an acceptable level of confidence [30]. Any trivial statistical model can capture correlation among sensors. For example, the temperature values read by geographically closely located sensors are likely to be correlated. In such a situation, the reading from one sensor could be used to improve the estimates of the other readings. In such a system, temperature measurements have both temporal and spatial correlations. The historical values measured by the sensors should help to estimate the temperature later in time. Such temporal correlations can be represented by a dynamic probabilistic model. In such a model, for each discrete time index t, one needs to estimate a probability density function (pdf) represented by $p(X_1^t, \ldots, X_n^t \mid o^{1\ldots t})$, which assigns a probability for each joint assignment to the attributes at t, given $O^{1\ldots t}$, all observations made up to time t. The evolution of this system over time allows to calculate the probability for each joint assignment to the attributes at time t+1 as $p(X_1^{t+1}, \ldots, X_n^{t+1} \mid o^{1\ldots t})$. Therefore, all the measurements made up to time t can be used to improve the estimate of the pdf at time t+1.

With the help of a transition model, one can calculate $p(X_1^{t+1}, \ldots, X_n^{t+1} \mid o^{1\ldots t})$ via a simple marginalization operation as

$$p(X_1^{t+1}, \ldots, X_n^{t+1} \mid o^{1\ldots t}) = \int p(X_1^{t+1}, \ldots, X_n^{t+1} \mid x_1^t, \ldots, x_n^t) p(x_1^t, \ldots, x_n^t \mid o^{1\ldots t}) dx_1^t \ldots dx_n^t \quad (12.3)$$

where it is assumed that the transition model $p(X^{t+1}|X^t)$ is the same for all times t. For example, the transition model needs to be different in different times of the day due to different types of variations (increase/decrease) happening in the temperature throughout the day.

Once the $p(X_1^{t+1}, \ldots, X_n^{t+1} \mid o^{1\ldots t})$ has been obtained, the measurements o^{t+1} made at time $t+1$ can be used to obtain $p(x_1^{t+1}, \ldots, x_n^{t+1} \mid o^{1\ldots(t+1)})$, the posterior distribution at time $t+1$ can be calculated given all measurements up to time $t+1$. The process is continued for time $t+2$, $t+3$, and so on. The pdf for the initial time $t = 0$, $p\left(X_1^0, \ldots, X_n^0\right)$ is initialized using the prior distribution for attributes $X_1, \ldots, X_n$. The process of inputting the estimate for density at time t via the transition model and then conditioning on the measurements at time t+1 is generally called filtering. Filtering enables to condition the estimates on the complete history of observations, which can considerably reduce the number of observations required for acquiring confident approximations for the queries on the system.

For Gaussian distributions, the filtering process is called Kalman filter [31]. In Kalman filtering, the transition model $p(X_1^{t+1}, \ldots, X_n^{t+1} \mid x_1^t, \ldots, x_n^t)$ is a learned data with two steps. First, a mean and covariance matrix need to be learned for the joint density $p(X_1^{t+1}, \ldots, X_n^{t+1}, x_1^t, \ldots, x_n^t)$. Once this is done, tuples can be formed as $\langle X_1^{t+1}, \ldots, X_n^{t+1}, x_1^t, \ldots, x_n^t \rangle$ from the attributes at every consecutive times t and t+1. These tuples are used to compute the joint mean vector and covariance matrix. Next, a conditioning rule is used to compute the transition model:

$$p(X^{(t+1)} \mid X^t) = \frac{p(X^{(t+1)}, X^t)}{p(X^t)} \quad (12.4)$$

When this transition model has been computed, one can answer queries in a similar fashion and thus can compute all of the operations required to answer the queries by performing only basic matrix operations.

A practical example of the use of filtering is human trajectory processing. Consider the scenario of a person carrying an iBeacon sensor (e.g., a smartphone) walking in a field of iBeacons. The signals transmitted by the iBeacons are received by the iBeacon sensor. An approximation of the location of the person at a particular time is constructed by triangulating the locations of the iBeacons, which the iBeacon sensor detected (see Figure 12.7). However, the location $P(x,y)$ obtained from such a triangulation is a rough approximation of the exact location of that person at a particular time. This is due to multiple reasons, such as signals emitted by different iBeacons are received by the iBeacon sensor with similar signal strength, at different times, low sampling frequency of iBeacon sensor, out-of-order arrival of events, etc. If the iBeacon sensors are operating with low sampling frequency, sudden changes made to the trajectory of the person are not properly captured (Figure 12.7).

If one plots the raw triangulated path of the person, it may create a rough trajectory that has significant deviations from the person's original trajectory. Hence, a trajectory smoothing and realignment technique needs to be used to correct the trajectory of the person.

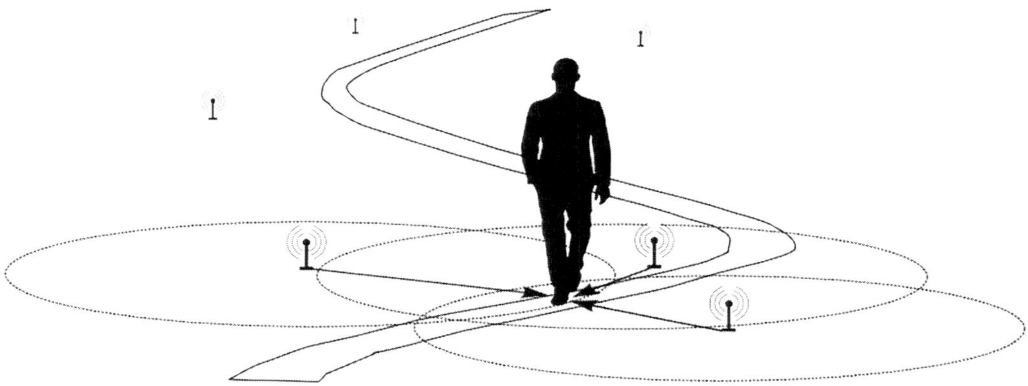

FIGURE 12.7 A person walking with an iBeacon sensor through a field of iBeacons. The signals sent from the iBeacons are received by the sensor and are used to construct an approximation of the location of the person carrying the iBeacon sensor.

12.5.1.3 Data Stream Compression and Redundancy Elimination

Events gathered from sensors can be compressed before they are sent to the data-processing system. Furthermore, sending redundant or useless data via the network can be avoided. In this way, the huge amounts of data that otherwise would have to be sent through the network could be eliminated.

In most of the environment monitoring applications, the captured data can be of high temporal or spatial correlation. Such applications could tolerate some loss of data accuracy [32]. The high temporal coherence indicates the presence of redundancy in the continuous data sequence, which creates unnecessary data transmission and energy consumption.

In one such scheme that involves bitmap-based event encoding scheme when an event arrives, the event's bit-map-based encoding is computed. The generated bitmap is used for traversing a tree-based index structure and finding the matching results. Sadoghi et al. developed a parallel compressed event matching (PCM) algorithm, which conducts subscription matching in parallel overcompressed events. These compressed events are produced by coalescing multiple bitmap-based event encodings into one [33] using bit-wise OR operations and these compressed events are used for traversing the index. The PCM algorithm can easily solve the matching problem for a set of events via single index traversal with a single pass over all relevant leaf nodes. Figure 12.8 depicts an overview of the PCM algorithm.

In order to gain the benefit of the use of any compressed event-matching algorithm, the compressed events must be similar. Accounting for the noise in the event stream and bringing similar events together that are close to each other (yet not adjacent) using an online stream reordering (OSR) technique needs to be employed. OSR algorithm has the ability of reasoning about stream heterogeneity and dynamically adapts to similarity among the events. Sadoghi et al. further proposed an adaptive parallel compressed matching algorithm (A-PCM) that first reorders the stream online using the OSR technique, and for each batch of events that OSR outputs, a similarity value is calculated. All the event batches that have lower similarity value compared to a predefined threshold are processed uncompressed using the standard matching algorithm while the others are processed using the compressed matching technique. It has been observed that A-PCM algorithm is mostly effective when the variance in the event stream is high.

Redundancy elimination is another important technique to be followed when implementing data summarization. Significant amount for work has been conducted on redundancy elimination in the domain of radio-frequency identification (RFID) stream processing. One of the key hindrances in the adoption of RFID technology is the unreliability of the data streams that are produced by RFID

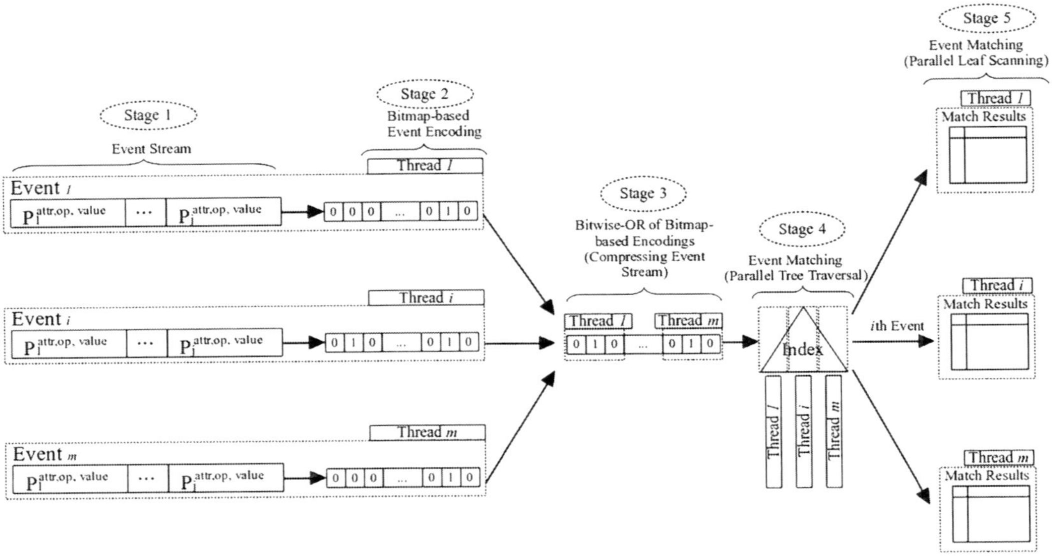

FIGURE 12.8 Parallel compressed matching (PCM) algorithm. (Adapted from M. Sadoghi and H. A. Jacobsen, 2014, Adaptive parallel compressed event matching, In *2014 IEEE 30th International Conference on Data Engineering*. Chicago, IL, pp. 364–375. doi: 10.1109/ICDE.2014.6816665.)

sensors [34]. A sliding window over the reader's data stream (i.e., smoothing filter) that estimates the value of lost readings from each RFID tag within a time window is utilized as the solution. The smoothing filter functionality can be expressed in CQL as,

SELECT distinct tag_id FROM rfid_readings_stream [ANGE '5 sec'] GROUP BY tag_id

Here, setting the smoothing window size is a challenging activity because one needs to balance two opposing application requirements "ensuring completeness" for the set of tag readings because of the reader unreliability and "capturing tag dynamics" because of the tag movement in and out of the reader's detection field. The smoothing window must be large enough to correct the reader unreliability so that the system could ensure the completeness property. However, using larger smoothing window reduces the accuracy of detecting the tag movements within the window resulting false positives.

12.5.2 System-Wide Scaling

The second approach that could be followed to handle large amounts of streaming IoT data is system-wide scaling, which means adjusting the system to handle the entire set of data generated from the IoT sensors. This requires provisioning of additional resources. Several techniques such as geo-distributed stream processing, elastic scaling of event-processing systems, etc. have been used in this context with proven results.

12.5.2.1 Geo-Distributed Stream Processing

Increased deployment of cost-efficient data centers around the globe has enabled geo-distributed stream processing to become a reality. Since IoT systems get deployed across different geographical areas, the analytics conducted on such geo-distributed IoT deployments need to be supported by geo-distributed stream-processing systems. Efficient event-transferring techniques such as batched event-transferring need to be employed in such geo-distributed stream-processing systems. Maintaining low response times is another significant challenge in geo-distributed stream processing.

JetStream is one such example for a geographically distributed data stream-processing system [35]. Bandwidth limitation is a critical factor when implementing a geo-distributed stream-processing system. Two techniques have been used by JetStream to overcome the issues of bandwidth limitation, which are explicitly defined in the programming model. First, a structured storage is operated by the system in the form of online analytical processing (OLAP) data cubes, which enables data to be analyzed where they get generated. Second, adaptive filtering and data transformations that adjust data quality to match the bandwidth availability have been used by JetStream.

Heintz et al. [36] have examined the characteristics of centralized versus edge computing in the context of geo-distributed data processing. The study has resulted saying neither of these two approaches is ideal for modern analytics requirements. Especially, the resource requirements of the queries could vary drastically. While some queries require large amounts of verbose data to be transferred across the wide area networks, most of the geo-distributed data streaming that involve IoT scenarios operate with relatively small amounts of raw data to be transferred from thousands of edge devices to a centralized location for processing. Hence, techniques need to be devised to automatically place data and computation based on characteristics of the query, the data, and the resources. Furthermore, identification of a proper set of operators to be placed at the center versus at the edge is another important task to be performed. In such a setup, for example, filter operators could be placed at the edge while aggregation at the edge may not be beneficial.

12.5.2.2 Elastic Scaling

Another approach for system-wide scaling is elastic scaling where the processing conducted by an event-processing system has been expanded to third-party compute clusters. The decision for expanding to external cluster can be taken based on considering the throughput and latency requirements of the jobs handled by the stream-processing system.

Elastic scaling in the resource-limited scenarios is often most interesting for IoT deployments. Most of the IoT systems need to operate with low resource levels. Resource limitations are associated with budget limitations, inadequate electricity supply, space limitations, etc. Local system resources are limited in most of the scenarios; hence, it is required to expand into external systems such as public clouds. When to provision resources is a critical question to be addressed in such scenarios. For example, virtual machines (VMs) need to be spawned in an elastic fashion to cater the real-time processing requirements [37]. Since commercial clouds incur usage cost, techniques need to be in place to keep the economic costs at minimum by formulating a trade-off between the latency and economic costs as an optimization problem.

One of the key hindrances for elastic scaling of real-time data-processing systems is the requirement for accessing shared state. For example, when some operator needs to be shifted to newly provisioned computing resource (e.g., a VM), it requires the existing state of the operator also to be migrated to the newly provisioned compute resource, which becomes virtually impossible if the shared state is very large. Efforts have been made to solve such issues by the introduction of global state managers [38,39].

12.5.3 Data Diversity

Semantic descriptions of data are an important aspect when dealing with the data deluge. IoT data often correlate with each other. Furthermore, the event field descriptions often have similarities between them. Semantics of the data streams produced by multiple different sensors can be considered to reduce the large amounts of data.

The use of semantic technologies such as RDF requires significant quantities of computing and communication resources, which are generally scarce in IoT devices [40]. This is one of the main issues that needs to be overcome when addressing the issue of data diversity. One example of application of semantic technologies in the context of IoT data processing can be pointed out from the marine and fishery domain. The water quality of fish farms can be monitored via IoT applications. Knowledge models need to be applied to analyze sensor data and emit warnings in the case of anomalous measures [40]. Sensor Markup Language (SenML) is a nonproprietary emerging standard for denoting device parameters and sensor measurements that could be used with such application. SenML is designed for resource-constrained devices and it supports compact data representations for JavaScript Object Notation (JSON) and Efficient XML Interchange (EXI). However, to gain the benefit from data produced by IoT devices that communicate via SenML, the SenML elements need to be mapped to an RDF model such as using a directed labeled graph [40].

The ability of automatic discovery and integration of sensor data on the fly is another important characteristic when addressing the data diversity of real-time IoT data processing. Difficulty of discovering the capabilities of the available infrastructure and integrating heterogeneous data sources are two of the challenges in this domain [14]. The ACEIS integration and automated discovery system for urban data streams is one example IoT data-processing system that takes this into consideration.

12.6 DATA ANALYSIS TECHNIQUES

The previous two sections of this chapter discussed about two of the most pressing issues to be addressed when conducting real-time big data processing in the IoT. This section will discuss data analysis techniques currently used with real-time IoT data analytics that needs to take the above-mentioned issues into consideration. The first two subsections describe CEP and time series processing aspects of real-time IoT data while the latter two sections discuss the use of intelligent techniques with real-time data processing to obtain on-the-fly insights on IoT data.

12.6.1 Complex Event-Processing Approach

CEP deals with a special type of events called complex event, which is an event derived from a group of events using either aggregation or derivation functions. For example, if event A happens and then event B happens, we conclude that event pattern A-> B leads to a complex event C. Conducting operations on complex events is called complex event processing. CEP engines, which are the softwares that do CEP, are capable of detecting complicated patterns, correlations, trends, etc. from data streams.

CEP engines have been used as one of the technologies to implement solutions for the challenges mentioned above. CEP engines detect the presence of complex events and produce output events only when such complex events are encountered. Furthermore, some of the modern CEP engines such as WSO2 Siddhi [41], SAP event stream processor, etc. have support for handling the disorder of data streams, missing events, and duplicated events. Some of these CEP engines support communication over lightweight protocols such as MQTT, CoAP, etc.

12.6.2 Time Series Processing

Almost all IoT devices collect data over time and the resulting data are time series data. Hence, the time series analysis methods and tools will play a key role in real-time IoT analytics. For example, if we are trying to detect equipments that are likely to fail among IoT-enabled devices in operation, we need to process reading collected from each device and trigger an alarm when it deviates from normal behavior. When applying the time series processing concepts in IoT scenarios, there are several key issues to be solved. These include handling some specific issues such as out-of-order events arrival, triggering events out from a window, etc.

Doing this would involve time series analysis, which fits well with time and window-based processing supported by real-time analytics. Specifically, technologies like CEP support these processing well.

Unlike other datasets, time series data are autocorrelated. That is the value at time t is affected strongly by the values at $t - 1$ and $t - 2$ and so on. Hence, the processing is often done using moving time window that keeps the recent data and processing. A very good example of this kind of processing is seen in stock markets, where most of the decisions are taken not based on point data but on data from a time window.

1. Detecting anomalous devices—time window operations such as moving average, z-score, etc. are major features used in anomaly detection.
2. Predicting the next value (load prediction)—the expected electrical load, stock price forecasting, etc.
3. Data correlation—correlating two time series is an expensive operation without time windows.
4. Detecting trends and patterns—CEP pattern operators, hard coding patterns.

For example, consider the case where we want to detect whether the electricity load has increased more than 30% within the last hour. When implementing an algorithm like this, it is very hard to partition the data as the condition could fall across a boundary of partitions. For instance, if we partition the data by the hour, we will miss an occurrence that starts at 8:54 and finishes at 9:03. Consequently, this nullifies the advantage of batch processing and limits it to a single machine. This can also lead to the condition where processing cannot keep up with the data.

In contrast, real-time stream processing operates on data event by event as they arrive. Hence, they process data in a sequence and do not face the above problem. Moreover, since stream processing starts processing once the event has arrived, it has much better chance of keeping up with high event rates than batch processing (i.e., than letting the data to collect and try to process them in batches). As we mentioned before, streaming technologies have demonstrated the ability to handle event rates close to millions of events per second.

Also, most use cases would need a deep understanding about time, and stream-processing systems support time natively. Often, the event receive time is not the same as the time the event has actually occurred. IoT use cases need to operate with external time specified in the event as an attribute. This leads to several challenges.

1. Events may arrive out-of-order, and it is the responsibility of the system to order them. This becomes complicated because there is a trade-off between accuracy (longer you wait for out-of-order events, better accuracy you will have) and responsiveness (time from event arrival to trigger).
2. System can only know the progress of time as the events arrive in the system. Hence, each event arrival shifts the time in the system, and any parallel processing components need to be notified about the time shift. For example, if data is processed as four partitions, each partition needs to be notified about the time shift.

Streaming systems such as CEP supports above complicated scenarios natively, saving the end user from wasting a lot of time and complexity.

12.6.3 Predictive Analytics for IoT

One of the most important aspects of IoT analytics is predicting what might happen in the future and being prepared to face the opportunities and threats. For example, this is heavily used in predictive maintenance of machinery, sending warning alerts when defined limits are about to be reached, in managing supply and demand of resources such as to autoscaling the system just when the load is about to shoot. In this section, we will first describe some of the example application use cases of predictive analytics for IoT. Next, we will investigate some key issues of applying predictive analytics for IoT in the real-time data-processing domain such as handling the missing values.

The most simple form of prediction is done by defining multiple levels of thresholds below the actual threshold such that when the reading reaches the low-level thresholds, they can be alerted as warnings. But this approach has many flaws because there can be many false positives. When the reading reaches the warning it will not reach the actual threshold. In some cases the rate of increase might be very low such that it will take a very long time from the warning signal to actually hit the threshold.

This can be combined with regression analytics, where algorithms like linear regression can be used to predict the future values based on the current rate of change of the reading and with this model we can approximate how long it will take to reach the threshold, and if the time to reach the threshold is below the expected level, then the warning can be raised. Second or higher derivations of reading can also be used to more accurately predict the time to reach the threshold.

There are only a few cases where we can come up with a mathematical model for prediction; in all other cases, machine learning plays a vital role by learning the system over time and forecasting results and categorizing them into meaningful groups. There are plenty of open-source machine-learning library/solutions such as R, python, and Spark MLlib.

The forecasting functionality of machine learning not only helps to predict the future readings but it can also be used to identify missing events due to temporary network outage of sensor failure. Probability-based predictions such as Markov chains can also be used to predict the possibility of the occurrence of the next event based on its current state. Such techniques have been employed for anomaly detection in data streams.

12.6.4 Streaming Machine Learning for IoT

The application of machine-learning techniques in real-time IoT data processing has become a necessity due to the inherent characteristics of IoT data streams. However, most of the current streaming machine-learning research is focused on theoretical aspects. For example, popular streaming ML frameworks such as SAMOA [42] data streams produced by IoT sensors may get distorted by noise. Hence, analytics conducted on such noisy data streams often consists of a lot of missing values. Furthermore, concept drift may be present in IoT data analytics systems.

The relation between the input data and the target variable changes over time due to the phenomenon of concept drift. Techniques such as incremental decision tree inducer for data streams can be used as a means of building new methods for dealing with concept drift.

12.7 SECURE REAL-TIME IoT DATA PROCESSING

The growth of IoT systems in different locations getting interconnected via communication networks has resulted in added potential for unauthorized access, abuse, or fraud, which could take place at any access point in the network. Since the Internet is an enormous public network, when abuse does occur, it can create a significant impact to the society. Security violations could appear at any level of an IoT data-processing system. Hence, information security and associated threat mitigation techniques have direct impact on shaping up the real-time IoT big data-processing applications. This section investigates some of the key concerns in this area.

Most of the IoT security challenges are associated with the wireless Internet security challenges. Wireless networks are more vulnerable to penetration (i.e., eavesdropping) because radio frequency bands are easy to scan. Local area networks (LANs) that use the 802.11b (Wi-Fi) standard can be easily penetrated by outsiders using laptops, wireless cards, external antennae, and freeware hacking software [43]. Therefore, how to securely connect a device to a network is a great challenge. The weakest link in the communication in most of the scenarios is device to the home network. The degree of infrastructure protection is highly affected by its heterogeneity. A secure communication channel needs to be established between highly constrained devices that use low-bandwidth standards (e.g., IEEE 802.15.4) and more powerful devices [44].

Other than general security threats such as the one described above, IoT introduces a completely new breed of security threats to daily appliances. Nonintrusive load monitoring (NILM) could be used for detailed tracking of residents of a housing complex, resulting in decreased privacy. If a hacker gains access to a home's smart meter, the hacker could cut off electricity to the security systems [45]. Another example is hackers gaining access to one's car, which has the ability of remote manipulation via cell phone. This will lead to hackers controlling the internal systems of the car.

Securing with noisy data is one approach that could be followed in IoT infrastructures to mitigate such threats. By exploiting the fact that certain communication channels are generally noisy, one can probably achieve secure encryption against adversaries [46]. Furthermore, techniques such as homomorphic encryption can be used for remote health data analysis applications, which allows for preventing eavesdropping in the cloud [47].

12.8 SUMMARY AND CONCLUSIONS

This chapter clarified the important role played by real-time big data-processing technologies in advancing the IoT. We described use cases where IoT has been used in daily life and the requirements for why real-time data processing is required in such IoT use cases. We presented details of novel real-time IoT data-processing architectures specifically tailored for IoT use cases. Furthermore, we provided the details of data collection protocols used in real-time IoT data-processing systems. Then we described how to respond to events in a timely fashion and also presented methods to follow for handling the massive amounts of streaming data produced by IoT. Furthermore, we presented different data analysis techniques that are followed in real-time IoT data-processing scenarios. Finally, we described some of the notable information security-related concerns when conducting real-time IoT data processing.

It became clear that while multiple data stream-processing systems and architectures have been proposed and implemented, very few, if any, stream-processing systems specifically targeted for IoT use cases exist. From the content presented in this chapter, it was clear that while techniques exist for handling data deluge, it is not clear what types of issues may occur in applying such techniques in real-world settings. For example, system-wide scaling may have multiple issues such as scalability, reliability/fault tolerance, information security, power consumption, etc., which need to be handled. Furthermore, dealing with the semantic information has been a significant challenge to conquer. However, only few works have been conducted to address the issue of data diversity. Streaming machine learning is still at its early stage. Hence, significant amount of work can be conducted with the application of streaming machine learning for IoT applications. Overall we believe that multiple works will appear in the near future, which will fill the gaps of current real-time big data-processing technologies for IoT.

REFERENCES

1. S. Perera, 2015, IoT *Analytics: Using Big Data to Architect IoT Solutions*, WSO2 White Paper, http://wso2.com/whitepapers/iot-analytics-using-big-data-to-architect-iot-solutions/
2. J. Tully, T. Friedman, B. J. Lheureux, C. Geschickter, and M. Hung, 2016, *Internet of Things Primer for 2016*, Gartner, Inc., Stamford, CT.
3. A. Noronha, R. Moriarty, K. O'Connell, and N. Villa, 2014, *Attaining IoT Value: How to Move from Connecting Things to Capturing Insights—Gain an Edge by Taking Analytics to the Edge*, Cisco Systems, Inc., San Jose, CA.

4. A. Noronha, R. Moriarty, K. O'Connell, and N. Villa, 2014, *Attaining IoT Value: How to Move from Connecting Things to Capturing Insights*, Cisco Systems, Inc., San Jose, CA.
5. M. Loukides and J. Bruner, 2015, *What Is the Internet of Things?* O'Reilly Media, Inc., Sebastopol, CA.
6. M. Dayarathna and T. Suzumura, 2013, Automatic optimization of stream programs via source program operator graph transformations. *Distributed and Parallel Databases*, 31(4), 543–599.
7. A. Biem, B. Elmegreen, O. Verscheure, D. Turaga, H. Andrade, and T. Cornwell, 2010, A streaming approach to radio astronomy imaging, In *2010 IEEE International Conference on Acoustics, Speech and Signal Processing*. Dallas, TX, pp. 1654–1657.
8. A. Biem, E. Bouillet, H. Feng, A. Ranganathan, A. Riabov, O. Verscheure, H. Koutsopoulos, and C. Moran, 2010, IBM infosphere streams for scalable, real-time, intelligent transportation services, In *Proceedings of the 2010 ACM SIGMOD International Conference on Management of data (SIGMOD'10)*. ACM, New York, NY, USA, pp. 1093–1104.
9. S. Jayasekara, S. Perera, M. Dayarathna, and S. Suhothayan, 2015, Continuous analytics on geospatial data streams with WSO2 complex event processor, In *Proceedings of the 9th ACM International Conference on Distributed Event-Based Systems (DEBS'15)*. ACM, New York, NY, USA, pp. 277–284.
10. M. Dayarathna, 2016, Comparing 11 IoT Development Platforms, https://dzone.com/articles/iot-software-platform-comparison
11. WSO2, Inc., 2015, WSO2 CEP TFL Demo, https://www.youtube.com/watch?v=mjPPbTFAqes
12. A. Yamaguchi, Y. Nakamoto, K. Sato, Y. Ishikawa, Y. Watanabe, S. Honda, and H. Takada, 2015, AEDSMS: Automotive embedded data stream management system, In *2015 IEEE 31st International Conference on Data Engineering*. Seoul, pp. 1292–1303. doi: 10.1109/ICDE.2015.7113377.
13. M. I. Ali, N. Ono, M. Kaysar, K. Griffin, and A. Mileo, 2015, A semantic processing framework for IoT-enabled communication systems, In *The Semantic Web - ISWC 2015—14th International Semantic Web Conference*. Bethlehem, PA, USA, October 11–15, 2015, Proceedings, Part II. pp. 241–258.
14. F. Gao, M. I. Ali, and A, Mileo, 2014, October. Semantic discovery and integration of urban data streams. In *Proceedings of the Fifth International Conference on Semantics for Smarter Cities-Volume 1280*. CEUR-WS. Org, pp. 15–30.
15. R. Bloor and R. Jozwiak, 2014, *A Database Platform for the Internet of Things*, The Bloor Group, Austin, TX.
16. A. Al-Fuqaha, M. Guizani, M. Mohammadi, M. Aledhari, and M. Ayyash, Internet of things: A survey on enabling technologies, protocols, and applications. *IEEE Communications Surveys & Tutorials*, 17(4), 2347–2376, Fourth quarter 2015. doi: 10.1109/COMST.2015.2444095.
17. OASIS Advanced Message Queuing Protocol (AMQP) Version 1.0. 29 October 2012, OASIS Standard. http://docs.oasis-open.org/amqp/core/v1.0/os/amqp-core-complete-v1.0-os.pdf.
18. OMG, 2016, What Is DDS?, http://portals.omg.org/dds/what-is-dds-3, accessed July 14, 2016.
19. N. De Caro, W. Colitti, K. Steenhaut, G. Mangino, and G. Reali, 2013, Comparison of two lightweight protocols for smartphone-based sensing, In *2013 IEEE 20th Symposium on Communications and Vehicular Technology in the Benelux (SCVT)*. Namur, pp. 1–6.
20. S. Perera, S. Sriskandarajah, M. Vivekanandalingam, P. Fremantle, and S. Weerawarana, 2014, Solving the grand challenge using an opensource CEP engine, In *Proceedings of the 8th ACM International Conference on Distributed Event-Based Systems (DEBS'14)*. ACM, New York, NY, USA, pp. 288–293.
21. B. He, M. Yang, Z. Guo, R. Chen, B. Su, W. Lin, and L. Zhou, 2010, Comet: Batched stream processing for data intensive distributed computing, In *Proceedings of the 1st ACM Symposium on Cloud computing (SoCC'10)*. ACM, New York, NY, USA, pp. 63–74. doi: http://dx.doi.org/10.1145/1807128.1807139.
22. M. Zaharia, T. Das, H. Li, S. Shenker, and I. Stoica, 2012, Discretized streams: An efficient and fault-tolerant model for stream processing on large clusters, In *Proceedings of the 4th USENIX Conference on Hot Topics in Cloud Computing (HotCloud'12)*. USENIX Association, Berkeley, CA, USA, pp. 10–10.
23. D. Sun, G. Zhang, S. Yang, W. Zheng, S. U. Khan, and K. Li, 2015, Re-Stream. *Information Sciences*, 319, 92–112. doi: 10.1016/j.ins.2015.03.027.
24. T. De Matteis and G. Mencagli, 2016, Keep calm and react with foresight: Strategies for low-latency and energy-efficient elastic data stream processing, In *Proceedings of the 21st ACM SIGPLAN Symposium on Principles and Practice of Parallel Programming (PPoPP'16)*. ACM, New York, NY, USA, Article 13, p. 12. doi: http://dx.doi.org/10.1145/2851141.2851148.

25. P. Bodık, C. Sutton, A. Fox, D. Patterson, and M. Jordan, 2007, Response-time modeling for resource allocation and energy-informed SLAs, In *Proceedings of the. Workshop on Statistical Learning Techniques for Solving Systems Problems (MLSys'07)*. Whistler, BC, Canada.
26. IDC, 2014, IDC Reveals Worldwide Internet of Things Predictions for 2015, https://www.idc.com/getdoc.jsp?containerId=prUS25291514
27. Dell, 2015, Dell Edge Gateway 5000 Series Spec Sheet.
28. F. Bonomi, R. Milito, J. Zhu, and S. Addepalli, 2012, Fog computing and its role in the Internet of things, In *Proceedings of the First Edition of the MCC Workshop on Mobile Cloud Computing (MCC'12)*. ACM, New York, NY, USA, pp. 13–16.
29. Cisco, 2015, *Cisco Fog Computing Solutions: Unleash the Power of the Internet of Things*, Cisco Systems, Inc., San Jose, CA.
30. A. Deshpande, C. Guestrin, S. R. Madden, J. M. Hellerstein, and W. Hong, 2004, Model-driven data acquisition in sensor networks, In *Proceedings of the Thirtieth International Conference on Very Large Data Bases—Volume 30 (VLDB'04)*. VLDB Endowment, Toronto, Canada, pp. 588–599.
31. R. E. Kalman, 1960, A new approach to linear filtering and prediction problems, The American Society of Mechanical Engineers, *Journal of Basic Engineering*, 82(1), 35–45. doi: 10.1115/1.3662552.
32. G. Wei, Y. Ling, B. Guo, B. Xiao, and A. V. Vasilakos, 2011, Prediction-based data aggregation in wireless sensor networks: Combining grey model and Kalman filter. *Computer Communications*, 34(6), 793–802, ISSN 0140-3664, http://dx.doi.org/10.1016/j.comcom.2010.10.003.
33. M. Sadoghi and H. A. Jacobsen, 2014, Adaptive parallel compressed event matching, In *2014 IEEE 30th International Conference on Data Engineering*. Chicago, IL, pp. 364–375. doi: 10.1109/ICDE.2014.6816665.
34. S. R. Jeffery, M. J. Franklin, and M. Garofalakis, 2008, An adaptive RFID middleware for supporting metaphysical data independence. *The VLDB Journal*, 17(2), 265–289. doi: http://dx.doi.org/10.1007/s00778-007-0084-8.
35. A. Rabkin, M. Arye, S. Sen, V. S. Pai, and M. J. Freedman, 2014, Aggregation and degradation in JetStream: Streaming analytics in the wide area, In *Proceedings of the 11th USENIX Conference on Networked Systems Design and Implementation (NSDI'14)*. USENIX Association, Berkeley, CA, USA, pp. 275–288.
36. B. Heintz, A. Chandra, and R. K. Sitaraman, 2015, Towards optimizing wide-area streaming analytics, In *2015 IEEE International Conference on Cloud Engineering (IC2E)*. Tempe, AZ, pp. 452–457. doi: 10.1109/IC2E.2015.53.
37. A. Ishii and T. Suzumura, 2011, Elastic stream computing with clouds, In *2011 IEEE International Conference on Cloud Computing (CLOUD)*. Washington, DC, pp. 195–202. doi: 10.1109/CLOUD.2011.11.
38. B. Gedik, S. Schneider, M. Hirzel, and K.-L. Wu, 2014, Elastic scaling for data stream processing. *IEEE Transactions on Parallel and Distributed Systems*, 25(6), 1447–1463. doi: http://dx.doi.org/10.1109/TPDS.2013.295.
39. J. Li, C. Pu, Y. Chen, D. Gmach, and D. Milojicic, 2016, Enabling elastic stream processing in shared clusters, In *2016 IEEE International Conference on Cloud Computing (CLOUD)*. San Francisco, CA, 2016, pp. 108–115.
40. E. Shakshuki, A. Yasar, X. Su, H. Zhang, J. Riekki, A. Keränen, J. K. Nurminen, and D. Libin, 2014, Connecting IoT sensors to knowledge-based systems by transforming SenML to RDF, In *The 5th International Conference on Ambient Systems, Networks and Technologies (ANT-2014); The 4th International Conference on Sustainable Energy Information Technology (SEIT-2014)*, Procedia Computer Science, Vol. 32, pp. 215–222, ISSN 1877-0509, http://dx.doi.org/10.1016/j.procs.2014.05.417.
41. S. Suhothayan, K. Gajasinghe, I. L. Narangoda, S. Chaturanga, S. Perera, and V. Nanayakkara, 2011, Siddhi: A second look at complex event processing architectures, In *Proceedings of the 2011 ACM Workshop on Gateway Computing Environments (GCE'11)*. ACM, New York, NY, USA, pp. 43–50.
42. G. De Francisci Morales and A. Bifet, 2015, SAMOA: Scalable advanced massive online analysis. *The Journal of Machine Learning Research*, 16(1), 149–153.
43. K. C. Laudon and J. P. Laudon, 2006, *Management Information Systems: Managing the Digital Firm*, Pearson/Prentice Hall, Upper Saddle River, NJ, ISBN-9780131538412.
44. R. Roman, P. Najera, and J. Lopez, 2011, Securing the Internet of Things. *Computer*, 44(9), 51–58. doi: 10.1109/MC.2011.291.

45. A. Grau, 2015, *How to Build a Safer Internet of Things: Today's IoT Is Full of Security Flaws. We Must Do Better*, http://spectrum.ieee.org/telecom/security/how-to-build-a-safer-internet-of-things.
46. U. Maurer, R. Renner, and S. Wolf, 2007, *Unbreakable Keys from Random Noise, Security with Noisy Data: On Private Biometrics, Secure Key Storage and Anti-Counterfeiting*, Springer, London, pp. 21–44. http://dx.doi.org/10.1007/978-1-84628-984-2_2.
47. D. Preuveneers and W. Joosen, 2016, Privacy-enabled remote health monitoring applications for resource constrained wearable devices, In *Proceedings of the 31st Annual ACM Symposium on Applied Computing (SAC'16)*. ACM, New York, NY, USA, 119–124. doi: http://dx.doi.org/10.1145/2851613.2851683.

13 End-to-End Security Framework for Big Sensing Data Streams

Deepak Puthal, Surya Nepal, Rajiv Ranjan, and Jinjun Chen

CONTENTS

ABSTRACT

Big data streaming has become an important paradigm for real-time processing of massive continuous data flows in large-scale sensing networks. While dealing with big sensing data streams from Internet of Things (IoT), a data stream manager (DSM) must always verify the authenticity, integrity, and confidentiality of the data to ensure end-to-end security as the medium of communication is wireless and untrusted. Malicious attackers could access and modify the data at any time/place from source to cloud data center. Existing technologies for data security verification are not suitable for data-streaming applications, as the verification should be performed in real time and which introduces a delay in the data stream. In this chapter, we will propose a Dynamic Prime-Number-Based Security Verification (DPBSV) framework for big data streams. Our framework is based on a common shared key that is updated dynamically by generating synchronized prime numbers. The common shared key updates at both ends, that is, source-sensing devices and DSM, without further communication after handshaking. Theoretical analyses and experimental results of our DPBSV framework show that it can significantly improve the efficiency of the verification process by reducing the time and utilizing a smaller buffer size in DSM. We have experimented the proposed scheme in a simulated environment and demonstrated the feasibility of the approach. We observed that the proposed scheme not only reduces the verification time or buffer size in DSM, but also strengthens the security of the data by constantly changing the shared keys.

13.1 INTRODUCTION

A number of application scenarios such as telecommunications, network security, large-scale sensor networks, etc. require real-time processing of data streams, where the applicability of the traditional "store-and-process" method is limited [1]. There are a wide range of applications that require cloud-based data stream processing (e.g., data from large-scale sensors, information monitoring, web exploring, data from social networks such as Twitter and Facebook, surveillance data analysis, financial data analysis) [2]. These applications produce high-volume, high-velocity, and real-time data as input, and hence require a novel paradigm for data processing. As a result, a new computing paradigm based on stream-processing engines (SPEs) has emerged. SPEs deal with specific types of challenges and are intended to process data streams with a minimal delay [3,4].

Some applications such as network monitoring and fraud detection produce data, which is beyond the capability of traditional data-processing infrastructures. These applications require real-time processing of very high-volume data streams (termed as *big data streams*). The complexity of big data is defined through V^4's: (1) *volume*—referring to terabytes, petabytes, or even exabytes (1000^6 bytes) of stored data, (2) *variety*—referring to the unstructured, semistructured, and structured data from various sources like social media (e.g., Twitter, Facebook), sensors, surveillances, image or video, medical records, etc., (3) *velocity*—referring to the high speed at which the data move in/out, and (4) *veracity*—referring to the quality of data. These features present significant opportunities and challenges for big data stream processing [2]. Big data stream is continuous in nature and it is important to perform the real-time analysis as the life time of the data is often very short (applications can access the data only once) [5,6].

Though processing big data streams has emerged as one of the important topics of research, secure data stream processing has received little attention from researchers. Some of these data streams arise from mission-critical applications (e.g., environmental monitoring, military application), where data streams need to be secured [7]. The problem is further exacerbated when thousands to millions of small sensors simultaneously produce data streams for real-time analytics [8]. The hard question is: can we efficiently undertake secure processing of thousands of data streams while meeting mission-critical data-processing constraints (e.g., minimizing data-processing overheads)? In addition, compared to the conventional store-and-process method, these sensors have limited processing power, storage, bandwidth, and energy [8,9].

One of the security threats is the man-in-middle attack, in which a malicious attacker can access or modify the data stream from sensors. This situation arises as it is not possible to monitor a large number of sensors deployed in untrusted environments [9]. The common approach is to apply a cryptographic model for securing the data streams. Keeping data encrypted is the most common and safe choice to secure data in transmission subject to safeguarding of encryption keys. There are two prominent cryptographic encryption algorithms available: asymmetric and symmetric. Asymmetric-key encryption algorithms (e.g., RSA, ElGamal, DSS, YAK, Rabin) perform a number of exponential operations over a large finite field. Therefore, they are approximately 1000 times slower than symmetric-key cryptography [10,11]. Efficiency can become a serious issue if asymmetric-key cryptography-based infrastructure such as the Public-Key Infrastructure (PKI) [12] is applied to big data streams. Thus, symmetric-key encryption is the most efficient cryptographic solution for such applications. However, symmetric-key algorithms (e.g., DES, AES, IDEA, RC_4) do not scale when subjected to the real-time, on-the-fly processing of big data streams.

In this chapter, we present the design and development of a Dynamic Prime-Number-Based Security Verification (DPBSV) scheme. Our scheme is based on the notion of a common shared key that is dynamically and periodically updated by generating synchronized prime numbers. The synchronized prime number enables reduction of the communication overhead without compromising security. Our scheme is suitable for big data streams as it verifies the security (confidentiality and integrity) on-the-fly (with minimum delay), hence leading to reduced communication overhead. The scheme uses much smaller key length (64 bits) as against symmetric cryptographic algorithms. This enables faster security verification processing of streams at data stream manager (DSM). The same level of security is maintained by updating the shared keys dynamically. Dynamic key generation is based on the random prime numbers, and is initialized and synchronized at sensors and DSM. We save on network overhead as our scheme does not require DSM and sensor node to communicate after the initial handshaking key step.

Our proposed scheme is efficient in comparison to Advanced Encryption Standard (AES), as it reduces the computational load and execution time significantly. The main contributions of the chapter can be summarized as follows:

- We present a secure big data stream-processing scheme.
- We design and develop an efficient DPBSV scheme for big data streams.
- We evaluate the DPBSV scheme both theoretically and empirically. Our analysis shows that it is efficient when applied to big data streams in comparison to standard AES.

The rest of this chapter is organized as follows. Section 13.2 provides the background on big data stream and corresponding security-related work. Section 13.3 provides a motivating example in big data streams as well as detailed analysis of our research problem. Section 13.4 describes the DPBSV key exchange scheme. Section 13.5 presents the security analysis of the scheme formally. Section 13.6 evaluates the performance and efficiency of the scheme through experimental results. Section 13.7 concludes the chapter.

13.2 PROPOSED SECURE DATA STREAM ARCHITECTURE

13.2.1 Big Data Stream

Data stream processing is an emerging computing paradigm that is particularly suitable for application scenarios where huge amounts of data (termed as big data) must be processed in near real time (with minimal delay). Unlike traditional batch-processing systems where query processing is done over archived (i.e., the data need to be stored based on a predefined schema prior to processing) data, SPE processes real-time time streaming data on-the-fly. The need for on-the-fly processing arises from the high-volume and high-velocity input data that cannot be persisted for later analysis for practical reasons (e.g., data storage overhead). DSM handles streams of tuples in a similar way to a conventional database system handling relations. In addition, DSM undertakes the security verification of the data blocks on-the-fly.

Cloud computing has become the platform of choice for processing big data due to its on-demand elasticity, extremely low latency, and massively parallel processing architecture [13]. It supports the most efficient way to obtain actionable information from big data streams [5,14–16]. Figure 13.1 shows our cloud-based architecture for big data stream-processing systems consisting of data sources, the cloud data centers, and the DSM framework. We refer to Reference 17 for further information on stream data processing in datacenter cloud. It is important to note that the security verification of streaming data has to be performed in real time with a fixed buffer size before the actual stream query processing step. Finally, the processed data are stored in the cloud storage. Queries

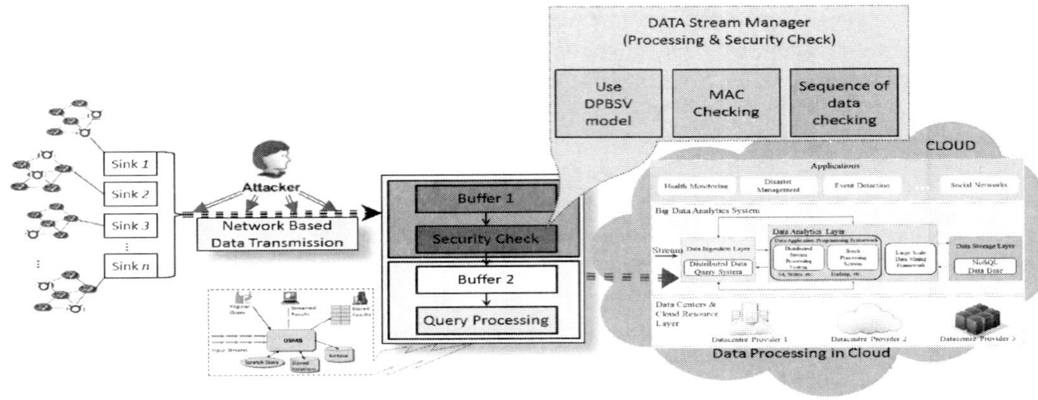

FIGURE 13.1 Overlay of our architecture from source-sensing devices to cloud data-processing center.

registered in DSM are defined as "continuous" since they are continuously applied to the streaming data flows. Results are sent to the user each time the streaming data satisfy the query predicate. The queries (including security verification operation) are defined as a directed acyclic graph where each node is an operator and edges define data flow.

It is clear from the above description that security verification is one of the critical requirements for big data stream processing. We note that the security verification step as proposed in our DSM framework adds to overall stream-processing time. Hence, the major challenge for DSM is to reduce this additional security verification overhead. This is critical for big data stream due to the high volume and high velocity. Hence, in our DSM approach, security verification is done on-the-fly (with minimal overhead).

13.2.2 Symmetric-Key Cryptography-Based Security Verification Methodology

The Data Encryption Standard (DES) has been a standard symmetric-key algorithm since 1977. However, it was cracked rather easily. In 2000, the AES [18] replaced the DES to meet the ever-increasing requirements of data security. The AES, also known as the Rijndael algorithm, is a symmetric block cipher that can encrypt data blocks of 128 bits using symmetric keys of 128, 192, or 256 bits [18,19]. AES was introduced to replace the Triple DES (3DES) algorithm. Hence, we have compared our proposed solution against AES.

Symmetric keys are smaller in size than asymmetric keys, so they have less computational burden. The 128-bit symmetric key provides the same strength of protection as a 3248-bit asymmetric key [11]. Since the aim is to perform the security verification on-the-fly (real-time), the symmetric-key cryptography becomes a natural choice due to its scalability. It is noted in the literature that symmetric-key cryptography is approximately 1000 times faster than strong public-key ciphers [10]. However, it is comparatively easy to read/modify the symmetric-key cryptography as it has small key size [10]. To circumvent this problem, we periodically apply a synchronized dynamic prime number (P_i) generation algorithm at both source and DSM. This algorithm leads to confusion for malicious attackers. The procedure *Prime* (P_i) is calculated and synchronized on both source and DSM ends. This intelligent modification makes the overall process of security verification faster and prevents potential attacks. We explain this algorithm in detail later in this chapter.

We assume that the deployed source nodes operate in two modes: trusted mode and untrusted mode. In the trusted mode, the nodes operate in a cryptographically secure space and adversaries cannot penetrate this space. Nodes can incorporate trusted platform module (TPM) to design the trusted mode of operation. The TPM is a dedicated security chip following the trust computing standard specification for cryptographic microcontroller system [20]. TPM provides a hardware-based trust, which contains cryptographic functionality such as key generation, store, and manage embedded in the chip. The detailed architecture can be found in Reference 20. We assume that the proposed *Prime* (P_i) and secret key calculation on source nodes are conducted in the trusted mode.

13.3 MOTIVATION AND PROBLEM ANALYSIS

The above discussion on the DSM framework architecture clearly outlines the following most important requirements as regards to the secure processing of the big data stream:

1. Security verification needs to be performed in real time (on-the-fly).
2. The verification framework has to deal with high-volume and high-velocity data.
3. Data items can be read once in the prescribed sequence.
4. Unlike the store-and-process paradigm, original data are not available for comparisons in the context of the stream-processing paradigm.

Based on the above features of big data stream, we have categorized existing security methods into two classes: communication security [21,22] and server side data security [23–26]. Communication security deals with handling security data in motion. On the other hand, server side data security is concerned with securing the data security when it is at rest. The security threats and solutions proposed in the literature are not suitable for secure processing of the big data streams for the reasons outlined below.

Communication security techniques are mainly proposed for network communication. Network communication-related attacks are broadly divided into two types: external and internal. To avoid such attacks, security solutions have been proposed for each individual TCP/IP layers. For the physical layer, the proposed solutions include spread jamming reports, accurate and complete design of the node physical package, etc.; for the data link layer, the proposed solutions include error correcting codes, collision detection and avoidance techniques, rate limiting, etc.; for the network layer, the proposed solutions include link layer encryption and authentication, multipath routing, identity verification and authenticated broadcast, etc.; and for the transport layer, the proposed solutions include packet authentication [21]. These solutions can avoid the communication threats but are not suitable for dealing with new challenges posed by big data stream.

The server side data security is mainly proposed for physical data centers, when data are at rest and accessed through applications. There are several potential attacks for such data such as data interruption, interception, privacy breach, impersonation, session hijacking, programming flaws, software modification, software interruption, defacement, disrupting communications, hardware interruption, hardware modification, etc. Several solutions have been proposed to protect data and cloud servers from attacks such as privacy in multitenant environments, data protection from disclosure, access control, software security, service availability, access control, application security, data security (e.g., data in transit, data at rest, reminisce), cloud management control security, virtual cloud protection, hardware security, hardware reliability, etc. [23–27]. However, these proposed solutions are tailored toward the store-and-process paradigm, and hence are not feasible for on-the-fly big data stream processing.

Existing symmetric cryptographic-based security solutions for data security are based on either static shared key or centralized dynamic key. In static shared key, we need to have a long key to defend from a potential attacker. The length of the key is always proportional to security verification time. Based on the requirement of big data stream processing (specified above), it is clear that security verification should be done in real time. For the dynamic key management solution, centralized rekeying processing and distribution of keys to all the sources is a time-consuming process. A big data stream is always continuous in nature and often huge in volume. This makes it impossible to pause the data movement while the rekeying, distribution, and synchronization processes finish. To address this problem, we are proposing a scheme for big data stream security verification without the need for rekeying. The benefits include reduction of the communication overhead and increase in the efficiency of the security verification process at DSM.

Our proposed scheme is as follows: we use a common shared key for both sensors and DSM. The key is updated dynamically by generating synchronized prime numbers without the need for communication between them. This reduces the communication overhead, as required by the rekeying process in existing methods, without compromising security. Owing to the reduced communication overhead, our scheme performs the security verification with minimum delay. The communication is required at the beginning for the initial key establishment and synchronization because DSM sends all the keys and key generation properties to the sources in this step. There is no further communication between the source sensor and DSM after handshaking, which increases the efficiency of the solution. Based on the shared key properties, individual source updates their dynamic key independently.

13.4 DYNAMIC PRIME-NUMBER-BASED SECURITY VERIFICATION

This section describes the DPBSV scheme. Similar to any secret key-based symmetric-key cryptography, the DPBSV scheme consists of four independent components: system setup, handshaking, rekeying, and security verification. Table 13.1 provides the notations used in describing the scheme. We next describe the scheme in detail.

TABLE 13.1
Notations

Acronym	Description
S_i	*i*th sensor's ID
K_i	*i*th sensor's secret key
K_{si}	*i*th sensor's session key
K_{enc}	Generated key for an authentication
K_{SH}	Secret shared key of sensors and DSM
K/K'	Encrypted with sensor's secret key for user authentication
$C/C'/C''$	Calculated hash value
r	Random number generated by sensors
t	Interval time to generate the prime number
P_i	Random prime number
K_d	Secret key of the DSM
k	Initial shared key for sensor and DSM for authentication
I_D	Encrypted data for integrity check
A_D	Secret key for authenticity check
$E()$	Encryption function
$H()$	One-way hash function
$Prime(P_i)$	Prime number generation function
$KeyGen$	Key generation procedure
$\oplus$	Bitwise X-OR operation
$\|\|$	Concatenation operation
$DATA$	Fresh data at sensor before encryption

13.4.1 DPBSV System Setup

We have made a number of realistic and practical assumptions while defining our scheme. First, we assume that DSM has deployed all the sensor's identities (IDs) and secret keys because the network is fully untrusted. We allow an increased number of key exchanges between the sensors and DSM for the initial session key establishment process to achieve stronger security. Our aim is to make this session more secure because we transmit all the secret information of key generation to sensors. We assume that both sensor node S_i and DSM have a secret shared key, that is, k.

Step 1: A sensor (S_i) generates a random number r and sends it to the DSM with its identity as $\{S_i, r\}$. There are n numbers of sensors deployed and those are $S_1, S_2, S_3, \ldots, S_n$, and S_i is the id of the ith sensor. In our scheme, sensors do not communicate with each other to reduce the communication overhead. The proposed scheme also updates the dynamic shared key on both ends to prevent potential attacks from traffic behavior analysis.

1. $S_i \rightarrow \text{DSM} : \{S_i, r\}$.

Step 2: Once the DSM receives the request from a sensor, it retrieves the corresponding sensor's secret key, that is, $K_i \leftarrow retrieveKey(S_i)$ first and then DSM selects a random session key K_{si}, that is, $K_{si} \leq ftarrowradomdKey()$. In order to share this session key with the corresponding sensor (S_i), DSM generates a key based on a selected session key and the corresponding sensor's private key $K_{\text{enc}} = K_{si} \oplus K_i$. Following the generated key (K_{enc}), DSM encrypts the generated key with the session key $K = E_k(K_{si}, K_{enc})$ and it performs the hash function $C = H(K_{\text{enc}}||K||r)$. Finally, DSM sends the value of C and K_{enc} to S_i.

$K_{\text{enc}} = K_{\text{si}} \oplus K_i$, from randomly selected session key K_{si}.

$$K = E_k(K_{si}, K_{enc})$$
$$C = H(K_{enc} \parallel K \parallel r)$$

2. $S_i \leftarrow \text{DSM} : \{C, K_{\text{enc}}\}$.

Step 3: The corresponding sensor gets its session key K_{enc} based on its own secret key $K_{si} = K_{enc} \oplus K_i$ and finds out the value of K' based on the value of K_{si} and K_{enc}, that is, $K' = E_k(K_{si}, K_{enc})$. Next, it computes the hash $H(K_{enc}\backslash parallelK'\backslash parallelr)$ and checks whether or not it is equal to C. If the hashes are equal and $K = K'$, S_i can authenticate DSM. However, if it is not equal, then S_i ends the protocol. Following the authentication, it transmits $C' = H(1||K_{enc}||K'||r)$ to DSM as follows.

$K_{si} = K_{enc} \oplus K_i$, to extract the session key for own.

$$K' = E_k(K_{si}, K_{enc})$$
$$C' = H(1 \parallel K_{enc} \parallel K' \parallel r)$$

3. $S_i \rightarrow \text{DSM} : \{C'\}$.

Step 4: After receiving C', DSM compares it with $H(1\backslash parallelK_{enc}\backslash parallelK\backslash parallelr)$ to check whether or not they are equal. If they are equal, DSM authenticates S_i. Otherwise, the protocol is terminated. After authentication by DSM and sensor, DSM and S can share the session key K_{si} and $C'' = H(2 \parallel K_{enc} \parallel K \parallel r)$.

$$C'' = H(2 \parallel K_{enc} \parallel K \parallel r)$$

4. $S_i \leftarrow \text{DSM} : \{C''\}$.

13.4.2 DPBSV Handshaking

DSM sends all its properties to sensors $\{S_1, S_2, S_2, \ldots, S_n\}$ based on their individual session key. Generally, the larger the prime number of secret shares used in the pairwise key establishment process, the better the security the pairwise key will achieve. However, using a larger prime number for the secret shares requires a greater computation time. In order to make the security verification lighter and faster, we reduce the prime number size. The dynamic prime number generation function is defined in Theorem 13.2 (described later in this chapter). We calculate the prime number on both sensor and DSM sides to reduce communication overhead and minimize the chances of disclosing the shared key.

Step 5: *Prime* (P_i) computes the relative prime number on both sides with a time interval t. In the handshaking process, it transmits all its procedures to generate the key and prime number such as (K_d, t, P_i, $Prime(P_i)$, K_{SH}, $KeyGen$).

5. $S_i \leftarrow$ DSM :$E_k(K_d, t, P_i, Prime(P_i), K_{SH}, KeyGen)$.

In this step, DSM sends all the parameters and properties of *KeyGen* to source sensors. The transferred information is stored in a trusted part of the sensor (e.g., TPM).

13.4.3 DPBSV Rekeying

We propose a novel rekeying mechanism that calculates prime numbers dynamically on both source sensors and DSM independently. In the proposed scheme, the small size of the key leads to faster security verification. However, a small key size can be relatively easy to crack. To counter this issue, the key pair is periodically updated. In the event of key compromise at sensors, DSM undertakes a key resynchronization process with the sensor as described next. The source sensor executes Step 3 to reinitialize and resynchronize the key pair with the DSM. We assume that the secret key information is managed by the sensor in a trusted fashion such as by employing the TPM hardware.

The following presents an alternative approach to rekeying and the corresponding analysis in terms of efficiency.

Step 6: The above-defined DPBSV handshaking process relays information related to the *Prime* (P_i) and KeyGen to the sensors. We next describe the secure data transmission and verification process based on the above functions and keys. As mentioned above, the proposed scheme applies the synchronized dynamic prime number generation *Prime* (P_i) on both sides, that is, sensors and DSM. At the end of the handshaking process, sensors have their own secret keys, initial prime number, and initial shared key generated by the DSM. The next cycle of the prime generation process is based on the value of the prime number and the specified time interval. Sensors generate the shared key $K_{SH} = H(E(P_i, K_d))$ using the prime number P_i and DSM secret key K_d. Each data block is associated with the authentication tag and contains two different parts. The first is the encrypted DATA based on its secret key K_i and shared key K_{SH} for integrity checking (i.e., $I_D = DATA \oplus K_{SH} \oplus K_i$), and the second part is concerned with the authenticity checking (i.e., $A_D = S_i \oplus K_{SH}$). The resulting data block is:

$$((DATA \oplus K_{SH} \oplus K_i) \parallel (S_i \oplus K_{SH}))$$

$$I_D = DATA \oplus K_{SH} \oplus K_i$$

$$A_D = S_i \oplus K_{SH}$$

6. $S_i \rightarrow$ DSM : $\{E_k(I_D || A_D)\}$.

13.4.4 DPBSV Security Verification

According to the features of big data streams, security verification should be performed in real time (with minimal delay). The next step explains how the DSM verifies the authenticity and integrity of each or selected data block.

Step 7: The DSM verifies whether the data were modified while in transit and was sent by an authenticated sensor node. The DSM first checks the authenticity and integrity of specific data block A_D. The approach selects the next block to be checked for authenticity and integrity based on specified random interval such as I_D (configurable variable). This random variable is calculated based on the corresponding prime number, that is, $j = P_i\%7$. The calculated values vary from 0 to 6, that is, the maximum interval of 6 blocks and if the value of j is 0, then it will verify every data block. For the authenticity check, the DSM decrypts A_D with shared key $S_i = A_D \oplus K_{SH}$. Once S_i is obtained, the DSM checks its source database and extracts the corresponding secret key K_i for the integrity check according to the value of j. Given K_i, the DSM decrypts data and checks Message Authentication Code (MAC) for integrity check $DATA = I_D \oplus K_{SH} \oplus K_i$.

$$S_i = A_D \oplus K_{SH}$$

$$DATA = I_D \oplus K_{SH} \oplus K_i$$

13.5 SECURITY ANALYSIS OF DPBSV

In this section, we provide a theoretical analysis of the proposed scheme and prove that it can ensure both authenticity and integrity of streaming data.

Assumption 13.1

No one can decrypt data that were encrypted by a symmetric-key algorithm, unless in possession of the session/shared key that was used to encrypt the data by the sensor.

Assumption 13.2

DSM is deployed on a trusted server.

Assumption 13.3

A sensor's secret key, *Prime* (P_i), and *secret key calculation* procedures are deployed on trusted hardware such as TPM; hence they are safe from intruders. Similar to most cryptological analysis of public-key communication protocols, we now define the attack models for the purpose of verifying authenticity and integrity.

Definition 13.1 (attack on authentication)

A malicious attacker M_a is an adversary capable of monitoring, intercepting, and introducing itself as an authenticated source node that can send data streams to the DSM.

Definition 13.2 (attack on integrity)

A malicious attacker M_i is an adversary capable of monitoring the data stream and is able to modify the stream while it is in transit.

Theorem 13.1

The security is not compromised by reducing the size of the shared secret key (K_{SH}).

TABLE 13.2
Notations Symmetric-Key (AES) Algorithm Takes Time to Get All Possible Keys Using Most Advanced Intel i7 Processor

Key length	8	16	32	64	128
Key domain size	256	65,536	4.295e+09	1.845e+19	3.4028e+38
Time (in nanosecond)	1435	1e+05	7.301e+09	3136e+19	5.7848e+35

Proof. We reduce the size of the prime number to make the key generation process faster. The ECRYPT II recommendations on key length say that a 128-bit symmetric key provides the same level of protection as a 3248-bit asymmetric key. Smaller keys can also provide desired security levels as long as they are not shared publically. An advanced processor (*Intel i7 processor*) takes about 1.7 nanoseconds to try out one key from one block. With this speed, it would take about $1.3 \times 10^{12} \times$ *the age of the universe* to check all the keys from the possible key set [11] of an asymmetric scheme. By reducing the size of the prime number, we speed up the security verification process at DSM (see Table 13.2). As shown in Table 13.2, a 64-bit symmetric key takes 3136e+19 nanoseconds (more than a month), so we safely concluded that updating the prime number every week (i.e., $t = 168$ hours) will not compromise the security of the system. The dynamic shared key is computed based on the prime number. Hence we conclude that an attacker cannot crack the shared key within the interval time t. Further, the shared key is updated without exchanging information between the sensors and DSM. This leads to confusion for adversaries who may try to intercept the data flow. The original key has been changed four times before an attacker knows that key and this knowledge is not known to the attackers. ■

Theorem 13.2

Dynamically generated prime number P_i in Algorithm 13.1 is always synchronized between the source sensors (S_i) and DSM.

Proof. The normal method to check the prime number is $6k + 1, \forall k \in N^+$ (an integer). Here, we initially initialize the value of k based on this primary test formula. Our prime generation method is based on the nth prime number generation and from the extended idea of Reference 28. In our scheme, the input P_i is the currently used prime number (initialized by DSM) and the return P_i is the calculated new prime number. Initially, P_i is initialized by DSM during the DPBSV handshaking process and the interval time is t. ■

From Algorithm 13.1, we calculate the new prime number P_i based on the previous one P_{i-1}. The complete process of the prime number calculation is based on the value of m, and m is initialized from the value k. The value of k is constant at source because it is calculated from the current prime number. This process is initialized during *DPBSV handshaking*. Since the value of k is the same on both sides, the procedure *Prime* (P_i) returns identical values. In Algorithm 13.1, the value of $S(m)$ is computed as follows [28]:

$$S_1(x) = \frac{(-1)}{(\sqrt{x}/6)+1} \sum_{k=1}^{(\sqrt{x}/6)+1} \frac{x}{6k+1} - \frac{x}{6k+1}$$

$$S_2(x) = \frac{(-1)}{(\sqrt{x}/6)+1} \sum_{k=1}^{(\sqrt{x}/6)+1} \frac{x}{6k-1} - \frac{x}{6k-1}$$

Algorithm 13.1
Dynamic Prime Number Generation

Prime (P_i)

1. $P_{i-1} = P_i$.
2. Set $k := \left\lceil \frac{P_{i-1}}{6} \right\rceil$.
3. Se $m := 6k + 1$.
4. If $m \geq 10^7$ then
5. $k := k/10^5 := k/10^5$
6. GO TO: 3
7. If $S(m) = 1$. then
8. GO TO: 14
9. Set $m := 6k + 5$
10. If $S(m) = 1$ then
11. GO TO: 14
12. $k := \lfloor k^3 + \sqrt{k} \rfloor \bmod 17 + k$
13. GO TO: 3
14. $P_i = m$
15. Return (P_i)//calculated new prime number

$$S(x) = \frac{S_1(x) + S_2(x)}{2}$$

If $S(x) = 1$, then x is prime, otherwise x is not prime.
$x \not\equiv 0 \bmod i \forall 1 \leq i \leq x - 1$, if x is prime.
Put the value of x as a prime number, then

$$\Rightarrow \frac{x}{6k+1} - \frac{x}{6k+1} = -1$$

$$\text{Same as } \frac{x}{6k-1} - \frac{x}{6k-1} = -1$$

$\forall k$ within the specified range, that is, 10^7, then

$$S_1(x) = \frac{(-1)}{(\sqrt{x}/6) + 1} \sum_{k=1}^{(\sqrt{x}/6)+1} (-1) = 1$$

The same $S_2(x)$ is also 1 and then

$$S(x) = \frac{S_1(x) + S_2(x)}{2} = 1$$

Hence, the property of $S(x)$ is proved.

Theorem 13.3

An *attacker* M_a cannot read the secret information from sensor node (S_i) or introduce itself as an authenticated node in DPBSV.

Proof. Following Definition 13.1, we know that an attacker M_a can gain access to the shared key K_{SH} by monitoring the network thoroughly, but M_a cannot get secret information such as *Prime* (P_i)

and *KeyGen*. Considering the computational hardness of secure modules (such as TPM), we know that M_a cannot get the secret information for P_i generation, K_i and *KeyGen*. So there are no possibilities for the malicious node to tap into the data stream; however, M_a can introduce himself/herself as the authenticated node and start sending false information to DSM. In our scheme, sensor (S_i) sends $((DATA \oplus K_{SH} \oplus K_i)\backslash parallel(S_i \oplus K_{SH}))$, where the second part of the data block ($S_i \oplus K_{SH}$) is used for authentication checks. DSM decrypts this part of the data block for the authentication check. DSM retrieves S_i after decryption and matches the corresponding S_i within its database. If the calculated S_i matches with the DSM database, it accepts; otherwise it rejects the node as source and marks it as not an authenticated sensor node. All required secured information for prime number and key generation procedure are stored in a trusted part of the sensor node (i.e., TPM). According to the features of TPM, the attacker cannot get the information from TPM as discussed before. Hence we conclude that *attacker* M_a cannot attack or get access to the big data stream. ■

Theorem 13.4

An *attacker* M_i cannot read the shared key K_{SH} within the time interval t in the DPBSV model.

Proof. Following Definition 13.2, we know that an attacker M_i has full access to the network to read the shared key K_{SH}, but M_i cannot get correct secret information such as K_{SH}. Considering the method described in Theorem 13.1, we know that M_i cannot get the currently used K_{SH} within the time interval t, because our proposed scheme calculates P_i randomly after time t and then uses the value of P_i sensor to generate K_{SH}. For more details on computation analysis, readers can refer to Theorem 13.1. ■

13.6 EXPERIMENT AND EVALUATION

In order to evaluate the efficiency and effectiveness of the proposed DPBSV scheme under adverse conditions, we observe each individual data block for authentication checks and selected data blocks for integrity attacks. The integrity attack verification interval is dynamic in nature and the data verification is done at the DSM only.

To validate our proposed scheme, we experimented with two different approaches by using different simulation environments. We first verify the security scheme using Scyther [29], and then measure the efficiency of the scheme using JCE (Java cryptographic environment) [30]. We also check the required buffer size to process our proposed scheme and compare with standard AES algorithm; this experiment is done in a MATLAB® simulation tool.

13.6.1 Security Verification

The scheme is written in the Scyther simulation environment using Security Protocol Description Language (.spdl). According to the features of Scyther, we define the role of S and D, where S is the sender (i.e., sensor nodes) and D is the recipient (i.e., DSM). Next, S and D have all the required information that are exchanged during the handshake process. This enables D and S to update their shared key. S sends the data packets to D, and D performs the security verification. In our simulation, we introduce two types of attacks by the adversaries, that is, attacks on integrity and authenticity. In our experiments, we evaluated all packets at D (DSM) for security verification. We experimented with 100 numbers of runs for each claim (also known as bounds) and found out the number of attacks at D as shown in Figure 13.2. Apart from these, we follow the default properties of Scyther.

13.6.1.1 Attack Model

Many types of cryptographic attack can be considered. In our case, we focus on integrity attack and authentication attacks as discussed above. In an integrity attack, an attacker can perform a brute

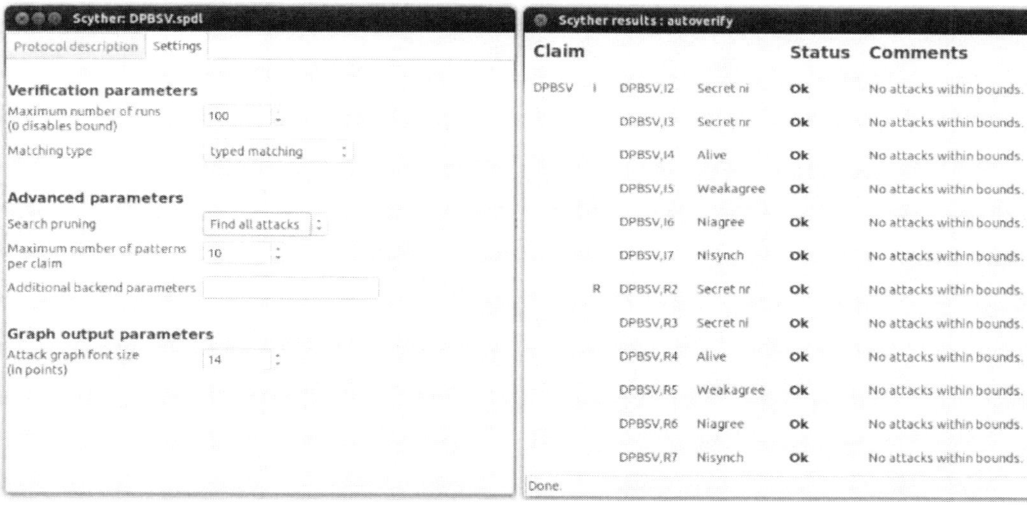

FIGURE 13.2 Scyther simulation environment with parameters and result page of success security verification at DSM.

force attack on captured packets by systematically testing every possible key, and we assumed that he/she is able to determine when the attack is successful. In an authentication attack, an attacker tries to get the behavior of the source node. We assume that he/she is able to determine the source node's behavior and the attacker can introduce an authenticated node and act as the original source node. In our concept, we are using a trusted module in the sensor to store the secret information and procedure for key generation and encryption (i.e., TPM).

13.6.1.2 Experiment Model

In practice, attacks may be more sophisticated and efficient than brute force attacks.

However, this does not affect the validity of the proposed DPBSV scheme as we are interested in efficient security verification without periodic key exchanges and successful attacks. Here, we model the process as described in the previous section and fixe the key size as 64 bits (see Table 13.2). We used Scyther, an automatic security protocols verification tool, to verify our scheme.

13.6.1.3 Results

We did our simulation using variable numbers of data blocks in each run. Our experiment ranges from 10 to 100 instances with 10 intervals. We check the authentication for each data block, whereas the integrity check is performed on the selected data blocks. Without encryption information, attackers cannot authenticate encrypted data blocks. Hence, we did not find any attacks for authentication checks. For integrity attacks, it is hard to get the shared key (K_{SH}), as the shared key (K_{SH}) is frequently changed based on the dynamic prime number P_i on both source sensor (S_i) and DSM. In the experiment, we did not encounter any attack in integrity check. Figure 13.2 shows the result of security verification experiments in the Scyther environment. From the observations above, we can conclude that our proposed scheme is secure.

13.6.2 Performance Comparison

13.6.2.1 Experiment Model

It is clear that the actual efficiency improvement brought about by our scheme depends highly on the size of key and rekeying without further communication between sensor and DSM. We have

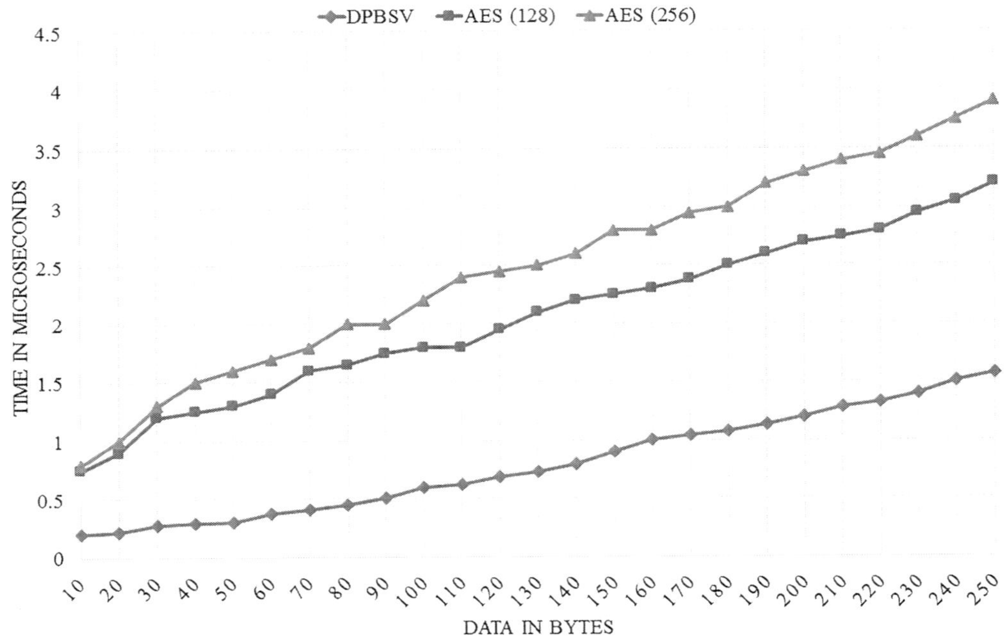

FIGURE 13.3 Performance of the proposed scheme compared in efficiency to 128-bit AES and 256-bit AES.

performed experiments with different sizes of data blocks. The results of our experiments are given below.

We compare the performance of our proposed scheme DPBSV with the AES, the standard symmetric-key encryption algorithm [18,19]. Our scheme was compared with two standard symmetric-key algorithms: 128-bit AES and 256-bit AES. This performance comparison experiment is carried out in JCE. This comparison is based on the features of JCE in Java virtual machine version 1.6 64 bit. JCE is the standard extension to the Java platform, which provides a framework implementation for cryptographic methods. We experimented with many-to-one communication. All sensor nodes communicate with the single node (DSM). All sensors have similar properties, whereas the destination node has the properties of DSM (more powerful to initialize the process). The processing time of data verification is measured at the DSM node. Our experimental results are shown in Figure 13.3; the result validates the theoretical analysis presented in Section 13.5.

13.6.2.2 Results

The performance of our scheme is better than the standard AES algorithm when different sizes of the data blocks are considered. Figure 13.3 shows the processing time of the proposed DPBSV scheme in comparison with base 128-bit AES and 256-bit AES for different sizes of data blocks. The performance comparison shows that our proposed scheme is more efficient and faster.

13.6.3 Required Buffer Size

13.6.3.1 Experiment Model

We experimented the features of the DSM buffer by using MATLAB as the simulation tool. This performance is based on the processing time performance calculated in Figure 13.3 (last subsection). Here, we compared our scheme with standard 128-bit AES and 256-bit AES, the same as the processing time performance comparison. DPBSV required minimum buffer size to process security

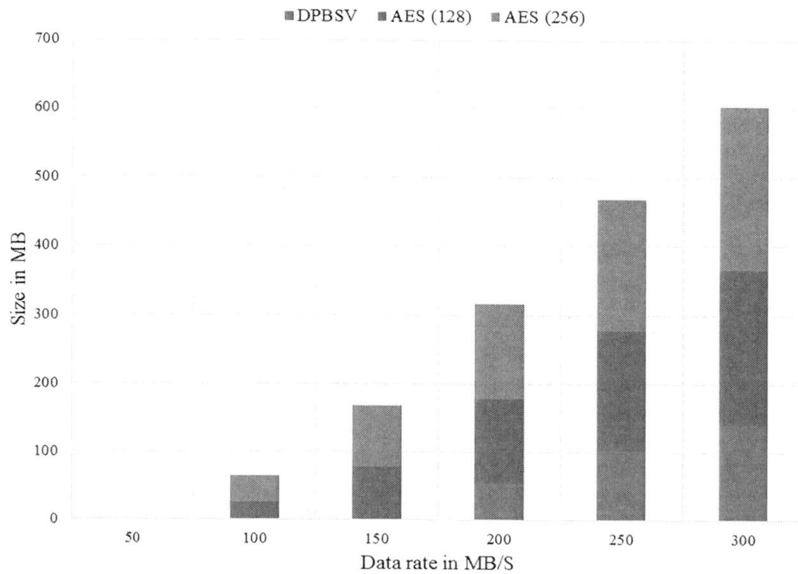

FIGURE 13.4 Performance comparison of minimum buffer size required to process the security verification with various data rates to DSM.

verification at DSM with various data rates starting from 50 to 300 MBpS with 50 MBpS interval. Performance comparison is done are to measure the efficiency of our proposed scheme (DPBSV).

13.6.3.2 Results

The performance of our scheme is better than the standard AES algorithm with different rates of data. Figure 13.4 shows the minimum buffer size required to process security at DSM and the proposed DPBSV scheme performance compared with base 128-bit AES and 256-bit AES. The performance comparison shows that our proposed scheme is efficient and requires less buffer to process security than the baseline AES protocols.

From the above three experiments, we conclude that our proposed DPBSV scheme is secured (from both authenticity and integrity attacks), efficient (compared to standard symmetric solutions, that is, 128/256-bit AES), and maintain end-to-end security in big sensing data stream.

13.7 CONCLUSIONS

In this chapter, we have proposed a novel authenticated key exchange scheme, namely, DPBSV, which aims to provide an efficient and fast (on-the-fly) security verification scheme and ensure end-to-end security in big data stream. Our scheme has been designed based on symmetric-key cryptography and random prime number generation. By theoretical analyses and experimental evaluations, we showed that our DPBSV scheme has provided significant improvement in the processing time, and prevented malicious attacks on authenticity and integrity. In our scheme, we decrease the communication and computation overhead by dynamic key initialization at both the sensor and DSM end, which in effect eliminates the need for rekeying and decreases the communication overhead.

REFERENCES

1. M. Stonebraker, U. Çetintemel, and S. Zdonik, The 8 requirements of real-time stream processing. *ACM SIGMOD Record*, 34(4), 42–47, 2005.

2. V. Gulisano et al., Streamcloud: An elastic and scalable data streaming system. *IEEE Transactions on Parallel and Distributed Systems*, 23(12), 2351–2365, 2012.
3. D. Carney et al., Monitoring streams: A new class of data management applications. In *Proceedings of the 28th International Conference on Very Large Data Bases*, pp. 215–226, 2002.
4. S. Chandrasekaran et al., TelegraphCQ: Continuous dataflow processing. In *Proceedings of the ACM SIGMOD International Conference on Management of Data*, pp. 668–668, 2003.
5. A. Bifet, Mining big data in real time. *Informatica (Slovenia)*, 37(1), 15–20, 2013.
6. M. Dayarathna and T. Suzumura, Automatic optimization of stream programs via source program operator graph transformations. *Distributed and Parallel Databases*, 31(4), 543–599, 2013.
7. R. V. Nehme et al., StreamShield: A stream-centric approach towards security and privacy in data stream environments. In *ACM SIGMOD*, pp. 1027–1030, 2009.
8. B. Sahoo, S. Rath, and D. Puthal, Energy efficient protocols for wireless sensor networks: A survey and approach. *International Journal of Computer Applications*, 44(18), 43–48, 2012.
9. I. F. Akyildiz et al., Wireless sensor networks: A survey. *Computer Networks*, 38(4), 393–422, 2002.
10. J. Burke, J. McDonald, and T. Austin, Architectural support for fast symmetric-key cryptography. *ACM SIGOPS Operating Systems Review*, 34(5), 178–189, 2000.
11. https://www.cloudflare.com (accessed on: 04.08.2014).
12. K. W. Park, S. S. Lim, and K. H. Park, Computationally efficient PKI-based single sign-on protocol, PKASSO for mobile devices. *IEEE Transactions on Computers*, 57(6), 821–834, 2008.
13. D. Puthal, B. P. S. Sahoo, S. Mishra, and S. Swain, Cloud computing features, issues, and challenges: A big picture. In *International Conference on Computational Intelligence and Networks (CINE)*, pp. 116–123, 2015.
14. H. Demirkan and D. Delen, Leveraging the capabilities of service-oriented decision support systems: Putting analytics and big data in cloud. *Decision Support Systems*, 55(1), 412–421, 2013.
15. J. Lu and D. Li, Bias correction in a small sample from big data. *IEEE Transactions on Knowledge and Data Engineering*, 25(11), 2658–2663, 2013.
16. J. M. Tien, Big data: Unleashing information. *Journal of Systems Science and Systems Engineering*, 22(2), 127–151, 2013.
17. R. Ranjan, Streaming big data processing in datacenter clouds. *IEEE Cloud Computing*, 1(1), 78–83, 2014.
18. PUB, NIST FIPS. 197: Advanced Encryption Standard (AES). *Federal Information Processing Standards Publication*, 197, 441–0311, 2001.
19. S. Heron, Advanced Encryption Standard (AES). *Network Security*, 2009(12), 8–12, 2009.
20. S. Nepal, J. Zic, D. Liu, and J. Jang, A mobile and portable trusted computing platform. *EURASIP Journal on Wireless Communications and Networking*, 2011(1), 1–19, 2011.
21. D. Puthal, Secure Data Collection and Critical Data Transmission Technique in Mobile Sink Wireless Sensor Networks. M.Tech. thesis, National Institute of Technology, Rourkela, 2012.
22. D. Puthal, S. Nepal, R. Ranjan, and J. Chen, Threats to networking cloud and edge datacenters in the Internet of things. *IEEE Cloud Computing*, 3(3), 64–71, 2016.
23. M. Benantar, R. H. High Jr, and M. K. Rathi, Method and system for maintaining client server security associations in a distributed computing system. U.S. Patent 6,141,758, October 31, 2000.
24. D. Zissis and D. Lekkas, Addressing cloud computing security issues. *Future Generation Computer Systems*, 28(3), 583–592, 2012.
25. C. Liu et al., Authorized public auditing of dynamic big data storage on cloud with efficient verifiable fine-grained updates. *IEEE Transactions on Parallel and Distributed Systems*, 25(9), 2234–2244, 2014.
26. C. Liu, R. Ranjan, C. Yang, X. Zhang, L. Wang, and J. Chen, MUR-DPA: Top-down levelled multi-replica Merkle hash tree based secure public auditing for dynamic big data storage on cloud. *IEEE Transactions on Computers*, 64(9), 2609–2622, 2015.
27. B. R. Kandukuri, V. R. Paturi, and A. Rakshit, Cloud security issues. In *IEEE International Conference on Services Computing (SCC'09)*, pp. 517–520, 2009.
28. I. Kaddoura and S. Abdul-Nabi, On formula to compute primes and the nth prime. *Applied Mathematical Science*, 6(76), 3751–3757, 2012.
29. Scyther, [Online] http://www.cs.ox.ac.uk/people/cas.cremers/scyther/
30. M. Pistoia et al., *Enterprise Java 2 Security: Building Secure and Robust J2EE Applications*. Addison Wesley Professional, 2004.

14 Considerations on the Use of Custom Accelerators for Big Data Analytics

Vito Giovanni Castellana, Antonino Tumeo, Marco Minutoli, Marco Lattuada, and Fabrizio Ferrandi

CONTENTS

ABSTRACT

Accelerators, including graphic processing units (GPUs) for general-purpose computation, many-core designs with wide vector units (e.g., Intel Phi), have become a common component of many high-performance clusters. The appearance of more stable and reliable tools that can automatically convert code written in high-level specifications with annotations (such as C or C++) to hardware description languages (high-level synthesis—HLS) is also setting the stage for a broader use of reconfigurable devices (e.g., field programmable gate arrays—FPGAs) in high-performance system for the implementation of custom accelerators, helped by the fact that new processors include advanced cache-coherent interconnects for these components. In this chapter, we briefly survey the status of the use of accelerators in high-performance systems targeted at big data analytics applications. Although the recent progress in the use of accelerators for this class of applications has been significant, we argue that, differently from scientific simulations, there are still gaps to close. This is particularly true for the "irregular" behaviors exhibited by emerging no-SQL and graph databases. We focus our attention on the limits of HLS tools for data analytics and graph methods, and discuss a new architectural template that better fits the requirement of this class of applications. We validate the new architectural templates by modifying the Graph Engine for Multithreaded System (GEMS) framework to support accelerators generated with such a methodology, and by testing it with queries coming from the Lehigh University Benchmark (LUBM). The architectural template enables better supporting the task- and memory-level parallelism present in graph methods by supporting a new control model and an enhanced memory interface. We show that our solution allows generating parallel accelerators, providing speed ups with respect to conventional HLS flows. We finally draw conclusions and present a perspective on the use of reconfigurable devices and design automation tools for data analytics.

14.1 INTRODUCTION

The emergence of big data analytics is determining profound changes in computing. Taming big data's 5 Vs, in fact, requires significant evolutions, if not true revolutions, in the conventional computing stack. To support the ever-increasing volume, velocity, and variety of data, enabling veracity and extraction of value from the data themselves, new solutions in software, runtimes, and hardware are required. The simple adaptation of current relational database infrastructures is not sufficient: they certainly have decades of history, research, and advancements, but also bring with them legacy approaches that do not cope well with the new issues introduced by big data. For example, tables may not be sufficient to express the variety of the data, and queries built along join and select procedures may not scale well with the volume of the data.

14.1.1 Big Data and Graphs

New data models, including graph databases based on the Resource Description Framework (RDF) and attributed graphs (which couple tables of attributes with vertices and edges), have appeared, together with related query languages (e.g., SPARQL and DATALOG).

Graphs appear a convenient way to store, process, and retrieve information for many of the emerging big data analytics datasets, such as security, communication, transportation and social networks, government and healthcare data, environmental science, biomedical research, and finance. Graph methods are inherently parallel, as they allow spawning concurrent activities for each vertex or edge, but they also present so-called *irregular behaviors*. They are basically pointer or linked list-based data structures, and require fine-grained data accesses. Large graphs exhibit poor spatial and temporal locality: an algorithm may move from a memory location to another one completely unrelated while following edges. They are usually synchronization intensive, because concurrent search activities may reach the same locations and need coordination. Additionally, it is difficult to partition a graph among concurrent activities on distributed memories without generating load imbalance, because certain vertices may have significantly more edges than others. Thus, they may be reached simultaneously by many activities. In general, they are characterized by limited arithmetic operations but an abundance of memory accesses. Current systems, instead, exploit processors with deep cache hierarchies and advanced prefetchers optimized for locality, high floating point performance, and, in clusters, interconnect networks that perform best with large, batched, data transfers.

14.1.2 Accelerating Graph Analytics

The emerging data models, the limitations of old frameworks, and the issues of commodity systems have led to the introduction of countless specialized software infrastructures. Open source RDF databases include Jena SDB [1] backed by relational databases; Jena TDB [1] backed by native, disk-based storage; Sesame [2] with support for layering on top of relational databases or a native backend; Virtuoso Open Source edition [3]; and 4store [4]. Research-level RDF database approaches include RDF-3X [5], Hexastore [6], YARS2 [7], SHARD [8], BitMat [9], and SPARQL queries on PIG [10]. Commercial RDF databases include Bigdata [11], BigOWLIM [12], and Virtuoso [3]. A number of these approaches leverage Map-Reduce frameworks to achieve scalability on clusters, or implement support for distributed cluster with the objective to increase performance, dataset size, or both [13–15]. The SPARK framework [16], on top of Hadoop or in standalone mode, together with the GraphX library, has also started to be employed to implement and query RDF databases. GEMS, the Graph Engine for Multithreaded Systems [17], is a software stack composed of three layers: a custom multithreaded runtime (GMT—Global Memory and Threading), a library of graph methods and related data structures, and a SPARQL-to-C++ compiler. The custom runtime at its basis enables irregular applications and, more specifically, graph methods, to scale in performance and size on commodity clusters by addressing through software approaches some of the shortcomings of current high-performance architectures with this type of applications. Specifically, it provides a global address space across cluster nodes (so that large datasets to be explored in memory do not need partitioning), lightweight software multithreading to tolerate latencies to access data on remote nodes, and messages aggregation to maximize utilization of the interconnect network of the cluster. The SPARQL-to-C++ compiler converts SPARQL queries into graph methods expressed in C++ that exploit the graph library at the lower level of the stack. GEMS is a first example of how hardware characteristics of systems need careful consideration for emerging big data analytics workloads. The original Cray Urika is an example of solutions that tried to go even further on the path of specialization. It employed the custom-designed Cray XMT 2 architecture (derived from the Tera MTA designs, systems implementing nodes with multithreaded processors, global address space, and synchronization at the level of the single memory word to better support throughput-based applications such as graph exploration) to implement graph databases, adapting existing open source frameworks. Cray has moved away from the use of custom architectures due to maintainability and cost issues, and introduced a Urika-GX [18], based on somewhat more commodity components (x86 nodes with the latest Cray Aries interconnect) and running Hadoop and Spark software frameworks. However, recognizing that these are not optimal for all type of workloads, it also supports the Cray Graph Engine (CGE), which again employs a custom runtime with features that can speed up graph methods.

While costs are a significant reason to implement data analytics frameworks using commodity systems, there is undeniably a need to better exploit the underneath hardware. Given the intense interest and focus on data analytics of the majority of large private and public institutions, custom, or semicustom, systems may still be justified if they can demonstrate higher performance, and the ability to manage larger datasets, without trading off too much flexibility.

Accelerators such as graphic processing units (GPUs) for general-purpose computations and as the Intel Phi are becoming more and more widespread in high-performance systems. Optimized for throughput computing, they allow increasing performance for massively parallel, arithmetic-intensive workloads, while remaining power efficient. By trading off latency for throughput, they also provide impressive amounts of memory bandwidth, which potentially make them an appealing platform also for applications different than scientific simulations. Because they find applications in a variety of markets (e.g., gaming), they have become a commodity component at affordable costs. Consequently, much work has been done to develop approaches for accelerating more unusual workloads for these architectures. We have seen approaches to accelerate conventional relational database operations, and more recently a large amount of research to accelerate a variety of graph methods [19–24], on single and multiple accelerators, even installed on distributed systems. A number of approaches try to accelerate graph methods by adopting Map-Reduce models. Lately, we have seen the appearance of the first graph databases (e.g., BlazeGraph) [25] able to exploit GPUs by building on existing MapReduce libraries of graph methods (MapGraph, in the case of BlazeGraph) [26].

When it comes to application-specific accelerators, reconfigurable devices, and in particular field programming gate arrays (FPGAs), are resurging. Owing to the end of Dennard's Scaling and slowing down of Moore's law, FPGAs have become more affordable to produce in large quantities with respect to general-purpose processors on Application Specific Integrated Circuits (ASICs), while reducing the spread in terms of efficiency. In fact, every production technology node becomes much more expensive to implement, and FPGAs, being mostly based on standard, heavily replicated cells (mainly Static Random Access Memories—SRAMs), can benefit from significantly increased densities, and an easier technology development process than processors, such as no need to develop custom logic cells, care specifically for hotspots, etc. And even if the final operating clock frequencies for the devices are different, FPGA-based designs are specialized after production on a case-by-case basis. They can even be reconfigured during system operation. An ASIC, instead, remains targeted for the specific function and cannot adapt, so that it effectively needs to address as many cases as possible, usually not always providing the highest efficiency. The latest industry developments, with a significant number of processor designs that integrate both general-purpose processors and reconfigurable logic (e.g., Xilinx Zynq platforms), initiatives to open coherent buses, interconnects, and protocols of general-purpose processors to accelerators (e.g., IBM's CAPI—Coherent Access Port Interface, and Intel's OmniPath, preceded by AMD's Hyper-Transports) and key acquisitions (Intel's acquisition of Altera and Micron's acquisitions of Pico and Convey), indicate a clear trend. The suitability for memory-intensive applications is also exemplified by the appearance of a number of FPGA devices integrating 3D stacked memories. FPGAs can thus represent more and more a very promising intermediate point between commodity-based accelerator and custom system for data analytics applications. However, there remains a significant productivity gap in the use of reconfigurable logic. Designing accelerators by employing Hardware Description Languages (HDL) is difficult and time-consuming. Hand-designed accelerators usually provide very high performance, but can address only a very specific set of algorithms. High-level synthesis (HLS) approaches, which generate HDL starting from descriptions in higher-level languages (such as C/C++), have been a research topic for many decades. However, they have historically targeted regular, compute-intensive applications, and have focused on the exploitation of instruction-level parallelism (ILP). Only recently have HLS approaches matured enough to start targeting task-level parallelism (TLP), which is preponderant in data analytics applications. A number of tools have started to support OpenMP or OpenCL (e.g., Convey's OpenHT, Xilinx Vivado HLS, and Altera HLS) [27–29] as a way to describe task parallel applications. However, these still better apply to compute-intensive and regular workloads, where memory patterns and forking/joining tasks are all precomputable during the synthesis phases. There is, however, still a large amount or research and explorations that need to be done to efficiently address issues of irregular and memory-intensive workloads, which instead present many unpredictable dynamic effects that are only manageable at runtime. Graph methods represent, again, a clear example. Because HLS tools basically are compilers, the nature of the data structures (mostly pointer-based) used in graph methods makes many of the compiler methods inefficient or inapplicable (e.g., alias analysis).

14.1.3 Chapter Organization

In this chapter, we present a case study that shows how HLS synthesis tools could be improved to better support data analytics applications. In particular, we focus on task parallelism extraction and the management of the memory system, which represent the most significant limitations of conventional HLS approaches. We present the case study in the context of the GEMS graph database, a real data analytics application. Progress still remains to be done, but we believe that this is a step in the direction of increasing the usability and applicability of custom accelerators based on FPGA technology for data analytics workloads, making them a viable platform. Section 14.2 of this chapter presents related works in the area of acceleration of analytics workloads with reconfigurable devices. Section 14.3 describes the general case study, where GEMS is modified to support query accelerators running on FPGA. Section 14.4 describes the proposed architecture design and its integration in an open source FPGA synthesis flow. Section 14.5 discusses experimental results obtained by generating accelerators for queries coming from the Lehigh University Benchmark (LUBM) [30]. Finally, Section 14.6 draws some conclusions and presents future prospects for the use of FPGA accelerators, and design automation tools, in data analytics.

14.2 RELATED WORK

Our case study touches many different aspects connected with the design of accelerators for reconfigurable devices. First and foremost, we have to look at platforms and related research for the acceleration of databases and data analytics. Then, because we look in particular to graph-based data models, we also need to look to more general solutions that try to speed up graph methods and workloads that exhibit an irregular behavior. Finally, because our main objective is not just to discuss the design of custom accelerators per se, but also to highlight the gaps in the approaches that could greatly increase the flexibility in the applicability of reconfigurable devices for accelerating data analytics, we need to discuss the current trends in HLS and contrast them with the requirements of data analytics code.

14.2.1 Accelerators for Databases, Data Analytics, and Graph Methods

In the last few years, an increasing number of commercial platforms for data analytics that implement reconfigurable devices have appeared. The most prominent examples are the Microsoft Catapult [31] project, which has integrated FPGAs in Microsoft-designed servers to improve performance, reduce power consumption, and provide new capabilities in the datacenter, and the Netezza's systems [32], now owned by IBM. Data analytics has also been an area of intense study and development for the Convey HC and MX hybrid platforms. These systems integrate high-density FPGAs with general-purpose processors, providing optimized high bandwidth, and host-coherent memory controllers. Convey HC and MX have been followed up, for cost reasons, by the Convey WX (Wolverine) accelerator, which is a PCI-Express drop-in solution that provides similar features.

These systems are the outcome of a large amount of research done to accelerate databases and data analytics, including operators and full queries. IBM has proposed an FPGA-based system to accelerate expensive operations in relational databases queries, including data decompression and predicate evaluation [33]. IBM has also explored FPGA support for DB2 with BLU acceleration: compression techniques, paired with the Column-Store approach, enable performing most SQL operations on the compressed values, so that they can be processed in a Single Instruction Multiple Data (SIMD) fashion. IBM looked at a similar approach also for GPUs [34]. The work from Halstead et al. [35] discusses FPGA acceleration of hash-joins on a Convey MX, exploiting multithreading and the support for atomic memory operations provided by the system. Casper and Olukotun [36] show the potential of hardware acceleration for in-memory databases with select, sort, and join operations. In Reference 37, we see an example of the integration of custom units on reconfigurable logic with general-purpose processors to accelerate analytics workloads.

Reference 38 presents a first example of compilation of queries to FPGA, targeted to streaming databases. The work from Takenaka et al. [39] presents a compiler-based approach that translates SQL-based queries for software-based complex event-processing systems in hardware. Dennl et al. [40] discuss acceleration of the SQL restrict and aggregate operators, employing partial dynamic reconfiguration to compose query-specific datapaths. The poster [41] hints at the potential of the use of HLS to fully implement queries for in-memory databases by employing Vivado HLS.

The approach that we discuss in this chapter goes a step further than these solutions. We focus on the acceleration of workloads in emerging data formats based on graph representations. In these situations, the acceleration of conventional relational and table-based operations only improves part of the problem. We, instead, look at techniques to support complete acceleration of SPARQL queries. To do so, we work in the context of the GEMS framework. In particular, the GEMS SPARQL-to-C++ compiler converts queries expressed in SPARQL into a set of graph pattern-matching routines. Our objective is, thus, to provide efficient ways to synthesize, and accelerate, those graph methods.

Prominent examples of designs to accelerate graph traversal and, in general, irregular kernels are the Breadth First Search (BFS) personalities for the Convey HC [42], and the Convey MX systems. The Convey MX, in particular, couples a multithreaded custom processor on the reconfigurable logic with an OpenMP programming environment (CHOMP—Convey Hybrid OpenMP) [43]. Betkaoui et al. [44] discuss reconfigurable hardware methodologies for efficient parallel processing of large-scale graph exploration. These, however, either are custom accelerators for a specific kernel, or employ general-purpose designs on the FPGA. Our approach exploits an HLS approach. In Reference 45, Halstead et al. discuss how to extend the ROCCC framework to support irregular applications, introducing multithreading to tolerate long memory access latencies. However, they do not address atomic memory operations and focus on the simple case study of pointer chasing.

14.2.2 Synthesis Approaches

Conventional HLS approaches and tools typically adopt the so-called finite-state machine (FSM) with Datapath (FSMD) model. This model works by analyzing the specification and by identifying the operations in the code, determining type and dependencies of these operations. Given *resource constraints*, that is, limitations on the number of functional units and requirements in terms of memory, they consequently generate a datapath and an FSM that, based on a static scheduling of the operations, executes them on the datapath. This model allows efficient extraction of ILP, but does not work well when the code exposes TLPs (such as, for example, independent iterations in a for loop). In fact, complexity of the FSM controller, which is typically centralized for the whole portion of code that gets synthesized, exponentially grows as it needs to manage concurrent tasks. As data analytics applications, and graph methods, present significant amounts of task parallelism, better solutions to manage task parallelism are required.

To improve the situation, the majority of the current HLS approaches look at decomposing the FSM to reduce its complexity. Among the variety of works, we highlight approaches that restructure the controller in a hierarchical way [46,47], even using State Charts descriptions [48]. Some solutions, like [49], employ a pseudo-distributed approach that enables supporting Speculative Functional Units (SFUs). The final architecture still relies on a static schedule, but a local controller dynamically checks results of SFUs without stalling the whole datapath. Our approach, instead, is completely orthogonal. It is built from the beginning with distributed controllers, and does not consider any fixed schedule, avoiding runtime conflicts on shared resources through arbiters.

Some other approaches try to solve the problem by synthesizing the tasks independently, and then managing their execution through custom schedulers or dedicated processors [50,51]. The design proposed in our case study, instead, does not require any additional control unit.

Various commercial and research HLS flows started considering parallel specifications as input descriptions. These include specifications annotated in CUDA, OpenMP, OpenCL, and pthreads [52,53]. LegUP [54] also supports OpenMP specifications, but requires the instantiation of an additional general-purpose processor for scheduling. These do not apply very well to data analytics applications in general, and in particular to graph methods. These may present several nested loops with significantly different number of iterations, and instances that, only due to data dependencies, can show significant load unbalance. The solutions that we present in our case do not require an additional processor, and can support any level of nested parallelism. OpenCL [55] is finding some success, also in commercial tools [27]. However, having been designed mainly for vector-based processors, it does not adapt well to irregular applications and graph methods.

14.3 CASE STUDY: GEMS ON FPGA

GEMS [17] implements an RDF database on a commodity cluster by mainly employing graph methods at all levels of his stack. To address the limitations of HPC systems, GEMS employs GMT, a custom runtime that provides a global address space across the cluster, so that data do not need to be partitioned, lightweight software multithreading, to tolerate data access latencies, and message aggregation, to improve network utilization with fine-grained transactions. A graph application programming interface (API) and a set of methods to ingest RDF triples and generate the related graph and dictionary, collectively named *SGLib*, are built with the functions provided by the runtime. On top of the whole system, a translator converts the query expressed in SPARQL to graph pattern-matching operations in C++. GEMS has demonstrated that by rethinking, and deeply customizing, the conventional database stack, it is possible to obtain promising scaling results for performance and size with emerging data models. Although running on commodity homogeneous clusters, GEMS' runtime tries to address in software issues that limit performance of graph methods and irregular applications on these architectures. The approach aims at exploiting in a useful way the surplus of computing power coming from today's HPC systems to address their limitations with specific workloads, without requiring, as in the past, fully custom systems.

We argue that the any novel data analytics infrastructure needs to start taking advantage of accelerators. The use of accelerators, in particular GPUs and vector processors, is now widespread in high-performance systems, because they allow to reach, although for specific workloads, high peak performance while maintaining power under control. However, because only certain workloads map well on these somewhat "commoditized" accelerators, further research is needed to understand if data analytics can really benefit from them. Researcher are making a significant effort to map in the most efficient way possible relevant algorithms such as graph algorithms on these architectures, with various degrees of success.

We also argue that reconfigurable devices such as FPGAs can represent a promising middle ground between fully custom designs and fully commodity systems, as shown by some available commercial platforms. To demonstrate the suitability of FPGAs for data analytics, we study a modification to the GEMS stack so that the SPARQL queries, after being converted to graph methods in a standard programming language, are executed directly on an FPGA-based accelerator, rather than through the intermediate library developed on GEMS' multithreaded runtime. We go further than approaches that exploit logic already implemented on the FPGA, being in the form of processors optimized for certain workloads (akin to GPUs or vector processors, only with different optimization points), or in the form of accelerators for specific recurrent functions for the query processing. We look at providing a way to synthesize completely custom accelerators for each query, expressed as set of graph pattern-matching operations, starting from their C code. The logic synthesis of the FPGA bitstream from the HDL code may require more times than the usual software compilation and optimization of queries performed in databases. However, the logic synthesis time is not a limiting factor. In fact, especially for databases supporting all the emerging data models that enable recognizing recurring patterns, analysts spend a great majority of the time running the same queries on dynamically changing data, rather than on changing and recompiling the queries.

We have modified the GEMS stack so that the SPARQL translator interacts with an HLS tool to generate the HDL code. The modified translator generates the C code that expresses the graph search. We also extended the intermediate SGLib, developing an alternate version of the graph API written in C that does not use the GMT runtime.

As the HLS tool, we have adopted the Bambu framework [56]. Bambu is a state-of-the-art HLS tool available under GPL. Bambu takes in input a C-code specification and synthesis objectives (e.g., target frequency and area), and outputs a Verilog implementation, directly synthesizable on a variety of devices from several vendors (Altera, Xilinx, Lattice). Bambu's conventional target architecture is an FSMD. Bambu's flow has three main components: front-end, synthesis, and back-end. The front-end phase processes the input specification, employing the GNU Compiler Collection (GCC). The front-end analyzes the input specifications and applies code transformations and optimizations (loop unrolling, function inlining, constant propagation, etc.). The process generates several graph-based Internal Representations (IR), such as Control Flow Graphs, Data Flow Graphs, Program Dependence Graphs, and Call Graphs. The synthesis phase takes those IRs in input and synthesizes the application one function at a time, following the structure of the call graph. This results in a modular, hierarchical design. The main activities that the flow performs, as in most HLS approaches, are operation scheduling, allocation and binding of functional units, registers, and interconnections. Finally, the back-end generates the final circuit description in Verilog, together with the simulation and synthesis scripts that enables Bambu to directly interface with third-party tools.

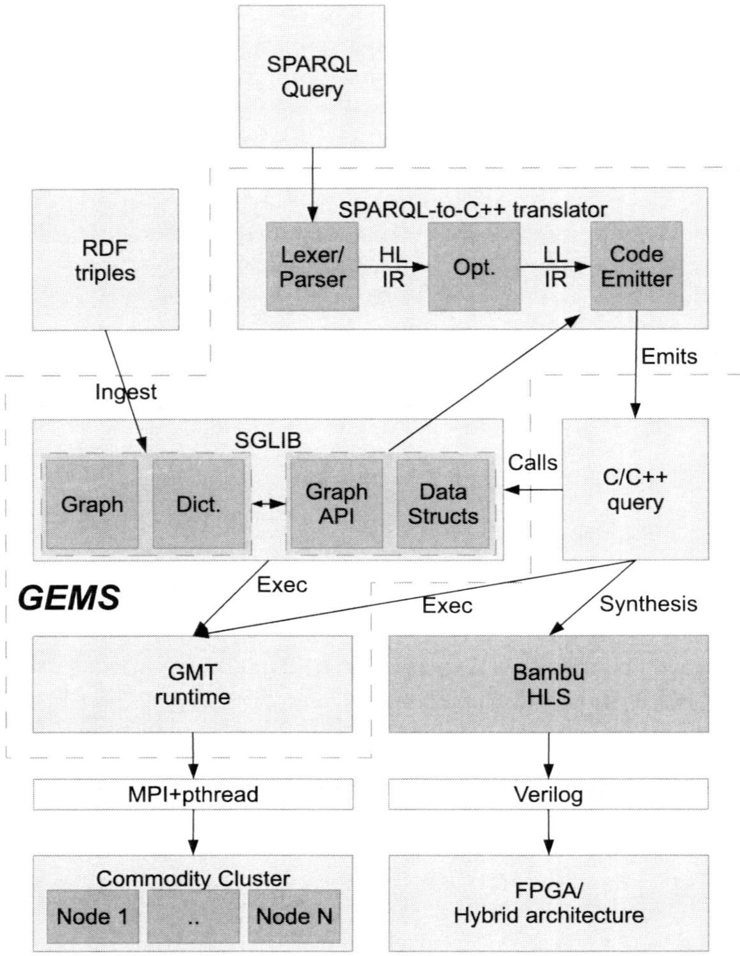

FIGURE 14.1 Structure of the GEMS stack and interaction with Bambu HLS.

Because the currently available version of Bambu is based around the FSMD model, we have heavily extended and modified the framework to support a different control model and the related novel synthesis techniques for the generation of the accelerators that can cope better with the requisites of graph methods and irregular workloads.

Figure 14.1 conceptually shows the modifications to the GEMS stack and the interaction with Bambu.

Figure 14.2 shows a sample SPARQL query, together with its graph pattern representation.

When processing this query, the custom SPARQL-2-C translator generates the C-code implementation as listed in Figure 14.3a.

Bambu processes the C query implementation generated by GEMS' SPARQL translator, in the form of pattern-matching functions. The pattern-matching function consists of a nest of parallel loops: each loop corresponds to matching a particular edge of the graph pattern that composes the query. In SPARQL queries, both vertices and edges may be either constant (represented through their value in the input data) or variable. The labels of constant elements, used the perform value checking during the query execution, act as input parameters for the search function. This allows supporting with just one procedure different queries that differ only for those labels. Figure 14.3 presents, as

(a)

```
SELECT ?x ?y
WHERE {
 ?y ub:subOrganizationOf
  <http://www.University0.edu> .
 ?y rdf:type ub:Department .
 ?x ub:worksFor ?y .
 ?x rdf:type ub:FullProfessor
}
```

(b)

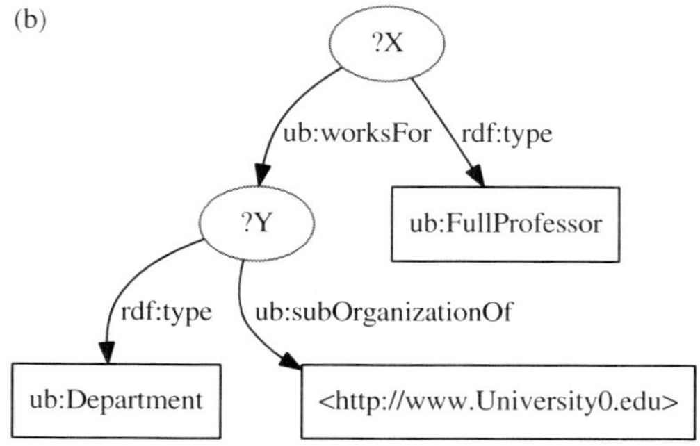

FIGURE 14.2 Example Query Q6: *full professors working at a department of University0.* (a) shows the query expressed in SPARQL, while (b) shows the equivalent graph pattern.

an example, query Q6 from the LUBM benchmark [30], together with its graph representation and a pseudocode describing the output of GEMS' modified translator.

Bambu processes the generated code and performs additional transformations to better expose TLP. In particular, Figure 14.3b shows how parallel loops are partially unrolled, with an unrolling factor equal to the number of kernel instances allocated in the synthesized architecture. Currently, the user must provide this number. The flow bounds all the kernel instances in the unrolled loop to different hardware modules during the synthesis, enabling concurrent execution.

14.4 PROPOSED ARCHITECTURE

As previously discussed, the majority of HLS techniques adopts the FSMD model for the target architecture. While very effective in exploiting ILP, this execution paradigm is inherently serial and does not efficiently exploit coarser granularities of parallelism, such as TLP. However, Graph methods and, in general, data analytics, although providing some ILP, typically have large amounts of dynamic TLP. Additionally, the conventional HLS techniques are optimized for applications with regular memory patterns and small datasets. Consequently, they just assume simple memory models where datasets are easily partitionable, and there is no need to synchronize parallel operations as they work on different data. This is not the case of graph methods: they do not have any locality, and a uniform partitioning of the dataset usually leads to load imbalance. In general, assuming a shared memory is the preferred abstraction to implement efficient graph algorithms, also in common programming languages. This is the same assumption made by GEMS' SPARQL translator. Because graph methods are also synchronization intensive, as concurrent activity may need to access the same elements simultaneously, the memory model also has to offer atomic memory operations. Since we have to generate the full architecture executing the graph algorithm, we need to couple this abstraction with an effective, and high-performance, architectural implementation. And, differently from all the other HLS synthesis approaches, we also need to provide support for atomic memory operations.

To overcome the limitations of the FSMD model, we have devised an adaptive distributed controller (DC) design able to manage concurrent execution flows, and thus execute parallel tasks. To provide adequate support to the memory model, we have designed an enhanced memory interface that, while providing an abstract shared memory view, implements multiple channels for multibanked/multiported memories and supports atomic memory operations.

14.4.1 Distributed Controller Architecture

The proposed design supports parallel execution and dynamic scheduling through the introduction of an adaptive DC [57]. The DC consists of a set of communicating modules, each one associated

```
void search(Graph * graph, NodeId var_2, Label
    p_var_3,
  LabelId p_var_4, LabelId p_var_5, LabelId p_var_7,
  LabelId p_var_8, LabelId p_var_9) {
 size_t in_degree_var_2 = getInDegree(graph, var_2);
 Edge * var_2_1_inEdges = getInEdges(graph, var_2);
 for(size_t i_var_3 = 0; i_var_3 < in_degree_var_2;
      i_var_3++) {
  LabelId var_3; //el. with label
      "ub:subOrganizationOf"
  var_3 = var_2_1_inEdges[i_var_3].property;
  NodeId var_1; //el. with label "?Y"
  var_1 = var_2_1_inEdges[i_var_3].node;
  if(var_3 == p_var_3) {
   size_t in_degree_var_1 = getInDegree(graph, var_1)
       ;
   Edge * var_1_3_inEdges = getInEdges(graph, var_1);
   for(size_t i_var_7 = 0; i_var_7 < in_degree_var_1;
        i_var_7++) {
    LabelId var_7; //el. with label "ub:worksFor"
    var_7 = var_1_3_inEdges[i_var_7].property;
    NodeId var_6; //el. with label "?X"
    var_6 = var_1_3_inEdges[i_var_7].node;
    if(var_7 == p_var_7) {
     size_t out_degree_var_6 = getOutDegree(graph,
          var_6);
     Edge * var_6_5_outEdges = getOutEdges(graph,
          var_6);
     for(size_t i_var_9 = 0; i_var_9 <
          out_degree_var_6; i_var_9++) {
      LabelId var_9; //el. with label "rdf::type"
      var_9 = var_6_5_outEdges[i_var_9].property;
      NodeId var_8; //el. with label
          "ub:FullProfessor"
      var_8 = var_6_5_outEdges[i_var_9].node;
      if((var_9 == p_var_9) && (var_8 == p_var_8)) {
       size_t out_degree_var_1 = getOutDegree(graph,
            var_1);
       Edge * var_1_7_outEdges = getOutEdges(graph,
            var_1);
       for(size_t i_var_5=0; i_var_5<out_degree_var_1
            ; i_var_5++) {
        LabelId var_5; //el. with label "rdf::type"
        var_5 = var_1_7_outEdges[i_var_5].property;
        NodeId var_4; //el. with label
            "ub:Department"
        var_4 = var_1_7_outEdges[i_var_5].node;
        if((var_5 == p_var_5) && (var_4 == p_var_4))
          insertResults(var_6);
       }
      }
     }
    }
   }
  }
 }
}
```

```
void kernel(size_t i_var3, Edge * var_2_1_inEdges
    , Graph * graph, NodeId var_2, Label
    p_var_3, LabelId p_var_4, LabelId p_var_5,
    LabelId p_var_7, LabelId p_var_8, LabelId
    p_var_9) {
 LabelId var_3; //el. with label
     "ub:subOrganizationOf"
 var_3 = var_2_1_inEdges[i_var_3].property;
 NodeId var_1; //el. with label "?Y"
 var_1 = var_2_1_inEdges[i_var_3].node;
 if(var_3 == p_var_3) {
  size_t in_degree_var_1 = getInDegree(graph,
      var_1);
  Edge * var_1_3_inEdges = getInEdges(graph,
      var_1);
  for(size_t i_var_7 = 0; i_var_7 <
      in_degree_var_1; i_var_7++) {
   // Same as Fig. 14.3a lines [15-40]
   ...
  }
 }
}


void search(Graph * graph, NodeId var_2, Label
    p_var_3, LabelId p_var_4, LabelId p_var_5,
    LabelId %p_var_7, LabelId p_var_8, LabelId
    p_var_9) {
 size_t in_degree_var_2 = getInDegree(graph,
     var_2);
 Edge * var_2_1_inEdges = getInEdges(graph, var_2
     );
 size_t i_var_3;

 for(i_var_3=0; i_var_3 < in_degree_var_2%4;
      i_var_3++) {
  kernel(i_var3, var_2_1_inEdges, graph, p_var_3,
       p_var_4, p_var_5, p_var_7, p_var_8,
      p_var_9);
 }

 for(; i_var_3 < in_degree_var_2%4; i_var_3+=4) {
  kernel(i_var3, var_2_1_inEdges, graph, p_var_3,
       p_var_4, p_var_5, p_var_7, p_var_8,
      p_var_9);
  kernel(i_var3+1, var_2_1_inEdges, graph,
      p_var_3, p_var_4, p_var_5, p_var_7,
      p_var_8, p_var_9);
  kernel(i_var3+2, var_2_1_inEdges, graph,
      p_var_3, p_var_4, p_var_5, p_var_7,
      p_var_8, p_var_9);
  kernel(i_var3+3, var_2_1_inEdges, graph,
      p_var_3, p_var_4, p_var_5, p_var_7,
      p_var_8, p_var_9);
 }
}
```

FIGURE 14.3 Pseudocode for the pattern-matching routines of example query Q6.

with an operation. The approach does not require the definition of any execution order (scheduling) at design time, and allows runtime exploitation of parallelism. The controller modules, called execution managers (EMs), start the execution of the associated operations as soon as all their dependencies are satisfied and resource conflicts are resolved. The minimum set of dependencies each operation is subject to, called activating conditions (ACs), is computed by analyzing the Extended Program Dependence Graph (EPDG) of the algorithm, which extends a typical Program Dependence Graph (PDG) with control-flow information, such as loops' back edges. ACs are expressed as logic functions, and specifically synthesized for each EM. Instead, dedicated arbiters, called resource managers (RMs), associated to shared resources manage resource conflicts: if multiple operations compete for a resource, the arbiter establishes which one executes first, according to a priority ordering. EMs communicate through a lightweight token-based schema: each EM receives a token signal whenever a dependency gets satisfied. When the controller has collected all the AC tokens (i.e., all dependencies are satisfied), it checks for resource availability. If the resource associated with the operation is free, execution starts. The approach does not introduce any communication overhead, because it does not use any sophisticated protocol. Since every operation and function is managed independently, the DC can efficiently control several concurrent execution flows. Obtaining the same behavior with centralized FSMs is possible, but not cheap: in fact, the complexity of an FSM controller, in terms of number of states and transitions, is exponential with respect to number of flows. This complexity would lead to unfeasible designs even for relatively small degrees of TLP. The complexity of the DC instead grows linearly with the number of operations, regardless of the latency of the operations and of number of concurrent flows. Figure 14.4 proposes an example of EPDG, annotated with ACs and binding information, and the associated parallel controller architecture. Operations 3, 4, 5 are bound

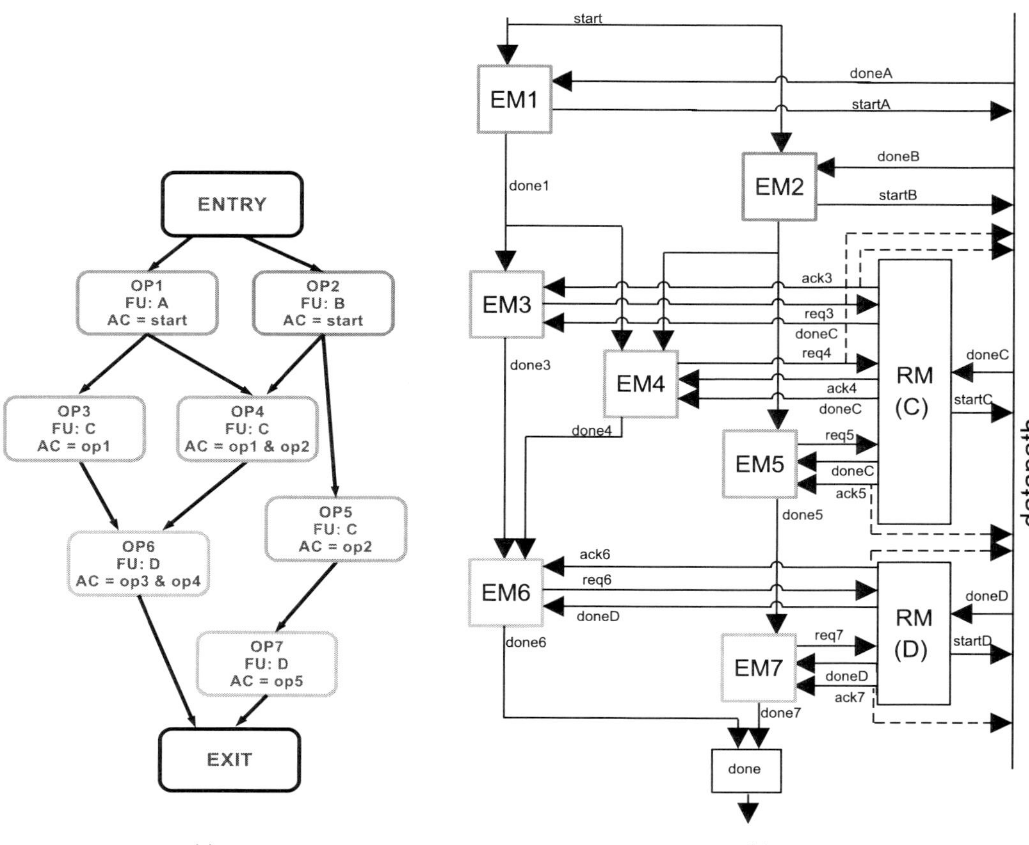

FIGURE 14.4 Example Extended Program Dependencies Graph (a) and corresponding Distributed Controller architecture (b).

to the same resource C, while operations 6, 7 are bound to D: the corresponding EMs interface with RMs to avoid structural conflicts. In this example, all the operations have unknown latency (e.g., external memory accesses, function calls, speculative operations) and the completion of their execution is notified through explicitly done signals from the datapath to the EMs. If the execution latency is known at design time, this signaling is not required, and the EMs directly manage the timing.

14.4.2 Memory Interface

In hardware synthesis, TLP is exploited by replicating the computing resources, substantially implementing *spatial* multithreading. Different hardware accelerators implement different tasks/threads. The final design allocates multiple instances of such accelerators. Our approach works in the same way by binding concurrent function calls to distinct hardware components, thus allowing parallel execution. However, not all the resources can be straightforwardly replicated. This is, in particular, the case with memory resources. In parallel applications, tasks usually share data, consequently requiring access to a shared memory. Thus, parallel execution of tasks requires managing concurrent memory operations. This is particularly important in memory-bound applications, because they may have limited ILP and as such not enough operations to completely hide memory latency. Employing caches across accelerators requires implementing coherency protocols, and caches are not effective with kernels that generally have poor spatial and temporal locality (such as graph methods). More suitable architectural approaches are mostly based on memory distribution and/or partitioning. These techniques enable memory operations to concurrently access data, but introduce additional challenges:

1. Memory addresses usually are not statically known, thus destination locations must be identified at runtime.
2. Tasks may try to access the same data in parallel, thus they may need synchronization.
3. Structural conflicts on shared memory resources have to be avoided.

In our approach, we address these issues by incorporating in the synthesized architectures an adaptive memory interface controller (MIC). The MIC completely manages concurrency and synchronization of the memory resources [58]. It dynamically maps memory operations across multiple, distributed and/or multiported memories, such as those available today in the latest hybrid systems that integrate general-purpose processors and FPGAs (Convey HC and MX).

Figure 14.5 shows a high-level schematic representation of the MIC. The MIC takes in input memory access requests from N ports, which have an address, a data, and an operation-type (load/-store) line. The MIC routes requests toward one of the M output ports by evaluating their addresses. It serves a request as soon as the corresponding port is available. In a similar way, it routes back M done signals (which notify termination of an operation) and the results (in case of loads) to the

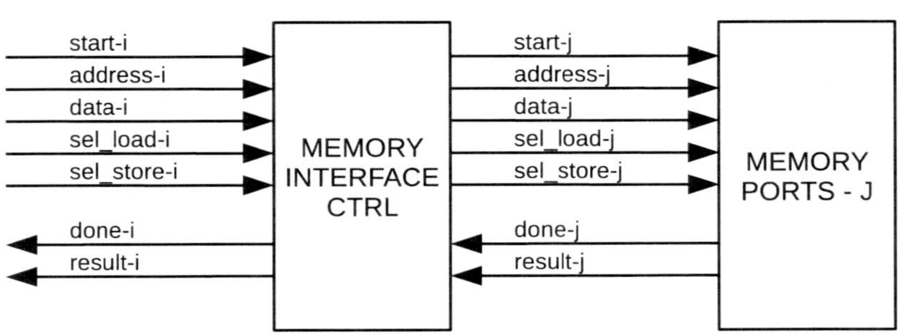

FIGURE 14.5 Top-level memory interface controller structure.

requesting operation. The memory is composed of M different and independent banks, and each output port accesses one bank. Each memory bank has nonoverlapping addresses. Accesses are routed toward a specific memory port at runtime, providing efficient support of the unpredictable memory access patterns typical in irregular applications. Customizable control logic, synthesized according to the particular scrambling function that distributes the data on the memory system, performs the routing. A lightweight arbitration scheme, which avoids any structural conflict on shared resources and does not introduce any further delay, provides concurrency management. For arbitration, we employ RMs also in the MIC, similarly to the DC. Access routing and resource availability checks both occur at runtime, enabling the MIC to issue concurrent memory operations, provided that they do not address the same memory locations. This improves system memory bandwidth utilization. Support of atomic memory operations, such as fetch-and-add and compare-and-swap, enables synchronization. The RMs reject further memory requests on a memory location accessed by an atomic memory operation, guaranteeing atomicity.

14.4.3 Synthesis Flow

As previously discussed, we have integrated these solutions in Bambu. To generate the DC architecture, we either designed novel synthesis techniques or heavily customized previous approaches. Having been designed around the FSMD model, the majority of HLS algorithms requires the definition of an execution schedule. The proposed architecture, instead, does not employ any predetermined execution ordering. In fact, the DCs dynamically execute operations. With respect to an FSMD synthesis flow, the proposed approach mandates additional front-end analysis steps to build the EPDG and compute the ACs. The approach also adopts custom algorithms for register [59] and module binding [60]. To integrate the MIC into the synthesis flow, instead, no significant changes to the synthesis algorithms are required.

14.5 EXPERIMENTAL RESULTS

We tested our approach by generating accelerators that implements queries from the LUBM benchmark. We consider seven queries from the set used in Reference 61. The objective of LUBM is to evaluate the performance of semantic web repositories in a standard and systematic way. It evaluates the performance considering queries over datasets originated from a single realistic ontology. LUBM consists of a university domain ontology, customizable and repeatable synthetic data, a set of test queries, and several performance metrics. We generated two different datasets: *LUBM-1*, consisting of 100,573 triples, and *LUBM-40*, consisting of 5,309,056 triples.

To evaluate the effectiveness of the proposed approach, we synthesized the queries with two different configurations. In the first (*serial*), the generated accelerator is serial (i.e., a single task). In the second, the generated accelerator is parallel, implementing four hardware kernels ($T = 4$) and a MIC with four memory channels ($M = 4$). We synthesized all the designs with Vivado 2015.1, targeting a Xilinx Virtex-7 xc7vx690t (the same device used in a Convey Wolverine WX690). We set a target frequency of 100 MHz for the synthesis. Table 14.1 reports the performance of the design in terms of execution latency (clock cycles) and maximum clock frequency.

In general, parallel accelerators ($T = 4$, $M = 4$) are able to provide speed ups with respect to the serial ones. With the small dataset, the average speed up is around 2.1, ranging from 1.03 (Q1) to 3.13 (Q3), depending on the query. With the large dataset, the average speed up is similar (2.05), with a minimum of 1.08 (Q1 and Q6) and a maximum of 3.13 (again Q3). The reasons for the minimal speed ups of query Q1 and Q6 with the large dataset reside in the structure of the query and the high dependency of graph-like methods from the dataset itself. In particular, the outer loops of Q1 and Q6 execute only a few iterations. Hence, these queries employ only a few tasks. Our current design implements a fork-join scheme that spawns a group of T tasks (identified from loop iterations) and assigns them to the T hardware kernels. The group of tasks runs to completion before a

TABLE 14.1
Execution Delays of LUBM Queries Q1–Q7 on Serial Accelerators and on Parallel Accelerators Generated with Our Methodology (4 Kernels, 4 Memory Channels)

	Serial			$T = 4, M = 4$				
	Latency (#Cycles)		Maximum Frequency (MHz)	Latency (#Cycles)		Maximum Frequency (MHz)	Speed Up	Speed Up
	LUBM-1	LUBM-40		LUBM-1	LUMB-40		LUBM-1	LUMB-40
Q1	5,339,286	1,082,526,974	130.34	5,176,116	1,001,581,548	113.37	1.03	1.08
Q2	141,022	7,359,732	143.66	54,281	2,801,694	130.11	2.60	2.63
Q3	5,824,354	308,586,247	121.27	1,862,683	98,163,298	114.53	3.13	3.14
Q4	63,825	63,825	143.20	42,851	42,279	122.97	1.49	1.51
Q5	33,322	33,322	133.92	13,442	13,400	138.31	2.48	2.49
Q6	674,951	682,949	136.76	340,634	629,671	113.26	1.98	1.08
Q7	1,700,170	85,341,784	131.98	694,225	35,511,299	106.71	2.45	2.40

TABLE 14.2
Area Occupation (in Terms of LUTs and FPGA slices) of the Serial Accelerators and of the Parallel Accelerators for LUBM Queries Q1–Q7

	Serial		$T = 4, M = 4$		Area Overhead	
	LUTs	Slices	LUTs	Slices	LUTs	Slices
Q1	5600	1802	13,469	4317	2.40	2.39
Q2	2690	824	5280	1607	1.96	1.95
Q3	5525	1775	13,449	4308	2.43	2.43
Q4	3477	1073	7806	2399	2.24	2.24
Q5	2785	848	5750	1738	2.06	2.05
Q6	4364	1369	10,600	3426	2.43	2.50
Q7	6194	1943	15,002	4953	2.42	2.55

Note: Area Overhead is the ratio of the area occupied by the parallel accelerators over the serial accelerators.

new group can start execution. Consequently, tasks of the same group could have different execution times, but the group terminates only when all the tasks have completed, leading to underutilization of hardware resources and memory bandwidth. The dataset dependency is highlighted by Q6, which takes almost the same time on the sequential architecture with both the dataset sizes. However, while the parallel accelerator reaches a speed up of 2 on the smaller dataset, on the larger dataset, it only provides minimal speed up due to data layout in memory that does not maximize concurrency. In fact, whenever one of the hardware kernels in the parallel accelerator tries to access a memory location concurrently accessed by another kernel, the MIC, by design, denies the request, and the kernel stalls. The parallel accelerators always meet the target frequency of 100 MHz, but they are on average 10% slower than the serial accelerators, with a maximum of around 20% for the biggest designs (Q7). With the smallest designs, the difference is obviously lower, and in one case (Q5), the parallel accelerator also reaches a slightly higher maximum frequency.

Table 14.2 reports the area of the synthesized accelerators in terms of number of look-up tables (LUTs) and slices. The results are post place and route. The occupation of the parallel accelerators goes from around 2 times to 2.5 times the occupation of the serial accelerators. While the kernels are replicated four times, the synthesis tool performs optimizations that make occupation a sublinear function of the number of hardware kernels.

Because we see an average speed up of 2, the average increase in area is somewhat balanced by the higher performance. Obviously, for queries with speed ups over 2.5, the parallel implementation is highly profitable, while for the others, although there is still an advantage in using the parallel controller, it does not outweigh the increased occupation.

14.6 CONCLUSIONS

In this chapter, we have discussed the prospectives on the use of accelerators for data analytics applications. We have presented the contrasts between the aspiration to reach high scalability in performance and size through the use of fully custom systems, from the hardware to the software, and the need to employ commodity hardware designs to contain costs. We have highlighted how the increasingly widespread use of accelerators such as GPUs and vector processors, now basically commodity resources for HPC systems, represents an opportunity for data analytics. We argued that the emerging class of accelerators employing reconfigurable devices such as FPGAs, although not as widespread as GPUs, may provide an opportunity to better customize systems for workloads that, presenting irregular behaviors, may not be as amenable as (for example) scientific simulations to more commodity accelerators. While there are still productivity gaps to bridge, tools that enable automatic generation of accelerators from specifications in high-level languages (HLS tools) have matured significantly. As a case study, we have presented a set of novel architectural templates and techniques to enhance the synthesis of parallel accelerators for data analytics applications. Our proposed approach allows, in particular, generating efficient accelerators for graph methods and applications that present irregular behaviors. These are present in many data analytics applications (e.g., graph databases) that exploit emerging data models such as RDF or attributed graphs, and are extremely different from the behaviors of more conventional, table-based, relational databases. We have detailed the approach and have discussed how it can be integrated into the GEMS' stack (an RDF graph database) to generate parallel accelerators for SPARQL queries. We have validated the approach by synthesizing SPARQL queries from LUBM.

We believe that these represent significant steps towards making FPGA-based accelerators viable for data analytics. Although there are still limitations to address, such as enabling better load balancing and providing scalability across multiple accelerators, these efforts show that there exists a promising intermediate step between a fully custom and a commodity system. Accelerator-based systems can provide performance and flexibility for data analytics applications, while still being affordable in terms of costs.

REFERENCES

1. Apache Jena. Home. Available at: https://jena.apache.org, 2014.
2. SesameRDF. Home. Available at: http://www.openrdf.org, 2014.
3. Virtuoso. Openlink Virtuoso Universal Server. Available at: http://virtuoso.openlinksw.com.
4. Steve Harris, Nick Lamb, and Nigel Shadbolt. 4store: The design and implementation of a clustered RDF store. In *5th International Workshop on Scalable Semantic Web Knowledge Base Systems (SSWS2009)*, pages 94–109, 2009.
5. Thomas Neumann and Gerhard Weikum. The RDF-3X engine for scalable management of RDF data. *The VLDB Journal*, 19(1):91–113, 2010.

6. Cathrin Weiss, Panagiotis Karras, and Abraham Bernstein. Hexastore: Sextuple indexing for semantic web data management. *Proceedings of the VLDB Endowment*, 1(1):1008–1019, 2008.
7. Andreas Harth, Jürgen Umbrich, Aidan Hogan, and Stefan Decker. YARS2: A federated repository for querying graph structured data from the web. In *ISWC'07/ASWC'07: 6th International Semantic Web and 2nd Asian Semantic Web Conference*, pages 211–224, 2007.
8. Kurt Rohloff and Richard E. Schantz. High-performance, massively scalable, distributed systems using the mapreduce software framework: The shard triple-store. In *PSI EtA '10: Programming Support Innovations for Emerging Distributed Applications*, pages 4:1–4:5, 2010.
9. Medha Atre, Vineet Chaoji, Mohammed J. Zaki, and James A. Hendler. Matrix bit loaded: A scalable lightweight join query processor for RDF data. In *Proceedings of the 19th International Conference on World Wide Web*, pages 41–50.
10. Spyros Kotoulas, Jacopo Urbani, Peter Boncz, and Peter Mika. Robust runtime optimization and skew-resistant execution of analytical sparql queries on pig. In *Proceedings of the 11th International Semantic Web Conference*, 2012.
11. BigDataDB. Bigdata®. Available at: http://www.blazegraph.com.
12. Ontotext. OWLIM|Ontotext. Available at: https://www.ontotext.com, 2014.
13. Apache Giraph. Available at: http://giraph.apache.org.
14. Graphlab. Available at: https://turi.com.
15. Grzegorz Malewicz, Matthew H. Austern, Aart J.C. Bik, James C. Dehnert, Ilan Horn, Naty Leiser, and Grzegorz Czajkowski. Pregel: A system for large-scale graph processing. In *SIGMOD'10: ACM International Conference on Management of Data*, pages 135–146, 2010.
16. Apache. Apache spark—Lightning-fast cluster computing. Available at: http://spark.apache.org.
17. Vito Giovanni Castellana, Alessandro Morari, Jesse Weaver, Antonino Tumeo, David Haglin, Oreste Villa, and John Feo. In-memory graph databases for web-scale data. *Computer*, 48(3):24–35, 2015.
18. Inc. Cray. Urika-gx agile analytics platform for big data. Available at: http://www.cray.com/products/analytics/urika-gx.
19. Gunrock, High-performance graph primitives on GPUs. Available at: https://github.com/gunrock/gunrock.
20. Massimo Bernaschi, Giancarlo Carbone, and Flavio Vella. Betweenness centrality on multi-GPU systems. In *Proceedings of the 5th Workshop on Irregular Applications—Architectures and Algorithms, IA3 2015*, Austin, Texas, USA, November 15, 2015, pages 12:1–12:4, 2015.
21. Adam McLaughlin and David A. Bader. Scalable and high performance betweenness centrality on the GPU. In *International Conference for High Performance Computing, Networking, Storage and Analysis, SC 2014*, New Orleans, LA, USA, November 16–21, 2014, pages 572–583, 2014.
22. Duane Merrill, Michael Garland, and Andrew Grimshaw. High-performance and scalable GPU graph traversal. *ACM Transactions on Parallel Computing*, 1(2):14:1–14:30, February 2015.
23. Md. Naim, Fredrik Manne, Mahantesh Halappanavar, Antonino Tumeo, and Johannes Langguth. Optimizing approximate weighted matching on NVIDIA Kepler K40. In *22nd IEEE International Conference on High Performance Computing, HiPC 2015*, Bengaluru, India, December 16–19, 2015, pages 105–114, 2015.
24. Jyothish Soman and Ankur Narang. Fast community detection algorithm with GPUs and multicore architectures. In *2011 IEEE International Parallel Distributed Processing Symposium (IPDPS)*, pages 568–579, 2011.
25. SYSTAP. Blazegraph. Available at: https://www.blazegraph.com/product/.
26. Zhisong Fu, Michael Personick, and Bryan Thompson. Mapgraph: A high level API for fast development of high performance graph analytics on GPUs. In *Proceedings of Workshop on GRAph Data Management Experiences and Systems, GRADES'14*, pages 2:1–2:6, 2014.
27. Altera SDK for OpenCL. Available at: http://www.altera.com.
28. Convey. Openht—Hybrid threading toolset. Available at: https://github.com/tonybrewer/openht.
29. Xilinx. Vivado high level synthesis. Available at: http://www.xilinx.com/products/design-tools/vivado/integration/esl-design.html.
30. Yuanbo Guo, Zhengxiang Pan, and Jeff Heflin. Lubm: A benchmark for OWL knowledge base systems. *Web Semantics*, 3(2–3):158–182, October 2005.

31. Andrew Putnam, Adrian M. Caulfield, Eric S. Chung, Derek Chiou, Kypros Constantinides, John Demme, Hadi Esmaeilzadeh et al. A reconfigurable fabric for accelerating large-scale datacenter services. In *2014 ACM/IEEE 41st International Symposium on Computer Architecture (ISCA)*, pages 13–24, June 2014.
32. IBM. Netezza analytics. Available at: https://www-01.ibm.com/software/data/puredata/analytics/ nztechnology/analytics.html.
33. Bharat Sukhwani, Hong Min, Mathew Thoennes, Parijat Dube, Balakrishna Iyer, Bernard Brezzo, Donna Dillenberger, and Sameh Asaad. Database analytics acceleration using FPGAs. In *Proceedings of the 21st International Conference on Parallel Architectures and Compilation Techniques, PACT'12*, pages 411–420, New York, NY, USA, 2012. ACM.
34. Sina Meraji, Berni Schiefer, Lan Pham, Lee Chu, Peter Kokosielis, Adam Storm, Wayne Young, Chang Ge, Geoffrey Ng, and Kajan Kanagaratnam. Towards a hybrid design for fast query processing in db2 with blu acceleration using graphical processing units: A technology demonstration. In *Proceedings of the 2016 International Conference on Management of Data, SIGMOD'16*, pages 1951–1960, 2016.
35. Robert J. Halstead, Bharat Sukhwani, Hong Min, Mathew Thoennes, Parijat Dube, Sameh Asaad, and Balakrishna Iyer. Accelerating join operation for relational databases with FPGAs. In *2013 IEEE 21st Annual International Symposium on Field-Programmable Custom Computing Machines (FCCM)*, pages 17–20, April 2013.
36. Jared Casper and Kunle Olukotun. Hardware acceleration of database operations. In *Proceedings of the 2014 ACM/SIGDA International Symposium on Field-Programmable Gate Arrays, FPGA'14*, pages 151–160, New York, NY, USA, 2014. ACM.
37. Lisa Wu, Andrea Lottarini, Timothy K. Paine, Martha A. Kim, and Kenneth A. Ross. Q100: The architecture and design of a database processing unit. In *Proceedings of the 19th International Conference on Architectural Support for Programming Languages and Operating Systems, ASPLOS'14*, pages 255–268, New York, NY, USA, 2014. ACM.
38. Rene Mueller, Jens Teubner, and Gustavo Alonso. Glacier: A query-to-hardware compiler. In *Proceedings of the 2010 ACM SIGMOD International Conference on Management of Data, SIGMOD'10*, pages 1159–1162, New York, NY, USA, 2010. ACM.
39. Takashi Takenaka, Masamichi Takagi, and Hiroaki Inoue. A scalable complex event processing framework for combination of sql-based continuous queries and c/c++ functions. In *2012 22nd International Conference on Field Programmable Logic and Applications (FPL)*, pages 237–242, August 2012.
40. Christopher Dennl, Daniel Ziener, and Jürgen Teich. Acceleration of SQl restrictions and aggregations through FPGA-based dynamic partial reconfiguration. In *2013 IEEE 21st Annual International Symposium on Field-Programmable Custom Computing Machines (FCCM)*, pages 25–28, April 2013.
41. Gorker Alp Malazgirt, Nehir Sonmez, Arda Yurdakul, Osman Unsal, and Adrian Cristal. Accelerating complete decision support queries through high-level synthesis technology (abstract only). In *Proceedings of the 2015 ACM/SIGDA International Symposium on Field-Programmable Gate Arrays, FPGA'15*, pages 277–277, New York, NY, USA, 2015. ACM.
42. Convey Computer. Convey computer doubles graph500 performance, develops new graph personality. Available at: http://www.conveycomputer.com.
43. Convey Computer. Convey MX Series. Architectural Overview. Available at: http://www.convey computer.com.
44. Brahim Betkaoui, Yu Wang, David B. Thomas, and Wayne Luk. A reconfigurable computing approach for efficient and scalable parallel graph exploration. In *2012 IEEE 23rd International Conference on Application-Specific Systems, Architectures and Processors (ASAP)*, pages 8–15, 2012.
45. Robert J. Halstead, Jason Villarreal, and Walid Najjar. Exploring irregular memory accesses on FPGAs. In *Proceedings of the First Workshop on Irregular Applications: Architectures and Algorithms, IAAA'11*, pages 31–34, 2011.
46. Alain Girault, Bilung Lee, and Edward A. Lee. Hierarchical finite state machines with multiple concurrency models. *IEEE Transactions on Computer-Aided Design of Integrated Circuits and Systems*, 18(6):742–760, June 1999.
47. Chris Papachristou and Yusuf Alzazeri. A method of distributed controller design for RTL circuits. *DATE'99: Design, Automation and Test in Europe*, pages 774–775, 1999.
48. Andrew Seawright and Wolfgang Meyer. Partitioning and optimizing controllers synthesized from hierarchical high-level descriptions. In *DAC'98: 35th Annual Design Automation Conference*, pages 770–775, 1998.

49. Alberto A. Del Barrio, Seda Ogrenci Memik, María C. Molina, José M. Mendias, and Román Hermida. A distributed controller for managing speculative functional units in high level synthesis. *IEEE Transactions on Computer-Aided Design of Integrated Circuits and Systems*, 30(3):350–363, March 2011.
50. Chao Huang, Srivaths Ravi, Anand Raghunathan, and Niraj K. Jha. Generation of heterogeneous distributed architectures for memory-intensive applications through high-level synthesis. *IEEE Transactions on Very Large Scale Integration (VLSI) Systems*, 15(11):1191–1204, 2007.
51. Faraydon Karim, Alain Mellan, Anh Nguyen, Utku Aydonat, and Tarek Abdelrahman. A multilevel computing architecture for embedded multimedia applications. *IEEE Micro*, 24(3):56–66, 2004.
52. David Bacon, Rodric Rabbah, and Sunil Shukla. FPGA programming for the masses. *Queue*, 11(2):40:40–40:52, February 2013.
53. Jason Cong, Bin Liu, Stephen Neuendorffer, Juanjo Noguera, Kees A. Vissers, and Zhiru Zhang. High-level synthesis for FPGAs: From prototyping to deployment. *IEEE Transactions on Computer-Aided Design of Integrated Circuits and Systems*, 30(4):473–491, 2011.
54. Jongsok Choi, Stephen Brown, and Jason Anderson. From software threads to parallel hardware in high-level synthesis for FPGAs. In *2013 International Conference on Field-Programmable Technology (FPT)*, pages 270–277, December 2013.
55. Tomasz S. Czajkowski, Utku Aydonat, Dmitry Denisenko, John Freeman, Michael Kinsner, David Neto, Jason Wong, Peter Yiannacouras, and Deshanand P. Singh. From OpenCL to high-performance hardware on FPGAs. In *FPL'12: 22nd International Conference on Field Programmable Logic and Applications*, pages 531–534, 2012.
56. Bambu: A Free Framework for the High-Level Synthesis of Complex Applications. Available at: http://panda.dei.polimi.it.
57. Christian Pilato, Vito Giovanni Castellana, Silvia Lovergine, and Fabrizio Ferrandi. A runtime adaptive controller for supporting hardware components with variable latency. In *AHS 2011: NASA/ESA Conference on Adaptive Hardware and Systems*, pages 153–160, 2011.
58. Vito Giovanni Castellana, Antonino Tumeo, and Fabrizio Ferrandi. An adaptive memory interface controller for improving bandwidth utilization of hybrid and reconfigurable systems. In *DATE 2014: Design, Automation and Test in Europe*, pages 1–4, 2014.
59. Vito Giovanni Castellana and Fabrizio Ferrandi. Scheduling independent liveness analysis for register binding in high-level synthesis. In *DATE 2013: Design, Automation and Test in Europe*, pages 1571–1574, 2013.
60. Vito Giovanni Castellana and Fabrizio Ferrandi. An automated flow for the high level synthesis of coarse grained parallel applications. In *2013 International Conference on Field-Programmable Technology (FPT)*, pages 294–301, December 2013.
61. Bin Shao, Haixun Wang, and Yatao Li. Trinity: A distributed graph engine on a memory cloud. In *Proceedings of the 2013 ACM SIGMOD International Conference on Management of Data*, pages 505–516. ACM, 2013.

15 Complex Mining from Uncertain Big Data in Distributed Environments

Problems, Definitions, and Two Effective and Efficient Algorithms

Alfredo Cuzzocrea, Carson Kai-Sang Leung, Fan Jiang, and Richard Kyle MacKinnon

CONTENTS

ABSTRACT

Big data refer to a wide variety of valuable data of different veracities that are generated or collected at a high velocity with volumes beyond the ability of commonly used software to manage, query, and process within a tolerable elapsed time. On the one hand, *big data analytics* incorporates various techniques from a broad range of fields, which include cloud computing, data mining, machine learning, mathematics, and statistics. For instance, data mining discovers implicit, previously unknown, and potentially useful information and/or knowledge from data. On the other hand, *uncertain big data management* represents an active and well-recognized research area where a relevant number of proposals converge. This is due to several reasons, but mostly dictated by the *emergence of big data trends* as well as the *explosion of cloud computing paradigms*. Within this wide research context, a leading role is played by the issue of *extracting useful knowledge from big data* being the uncertain big data setting a critical case to be considered. In our research, we specially focus on two well-known distinct first-class data-mining problems over uncertain big data, namely: (i) *frequent itemset mining from uncertain big data* and (ii) *constrained mining from uncertain big data*. We recognize that these subproblems converge into a general problem that we name as *complex mining from uncertain big data*, for which a plethora of real-life applications and systems can be found. Inspired by these relevant research challenges, we provide in this chapter the following contributions: (i) a comprehensive overview of state-of-the-art literature in the context of the research problem of complex mining from uncertain big data, (ii) an effective and efficient algorithm for supporting *tree-based constrained mining of uncertain big data in distributed environments*, as well as (iii) another effective and efficient algorithm for supporting *MapReduce-based constrained mining of uncertain big transactional data in cloud environments*.

15.1 INTRODUCTION

Big data [1–3] refer to high-value data with different veracities (e.g., precise, imprecise, or uncertain data) and high volumes beyond the ability of commonly used software to manage, query, and process within a tolerable elapsed time. These high volumes of valuable data can be easily collected or generated at a high velocity from a wide variety of data sources (which may lead to a wide variety of data types and/or formats) in various real-life applications such as bioinformatics, graph management, sensor and stream systems, smart worlds, social networks, as well as the Web [4–9]. The characteristics of these big data can be described by the following "5V's":

1. *Value*, which focuses on the usefulness of data
2. *Variety*, which focuses on differences in types, contents, or formats of data
3. *Velocity*, which focuses on the speed at which data are collected or generated
4. *Veracity*, which focuses on the quality of data (e.g., uncertainty, messiness, or trustworthiness of data)
5. *Volume*, which focuses on the quantity of data

Rich sets of useful information and knowledge are embedded in the big data (e.g., biological data, medical images, streams of advertisements, surveillance videos, business transactions, financial charts, social media data, web logs, texts, and documents). Owing to the "5V's" characteristics of big data, new forms of algorithm are needed for managing, querying, and processing these big data so as to enable enhanced decision making, insight, process optimization, data mining, and knowledge discovery. This drives and motivates research and practices in data science, which aims to develop systematic or quantitative data analytic algorithm to analyze (e.g., inspect, clean, transform, and model) and mine big data.

On the one hand, *big data analytics* [10–15] incorporates various techniques from a broad range of fields, which include cloud computing, data mining, machine learning, mathematics, and statistics. Data mining aims to extract implicit, previously unknown, and potentially useful information from data. With "5V's" characteristics of big data, it is natural to handle the data in a cloud computing environment as a cloud environment represents a "natural" context for big data by providing high performance, reliability, availability, transparency, abstraction, and/or virtualization. Various approaches—ranging from mathematical models to approximation models, from resource-constrained paradigms to memory-bounded methods—can be applied in cloud computing environments. Over the past few years, algorithms for handling big data according to a "systematic" view of the problem (e.g., MapReduce algorithms) are gaining momentum. *MapReduce* [16] is a high-level programming model for handling high volumes of big data by using parallel and distributed computing [17–20] on clouds [21–23], which consist of a master node and multiple worker nodes. As implied by its name, MapReduce involves two key functions: (i) the "map" function and (ii) the "reduce" function both commonly used in functional programming languages such as LISP for list processing:

1. The mapper applies a *mapping function* to each value in the *list of values* and returns the resulting list.
2. The reducer applies a *reducing function* to combine all the values in the *list of values* and returns the combined result.

An advantage of using the MapReduce model is that users only need to focus on (and specify) these "map" and "reduce" functions—without worrying about implementation details for the following:

- Handling machine failures
- Managing intermachine communication
- Partitioning the input data
- Scheduling and executing the program across multiple machines

On the other hand, *uncertain big data management* (e.g., [24–30]) represents an active and well-recognized research area where a relevant number of proposals converge. This is due to several reasons, but mostly dictated by the *emergence of big data trends* as well as the *explosion of cloud computing paradigms* (e.g., [31–35]). Within this wide research context, a leading role is played by the issue of *extracting useful knowledge from big data* (e.g., [36–40]) being the uncertain big data setting a critical case to be considered. In our research, we specially focus on two well-known distinct first-class data-mining problems over uncertain big data, namely:

1. Frequent itemset mining from uncertain big data
2. Constrained mining from uncertain big data

We recognize that these subproblems converge into a general problem that we name as *complex mining from uncertain big data*, for which a plethora of real-life applications and systems can be found. Some examples are (i) *healthcare management* (e.g., [41]), (ii) *advanced Web applications* (e.g., [42,43]), (iii) *traffic flow prediction* (e.g., [44,45]), (iv) *reservation management on optical grids* (e.g., [46]), as well as (v) *mobile web and social networking* (e.g., [47,48]).

Inspired by these relevant research challenges, we provide in this chapter the following contributions:

1. A comprehensive overview of state-of-the-art literature in the context of complex mining from uncertain big data, by respectively focusing on problems and definitions of *frequent itemset-mining from uncertain big data* and *constrained mining from uncertain big data*
2. An effective and efficient algorithm for supporting *tree-based constrained mining of uncertain big data in distributed environments* (like clouds, indeed, or even wireless sensor big data networks), which is capable of dealing with *input constraints*, thus finally devising an innovative constrained frequent itemset-mining framework for uncertain big data
3. An effective and efficient algorithm for supporting *MapReduce-based constrained mining over uncertain big transactional data in cloud environments*, which allows users to query big data by specifying *constraints* that express their interests, and it also processes user-specified constraints to discover useful information and knowledge from uncertain big data

The remainder of this chapter is organized as follows. In Section 15.2, we provide problems, definitions, and motivations of complex mining from uncertain big data in distributed environments (like clouds). Section 15.3 contains the necessary background on research areas that are critical for our work. In Section 15.4, we introduce the first algorithm embedded in our framework for supporting complex mining from uncertain big data, that is, the one that focuses on frequent itemset mining. Section 15.5 illustrates the MapReduce-based algorithm for supporting constrained mining over uncertain big data, which represents the second algorithm embedded in our proposed framework. In Section 15.6, we describe our extensive experimental campaign that clearly shows the benefits coming from our proposal. Finally, Section 15.7 contains conclusions and future work of our research. This chapter significantly extends our previous studies [17,49], by providing a unified conceptual view of the general issue of supporting complex mining from uncertain big data in distributed environments.

15.2 COMPLEX MINING FROM UNCERTAIN BIG DATA: PROBLEMS AND DEFINITIONS

As described in Section 15.1, our general focus is on the problem of supporting complex mining over uncertain big data, by specifically focusing on the issue of providing frequent itemset mining over uncertain big data and the issue of providing constrained mining over uncertain big data, respectively. In this section, we provide foundations, definitions, and motivations of complex mining from uncertain big data for distinct applicative settings.

15.2.1 FREQUENT ITEMSET MINING

Data mining aims to discover implicit, previously unknown, and potentially useful information that is embedded in data. As a common data-mining task, *frequent itemset mining* [50–52] looks for *itemsets* (i.e., sets of items) that are frequently co-occurring together. The mined frequent itemsets can be used in the discovery of correlation or casual relations, analysis of sequences, and formation of association rules.

The research problem of finding frequent itemsets has been the subject of numerous studies [53–55] since its introduction [56]. In early days, many algorithms were Apriori-based [57], which depends on a generate-and-test paradigm to find all frequent itemsets by first generating candidates and then checking their support (i.e., their occurrences) against the traditional databases containing precise data (e.g., traditional databases of shopper market basket transactions). To avoid the generate-and-test paradigm, the FP-growth algorithm [58] was proposed. Such a tree-based algorithm constructs an extended prefix-tree structure, called frequent pattern tree (FP-tree), to capture the contents of the transaction database. Rather than employing the generate-and-test strategy of Apriori-based algorithms, FP-growth focuses on frequent pattern growth [59,60]—which is a restricted test-only approach (i.e., does not generate candidates, and only tests for support).

15.2.2 Frequent Itemset Mining from Uncertain Data

With the aforementioned traditional databases of precise data, users definitely know whether an item is present in (or is absent from) a transaction. In contrast, data in many real-life applications are riddled with uncertainty [61–66]. It is partially due to inherent measurement inaccuracies, sampling and duration errors, network latencies, and intentional blurring of data to preserve anonymity. As such, the presence or absence of items in a dataset is uncertain. Moreover, with the increasing number of uncertain objects for sensor devices and noisy data management technologies such as DUST [67] in recent years, *uncertain data-mining* [68–72] is in demand. As a concrete example, a physician may highly suspect (but cannot guarantee) that a coughing patient suffers from the Middle East respiratory syndrome (MERS). The uncertainty of such suspicion can be expressed in terms of existential probability (e.g., a 60% likelihood of suffering from the MERS). With this notion, each item in a transaction t_j in databases containing precise data can be viewed as an item with a 100% likelihood of being present in t_j. To find frequent itemsets from these uncertain data, several uncertain data-mining algorithms (e.g., U-Apriori [73], UF-growth [74], tube-growth [75], and BLIMP-growth [76] algorithms) have been proposed. Among them, UF-growth, tube-growth, and BLIMP-growth capture the contents of the uncertain data in a tree structure, from which frequent itemsets can be mined recursively.

15.2.3 Constrained Frequent Itemset Mining from Uncertain Data

For many real-life applications, users look for all frequent itemsets. Correspondingly, many frequent itemset-mining algorithms, regardless of whether they are Apriori-based or tree-based, provide little or no support for user focus when mining precise or uncertain data. However, for some other real-life applications, users may have some particular phenomena in mind on which to focus the mining (e.g., a physician may want to find only those patients who are suffering from MERS, medical analysts may want to find only those lab test records belonging to patients suspected to suffer from asthma instead of all the patients). Without user focus, the user often needs to wait for a long period of time for numerous frequent itemsets, out of which only a tiny fraction may be interesting to the user. Hence, *constrained frequent itemset mining* [77,78], which aims to find those frequent itemsets that satisfy the user-specified constraints, is needed. CAP [79], DCF [80], and $\mathcal{FIC}$ [81] are examples of algorithms that mine constrained frequent itemsets from traditional precise data.

15.2.4 Constrained Frequent Itemset Mining from Distributed Uncertain Data

With advances in technology, one can easily collect high volumes of massive data [12,82] from not only a single source but multiple sources. For example, in recent years, sensor networks have been widely used in many application areas such as agricultural, architectural, environmental, and structural surveillance. Sensors distributed in these networks serve as good sources of data. However, sensors usually have limited communication bandwidth, transmission energy, and computational power. Thus, data are not usually transmitted to a single distant centralized processor to perform the data-mining task. Instead, data are transmitted to their local (e.g., closest) processors within a distributed environment [83]. As this requires massive computing power (e.g., [84]), this calls for *parallel and distributed mining* [85–87]. For example, *parallel and distributed frequent itemset-mining* [20,88] searches for implicit, previously unknown, and potentially useful frequent itemsets that might be embedded in the distributed data.

Some examples of Apriori-based distributed algorithms that find frequent itemsets in a distributed environment include Count Distribution, Data Distribution, and Candidate Distribution [89], as well as FDM [90]. Similarly, Parallel-HFP-Leap [91] also finds frequent itemsets in a distributed environment, but it is a tree-based algorithm. However, regardless of whether they are Apriori-based or tree-based, all these distributed frequent itemset-mining algorithms do not handle constraints nor do they mine uncertain data. On the other hand, CAP, DCF, and $\mathcal{FIC}$ all find *constrained* frequent itemsets, but they mine a centralized database of precise data. Similarly, the U-Apriori and UF-growth algorithms both mine a centralized database of *uncertain* data for all (unconstrained) frequent itemsets instead of only those constrained ones. Recently, Kozawa et al. [92] used general-purpose computation on GPU in an attempt to accelerate uncertain data mining. However, they aimed to find all (unconstrained) *probabilistic-frequent* itemsets instead of constrained *frequent* ones. In other words, these existing mining algorithms fall short in different aspects.

Hence, a natural question to ask is: Is it possible to mine *uncertain* data for only those frequent itemsets that satisfy user-specified *constraints* in a *distributed* environment? In response to this question, we conducted a feasibility study. Its preliminary results [93,94] show the possibility of mining constrained frequent itemsets from distributed uncertain data. In this chapter, we propose an effective and efficient algorithm for tree-based mining of uncertain data in a distributed environment for frequent itemsets that satisfy user-specified constraints. Here, our *key contribution* is the nontrivial integration of (i) constrained mining, (ii) parallel and distributed mining, (iii) uncertain data mining, (iv) tree-based mining, and (v) frequent itemset mining. The resulting tree-based algorithm efficiently mines from distributed uncertain data for only those constrained frequent itemsets. It avoids the candidate generate-and-test paradigm, handles uncertain data, pushes user constraints inside the mining process, avoids unnecessary computation, and finds only those itemsets satisfying the constraints in a distributed environment.

15.2.5 MapReduce-Based Constrained Frequent Itemset Mining from Uncertain Big Data

Several algorithms have been proposed over the past few years to use the MapReduce model—which mines the search space with parallel, distributed, or cloud computing—for big data analytics tasks like classification [95] and clustering [96]. In contrast, we focus on another big data analytics task—namely, association rule mining [57], which discovers interesting knowledge in the form of association rules $A \Rightarrow C$ revealing associative relationships between (i) shopper market baskets A and C of frequently purchased merchandise items or (ii) collections A and C of frequently co-located events.

By applying association rule mining to valuable big market basket data, data scientists can help shop owners/managers find interesting or popular patterns that reveal customer purchase behavior. The research problem of association rule mining usually consists of two key steps:

1. Mining of frequent patterns [97]
2. Formation of association rules (by using the mined frequent patterns as antecedents and consequences of the rules)

Recall from Section 15.2.3 that CAP [79], DCF [80], and $\mathcal{FIC}$ [81] are examples of algorithms that mine constrained frequent itemsets from traditional precise data. To mine constrained frequent itemsets from big data, BigSAM [98] exploits a special class of constraints called SAM constraints. Such exploitation helps reduce the search space when mining itemsets satisfying user-specified SAM constraints. However, many commonly used constraints (e.g., sum($X.Price$) $\leq$ \$150, which finds every combination X of items with a total price at most \$150) do not belong to the class of SAM constraints. In the current chapter, we explore another class of constraints, called antimonotone (AM) constraints, to which commonly used constraints belong. We explore two subclasses of AM constraints: (i) the frequency constraint and (ii) nonfrequency AM constraints.

In this respect, our *key contribution* is our second effective and efficient algorithm called MrCloud—which uses the MapReduce model in cloud environments for managing, querying, and processing uncertain big data. More specifically, MrCloud manages transactions of uncertain big data, allows users to query these big data by specifying AM constraints expressing their interests, and processes the user-specified constraints to discover useful information and knowledge in the form of frequent patterns from the uncertain big data.

15.3 BACKGROUND

Three well-defined research areas are critical for our work, namely:

1. *Frequent itemset mining from uncertain data*
2. *Constrained mining*
3. *Big data mining with the MapReduce model*

In the following, we provide the necessary background for all these areas.

15.3.1 Mining Frequent Itemsets from Uncertain Data

The research problem of frequent itemset mining was first introduced [56] in 1993. The corresponding algorithm—namely, Apriori—mined all frequent itemsets from a transaction database (TDB) consisting of *precise data*, in which the contents of each transaction are precisely known. Specifically, if a transaction t_i contains an item x (i.e., $x \in t_i$), then x is precisely known to be present in t_i. On the other hand, if a transaction t_i does not contain an item y (i.e., $y \notin t_i$), then y is precisely known to be absent from t_i. However, this is not the case for probabilistic databases consisting of uncertain data. A key difference between precise and uncertain data is that each transaction of the latter contains items and their *existential probabilities*. The existential probability $P(x, t_i)$ of an item x in a transaction t_i indicates the likelihood of x being present in t_i. For a real-life example, each transaction t_i represents a patient's visit to a physician's office. Each item x within t_i represents a potential disease, and is associated with $P(x, t_i)$ expressing the likelihood of a patient having that disease x in t_i (say, in t_1, the patient has a 60% likelihood of having asthma, and a 90% likelihood of catching a cold regardless of having asthma or not). With this notion, each item in a transaction t_i in datasets of precise data can be viewed as an item with a 100% likelihood of being present in t_i.

Given an item x and a transaction t_i, there are two possible worlds when using the *possible world interpretation* of uncertain data [99,100]:

1. The possible world W_1 where $x \in t_i$
2. The possible world W_2 where $x \notin t_i$

Although it is uncertain which of these two worlds is the *true world*, the probability of W_1 being the true world is $P(x, t_i)$ and that of W_2 is $1 - P(x, t_i)$.

Definition 15.1

Let (i) $\texttt{Item}$ be a set of m domain items and (ii) $X = \{x_1, x_2, \ldots, x_k\}$ be a k-itemset (i.e., a pattern consisting of k items), where $X \subseteq \texttt{Item}$ and $1 \leq k \leq m$. Then, a transactional database is the set of n transactions, where each transaction $t_j \subseteq \texttt{Item}$ (for $1 \leq j \leq n$). The projected database of X is the set of all transactions containing X. Each item x_i in a transaction $t_j = \{x_1, x_2, \ldots, x_h\}$ in an uncertain database is associated with an *existential probability* $P(x_i, t_j)$, which represents the likelihood of the presence of x_i in t_j [100], with value:

$$0 < P(x_i, t_j) \leq 1 \tag{15.1}$$

The *existential probability* $P(X, t_j)$ *of a pattern* X *in* t_j is then the product of the corresponding existential probabilities of every item x_i within X when these items are independent [101,102]:

$$P(X, t_j) = \prod_{x_i \in X} P(x_i, t_j) \tag{15.2}$$

Finally, the *expected support expSup (X)* of X is the sum of $P(X, t_j)$ over all n transactions in the database:

$$expSup(X) = \sum_{j=1}^{n} P(X, t_j) = \sum_{j=1}^{n} \left(\prod_{x_i \in X} P(x_i, t_j) \right) \tag{15.3}$$

With this notion of expected support, existing tree-based algorithms—such as UF-growth [74], tube-growth [75], and BLIMP-growth [76]—mine frequent patterns from uncertain data by first scanning the uncertain database once to compute the expected support of all domain items (i.e., singleton patterns). Infrequent items are pruned as their extensions/supersets are guaranteed to be infrequent. The algorithms then scan the database a second time to insert all transactions (with only frequent items) into a tree (e.g., UF-tree [74], TPC-tree [75], or BLIMP-tree [76]). Each node in the tree captures (i) an item x, (ii) its existential probability $P(x, t_j)$, and (iii) its occurrence count. At each step during the mining process, the frequent patterns are expanded recursively.

Definition 15.2

A pattern X is *frequent* in an uncertain database if $expSup(X) \geq minsup$. Given a database and *minsup*, the research problem of frequent pattern mining from uncertain data is to discover from the database a complete set of frequent patterns having expected support $\geq minsup$.

15.3.2 Constrained Mining

An existing constrained frequent itemset-mining framework [78–80] allows the user to use a rich set of SQL-style constraints to specify his interest for guiding the mining process so that only those frequently occurring sets of market basket items that satisfy the user constraints are found. This avoids unnecessary computation for mining those uninteresting frequent itemsets. These user-specified constraints can be imposed on items, events, or objects in various domains, including shopper market baskets, meteorological records, and event planning calendars. In general, these constraints can be categorized into following two subclasses of constraints, which can be further subdivided into several overlapping classes according to the properties that they possess:

1. Frequency constraints include the following:
   - $C_1 \equiv sup(X) \geq minsup$ expresses the user interest in finding frequent patterns from precise data, that is, every pattern X with actual support (or frequency) meeting or exceeding the user-specified minimum support threshold *minsup*.
   - $C_2 \equiv expSup(X) \geq minsup$ expresses the user interest in finding frequent patterns from uncertain data, that is, every pattern X with expected support meeting or exceeding the user-specified minimum support threshold *minsup*.

2. Nonfrequency constraints, with examples include the following:
   - $C_3 \equiv max(X.Price) \leq \$25$ expresses the user interest in finding every frequent itemset X such that the maximum price of all market basket items in each X is at most \$25.
   - $C_4 \equiv min(X.RewardPoints) \geq 2000$ expresses the user interest in finding every pattern X such that the minimum reward points earned by travelers among all airports visited are at least 2000.
   - $C_5 \equiv X.Location =$ Europe expresses the user interest in finding every pattern X such that all places in X are located in Europe.
   - $C_6 \equiv min(X.Price) \leq \$30$ says that the minimum price of all items in an itemset X is at most \$30.
   - $C_7 \equiv avg(X.Price) \leq \$30$ says that the average price of all items in X is at most \$30.
   - $C_8 \equiv sum(X.Price) \leq \$150$ says that the total price of all items in X is at most \$150.
   - $C_9 \equiv sum(X.Rainfall) \geq 90$ mm says that the total rainfall among all meteorological records in X is at least 90 mm.

The above constraints can be categorized into several overlapping classes according to the properties that they possess. One of these properties is *succinctness* [78].

Definition 15.3

Let `Item` be the set of domain items. Then, an itemset $SS_j \subseteq$ `Item` is a *succinct set* if SS_j can be expressed as a result of selection operation $\sigma_p(\texttt{Item})$, where σ is the usual SQL-style selection operator and p is a selection predicate. A powerset of items $SP \subseteq 2^{\texttt{Item}}$ is a *succinct powerset* if there is a fixed number of succinct sets $SS_1, \ldots, SS_k \subseteq$ `Item` such that SP can be expressed in terms of the powersets of $SS_1, \ldots, SS_k$ using set union and/or set difference operators. A constraint C is *succinct* provided that the set of itemsets satisfying C is a succinct powerset.

It is important to note the following two observations about succinct constraints:

1. *A majority of user-specified constraints are succinct.* Among the aforementioned nonfrequency constraints, (i) $C_3 \equiv max(X.Price) \leq \$25$, (ii) $C_4 \equiv min(X.RewardPoints) \geq 2000$, (iii) $C_5 \equiv X.Location =$ Europe, and (iv) $C_6 \equiv min(X.Price) \leq \$30$ are *succinct*. For any *succinct* constraints, one can directly generate precisely all and only those itemsets satisfying the constraints without generating and excluding itemsets not satisfying the constraints. Hence, one can use member generating functions [80] to precisely generate constrained itemsets.

   For instance, $C_3 \equiv max(X.Price) \leq \$25$ is succinct because any itemset satisfying C_3 can be expressed as a member in the succinct powerset $2^{\sigma_{Price \leq \$25}(\texttt{Item})}$. In other words, itemsets satisfying C_3 can be precisely generated by combining any market basket items having price $\leq \$25$, thereby avoiding the substantial overhead of the generation and exclusion of invalid itemsets.

   Similarly, itemsets satisfying $C_6 \equiv min(X.Price) \leq \$30$ can be precisely generated by combining at least one market basket item having price $\leq \$30$ with some optional items (of any price values).
2. *Many nonsuccinct constraints can be induced into weaker constraints that are succinct.* As an example, nonsuccinct constraint $C_7 \equiv avg(X.Price) \leq \$30$ can be induced into a succinct constraint $C_6 \equiv min(X.Price) \leq \$30$ as all frequent itemsets satisfying C_7 must satisfy C_6.

Besides succinctness, there are some other properties possessed by constraints. One of them is *antimonotonicity* [78].

Definition 15.4

A constraint C is *anti-monotone (AM)* if and only if all subsets of an itemset satisfying C also satisfy C. Equivalently, a constraint C' is AM if and only if all supersets of an itemset violating C' also violate C'.

With this additional property (i.e., antimonotonicity), succinct constraints can be further divided into the following two subclasses:

1. Succinct antimonotone (SAM) constraints
2. Succinct non-antimonotone (SUC) constraints

Among the aforementioned nonfrequency constraints, (i) $C_3 \equiv max(X.Price) \leq \$25$, (ii) $C_4 \equiv min(X.RewardPoints) \geq 2000$, and (iii) $C_5 \equiv X.Location$ = Europe are *SAM constraints*. For instance, for any itemset X satisfies C_3, subsets of X formed by removing items (having either the maximum price or not) from X would not possess a higher maximum price (i.e., maximum price of all market basket items in these subsets $\leq \$25$). Note that supersets of any itemset violating the SAM constraints also violate the constraints (e.g., if an itemset X contains an item having price > \$25, then X violates C_3 and so does every superset of X).

In contrast, $C_6 \equiv min(X.Price) \leq \$30$ is a *SUC constraint* because it does not possess such an antimonotonicity property. For instance, if the minimum price of all items contained within X is higher than \$30, then X violates C_6 but there is no guarantee that all supersets of X would violate C_6. As an example, let $y.Price$ be \$50 and $z.Price$ be \$10. Then, $X \cup \{y\}$ and $X \cup \{z\}$ are both supersets of X. Among them, the former (i.e., $X \cup \{y\}$) still violates C_6 but the latter (i.e., $X \cup \{z\}$) satisfies C_6.

Definition 15.5

A pattern X is *valid* in a database if such a pattern also satisfies the user-specified constraints. Given (i) a database, (ii) user-specified *minsup*, and (iii) user-specified constraints, the research problem of *constrained pattern mining from uncertain data* is to discover from the database a complete set of patterns satisfying the user-specified constraints (i.e., valid patterns).

15.3.3 Big Data Mining with the MapReduce Model

MapReduce [16] is a high-level programming model for processing vast amounts of data. It usually uses parallel and distributed computing on clouds of nodes (i.e., computers). As implied by its name, MapReduce involves two key functions: "map" and "reduce."

First, the input data are read, divided into several partitions (subproblems), and assigned to different processors. Each processor executes the map function on each partition (subproblem). The map function takes a pair of $\langle key, value\rangle$ and returns a list of $\langle key, value\rangle$ pairs as an intermediate result:

$$\text{map: } \langle key_1, value_1\rangle \mapsto \text{list of } \langle key_2, value_2\rangle$$

where (i) key_1 and key_2 are keys in the same or different domains and (ii) $value_1$ and $value_2$ are the corresponding values in some domains.

Afterward, the pairs returned by the map function are shuffled and sorted. Each processor then executes the reduce function on (i) a single key from this intermediate result together with (ii) the list of all values that appear with this key in the intermediate result. The reduce function "reduces"—by combining, aggregating, summarizing, filtering, or transforming—the list of values associated with a given key (for all k keys) and returns a single (aggregated or summarized) value:

$$\text{reduce: } \langle key_2, \text{list of } value_2\rangle \mapsto value_3$$

where (i) key_2 is a key in some domains and (ii) $value_2$ and $value_3$ are the corresponding values in some domains. Examples of MapReduce applications include the construction of an inverted index as well as the word counting of a document for data processing [16].

To mine frequent patterns from precise data using the MapReduce model, three Apriori-based algorithms called SPC, FPC, and DPC [103] were proposed. Among them, SPC uses single-pass counting to find frequent patterns of cardinality k at the k-th pass (i.e., the k-th database scan) for $k \geq 1$. FPC uses fixed-passes combined-counting to find all patterns of cardinalities k, $(k+1)$, …, $(k+m)$ in the same pass or database scan. On the one hand, this fixed-passes technique fixes the number of required passes from k_{max} (where k_{max} is the maximum cardinality of all frequent patterns that can be mined from the precise data) to a user-specified constant. On the other hand, owing to combined-counting, the number of generated candidates is higher than that of SPC. In contrast, DPC uses dynamic-passes combined-counting, which takes the benefits of both SPC and FPC by taking into account the workloads of nodes when mining frequent patterns with MapReduce. In addition, a parallel randomized algorithm called PARMA [104] was proposed for mining approximations to the top-k frequent patterns and association rules from precise data by using MapReduce.

As a preview, our MrCloud algorithm also uses MapReduce. However, unlike SPC, FPC, or DPC [103] (which use the Apriori-based approach to mine frequent patterns from precise data), our MrCloud uses a tree-based approach to mine frequent patterns from uncertain data—which deals with a much larger search space than that for mining precise data due to the presence of the existential probability values. Moreover, unlike PARMA (which mines all of the approximately frequent patterns from precise data), our data analytic algorithm mines some—specifically, those interesting patterns that satisfy the user-specified constraints—of the truly frequent patterns from uncertain data.

15.4 AN EFFECTIVE AND EFFICIENT TREE-BASED ALGORITHM FOR SUPPORTING CONSTRAINED MINING FROM UNCERTAIN BIG DATA IN DISTRIBUTED ENVIRONMENTS

Without loss of generality, we assume to have p sites/processors and $m = m_1 + m_2 + \cdots + m_p$ sensors in a distributed network such that m_1 wireless sensors transmit data to their closest or designated site/processor P_1, m_2 sensors transmit data to the site/processor P_2, and so on. With this setting, our proposed algorithm finds constrained itemsets that are frequent in the entire wireless sensor network. Depending on the properties of constraints (i.e., whether the constraints are succinct or not), different procedures are carried out.

15.4.1 Finding Frequent Itemsets That Satisfy Succinct Constraints

In this section, we describe our proposed algorithm for supporting frequent itemset mining from uncertain big data in distributed environments. In particular, we show how the algorithm first finds (i) itemsets that satisfy *succinct* constraints and are locally frequent with respect to site/processor P_i (in Section 15.4.1.1) and then finds (ii) those that satisfy succinct constraints and are globally frequent with respect to all sites/processors in the entire wireless sensor network (in Section 15.4.1.2). As a preview, in Section 15.4.2, we will show how our proposed algorithm discovers frequent itemsets that do *not* satisfy succinct constraints.

15.4.1.1 Finding Locally Frequent Itemsets That Satisfy Succinct Constraints

Given m_i sensors transmitting data to the processor P_i, a local database TDB_i of uncertain data can be created for P_i. We aim to find itemsets that are both (i) frequent to P_i and (ii) satisfying a succinct (SAM or SUC) constraint C. For uncertain data, we use the "possible world" interpretation of uncertain data. We find constrained locally frequent itemsets from uncertain data in the following steps:

1. *Identification of items satisfying the constraints*: Let $\texttt{Item}^{\text{M}}$ be the collection of mandatory items—that is, the collection of domain items that individually satisfy the SAM or SUC constraint C; let $\texttt{Item}^{\text{O}}$ be the collection of optional items—that is, the collection of domain items that individually violate C.

   Then, for any SAM constraint C_{SAM}, an itemset X satisfying C_{SAM} cannot contain any item from $\texttt{Item}^{\text{O}}$ due to the antimonotonicity property. So, any itemset X satisfying C_{SAM} must consist of *only* items that individually satisfy C_{SAM}. In other words, any itemset X satisfying C_{SAM} must be generated by combining items from $\texttt{Item}^{\text{M}}$ (i.e., $X \subseteq \texttt{Item}^{\text{M}}$). Owing to the succinctness property, items in $\texttt{Item}^{\text{M}}$ can be efficiently enumerated (from the list of domain items) by selecting only those items that individually satisfy C_{SAM}. See Example 15.1.

EXAMPLE 15.1

Let us consider an illustrative sample set of an uncertain database (as shown in Table 15.1) and its auxiliary information (as shown in Table 15.2) about shopper market basket data. In this uncertain database, each transaction contains items and their corresponding existential probabilities. For example, there are five domain items a, b, c, d, and e in the first transaction t_1, where the existential probabilities of these items are 0.7, 0.8, 0.8, 1.0, and 0.2, respectively. Note that (i) different items may have the same existential probabilities (e.g., the existential probabilities of two different items b and c in t_1 have the same value 0.8) but (ii) the existential probabilities of the same item may vary from one transaction to another (e.g., the existential probability of item e is 0.2 in transaction t_1 but it is 0.1 in t_2). Let constraint C_{SAM} be the SAM constraint $C_3 \equiv max(X.Price) \leq \$25$. Our proposed algorithm checks each of the six domain items against the constraint C_{SAM}. It first enumerates the valid items a, b, and f (i.e., items with individual price $\leq$ \$25).

TABLE 15.1
An Illustrative Sample Set of an Uncertain Database on Shopper Market Baskets

TID	Content
t_1	$\{a{:}0.7, b{:}0.8, c{:}0.8, d{:}1.0, e{:}0.2\}$
t_2	$\{a{:}0.7, b{:}0.8, d{:}1.0, e{:}0.1, f{:}0.4\}$
t_3	$\{a{:}0.8, c{:}0.5, e{:}0.3, f{:}0.4\}$
t_4	$\{b{:}0.8, c{:}0.8, d{:}1.0\}$
t_5	$\{c{:}0.8, d{:}1.0\}$

TABLE 15.2
Auxiliary Information for the Uncertain Data in Table 15.1

Item	Price
a	\$10
b	\$20
c	\$100
d	\$50
e	\$75
f	\$25

So, $\text{Item}^M = \{a, b, f\}$. Once we have identified the domain items that satisfy the SAM constraint C_{SAM}, these items serve as building blocks for all constrained frequent itemsets satisfying C_{SAM} because all constrained frequent itemsets must comprise only those Item^M items.

Next, for any SUC constraint C_{SUC}, any itemset X satisfying C_{SUC} is composed of mandatory items (i.e., items that individually satisfy C_{SUC}) and possibly some optional items (regardless of whether or not they satisfy C_{SUC}). Note that, although C_{SUC} possesses the succinctness property (i.e., one can easily enumerate all and only those itemsets that are guaranteed to satisfy C_{SUC}), it does not possess the antimonotonicity property. So, if an itemset violates C_{SUC}, there is no guarantee that all or any of its supersets would violate C_{SUC}. Hence, not all itemsets satisfying C_{SUC} are composed of only domain items that individually satisfy the constraints (as for SAM constraints). Instead, any itemset X satisfying C_{SUC} must be generated by combining at least one Item^M item and possibly some Item^O items. Owing to succinctness, items in Item^M and in Item^O can be efficiently enumerated. See Example 15.2.

EXAMPLE 15.2

Consider the same illustrative sample set of an uncertain database (as shown in Table 15.1) and its auxiliary information (as shown in Table 15.2) in Example 15.1. Let constraint C_{SUC} be the SUC constraint $C_6 \equiv min(X.Price) \leq \$30$. Our proposed algorithm checks each of the six domain items against C_{SUC}. It first enumerates the valid items a, b, and f (i.e., items with individual price $\leq \$30$), giving $\text{Item}^M = \{a, b, f\}$. The remaining domain items then belong to Item^O (i.e., items with individual price $> \$30$). Once we have classified the domain items into (i) the Item^M items (which satisfy C_{SUC}) and (ii) the Item^O items (which violate C_{SUC}), all these items serve as building blocks for all constrained frequent itemsets satisfying C_{SUC} because all constrained frequent itemsets must comprise at least one Item^M item and may contain some additional Item^M or Item^O items.

2. *Construction of a UF-Tree*: Once the domain items are classified into Item^M and Item^O items (no Item^O items for C_{SAM}), our algorithm then constructs a UF-tree, which is built in preparation for mining constrained frequent itemsets from uncertain data. It does so by first scanning the TDB of uncertain data once. It accumulates the expected support of each of the items in order to find all *frequent* domain items. Among these items, the algorithm discards those infrequent ones and only captures those frequent ones in the UF-tree. Note that any infrequent Item^M or Item^O items can be safely discarded because any itemset containing an infrequent item is also infrequent.

   Once the frequent Item^M and Item^O items are found, our algorithm arranges these two kinds of items in such a way that Item^M items appear *below* Item^O items (i.e., Item^M items are closer to the leaves, and Item^O items are closer to the root). Among all the items in Item^M, they are sorted in nonascending order of accumulated expected support. Similarly, among all the items in Item^O, they are also sorted in nonascending order of accumulated expected support. The algorithm then scans the TDB the second time and inserts each transaction of the TDB into the UF-tree. Here, the new transaction is merged with a child (or descendant) node of the root of the UF-tree (at the highest support level) only if the same item *and the same expected support* exist in both the transaction and the child (or descendant) nodes.

   For SAM constraints, the corresponding UF-tree captures only those frequent Item^M items; for SUC constraints, the corresponding UF-tree captures both the frequent Item^M items and the frequent Item^O items. With such a tree construction process, the UF-tree possesses the property that *the occurrence count of a node is at least the sum of occurrence counts of all its child nodes*. See Example 15.3.

EXAMPLE 15.3

Let us continue with Example 15.2, and let the user-specified support threshold *minsup* be set to 1.0. Our algorithm builds the UF-tree that captures the frequent items satisfying the SUC constraint $C_6 \equiv min(X.Price) \leq \$30$ as follows. First, the algorithm scans the uncertain data once and accumulates the expected support of each $\texttt{Item}^{\texttt{M}}$ item as well as each $\texttt{Item}^{\texttt{O}}$ item. Hence, it finds all frequent $\texttt{Item}^{\texttt{M}}$ items and sorts them in descending order of (accumulated) expected support. It also finds all frequent $\texttt{Item}^{\texttt{O}}$ items and sorts them in descending order of (accumulated) expected support. Among the two kinds of items, $\texttt{Item}^{\texttt{O}}$ are arranged on top (near the root) of $\texttt{Item}^{\texttt{M}}$ items (which are near the leaves). Specifically, our algorithm obtains $\texttt{Item}^{\texttt{O}}$ items d, c, and e (with their corresponding accumulated expected support values of 4.0, 2.9, and 0.6), which are sorted in descending order of their expected support values. Among these $\texttt{Item}^{\texttt{O}}$ items, e (having accumulated expected support of $0.6 < minsup$) is removed. Then, the algorithm represents the frequent $\texttt{Item}^{\texttt{O}}$ items and their expected support as d:4.0 and c:2.9. The expected support of each of these frequent $\texttt{Item}^{\texttt{O}}$ items $\geq minsup$. Similarly, the algorithm also obtains $\texttt{Item}^{\texttt{M}}$ items b, a, and f (with their corresponding accumulated expected support values of 2.4, 2.2, and 0.8), which are also sorted in descending order of their expected support values. Among these $\texttt{Item}^{\texttt{M}}$ items, f (having accumulated expected support of $0.8 < minsup$) is removed. Then, the algorithm represents the frequent $\texttt{Item}^{\texttt{M}}$ items and their expected support as b:2.4 and a:2.2. The expected support of each of these frequent $\texttt{Item}^{\texttt{M}}$ items $\geq minsup$.

Next, our algorithm scans the uncertain data the second time and inserts each transaction into the UF-tree. The algorithm first inserts frequent items from the first transaction t_1 into the tree. It then inserts the frequent items from the second transaction t_2 into the UF-tree. Since the expected support of d in t_2 is the same as that in an existing branch (i.e., the branch for t_1), this node can be shared. So, the algorithm increments the occurrence count for the tree node (d:1.0) to 2, and adds the remainder of t_2—namely, $\langle$(b:0.8):1, (a:0.7):1$\rangle$—as a child of the node (d:1.0):2. To capture the third transaction t_3, our algorithm inserts $\langle$(c:0.5):1, (a:0.8):1$\rangle$ into the tree. For the fourth transaction t_4, the algorithm increments the occurrence count for each tree node in an existing path $\langle$(d:1.0):2, (c:0.8):1, (b:0.8):1$\rangle$ by 1. Finally, our algorithm increments the occurrence count for the tree nodes in an existing path to get $\langle$(d:1.0):3, (c:0.8):2$\rangle$ by 1 for the fifth transaction t_5. Hence, at the end of the tree construction process, we get the UF-tree shown in Figure 15.1a capturing the contents of the uncertain data.

3. *Mining of Constrained Frequent Itemsets from the UF-Tree:* Once the UF-tree is constructed with the item-ordering scheme where $\texttt{Item}^{\texttt{O}}$ items are above $\texttt{Item}^{\texttt{M}}$ items, our proposed algorithm extracts appropriate paths to form a projected database for each $x \in \texttt{Item}^{\texttt{M}}$. The algorithm does not need to form projected databases for any $y \in \texttt{Item}^{\texttt{O}}$ because all itemsets satisfying C_{SUC} must be "extensions" of an item from $\texttt{Item}^{\texttt{M}}$ (i.e., all valid itemsets must be grown from $\texttt{Item}^{\texttt{M}}$ items) and no $\texttt{Item}^{\texttt{O}}$ items are kept in the UF-tree for C_{SAM}.

   When forming each $\{x\}$-projected database and constructing its UF-tree, our algorithm does not need to distinguish those $\texttt{Item}^{\texttt{M}}$ items from $\texttt{Item}^{\texttt{O}}$ items in the UF-tree for the $\{x\}$-projected database. Such a distinction between two kinds of items is only needed for the UF-tree for the TDB (for SUC constraints only) because, once we found at least one valid item $x \in \texttt{Item}^{\texttt{M}}$, for any v satisfying C_{SUC},

$$v = \{x\} \cup \text{others} \tag{15.4}$$

   where (i) $x \in \texttt{Item}^{\texttt{M}}$ and (ii) others $\subseteq \left(\texttt{Item}^{\texttt{M}} \cup \texttt{Item}^{\texttt{O}} - \{x\}\right)$.

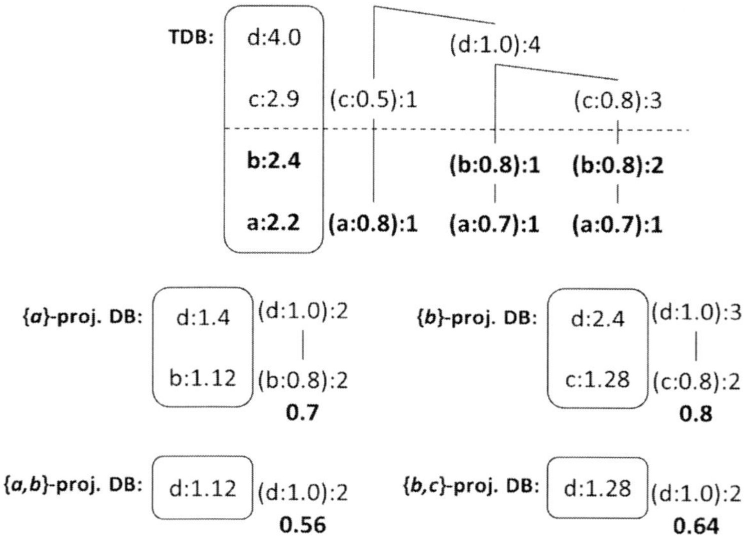

FIGURE 15.1 The UF-trees used in our proposed algorithm (Examples 15.3 and 15.4).

After constructing projected UF-trees for each $x \in \texttt{Item}^{\text{M}}$, our proposed algorithm mines all frequent itemsets that satisfy C_{SUC} in the same manner as it mines those satisfying C_{SAM}. See Example 15.4.

EXAMPLE 15.4

Let us continue with Example 15.3. Once the UF-tree is constructed, our proposed algorithm recursively mines constrained locally frequent itemsets from this tree with $minsup = 1.0$ as follows. From the header table (from top to bottom) containing two $\texttt{Item}^{\text{O}}$ items $d: 4.0 = (4 \times 1.0)$ and $c: 2.9 = (1 \times 0.5) + (3 \times 0.8)$ as well as two $\texttt{Item}^{\text{M}}$ items $b: 2.4 = (1 \times 0.8) + (2 \times 0.8)$ and $a: 2.2 = (1 \times 0.8) + (1 \times 0.7) + (1 \times 0.7)$, the algorithm first finds two constrained frequent itemsets $\{b\}$ and $\{a\}$ with expected support values of 2.4 and 2.2, respectively.

Then, our algorithm recursively mines constrained frequent itemsets from this UF-tree with $minsup = 1.0$ as follows. From the UF-tree shown in Figure 15.1a, our algorithm starts with $a \in \texttt{Item}^{\text{M}}$ and constructs a UF-tree for the $\{a\}$-projected database. The resulting tree, as shown in Figure 15.1b, consists of a single path—namely, $\langle(d{:}1.0){:}2, (b{:}0.8){:}2\rangle$ with the expected support of $\{a\}$ equal to $\mathbf{0.7}$ (implying that d or b occurs together with a twice in the original database). The expected support values of $\{a, b\} = 2 \times \mathbf{0.7} \times 0.8 = 1.12$ and of $\{a, d\} = 2 \times \mathbf{0.7} \times 1.0 = 1.4$. Thus, both $\{a, b\}$ and $\{a, d\}$ are frequent.

The algorithm then extracts from this single-path tree to form a UF-tree for the $\{a, b\}$-projected database. The resulting tree, as shown in Figure 15.1c, consists of a single node $(d{:}1.0){:}2$ with the expected support of $\{a, b\}$ equal to $\mathbf{0.56} = 0.7 \times 0.8$ (implying that $\{d\}$ occurs together with $\{a, b\}$ twice in the original database). Itemset $\{a, b, d\}$, with its expected support equals $2 \times \mathbf{0.56} \times 1.0 = 1.12$, is frequent. This marks the end of the extensions of $\{a\}$.

Then, the algorithm considers the next item in $\texttt{Item}^{\text{M}}$ (i.e., b) and constructs a UF-tree for the $\{b\}$-projected database. The resulting tree, as shown in Figure 15.1d, consists of a single path—namely, $\langle(d{:}1.0){:}3, (c{:}0.8){:}2\rangle$ with the expected support of b equal to $\mathbf{0.8}$ (implying that $\{b, d\}$ occurs three times and $\{b, c\}$ occurs twice in the original database). The expected support values of $\{b, c\} = 2 \times \mathbf{0.8} \times 0.8 = 1.28$ and of $\{b, d\} = 3 \times \mathbf{0.8} \times 1.0 = 2.4$. So, they are both frequent.

The algorithm then extracts from this single-path tree to form a UF-tree for the $\{b, c\}$-projected database. The resulting tree, as shown in Figure 15.1e, consists of a single node $(d{:}1.0){:}2$ with expected support of $\{b, c\}$ equal to $\mathbf{0.64} = 0.8 \times 0.8$ (implying that d occurs together with $\{b, c\}$ twice in the original database). Itemset $\{b, c, d\}$, with its expected support equal to $2 \times \mathbf{0.64} \times 1.0 = 1.28$, is frequent.

Since no more items belong to $\texttt{Item}^{\texttt{M}}$, this marks the end of the mining process. Our proposed algorithm recursively finds the following eight locally frequent itemsets that satisfy the SUC constraint $C_6 \equiv min(X.Price) \leq \$30$ from uncertain data: $\{a\}$:2.2, $\{a, b\}$:1.12, $\{a, b, d\}$:1.12, $\{a, d\}$:1.4, $\{b\}$:2.4, $\{b, c\}$:1.28, $\{b, c, d\}$:1.28, and $\{b, d\}$:2.4.

15.4.1.2 Finding Globally Frequent Itemsets That Satisfy Succinct Constraints

Once the constrained locally frequent itemsets are found from distributed uncertain data, the next step is to find the constrained globally frequent itemsets among those constrained locally frequent itemsets. Note that it is not a good idea to transmit all data in TDB_i from each site/processor P_i to a centralized site/processor Q, where all data are merged to form a global database $TDB = \bigcup_i TDB_i$ from which constrained globally frequent itemsets are found. The problem with such an approach is that it requires lots of communication for transmitting data from each site. This problem is worsened when TDB_i's are huge; wireless sensors can generate huge amounts of data. Moreover, such an approach does not make use of constrained locally frequent itemsets in finding constrained globally frequent itemsets.

Similarly, it is also not a good idea to ask each site to transmit all its constrained locally frequent itemsets to a centralized site, where the itemsets are merged. The merge result is a collection of global candidate itemsets. The problem is that if a constrained itemset X is locally frequent at a site P_1 but not at another site P_2, then we do not have the frequency of X at P_2. Lacking this frequency information, one may not be able to determine whether X is globally frequent or not.

Instead, our proposed algorithm does the following. Each site/processor P_i (for $1 \leq i \leq p$) applies constraint checking and frequency checking to find locally frequent $\texttt{Item}_i^{\texttt{M}}$ items (and $\texttt{Item}_i^{\texttt{O}}$ items for C_{SUC}), which are then transmitted to a centralized site/processor Q. It takes the union of these items, and broadcasts the union to all P_i's. Each P_i then extracts these items (potentially globally frequent items) from transactions in TDB_i and puts them into a UF-tree. Note that all globally frequent itemsets must be composed of only the items from this union because of the following:

- If an item A is globally frequent, then A must be locally frequent in at least one of P_i's.
- If an item B is locally infrequent in *all* the P_i's, then B is guaranteed to be globally infrequent.

At each site P_i, the UF-tree contains (i) items that are locally frequent with respect to P_i and (ii) items that are potentially globally frequent but locally infrequent items with respect to P_i. Then, our algorithm recursively applies the usual tree-based mining process (e.g., UF-growth) to each α-projected database (where locally frequent $\alpha \subseteq \texttt{Item}_i^{\texttt{M}}$) of the UF-tree at P_i to find *constrained locally frequent itemsets* (with local frequency information). These itemsets are then sent to Q, where the local frequencies are summed. As a result, *constrained globally frequent itemsets* can be found. If the sum of available local frequencies of a constrained itemset X meets the minimum support threshold, then X is globally frequent. For the case where a constrained itemset is locally frequent at a site P_1 but not at another site P_2, then Q sends a request to P_2 for finding its local frequency. It is guaranteed that such frequency information can be found by traversing appropriate paths in the UF-tree at P_2 (because the UF-tree keeps all potential globally frequent items).

15.4.1.3 Summary

Given p sites/processors in a distributed environment (e.g., a wireless sensor network), our algorithm makes use of (i) the constrained locally frequent itemsets and (ii) the UF-trees that keep all potentially global frequent items to efficiently find constrained globally frequent itemsets (with respect to the entire distributed environment). Again, succinct constraints are pushed inside the mining process; the computation is proportional to the selectivity of succinct constraints. Moreover, our proposed algorithm does not require lots of communication among processors (e.g., it does not need to transmit TDB_i).

15.4.2 Finding Frequent Itemsets That Satisfy Nonsuccinct Constraints

In Section 15.4.1, we showed how our proposed distributed mining algorithm finds frequent itemsets that satisfy *succinct* constraints. Recall from Section 15.3.2 that, although a majority of constraints are succinct, there are a few constraints that are *not* succinct. In this section, we discuss how we modify the proposed distributed mining algorithm for finding frequent itemsets that do *not* satisfy succinct constraints.

15.4.2.1 Finding Frequent Itemsets That Satisfy Inductive Succinct Constraints

For a constraint C that is not succinct, our proposed distributed mining algorithm first tests to see if such a nonsuccinct constraint C can be induced into a succinct constraint C'. If so, the algorithm carries out the following steps:

1. The algorithm induces C into C'.
2. The algorithm applies the same mining procedures as described in Section 15.4.1 but using the induced constraint C' (instead of the original constraint C). In other words, the algorithm finds locally frequent itemsets that satisfy C', from which globally frequent itemsets that satisfy C' can be found.
3. For each globally frequent itemset X that satisfy C', the algorithm tests to see if X also satisfies the original nonsuccinct C and returns X to users if it satisfies C.

EXAMPLE 15.5

Given a user-specified constraint $C_7 \equiv avg(X.Price) \leq \$30$, our algorithm induces C_7 into a succinct constraint $C_6 \equiv min(X.Price) \leq \$30$ and finds all globally frequent itemsets that satisfy C_6. Afterward, the algorithm tests these itemsets and returns only those that satisfy C_7.

15.4.2.2 Finding Frequent Itemsets That Satisfy Antimonotone Constraints

Recall from Section 15.3.2 that a constraint C_{AM} is antimonotone (AM) if all subsets of an itemset satisfying C_{AM} also satisfy C_{AM}. Hence, for a constraint C that is not succinct and cannot be induced into a succinct constraint, our proposed distributed mining algorithm tests to see if such a nonsuccinct constraint C is AM. If so, the algorithm carries out mining procedures that are similar (but not identical) to those described in Section 15.4.1. Specifically, the algorithm takes the following steps to find constrained locally frequent itemsets:

1. The algorithm identifies frequent items satisfying C in the same way as described in Section 15.4.1.1.
2. The algorithm constructs a UF-tree in the same way as described in Section 15.4.1.1.
3. The algorithm mines those frequent itemsets that satisfy C from the UF-tree. Here, unlike the usual Step 3 in which no constraint checking is needed when forming a projected database and constructing a smaller UF-tree for a frequent itemset X, the algorithm needs to apply additional constraint checking (to see if X satisfies C).

   On the one hand, if X satisfies C, the algorithm forms an X-projected database and constructs a smaller UF-tree capturing such an X-projected database.

On the other hand, if X violates C, the algorithm does not form an X-projected database and any supersets of X can be pruned/ignored because these *supersets of* X are guaranteed to violate C (whenever X itself violates C).

4. Once the *locally* frequent itemsets that satisfy C are found, the algorithm finds *globally* frequent itemsets that satisfy C in the same way as described in Section 15.4.1.2.

EXAMPLE 15.6

Given a user-specified constraint $C_8 \equiv sum(X.Price) \leq \$150$, our algorithm constructs a UF-tree capturing all frequent items. During the mining process, the algorithm recursively applies constraint checking to see if an itemset X satisfies C_8. If it does, the algorithm forms an X-projected database and constructs its corresponding UF-tree for extensions of X; otherwise, the algorithm prunes X. Consequently, the algorithm finds all globally frequent itemsets that satisfy C_8.

15.4.2.3 Finding Frequent Itemsets in a Postprocessing Step

Finally, for a constraint C that is (i) neither succinct nor AM and (ii) cannot be induced into succinct constraints, our proposed distributed mining algorithm carries out the following steps:

1. The algorithm applies the same mining procedures as described in Section 15.4.1, but using no constraint. In other words, the algorithm finds locally frequent itemsets, from which globally frequent itemsets can be found.
2. For each globally frequent itemset X, the algorithm carries out a postprocessing step to test if X satisfies the original nonsuccinct C and returns X to users if it satisfies C.

EXAMPLE 15.7

Given a user-specified constraint $C_9 \equiv sum(X.Rainfall) \geq 90$ mm, our algorithm first finds all globally frequent itemsets, which include those that satisfy C_9 and those that do not. Then, the algorithm carries out a postprocessing step to test these itemsets and returns only those that satisfy C_9.

15.4.2.4 Summary

Given p sites/processors in a distributed environment (e.g., a wireless sensor network), our proposed distributed mining algorithm first finds constrained locally frequent itemsets depending on the following classes of the constraint C:

- If C is succinct (SAM or SUC), then our algorithm carries out the steps as described in Section 15.4.1.
- If C is not succinct but can be induced into succinct constraints, then our algorithm carries out the steps as described in Section 15.4.2.1.
- If C is AM but not succinct, then our algorithm carries out the steps as described in Section 15.4.2.2.
- If C is neither succinct nor AM and cannot be induced into succinct constraints, then our algorithm carries out the steps as described in Section 15.4.2.3.

Afterward, our proposed distributed mining algorithm effectively and efficiently finds constrained globally frequent itemsets (with respect to the entire distributed environment) from the UF-trees capturing all potentially global frequent items.

15.5 MRCLOUD: AN EFFECTIVE AND EFFICIENT MAPREDUCE-BASED ALGORITHM FOR SUPPORTING CONSTRAINED MINING FROM UNCERTAIN BIG DATA IN CLOUD ENVIRONMENTS

Given (i) uncertain big data, (ii) user-specified *minsup*, and (iii) a user-specified constraint C (e.g., an AM constraint), the research problem of constrained frequent pattern mining from uncertain big data is to discover from big data a complete set of patterns having expected support $\geq$ *minsup* and satisfying C (i.e., valid frequent patterns). In this section, we introduce our data analytic algorithm—called *MrCloud*—that uses *M*ap*R*educe for managing, querying, and processing uncertain big data in *Cloud* environments. Specifically, our algorithm manages transactions of uncertain big data, allows users to query these big data by specifying constraints expressing their interests, and processes the user-specified constraints to discover useful information and knowledge from the uncertain big data.

15.5.1 MANAGING UNCERTAIN BIG DATA

To manage uncertain big data, our MrCloud algorithm keeps track of both (i) the transactions of uncertain data and (ii) an auxiliary file capturing information about domain items in uncertain data. Here, items in each transaction of uncertain data are associated with existential probability values expressing the likelihood of these items in the transaction in the form of a set of every item x_i with its existential probability value $P(x_i, t_j)$, as follows:

$$\{x_i : P(x_i, t_j)\} \tag{15.5}$$

See Table 15.3 for an illustrative sample capturing transactions of uncertain data collected about the airports visited by travelers. Also see Table 15.4 for the auxiliary information about reward points

TABLE 15.3
An Illustrative Sample Set of Uncertain Big Data

TID	Content
t_1	{AMS: 0.9, BCN: 1.0, CPH: 0.5, DEL: 0.9, EDI: 1.0, FRA: 0.2}
t_2	{AMS: 0.8, BCN: 0.8, CPH: 1.0, EDI: 0.2, FRA: 0.2, IST: 0.6}
t_3	{AMS: 0.4, FRA: 0.2, GUM: 1.0, HEL: 0.5}

TABLE 15.4
Auxiliary Information for the Uncertain Big Data in Table 15.3

IATA Code	Airport	Reward Points
AMS	Amsterdam	2400
BCN	Barcelona	3000
CPH	Copenhagen	2600
DEL	Delhi	3200
EDI	Edinburgh	2000
FRA	Frankfurt	2200
GUM	Guam	1800
HEL	Helsinki	2800
IST	Istanbul	1600

TABLE 15.5
Classification of Some AM and Non-AM Constraints

Classification	Constraints
AM	$X.attribute\ \theta\ constant$, where $\theta \in \{>, \geq=, \leq, <\}$
	$max(X.attribute)\ \theta\ constant$, where $\theta \in \{=, \leq, <\}$
	$min(X.attribute)\ \theta\ constant$, where $\theta \in \{>, \geq, =\}$
	$sum(X.attribute)\ \theta\ constant$, where $\theta \in \{\leq, <\}$
	$C_1 \wedge C_2$, where C_1 and C_2 are AM constraints
	$C_1 \vee C_2$, where C_1 and C_2 are AM constraints
Non-AM	$max(X.attribute)\ \theta\ constant$, where $\theta \in \{>, \geq\}$
	$min(X.attribute)\ \theta\ constant$, where $\theta \in \{\leq, <\}$
	$sum(X.attribute)\ \theta\ constant$, where $\theta \in \{>, \geq\}$
	$avg(X.attribute)\ \theta\ constant$, where $\theta \in \{>, \geq, =, \leq, <\}$

that can be earned by travelers visiting those airports. For instance, t_1 captures the uncertain data that a traveler may have visited six airports (namely, AMS, BCN, CPH, DEL, EDI, and FRA). Among them, it is 100% sure that he has visited BCN and EDI (where he earned 3000 and 2000 points, respectively). There is a 90% chance that he has visited AMS or DEL (where he would earn 2400 and 3200 points, respectively), 50% chance that he has visited CPH (where he would earn 2600 points), and only 20% chance that he has visited FRA (where he would earn 2200 points).

15.5.2 Querying Uncertain Big Data

Once our MrCloud algorithm managed uncertain big data, it allows users to query the data. Users can express their interests by selecting one of SQL-style constraints in the form of (i) "$X.attribute\ \theta\ constant$," (ii) "$agg(X.attribute)\ \theta\ constant$," and (iii) their logical combinations via the conjunction operator "AND" ($\wedge$) or the disjunction operator "OR" ($\vee$), where (i) agg is an aggregate function including max, min, sum, and (ii) θ is a comparison operator including $>, \geq, =, \leq, <$. Examples are not confined to the aforementioned frequency or nonfrequency constraints (as shown in Section 15.3.2); users can also specify AM constraints involving more than one aggregate function. The following is an example:

- $C_{10} \equiv difference(X.Price) = max(X.Price) - min(X.Price) \leq \$10$ says that the difference between the maximum and minimum prices in X is at most \$10 (which involves the difference between two aggregate functions maximum and minimum).

Moreover, users can also specify constraints involving more than one constraint. Examples include the following:

- $C_{11} \equiv (C_4 \wedge C_5) \equiv [min(X.RewardPoints) \geq 2000] \wedge [X.Location = \text{Europe}]$ expresses the user interest in finding every pattern X such that the minimum reward points earned by travelers among all European airports visited are at least 2000 (which involves a logical conjunction "AND" of two AM constraints).

Since the users specify their constraints by selecting one of the SQL-style constraints, MrCloud can easily determine whether the user-specified constraints are AM or not. Table 15.5 shows examples of the classification.

15.5.3 Processing Uncertain Big Data

Once the users queried uncertain big data by specifying their constraints that express their interest, our MrCloud algorithm processes these user-specified queries to find frequent patterns that satisfy these user-specified constraints. Given (i) an implicit frequency constraint $C_2 \equiv expSup(X) \geq minsup$ and (ii) an explicit user-specified constraints, MrCloud explores the antimonotonicity of these constraints in pruning the search space. More specifically, the implicit frequency constraint satisfies the antimonotonicity, as described in the following:

- If a pattern X is frequent (i.e., $expSup(X) \geq minsup$), then all subsets of X are guaranteed to satisfy the AM constraints because $expSup(X') \geq expSup(X) \geq minsup$ for every subset $X' \subseteq X$.
- If a pattern Y is infrequent (i.e., $expSup(Y) < minsup$), then all supersets of Y are guaranteed to be infrequent because $expSup(Y') < expSup(Y) < minsup$ for every superset $Y' \supseteq Y$. Thus, every superset Y' of Y can be pruned.

However, if a pattern X is frequent, then some supersets of X may be frequent while some other may not be frequent. Thus, frequency checking is needed to be applied to every superset of X.

Similarly, if the user-specified constraint satisfies the antimonotonicity, then we can prune the search space due to the following:

- If a pattern X satisfies AM constraints, then all subsets of X are guaranteed to satisfy the AM constraints.
- If a pattern Y does not satisfy AM constraints, then all supersets of Y are guaranteed not to satisfy the AM constraints and thus can be pruned.

However, if a pattern X satisfies AM constraints, then some supersets of X may satisfy the AM constraints while some other may not satisfy the AM constraints. Thus, constraint checking is needed to be applied to every superset of X.

These observations about AM constraints hold not only for constraints involving one AM constraint but also constraints involving multiple AM constraints due to the following:

1. *If constraints C_a and C_b are AM, then the constraint $(C_a \wedge C_b)$ is also AM.* For AM constraints C_a and C_b, if a pattern X satisfies C_a and C_b, then all subsets of X are guaranteed to satisfy C_a and satisfy C_b. In other words, all subsets of X are guaranteed to satisfy $(C_a \wedge C_b)$. Conversely, if a pattern Y does not satisfy C_a and does not satisfy C_b, then all supersets of Y are guaranteed not to satisfy C_a and not to satisfy C_b. In other words, all supersets of Y are guaranteed not to satisfy $(C_a \wedge C_b)$. Thus, $(C_a \wedge C_b)$ is also AM.
2. *If constraints C_a or C_b are AM, then the constraint $(C_a \vee C_b)$ is also AM.* For AM constraints C_a or C_b, if a pattern X satisfies C_a and C_b, then all subsets of X are guaranteed to satisfy C_a or satisfy C_b. In other words, all subsets of X are guaranteed to satisfy $(C_a \vee C_b)$. Conversely, if a pattern Y does not satisfy C_a or does not satisfy C_b, then all supersets of Y are guaranteed not to satisfy C_a or not to satisfy C_b. In other words, all supersets of Y are guaranteed not to satisfy $(C_a \vee C_b)$. Thus, $(C_a \vee C_b)$ is also AM.

On the other hand, if the explicit user-specified constraints do not satisfy antimonotonicity, our MrCloud first discovers all frequent patterns and then verifies the validity of each of these discovered patterns to see if it satisfies the user-specified constraints at a postprocessing step.

To process uncertain big data, our MrCloud algorithm first reads and divides the uncertain big data into several partitions and assigns them to different processors. The map function (denoted as map_1) receives ⟨transaction ID, content of that transaction⟩ as input. To facilitate time-efficient and space-efficient constrained frequent pattern mining, MrCloud pushes the user-specified nonfrequency AM constraints C_{AM} early in the mining process by pushing them into the map$_1$ function. So, for every transaction t_j, the map$_1$ function performs constraint checking for C_{AM} and emits an $\langle x, P(x, t_j)\rangle$ pair for each occurrence of valid item $x \in t_j$ (i.e., those domain items satisfying the nonfrequency AM constraints), as follows:

$$\begin{aligned} \text{map}_1\text{:}&\langle \text{ID of transaction } t_j, \text{ content of } t_j\rangle \\ &\mapsto \text{ list of } \langle \text{valid } x, P(x, t_j)\rangle \end{aligned} \tag{15.6}$$

In other words, by specifying the following, the map$_1$ function produces a list of $\langle$valid $x, P(x, t_j)\rangle$ pairs with many different valid x and $P(x, t_j)$ for the keys and values:

for each $t_j \in$ partition of the uncertain big data **do**
  for each item $x \in t_j$ **and** $\{x\}$ satisfies C_{AM} **do**
    emit $\langle x, P(x, t_j)\rangle$.

Afterward, these $\langle$valid $x, P(x, t_j)\rangle$ pairs are shuffled and sorted. Each processor then executes the reduce function (denoted as reduce$_1$) on the shuffled and sorted pairs to obtain the expected support of x. Recall that each item in the uncertain big data is associated with an existential probability value. The reduce$_1$ function computes the expected support of all domain items (i.e., singleton patterns) by using MapReduce with Equation 15.3, which can be simplified to become the following when computing singleton patterns:

$$expSup(\{x\}) = \sum_{j=1}^{n} P(x, t_j) \tag{15.7}$$

where $P(x, t_j)$ is an existential probability of item x in transaction t_j. In other words, the reduce$_1$ function sums all existential probabilities of x for each valid x to compute its expected support:

$$\begin{aligned} \text{reduce}_1\text{:}&\langle \text{valid } x, \text{ list of } P(x, t_j)\rangle \\ &\mapsto \text{ list of } \langle \text{valid frequent } \{x\}, expSup(\{x\})\rangle \end{aligned} \tag{15.8}$$

More specifically, the reduce$_1$ function finds those items satisfying the frequency constraints by specifying the following:

for each $x \in \langle$valid x, list of $P(x, t_j)\rangle$ **do**
  set $expSup(\{x\}) = 0$;
  for each $P(x, t_j) \in$ list of $P(x, t_j)$ **do**
    $expSup(\{x\}) = expSup(\{x\}) + P(x, t_j)$;
  if $expSup(\{x\}) \geq minsup$ **then**
    emit $\langle \{x\}, expSup(\{x\})\rangle$

For the explicit user-specified nonfrequency non-AM constraints C_{nonAM}, our MrCloud verifies the validity of each discovered frequent $\{x\}$ returned by the reduce$_1$ function to see if it satisfies the user-specified constraints. Consequently, we obtain all valid frequent singletons (i.e., domain items that satisfy the user-specified constraints) and their associated existential support values.

MrCloud then proceeds to the next step, which is computationally intensive, by rereading each transaction in the uncertain big data to form an $\{x\}$-projected database (i.e., a collection of all prefixes of transactions ending with x) for each valid frequent singleton $\{x\}$ returned by the reduce$_1$ function. This second map function (denoted as map$_2$) is defined as follows:

$$\begin{aligned} \text{map}_2\text{:}&\langle \text{ID of transaction } t_j, \text{ content of } t_j\rangle \\ &\mapsto \text{ list of } \langle \text{valid frequent } \{x\}, \text{ part of } t_j \text{ with } x\rangle \end{aligned} \tag{15.9}$$

It can be specified as follows:

for each $t_j \in$ partition of the uncertain big data **do**
  for each $\{x\} \in \langle\{x\}, expSup(\{x\})\rangle$ **do**
    if prefix of t_j ending with x contains items besides x **then**
      emit $\langle\{x\}$, prefix of t_j ending with $x\rangle$

The worker node corresponding to each partition helps to form an $\{x\}$-projected database for every valid frequent item x in the transactions assigned to that partition. The $\{x\}$-projected database consists of prefixes of relevant transactions (from the uncertain big data) that end with x. More precisely, the worker node outputs $\langle\{x\}$, portion of t_j for forming the $\{x\}$-projected database$\rangle$ pairs.

Then, the reduce function reduce$_2$ is defined as follows:

$$\begin{aligned} \text{reduce}_2\text{: } & \langle\text{valid frequent } \{x\}, \{x\}\text{-projected database}\rangle \\ & \mapsto \text{ list of } \langle\text{valid frequent } X, expSup(X)\rangle \end{aligned} \tag{15.10}$$

It shuffles and sorts these pairs of $\{x\}$-projected databases, from which valid frequent nonsingleton patterns can be found and their expected support values can be computed. As any nonsingleton patterns containing valid singleton items are not guaranteed to be valid, additional constraint check on AM constraints C_{AM} is required when forming the projected database in mining valid frequent patterns. So, the worker node corresponding to each projected database then builds appropriate trees (e.g., UF-tree, TPC-tree, or BLIMP-tree)—based on the projected databases assigned to the worker node—to mine every valid frequent nonsingleton pattern X (with cardinality k, where $k \geq 2$). The worker node also outputs $\langle X, expSup(X)\rangle$, that is, every valid frequent nonsingleton pattern with its expected support:

for each $x \in \{x\}$-projected database **do**
  build a tree for $\{x\}$-projected database to find X;
  if X satisfies C_{AM} **and** $expSup(X) \geq minsup$ **then**
    emit $\langle X, expSup(X)\rangle$

Again, for the explicit user-specified nonfrequency non-AM constraints C_{nonAM}, our MrCloud verifies the validity of each discovered frequent X returned by the reduce$_2$ function to see if it satisfies the user-specified constraints.

EXAMPLE 15.8

Let us consider an illustrative sample set of an uncertain big database (as shown in Table 15.3) and its auxiliary information (as shown in Table 15.4) with (i) the user-specified $minsup$=0.9 and (ii) a user-specified constraint $C_{11} \equiv [min(X.RewardPoints) \geq 2000] \wedge [X.Location = \text{Europe}]$ (which expresses the user interest in finding every pattern X such that the minimum reward points earned by travelers among all European airports visited are at least 2000). Based on the auxiliary information, we learn that airports AMS, BCN, CPH, EDI, FRA, and HEL (but not DEL, GUM, or IST) satisfy C_{10}. More specifically, (i) both DEL and GUM are not in Europe and (ii) travelers visiting either GUM or IST would not be able to earn at least 2000 reward points.

Then, for the first transaction t_1, the map$_1$ function outputs only ⟨AMS, 0.9⟩, ⟨BCN, 1.0⟩, ⟨CPH, 0.5⟩, ⟨EDI, 1.0⟩, and ⟨FRA, 0.2⟩. Similarly, for the second transaction t_2, the map$_1$ function outputs ⟨AMS, 0.8⟩, ⟨BCN, 0.8⟩, ⟨CPH, 1.0⟩, ⟨EDI, 0.2⟩, and ⟨FRA, 0.2⟩. For the third transaction t_3, the map$_1$ function outputs only ⟨AMS, 0.4⟩, ⟨FRA, 0.2⟩, and ⟨HEL, 0.5⟩. These output pairs are then shuffled and sorted.

Note that the map$_1$ function does not output ⟨DEL, 0.9⟩ for t_1 because {DEL} does not satisfy C_{10}. Moreover, it also does not output ⟨IST, 0.6⟩ for t_2 or ⟨GUM, 1.0⟩ for t_3 because both {IST} and {GUM} also do not satisfy C_{10}.

Afterward, the $reduce_1$ function first reads ⟨AMS, [0.9, 0.8, 0.4]⟩, ⟨BCN, [1.0, 0.8]⟩, ⟨CPH, [0.5, 1.0]⟩, ⟨EDI, [1.0, 0.2]⟩, ⟨FRA, [0.2, 0.2, 0.2]⟩, and ⟨HEL, [0.5]⟩; the function then outputs ⟨{AMS}, 2.1⟩, ⟨{BCN}, 1.8⟩, ⟨{CPH}, 1.5⟩, and ⟨{EDI}, 1.2⟩ (i.e., valid frequent singletons and their corresponding expected support).

Also note that, although the $reduce_1$ function reads ⟨FRA, [0.2, 0.2, 0.2]⟩ and ⟨HEL, [0.5]⟩, it does not output ⟨{FRA}, 0.6⟩ or ⟨{HEL}, 0.5⟩ because valid singletons {FRA} and {HEL} are infrequent.

After rereading the first transaction t_1, the map_2 function outputs ⟨{BCN}, {AMS: 0.9, BCN: 1.0}⟩ (where {AMS: 0.9, BCN: 1.0} is a prefix of t_1 ending with item BCN), ⟨{CPH}, {AMS: 0.9, BCN: 1.0, CPH: 0.5}⟩, and ⟨{EDI}, {AMS: 0.9, BCN: 1.0, CPH: 0.5, EDI: 1.0}⟩ (where {AMS: 0.9, BCN: 1.0, CPH: 0.5, EDI: 1.0} contains only valid frequent items—i.e., it does not contain invalid item DEL). Similarly, after rereading the second transaction t_2, the map $function_2$ outputs ⟨{BCN}, {AMS: 0.8, BCN: 0.8}⟩, ⟨{CPH}, {AMS: 0.8, BCN: 0.8, CPH: 1.0}⟩, and ⟨{EDI}, {AMS: 0.8, BCN: 0.8, CPH: 1.0, EDI: 0.2}⟩. After rereading the third transaction t_3, the map_2 function does not output anything. All output pairs are then shuffled and sorted.

Note that the map_2 function does not output ⟨{AMS}, {AMS: 0.9}⟩ for t_1 because {AMS: 0.9} does not contain any valid frequent item other than AMS itself (i.e., singleton prefix of transactions does not contribute to the mining of nonsingletons). The same comments apply to not outputting ⟨{AMS}, {AMS: 0.8}⟩ for t_2 or ⟨{AMS}, {AMS: 0.4}⟩ for t_3. Moreover, recall that the $reduce_1$ function outputs ⟨{AMS}, 2.1⟩, ⟨{BCN}, 1.8⟩, ⟨{CPH}, 1.5⟩, and ⟨{EDI}, 1.2⟩ (as FRA and HEL are infrequent and GUM is invalid). Hence, the map_2 function does not output anything for FRA, GUM, or HEL (i.e., not outputting ⟨{FRA}, {AMS: 0.9, BCN: 1.0, CPH: 0.5, EDI: 1.0, FRA: 0.2}⟩ for t_1; {AMS: 0.8, BCN: 0.8, CPH: 1.0, EDI: 0.2, FRA: 0.2}⟩ for t_2; ⟨{FRA}, {AMS: 0.4, FRA: 0.2}⟩; or ⟨{HEL}, {AMS: 0.4, FRA: 0.2, HEL: 0.5}⟩ for t_3).

Afterward, the $reduce_2$ function reads ⟨{BCN}, {BCN}-projected database⟩. Based on this {BCN}-projected database (which consists of two subtransactions {AMS: 0.9, BCN: 1.0} and {AMS: 0.8, BCN: 0.8}), a tree is built. Consequently, valid frequent pattern {AMS, BCN} with an expected support of 1.54 is found. Similarly, the $reduce_2$ function reads ⟨{CPH}, {CPH}-projected database⟩. It builds a tree based on this {CPH}-projected database (which consists of two subtransactions {AMS: 0.9, BCN: 1.0, CPH: 0.5} and {AMS: 0.8, BCN: 0.8, CPH: 1.0}), and finds valid frequent patterns {AMS, CPH}, {AMS, BCN, CPH}, and {BCN, CPH} with expected support values of 1.25, 1.09, and 1.3, respectively. The $reduce_2$ function then reads ⟨{EDI}, {EDI}-projected database⟩. It builds a tree based on this {EDI}-projected database (which consists of two subtransactions {AMS: 0.9, BCN: 1.0, CPH: 0.5, EDI: 1.0} and {AMS: 0.8, BCN: 0.8, CPH: 1.0, EDI: 0.2}), and finds valid frequent patterns {AMS, EDI} and {BCN, EDI} with expected support values of 1.06 and 1.16, respectively.

Recall from Example 15.8 that the set of map_1 and $reduce_1$ functions discover four valid frequent singletons (with their corresponding expected support values): ⟨{AMS}, 2.1⟩, ⟨{BCN}, 1.8⟩, ⟨{CPH}, 1.5⟩, and ⟨{EDI}, 1.2⟩. Here, the set of map_2 and $reduce_2$ functions discover six additional valid frequent nonsingleton patterns (with their corresponding expected support values): ⟨{AMS, BCN}, 1.54⟩, {AMS, BCN, CPH}, 1.09⟩, ⟨{AMS, CPH}, 1.25⟩, ⟨{AMS, HEL}, 1.06⟩, ⟨{BCN, CPH}, 1.3⟩, and ⟨{BCN, EDI}, 1.16⟩. Hence, MrCloud finds a total of 10 patterns satisfying both frequency constraint $C_2 \equiv expSup(X) \geq minsup$ and nonfrequency AM constraint $C_{11} \equiv [min(X.RewardPoints) \geq 2000] \wedge [X.Location = \text{Europe}]$ involving a logical conjunction of two nonfrequency AM constraints.

15.6 EXPERIMENTAL ASSESSMENT AND ANALYSIS

In order to assess and analyze the performance of our proposed algorithms for supporting complex mining from uncertain big data, we conducted extensive experimental campaigns. Derived results clearly show the benefits coming from our proposals. In this section, we provide experimental evidence for both our algorithms.

15.6.1 Experimenting the Tree-Based Algorithm for Supporting Constrained Mining from Uncertain Big Data in Distributed Environments

In this section, we focus the attention on the experimental assessment and analysis of the first algorithm embedded in our framework for supporting complex mining from uncertain big data.

To evaluate our proposed algorithm, we used many different datasets, including IBM synthetic data, real-life databases from the UC Irvine Machine Learning Depository (e.g., mushroom data), as well as those from the *Frequent Itemset-Mining Implementation* (FIMI) Dataset Repository.* For instance, IBM synthetic datasets used in our experiments were generated by the program developed at IBM Almaden Research Center [57]. The datasets contain 100 K to 10 M records with an average transaction length of 10 items, and a domain of 1000 items. We assigned to each item an existential probability in the range of (0,1]. All experiments were run in a time-sharing environment in a 2.4 GHz machine. The reported figures are based on the average of multiple runs. Runtime includes CPU and I/Os for constraint checking, UF-tree construction, and frequent itemset-mining steps.

In Experiment 15.1, we evaluated the functionality of our proposed algorithm, which was implemented in C++. For instance, we used (i) a dataset of uncertain data and (ii) a *constraint with 100% selectivity* (so that every item is selected). With this setting, we compared our algorithm (which mines *constrained* frequent itemsets from uncertain data) with U-Apriori [73] and UF-growth [74] (which mine *unconstrained* frequent itemsets from uncertain data). Experimental results on the IBM dataset showed that, in terms of accuracy, our algorithm returned the *same* mining results—that is, the *same* collection of frequent itemsets—as those returned by U-Apriori and UF-growth.

However, it is important to note that both U-Apriori and UF-growth are confined to finding frequent itemsets from a centralized dataset of uncertain data when the user-specified constraints are of a single selectivity of 100%, whereas our proposed algorithm is more flexible as it is capable of finding frequent itemsets from *distributed* uncertain data with constraints of *any selectivity*.

As for the runtimes among these three algorithms, our algorithm took the shortest amount of time to mine frequent itemsets because it pushes user-specified constraints into the mining process. The higher the selectivity of the constraints, the longer was the runtime for our algorithm. Both U-Apriori and UF-growth were not designed to handle constraints, let alone pushing the constraints into the mining. To handle constraints, U-Apriori and UF-growth first ignored the constraints and found all frequent itemsets. Then, they applied constraint checking as a postprocessing step to prune those

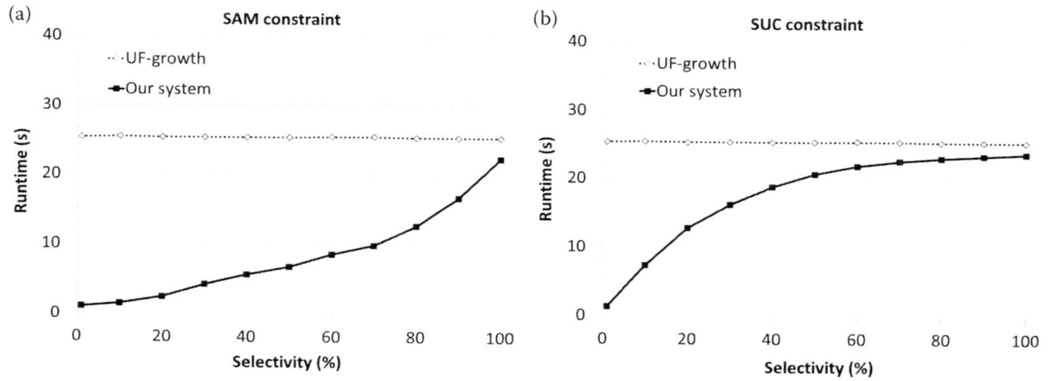

FIGURE 15.2 Experiment 15.1: Runtime of our algorithm versus existing algorithms (e.g., UF-growth [74]).

* http://fimi.ua.ac.be/

infrequent itemsets. Hence, the runtime of these two existing algorithms were independent of the selectivity of the SAM and SUC constraints. See Figure 15.2.

In Experiment 15.2, we continued with our functionality evaluation. Specifically, we used (i) a constraint and (ii) a dataset of uncertain data consisting of items *all with existential probability of 1* (indicating that all items are definitely present in the database). With this setting, we compared our algorithm (which mines constrained frequent itemsets from *uncertain* data) with some existing algorithms that mine constrained frequent itemsets from *precise* data (e.g. CAP [79]). We observed from the experimental results that our algorithm returned the *same* mining results—that is, the *same* collection of frequent itemsets—as those returned by CAP. In other words, our algorithm is as accurate as CAP.

However, regarding the flexibility, CAP is confined to finding frequent itemsets from a centralized dataset of uncertain data when existential probability of all items is of 1. In contrast, our proposed algorithm is capable of finding frequent itemsets from distributed uncertain data containing items with *various existential probability values* ranging from 0 to 1.

In Experiment 15.3, we measured the amount of communication/data transmitted between the distributed sites P_i's and their centralized site Q. Figure 15.3 shows the results for both IBM synthetic dataset and UCI real-life mushroom dataset. Note that the amount of transmitted data decreased when the selectivity of constraints decreased. The reason is that, as the constraint selectivity decreased, fewer frequent itemsets satisfied the constraints. Hence, less data were transmitted.

Between the SAM and SUC constraints, frequent itemsets satisfying SAM constraints consist of only those domain items that individually satisfy the constraints. Hence, the amount of data transmitted grew exponentially when selectivity increased linearly. In contrast, frequent itemsets

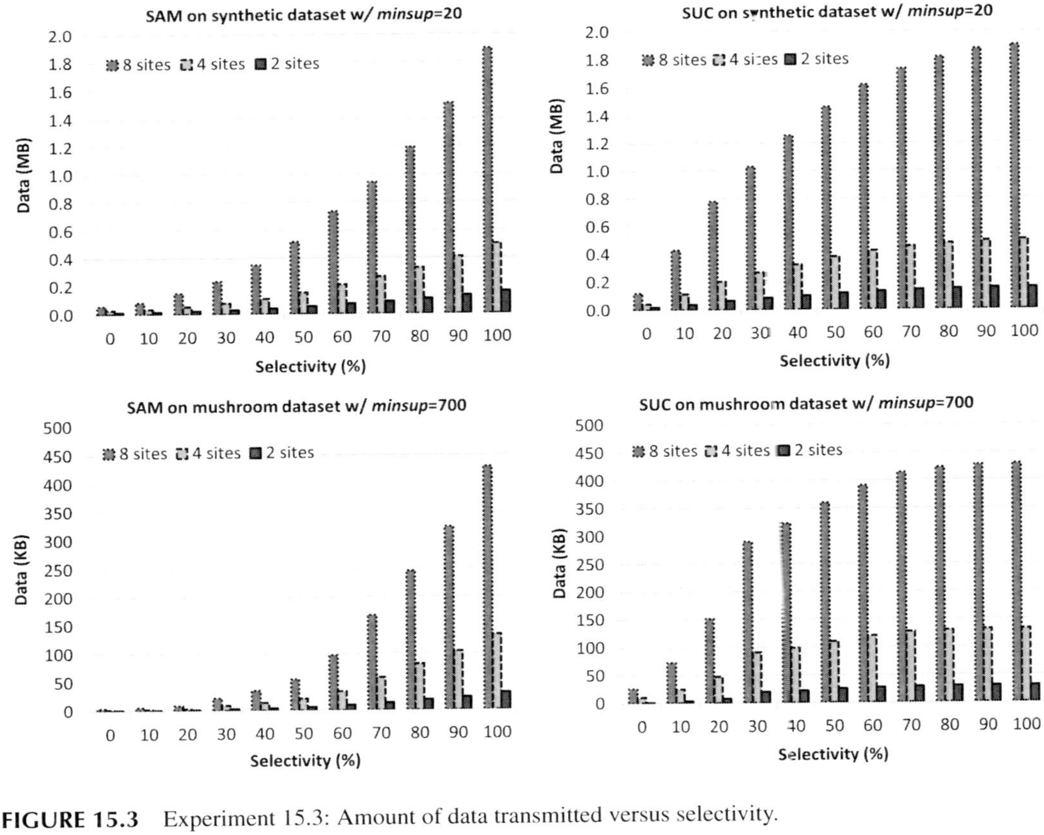

FIGURE 15.3 Experiment 15.3: Amount of data transmitted versus selectivity.

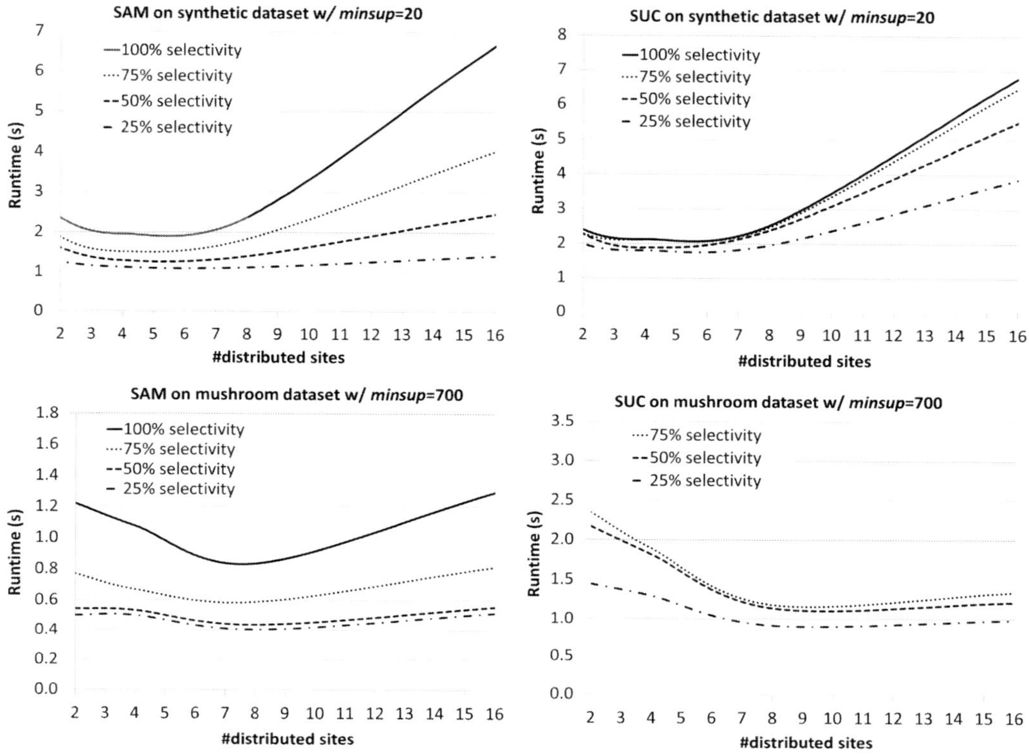

FIGURE 15.4 Experiment 15.4: Runtime versus number of sites.

satisfying SUC constraints consist of (i) those domain items that individually satisfy the constraints and (ii) optional items. Hence, the amount of data transmitted grew rapidly at the beginning (i.e., when selectivity was low). When selectivity kept increasing, the amount of data transmitted gradually became stable (as domain items in frequent itemsets are either in required or optional).

In Experiment 15.4, we evaluated the effects of varying the number of distributed sites. Recall from Figure 15.3 that, when more sites were in the distributed network, our algorithm transmitted more data because an addition of a site implies transmission of an additional set of locally frequent items and locally frequent itemsets. In other words, more sites in the network led to extra communication time. However, more sites led to smaller UF-trees that were built and mined at each site. Regarding runtime, there was trade-off between the communication cost and the tree construction/mining cost. We observed from Figure 15.4a and b that, when the number of sites increased from 1 to 2 and to 4, the mining on the synthetic dataset was distributed among multiple sites. As a result, less work was required at each individual site, where smaller UF-trees were built and mined. So, runtimes decreased. However, when the number of sites grew from 4 to 8 and to 16, the overhead due to extra communication cost offset the benefits of using extra sites. Consequently, runtimes increased. Figure 15.4c and d shows similar observation on mining the real-life mushroom databases except that (i) the runtimes decreased when the number of sites increased from 2 to 4 and to 8 and (ii) the times increased when the number of sites grew from 8 to 16.

In Experiment 15.5, we examined the effect of the distribution of existential probabilities of items. Recall that nodes are merged in a UF-tree if they contain the same item and same existential probability values. So, we divided the precision of existential probability values into 2%, 5%, and 10%. Figure 15.5 shows three versions of an IBM synthetic dataset having existential probability values in the range [10%, 100%]. When the precision is 2%, all existential probability values are multiples

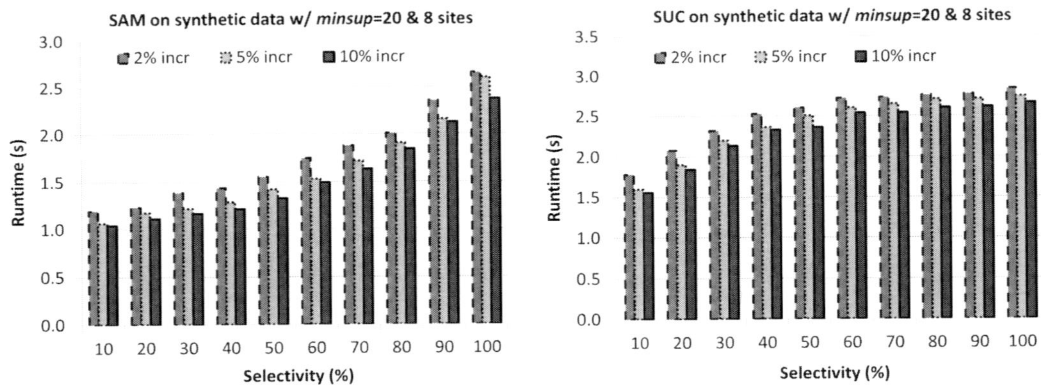

FIGURE 15.5 Experiment 15.5: Runtime versus probability distribution.

of 2% within that range (e.g., 10%, 12%, 14%, 16%, . . ., 98%, 100%) for a total of 46 unique existential probability values. Similarly, when the precision is 5% (or 10%), there are 19 (or 9) unique existential probability values. When items took on only a few unique existential probability values, UF-trees became smaller and thus took shorter runtimes.

In Experiment 15.6, we also tested the effect of *minsup*. When *minsup* increased, fewer itemsets had expected support $\geq$ *minsup*, and thus shorter runtimes were required for the experiment.

All these experimental results showed the importance and the benefits of using our proposed distributed algorithm in mining constrained frequent itemsets from uncertain data.

15.6.2 Experimenting the MapReduce-Based Algorithm for Supporting Constrained Mining over Uncertain Big Data in Cloud Environments

In this section, we focus the attention on the experimental assessment and analysis of the second algorithm embedded in our framework for supporting complex mining from uncertain big data.

We evaluated our proposed data analytic algorithm MrCloud in mining user-specified constraints from uncertain big data. We used various benchmark datasets, which include real-life datasets (e.g., accidents, connect4, and mushroom) from the *UCI Machine Learning Repository** and the FIMI Repository. We also used IBM synthetic datasets, which were generated using the IBM Quest Dataset Generator [57]. For our experiments, the generated data ranges from 2 M to 10 M transactions with an average transaction length of 10 items from a domain of 1 K items. As the above real-life and synthetic datasets originally contained only precise data, we assigned to each item contained in every transaction an existential probability from the range (0, 1].

All experiments were run using either (i) a single machine with an Intel Core i7 4-core processor (1.73 GHz) and 8 GB of main memory running a 64-bit Windows 7 operating system or (ii) the Amazon Elastic Compute Cloud (EC2) cluster—specifically, 11 High-Memory Extra Large (m2.xlarge) computing nodes.†

We implemented existing mining framework [78–80], UF-growth [74], tube-growth [75], BLIMP-growth [76], and our data analytic algorithm MrCloud all in the Java programming language. The stock version of Apache Hadoop 2.7.2 was used.

In Experiment 15.7, we demonstrated the functionality and capability of MrCloud by using (i) a database consisting of items all with existential probability value of 1.0 (indicating that all items are definitely present in the database) and (ii) a user-specified AM constraint. Experimental results show

* http://archive.ics.uci.edu/ml/
† http://aws.amazon.com/ec2/

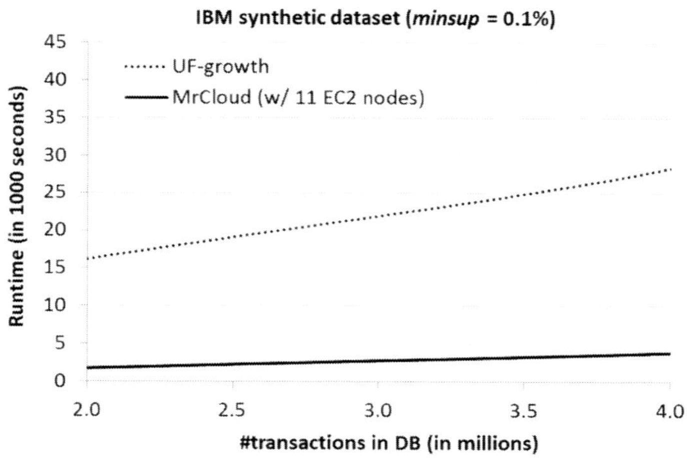

FIGURE 15.6 Experiment 15.9: Runtime versus #transactions.

that, in terms of accuracy, our data analytic algorithm returned the same collection of valid frequent patterns as those returned by the existing mining framework [78–80] for finding valid frequent patterns from precise data. Note that, in terms of flexibility, MrCloud is not confined to finding valid frequent patterns from a database in which existential probability values of all items are 1.0. MrCloud is capable of finding valid frequent patterns from any database, in which existential probability values of all items are ranging from 0 to 1.

In Experiment 15.8, we experimented with (i) an uncertain database and (ii) a user-specified AM constraint with 100% selectivity (so that every item is selected). Experimental results show that, in terms of accuracy, MrCloud returned the same collection of frequent patterns as those returned by UF-growth [74], tube-growth [75], and BLIMP-growth [76]. Note that, in terms of flexibility, MrCloud is not confined to handling AM constraints with 100% selectivity. MrCloud is capable of handling AM constraints with any selectivity.

In Experiment 15.9, we demonstrated the efficiency of MrCloud. Figure 15.6 shows that MrCloud took much shorter runtimes than the runtimes required by the existing UF-growth algorithm [74] when handling AM constraints with 100% selectivity because UF-growth was not designed to handle different selectivity of constraints. Hence, for a fair comparison, we used 100% selectivity for this experiment.

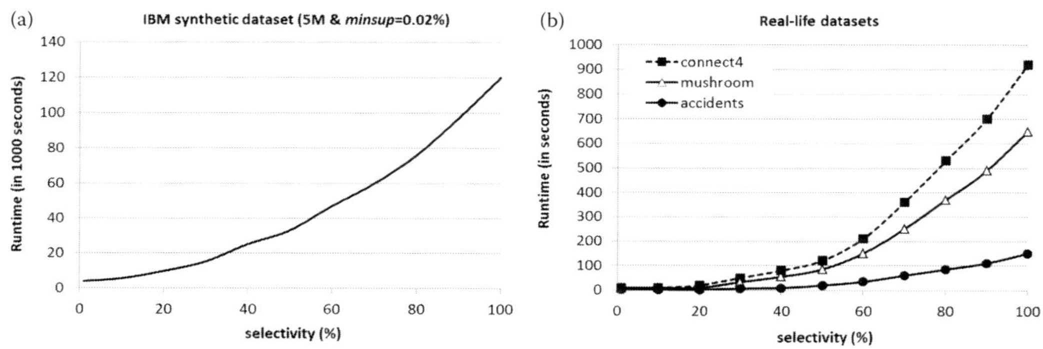

FIGURE 15.7 Experiment 15.10: Runtime versus selectivity on (a) synthetic dataset and (b) real-life datasets.

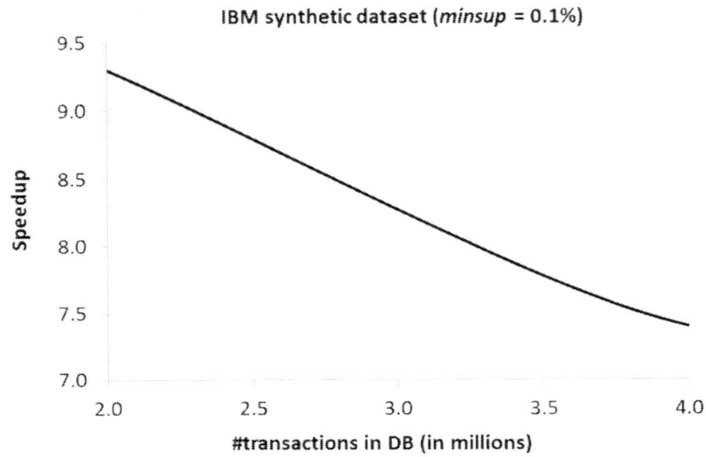

FIGURE 15.8 Experiment 15.11: Speedup versus #transactions.

In Experiment 15.10, we showed how the runtimes for MrCloud decreased when the selectivity increased (i.e., fewer patterns were selected). For the current experiment, MrCloud was run in the aforementioned EC2 cluster. As a MapReduce-based algorithm, MrCloud takes advantage of all 11 nodes in the EC2 cluster. In contrast, as a non-MapReduce-based algorithm, UF-growth was run on a single machine (i.e., does not take advantage of multiple nodes). This explains why MrCloud is faster than UF-growth. Moreover, the figure shows the scalability of MrCloud. When the number of transactions in the IBM synthetic dataset increased, the runtimes required by both MrCloud and UF-growth also increased. However, MrCloud required significantly lower runtimes than UF-growth. The same comments apply to other tested datasets (e.g., real-life accidents, connect4, and mushroom datasets). Figure 15.7a shows the benefits of constraint pushing in the big data-mining process than applying constraint pushing as a postprocessing step in the IBM synthetic dataset, while Figure 15.7b shows those for the three real-life accidents, connect4, and mushroom datasets. Both figures show that, when selectivity decreased (i.e., fewer frequent patterns satisfy the constraints), runtimes also decreased, because (i) fewer pairs were returned by the map function, (ii) fewer pairs were shuffled and sorted by the reduce function, and/or (iii) fewer constraint checks were performed.

In Experiment 15.11, we examined the speedup of MrCloud. Figure 15.8 shows that MrCloud led to high speedup (e.g., more than seven times for the IBM synthetic dataset) even with just 11 nodes when compared with UF-growth [74].

In Experiment 15.12, we examined the efficiency of MrCloud with respect to different values of *minsup*. Figure 15.9a shows the efficiency of MrCloud for the real-life accidents dataset: The runtimes of MrCloud decreased when the user-specified *minsup* increased. Consistent results are shown in Figure 15.9b and c for the real-life connect4 and mushroom datasets, respectively.

15.7 CONCLUSIONS AND FUTURE WORK

Big data are everywhere. Existing big data analytic algorithms discover frequent patterns from precise databases. However, there are situations in which data are uncertain. As items in each transaction of these uncertain data are usually associated with existential probabilities expressing the likelihood of these items to be present in the transaction, the corresponding search space for uncertain data is much larger than that for precise data. This matter is worsened when we are dealing with uncertain big data. Furthermore, in many real-life applications, users may be interested in only a tiny portion of this large search space, for instance like it happens with amounts of uncertain data obtained from

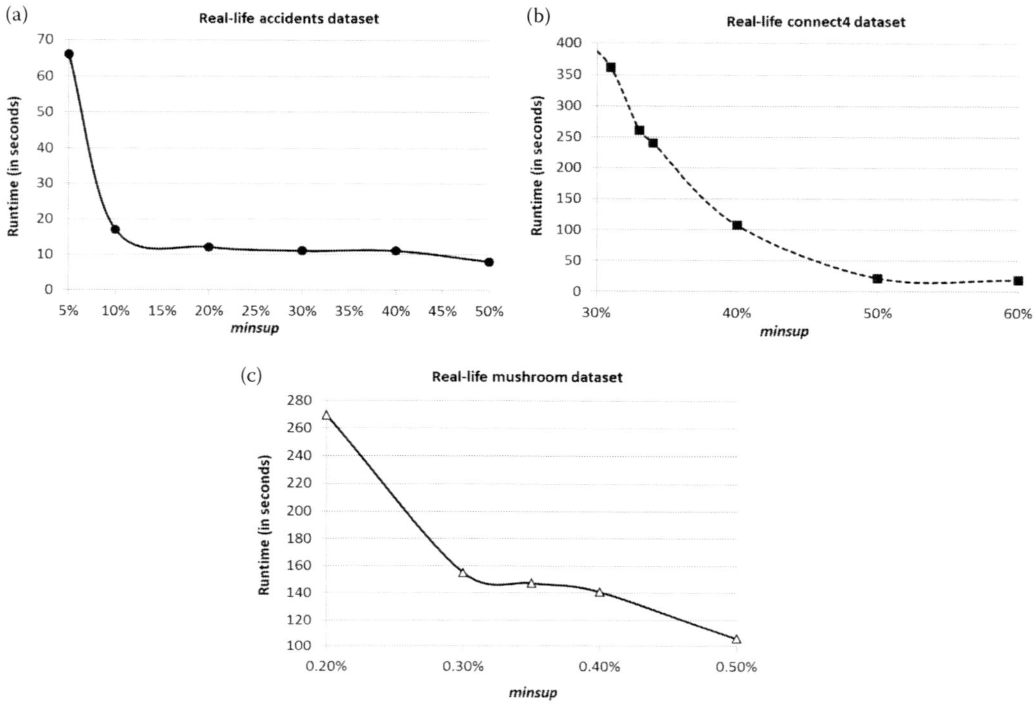

FIGURE 15.9 Experiment 15.12: Runtime versus *minsup* on (a) accidents, (b) connect4, and (c) mushroom datasets.

various sources such as networks of distributed wireless sensors, which have increased over the past few years. On the other hand, there are many real-life applications in which users are interested in only some subsets of all the frequent itemsets that can be mined from these high volumes of massive distributed uncertain data.

Inspired by these considerations, in this chapter, we have proposed a framework for supporting complex miming from uncertain big data targeted to distributed environments, which embeds the following two distinctive algorithms: (i) an algorithm for supporting tree-based mining of uncertain big data in distributed environments like clouds and even wireless sensor big data networks and (ii) a MapReduce-based algorithm for supporting constrained mining over uncertain big (transactional) data in cloud environments.

To find frequent itemsets that satisfy the user-specified constraints from these distributed uncertain data, the first algorithm introduces a tree-based mining approach, which is a nontrivial integration of constrained mining, parallel and distributed mining, uncertain data mining, and tree-based frequent itemset mining. The deriving algorithm handles different types of user-specified constraints. For instance, our algorithm first identifies domain items that satisfy succinct constraints at each distributed site and then constructs a UF-tree, from which constrained locally frequent itemsets can be mined recursively. To return to the user each constrained globally frequent itemset, its local frequencies at all sites are summed. Missing frequencies can be computed by traversing appropriate paths in essential UF-trees. In addition to succinct constraints, our algorithm also handles nonsuccinct constraints such as inductive succinct constraints and AM constraints.

MrCloud, the second algorithm embedded in our framework, allows users to query uncertain big data by expressing their interest, and processes the user-specified query by using the MapReduce model in cloud environments, thus avoids wasting lots of time and space by first discovering all frequent patterns and then pruning uninteresting ones at a postprocessing step. As an output, MrCloud discovers from uncertain big data all and only those patterns that are interesting to the users.

In addition to this, a comprehensive experimental campaign has clearly shown the effectiveness and the efficiency of our framework for supporting complex miming from uncertain big data in distributed environments.

Future work is mainly oriented to extend our framework to provide innovative adaptiveness metaphors. It is inspired by both traditional (e.g., [105]) and recent (e.g., [106]) studies.

REFERENCES

1. Cuzzocrea, A., D. Sacca, and J.D. Ullman. 2013. Big data: A research agenda. In *Proceedings of the IDEAS 2013*, Barcelona, Spain (pp. 198–203).
2. Kejariwal, A. 2012. Big data challenges: A program optimization perspective. In *Proceedings of the CGC 2012*, Xiangtan, China (pp. 702–707).
3. Madden, S. 2012. From databases to big data. *IEEE Internet Computing* 16(3):4–6.
4. Cuzzocrea, A., L. Bellatreche, and I. Song. 2013. Data warehousing and OLAP over big data: Current challenges and future research directions. In *Proceedings of the DOLAP 2013*, San Francisco, CA, USA (pp. 67–70).
5. Dubois, P.M.J., Z. Han, F. Jiang, and C.K. Leung. 2016. An interactive circular visual analytic tool for visualization of web data. In *Proceedings of the IEEE/WIC/ACM WI 2016*, Omaha, NE, USA (pp. 709–712).
6. Jiang, F., K. Kawagoe, and C.K. Leung. 2015. Big social network mining for "following" patterns. In *Proceedings of the C3S2E 2015*, Yokohama, Japan (pp. 28–37).
7. Kawagoe, K., and C.K. Leung. 2015. Similarities of frequent following patterns and social entities. *Procedia Computer Science* 60:642–651.
8. Leung, C.K., and F. Jiang. 2015. Big data analytics of social networks for the discovery of "following" patterns. In *Proceedings of the DaWaK 2015*, Valencia, Spain (pp. 123–135).
9. Ting, H.F., L.K. Lee, H.L. Chan, and T.W. Lam. 2011. Approximating frequent items in asynchronous data stream over a sliding window. *Algorithms* 4(3):200–222.
10. Cuzzocrea, A. 2013. Analytics over big data: Exploring the convergence of data warehousing, OLAP and data-intensive cloud infrastructures. In *Proceedings of the IEEE COMPSAC 2013*, Kyoto, Japan (pp. 481–483).
11. Kumar, A., F. Niu, and C. Re. 2013. Hazy: Making it easier to build and maintain big-data analytics. *ACM Queue* 11(1):30.
12. Leung, C.K., and Y. Hayduk. 2013. Mining frequent patterns from uncertain data with MapReduce for big data analytics. In *Proceedings of the DASFAA 2013, Part I*, Wuhan, China (pp. 440–455).
13. Leung, C.K., and F. Jiang. 2014. A data science solution for mining interesting patterns from uncertain big data. In *Proceedings of the IEEE BDCloud 2014*, Sydney, Australia (pp. 235–242).
14. Leung, C.K., F. Jiang, H. Zhang, and A.G.M. Pazdor. 2016. A data science model for big data analytics of frequent patterns. In *Proceedings of the IEEE DASC-PICom-DataCom-CyberSciTech 2016*, Auckland, New Zealand (pp. 866–873).
15. Leung, C.K., and R.K. MacKinnon. 2014. Reducing the search space for big data mining for interesting patterns from uncertain data. In *Proceedings of the IEEE BigData Congress 2014*, Anchorage, AK, USA (pp. 315–322).
16. Dean, J., and S. Ghemawat. 2008. MapReduce: Simplified data processing on large clusters. *Communications of the ACM* 51(1):107–113.
17. Cuzzocrea, A., C.K. Leung, and R.K. MacKinnon. 2014. Mining constrained frequent itemsets from distributed uncertain data. *Future Generation Computer Systems* 37:117–126.
18. Leung, C.K., R.K. MacKinnon, and F. Jiang. 2014. Distributed uncertain data mining for frequent patterns satisfying anti-monotonic constraints. In *Proceedings of the IEEE AINA Workshops 2014*, Victoria, BC, Canada (pp. 1–6).
19. Leung, C.K., and H. Zhang. 2016. Management of distributed big data for social networks. In *Proceedings of the IEEE/ACM CCGrid 2016*, Cartagena, Colombia (pp. 639–648).

20. Zaki, M.J. 1999. Parallel and distributed association mining: A survey. *IEEE Concurrency* 7(4):14–25.
21. Ibrahim, A., H. Jin, A. Yassin, and D. Zou. 2012. Towards privacy preserving mining over distributed cloud databases. In *Proceedings of the CGC 2012*, Xiangtan, China (pp. 130–136).
22. Ismail, L., and L. Zhang. 2012. Modeling and performance analysis to predict the behavior of a divisible load application in a cloud computing environment. *Algorithms* 5(2):289–303.
23. Wang, L., Y. Wang, and Y. Xie. 2015. Implementation of a parallel algorithm based on a Spark cloud computing platform. *Algorithms* 8(3):407–414.
24. Bendler, J., S. Wagner, T. Brandt, and D. Neumann. 2014. Taming uncertainty in big data—Evidence from social media in urban areas. *Business & Information Systems Engineering* 6(5):279–288.
25. He, Q., H. Wang, F. Zhuang, T. Shang, and Z. Shi. 2015. Parallel sampling from big data with uncertainty distribution. *Fuzzy Sets and Systems* 258:117–133.
26. Li, X., Y. Wang, X. Li, X. Wang, and J. Yu. 2014. GDPS: An efficient approach for skyline queries over distributed uncertain data. *Big Data Research* 1:23–36.
27. Li, Y., R. Wang, and S.C.K. Shiu. 2015. Interval extreme learning machine for big data based on uncertainty reduction. *Journal of Intelligent and Fuzzy Systems* 28(5):2391–2403.
28. Nguyen, H.T.H., and J. Cao. 2015. Trustworthy answers for top-k queries on uncertain big data in decision making. *Information Sciences* 318:73–90.
29. Strauss, S. 2015. Datafication and the seductive power of uncertainty—A critical exploration of big data enthusiasm. *Information* 6(4):836–847.
30. Wang, R., Y.L. He, C.Y. Chow, F.F. Ou, and J. Zhang. 2015. Learning ELM-tree from big data based on uncertainty reduction. *Fuzzy Sets and Systems* 258(1):79–100.
31. Collins, E. 2014. Intersection of the cloud and big data. *IEEE Cloud Computing* 1(1):84–85.
32. de Assuncao, M.D., R.N. Calheiros, S. Bianchi, M.A.S. Netto, and R. Buyya. 2015 Big data computing and clouds: Trends and future directions. *Journal of Parallel and Distributed Computing* 79–80:3–15.
33. Dong, F., and A. Malloy. 2015. Recent research advances in cloud computing and big data. *Concurrency and Computation: Practice and Experience* 27(18):5574–5576.
34. Fernandez, A., S. del Rio, V. Lopez, A. Bawakid, M.J. del Jesus, J.M. Benitez, and F. Herrera. 2014. Big data with cloud computing: An insight on the computing environment, MapReduce, and programming frameworks. *Wiley Interdisciplinary Review: Data Mining and Knowledge Discovery* 4(5): 380–409.
35. Hashem, I.A.T., I. Yaqoob, N.B. Anuar, S. Mokhtar, A. Gani, and S.U. Khan. 2015. The rise of 'big data' on cloud computing: Review and open research issues. *Information Systems* 47:98–115.
36. Cuzzocrea, A. 2014. Big data mining or turning data mining into predictive analytics from large-scale 3Vs data: The future challenge for knowledge discovery. In *Proceedings of the MEDI 2014*, Larnaca, Cyprus (pp. 4–8).
37. Fan, W., and A. Bifet. 2012. Mining big data: Current status, and forecast to the future. *ACM SIGKDD Explorations* 14(2):1–5.
38. Lin, J.J., and D.V. Ryaboy. 2012. Scaling big data mining infrastructure: The twitter experience. *ACM SIGKDD Explorations* 14(2):6–19.
39. Simmen, D.E., K. Schnaitter, J. Davis, Y. He, S. Lohariwala, A. Mysore, V. Shenoi, M. Tan, and Y. Xiao. 2014. Large-scale graph analytics in aster 6: Bringing context to big data discovery. *PVLDB* 7(13):1405–1416.
40. Wu, X., X. Zhu, G.Q. Wu, and W. Ding. 2014. Data mining with big data. *IEEE Transactions on Knowledge and Data Engineering* 26(1):97–107.
41. Chen, J., K. Li, Z. Tang, K. Bilal, and K. Li. 2016. A parallel patient treatment time prediction algorithm and its applications in hospital queuing-recommendation in a big data environment. *IEEE Access* 4(1):1767–1783.
42. Jiang, F., C.K. Leung, and A.G.M. Pazdor. 2016. Web page recommendation based on bitwise frequent pattern mining. In *Proceedings of the IEEE/WIC/ACM WI 2016*, Omaha, NE, USA (pp. 632–635).
43. Zhang, Z., H. Fang, and H. Wang. 2016. A new MI-based visualization aided validation index for mining big longitudinal web trial data. *IEEE Access* 4:2272–2280.
44. Chowdhury, N.K., and C.K. Leung. 2011. Improved travel time prediction algorithms for intelligent transportation systems. In *Proceedings of the KES 2011, Part II*, Kaiserslautern, Germany (pp. 355–365).
45. Xia, D., H. Li, B. Wang, Y. Li, and Z. Zhang. 2016. A Map Reduce-based nearest neighbor approach for big-data-driven traffic flow prediction. *IEEE Access* 4:2920–2934.

46. Abouelela, M., and M. El-Darieby. 2016. Scheduling big data applications within advance reservation framework in optical grids. *Applied Soft Computing* 38(1):1049–1059.
47. Lee, W., C.K. Leung, and J.J.H. Lee. 2011. Mobile web navigation in digital ecosystems using rooted directed trees. *IEEE Transactions on Industrial Electronics* 58(6):2154–2162.
48. Yang, X., R. Lu, H. Liang, and X. Tang. 2016. SFPM: A secure and fine-grained privacy-preserving matching protocol for mobile social networking. *Big Data Research* 3:2–9.
49. Jiang, F., and C.K. Leung. 2015. A data analytic algorithm for managing, querying, and processing uncertain big data in cloud environments. *Algorithms* 8(4):1175–1194.
50. Cameron, J.J., A. Cuzzocrea, F. Jiang, and C.K. Leung. 2013. Mining frequent itemsets from sparse data streams in limited memory environments. In *Proceedings of the WAIM 2013*, Beidaihe, China (pp. 51–57).
51. Cem, E., and O. Ozkasap. 2013. ProFID: Practical frequent items discovery in peer-to-peer networks. *Future Generation Computer Systems* 29(6):1544–1560.
52. Leung, C.K., and C.L. Carmichael. 2010. Exploring social networks: A frequent pattern visualization approach. In *Proceedings of the SocialCom 2010*, Minneapolis, MN, USA (pp. 419–424).
53. Cameron, J.J., A. Cuzzocrea, F. Jiang, and C.K. Leung. 2014. Frequent pattern mining from dense graph streams. In *Proceedings of the EDBT/ICDT 2014 Workshops*, Athens, Greece (pp. 240–247).
54. Chorley, M.J., G.B. Colombo, S.M. Allen, and R.M. Whitaker. 2013. Visiting patterns and personality of foursquare users. In *Proceedings of the IEEE CGC 2013*, Karlsruhe, Germany (pp. 271–276).
55. Cuzzocrea, A., F. Jiang, W. Lee, and C.K. Leung. 2014. Efficient frequent itemset mining from dense data streams. In *Proceedings of the APWeb 2014*, Changsha, China (pp. 593–601).
56. Agrawal, R., T. Imielinski, and A. Swami. 1993. Mining association rules between sets of items in large databases. In *Proceedings of the ACM SIGMOD 1993*, Washington, DC, USA (pp. 207–216).
57. Agrawal, R., and R. Srikant. 1994. Fast algorithms for mining association rules. In *Proceedings of the VLDB 1994*, Santiago de Chile, Chile (pp. 487–499).
58. Han, J., J. Pei, Y. Yin, and R. Mao. 2004. Mining frequent patterns without candidate generation: A frequent-pattern tree approach. *Data Mining and Knowledge Discovery* 8(1):53–87.
59. Ke, J., Y. Zhan, X. Chen, and M. Wang. 2013. The retrieval of motion event by associations of temporal frequent pattern growth. *Future Generation Computer Systems* 29(1):442–450.
60. Leung, C.K., and S.K. Tanbeer. 2013. PUF-tree: A compact tree structure for frequent pattern mining of uncertain data. In *Proceedings of the PAKDD 2013, Part I*, Gold Coast, Australia (pp. 13–25).
61. Cameron, J.J., and C.K. Leung. 2011. Frequent patterns from precise and uncertain data. *Computing and System Journal (RSC)* 1(1):3–22.
62. Cuzzocrea, A. 2011. Retrieving accurate estimates to OLAP queries over uncertain and imprecise multidimensional data streams. In *Proceedings of the SSDBM 2011*, Portland, OR, USA (pp. 575–576).
63. Cuzzocrea, A. 2013. Approximate OLAP query processing over uncertain and imprecise multidimensional data streams. In *Proceedings of the DEXA 2013, Part II*, Prague, Czech Republic (pp. 156–173).
64. Cuzzocrea, A., F. Furfaro, F., and D. Sacca. Hand-OLAP: A system for delivering OLAP services on handheld devices. In *Proceedings of the ISADS 2003*, Pisa, Italy (pp. 80–87).
65. Leung, C.K., and B. Hao. 2009. Mining of frequent itemsets from streams of uncertain data. In *Proceedings of the IEEE ICDE 2009*, Shanghai, China (pp. 1663–1670).
66. Tong, W., C.K. Leung, D. Liu, and J. Yu. 2015. Probabilistic frequent pattern mining by PUH-Mine. In *Proceedings of the APWeb 2015*, Guangzhou, China (pp. 781–793).
67. Sarangi, S.R. and K. Murthy. 2010. DUST: A generalized notion of similarity between uncertain time series. In *Proceedings of the ACM KDD 2010*, Washington, DC, USA (pp. 383–392).
68. Bernecker, T., H.-P. Kriegel, M. Renz, F. Verhein, and A. Zuefle. 2009. Probabilistic frequent itemset mining in uncertain databases. In *Proceedings of the ACM KDD 2009*, Paris, France (pp. 119–127).
69. Jiang, F., and C.K. Leung. 2013. Stream mining of frequent patterns from delayed batches of uncertain data. In *Proceedings of the DaWaK 2013*, Prague, Czech Republic (pp. 209–221).
70. Leung, C.K., A. Cuzzocrea, and F. Jiang. 2013. Discovering frequent patterns from uncertain data streams with time-fading and landmark models. *Transactions on Large-Scale Data- and Knowledge-Centered Systems* 8:174–196.
71. Leung, C.K., and R.K. MacKinnon. 2015. Balancing tree size and accuracy in fast mining of uncertain frequent patterns. In *Proceedings of the DaWaK 2015*, Valencia, Spain (pp. 57–69).
72. Tong, Y., L. Chen, Y. Cheng, and P.S. Yu. 2012. Mining frequent itemsets over uncertain databases. *PVLDB* 5(11):1650–1661.

73. Chui, C., B. Kao, and E. Hung. 2007. Mining frequent itemsets from uncertain data. In *Proceedings of the PAKDD 2007*, Nanjing, China (pp. 47–58).
74. Leung, C.K., M.A.F. Mateo, and D.A. Brajczuk. 2008. A tree-based approach for frequent pattern mining from uncertain data. In *Proceedings of the PAKDD 2008*, Osaka, Japan (pp. 653–661).
75. Leung, C.K., R.K. MacKinnon, and S.K. Tanbeer. 2014. Fast algorithms for frequent itemset mining from uncertain data. In *Proceedings of the IEEE ICDM 2014*, Shenzhen, China (pp. 893–898).
76. Leung, C.K., and R.K. MacKinnon. 2014. BLIMP: A compact tree structure for uncertain frequent pattern mining. In *Proceedings of the DaWaK 2014*, Munich, Germany (pp. 115–123).
77. Grahne, G., L.V.S. Lakshmanan, and X. Wang. 2000. Efficient mining of constrained correlated sets. In *Proceedings of the IEEE ICDE 2000*, Long Beach, CA, USA (pp. 512–521).
78. Leung, C.K. 2009. Frequent itemset mining with constraints. In *Encyclopedia of Database Systems* (pp. 1179–1183).
79. Ng, R.T., L.V.S. Lakshmanan, J. Han, and A. Pang. 1998. Exploratory mining and pruning optimizations of constrained associations rules. In *Proceedings of the ACM SIGMOD 1998*, Seattle, WA, USA (pp. 13–24).
80. Lakshmanan, L.V.S., C.K. Leung, and R.T. Ng. 2003. Efficient dynamic mining of constrained frequent sets. *ACM Transactions on Database Systems* 28(4):337–389.
81. Pei, J., J. Han, and L.V.S. Lakshmanan. 2004. Pushing convertible constraints in frequent itemset mining. *Data Mining and Knowledge Discovery* 8(3):227–252.
82. Cuzzocrea, A., and P. Serafino. 2009. LCS-Hist: Taming massive high-dimensional data cube compression. In *Proceedings of the EDBT 2009*, Saint Petersburg, Russia (pp. 768–779).
83. Bonifati, A., and A. Cuzzocrea. 2006. Storing and retrieving XPath fragments in structured P2P networks. *Data & Knowledge Engineering* 59(2):247–269.
84. Yu, B., A. Cuzzocrea, D.H. Jeong, and S. Maydebura. 2012. On managing very large sensor-network data using Bigtable. In *Proceedings of the IEEE/ACM CCGrid 2012*, Ottawa, ON, Canada (pp. 918–922).
85. Faro, A., D. Giordano, and F. Maiorana. 2011. Mining massive datasets by an unsupervised parallel clustering on a GRID: Novel algorithms and case study. *Future Generation Computer Systems* 27(1):711–724.
86. Secretan, J., M. Georgiopoulos, A. Koufakou, and K. Cardona. 2010. APHID: An architecture for private, high-performance integrated data mining. *Future Generation Computer Systems* 26(7):891–904.
87. Swain, M.T., C.G. Silva, N. Loureiro-Ferreira, V. Ostropytskyy, J. Brito, O. Riche, F. Stahl, W. Dubitzky, and R.M.M. Brito. 2010. P-found: Grid-enabling distributed repositories of protein folding and unfolding simulations for data mining. *Future Generation Computer Systems* 26(3):424–433.
88. Schuster, A., R. Wolff, and D. Trock. 2005. A high-performance distributed algorithm for mining association rules. *Knowledge and Information Systems* 7(4):458–475.
89. Agrawal, R., and J. Shafer. 1996. Parallel mining of association rules. *IEEE Transactions on Knowledge and Data Engineering* 8(6):962–969.
90. Cheung, D.W., J. Han, V.T. Ng, A.W. Fu, and Y. Fu. 1996. A fast distributed algorithm for mining association rules. In *Proceedings of the PDIS 1996*, Miami Beach, FL, USA (pp. 31–42).
91. El-Hajj, M., and O.R. Zaiane. Parallel leap: Large-scale maximal pattern mining in a distributed environment. In *Proceedings of the ICPADS 2006*, Minneapolis, MN, USA (pp. 135–142).
92. Kozawa, Y., T. Amagasa, and H. Kitagawa. 2012. GPU acceleration of probabilistic frequent itemset mining from uncertain databases. In *Proceedings of the ACM CIKM 2012*, Maui, HI, USA (pp. 892–901).
93. Cuzzocrea, A., and C.K. Leung. 2011. Distributed mining of constrained frequent sets from uncertain data. In *Proceedings of the ICA3PP 2011, Part I*, Melbourne, Australia (pp. 40–53).
94. Cuzzocrea, A., and C.K. Leung. 2012. Frequent itemset mining of distributed uncertain data under user-defined constraints. In *Proceedings of the SEBD 2012*, Venice, Italy (pp. 243–250).
95. Alvi, A.K., and M. Zulkernine. 2011. A natural classification scheme for software security patterns. In *Proceedings of the IEEE DASC 2011*, Sydney, Australia (pp. 113–120).
96. Meng, Q., and P.J. Kennedy. 2012. Determining the number of clusters in co-authorship networks using social network theory. In *Proceedings of the CGC 2012*, Xiangtan, China (pp. 337–343).
97. Fariha, A., C.F. Ahmed, C.K. Leung, M. Samiullah, S. Pervin, and L. Cao. 2015. A new framework for mining frequent interaction patterns from meeting databases. *Engineering Applications of Artificial Intelligence* 45:103–118.

98. Jiang, F., C.K. Leung, and R.K. MacKinnon. 2014. BigSAM: Mining interesting patterns from probabilistic databases of uncertain big data. In *Proceedings of the PAKDD 2014 Workshops*, Tainan, Taiwan (pp. 780–792).
99. Aggarwal, C.C., Y. Li, J. Wang, and J. Wang. 2009. Frequent pattern mining with uncertain data. In *Proceedings of the ACM KDD 2009*, Paris, France (pp. 29–37).
100. Leung, C.K. 2011. Mining uncertain data. *WIREs Data Mining and Knowledge Discovery* 1(4):316–329.
101. Leung, C.K. 2013. Mining frequent itemsets from probabilistic datasets. In *Proceedings of the EDB 2013*, Jeju Island, South Korea (pp. 137–148).
102. Leung, C.K. 2014. Uncertain frequent pattern mining. In *Frequent Pattern Mining* (pp. 417–453).
103. Lin, M.Y., P.Y. Lee, and S.C. Hsueh. 2012. Apriori-based frequent itemset mining algorithms on MapReduce. In *Proceedings of the ACM ICUIMC 2012*, Kuala Lumpur, Malaysia (art. 76)
104. Riondato, M., J. DeBrabant, R. Fonseca, and E. Upfal. 2012. PARMA: A parallel randomized algorithm for approximate association rules mining in MapReduce. In *Proceedings of the ACM CIKM 2012*, Maui, HI, USA (pp. 85–94).
105. Cannataro, M., A. Cuzzocrea, and A. Pugliese. 2002. XAHM: An adaptive hypermedia model based on XML. In *Proceedings of the SEKE 2002*, Ischia, Italy (pp. 627–634).
106. Pop, F., and M. Potop-Butucaru. 2016. ARMCO: Advanced topics in resource management for ubiquitous cloud computing: An adaptive approach. *Future Generation Computer Systems* 54:79–81.

16 Clustering in Big Data

Min Chen, Simone A. Ludwig, and Keqin Li

CONTENTS

ABSTRACT

The need to understand large, complex, information-rich data sets is common to all fields of studies in this current information age. Given this tremendous amount of data, efficient and effective tools need to be present to analyze and reveal valuable knowledge that is hidden within the data. Clustering analysis is one of the popular approaches in data mining and has been widely used in big data analysis. The goal of clustering involves the task of dividing data points into homogeneous groups such that the data points in the same group are as similar as possible and data points in different groups are as dissimilar as possible. The importance of clustering is documented in pattern recognition, machine learning, image analysis, information retrieval, etc.

Due to the difficulties of parallelization of the clustering algorithms and the inefficiency at large scales, challenges for applying clustering techniques in big data have arisen. The question is how to deploy clustering algorithms to this tremendous amount of data to get the clustering result within a reasonable time. This chapter provides an overview of the mainstream clustering techniques proposed over the past decade and the trend and progress of clustering algorithms applied in big data. Moreover, the improvement of clustering algorithms in big data is introduced and analyzed.

The possible future for more advanced clustering techniques is illuminated on the basis of today's information era.

16.1 INTRODUCTION

16.1.1 Application Background

An overwhelming flow of data in a structured, unstructured, or heterogeneous format has been accumulated due to the continuous increase in the volume and detail of data captured by organizations, such as social media, government, industry, and science. These massive quantities of data are produced because of the growth of the Web, the rise of social media, the use of mobile, and the information of Internet of Things (IoT) by and about people, things, and their interactions. The big data era has arrived. Big data becomes the most influential force in daily life. According to the IDC reports, the digital universe is doubling in size every 2 years and it will reach 44 zettabytes by 2020 [1].

How to store huge amounts of data is not the biggest problem anymore. But how to design solutions to understand this big amount of data is a major challenge. Operations such as analytical operations, process operations, retrieval operations are very difficult and hugely time consuming because of this massive volume of data. One solution to overcome these problems is the use of data-mining techniques in discovering knowledge from big data. Data mining [2] is called exploratory data analysis, among other things. It is an analytic process designed to explore data. Data mining aims to search for consistent patterns or systematic relationships between variables. It then validates the findings by applying the detected patterns to new subsets of data. Although the hidden patterns are derived from heterogeneous data in big data mining, these hidden patterns can still be reviewed as structured knowledge. The structured knowledge is combined with human knowledge of decision makers that are heterogeneous or unstructured and upgraded into intelligent knowledge [3].

16.1.2 Big Data Challenge

The term of big data [4] that refers to large database has a comprehensive definition through the 3Vs of big data: volume, variety, and velocity. Garter [5] extended this 3Vs model to a 4Vs mode by including a new "V": value. More recently, this model has been updated to 5Vs [6]: volume, velocity, variety, veracity, and value. Where *volume* refers to the vast amounts of data generated every second. *Velocity* refers to the speed at which new data is generated and the speed at which data moves around. *Variety* refers to the different types of data, such as structured, unstructured, and heterogeneous data, and different source of data that can be used. *Veracity* refers to the messiness or trustworthiness of the data. Quality and accuracy are less controllable with different forms of big data. *Value* refers to how the data can be turned into value. It is the process of discovering hidden values of big data sets, which then documents and socializes as realized values. Challenges of big data have been arisen because of its 5Vs characteristics [7]:

Volume: Massive data has been produced by the increased use of emails, twitter messages, photos, video clips, and sensor data. This massive data is too large to store and is hard to analyze using traditional database technology. The challenge is how to determine the relevance within large data volumes and how to extract valuable information from the relevant data.

Velocity: Another change of big data is how to response quickly to data and deal with it in a reasonable time. Techniques on analyzing the data while it is being generated without ever putting it into databases are urgent in the field of big data study.

Variety: Data comes from different sources with different specifications such as Twitter, Facebook, LinkedIn, and instant messaging in a complex and heterogeneous format.

Another challenge issue is how to manage, merge, and govern the different forms of data.

Complexity: Quality and accuracy are less controllable due to the different sources and different structures of data. It becomes really complicate to connect and associate from heterogeneous data to extract useful information and thus improvements on exploiting this huge amount of data are very wide and dispersed. Data complexity increases with the increase in volume. The traditional data managements with relational database tools are no longer sufficient to meet the requirements to capture, store, and further analyze big data.

16.1.3 Big Data Clustering Analysis

The speed of information growth exceeds Moore's Law at the beginning of this new century. Given this tremendous amount of data, efficient and effective tools need to be present to analyze and reveal valuable knowledge that is hidden within the data. Techniques from data mining are well-known knowledge discovery tools for this purpose. Clustering is one of the popular approaches in data mining and has been widely used in big data analysis. The goal of clustering involves the task of dividing data points into homogeneous groups such that the data points in the same group are as similar as possible and data points in different groups are as dissimilar as possible.

However, conventional clustering techniques cannot cope with this huge amount of data because of their high complexity and computational cost [8]. The question for big data clustering is how to scale up and speed up clustering algorithms with minimum sacrifice to the clustering quality. Therefore, an efficient processing model with a reasonable computational cost of this huge, complex, dynamic, and heterogeneous data is needed in order to exploit this huge amount of data. Single-machine clustering techniques and multiple-machine clustering techniques are two most popular big data clustering techniques. Single-machine clustering algorithms run in one machine and can use resources of just one single machine while the multimachine clustering [8] techniques run in several machines and can have access to more resources. Multimachine clustering techniques become more popular due to the better scalability and faster response time to the users.

16.1.4 Chapter Organization

The rest of the chapter is organized as follows: the main stream clustering algorithms and key technologies for clustering in big data are introduced in Section 16.2. The instances of clustering techniques that have been used in single-machine clustering and multimachine clustering are illustrated in Section 16.3. The applications of big data clustering including image segmentation, load balancing in parallel computing, genetic mapping, and community detention are discussed in Section 16.4. Finally, the chapter is concluded in Section 16.5.

16.2 OVERVIEW OF CLUSTERING TECHNIQUES IN BIG DATA

16.2.1 General Information of Clustering Analysis

Clustering is one of the most fundamental tasks in exploratory data analysis that groups similar data points in an unsupervised process. Clustering techniques have been exploited in many fields including in many areas, such as data mining, pattern recognition, machine learning, biochemistry, and bioinformatics [9]. The main process of clustering algorithms is to divide a set of unlabeled data objects into different groups. The cluster membership measure is based on a similarity measure. In order to obtain high-quality partition, the similarity measure between the data objects in the same group is to be maximized and the similarity measure between the data objects from different groups is to be minimized. Most of the clustering task uses an iterative process to find locally or globally optimal solutions from high-dimensional data sets. In addition, there is no unique clustering solution for real-life data and it is also hard to interpret the "cluster" representations [9]. Therefore, clustering task requires many experiments with different algorithms or with different features of the same data set. Hence, how to save computational complexity is a significant issue for the clustering algorithms. Moreover, clustering very large data sets that contain large numbers of records with high dimensions is considered a very important issue nowadays. Most conventional clustering algorithms suffer from the problem that they do not scale with larger sizes of data sets, and most of them are computationally expensive in memory space and time complexities. For these reasons, the parallelization of clustering algorithms is a practical approach to overcome the aforementioned problems, and the parallel implementation of clustering algorithms is somewhat inevitable.

More importantly, clustering analysis is distinguished with other analysis [9]. Clustering analysis is called unsupervised learning. The main goal is to divide a set of unlabeled data sets into several groups based on the conceptual or hidden properties of the input data sets. In the other word, clustering analysis is unsupervised "nonpredictive" learning. It divides the data sets into several clusters on their subjective measurements. It is unlike supervised learning and it is not based on the "trained characterization." In general, there are a set of desirable features for a clustering algorithm [9,10]: *scalability*, the temporal and spatial complexity of the algorithm should not explode on large data sets; *robustness*, the outliers in the data set should be detected during the process; *order insensitivity*, the ordering of the input data should not affect the outcome of the algorithm; *minimum user-specified input*, the number of user-specified parameters should be minimized; *arbitrary-shaped clusters*, the clusters can be shaped arbitrary; and *point proportion admissibility*, different clustering algorithms produce different results with different features. Hence, a clustering algorithm should be chosen such that duplicating data set and re-clustering task should not change the clustering results.

16.2.2 Mainstream Clustering Algorithms

Depending on the data properties or the purpose of clustering, different types of clustering algorithms have been developed [10]:

Partitioning: clustering requires a fixed number of clusters to be specified a priori. Objective functions such as square error function are used as a criterion in the optimization process of data partitioning. Partitioning clustering uses an iterative process to optimize the cluster centers, as well as the number of clusters.

Hierarchical: clustering does not specify the number of clusters, and the output is independent of the initial condition. However, the hierarchical clustering is static, that is, the data points assigned to a cluster cannot be reassigned to another cluster. In addition, it will fail to separate overlapping clusters due to the lack of information regarding the global shape or size of the clusters.

Density-based: clustering separates data objects based on their regions of density, connectivity, and boundary. The clusters are defined as connected dense component which can grow in any direction that density leads to. Density-based clustering is good for discovering clusters of arbitrary shapes and it can provide a natural protection against outliers.

Grid-based: clustering divides the space of data objects into grids. It is capable to go through the data set once to compute the statistical values for the grids with a fast-processing time. However, the performance of grid-based clustering depends on the size of the grid; it is insufficient to obtain the required clustering quality for highly irregular data distributions.

Model-based: clustering assumes that the data is generated by a mixture of underlying probability distributions. It is a method which is used to optimize the fit between the given data and the predefined mathematical model. One advantage of model-based clustering is that it can automatically determine the number of clusters based on standard statistics.

Evolutionary: clustering approaches use genetic algorithm, particle swarm optimization, and other evolutionary approach for clustering task. For example, genetic algorithm uses evolutionary operators (such as selection, crossover, and mutation) and a population to obtain the optimal partition of the input data. Evolutionary approaches are stochastic and use an iterative process. These algorithms start with a random population of solutions, which is a valid partition of data with a fitness value. In the iterative step, the evolutionary operators are applied to generate the new population. A population's likelihood of surviving into the next iteration is determined by a fitness function. The iterative step is repeated until it finds the required solution meeting some stop criteria.

16.2.3 Key Technologies for Clustering in Big Data

Unlike traditional clustering algorithms, the volume of data must be taken into account when clustering big data because this requires substantial changes in the architecture of a storage system. In addition, most of traditional clustering algorithms are designed to handle either numeric or categorical data with limited size. On the other hand, big data clustering deals with different types of data such as image, video, sensors, mobile devices, text, etc. [11,12]. Moreover, the velocity of big data requires that the big data clustering techniques have a high demand for the online processing of data. At the high level of the five categories of clustering algorithms, most of the algorithms have a similar procedure. These algorithms start with some random initialization and follow with some iterative process until some convergence criteria are met. For example, partitioned clustering such as k-means algorithm starts with randomly choosing k centroids and reassigns each data point to the closest cluster centroids in an iterative process. Thus, the issue of the big data clustering is how to speed up and scale up the clustering algorithms with the minimum sacrifice to the clustering quality. There are three ways to speed up and scale up big data clustering algorithms.

The first way is to reduce the iterative process using sampling-based algorithms. Sampling-based algorithms perform clustering algorithms on a sample of the data sets instead of performing on the whole data set. Complexity and memory space needed for the process decrease in sampling-based algorithms because computation needs to take place only for smaller sample data sets. PAM, CLARA, and CLARANS [9–12] are proposed to fight with the exponential search space in the k-medoid clustering problem.

The second way is to reduce the data dimension using randomized techniques. Dimensionality of the data set is another aspect, which influences the complexity and speed of clustering algorithms. Random projection and global projection are used to project data set from a high-dimensional space to a lower-dimensional space [8,12]. CX/CUR, CMD, and Colibri [8,12] are dimension reduction techniques, which are proposed to reduce long execution time of big data clustering.

The last way is to apply parallel and distributed algorithms, which use multiple machines to speed up the computation in order to increase the scalability. Parallel processing applications include conventional parallel application and data-intensive applications. The conventional parallel applications assume that data can be fit into the memory of distributed machines. Data-intensive applications are I/O bound and devote the largest fraction of execution time to movement of data. OpenMP, MPI [13], and MapReduce are common parallel processing models for computing data-intensive applications.

16.3 INSTANCES OF CLUSTERING TECHNIQUES IN BIG DATA

In this section, we will list some clustering techniques, which are designed for large-scale data sets. There are mainly two types of techniques based on the number of computer nodes that have been used: single-machine techniques and multimachine techniques. Due to the nature of scalability and faster response time to the users, multimachine clustering techniques have attracted more attention. A list of common big data clustering techniques is shown in Figure 16.1.

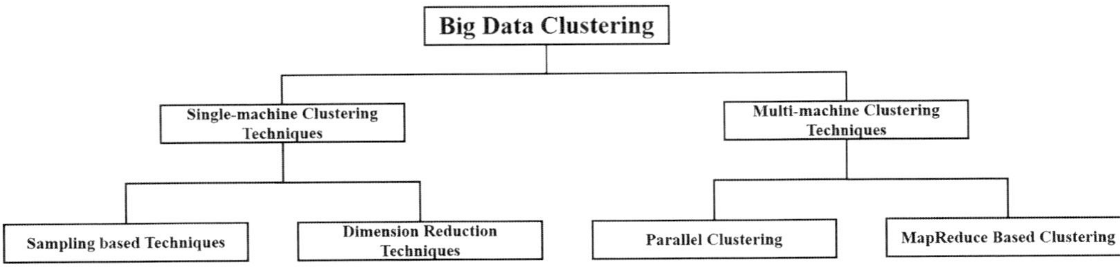

FIGURE 16.1 List of big data clustering techniques.

16.3.1 Single-Machine Clustering Techniques

Single-machine clustering techniques run in one machine and the data has been stored in another machine. Sampling-based techniques and dimension reduction techniques are two common strategies for single-machine techniques.

16.3.1.1 Sampling-Based Techniques

The problem of scalability in clustering algorithms is in terms of computing time and memory requirements. Sampling-based algorithms handle one sample of the data sets at a time, and then generalize it to whole data set. Most of these algorithms are partitioning-based algorithms.

CLARANS is an example of k-medoid methods, which has been extended to spatial very large database (VLDB) [9–12]. Before CLARANS, PAM (partitioning around medoids) and CLARA are the two early versions of k-medoid methods. PAM is one of the first k-medoid algorithms that are introduced. It is more robust than k-means in the presence of noise and outlier detection. PAM combines relocation of points between perspective clusters with re-nominating the points as potential medoids in an iterative process. The objective function is adopted to guide the process. The space complexity of PAM is $O(n^2)$ because it needs to store the entire pairwise dissimilarity matrix between objects in central memory. Hence, PAM becomes impractical in large data sets. Unlike PAM, CLARA is proposed to avoid this problem. CLARA uses five samples and each sample has $O(k)$ points. PAM will be applied to each sample, and CLARA retains the best medoids using the objective function. The whole data set is assigned to resulting medoids for final partition. Both space complexity and time complexity are linear, not quadratic.

CLARANS is proposed to improve efficiency in comparison to CLARA. CLARANS uses random search to generate neighbors by starting with a set of medoids. If a neighbor represents a better partition, then the process continues with the same set of medoids. Otherwise, the algorithms restart with a local minimum that is found. The best medoids are returned for the formation of a resulting partition. The time complexity of CLARANS is $O(n^2)$.

16.3.1.2 Dimension Reduction Techniques

The complexity and the speed of clustering algorithm are influenced by the number of instances in the data set. However, objects in data mining could consist of hundreds of attributes. High dimensionality of the data set is another influential aspect, and clustering in such high-dimensional spaces requires more complexity and longer execution time [8,12]. One approach to dimension reduction is projection. A data set can be projected from a high-dimensional space to a lower-dimensional space. PCA (principal component analysis) is one method used to reduce the dimensionality of a data set [14]. It provides simpler representation of data, reduction in memory, and faster execution time. One approach to dimension reduction is subspace clustering. Subspace clustering seeks to find clusters in different subspaces within a data set. Many dimensions are irrelevant in high-dimensional data. Subspace clustering algorithms localize the search for relevant dimensions, allowing them to find clusters that exist in multiple subspaces. CLIQUE is one of the algorithms proposed to find clusters

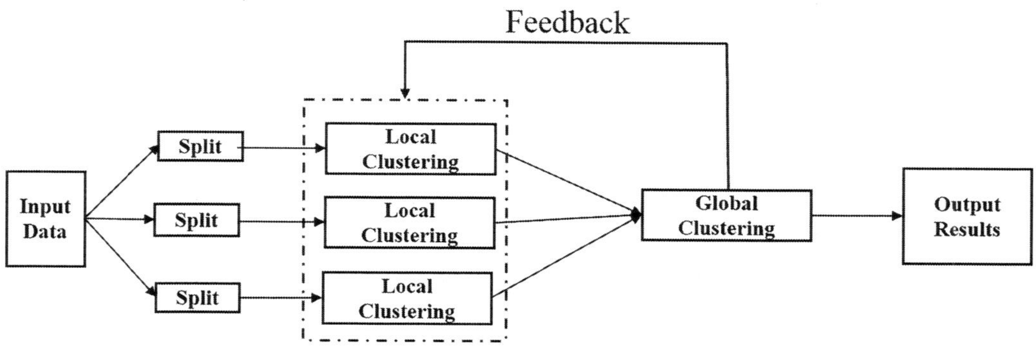

FIGURE 16.2 General framework of most parallel and MapReduce clustering.

within subspaces of data set [15]. CLIQUE combines density- and grid-based clustering. CLIQUE operates on high-dimensional data by not operating all the dimensions at once but by processing a single dimension at first step and then grows upward to the higher one. The last way to address the problem of dimension reduction is co-clustering. Traditional clustering focuses only on features while co-clustering focuses on both data points and features. Dual regularized co-clustering (DRCC) [16] method based on semi-nonnegative matrix tri-factorization is a co-clustering algorithm. It generates a data graph and a feature graph to explore the geometric structure of data manifold and feature manifold.

16.3.2 Multiple-Machine Clustering Techniques

In this age of data explosion, parallel processing is essential to process a massive volume of data in a timely manner. Because the growth of data size is a lot faster than memory and processor advancements, single-machine clustering techniques with a single processor and a memory cannot handle the tremendous amount of data. Algorithms that can be run on multiple machines are needed. Unlike single-machine techniques, multiple-machine clustering techniques divide the huge amount of data into small pieces. These small pieces of data can be loaded on different machines and the huge problem can be solved using processing power of these machines. Parallel processing applications include conventional parallel applications and data-intensive applications. The conventional parallel applications assume that data can be fit into the memory of distributed machines. Data-intensive applications are I/O bound and devote the largest fraction of execution time to the movement of data. OpenMP, MPI [13], and MapReduce are common parallel processing models for computing data-intensive applications. Here, we only discuss the conventional parallel and MapReduce clustering algorithms.

Both parallel and MapReduce clustering algorithms follow the general framework illustrated in Figure 16.2. First, the input data are partitioned and distributed over different machines. Second, each machine performs local clustering on its own split of the input data. Third, the information of machine is aggregated globally to produce global clusters for the whole data set. The global cluster is sent back to each machine as a start point for new local clustering. This process continues until the stop criteria have been met. Finally, the final results of the global clusters are generated.

16.3.2.1 Parallel Clustering

Three main strategies in the parallelism used in data-mining algorithms can be identified as the followings [10]: (1) *independent parallelism*, the whole data is operated in each processor and no communication between processors; (2) *task parallelism*, different algorithms are operated on each processor; and (3) *SPMD (single program multiple data) parallelism*, the same algorithm is executed on multiple processors with different partitions. The results are exchanged in order to cooperate with

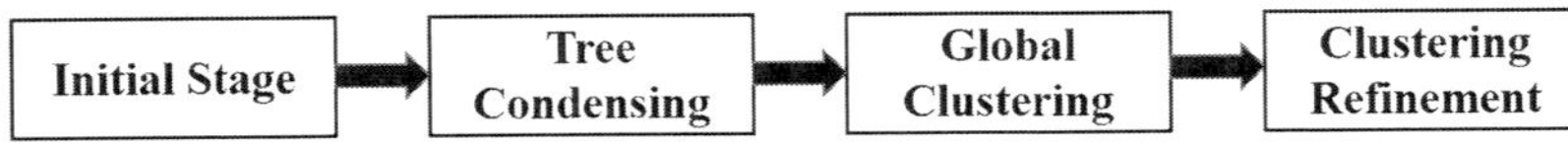

FIGURE 16.3 Flow chart of BIRCH algorithm.

each other. The combination of task and SPMD parallelism with master–slave architecture is the common strategy.

16.3.2.1.1 Parallel Partitioning Clustering Algorithms

k-means algorithm is one of the most popular partitioning clustering algorithms. A parallel implementation of *k*-means is introduced in Reference 17. The parallel *k*-means algorithm is developed on the message-passing model of a network of workstations (NOWs). Besides parallel *k*-means, a parallel CLARANS algorithm using PVM (parallel virtual machine) is introduced in Reference 18. PVM uses a master–slave paradigm. Master program can assign tasks to other slaves, and the communication between computers is based on the message passing.

16.3.2.1.2 Parallel Hierarchical Clustering Algorithm

The network topology of processors and the splitting data accessing have been used in the parallelization of hierarchical clustering algorithms. A parallel BIRCH [19] called PBIRCH is a hierarchical clustering algorithm applied to the SPMD model with message passing. PBIRCH divides the data equally into the processors, and *k*-means algorithm is applied in the initial stage. The *k* initial centroids are broadcasted to each processor, and a CF-tree is constructed accordingly. The centroids of the local clusters are used to compute the global centroids. Each processor recalculates the centroids, and the processes are repeated until it converges. In Figure 16.3, BIRCH scans the input data and builds the CF tree. The initial CF-tree might not be accurate due to the skewed input order or the splitting effect by the page size. A tree condensing step might be applied to address this issue. The global clustering clusters all the subclusters in the leaf nodes, which is done by an agglomerative hierarchical clustering algorithm. The clustering results reassign all the data points based on the results by global clustering step.

16.3.2.1.3 Parallel Density-Based Clustering Algorithm

PDBSCAN [20] is a parallel version of DSBSCAN algorithm. DSBSCAN is a density-based clustering algorithm. The main objective of density-based clustering is discovery of clusters of arbitrary shapes. PDBSCAN with master–slave configuration includes three steps. The first step divides the input data into several partitions and distributes them to different nodes. The second step concurrently clusters the partition using DBSCAN. The last step accumulates the local clusters and calculates the global clusters for the whole data.

16.3.2.1.4 Parallel Graph-Based Clustering Algorithm

The goal of graph partitioning is to find the good cluster of vertices. The parallelization of METIS is ParMETIS, which is a multilevel partitioning algorithm [21]. ParMETIS includes three phases. The first phase is coarsening phase. It tries to find the maximal matching on the original graph such that the vertices that are matched create a small enough graph. The second phase is partitioning phase. The coarsened graph from previous phases clusters in *k*-way using multilevel recursive bisection algorithm. A greedy algorithm is applied to project back the partitioning from second phases to the original graph in the last phase.

16.3.2.1.5 GPU-Based Parallel Clustering

The use of GPU instead of CPU speeds up the computation in parallel computing. GPUs are consisted of thousands of cores, and CPUs have only several processing cores (see Figure 16.4). GPUs are

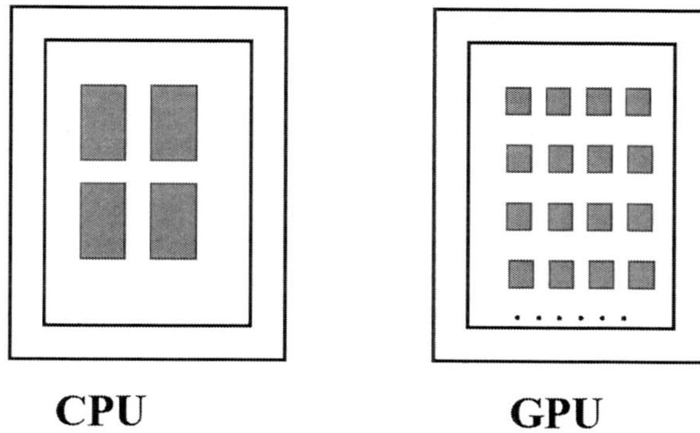

FIGURE 16.4 Difference between CPU and GPU. CPU has several cores while GPU consists of hundreds of cores.

much more powerful and faster than CPUs. A G-DBSCAN [22] is a GPU-based parallel algorithm. G-DBSCAN has two parallelized steps. A graph where the edges are created based on a predefined threshold is constructed in the first step. The second step uses breadth-first search (BFS) to traverse the graph to identify the clusters. Results show that G-DBSCAN is 112 times faster than DBSCAN.

16.3.2.2 MapReduce-Based Clustering

MapReduce is one of the most efficient big data solutions, which enables to process a massive volume of data in parallel with many low-end computing nodes. This programming paradigm is a scalable and fault-tolerant data-processing tool that was developed to provide significant improvements in large-scale data-intensive applications in clusters. MapReduce has gained significant momentum from industry and academia by virtue of its simplicity, scalability, and fault tolerance [23].

MapReduce model hides details of parallel execution, which allows users to focus only on data-processing strategies. The MapReduce model consists of two basic elements [24]: mappers and reducers. The idea of this programming model is to design mappers (or map function), which can be used to generate a set of intermediate key/value pairs. The reducer (or reduce function) is used as a shuffling or combining function to merge all of the intermediate values that are associated with the same intermediate key. The main aspect of the MapReduce algorithm is that if every map and reduce is independent of all other ongoing maps and reduces, then the operations can be run in parallel on different keys and lists of data.

The process of MapReduce approach can be decomposed as follows: (1) Prepare input data: MapReduce utilizes the Google File System (GFS or HDFS) as an underlying storage layer to read input and store output [23]. GFS is a chunk-based distributed file system that supports fault tolerance by data partitioning and replication. The big data is divided into small chunk on different worker nodes. (2) The map step: The map function of each note is applied to local data and the output is written to a temporary storage space. (3) The sort and send step: The output from Step 2 is sorted with key such that all data belonging to one key are located on the same node. The sorted results are sent to reduce processors. (4) The reduce step: Each group of output data (per key) is processed in parallel on each reduce node. The user-provided reduce function is executed once for each key value produced by the map step. (5) Produce the final output: The MapReduce system collects all of the reduce outputs and sorts them by key to produce the final output. The results are stored in the GFS.

16.3.2.2.1 MapReduce-Based Partitioning Clustering Algorithms

PKMeans [25] is a distributed version of *k*-means algorithm using MapReduce framework to speed up and scale up the process. The PKMeans follows the general framework illustrated in Figure 16.5. The data is implicitly partitioned in the distributed file system. The local clustering is performed in

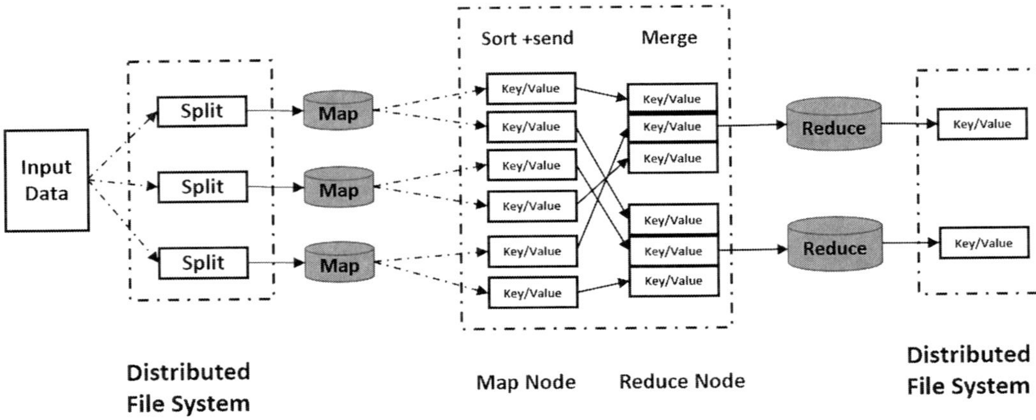

FIGURE 16.5 General framework of a MapReduce system.

the map step using *k*-means algorithm. The global clustering is performed in the merge and reduce step. The outputs of the reduce step are the centroids of clusters, which are sent back to the map step for the next iteration. The process is iterated until it converges. The speed up and size up of PKMeans are near linear and the scale up is also good.

16.3.2.2.2 MapReduce-Based DBSCAN

MapReduce-based DBSCAN [26] is a density-based clustering algorithm implemented using MapReduce. Existing parallel DBSCAN has three major drawbacks. First, they cannot properly balance the load among parallel tasks. Second, the scalability of these algorithms is limited because all critical subprocedures are not parallelized. Third, these algorithms are not less portable to emerging parallel processing paradigms because they are not designed for shared-nothing environments. In MR-DBSCAN, all the critical subprocedures are parallelized to ensure scalability. A novel cost-based data partitioning method is proposed to achieve desirable load balancing on heavily skewed data. Results show that the MR-DBSCAN has good speed up and scale up. It is a lot faster than the exiting parallel DBSCAN.

16.3.2.2.3 MapReduce-Based Evolutionary Algorithm

The inherent parallel nature of evolutionary algorithms makes them optimal candidates for parallelization. A scalable MR-CPSO algorithm using the MapReduce framework to overcome the inefficiency of PSO clustering for large data sets is proposed in Reference 27. MR-CPSO algorithm using the MapReduce methodology has been successfully parallelized. MR-CPSO is a partitioning clustering algorithm similar to the *k*-means approach. The clustering task in MR-CPSO is formulated as an optimization problem to obtain the best solution based on the minimum distances between the data points and the cluster centroids.

16.4 APPLICATION

16.4.1 Image Segmentation

Image segmentation is a necessary first process in image understanding and computer vision by correctly classifying the pixels of an image in decision-oriented applications [28]. The essential goal of image segmentation is to partition an image into uniform and homogeneous attribute regions based on some likeness measure, such as gray level, color, tone, texture, etc. Due to the variety and complexity of images, image segmentation is still a very challenging research topic. Basically, segmentation approaches for images are based on the discontinuity and similarity of image intensity values. Discontinuity is an approach which partitions an image based on abrupt changes. According to the predefined criteria, the similarity approach is based on partitioning an image into similar regions.

Big data image segmentation is a strategy in image analysis, which is emerged especially in the medicine area [4]. Different algorithms for big data image segmentation have been executed on the parallel computing strategy to achieve effective results. Researchers have proposed a variety of techniques to tackle the challenging problem of image segmentation. Because of the complexity of image segmentation and given that only partial prior knowledge is provided, the segmentation result would be poor if a supervised method was adopted. Thus, the unsupervised method is a better choice to solve such a problem. Clustering as an unsupervised learning strategy has been used for solving automatic grouping of images and image segmentation problem. In addition, clustering can also organize and retrieve image databases in an efficient way.

Partitioning clustering is the most popular technique for big data image segmentation due to the simplicity of implementation. In Reference 29, a distributed c-means algorithm is proposed for big data image segmentation and has been applied for magnetic resonance image (MRI) segmentation. The algorithm is implemented on a parallel and distributed machine based on mobile agents. The approach is implemented on a multiagent platform. The proposed algorithm is executed on Mobile Classification Agents on different nodes on their data at the same time. The results are provided to Mobile Host Agent to further compute the global results until the stop criteria have met. The output segmented images are provided from the Mobile Classification Agents. The algorithm is applied on MRI cerebral image and the results show that the complexity of the parallel program has been reduced using the multiagent platform. In addition, it overcomes the big data challenges and offers a high-performance computing tool using a multiagent system.

16.4.2 Load Balancing in Parallel Computing

In the big data era, the rapid and scalable deployment of virtual Web stores, media outlets, and other online sites or services is a problem of considerable practical interest. In a cloud-based architecture, a set of hosted resources such as processors, operating systems, software, and other components can be combined or strung together to form virtual machines. The key is how to allocate the resources to support these virtual machines and reduce the response time. Load balancing [30] is an important problem of heterogeneous computer networks in cloud computing. The main concern of load balancing is how to distribute resources among the users such that no node is overloaded or sitting idle. Traditional parallel computing and grid computing environments load-balancing algorithms can be classified into three ways [31]:

1. *Static load balance algorithms*: These algorithms are suitable for small distributed environments. The decisions related to balancing of load will be made at compile time when resource requirements are estimated. The advantage of static load balance algorithms is the simplicity with regard to both implementation and overhead.
2. *Dynamic load balance algorithms*: The distribution of work load for dynamic load balance algorithms is changed at run-time. The communication delays and execution time have been reduced since they use current load information when making distribution decisions.
3. *Mixed load balance algorithms*: These algorithms are a mix of static and dynamic load balance algorithms. They focus on how to symmetrically assign computing task and how to reduce communication cost of symmetrical distributed computing nodes.

In a distributed system environment, load balance algorithms focus on reducing the job response time by distributing the total load of system. There are many load-balancing algorithms available. Depending on the requirement, clustering algorithms play an important role in realizing cloud computing to implement the load-balance of accessing resources. Active clustering [32] is a clustering-based dynamic load-balancing algorithm. It groups similar nodes together using local re-wiring and then works on these clusters. It uses the concept of matchmaker node to create a cluster. The active clustering adopts the iterative nature of hierarchical clustering algorithms. In the iterative process, the algorithm assumes that there are two types of nodes. First node selects a matchmaker node that is of a different type. This matchmaker node connects with its neighbor node that is of same type as the first node. The process repeats until the matchmaker node gets detached. The performance of the system is enhanced with high resources, thereby increasing the throughput by using these resources effectively. However, the algorithm is degraded due to the increase of system diversity. Hence, there is a strong need for an efficient load-balancing mechanism in cloud computing.

16.4.3 Genetic Mapping

Genetic maps are important component in plant science. A genetic map serves many practical biological purposes and is a key tool in both classical and modern plant research. A genetic map is a list of genetic elements ordered according to their co-segregation patterns [33]. The essential concept of a genetic map is the linkage group. The linkage group collects genetic markers that are found on a single chromosome. The number of linkage groups equals to the number of chromosomes in the species. Genetic markers are clustered into the linkage groups. In order to group genetic makers into linkage groups, it needs to compute pairwise similarities between all pairs of markers and then use various standard clustering algorithms for clustering. A similarity matrix with the similarity scores is an input for clustering algorithms with a complexity of $O(m^2)$ for m markers.

The bottleneck for genetic mapping therefore is how to efficiently find the linkage groups using clustering algorithms. Moreover, conventional genetic mapping tools were designed for small data sets and can only handle up to 10,000 markers. In Reference 34, a fast clustering algorithm called BubbleCluster is proposed to exploit the structure of genetic makers. The BubbleCluster algorithm consists of three phases. The first phase is the most important. It exploits the structure of genetic linkage groups to quickly cluster high-quality makers as a skeleton. The second phase uses the skeleton obtained from the first phase to cluster noisier low-quality makers. Small clusters found from previous phases are merged with large clusters. This algorithm exploits the underlying linear structure of chromosomes to avoid the quadratic pairwise calculation.

16.4.4 Community Detection

Community detection is a useful tool to partition the nodes of an observed network into groups. A "network community" is typically thought of as a group of nodes such that the connection of the nodes is dense within groups but sparser between them [35]. Community detection is potentially very useful. A good partition can be considered as a hint of underlying semantic structure or possible mechanisms of network formation. Researchers in computer science, mathematics, physics, statistics, and bioinformatics use community detection algorithms to better understand the large-scale structure of the interaction between groups in social and biological systems. For example, knowing the groups or communities within a social network such as LinkedIn can be used to infer about the trends of collaboration between individuals in industry as well as in academia. It helps to better understand the function of key biological process by uncovering the nature of interactions between groups of proteins in a protein–protein interaction network. Hence, community detection has received a great deal of attention in real-world graphs such as large social networks, Web graphs, and biological networks.

Community detection is similar to clustering where both use a data-mining technique to partition a network into groups based on the similarity measurement. In Reference 36, a fast parallel modularity optimization algorithm (FPMQA) for community detection is introduced. An interested social network called Interest Network links two IDs if both IDs have participated to the discussion about one or more topics. The initial network is updated using the attitude consistency of the connected ID pairs. FPMQA is then used to conduct community detection. FPMQA assumes that the each node is a separate community in a network and it then finds the pairs of communities with the local maximum. FPMQA uses the parallel manner to merge the corresponding community pairs into one community. Compared to conventional approaches, FPMQA reduces the running time of community detection and uses the reliable ground truths to evaluate detected communities.

16.5 CONCLUDING REMARKS

In this chapter, we reviewed the literatures about clustering in big data and the corresponding clustering algorithms. Clustering algorithms are categorized to six classifications: partitioning, hierarchical, density-based, model-based, grid-based, and evolutionary algorithms. The most popular clustering algorithms are partitioning and hierarchical algorithms and many of parallel versions of the algorithms have been developed. The traditional single-machine techniques are not powerful enough to handle the huge volume of data accumulated nowadays. Parallelism in the clustering algorithms is important for multimachine techniques. Parallel clustering is potentially useful for big data clustering. But the complexity of implementing such algorithms is a challenge for researchers. Hence, MapReduce has gained significant momentum from industry and academia by virtue of its simplicity, scalability, and fault tolerance. Big data clustering as an essential task in big data mining is not limited in image segmentation, load balance, genetic maps, and community detection.

REFERENCES

1. Executive summary: Data growth, business opportunities, and the IT imperatives. An ICD report. Retrieved from www.emc.com/leadership/digital-universe/2014iview/executive-summary.htm
2. Edelstein, H. A. 1999. *Introduction to Data Mining and Knowledge Discovery* (3rd ed.). Two Crows Corp, Potomac, MD.
3. Xu, Z., & Shi, Y. 2015. Exploring big data analysis: Fundamental scientific problems. *Annals of Data Science*, 2(4), 363–372.
4. Chen, C. P., & Zhang, C. Y. 2014. Data-intensive applications, challenges, techniques and technologies: A survey on big data. *Information Sciences*, 275, 314–347.
5. Laney, D. 2001. 3D data management: Controlling data volume, velocity and variety. Technical Report 949, META Group. Retrieved from https://blogs.gartner.com/doug-laney/files/2012/01/ad949-3D-Data-Management-Controlling-Data-Volume-Velocity-and-Variety.pdf
6. Demchenko, Y., Grosso, P., De Laat, C., & Membrey, P. 2013, May. Addressing big data issues in scientific data infrastructure. In *Proceedings of the 2013 International Conference on Collaboration Technologies and Systems (CTS)* (pp. 48–55). IEEE, Chicago, IL.
7. Fahad, A., Alshatri, N., Tari, Z., Alamri, A., Khalil, I., Zomaya, A. Y., & Bouras, A. 2014. A survey of clustering algorithms for big data: Taxonomy and empirical analysis. *IEEE Transactions on Emerging Topics in Computing*, 2(3), 267–279.
8. Shirkhorshidi, A. S., Aghabozorgi, S., Wah, T. Y., & Herawan, T. 2014, June. Big data clustering: A review. In *International Conference on Computational Science and Its Applications* (pp. 707–720). Springer International Publishing, Portugal.
9. Kaufman, L., & Rousseeuw, P. J. 2009. *Finding Groups in Data: An Introduction to Cluster Analysis* (Vol. 344). John Wiley & Sons, Hoboken, NJ.
10. Kim, W. 2009. *Parallel Clustering Algorithms: Survey*. CSC 8530 Parallel Algorithms, Spring 2009.
11. Aggarwal, C. C., & Reddy, C. K. (Eds.). 2013. *Data Clustering: Algorithms and Applications*. CRC Press, London, UK.
12. Ng, R. T., & Han, J. 2002. CLARANS: A method for clustering objects for spatial data mining. *IEEE Transactions on Knowledge and Data Engineering*, 14(5), 1003–1016.
13. Zhang, J. 2013. A parallel clustering algorithm with MPI–Kmeans. *Journal of Computers*, 8(1), 10–17.
14. Jolliffe, I. 2002. *Principal Component Analysis*. John Wiley & Sons. http://ai2-s2-pdfs.s3. amazonaws.com/9856/3b4a26779ebf1fcb145f13713cc5fdba87b4.pdf.

15. Yadav, J., & Kumar, D. 2014. Subspace clustering using CLIQUE: An exploratory study. *International Journal of Advanced Research in Computer Engineering & Technology*, 3(2), 372–378.
16. Gu, Q., & Zhou, J. 2009, June. Co-clustering on manifolds. In *Proceedings of the 15th ACM SIGKDD International Conference on Knowledge Discovery and Data Mining* (pp. 359–368). ACM.
17. Kantabutra, S., & Couch, A. L. 2000. Parallel k-means clustering algorithm on NOWs. *NECTEC Technical Journal*, 1(6), 243–247.
18. Zhang, Y. P., Sun, J. Z., Zhang, Y., & Zhang, X. 2004, August. Parallel implementation of CLARANS using PVM. In *Proceedings of 2004 International Conference on Machine Learning and Cybernetics* (Vol. 3, pp. 1646–1649). IEEE, Shanghai, China.
19. Garg, A., Mangla, A., Gupta, N., & Bhatnagar, V. 2006, December. PBIRCH: A scalable parallel clustering algorithm for incremental data. In *2006 10th International Database Engineering and Applications Symposium (IDEAS'06)* (pp. 315–316). IEEE, Delhi, India.
20. Xu, X., Jäger, J., & Kriegel, H. P. 1999. A fast parallel clustering algorithm for large spatial databases. In *Data Mining and Knowledge Discovery* (pp. 263–290). Springer, Netherlands.
21. Karypis, G., Schloegel, K., & Kumar, V. 2003. ParMETIS: Parallel graph partitioning and sparse matrix ordering library. Version, 2. University of Minnesota.
22. Andrade, G., Ramos, G., Madeira, D., Sachetto, R., Ferreira, R., & Rocha, L. 2013. G-DBSCAN: A GPU accelerated algorithm for density-based clustering. *Procedia Computer Science*, 18, 369–378.
23. Shim, K. 2012. MapReduce algorithms for big data analysis. *Proceedings of the VLDB Endowment*, 5(12), 2016–2017.
24. Wu, X., Zhu, X., Wu, G. Q., & Ding, W. 2014. Data mining with big data. *IEEE Transactions on Knowledge and Data Engineering*, 26(1), 97–107.
25. Zhao, W., Ma, H., & He, Q. 2009, December. Parallel k-means clustering based on MapReduce. In *IEEE International Conference on Cloud Computing* (pp. 674–679). Springer, Berlin, Germany.
26. He, Y., Tan, H., Luo, W., Feng, S., & Fan, J. 2014. MR-DBSCAN: A scalable MapReduce-based DBSCAN algorithm for heavily skewed data. *Frontiers of Computer Science*, 8(1), 83–99.
27. Aljarah, I., & Ludwig, S. A. 2012, November. Parallel particle swarm optimization clustering algorithm based on MapReduce methodology. In *2012 Fourth World Congress on Nature and Biologically Inspired Computing (NaBIC)* (pp. 104–111). IEEE, Mexico City, Mexico.
28. Gong, M., Liang, Y., Shi, J., Ma, W., & Ma, J. 2013. Fuzzy c-means clustering with local information and kernel metric for image segmentation. *IEEE Transactions on Image Processing*, 22(2), 573–584.
29. Benchara, F. Z., Youssfi, M., Bouattane, O., Ouajji, H., & Bensalah, M. O. 2015. Distributed C-means algorithm for big data image segmentation on a massively parallel and distributed virtual machine based on cooperative mobile agents. *Journal of Software Engineering and Applications*, 8(3), 103.
30. Kansal, N. J., & Chana, I. 2012. Cloud load balancing techniques: A step towards green computing. *International Journal of Computer Science Issues*, 9(1), 238–246.
31. Moharana, S. S., Ramesh, R. D., & Powar, D. 2013. Analysis of load balancers in cloud computing. *International Journal of Computer Science and Engineering*, 2(2), 101–108.
32. Uma, J., Ramasamy, V., & Kaleeswaran, A. 2014. Load balancing algorithms in cloud computing environment—A methodical comparison. *International Journal of Advanced Research in Computer Engineering & Technology (IJARCET)*, 3, 272–275.
33. Cheema, J., & Dicks, J. 2009. Computational approaches and software tools for genetic linkage map estimation in plants. *Briefings in Bioinformatics*, 10(6), 595–608.
34. Strnadová, V., Buluç, A., Chapman, J., Gilbert, J. R., Gonzalez, J., Jegelka, S., & Oliker, L. 2014, November. Efficient and accurate clustering for large-scale genetic mapping. In *2014 IEEE International Conference on Bioinformatics and Biomedicine (BIBM)* (pp. 3–10). IEEE, UK.
35. Leskovec, J., Lang, K. J., & Mahoney, M. 2010, April. Empirical comparison of algorithms for network community detection. In *Proceedings of the 19th International Conference on World Wide Web* (pp. 631–640). ACM, Raleigh, NC.
36. Bu, Z., Zhang, C., Xia, Z., & Wang, J. 2013. A fast parallel modularity optimization algorithm (FPMQA) for community detection in online social network. *Knowledge-Based Systems*, 50, 246–259.

17 Large Graph Computing Systems

Chengwen Wu, Guangyan Zhang, Keqin Li, and Weimin Zheng

CONTENTS

ABSTRACT

Large graph computing system is a key tool in big data computing. It can be applied to a variety of big data applications, such as social networks, web page search, and protein interactions. However, the unstructured graph data make data access nonuniform, which poses a great challenge for building an efficient large graph computing system. Fortunately, a lot of large graph computing frameworks have been proposed recently to alleviate the above problems. In general, these frameworks can be categorized into single-node in-memory system, distributed shared memory system, and single-node out-of-core system. Besides, there are some other solutions that utilize flash SSD and GPU to speed up large graph computing. In this chapter, we will review these typical large graph computing systems from a system perspective.

17.1 INTRODUCTION

17.1.1 Application Background

Many practical problems can be expressed as graphs, which consist of a set of vertices and some edges between them. In detail, the vertices can be viewed as entities, and the edges can be used to represent the relationship between two entities. We are now living in the era of big data. A variety of data with different formats are generated quickly, and are growing in both size and complexity. It is a nontrivial work to process, store, and analyze these big data. To extract values from it, efficient analysis frameworks are required.

MapReduce [1] is a parallel programming model that can handle a lot of big data problems efficiently, but its performance on graph algorithms is poor, because the iterative nature of graph algorithms will cause a lot of communication and synchronization overhead if MapReduce model is used. Parallel Boost Graph Library (Parallel BGL) [2] and CGMGraph [3] are two parallel graph libraries based on Message Passing Interface (MPI), and a number of graph algorithms can be implemented by using their Application Programming Interfaces (APIs). But these two libraries do not support fault tolerance, which means it is impractical for them to be employed in a huge cluster environment, where machines may fail frequently. Some other works focus on optimizing a single graph algorithm, which are not general solution for all algorithms.

17.1.2 Large Graph Computing Systems

Based on above facts, a lot of distributed graph computing systems have been proposed in recent years, including Pregel [4], and its open source clones Giraph [5] and Hama [6], GraphLab [7], PowerGraph [8], and GraphX [9]. These systems adopt the philosophy of "think like a vertex" (vertex-centric computing model), where each vertex receives messages from other vertices, updates its value based on user-defined logic, and then sends its newly updated value to its outgoing neighbor vertices. The vertex-centric computing model is easy for users to design and implement scalable graph algorithms. In addition to the vertex-centric computing model, PowerGraph supports edge-centric computing model, where for the edge to be addressed, it first gathers updates that are generated in the last iteration for each vertex, and applies the new value, and then for each edge to be addressed, spreads the new value of the source vertex to destination vertex. Reference 10 adopts a block-centric computation model. PathGraph [11] exploits a path-centric computation model. These systems trade a comparatively long partition time for the better locality of graph data when using their computing model.

A distributed graph computing system scales well with the increase of the graph size, but its hardware cost is relatively high. Besides, to build a robust and efficient system, load balance, fault tolerance, synchronization, and coordination are the challenges that need to be carefully addressed. Moreover, for ordinary users, it is a nontrivial work to build the environment, implement graph algorithms, debug, and tune the performance on a distributed system. Hence, some researchers have started to explore the solution of large graph computation on a single machine (we ignore the in-memory systems on a single machine in this chapter), and a lot of systems have been proposed, such as GraphChi [12], X-Stream [13], PathGraph, VENUS [14], and GridGraph [15]. These systems use disks to scale when processing large graphs, so their bottleneck lies in the disk access I/O. What is worse, the data locality of graph computation is poor. To make efficient large graph computing on a single machine possible, they usually preprocess the graph data, and based on the preprocessing scheme, the corresponding computation model is used, so that good data locality during the computation can be guaranteed. According to the experiment results of GraphChi, to run the PageRank algorithm on a Twitter graph of 1.5 billion edges, it takes Spark with 50 machines (100 CPU cores) 8.1 min, while GraphChi only needs 13 min on MacMini of 8GB RAM and a 256GB SSD (solid-state drive). However, a single machine large graph computation system also has its limitation, for example, when the graph size is extremely large, it usually fails to process it or the performance is unacceptable.

There are some other solutions targeting at the heterogeneous systems. The representative systems are TurboGraph [16], FlashGraph [17], TOTEM [18], and Cusha [19]. SSD has different performance characteristics with HDD (hard disk drive), so TurboGraph and FlashGraph exploit some novel schemes optimized specially for SSD. A graphics processing unit (GPU) is a part of most computer systems, which has much better parallel processing capability than CPU, and can be used to offload computation tasks, but its logical processing is short. As for the characteristics of GPU, TOTEM and Cusha proposed approaches to maximize the performance of the GPU when doing graph computation.

17.1.3 Chapter Organization

The chapter is organized as follows: Section 17.2 lists some challenges of large graph computation. In Section 17.3, we introduce the representative distributed graph computing systems and their key techniques. Section 17.4 shows the representative single machine graph computing systems and their key techniques. Section 17.5 describes the representative heterogeneous graph computing systems and their key techniques. We finally conclude the chapter in Section 17.6.

17.2 CHALLENGES OF LARGE GRAPH COMPUTATION

Efficient large graph computation is challenging. First, large graph computation is a branch of big data computation, which faces the common challenges as many other big data problems. Second, graph computation has its own characteristics, such as poor data locality, nonstructured graph data, which pose new challenges to large graph computation. In this section, we will discuss the challenges of large graph computation in detail.

17.2.1 Big Volume and Nonstructured Data

First of all, graph data is a kind of big data, which satisfies the basic features (i.e., volume, velocity, and variety) of big data. The volume of graph data is huge and is growing rapidly. The web pages indexed by Google in 1998 were around one million, and quickly reached one billion in 2000. In 2014, it indexed around 30 trillion web pages [20]. Facebook achieved one billion users in October 2012. Obviously, large graphs are usually beyond the memory size of a single machine. Careful design is required on either scale out by using clusters or scale up on disks. Another issue is the variety of graph data, which comes from the annotating and combining data sets. That means vertices and edges can be labeled as arbitrary properties. For example, edges can be labeled to define the nominal difference between two vertices (A is the fan of B) or can carry the weight to show the degree of difference (need to walk 15 miles from A to B).

In addition to the challenges from volume, velocity, and variety, the difficulties brought by the unstructured feature of graph data also require to be addressed before we start to build an efficient graph computing system. There is no canonical definition of the unstructured data, but generally, the elements within the unstructured data have no structure. For example, social graphs and road graphs have completely different structures, and even with the social graphs, different types of social graphs are also varied. Moreover, within a graph, different vertices are varied in its number of edges and the vertices they connect to. The unstructured data have poor data locality, and the graph algorithms are data driven, which will result in suboptimal performance if the data are not well preprocessed.

17.2.2 Parallel Graph Processing

Parallel computing is essential for efficient large graph computing, but also offers challenges. First, we need to deal with task assignment, which corresponds to graph partitioning. Note that an optimal graph partition requires that the tasks are equal-sized with minimum shared vertices (edge cut) or shared edges (vertex cut), but this is an NP-hard problem. Besides, tasks are usually dependent, so that we have to take the synchronization overhead into consideration. For a distributed system, the overhead mainly comes from the communication among machines, while in a single machine of NUMA architecture, the impact is particularly significant.

When processing a problem in parallel, load balance is an important factor that affects the overall performance. However, in the field of graph computing, most real graphs follow the phenomenon of power law [21], which indicates that the degrees of different vertices are varied significantly in a graph. Therefore, load balance is another challenge we face to build an efficient parallel graph system.

In a distributed system, fault tolerance is important and necessary to maintain the system available. However, it will incur extra overhead not only at the normal computation stage, but also at the recovery stage. A good fault tolerance should have little impacts on the system performance at both stages.

17.3 REPRESENTATIVE DISTRIBUTED LARGE GRAPH COMPUTING SYSTEMS AND OPTIMIZATION TECHNIQUES

In this section, we introduce three representative distributed graph computing systems, and then we summarize some optimization techniques that are used in distributed systems.

17.3.1 Pregel

Pregel was presented by Google in 2010, which aims to replace MapReduce to do efficient and reliable graph computing in a distributed environment. It borrows the ideas of BSP (Bulk Synchronous Parallel) [22] model to implement its computation and communication model. Specifically, the computation of Pregel consists of a sequence of iterations. An iteration is called a superstep, where vertices are processed in parallel. Besides, Pregel adopts vertex-centric computation model, so that, during a superstep, each vertex will receive the messages that were sent by its in-neighbors at the last superstep, and then updates its own state based on user-defined compute logic, and finally sends the new state along its outgoing edges.

In Pregel, an algorithm terminates when every vertex votes to halt (as shown in Figure 17.1), and no messages are passed in the current superstep. At the beginning, every vertex is in the active state, which will execute the compute logic defined by users. A vertex goes into inactive state by voting to halt; this means that the vertex will not do any computation unless it receives new messages from other vertices. Those vertices that reactivated by the messages must explicitly deactivate themselves again after they complete the computation in the superstep.

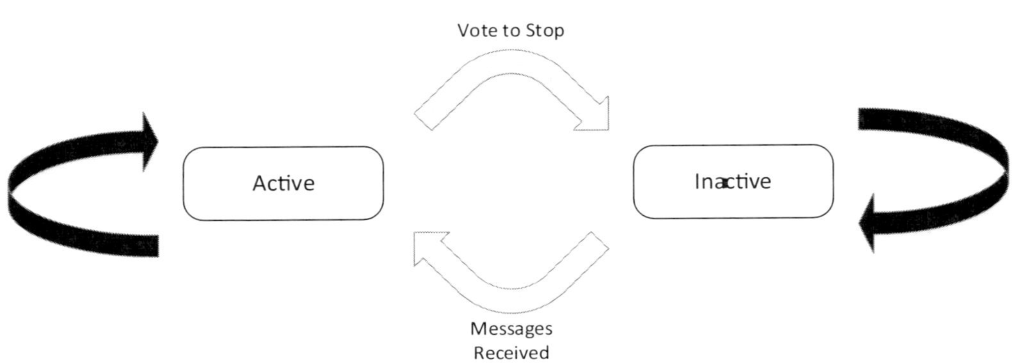

FIGURE 17.1 Vertex state machine.

```
class PageRankVertex : public Vertex<double, void, double> {
 public: virtual void Compute(MessageIterator* msgs) {
        if (superstep() >= i) {
            double sum = 0;
            for (; !msgs->Done(); msgs->Next())
                sum += msgs->Value();
            *MutableValue() = 0.15/NumVertices() + 0.85 * sum;
        }
        if (superstep() < 30) {
            const int64 n = GetOutEdgeIterator().size();
            SendMessageToAllNeibhbors(GetValue()/n);
        }
        else {
            VoteToHalt();
        }
 }
};
```

FIGURE 17.2 PageRank implemented in Pregel.

In Figure 17.2, we illustrate an implementation of PageRank in Pregel. In a superstep, the vertex program first iterates all the messages sent in the previous superstep, which contain the sum of PageRanks of all in-neighbors. Then, the new PageRank value is computed, which is sent to its out-neighbors.

Pregel partitions graph into different parts, each part consists of a set of vertices and all their outgoing edges. The partition scheme is based on the vertex ID, so that we can easily imply which partition a vertex belongs to. The default partition function is hash(N), where N is the number of the partitions, and users can design their own partition scheme to replace the default partition function.

Communication between vertices is completed by messages. During a superstep, a vertex may receive many messages from its in-neighbors. All messages are guaranteed to be delivered and not to be duplicated, which will be available in the next superstep as the input of the vertex's update function. Note that in a distributed environment, the communication overhead between machines may be the main bottleneck of the performance. To improve the performance, Pregel provides combiner function for users, by which users can combine messages sent to a vertex into a single message to reduce the number of messages to be sent; however, owing to the un-order characteristic of messages, the combiners can only be used for commutative and associative operations.

Pregel's fault-tolerant mechanism is implemented by checkpoint. At the beginning of a superstep, the master instructs every worker to save their partitions to the persistent storage, which includes vertex value, edge value, and incoming messages, and so on. The master uses ping messages to detect worker failures. When workers fail, the master will reassign the partitions owed by these workers to the currently available workers in the cluster, reload the partition state from the most recent state, and compute the lost steps to the current step. To balance the overhead between the recovery overhead and checkpoint overhead, Pregel sets the checkpoint frequency according to the mean time to failure model.

17.3.2 GraphLab

GraphLab (we describe the distributed version here) is an asynchronous distributed shared memory graph system in which the vertex program can directly access the information of its current vertex, adjacent edges, and adjacent vertices. Its main purpose is to provide an asynchronous, dynamic, graph-parallel computation that can execute many Machine-Learning and Data Mining (MLDM) algorithms efficiently on a cluster.

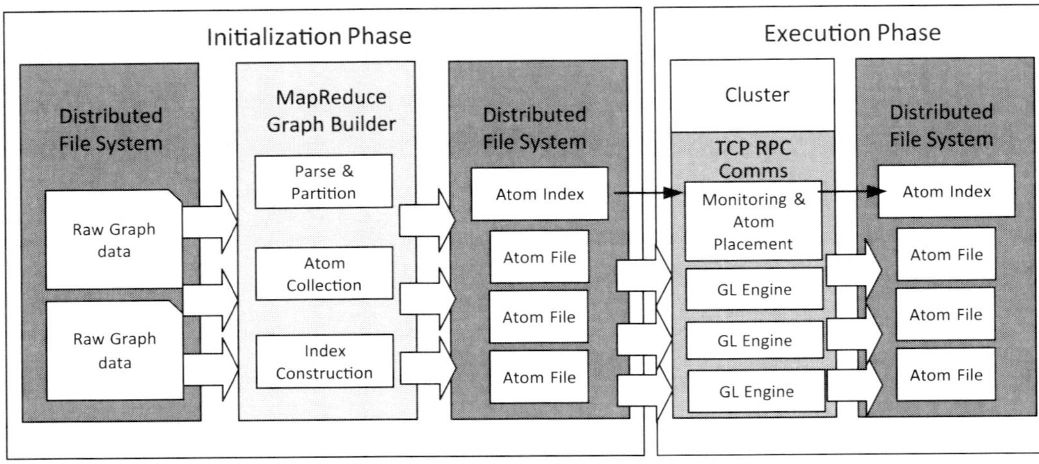

FIGURE 17.3 GraphLab system overview.

Many MLDM algorithms can be modeled by using graph data; in this way, data dependencies can be expressed, and we are able to extract more singles from the noise data. Besides, most MLDM algorithms iteratively update a set of parameters, and these updates depend on the underlying graph structure (the same algorithm on different graph data structure may output varied parameters). Synchronous systems such as Pregel update all parameters at the end of an iteration in parallel, where the input data are the parameters received from the last iteration, while GraphLab updates the parameters asynchronously by using the most recent parameter values. Synchronous computation can result in performance degradation, since the runtime of each computation phase is determined by the slowest machine when synchronous computation is used, and the slow machine can be caused by various factors, such as load, network, and hardware variety. In addition, the vertex itself has different complexity and convergence (depending on the data) in the algorithm, which can produce the varied runtime. Therefore, GraphLab exploits the asynchronous computation mode, with which a lot of MLDM algorithms can benefit a lot from, such as belief propagation, PageRank.

The parameters of many MLDM algorithms converge asymmetrically, which means some parameters converge quickly in a few iterations, while others converge very slowly over many iterations. To optimize the performance, GraphLab adopts a dynamic scheduling scheme, which focuses on these more challenging parameters (converge slow parameters) to accelerate the convergence. Although Pregel supports dynamic computation by allowing some vertices to skip some supersteps, its effectiveness is very limited compared to the priority computation of GraphLab.

Parallel processing is a necessity for efficient large graph computing. However, for some MLDM algorithms, serializability is required to help speed up the convergence or ensure the correctness of algorithms. To address the problem, GraphLab ensures that every parallel processing has an equivalent sequential execution by introducing sort consistency models with different levels, where users can choose the corresponding model based on their algorithms.

Figure 17.3 shows the overview of GraphLab. The system first loads row graph data from a distributed file system, and then graph partition is conducted. If hashed partitioning is used, the process will be done by MapReduce framework, where a map is performed over each vertex and edge, and each reducer accumulates the atom file, which will then be uploaded to the distributed file system. In the execution phase, the atom files will be assigned to the machines in the cluster, and these perform the corresponding computation in parallel (Figure 17.3).

GraphLab introduces the Gather, Apply, and Scatter (GAS) computation model. In the gather phase, the vertex program reads the information from its in-neighbors along its in-edges, and the update value is generated and applied to the vertex. Figure 17.4 shows the PageRank implemented

```
PageRank (Scope scope) {
    float accum = 0;
    foreach (nbr in scope.in_nbrs) {
        accum += nbr.val / nbr.out_nbrs;
    }
    vertex.val = 0.15 + 0.85 * accum;
}
```

FIGURE 17.4 PageRank in GraphLab.

in GraphLab; the vertex program directly reads the neighbor vertices' state to compute the sum. Once the new sum is updated to the vertex, its value can be read by other vertex programs.

Pregel employs the synchronous checkpoint, which suspends all the computation and flushes the communication channels when constructing the snapshot. This synchronous mechanism is inefficient for GraphLab as the synchronous computation. Therefore, GraphLab uses asynchronous checkpoint (Chandy–Lamport algorithm [23]) to implement the fault-tolerant mechanism, which incrementally constructs a snapshot without suspending the computation. When a failure occurs, the system can recover from the last checkpoint.

17.3.3 PowerGraph

Most real graphs present a power-law degree distribution, which implies that most vertices have relatively small numbers of neighbors while a small fraction of vertices have very large number of neighbors. This phenomenon brings challenges to the efficient distributed parallel graph processing, for instance, the imbalanced workloads between the workers, the communication asymmetry, and imbalanced worker storage.

To address these challenges, Gonzalez et al. [8] present PowerGraph (included in GraphLab version 2.2), which exploits vertex-cut graph partition to ensure balanced computation and communication. Moreover, PowerGraph combines the best features of Pregel and GraphLab, so that it supports BSP computation model, as well as the computation-efficient asynchronous computation model.

Figure 17.5 shows the communication model of PowerGraph, where a vertex with high degree is split into multiple parts, and each part contains part of the edges and is stored on a machine in the cluster. During the computation, the vertex program runs on each part in parallel, and the accumulator and the updated vertex data are exchanged via network communication. In this way, edge data of high-degree vertex can be evenly assigned across the machines in the cluster. Moreover, a vertex program can also span among the machines, which helps improve work balance and reduce communication. Since there exists communications between the vertex data (master) and its replicas (mirrors), and the vertex replicas will increase the storage overhead of the system, the number of split is carefully determined to reduce such network and storage overhead.

17.3.4 Optimization Techniques

Based on the above system architectures, some works propose optimization techniques, which improve the system performance significantly.

Pregel and GraphLab employ a vertex-centric programing model, which is easy for users to implement a lot of graph algorithms. However, this model hides the partition information from users, which may result in heavy network (Pregel) or scheduling (GraphLab) overhead. To optimize the performance, Tian et al. proposed Giraph++, which exploits a new "think like a graph" (graph-centric) computation model. Giraph++ exposes the partition information to users, with which graph algorithms can be optimized.

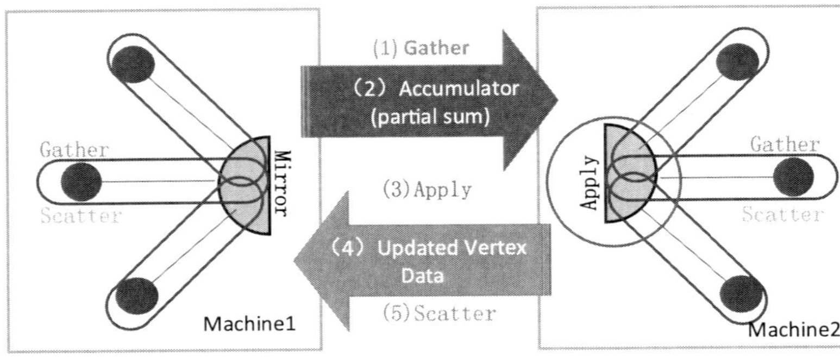

FIGURE 17.5 Communication pattern of PowerGraph.

Xue et al. [24] found that most existing distributed graph computing systems (such as Pregel) are inefficient in their memory usage, since they do not allow jobs to share graph data. As shown in Figure 17.6a, when running concurrent jobs, each job maintains a separate graph data, though the graph data may be duplicate. To solve the problem, they propose Seraph, which decouples the graph data and the job-specific data, so that graph data can be shared among the jobs (shown in Figure 17.6b); thus, memory usage can be reduced greatly. Moreover, Seraph exploits delta graph checkpointing and state regeneration to implement efficient fault tolerance mechanism.

In terms of processing natural graph with skewed degree distribution, Pregel and GraphLab will incur load imbalance and heavy data contention, while PowerGraph suffers from high vertex communication overhead, even for the low-degree vertices. PowerLyra [25] improves the performance in processing skewed graph through dynamically applying different computation and partition strategies for vertices with different degrees. PowerLyra follows the computation model of PowerGraph in the process of high-degree vertices, which guarantees high parallelism. For the low-degree vertices, by preserving vertices and along with their one-direction edges (in or out-edges), PowerLyra

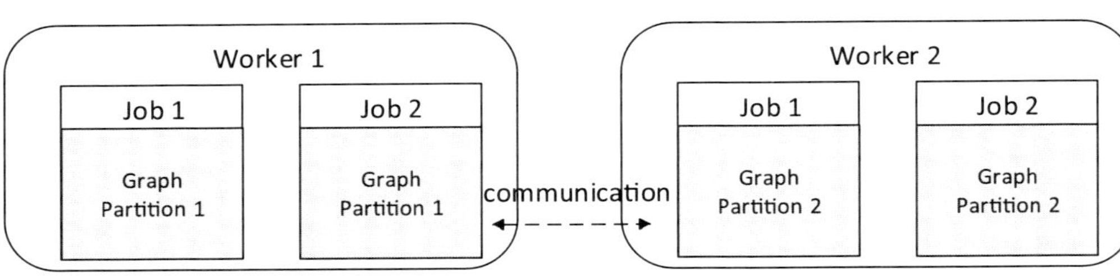

(a) Existing Graph Systems

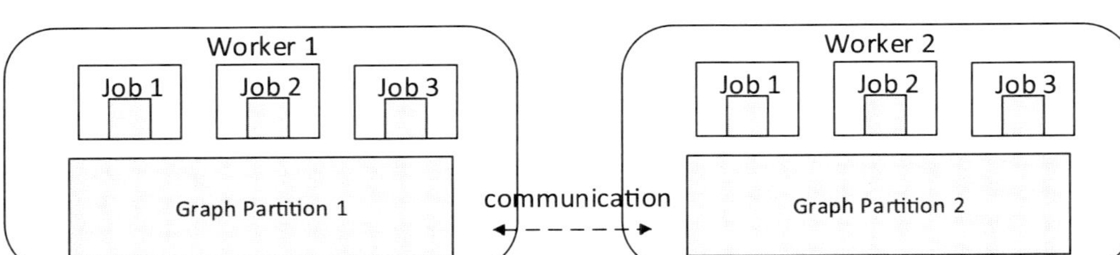

(b) Seraph

FIGURE 17.6 Manner of executing concurrent jobs. (a) Existing graph systems. (b) Seraph.

performs local gathering, and distributed scattering to minimize the communication overhead. As for the partition scheme, PowerLyra uses edge cut for low-degree vertex and reserve one-direction edges for them; vertex cut was used to partition the vertices of high degree, whose edges are spanned across many machines for the consideration of parallelism.

Synchronous and asynchronous checkpoints require to save the current vertex state to reliable persistent storage (e.g., distributed file systems) and this state information will be loaded from the storage and the missing steps where faults occurred for the recovery will be recomputed. This process is costly for normal execution as well as the recovery stage. Wang et al. [26] introduced Imitator, which supports an efficient fault-tolerant mechanism by replicating vertex state to their replicas. In existing vertex-centric distributed graph computing systems, vertex replicas are originally used for the local access of vertex state. Therefore, Imitator borrows the idea of fault tolerance of distributed file system (DFS) to reuse these replicas for the backup of vertex data, and synchronization messages between the master vertex and its mirrors can be used to keep the mirrors at the fresh state. In this way, fault tolerance can be implemented with very low storage overhead. Moreover, replicas of a vertex are spread across many machines, which means the recovery can be done in parallel, and this process can be done fast since the state is read from Dynamic Random Access Memory (DRAM) instead of disk-based storage.

17.4 REPRESENTATIVE SINGLE-NODE LARGE GRAPH COMPUTING SYSTEMS AND OPTIMIZATION TECHNIQUES

Two representative single-node large graph computing systems based on disks are introduced in this section, and then some optimization techniques on this field are given.

17.4.1 GraphChi

GraphChi is a disk-based vertex-centric large graph computing system on a single machine. To process a large graph with billion edges, it is necessary to use disk to extend the memory. However, without careful design, a lot of random I/Os will be generated due to the nonstructured feature of graph data and poor locality of graph algorithm; thus, the performance of processing large graphs would be unacceptable.

To enable the efficient large graph processing based on disks, GraphChi first conducts a preprocess to arrange the location of graph data on the disks, and then a novel computation model is used to do the execution, which makes the access to storage sequentially with only a few random accesses. Further, GraphChi's computation model is asynchronous, which helps speed up the convergence of some algorithms. Besides, the selective scheduling employed in GraphChi can mitigate I/O amount for traversal algorithms, which further boosts the performance.

In the preprocessing phase, GraphChi first splits vertices into vertex subsets (intervals) based on the rule that the number of in-edges of each interval is roughly equal and can fit into the memory. Then, according to the intervals, GraphChi partitions edges into shards, and each shard stores all the in-edges of the interval. Within a shard, the edges are sorted according to their source vertex ID. Based on the preprocessing scheme, the Parallel Sliding Window (PSW) method is used to load the graph from disks and computation for vertices is done in parallel. As shown in Figure 17.7, the vertices of the graph are split into four intervals, where each interval associates a shard (a set of edges). In an iteration, PSW executes the computation in intervals by processing the vertices one interval at a time. When executing an interval, all the in-edges of that interval will be loaded from the disks sequentially to the memory, and since the edges are ordered by their source vertex ID in a shard, the out-edges of the interval are located in a block in other shards, so that another 3 (4-1) sequential accesses in the example of Figure 17.7 are required to load the out-edges in an interval. The experimental results show that GraphChi runs on a personal computer and has comparable or even better performance than the distributed system with a number of machines.

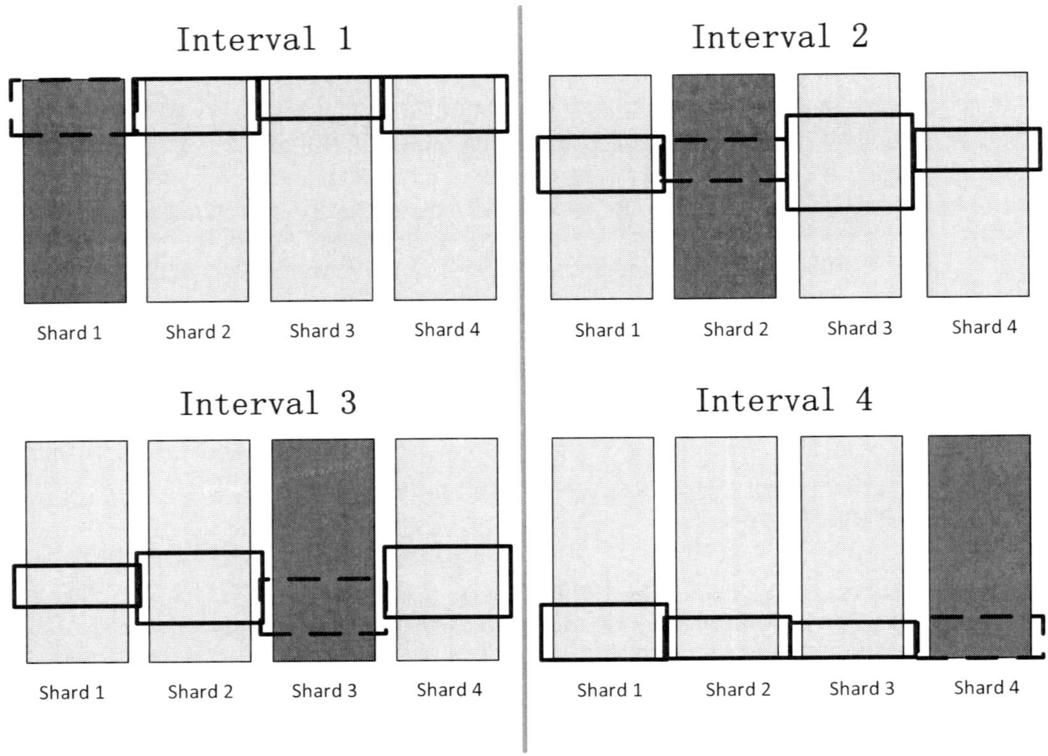

FIGURE 17.7 Visualization of the stages of one iteration of the Parallel Sliding Windows method.

17.4.2 X-Stream

GraphChi achieves good performance on large graph computing by using disks on a single machine. However, its preprocessing overhead is expensive, which requires to sort the edges within a shard to reduce random accesses to edges on storage. X-Stream presents an edge-centric computation model, which needs no preprocessing model, and takes full advantage of the sequential bandwidth of disks.

X-Stream is also a disk-based large graph computing system on a single machine. But different from GraphChi's vertex-centric computation model, it adopts an edge-centric computation model and computational states are maintained on the vertices. Its computational model is shown in Figure 17.8. In the scatter phase, X-Stream iterates all the edges and sends the update over the edge, and then in gather phase, iterates the updates and applies the update to the corresponding vertex. This edge-centric approach accesses edges sequentially to make better use of the disk's bandwidth. However, it incurs random access on the vertex state. To mitigate this overhead, streaming partition approach is used, which partitions vertices into subsets, so that the states of a subset can fit in high-speed memory (cache) for in-memory graphs, and main memory for out-of-core graphs. Each vertex subsets associates an edge partition, which stores all the out-edges of that vertex subset. Figure 17.9 shows the edge-centric computation model with streaming partitions. In the scatter phase, X-Stream processes all the streaming partitions, and for each partition, it loads the vertex subset, and then streams the edges on the storage to generate updates, and writes them to output buffer (Uout). X-Stream appends the update of a edge to corresponding destination partition's local input buffer (Uin). In the gather phase, it reads the update value from Uin and updates the vertex state.

```
edge_scatter (edge e)
  send update over e;

update_gather (update u)
  apply update u to u.destination;

while not done
  for each edege e
    edge_scatter(e);
  for each update u
    update_gather(u);
```

FIGURE 17.8 Edge-centric computation model.

```
Scatter phase:
for each streaming partition p
   read in vertex set of p;
   for each edge e in edge list of p
       edge_scatter(e): append update to Uout;

Shuffle phase:
for each update u in Uout
   let p = partition containing target of u;
   append u to Uin(p);
destroy Uout;

Gather phase:
for each streaming partition p
    read in vertex set of p;
    for each update u in Uin(p)
        edge_gather(u);
     destroy Uin(p);
```

FIGURE 17.9 Edge-centric computation model with streaming partition.

17.4.3 Optimization Techniques

There are some other works that present optimization techniques to optimize the performance of a single machine graph computing system based on disks.

GraphChi has the drawbacks of long preprocessing time and separated load and computation phases. Cheng et al. [14] proposed VENUS, which adopts a novel computation model. In detail, their computation model supports vertex-centric computation with streamlined processing. First, a new sharding model (preprocessing) is used, where vertices are split into disjoint intervals, for each interval, a g-shard and v-shard are created. The g-shard stores the in-edges of the interval, while the v-shard contains all vertices in that g-shard, including the source and destination of each edge. The in-edges of a g-shard are ordered by their destination vertex. Note that, since the update of a vertex can be done when all in-edges of that vertex are loaded into the memory, there is no need to load the whole subgraph (edges in an interval). Based on that, the interval is split to ensure that v-shard can be fit in the memory. Second, based on the sharding model, the streamlined computation model is proposed. As shown in Figure 17.10, the execution begins when the v-shard is loaded into the memory, and the update of vertex starts when all its in-edges are read from storage, and the load process of other vertices' in-edges is conducted at the same time to parallelize I/O and computation, while GraphChi needs both the out-edges and in-edges to update the value, and cannot parallelize I/O and computations like VENUS.

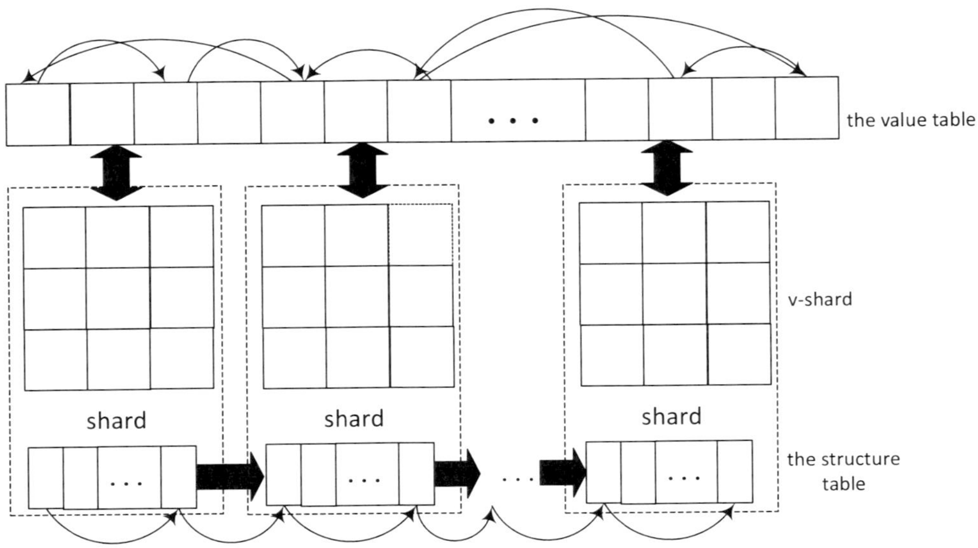

FIGURE 17.10 Vertex-centric streamlined processing.

In X-Stream, update values in the scatter phase can be as large as |E|, which may incur a large amount of I/Os and result in suboptimal performance. Zhu et al. [15] proposed GridGraph, which splits the vertices into P equal-sized vertex chunks; each vertex chunk contains vertices within a continuous range. Then the edges are partitioned into P × P blocks (grids), and an edge is distributed to a gird based on the rule that the source vertex determines the row block, while the destination vertex determines the column block. Figure 17.11 shows an example of GridGraph's partition scheme. Based on this storage layout, a novel dual sliding window computation model is used. Figure 17.12 shows the PageRank algorithm of the example graph (Figure 17.11) by using the computation model. We use this example to illustrate the dual sliding window computation model. To update a vertex's pagerank value, GridGraph sequentially reads the edges of the block at the column-oriented target, and the vertex values of source chunk and destination chunk are loaded in the memory, so updates can be applied to the destination vertex in place, which avoids the overhead write to local buffer or the disks in the worst case. Further, selective scheduling is employed to skip unnecessary blocks for algorithms such as BFS (breadth first search) and WCC (weakly connected component) to boost the performance.

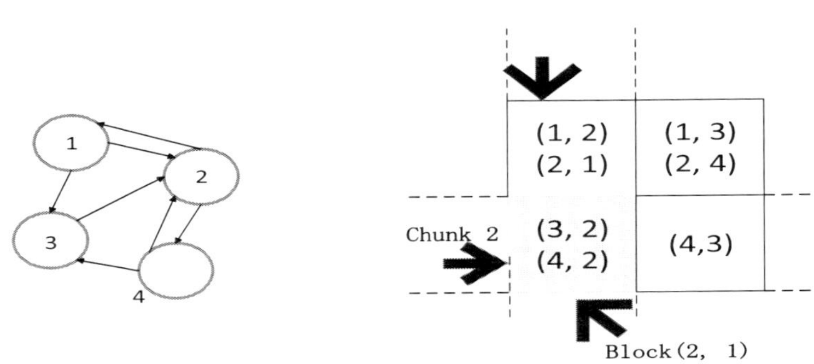

FIGURE 17.11 An example of GridGraph's partition scheme.

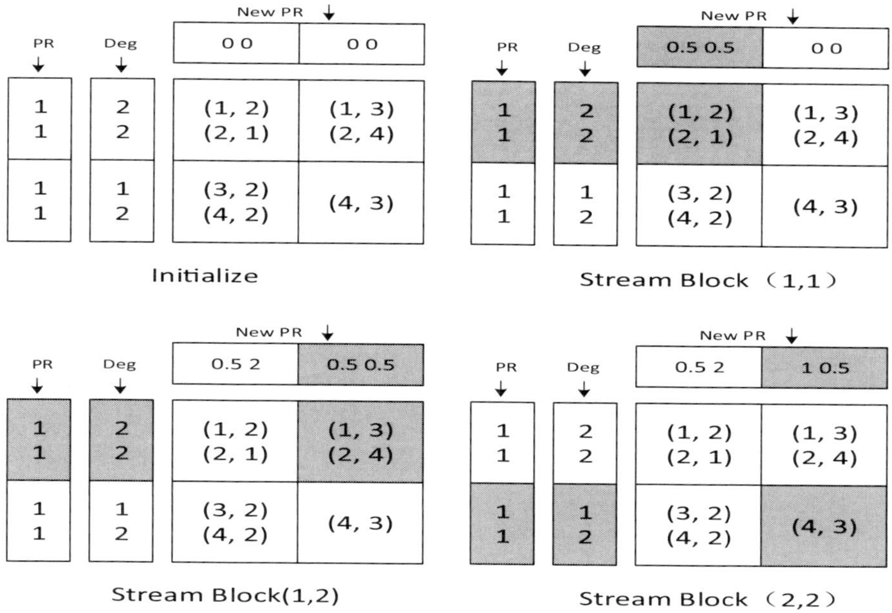

FIGURE 17.12 Illustration of dual sliding windows. It shows the first iteration of PageRank on the example graph.

17.5 REPRESENTATIVE HETEROGENEOUS LARGE GRAPH COMPUTATION SYSTEMS AND OPTIMIZATION TECHNIQUES

In this section, we introduce two heterogeneous graph computation systems based on SSDs and GPU, respectively.

17.5.1 FLASHGRAPH

FlashGraph is a single machine large graph computing system based on an array of SSDs. Besides, FlashGraph is a semiexternal system, which maintains algorithmic vertex state in the memory, and edge data on storage. In addition, algorithms implemented in FlashGraph are executed by reading/writing vertices and reading edges. In this way, bad write performance and endurance of SSDs can be avoided. FlashGraph provides performance comparable to in-memory systems, and outperforms out-of-core systems. Moreover, FlashGraph adopts a vertex-centric computation model, and requests the edge lists on demand; this is because the performance gap between the sequential access and random access of SSD is much smaller than that of HHD.

To provide performance comparable to in-memory systems, FlashGraph uses an array of SSDs to achieve the high throughput and low latency to storage. But the throughput and I/O latency of SSDs is still far beyond that of DRAM. To overcome these challenges, FlashGraph is built on SAFS (set-associative file system), which is used to refactor I/O scheduling, data placement, and data caching for the extreme parallelism of modern NUMA multiprocessors.

Figure 17.13 shows the architecture of FlashGraph. The edge data are stored on SSDs, which are accessed selectively, and a compact edge data format is applied to reduce the I/O amount. The SSDs are managed by SAFS; to improve the performance, an asynchronous user-task I/O interface is added to SAFS, which allows general-purpose computation in the page cache, so the overhead of accessing data in page cache and memory consumption can be reduced. Besides, it overlaps the I/O and computation. The graph engine is responsible for the schedules of vertex programs; to optimize

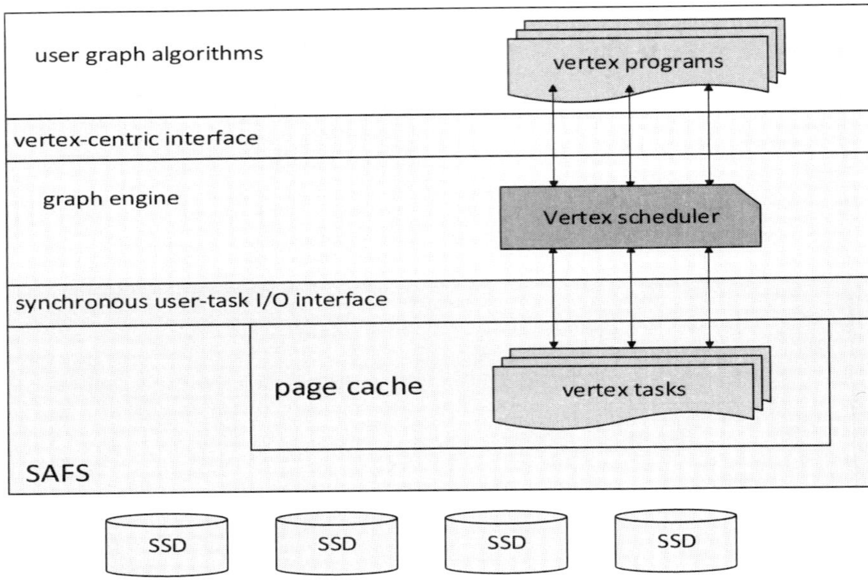

FIGURE 17.13 Architecture of FlashGraph.

the performance, the engine will merge the adjacent I/O requests of vertex programs, which not only reduces the I/O amount but also performs I/O sequentially. FlashGraph exposes vertex-centric interface to users, with which a variety of graph algorithms can be expressed.

17.5.2 TOTEM

The hybrid systems with processing units of different characteristics optimized for both sequential processing and bulk processing (e.g., GPU) have the potential to enable efficient large graph processing. However, before that, some challenges need to be addressed, for example, the graph partition and load assignment for assistant processing units.

TOTEM exploits a low time and space complexity graph partitioning algorithm based on vertex connectivity. Besides, in the CPU–GPU hybrid system, the communication of graph processing can be significantly reduced by aggregating and batching messages (assisted by the high bandwidth of the PCI-E bus that typically connects discrete GPUs); in this case, computation is the main bottleneck. The vertex connectivity here is quantized by vertex degree. By doing so, most graphs can be partitioned into different degrees of parallelism, which match the different processing elements with varied processing ability, and are more likely to result in balanced workloads among the processing units. One straight idea of implementing the partition scheme is to sort the vertices according to their degree in place, which results in $O(|V| \log |V|)$ time complexity. However, there is no need to sort the vertices completely; a partial sort can be applied (i.e., finding the degree values that divide the graph into the desired partitions), which takes $O(|V|)$ time complexity.

TOTEM offloads low-degree vertices to GPU for the computation; this is because low-degree vertices have a few connected edges, which are a good choice for memory-limited GPU. Besides, most natural graphs follow power-law degree distribution, where most vertices have a few edges, and few vertices adjacent to a large number of edges. Therefore, offloading many low-degree vertices to GPU and placing a few high-degree vertices on CPU matches the level of parallelism offered by the processing element. Moreover, this assignment achieves good load balance across the cores.

17.6 SUMMARY

In this chapter, we introduce the representative distributed, single node based on disks, and heterogeneous large graph computing systems. For the distributed large graph computing systems, the partition scheme, communication model, and fault tolerance are three important aspects that affect the system's performance significantly. For the single-node large graph computing systems based on disks, I/Os are the main bottleneck; to boost the performance, we should concentrate on the data layout and data format on the storage. Of course, a proper computation model based on the layout and format should also be carefully designed. For the heterogeneous large graph computing systems based on SSDs, we need to keep the characteristics of SSDs in mind, for example, the I/O parallelism, small performance gap between sequential access and random access, and wear out, to design the system, which can take fully advantage of the good features of SSDs and avoid or reduce impacts brought by the bad side. As for the heterogeneous CPU–GPU, we should fully make better use of the high parallelism offered by GPU, and consider its limited memory size to offload proper tasks to it; besides, the work load balance among the cores is also the key factor we need to take into consideration.

The research field of large graph computing system has experienced good developments and some breakthroughs, but as we described above, there still remains some open issues to be addressed in all kinds of systems. And we look forward to more research work in this direction.

REFERENCES

1. Dean J, Ghemawat S. MapReduce: Simplified data processing on large clusters. *Communications of the ACM*, 2008, 51(1): 107–113.
2. Gregor D, Lumsdaine A. The parallel BGL: A generic library for distributed graph computations. *Proceedings of Parallel Object-Oriented Scientific Computing (POOSC)*, Glasgow, UK, 2005.
3. Chan A, Dehne F, Taylor R. CGMGRAPH/CGMLIB: Implementing and testing CGM graph algorithms on PC clusters and shared memory machines. *International Journal of High Performance Computing Applications*, 2005, 19(1): 81–97.
4. Malewicz G, Austern M, Bik A J C et al. Pregel: A system for large-scale graph processing. *Proceedings of ACM Special Interest Group on Management of Data*, Indianapolis, IN, USA, 2010: 135–146.
5. https://giraph.apache.org/
6. http://hama.apache.org/
7. Low Y C, Bickson D, Gonzalez J et al. Distributed GraphLab: A framework for machine learning in the cloud. *Proceedings of the VLDB Endowment (PVLDB)*, 2012, 5(8): 716–727.
8. Gonzalez J E, Low Y C, Gu H J et al. Powergraph: Distributed graph-parallel computation on natural graphs. *Proceedings of the 10th USENIX Symposium on Operating Systems Design and Implementation*, Hollywood, CA, USA, 2012: 17–30.
9. Gonzalez J E, Xin R S, Dave A et al. Graphx: Graph processing in a distributed dataflow framework. *Proceedings of the 11th USENIX Symposium on Operating Systems Design and Implementation*, Broomfield, CO, USA, 2014: 599–613.
10. Yan D, Cheng J, Lu Y et al. Blogel: A block-centric framework for distributed computation on real-world graphs. *Proceedings of the VLDB Endowment (PVLDB)*, 2014, 7(14): 1981–1992.
11. Yuan P P, Zhang W Y, Xie C F et al. Fast iterative graph computation: A path centric approach. *Proceedings of the International Conference for High Performance Computing, Networking, Storage and Analysis*, Piscataway, NJ, USA, 2014: 401–412.
12. Kyrola A, Blelloch G, Guestrin C et al. GraphChi: Large-scale graph computation on just a PC. *Proceedings of the 10th USENIX Symposium on Operating Systems Design and Implementation*, Hollywood, CA, USA, 2012: 31–46.
13. Roy A, Mihailovic I, Zwaenepoel W. X-stream: Edge-centric graph processing using streaming partitions. *Proceedings of ACM Symposium on Operating Systems Principles*, Farmington, PA, USA, 2013: 472–488.

14. Cheng J F, Liu Q, Li Z G et al. VENUS: Vertex-centric streamlined graph computation on a single PC. *Proceedings of the 31st IEEE International Conference on Data Engineering*, Seoul, Korea, 2015: 1131–1142.
15. Zhu X W, Han W T, Chen W G. Grid Graph: Large-scale graph processing on a single machine using 2-level hierarchical partitioning. *Proceedings of the 2015 USENIX Conference on Usenix Annual Technical Conference*, Santa Clara, CA, USA, 2015: 375–386.
16. Han W S, Lee S, Park K et al. TurboGraph: A fast parallel graph engine handling billion-scale graphs in a single PC. *Proceedings of the 19th ACM SIGKDD Conference on Knowledge Discovery and Data Mining*, Chicago, USA, 2013: 77–85.
17. Zheng D, Mhembere D, Burns R et al. FlashGraph: Processing billion-node graphs on an array of commodity SSDs. *Proceedings of the 13th USENIX Conference on File and Storage Technologies*, Santa Clara, CA, USA, 2015: 45–58.
18. Gharaibeh A, Costa L B, Santos-Neto E et al. On graphs, GPUs, and blind dating: A work load to processor matchmaking quest. *Proceedings of IEEE the 27th International Symposium on Parallel and Distributed Processing*, Washington DC, USA, 2013: 851–862.
19. Khorasani F, Vora K, Gupta R et al. CuSha: Vertex-centric graph processing on GPUs. *Proceedings of the International ACM Symposium on High-Performance Parallel and Distributed Computing*, Vancouver, Canada, 2014: 239–252.
20. http://www.statisticbrain.com/total-number-of-pages-indexed-by-google/
21. Baraba'si A L, Albert R. Emergence of scaling in random networks. *Science*, 1999, 286(5439): 509–512.
22. Valiant Leslie G. A bridging model for parallel computation. *Communications of the ACM*, 1990, 33(8): 103–111.
23. Chandy K M, Lamport L. Distributed snapshots: Determining global states of distributed systems. *ACM Transactions on Computer Systems*, 1985, 3(1): 63–75.
24. Xue J, Yang Z, Qu Z et al. Seraph: An efficient, low-cost system for concurrent graph processing. *Proceedings of the 23rd International Symposium on High-Performance Parallel and Distributed Computing*, Vancouver, BC, Canada, 2014: 227–238.
25. Chen R, Shi J, Chen Y et al. PowerLyra: Differentiated graph computation and partitioning on skewed graphs. *Proceedings of the 10th European Conference on Computer Systems*, Bordeaux, France, 2015: 1–15.
26. Wang P, Zhang K, Chen R et al. Replication-based fault-tolerance for large-scale graph processing. *44th Annual IEEE/IFIP International Conference on Dependable Systems and Networks*, Atlanta, GA, 2014: 562–573.

18 Big Data in Genomics

Huaming Chen, Jiangning Song, Jun Shen, and Lei Wang

CONTENTS

ABSTRACT

The leverage of high-throughput technologies in biology area brings the academia and industry an enormous amount of "omics" data. These data include genomics data and proteomics data. In this chapter we consider mostly on the genomics data. Benefited from the development of "Big Data" area and also the domain knowledge driven by genomics data, two subsequent areas including precision medicine and cancer genomics, are discussed in this chapter. Meanwhile, we consider genomics data from the "Big Data" landscape and give a comprehensive "life cycle" on these data. Two significant and state-of-the-art cases in genomics data study are also presented. These two cases, which are ENCODE and CGHub, show inspiring and interesting results by the integration of big data analytics technology in genomics data. As the life science, biomedicine and health care sectors are at a turning point into data intensive science. Since we could benefit from the overwhelming genomics data, big data analytics shows us a promising potential to deliver a better understanding and improvement of our life.

18.1 INTRODUCTION

In recent years, bioinformatics has drawn much attention from the academia and industry. The many advanced tools and in-depth analyses provide a deeper understanding of the internal and correlated meanings of different mechanisms of the molecular systems on the Earth. With high-throughput technologies, the increasing amount of "omics" data, including proteomics and genomics, have boosted this even further. An upsurge of interest for data analytics in bioinformatics comes as no surprise to researchers from a variety of disciplines. Specifically, the astonishing rate at which genomics and

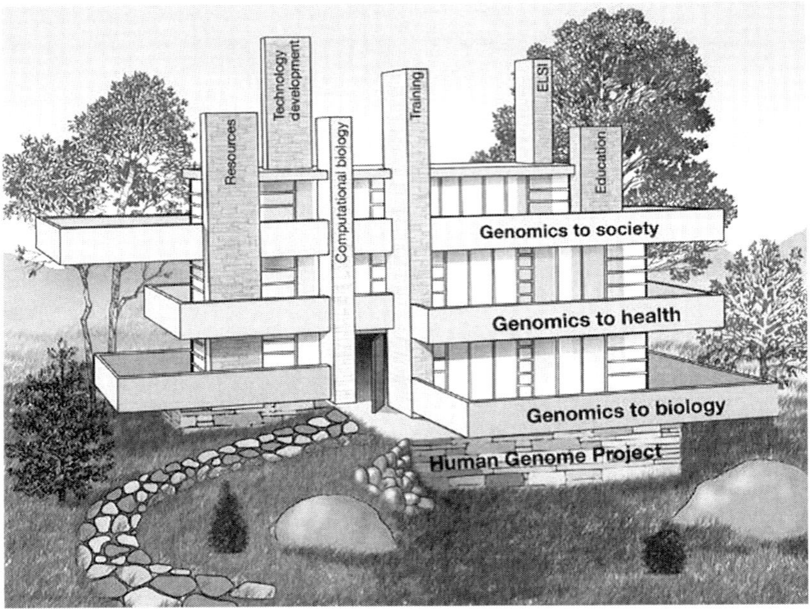

FIGURE 18.1 The future of genomics rests on the foundation of the Human Genome Project. (From Francis S. Collins et al. *Nature*, 422(6934):835–847, 2003.)

genetic data are generated leads the researchers into the realm of "big data." This chapter is dedicated to providing an update of the genomics background and the state-of-the-art developments in the genomics area from the perspective of big data analytics.

18.1.1 History of Genomics

The study of genomics started since the 1990s when the Human Genome Project (HGP) launched its research on a complete sequence of all three billion base pairs in the human genome. The experimental genomics, which provides the veracious data of life at the molecular level, promises to revolutionize the way in which cells and cellular processes have been studied [1]. The HGP was designed as a three-step program to produce genetic maps, physical maps, and then the complete nucleotide sequence map of human chromosomes [2]. Besides the development of sequencing and genotyping technologies in the past few decades, computational biology has become intrinsic to modern biological research [3].

The main contribution of HGP is the generation of large, publicly available, and comprehensive genomics data [3]. On April 14, 2003, the USA's National Human Genome Research Institute (NHGRI), the Department of Energy (DOE), and their partners in the International Human Genome Sequencing Consortium announced the successful completion of the HGP within the state-of-the-art technology [4]. Not only human beings but also other species are being sequenced. In 1995, the first bacterium genome sequence was completed, namely, *Haemophilus influenza. Saccharomyces cerevisiae* (a type of beer yeast) was completely sequenced in 1996. In 2000, *Drosophila melanogaster*, the well-known fruit fly, had its full genome sequence of the model organism completed. The latest sequenced species in records is Zebrafish, which was completed in 2013. So far, increasingly different types of life on Earth are being sequenced, which means that more and more corresponding genomics and proteomics data have been recorded. As shown in Figure 18.1, it details the future of genomics firmly resting on the foundation of HGP [3]. Three themes are presented: the genomics to biology, the genomics to health, and the genomics to society. There are six critically important components relevant to the themes, which are resources, technology development, computational biology, training, ELSI (ethical, legal, and social implications), and education.

It has been a promising research area that integrates computational and experimental technology components [3]. The emergent availability of massive biological data has necessitated the involvement of a bunch of computational technologies, including the big data analytics tools, data mining, and machine learning, to cooperatively handle these data. The key issue in the next-generation biomedical research is how to address the computational technology toward developing data-driven decision support systems, in order to help biologists either design further experiments or conduct data analysis.

18.1.2 Genomics Data

With the impressive drop in cost of high-throughput instruments, there are now many biology labs that are able to produce data as quickly and vastly as they want. Comparing genomics data with other major areas of "big data," such as proteomics data, astronomy data, particle physics data, website resources (such as YouTube, Twitter), and so on, it is very critical to have an insightful view about genomics via big data analytics [5], as genomics data are being produced at an extraordinary speed and has its specific domain knowledge.

Every year, over 25 zetabytes (ZB) of data are being produced in the field of astronomy [5]. The same phenomenon occurs in particle physics, which produces massive quantities of raw data. However, very less data are kept for storing and further analysis after data cleansing and preprocessing. In the genomics area, around 1 ZB data are generated annually. There are more than 7000 recorded high-throughput instruments all over the world. These instruments are located in nearly 1000 sequencing centers [5]. It is approximated that over the next 10 years, the sequencing genomics data of over 1.2 million reported species of plants and animals would be encompassed.

Genomics data refer to the genome and DNA/RNA data of the organism. Typically, it is the representation in an alphabetical array for every sequence. It is a chemical and mechanical process essentially to "digitize" the information present in the DNA and RNA. Besides these data, other available omics data, which include transcriptomics, methylomics, and metabolomics data, could be integrated hierarchically to improve our further understanding from the genotype to the phenotype [6]. Either for considering individual data type for specific domain study or integrating related data types for knowledge discovery between different domains, a data-driven framework built upon a comprehensive representation of biology is desired to ease the upsurge of data and facilitate bioinformatics research.

For example, in one of our recent work, considering that the proteomics data is publicly available and is an expression of genomics data, we had drilled big data analytics into the proteomics area to facilitate the experimental research of biologists. To be specific, among proteomics research, direct benefit from proteomics would be infectious diseases. Thus, in our work, where pathogen–host protein–protein interaction (PHPPI) is considered as the key infection process at the molecular level, a proper representation of the proteomics data would introduce a high dimensionality issue, while a highly skewed ratio between positive and negative PHPPIs exists in a big dataset [7]. The highly skewed ratio is normally set to be 1:100 to 1:500. Considering the variety of infectious diseases and the rising number of proteomics data, a powerful and comprehensive model is desired in this area to help biologists to analyze these proteomics data.

These omics data, including genomics, proteomics, and so on, have revolutionized system biology for a better understanding of biological mechanisms [8]. Bottlenecks and opportunities are posed by a growing gap between the abilities in generating and interpreting these data. The cost and difficulties in quantitative experiment have been relatively controllable nowadays, whereas the challenges are brought in the data analysis stage, which involves data management, integration, analysis, and interpretation [9]. Now it has become even more challenging, as precision medicine is gaining intensive attentions recently, and the cooperation of big data analytics with researchers on personalized medicine has also become very promising.

18.1.3 Challenges Ahead

While extensive specialized analyses are required when data become extremely large, different big data areas have different domain knowledge. The interpretation of genomics sequences and analysis of DNA expression, and the research of mutations and developments at the molecular level are the main vision of genomics [5]. Incorporated with big data analytics technologies, an integration of biology domain expertise, data science, machine learning, and even an infrastructure with powerful computation capability are required to achieve these goals. There is no clear consensus among and within biologists and bioinformatics researchers nowadays to best describe the process of leveraging the available omics data to interpret such a domain knowledge, which could be either discovering previously unknown insights or looking for specific patterns [10], such as recognizing the locations of transcription start sites [11]. Today, many research institutions and companies are utilizing their specialty domain knowledge to define and explore their own big data solutions for analyzing these omics data for further research and application [12,13].

Since profiling genomics data is no longer a bottleneck for biology study, an efficient framework for data storage, transfer, and analysis is desired. Unlike the traditional dataset, a single genome sequencing file could be several gigabytes; meanwhile, the worldwide distribution of high-throughput instruments would have facilitated research on formulating a fast and qualified system for cooperation. These specifications in the genomics area call for more considerations in data acquisition, data transfer, data storage, and data analysis.

The next section provides an in-depth view of the genomics area and its knowledge delivered by cooperation with big data analytics technology. In the third section, we will detail the current research on data science in the genomics area.

18.2 DOMAIN KNOWLEDGE DRIVEN BY GENOMICS DATA: IN-DEPTH VIEW

The general definition of "big data" includes using inductive statistics and concepts from nonlinear system identification to infer laws (regressions, nonlinear relationships, and causal effects) from large dataset to reveal relationships, dependencies, and to perform predictions of outcomes and behaviors. By now, the DNA data deluge comes from thousands of sources. More than 7000 sequencing instruments are dispersed around the world, generating genomics data, and sooner or later, there will be tens of thousands of profiling instruments. As a consequence, both the storage and computation burden have been increasing dramatically. In spite of these challenges, how to narrow the gap and build an efficient connection between genomics data and the domain knowledge we want to discover is an urgent research problem. Precision medicine and cancer genomics are two major subareas that we would like to discuss in this section.

18.2.1 Knowledge for Precision Medicine

As genomics data pile up at an extraordinary speed and volume, biomedicine area is increasingly turning into cross-disciplines of data science [10,14,15]. Specifically, it delivers a promising fortune toward precision and personalized research, which means a P4 medicine: predictive, preventive, participatory, and personalized [16].

On January 20, 2015, U.S. President Barack Obama announced a program to launch a new Precision Medicine Initiative, which takes a closer look at curing diseases like cancer and diabetes. The ultimate goal is to generate a medical solution according to the personalized information to keep the human body healthy. According to the definition of precision medicine in Reference 17, besides other biological databases, it is important to consider individual information to pose a possible precaution

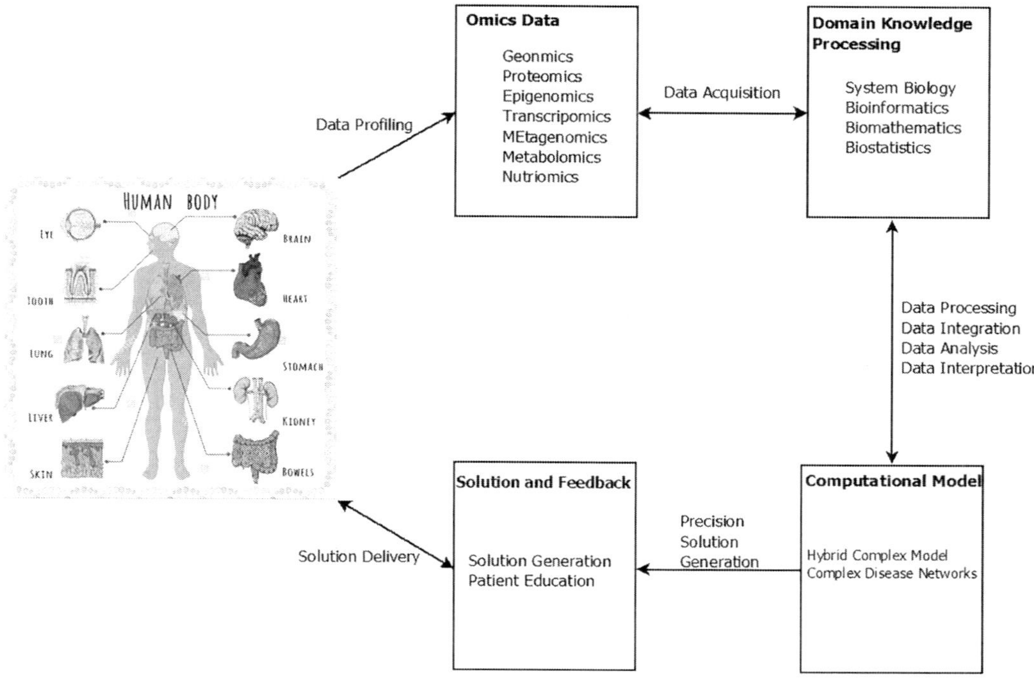

FIGURE 18.2 Basic framework of personalized medicine. (From Akram Alyass et al. *BMC Medical Genomics*, 8(1):33, 2015.)

and treatment solution against diseases. Even though the development of high-throughput technologies has lowered the cost of data acquisition, the development of electronic medical system is still on its early stage for data acquisition. Currently, there are two main components being discussed in precision medicine: a near-term in personalized therapeutic solution for specific disease and a long-term in knowledge extraction for better health [12]. A basic framework of personalized medicine, as shown in Figure 18.2, was proposed. The accumulated genomics data also simulate the development of system biology, which is an integrative research strategy for tackling the complexity of biological systems and interpreting their behavior and interactions across all organization levels [18]. The precision medicine benefits from the overwhelming medical data, which establishes a new link between genes, biologic functions, and the related diseases [18–21]. Analogous to the proteomics area, assembling genomics data in system biology could deliver a trustful graphical representation of biological interaction maps, and further compute a predictive and dynamic model of organisms and diseases. The advancement in identifying the interactions between proteins reduced the false-positive rate and improved the quality of curated datasets [22,23]. In cooperation with genomics data, a study that utilized machine-learning methods to recognize the locations of transcription start sites in a genome sequence [11] has been a great start. Similar studies are supposed to be conducted on splice sites, promoters, or positioned nucleosomes identification [24–27].

The genomics-related medicine research is known as "genomics medicine" [28], which has a consensus definition "using an individual patients genotypic information in their clinical care" [29]. However, the approach to an effective precision medicine solution is currently in its very early stage of development incorporating with genomics data. The private protocol issues would be a hindrance in both the electronic medical system development and genomics data sequencing stage.

In order to generate a precision medicine solution, not only genomics data would be involved, but also other omics data, especially the electronic medical records. This particular vision provides a hierarchical framework as the physiology and pathophysiology do, in which there is a belief that "genetic can be used to definitely explain features that our genome might accurately indicate the individual risk of developing diseases" [30]. Some specific examples in therapy-related study have been done, such as the discussion of the relevance of CYP2D6 in breast cancer tamoxifen therapy decision [31], which tried to interpret the genotype–phenotype association of cancer.

A rational scheme of precision medicine would require each person's genomics profile, which raises not only ethical or legal issues, but also the modeling, computing, and analyzing ability problems. Even though almost 2000 clinical conditions are achieved with genetic testing nowadays, the effective electronic health records (EHRs) still need to be further developed, in an efficient way, which would accordingly produce a comprehensive and individual-specific data [32]. The ultimate goal for precision medicine would be aiming to deliver the exact right treatment at a right dose at a right time, with minimum illness consequences and maximum efficacy [33,34].

18.2.2 Knowledge for Cancer Genomics

Among the overwhelming amount of genomics data, big data analytics provides a novel paradigm to retrieve information into the related domain knowledge. Besides the precision medicine area, several other research areas, such as functional traits research [35], rice genome project [36], and plant genome annotation and function prediction [37], have been raised associating with the boosting genomics data. In this section, we will discuss another major area: cancer genomics, which covers the study of cancer mechanism, mutation prevention and detection, and cancer treatment. As an important step toward precision medicine, cancer genomics study is one of the most important discovery science areas [38]. A proposed paradigm from cancer genomics to precision medicine is shown in Figure 18.3. The gap between cancer genomics and precision medicine is wide, and bridging this gap is far from straightforward. The major ethical proof, data profiling and annotation, and the integration of domain knowledge are the first layer hurdles. Proper patient consents are required to proceed to data generation and computational analyses. Furthermore, an efficient knowledge-based system to process data to achieve functional and mechanistic studies is desired. Since cancer is considered as a disease of genome mutation, the more biologists learn from cancer tumors, the more they put the belief in the finding that each single cancer tumor is a representation of one specific set of genome changes. Even though its effect in clinic is currently limited because of the gap between cancer study and therapeutic decision, cancer genomics is considered to affect every corner of cancer research and would be extended as a critical link for personalized cancer medicine [39,40].

Most of the data science research on cancer genomics area are currently conducted on pattern detection problems. Our previous work once aimed to achieve a fast and accurate cancer subtype classification on genomics dataset. Machine-learning technology is the most popular method in classification. Specifically, extreme learning machines (ELM), support vector machine (SVM), general vector machine (GVM), and the state-of-the-art deep learning methods have been deployed to tackle the gene expression data classification problem [41,42]. In the classification problem of cancer genomics dataset, the small quantity of samples and high dimensionality are two main hindrances for learning model development. As cancer genomics data piling, a relatively big dataset with high dimension would appear in the near future, which is supposed to be an important but also a challenging branch of machine-learning application in the big data area.

There are two major consortia in the cancer genomics area, which are The Cancer Genome Atlas (TCGA) Research Network and the International Cancer Genome Consortium (ICGC). Both tumor and healthy cells from over 1000 patients have been sequenced and molecular differences have been recorded in TCGA across 34 cancer types. These data are currently held at the Cancer Genomics Hub at the University of California, Santa Cruz (UCSC). Also, for ICGC, more than 666 terabytes of data have been profiled. The recent ICGC data release is version 21, which contains 68 different cancer projects covering 18,677 donors. These data are housed on separate repositories, such as the European Genome-phenome Archive (EGA-Hinxton), Pan-Cancer Analysis of Whole Genomes

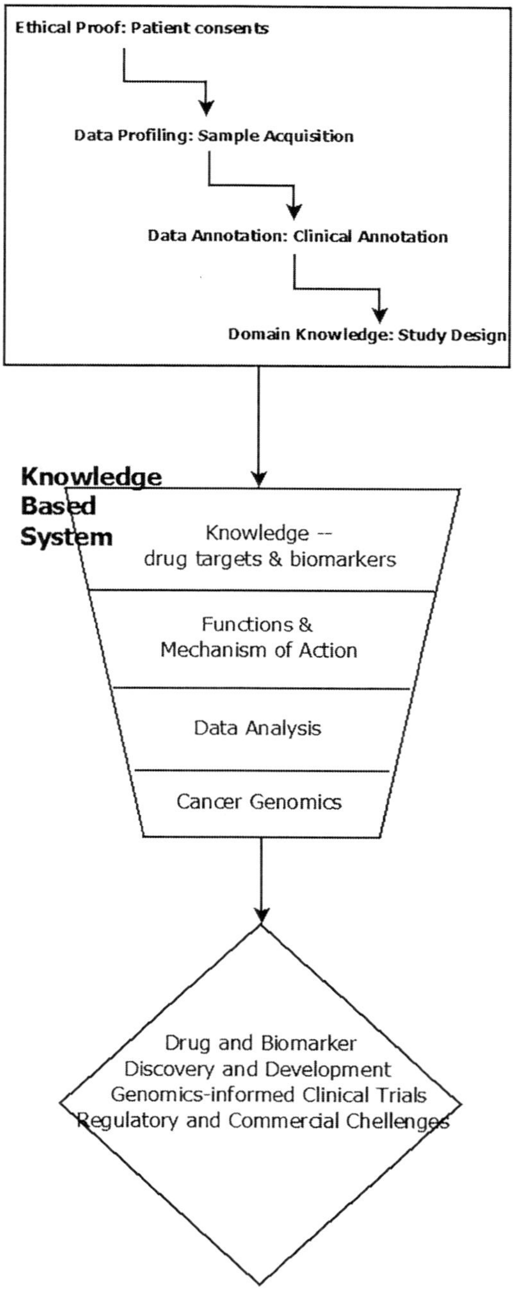

FIGURE 18.3 From cancer genomics to personalized medicine. (From Lynda Chin et al. *Nature Medicine*, 17(3):297–303, 2011.)

(PCAWG), Genomic Data Commons in the University of Chicago (GDC), and so on. As a benefit of cloud computing technologies, more and more data are now being transferred to Amazon Web Services (AWS). Figure 18.4 shows a statistic diagram of ICGC. Meanwhile, the Broads Genome Data Analysis Center (GDAC) is another genome data center that processes TCGA data through

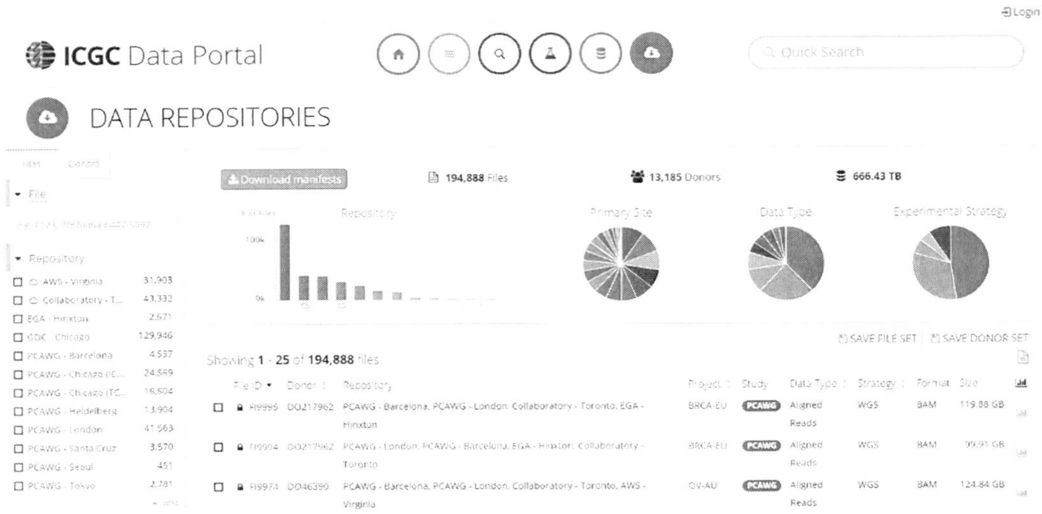

FIGURE 18.4 A statistic diagram from ICGC data portal.

their computational framework to generate analysis reports. This pipeline shown in Figure 18.5 in the computational framework is called Firehose.

However, most of the ongoing work still focuses on data acquisition and storage. Especially for some controlled data, the ethical and legal policies still need more consolidation efforts and a proper protocol to process. An in-depth analysis, such as a specific discovery, which is previously unreported loss-of-function mutations in HLA-A gene in over 170 squamous cell lung cancers by "The Cancer Genome Atlas Research Network" (TCGA) [43], has shown the power and importance of network collaboration. Beyond TCGA, these data would need to be more publicly available to researchers all over the world to facilitate the analysis.

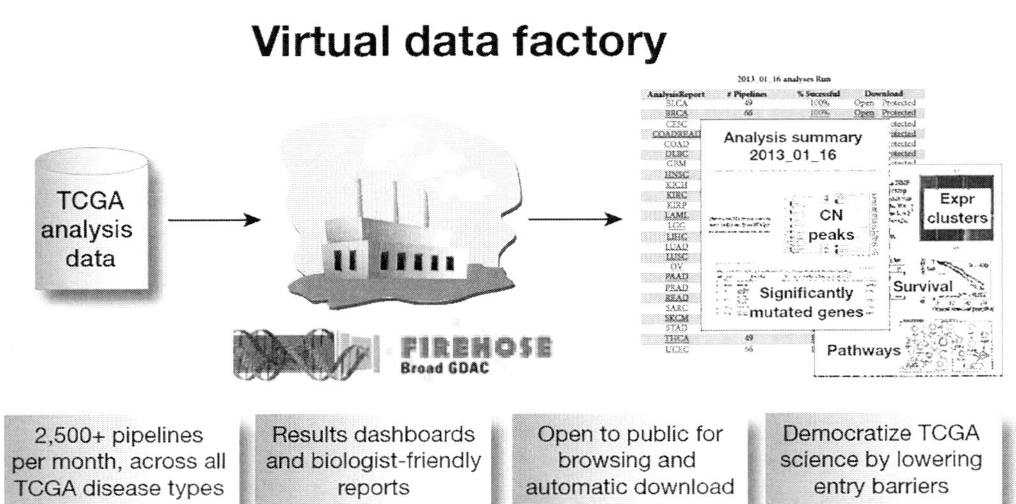

FIGURE 18.5 Broads genome data analysis center: Firehose. (From Vivien Marx. *Nature Methods*, 10(4):293–297, 2013.)

With the benefits from high-throughput technologies, cancer genomics is able to compare the genomics sequences, epigenomics profiles, and even the transcriptomics data between tumor cells and normal cells [44]. As the increasing research on genomics aberrations inspires to target on the ultimate goal, that is, personalized cancer medicine, the future focus of cancer genomics falls on the identification of new genetic aberrations [45], which is the critical aspect in revealing the cancer mechanism. Specifically, as cancer mostly occurs due to somatic mutations in genome with additional contributions from epigenetic and transcriptomics alterations, one of the in-depth analyses is mainly focused on the somatic mutations in cancer genomics data. This awareness focusing on somatic mutations research has promised us within the reach of personalized cancer medicine [46], in which three main challenges are considered as the key hurdles. The first issue is to identify the somatic mutations from the short sequence reads, the second issue is to distinguish the responsible but small somatic mutation for the development and progression of cancer, and the last one is to determine the developing biological pathways and processes that are expressed by these somatic mutations [45].

Along with the studies on cancer mechanism via cancer genomics, research on cancer treatments is another main area in cancer genomics. Through the enhanced understanding of molecular mechanisms of cancer, it is meaningful to translate the genomics data to improve cancer prevention, early detection, diagnosis, and treatment [47]. This would also be the link between cancer genomics and precision medicine, especially personalized cancer medicine, in modern oncology. Since very tiny changes in DNAs and RNAs could possibly introduce large-scale effects on the phenotype [48], the more we know by extracting from cancer genomics, the deeper and closer we are able to get a precision treatment.

Early-stage research is ongoing in the area of associating the high or low levels of gene expression with profiles of increased sensitivity or resistance to specific compounds [39,49]. As TCGA and ICGC are generating an overwhelming amount of cancer genomics data, both whole genome sequencing and targeted genome sequencing are promising to reveal individual genomics variants information [40,45]. The research on cancer treatments associated with genomics aims to detect the molecularly targeted therapies based on the genomics alterations in patient's tumor, from the perspectives of initiation and progression of cancer [50,51]. A specific research based on integration of analyzing complex cancer genomics and clinical profiles is introduced in Reference 52. Focusing on visualization and analysis of multidimensional cancer genomics data, Reference 52 provides a portal, namely, cBioPortal, to process the overwhelming surge of multidimensional genomics data. Currently, the users are able to view some basic patterns in gene alterations across samples in a cancer study, even to link the patterns to clinical outcomes when the related data are available. Yet, the future direction for cBioPortal is to include more genomics data types and clinical attributes. The related genomics data types include somatic mutations, DNA copy-number alterations (CNAs), mRNA and micro-RNA (miRNA) expression, DNA methylation, and proteomics data. The feature of batch download of complete datasets is also anticipated.

The gap between the study of precision medicine and cancer genomics is wide, and currently the research strength on translating genomics data from genotype to phenotype could not yet reduce the gap and bind these two areas together. This intrigues the introduction of data science, especially big data-related research, into this domain. Focusing on the early stage of big data analytics in the genomics area, we will provide a discussion about data management and analysis in genomics data in the next section.

18.3 EMERGING BIG DATA LANDSCAPE IN GENOMICS

As discussed in the earlier sections, to adapt big data analytics technologies in the genomics area, a scientific community consisting of bioinformatics, biomathematics, and biostatistics would be desired to transfer the genomics data to its biological meaning, which targets both precision medicine and cancer genomics areas [8]. At the turning point toward a data-intensive research in the bioinformatics area, we are able to decipher the potential clues on the mechanisms underlying disease initiation and progression, as well as providing further novel strategies for efficient prevention and treatment [8,9,53]. Inside these expectations, the effort in drilling the big data analytics technology into genomics data entails many challenges and future research directions. Although there are very few studies to reveal and establish a general or specific model on discovering the inner value out of genomics data for further study of disease mechanism, interventions, and treatments, the bottleneck has been shifted from the genomics data profiling to data management, which includes acquisition, transfer, and storage.

A basic "life cycle" of a dataset encompasses data acquisition, data transfer, data storage, and data analysis. In bioinformatics, the typical initialized dataset size was about 2.5 gigabyte in the year 2000, which was publicly available on the file transfer protocol site of the University of California, Santa Cruz [54]. In 2012, the dataset size was reported to be approximately 170 terabyte in the Cancer Genomics Hub (CGHub) [55,56]. Beyond the size of dataset, the computational infrastructure and software tools need to meet the requirement of the analysis tasks. Comparing with the data in astronomy, the data in genomics is much more heterogeneous [5], which brings more challenges when considering that even a single human sequencing genome is around 140 gigabyte in size nowadays.

Utilizing and optimizing the technologies in the big data area for genomics require special expertise and experiences in data sciences. As stated above, data are the key to interpret these inner meanings. In this section, the emerging big data landscape in genomics would introduce several novel ideas to overcome the challenges in dataset transfer, storage, and computation.

18.3.1 Data Acquisition

According to the facilities recorded in Reference 47, currently there are 7389 high-throughput "next-generation" sequencing machines situated in 1027 centers, out of which most of the machines are situated in the United States (5492 machines). These machines are the main data acquisition access of genomics. Since most machines are located in the United States, these sequencing data are mostly archived in Sequence Read Archive (SRA) maintained by the United States National Institutes of Health/National Center for Biotechnology Information (NIH/NCBI). Besides these direct sequencing data, the TCGA and ICGC also archive the cancer genomics data from both tumor and healthy cells. The genomics data are heterogeneous and the research focus of these centers differs from each other. Currently the genomics data are highly distributed and stored in different satellite sites as a consequence of the location distribution.

For the highly distributed data sites, a comprehensive dataset repository in one single site seems to be impossible in a short term. Besides the data transfer to AWS, there is also an ongoing project in ICGC that transfers data from different satellite sites to a single controllable repository, which is considered as a much more efficient way to maintain and distribute the data [13]. However, for other big data areas, the data acquisition accesses and acquisition differ a lot [5]. In the astronomy area, the astronomical data are acquired by limited specialist facilities [57,58], while in the video area, most of the video data comes from YouTube streaming clips under several standard protocols. The fMRI (functional magnetic resonance imaging) images are collected with controllable converted formats by some centralized facilities.

Data quality control is an important aspect for genomics data, since these data are generally unaligned and noisy. In some occasions, data value would be even missing. The electronic internal fluctuations of the instruments result in a nonconsistent performance across the profiling process. Considering the published dataset, the Genomics of Drug Sensitivity in Cancer project, it contains 639 cancer cell lines, which are described by a set of genomics features [39]. However, the data-missing problem reduces the available training dataset from 639 to 608, which results in less data samples. To uncover the knowledge beneath these data, a simple target toward data analysis is not enough since the data consist of multiple levels for their own corresponding meanings, including DNA sequencing data, RNA expression data, miRNA data, and so on.

To accommodate these problems, completing the missing data via data analytics method and designing a rational data integration model from multiple levels are required. A hybrid understanding on these data is critical in the data acquisition stage and may lead to a more meaningful and better knowledge discovery.

18.3.2 Data Transfer

It becomes increasingly challenging for a single facility to host its own data on a single machine since the upsurge speed of data is exceeding the Moore's law. Over the next 10 years, the sequencing speed and capacity are expected to grow continually. As collaborations are more common nowadays, the data in TCGA and ICGC are deposited in the corresponding portal and also every collaborator houses their own data. Considering the heterogeneity in omics data, the various communities supported by different foundering agencies also generate their own omics data [59]. An increasing motivation to share and transfer the data from the data portal to scientists at high speed has been significantly raised.

As a starting maneuver, some ICGC data are deposited in the European Genome Phoneme Archive [13]. Meanwhile, each ICGC collaboration country (since PCAWG is distributed by countries) and AWS also house their own data. Yet, the network issues have been occasionally occurring and brought inconvenience to scientists. Thus, now, a centralized database is being built to host all the interpreted data. This centralized database is chosen to be located in the Ontario Institute for Cancer Research (OICR). With such a strategy that centralized administering data by one single portal site, a faster and more stable connectivity is critical in data transfer. Currently, the Beijing Genomics Institute (BGI) in Shenzhen, China, is able to generate 6 terabytes of genomics data per day. BGI can transfer about 1 terabyte per day to its customer. By exploring a variety of technologies for data transfer over the Internet, BGI has a vision that their transferred ability could reach 24 gigabyte every 30 seconds when transferring data from China to University of California, San Diego (UCSD) [60]. However, this technology, namely, FASP, also requires the operators to maintain an extremely large bandwidth, which makes the transfer of data expensive in the genomics area.

An improvement on the Internet protocol itself would be a direct solution for big data transfer in genomics, such as Internet2 [61]. Aside from protocol technology, data compression on the DNA sequence reads, specifically in the FASTQ format, is another aspect to speed up the data transfer [55,62–65]. FASTQ format is a standard format for storing both a biological sequence and its corresponding quality scores. Another method to boost the data transfer speed would be realized via the efficient data distribution [55,63,66].

However, data transfer could be one of the less critical bottlenecks to apply big data analytics in genomics, while data storage strategy is supposed to significantly affect the performance of data processing. Since a single genome data file could be several gigabytes and also the data are highly distributed all over the world, the data analysis neither on the cloud nor the local storage in a raw data format could be limited. This introduces the discussion of the genomics data storage.

18.3.3 Data Storage

Petabyte-level storage management is required nowadays to tackle the storage demands in many big data areas. In the genomics area, the huge demand for storage mainly comes from the raw genomics data. Since the storage issue has been identified and shifted from the physical storage issues to the data itself, nowadays, shipping is still the main method to transfer large quantities of

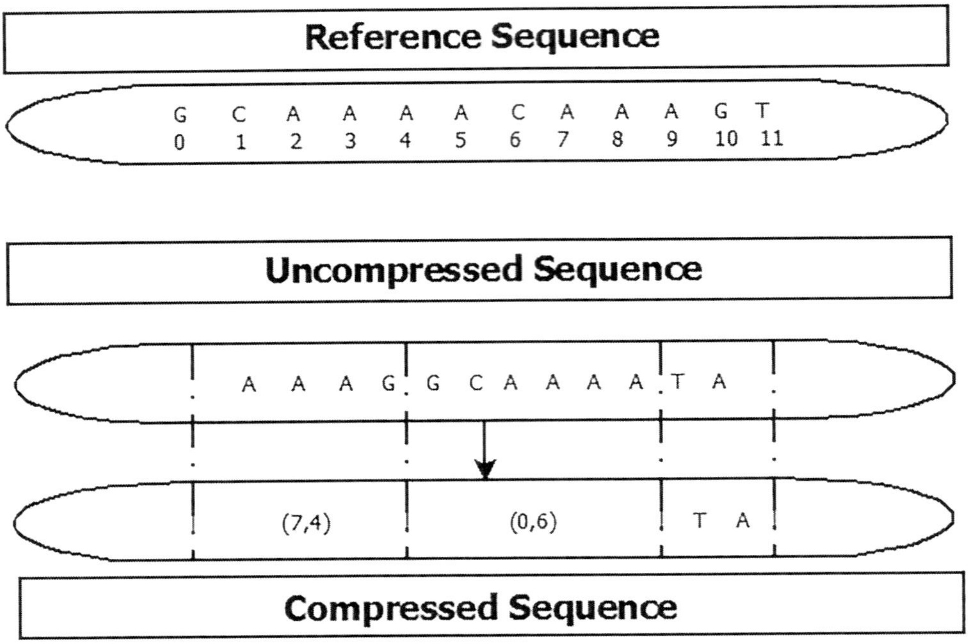

FIGURE 18.6 A referential compression sequence. (From Sebastian Wandelt. *Datenbank-Spektrum*, 12(3):161–171, 2012.)

sequence data [67]. Thus, an efficient method to store the genomics data remains a major challenge for genomics data.

A method that encodes the difference between a logging genome sequence and a recorded reference genome sequence was introduced in Reference 68. Considering that a single human genome that might occupy three gigabytes of storage, it would be 150 terabyte when it might reach 50,000 human genomes [67]. Different from traditional data compression algorithms, bioinformatics utilizes a referential data compression algorithm to avoid a huge decompression time consumption and keep the absolute fidelity of the raw sequence data [5,69,70]. A simple example for referential compression sequence is shown in Figure 18.6. A developed algorithm based on this compression schema could reach an evolutionary compression rate of 400:1 or even higher [67,68]. Shown as Figure 18.6, the reference sequence is set to be "GCAAAACAAAGT" while normally we used the Revised Cambridge Reference Sequence (rCRS). It is represented by its coordinate positions. For the uncompressed sequence, "AAAGGCAAAATA," the matches (7,4) and (0,6) indicate the segments of "AAAG" and "GCAAAA" by the start position and the length of the segments. The last segment, which is "TA," is stored in its raw data format since there is no good matching in the reference sequence.

To achieve an optimal compression algorithm and develop it into a standard is a promising effort to facilitate the storage of genomics data efficiently. However, using the compression strategy on genomics data to resolve the data storage problem remains open and a challenge for researchers [67]. A balance between compression speed and compression rate is one of the critical issues. Another issue after the data compression is about how to utilize these compressed sequences directly. Despite the data compression aspect in storage, data reduction is also a main aspect in data storage, which introduces great opportunities for a direct understanding of the raw genomics data. As soon as the real-time abstraction method becomes mature, these raw data will be redundant and no longer need to be stored in their raw representation method.

18.3.4 Data Analysis

Data analysis is the final stage that matters the most. It is the primary challenge when the researchers aim to learn knowledge from the massive genomics data. A functional data analysis comprises data visualization, data relationship network mapping, data relationship rules extraction, and data prediction. Genomics data is heterogeneous and high dimensional, it fits perfectly with the four "Vs" definition of big data: which are high volume, high velocity, high variety, and high veracity [71–73].

As data science is now flourishing with overwhelming data, various frameworks and tools have been developed. Taking TCGA as an example, every two weeks, the Broads Genome Data Analysis Center (GDAC) processes the TCGA data by the computational framework Firehose and releases a brief analysis report, profiling the significant alterations, and correlating methylation status with clinical features and mutated genes. Meanwhile, another framework, namely, SeqWare, takes consideration of a small portion of ICGC data to release a report.

One important aspect of data analysis is data visualization. In the knowledge extraction phase, a useful and important step is offering an intuitive visualization of the genomics data to display the different types of alterations. As long as the visualization techniques are employed in many areas, several tools such as Circos, Gitools, the UCSC Cancer Genomics Browser, the Cancer Genome Workbench, and the cBio Cancer Genomics Portal are developed [44,74–78]. The visualization techniques offer a visual exploration mostly for the cancer genomics area, in which the concerned data could reveal the cancer initialization genes and pathways. Several examples have been visualized in Reference 37, which are distinguishing the alterations in cancer-driven genome data in tumors, studying the cause–effect relationships between different alteration types data in tumor samples, stratifying the tumor samples based on clinical annotations data, and mapping the global alteration profile patterns on the rearrangement of large chromosomal regions data. Visualization of cancer genomics data is critical to translate knowledge of cancer genomics data into a possible personalized cancer medicine, which provides challenges and opportunities for the complex genomics data.

Since machine-learning methods have been extensively employed in almost every scientific and engineering area, it has been considered as the next powerful toolbox to interpret the genomics data and act as an important piece of precision medicine [79–82]. An example utilizing machine learning in genomics is to learn to recognize the locations of transcription start sites (TSSs) in a genome sequence [11,26]. As a blend of machine learning and bioinformatics, it develops into several special learning models considering the application situations in the genomics area, including supervised learning and unsupervised learning.

As quoted from the "no free lunch theorems" [83], there is not an exactly perfect machine-learning algorithm working for all applications. In the bioinformatics area, especially in the genomics area, the various types of biology knowledge at hand are critical in selecting a proper model. However, mostly it is implicit in mapping the prior knowledge into the framing of the machine-learning problem [26]. For example, there was a study to quantitatively link the genomics data with its functional traits by utilizing the whole genome sequence data from the related microbial communities [35]. In Reference 80, both the multilayer perceptron (MLP) and radial basis function neural networks (RBFNN) have been employed to predict the probability of membership of one individual in a phenotypic class of interest using genomics and phenotypic data.

Along with several other issues, such as handling of heterogeneous data [84–89], feature selection, imbalanced datasets, and the missing data considering different data sources, using the machine-learning methods to provide a comprehensive analysis and prediction in the genomics area remains challenging, yet promising [90,91].

In a nutshell, the ultimate goal for big data analytics in the genomics area is to be able to interpret genomics sequence, and further reach out to answer the relationship between genotype and phenotype data. To accomplish this goal, a hybrid understanding and cooperation from different domains, including data science, computer science, genomics specialist, and so on [59,92–95], are required.

In the next section, we will discuss two major projects: ENCODE project and CGHub project, to show how big data analytics could facilitate genomics research.

18.4 CASES IN GENOMICS ANALYTICS AND BIOINFORMATICS

Several research have achieved inspiring and interesting results from the analyses of big data in genomics. In this section, we will review some state-of-the-art achievements. One is the ENCODE project [92] and the other is the CGHub project [55,56].

18.4.1 ENCODE

The ENCODE (the encyclopedia of DNA Elements) project aims to project all the human genome to their corresponding functional elements. Launched in 2003, ENCODE involved more than 400 leading scientists and processed more than 11,972 files, with a size of more than 15 terabyte. The NHGRI established a worldwide research consortium.

Started with two phases simultaneously, a pilot phase and a technology development phase, currently, ENCODE is on its third phase, the production phase. The pilot phase tested and compared existing methods to rigorously analyze a defined portion of the human genome sequence, while the technology development phase scaled the ENCODE project to a production phase on the entire genome along with additional pilot-scale studies. The report of the pilot phase was published in June 2007 [96]. The findings highlighted the success of the project to identify and characterize functional elements in the human genome. The technology development phase has also been a success with the promotion of several new technologies to generate high-throughput data on functional elements.

The successes of the pilot phase and technology development phase stimulate the NHGRI to fund more studies in order to scale the ENCODE project to a production phase. Meanwhile, the production phase starts to include a Data Coordination Center, which is located at the University of California, Santa Cruz, to offer a storage, analysis, and service of the ENCODE data. Currently, there are over 440 scientists from 32 laboratories participating in the ENCODE project and the tasks are also assigned over different subgroups in the ENCODE Consortium, namely, Production Centers, Data Coordination Center, Data Analysis Center, Computational Analysis Awards, and Technology Development Effort.

The pilot phase targeted to identify gaps in current tools and data for detecting functional sequences, and also evaluate the efficiency of the available methods in a large-scale scenario. This phase involved both computational and experimental methods to annotate the human genome. The findings promoted the knowledge of human genome functions [96]. The targeted 1% of the human genome were studied from multiple and diverse experiments. The genome transcribed process, transcriptional regulation, a sophisticated view of chromatin structure, and data integration for new mechanistic and evolutionary insights of human genome functions were reported. The pilot phase helps define a more comprehensive pathway to understand the functional elements of the human genome.

In September 2007, the production phase was initiated in the ENCODE project. As a benefit from the pilot phase and technology development phase, an organized framework for genomics study was established, in which raw sequence data acted as the bottom layer with the annotation layers above [97]. The data model has facilitated the research on knowledge mining of the human genome [92,98–103]. As the data are continually accumulated, the real improvements start when the various datasets are layered together [104] to tackle much more complex genome mechanisms and diseases. Figure 18.7 shows a diagram of the ENCODE project. Currently, 13 of 60 known histone modifications and 120 of 1800 transcription factors are examined, which benefits a lot for the complex genome mechanisms study about the genotype–phenotype relationships. The view of genomics data from the biologists' side has been changed and revolutionized toward a data-intensive research when various data are tiered together in the ENCODE project.

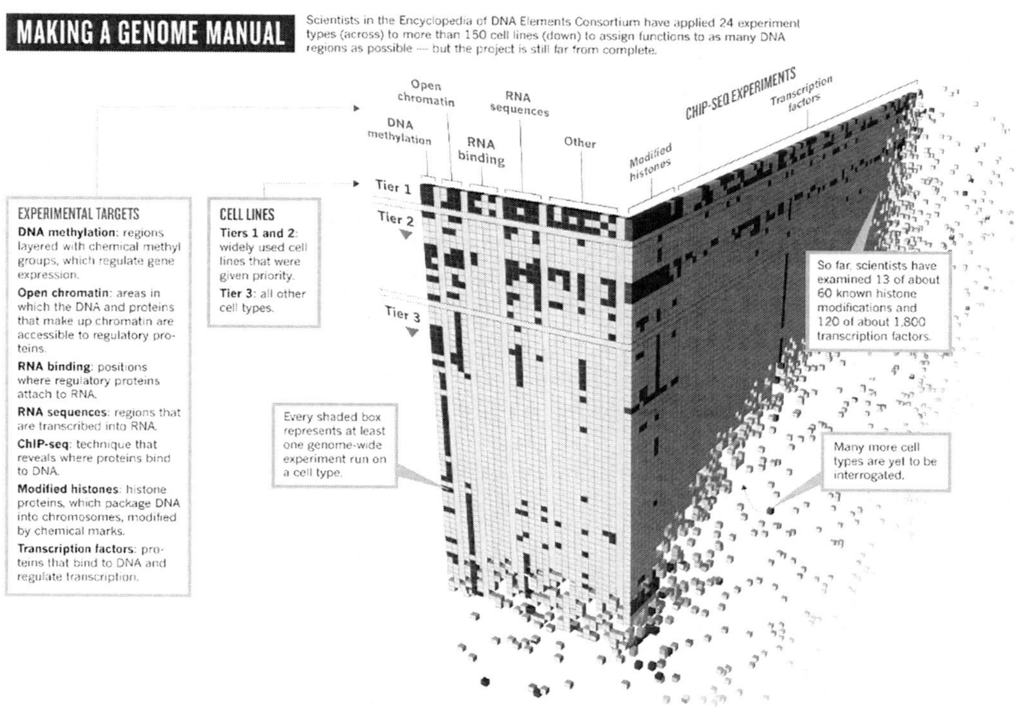

FIGURE 18.7 A diagram of ENCODE project. (From Brendan Maher. *Nature*, 489(7414):46, 2012.)

As the ENCODE project is currently on its way to the discovery of the functional elements of the human genome, the subgroup ENCODE Data Coordination Center (DCC) plays a key role in this project. A well-organized data transfer capability and a well-developed data visualization tool are the basic requirements in the ENCODE consortium. An available ENCODE data site on UCSC Genome Center is http://genome.ucsc.edu/ENCODE/. For cancer genomics research, another site named Cancer Genomics Hub in UCSC has already had a massive impact toward overcoming cancer through the power of torrential data [55,56].

18.4.2 CGHub

Under a contract with the National Cancer Institute (NCI), the Cancer Genomics Hub (CGHub) is an online repository of the sequence data, including the Cancer Genomics Atlas (TCGA), the Cancer Cell Line Encyclopedia (CCLE), and the Therapeutically Applicable Research to Generate Effective Treatments (TARGET) projects. Among the repository, there are more than 1.4 petabyte data.

Figure 18.8 shows the general TCGA data flow. Cancer genomics is the main focus area in CGHub. Considering data acquisition and data transfer issues mentioned in Section 18.3, a specially enhanced protocol and a well-designed data organization method have been developed.

To achieve a higher and better network service, CGHub utilized the Annai GeneTorrent (GT) protocol. It is an enhanced version of the BitTorrent (BT) protocol. Combined with the IBM General Purpose Filesystem (GPFS), CGHub is able to transfer data in a highly parallel and secure mode.

Since the data storage on CGHub is mostly patient-derived cancer genomics data, it is highly confidential. Only authorized researchers are able to access the data. In the system design phase, CGHub deployed a separate authentication and authorization component solution, which is a single-sign-on

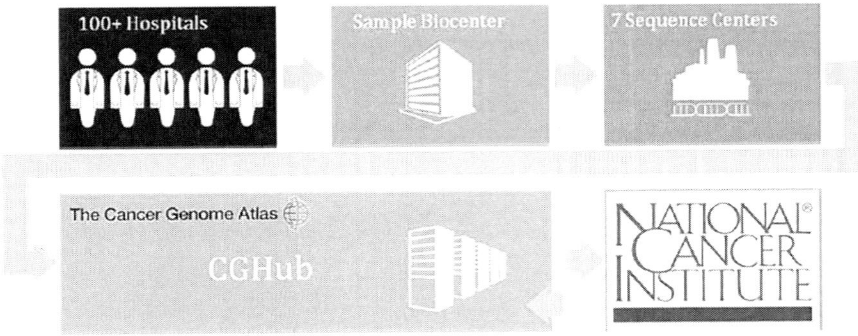

FIGURE 18.8 General TCGA data flow in CGHub. (From Christopher Wilks, Melissa S. Cline, Erich Weiler et al. *Database*, 2014:bau093, 2014.)

(SSO) architecture, and the full authorization is under the control of the NCI-appointed Data Access Committee (DAC).

To be a secure repository for the cancer genomics data, both the storage and transmission need to be encrypted. In CGHub, the SHA-1 (160 bits) hash and encryption are implemented for each single genomics sequence file. The genomics data are stored under the definition of the Sequence Read Archive Metadata XML schema, which is popular in the cancer genomics community. Including the available commands and interfaces, CGHub is an integrated system to provide confidential and interact service for cancer genomics researchers. As an extension of future development on CGHub, the expansion of data acquisition and storage issues are the promising research areas. Besides these, more help will come from the efforts on data transfer, such as deploying the Internet2 technology to increase the internet speed [13].

However, to address a possible solution on either precision medicine or cancer genomics, not a single site or single technology would be able to achieve them all [105,106]. DISSECT is now able to analyze a wide range of genomics data using the distributed-memory parallel computational architectures of computer clusters [105]. Even though the data are under restricted conditions, DISSECT shows an ability of achieving the same performance on large sample sizes. From the data sharing aspect, an omics data sharing mechanism is inevitably needed in the long run [107]. The genomics data are stored worldwide in many data centers. To reveal the genotype–phenotype relationships, the BD2K architecture is proposed to combine the separate genomics data repositories and deliver an open source software stack [107]. A cohesive genomics informatics ecosystem is desired and is developing very quickly.

18.5 SUMMARY

To utilize the big genomics data is challenging for our life and also research from every aspect. The life science, biomedicine, and healthcare sectors are currently at a turning point into a data-intensive science with the benefit from the overwhelmingly available data. When we are talking about big data analytics, the vision is not only about a research output but also the economic outcome and other benefits, specifically concerning human life. The genomics data lead us to a new era to play with heterogeneous data and domain knowledge in order to extract insightful knowledge for improving a better life.

As an emerging big data area, the knowledge discovery process of genomics data not only requires abundant data but also leverages the corresponding domain knowledge. In this chapter, two main concerning areas are discussed: precision medicine and cancer genomics. There is a scarcity of studies on the well-designed framework by now, which is both time-consuming and costly. A hybrid education and cooperation is highly demanded to leverage the data. Figure 18.9 shows a basic framework

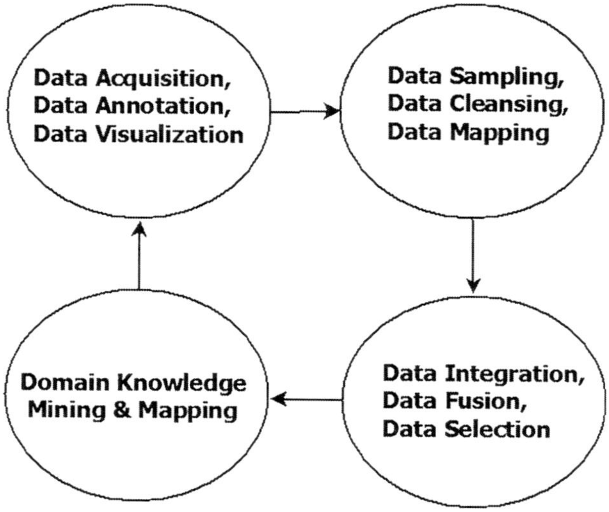

FIGURE 18.9 Proper framework for knowledge discovery in genomics.

for data science application. Several aspects must be considered during the research development, which are interpretability (being able to interpret the data clearly), reproducibility (could be mirrored to other research), simplicity (ease to deploy), and affinity (efficient utilization of the computation power).

Besides the domain knowledge involved in this chapter, we have reviewed the current international efforts in big data analytics in genomics data. In big data analytics, data matter the most, which introduces the issues of acquisition, storage, transfer, and analysis. As long as an urgent desire for efficient data operations before the specific analysis, the data operation problem is considered from several aspects: data acquisition, data transfer, and data storage. The highly distributed and heterogeneous characters of genomics data result in the specific requirement for data integration. Since both structured and unstructured data exist in the genomics area, an analysis either on the cloud side or in the local system involves a hybrid understanding of the cross-discipline areas.

We have also introduced some of our work [7,41] in big data analytics on genomics and proteomics. The ENCODE project and CGHub system were presented to give an understanding about how we take care of genomics data and how the data are revolutionizing our understanding of life. Technically, the legal and ethical issues are the first to be considered in the genomics area. Beyond further research of the genomics data, a basic pipeline to deal with the data operation issues (focusing on data acquisition, transfer, and storage) and also a general framework toward data analysis are desired to facilitate the international cooperation and research.

We have just reached a turning point toward the data-intensive life and research. Among these complex and unknown data, big data analytics has the potential to deliver a better understanding and improvement of our life. As in a nascent stage, the combination of big data analytics technologies and the surge of veracious data entail a lot of challenges and research visions.

REFERENCES

1. David J. Lockhart and Elizabeth A. Winzeler. Genomics, gene expression and DNA arrays. *Nature*, 405(6788):827–836, 2000.
2. Eric S. Lander. The new genomics: Global views of biology. *Science*, 274(5287):536, 1996.
3. Francis S. Collins, Eric D. Green, Alan E. Guttmacher, and Mark S. Guyer. A vision for the future of genomics research. *Nature*, 422(6934):835–847, 2003.

4. Human Genome Project Completion: Frequently Asked Questions. https://www. genome.gov/11006943/. Accessed: 2016-08-15.
5. Zachary D. Stephens, Skylar Y. Lee, Faraz Faghri, Roy H. Campbell, Chengxiang Zhai, Miles J. Efron, Ravishankar Iyer, Michael C. Schatz, Saurabh Sinha, and Gene E. Robinson. Big data: Astronomical or genomical? *PLoS Biol*, 13(7):e1002195, 2015.
6. Marylyn D. Ritchie, Emily R. Holzinger, Ruowang Li, Sarah A. Pendergrass, and Dokyoon Kim. Methods of integrating data to uncover genotype-phenotype interactions. *Nature Reviews Genetics*, 16(2):85–97, 2015.
7. Huaming Chen, Jun Shen, Lei Wang, and Jiangning Song. Towards data analytics of pathogen–host protein–protein interaction: A survey. In *Big Data (BigData Congress), 2016 IEEE International Congress on*, San Francisco, California, USA, pp. 377–388, IEEE.
8. Akram Alyass, Michelle Turcotte, and David Meyre. From big data analysis to personalized medicine for all: Challenges and opportunities. *BMC Medical Genomics*, 8(1):33, 2015.
9. Elaine R. Mardis. The 1,000 genome, the 100,000 analysis? *Genome Medicine*, 2(11):1, 2010.
10. Andreas Holzinger, Matthias Dehmer, and Igor Jurisica. Knowledge discovery and interactive data mining in bioinformatics state-of-the-art, future challenges and research directions. *BMC Bioinformatics*, 15(6):1, 2014.
11. Uwe Ohler, Guo-chun Liao, Heinrich Niemann, and Gerald M. Rubin. Computational analysis of core promoters in the drosophila genome. *Genome Biology*, 3(12):1, 2002.
12. Francis S. Collins and Harold Varmus. A new initiative on precision medicine. *New England Journal of Medicine*, 372(9):793–795, 2015.
13. Vivien Marx. Drilling into big cancer-genome data. *Nature Methods*, 10(4):293–297, 2013.
14. Wylie Burke and Bruce M. Psaty. Personalized medicine in the era of genomics. *JAMA*, 298(14):1682–1684, 2007.
15. Vasant Dhar. Data science and prediction. *Communications of the ACM*, 56(12):64–73, 2013.
16. Leroy Hood and Stephen H. Friend. Predictive, personalized, preventive, participatory (p4) cancer medicine. *Nature Reviews Clinical Oncology*, 8(3):184–187, 2011.
17. National Research Council (US) Committee on A Framework for Developing a New Taxonomy of Disease et al. *Toward Precision Medicine: Building a Knowledge Network for Biomedical Research and a New Taxonomy of Disease*. National Academies Press (US), Washington, DC, 2011.
18. Charles Auffray, Zhu Chen, and Leroy Hood. Systems medicine: The future of medical genomics and healthcare. *Genome Medicine*, 1(1):1, 2009.
19. Cosmas Giallourakis, Charlotte Henson, Michael Reich, Xiaohui Xie, and Vamsi K. Mootha. Disease gene discovery through integrative genomics. *Annual Review of Genomics and Human Genetics*, 6:381–406, 2005.
20. Justin Lamb, Emily D. Crawford, David Peck, Joshua W. Modell, Irene C. Blat, Matthew J. Wrobel, Jim Lerner, Jean-Philippe Brunet, Aravind Subramanian, Kenneth N. Ross et al. The connectivity map: Using gene-expression signatures to connect small molecules, genes, and disease. *Science*, 313(5795):1929–1935, 2006.
21. Mingyu Liang. Integrative pathway knowledge bases as a tool for systems molecular medicine. *Physiological Genomics*, 30(3):209–212, 2007.
22. Pedro Beltrao, Christina Kiel, and Luis Serrano. Structures in systems biology. *Current Opinion in Structural Biology*, 17(3):378–384, 2007.
23. Jean-François Rual, Kavitha Venkatesan, Tong Hao, Tomoko Hirozane-Kishikawa, Amélie Dricot, Ning Li, Gabriel F. Berriz, Francis D. Gibbons, Matija Dreze, Nono Ayivi-Guedehoussou et al. Towards a proteome-scale map of the human protein–protein interaction network. *Nature*, 437(7062):1173–1178, 2005.
24. Philipp Bucher. Weight matrix descriptions of four eukaryotic RNA polymerase II promoter elements derived from 502 unrelated promoter sequences. *Journal of Molecular Biology*, 212(4):563–578, 1990.
25. Sven Degroeve, Bernard De Baets, Yves Van de Peer, and Pierre Rouzé. Feature subset selection for splice site prediction. *Bioinformatics*, 18(Suppl 2):S75–S83, 2002.
26. Maxwell W. Libbrecht and William Stafford Noble. Machine learning applications in genetics and genomics. *Nature Reviews Genetics*, 16(6):321–332, 2015.

27. Eran Segal, Yvonne Fondufe-Mittendorf, Lingyi Chen, AnnChristine Thåström, Yair Field, Irene K. Moore, Ji-Ping Z. Wang, and Jonathan Widom. A genomic code for nucleosome positioning. *Nature*, 442(7104):772–778, 2006.
28. Dan M. Roden and Rachel F. Tyndale. Genomic medicine, precision medicine, personalized medicine: What's in a name? *Clinical Pharmacology & Therapeutics*, 94(2):169–172, 2013.
29. Teri A. Manolio, Rex L. Chisholm, Brad Ozenberger, Dan M. Roden, Marc S. Williams, Richard Wilson, David Bick, Erwin P. Bottinger, Murray H. Brilliant, Charis Eng et al. Implementing genomic medicine in the clinic: The future is here. *Genetics in Medicine*, 15(4):258–267, 2013.
30. John H. Coote and Michael J. Joyner. Is precision medicine the route to a healthy world? *The Lancet*, 385(9978):1617, 2015.
31. James M. Rae, Meredith Regan, Brian Leyland-Jones, Daniel F. Hayes, and Mitch Dowsett. Cyp2d6 genotype should not be used for deciding about tamoxifen therapy in postmenopausal breast cancer. *Journal of Clinical Oncology*, 31(21):2753–2755, 2013.
32. Maren T. Scheuner, Han de Vries, Benjamin Kim, Robin C. Meili, Sarah H. Olmstead, and Stephanie Teleki. Are electronic health records ready for genomic medicine? *Genetics in Medicine*, 11(7):510–517, 2009.
33. Suzette J. Bielinski, Janet E. Olson, Jyotishman Pathak, Richard M. Weinshilboum, Liewei Wang, Kelly J. Lyke, Euijung Ryu, Paul V. Targonski, Michael D. Van Norstrand, Matthew A. Hathcock et al. Preemptive genotyping for personalized medicine: Design of the right drug, right dose, right time using genomic data to individualize treatment protocol. *Mayo Clinic Proceedings*, 89:25–33, 2014.
34. Reza Mirnezami, Jeremy Nicholson, and Ara Darzi. Preparing for precision medicine. *New England Journal of Medicine*, 366(6):489–491, 2012.
35. Wei Zhang, Erliang Zeng, Dan Liu, Stuart Jones, and Scott Emrich. A machine learning framework for trait based genomics. In *Computational Advances in Bio and Medical Sciences (ICCABS), 2012 IEEE 2nd International Conference on*, Las Vegas, NV, USA, pp. 1–6. IEEE, 2012.
36. Jia-Yang Li, Jun Wang, and Robert S. Zeigler. The 3,000 rice genomes project: New opportunities and challenges for future rice research. *GigaScience*, 3(1):1, 2014.
37. Chuang Ma, Hao Helen Zhang, and Xiangfeng Wang. Machine learning for big data analytics in plants. *Trends in Plant Science*, 19(12):798–808, 2014.
38. Lynda Chin, Jannik N. Andersen, and P. Andrew Futreal. Cancer genomics: From discovery science to personalized medicine. *Nature Medicine*, 17(3):297–303, 2011.
39. Mathew J. Garnett, Elena J. Edelman, Sonja J. Heidorn, Chris D. Greenman, Anahita Dastur, King Wai Lau, Patricia Greninger, I. Richard Thompson, Xi Luo, Jorge Soares et al. Systematic identification of genomic markers of drug sensitivity in cancer cells. *Nature*, 483(7391):570–575, 2012.
40. Bryndis Yngvadottir, Daniel G. MacArthur, Hanjun Jin, and Chris Tyler-Smith. The promise and reality of personal genomics. *Genome Biology*, 10(9):1, 2009.
41. Huaming Chen, Hong Zhao, Jun Shen, Rui Zhou, and Qingguo Zhou. Supervised machine learning model for high dimensional gene data in colon cancer detection. In *2015 IEEE International Congress on Big Data*, New York, USA, pp. 134–141. IEEE, 2015.
42. Rasool Fakoor, Faisal Ladhak, Azade Nazi, and Manfred Huber. Using deep learning to enhance cancer diagnosis and classification. In Proceedings of the International Conference on Machine Learning, Atlanta, USA, 2013.
43. Cancer Genome Atlas Research Network et al. Comprehensive genomic characterization of squamous cell lung cancers. *Nature*, 489(7417):519–525, 2012.
44. Michael P. Schroeder, Abel Gonzalez-Perez, and Nuria Lopez-Bigas. Visualizing multidimensional cancer genomics data. *Genome Medicine*, 5(1):1, 2013.
45. Ben Tran, Janet E. Dancey, Suzanne Kamel-Reid, John D. McPherson, Philippe L. Bedard, Andrew M.K. Brown, Tong Zhang, Patricia Shaw, Nicole Onetto, Lincoln Stein et al. Cancer genomics: Technology, discovery, and translation. *Journal of Clinical Oncology*, 30(6):647–660, 2012.
46. Benjamin J. Raphael, Jason R. Dobson, Layla Oesper, and Fabio Vandin. Identifying driver mutations in sequenced cancer genomes: Computational approaches to enable precision medicine. *Genome Medicine*, 6(1):1, 2014.
47. National Cancer Institute: Office of Cancer Genomics. http://ocg.cancer.gov/. Accessed: 2016-08-15.
48. Paul S. Meltzer. Cancer genomics: Small RNAs with big impacts. *Nature*, 435(7043):745–746, 2005.

49. Michael P. Menden, Francesco Iorio, Mathew Garnett, Ultan McDermott, Cyril H. Benes, Pedro J. Ballester, and Julio Saez-Rodriguez. Machine learning prediction of cancer cell sensitivity to drugs based on genomic and chemical properties. *PLoS One*, 8(4):e61318, 2013.
50. Douglas Hanahan and Robert A. Weinberg. Hallmarks of cancer: The next generation. *Cell*, 144(5):646–674, 2011.
51. Roychowdhury Sameek and Arul M. Chinnaiyan. Translating genomics for precision cancer medicine. *Annual Review of Genomics and Human Genetics*, 15:395–415, 2014.
52. Jianjiong Gao, Bülent Arman Aksoy, Ugur Dogrusoz, Gideon Dresdner, Benjamin Gross, S. Onur Sumer, Yichao Sun, Anders Jacobsen, Rileen Sinha, Erik Larsson et al. Integrative analysis of complex cancer genomics and clinical profiles using the cBioPortal. *Science Signaling*, 6(269):11, 2013.
53. Leroy Hood and Mauricio Flores. A personal view on systems medicine and the emergence of proactive p4 medicine: Predictive, preventive, personalized and participatory. *New Biotechnology*, 29(6):613–624, 2012.
54. W. James Kent and David Haussler. Assembly of the working draft of the human genome with gigassembler. *Genome Research*, 11(9):1541–1548, 2001.
55. Christopher Wilks, Melissa S. Cline, Erich Weiler, Mark Diehkans, Brian Craft, Christy Martin, Daniel Murphy, Howdy Pierce, John Black, Donavan Nelson et al. The cancer genomics hub (cghub): Overcoming cancer through the power of torrential data. *Database*, 2014:bau093, 2014.
56. Christopher Wilks, Dan Maltbie, Mark Diekhans, and David Haussler. Cghub: Kick-starting the worldwide genome web. *Proceedings of the Asia-Pacific Advanced Network*, 35:1–13, 2013.
57. Peter E. Dewdney, Peter J. Hall, Richard T. Schilizzi, and T. Joseph L.W. Lazio. The square kilometre array. *Proceedings of the IEEE*, 97(8):1482–1496, 2009.
58. Cameron Kiddle, A.R. Taylor, Jim Cordes, Olivier Eymere, Victoria Kaspi, Dan Pigat, Erik Rosolowsky, Ingrid Stairs, and A.G. Willis. Cyberska: An on-line collaborative portal for data-intensive radio astronomy. In *Proceedings of the 2011 ACM Workshop on Gateway Computing Environments*, Seattle, WA, USA, pp. 65–72, ACM, 2011.
59. Dawn Field, Susanna-Assunta Sansone, Amanda Collis, Tim Booth, Peter Dukes, Susan K. Gregurick, Karen Kennedy, Patrik Kolar, Eugene Kolker, Mary Maxon et al. 'omics data sharing. *Science*, 326(5950):234–236, 2009.
60. Vivien Marx. Biology: The big challenges of big data. *Nature*, 498(7453):255–260, 2013.
61. Rick Summerhill. The new Internet2 network. In *6th GLIF Meeting*, Tokyo, Japan, 2006.
62. James K. Bonfield and Matthew V. Mahoney. Compression of FASTQ and SAM format sequencing data. *PloS One*, 8(3):e59190, 2013.
63. Anthony J. Cox, Markus J. Bauer, Tobias Jakobi, and Giovanna Rosone. Large-scale compression of genomic sequence databases with the burrows–wheeler transform. *Bioinformatics*, 28(11):1415–1419, 2012.
64. Sebastian Deorowicz and Szymon Grabowski. Compression of DNA sequence reads in FASTQ format. *Bioinformatics*, 27(6):860–862, 2011.
65. Zexuan Zhu, Yongpeng Zhang, Zhen Ji, Shan He, and Xiao Yang. High-throughput DNA sequence data compression. *Briefings in Bioinformatics*, page bbt087, 2013.
66. Morgan G.I. Langille and Jonathan A. Eisen. Biotorrents: A file sharing service for scientific data. *PLoS One*, 5(4):e10071, 2010.
67. Sebastian Wandelt, Astrid Rheinländer, Marc Bux, Lisa Thalheim, Berit Haldemann, and Ulf Leser. Data management challenges in next generation sequencing. *Datenbank-Spektrum*, 12(3):161–171, 2012.
68. Marty C. Brandon, Douglas C. Wallace, and Pierre Baldi. Data structures and compression algorithms for genomic sequence data. *Bioinformatics*, 25(14):1731–1738, 2009.
69. Markus Hsi-Yang Fritz, Rasko Leinonen, Guy Cochrane, and Ewan Birney. Efficient storage of high throughput DNA sequencing data using reference-based compression. *Genome Research*, 21(5):734–740, 2011.
70. Po-Ru Loh, Michael Baym, and Bonnie Berger. Compressive genomics. *Nature Biotechnology*, 30(7):627–630, 2012.
71. Aaron Golden, S. George Djorgovski, and John M. Greally. Astrogenomics: Big data, old problems, old solutions? *Genome Biology*, 14(8):1, 2013.
72. Michael C. Schatz. Computational thinking in the era of big data biology. *Genome Biology*, 13(11):1, 2012.

73. Oswaldo Trelles, Pjotr Prins, Marc Snir, and Ritsert C. Jansen. Big data, but are we ready? *Nature Reviews Genetics*, 12(3):224–224, 2011.
74. Ethan Cerami, Jianjiong Gao, Ugur Dogrusoz, Benjamin E. Gross, Selcuk Onur Sumer, Bülent Arman Aksoy, Anders Jacobsen, Caitlin J. Byrne, Michael L. Heuer, Erik Larsson et al. The cBio cancer genomics portal: An open platform for exploring multidimensional cancer genomics data. *Cancer Discovery*, 2(5):401–404, 2012.
75. Martin Krzywinski, Jacqueline Schein, Inanc Birol, Joseph Connors, Randy Gascoyne, Doug Horsman, Steven J. Jones, and Marco A. Marra. Circos: An information aesthetic for comparative genomics. *Genome Research*, 19(9):1639–1645, 2009.
76. Christian Perez-Llamas and Nuria Lopez-Bigas. Gitools: Analysis and visualisation of genomic data using interactive heat-maps. *PloS One*, 6(5):e19541, 2011.
77. Jinghui Zhang, Richard Finney, Michael Edmonson, Carl Schaefer, William Rowe, Chunhua Yan, Robert Clifford, Sharon Greenblum, Gang Wu, Hongen Zhang et al. The cancer genome workbench: Identifying and visualizing complex genetic alterations in tumors. *NCI Nature Pathway Interaction Database*, 10, 2010. doi: 10.1038/pid.2010.1.
78. Jingchun Zhu, J. Zachary Sanborn, Stephen Benz, Christopher Szeto, Fan Hsu, Robert M. Kuhn, Donna Karolchik, John Archie, Marc E. Lenburg, Laura J. Esserman et al. The UCSC cancer genomics browser. *Nature Methods*, 6(4):239–240, 2009.
79. Manuel Galli, Italo Zoppis, Andrew Smith, Fulvio Magni, and Giancarlo Mauri. Machine learning approaches in MALDI-MSI: Clinical applications. *Expert Review of Proteomics*, 13(7):685–696, 2016.
80. Juan Manuel González-Camacho, José Crossa, Paulino Pérez-Rodríguez, Leonardo Ornella, and Daniel Gianola. Genome-enabled prediction using probabilistic neural network classifiers. *BMC Genomics*, 17(1):1, 2016.
81. Bevan E. Huang, Widya Mulyasasmita, and Gunaretnam Rajagopal. The path from big data to precision medicine. *Expert Review of Precision Medicine and Drug Development*, 1(2):129–143, 2016.
82. Rosa S. Kim, Nicolas Goossens, and Yujin Hoshida. Use of big data in drug development for precision medicine. *Expert Review of Precision Medicine and Drug Development*, 1(3):245–253, 2016.
83. David H. Wolpert and William G. Macready. No free lunch theorems for optimization. *IEEE Transactions on Evolutionary Computation*, 1(1):67–82, 1997.
84. Lisa M. Breckels, Sean B. Holden, David Wojnar, Claire M. Mulvey, Andy Christoforou, Arnoud Groen, Matthew W.B. Trotter, Oliver Kohlbacher, Kathryn S. Lilley, and Laurent Gatto. Learning from heterogeneous data sources: An application in spatial proteomics. *PLoS Computational Biology*, 12(5):e1004920, 2016.
85. Nanye Long, Daniel Gianola, Guilherme J.M. Rosa, Kent A. Weigel, and Santiago Avendano. Machine learning classification procedure for selecting SNPs in genomic selection: Application to early mortality in broilers. *Journal of Animal Breeding and Genetics*, 124(6):377–389, 2007.
86. Lourdes Peña-Castillo, Murat Tasan, Chad L. Myers, Hyunju Lee, Trupti Joshi, Chao Zhang, Yuanfang Guan, Michele Leone, Andrea Pagnani, Wan Kyu Kim et al. A critical assessment of mus musculus gene function prediction using integrated genomic evidence. *Genome Biology*, 9(1):1, 2008.
87. Ian Walsh, Gianluca Pollastri, and Silvio C.E. Tosatto. Correct machine learning on protein sequences: A peer-reviewing perspective. *Briefings in Bioinformatics*, page bbv082, 2015.
88. Todd Wasson and Alexander J. Hartemink. An ensemble model of competitive multi-factor binding of the genome. *Genome Research*, 19(11):2101–2112, 2009.
89. Roger Pique-Regi, Jacob F. Degner, Athma A. Pai, Daniel J. Gaffney, Yoav Gilad, and Jonathan K. Pritchard. Accurate inference of transcription factor binding from DNA sequence and chromatin accessibility data. *Genome Research*, 21(3):447–455, 2011.
90. Leonardo Ornella, P Pérez, Elizabeth Tapia, Jose M. González-Camacho, Juan Burgueño, Xuecai Zhang, Sukhwinder Singh, Felix Manuel San Vicente, David Bonnett, Susanne Dreisigacker et al. Genomic-enabled prediction with classification algorithms. *Heredity*, 112(6):616–626, 2014.
91. Isabela SantAnna, Rafael S. Tomaz, Gabi N. Silva, Moyses Nascimento, Leonardo L. Bhering, and Cosme D. Cruz. Superiority of artificial neural networks for a genetic classification procedure. *Genetics and Molecular Research*, 14(3):9898–906, 2015.
92. ENCODE Project Consortium et al. An integrated encyclopedia of DNA elements in the human genome. *Nature*, 489(7414):57–74, 2012.

93. Michael I. Jordan and Tom M. Mitchell. Machine learning: Trends, perspectives, and prospects. *Science*, 349(6245):255–260, 2015.
94. Aisling ODriscoll, Jurate Daugelaite, and Roy D. Sleator. Big data, Hadoop and cloud computing in genomics. *Journal of Biomedical Informatics*, 46(5):774–781, 2013.
95. Xindong Wu, Xingquan Zhu, Gong-Qing Wu, and Wei Ding. Data mining with big data. *IEEE Transactions on Knowledge and Data Engineering*, 26(1):97–107, 2014.
96. Ewan Birney, John A. Stamatoyannopoulos, Anindya Dutta, Roderic Guigó, Thomas R. Gingeras, Elliott H. Margulies, Zhiping Weng, Michael Snyder, Emmanouil T. Dermitzakis, Robert E. Thurman et al. Identification and analysis of functional elements in 1% of the human genome by the encode pilot project. *Nature*, 447(7146):799–816, 2007.
97. Mark Gerstein. Genomics: Encode leads the way on big data. *Nature*, 489(7415):208–208, 2012.
98. Sarah Djebali, Carrie A. Davis, Angelika Merkel, Alex Dobin, Timo Lassmann, Ali Mortazavi, Andrea Tanzer, Julien Lagarde, Wei Lin, Felix Schlesinger et al. Landscape of transcription in human cells. *Nature*, 489(7414):101–108, 2012.
99. Mark B. Gerstein, Anshul Kundaje, Manoj Hariharan, Stephen G. Landt, Koon-Kiu Yan, Chao Cheng, Xinmeng Jasmine Mu, Ekta Khurana, Joel Rozowsky, Roger Alexander et al. Architecture of the human regulatory network derived from encode data. *Nature*, 489(7414):91–100, 2012.
100. Shane Neph, Jeff Vierstra, Andrew B. Stergachis, Alex P. Reynolds, Eric Haugen, Benjamin Vernot, Robert E. Thurman, Sam John, Richard Sandstrom, Audra K. Johnson et al. An expansive human regulatory lexicon encoded in transcription factor footprints. *Nature*, 489(7414):83–90, 2012.
101. Amartya Sanyal, Bryan R. Lajoie, Gaurav Jain, and Job Dekker. The long-range interaction landscape of gene promoters. *Nature*, 489(7414):109–113, 2012.
102. Robert E. Thurman, Eric Rynes, Richard Humbert, Jeff Vierstra, Matthew T. Maurano, Eric Haugen, Nathan C. Sheffield, Andrew B. Stergachis, Hao Wang, Benjamin Vernot et al. The accessible chromatin landscape of the human genome. *Nature*, 489(7414):75–82, 2012.
103. Kevin Y. Yip, Chao Cheng, Nitin Bhardwaj, James B. Brown, Jing Leng, Anshul Kundaje, Joel Rozowsky, Ewan Birney, Peter Bickel, Michael Snyder et al. Classification of human genomic regions based on experimentally determined binding sites of more than 100 transcription-related factors. *Genome Biology*, 13(9):1, 2012.
104. Brendan Maher. Encode: The human encyclopaedia. *Nature*, 489(7414):46, 2012.
105. Oriol Canela-Xandri, Andy Law, Alan Gray, John A. Woolliams, and Albert Tenesa. A new tool called dissect for analysing large genomic data sets using a big data approach. *Nature Communications*, 6:10162, 2015.
106. Emily R. Holzinger, Scott M. Dudek, Alex T. Frase, Brooke Fridley, Prabhakar Chalise, and Marylyn D. Ritchie. Comparison of methods for meta-dimensional data analysis using in silico and biological data sets. In *2012 European Conference on Evolutionary Computation, Machine Learning and Data Mining in Bioinformatics*, Málaga, Spain, pp. 134–143. Springer.
107. Benedict Paten, Mark Diekhans, Brian J. Druker, Stephen Friend, Justin Guinney, Nadine Gassner, Mitchell Guttman, W. James Kent, Patrick Mantey, Adam A. Margolin et al. The nih bd2k center for big data in translational genomics. *Journal of the American Medical Informatics Association*, 22(6):1143–1147, 2015.

19 Maximizing the Return on Investment in Big Data Projects

An Approach Based upon the Incremental Funding of Project Development

Antonio Juarez Alencar, Mauro Penha Bastos, Eber Assis Schmitz, Monica Ferreira da Silva, and Petros Sotirios Stefaneas

CONTENTS

ABSTRACT

Big data has created a foundation upon which competitive advantage can be created, sustained, and increased. However, it is the case that big data project managers are frequently unaware that financial planning is paramount to ensure return on investment. Otherwise, their projects may require more capital investment than they should and yield less financial returns. As a result, some of the projects they are responsible for may become unattractive or unfeasible from the financial point of view and have to be abandoned. This chapter presents a method to maximize the return on investment in big data projects. The method takes advantage of the fact that these projects are often divided into interrelated subprojects. Moreover, it acknowledges the fact that not all subprojects are necessarily going to be run. In addition, the order in which these subprojects are actually run may alter the financial value of big data projects as a whole. All of this provides big data project managers with a tool that allows them to make better financial decisions and increase the chances of having their projects selected for implementation.

19.1 INTRODUCTION

In recent years, a huge flow of structured and unstructured data has been made available for analysis to organizations in both the private and public sectors. According to Chen et al. (2014) and Rao and Ali (2015), the bulk of this data comes from

1. The business transactions that are recorded in computerized information systems on a daily basis,
2. The search engines that look for information over the Internet,
3. The social networks that connect people all over the world, and
4. The physical objects (appliances, sensors, cameras, machines, etc.) that are connected to the Internet in increasing numbers.

The term *big data* is frequently used to refer to this huge amount of data.

It is rightfully claimed by many that big data has become a basis for gaining competitive advantage, underpinning innovation, sales growth, increased productivity, and enhanced consumer satisfaction (Tien, 2015). Nevertheless, the business value of big data does not stem from the amount of data that an organization has at its disposal, but from what it does with it. In this respect, using currently available technology, one can gather data from a variety of sources. This data can then be analyzed to provide answers that enable cost reduction, revenue increase, shortening process time, speeding up product development, and optimizing advertising (Fosso et al., 2015).

As a result, many big data projects are currently being run by organizations of all types and sizes. These projects cover a variety of different business and research areas such as financial services (Bedeley & Iyer, 2014), city planning (Sullivan & Mitra, 2014), bioinformatics (Shahzad & Ahsan, 2014), ecology (Hampton et al., 2013), and health care (Groves et al., 2013), among others. According to Jeff Kelly, a research analyst with Wikibon (www.wikibon.org), the big data market is likely to exceed US$ 50 billion by 2017 (Kelly, 2014).

Nevertheless, it is a well-established economic principle that everything costs something (Shiffman & Jochum, 2011). Moreover, every rational investment decision has to take into account all the opportunities that are currently available to investors. Therefore, besides being profitable, an investment opportunity has to be attractive from the financial point of view, that is, it has to provide more financial benefits than other investment opportunities (Melicher & Norton, 2013).

However, it is frequently the case that big data project managers are unaware of the effect of financial planning on the projects under their responsibility. As a result, many big data projects tend to require more capital investment than they should and yield less return on investment. Moreover, they are likely to be more exposed to financial risk. All of this may turn financially viable projects into unfeasible or unattractive endeavors, which have to be abandoned (Chen et al., 2015; Dutta & Bose, 2015).

This chapter presents a method to analyze big data projects from the financial point of view. The method takes into account that big data projects are frequently divided into a portfolio of interrelated subprojects to facilitate understanding, planning, and execution (Kerzner, 2013). Moreover, it identifies the subproject running order that maximizes the return on the investment that is about to be made. Finally, it takes into account that it may be more profitable not to run all the subprojects in the portfolio. This tends to make big data projects more attractive and valuable, increasing their chances of being selected for implementation.

The remainder of this chapter is organized as follows. Section 19.2 presents the concepts and techniques that are required to comprehend the subsequent sections. Section 19.3 discusses works that are related to the content of this chapter. Section 19.4 introduces the method with the help of a real-world inspired example. Section 19.5 summarizes the method. Finally, Section 19.6 presents the conclusions of this chapter.

19.2 CONCEPTUAL BACKGROUND

According to the Project Management Institute (www.pmi.org), a project is a temporary undertaking that aims to create a unique product, service, or result. In this context, a subproject is a project partition of reduced scope, containing strongly related activities (PMI, 2013).

The idea of dividing a project into subprojects is not new. It is believed that the Egyptians used it to expedite the construction of the pyramids in the Giza Plateau, about 5000 years ago (El-Mehalawi, 2010; Hodgson & Cicmil, 2006). In this respect, the use of subprojects tends to facilitate understanding, planning, execution, and monitoring. Moreover, it is likely to make the estimates of cost and duration more accurate (Kerzner, 2013).

According to Denne and Cleland-Huang, there are two kinds of subprojects into which a project can be divided (Alencar et al., 2012a). The first, called *minimum marketable feature* or *MMFs*, yield direct financial returns when they are completed. The second, called *architectural elements* or *AEs*, yield no direct financial returns. However, they are necessary for the completion of other subprojects. Although the ideas of Denne and Cleland-Huang were originally expressed in terms of software modules, they are extended here to encompass projects and subprojects.

19.2.1 Dependency Relations among Subprojects

Although AEs and MMFs are usually self-contained units, it might be the case that a subproject can only be run when another is completed. This creates a dependency relation among subprojects, which is frequently modeled with the support of a network diagram (Kerzner, 2013).

For instance, consider a portfolio of subprojects $SP = \{sp1, sp2, \ldots, sp10\}$ into which a project P has been divided. Let us assume that *sp2* can only run when *sp1* is completed and that the same applies to *sp3* and *sp6* in regard to *sp2*. Moreover, take into account that *sp4* can only be run after the competition of *sp3* and that *sp5* cannot be run before *sp4* is finished. Furthermore, consider that *sp7* can only be after *sp6* is completed and that the same thing can be said about *sp8* in regard to *sp7*. In addition, acknowledge that *sp9* and *sp10* do not depend on the completion of one another to run. However, they have to wait for the completion of all the other subprojects in the portfolio before they can be run. The network diagram presented in Figure 19.1 specifies these dependency relations.

In Figure 19.1, *Begin* and *End* are dummy subprojects. They require no capital investment to be run. In addition, they take no time to be completed and yield no results. Moreover, an arrow going from a subproject to another, for example, $sp1 \rightarrow sp2$, indicates that the latter can only be run when

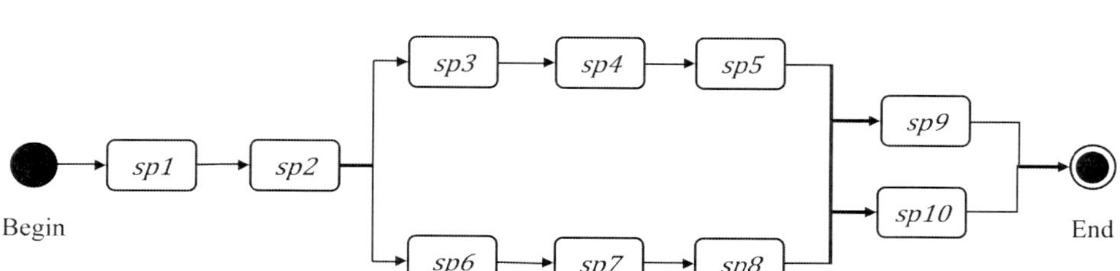

FIGURE 19.1 Network diagram.

the former is completed. See Kerzner (2013) and Nuguti (2015) for thorough but gentle introductions to the use of network diagrams to manage projects.

19.2.2 Project Financing

As everything costs something (Shiffman & Jochum, 2011), with the exception of dummy subprojects like *Begin* and *End*, every subproject requires capital investment to be run. In addition, some subprojects may produce a flow of financial inputs when they are completed. The financial inputs and outputs of a subproject describe a cash flow. For instance, Table 19.1 presents the cash flow of the subprojects of project *P* introduced in Figure 19.1.

In Table 19.1, *Id* is used to recognize that each subproject has a unique identifier. *Type* indicates whether a subproject is an AE or an MMF. *Period* refers to an arbitrary length of time of equal duration, for example, days, weeks, quarters, etc. *MkSp*, which stands for makespan, indicates the number of periods that a subproject requires to be completed. For example, all subprojects in Table 19.1 require just one period to be completed.

The numbers presented in Table 19.1 from column 1 to 24 are the subprojects' financial inputs and outputs. These numbers are introduced in thousand units of an arbitrary currency, that is, American dollar, euros, yens, British pounds, etc. The symbol $ is used to designate values of that currency. Positive values are financial inputs (i.e., revenues) while negatives values are financial outputs (i.e., expenses).

For example, Table 19.1 registers an output of $100 K (one hundred thousand monetary units) in the first period in respect to subproject *sp5*. This is the capital investment that is required to run that subproject. In periods 2 and 3, *sp5* yields outputs of $10 K and $20 K, respectively. From period 4 to 24, it yields a steady output of $60 K per period. Therefore, *sp5* is an MMF. Subprojects *sp8*, *sp9*, and *sp10* follow the same pattern and are also MMFs. The remaining subprojects in Table 19.1 are all AEs, that is, *sp1*, *sp2*, *sp3*, *sp4*, *sp6*, and *sp7*.

It should be noted that the flow of inputs and outputs described in Table 19.1 ends at period 24. By the end of that period, the final products yielded by the subprojects *sp1*, *sp2*, ..., *sp10* are out of date and a new solution is expected to take over. The length of time from period 1 to 24 is called *window of opportunity* or *WO* for short.

It is a well-established financial principle that monetary values associated with different periods do not have the same worth. The reasons for this are quite simple. For example, money can be invested and provide financial return. In particular, it can be lent and yield interest. Moreover, its value can

TABLE 19.1
Subprojects' Cash Flow

Subproject			Period								
Id	**Type**	***MkSp***	**1**	**2**	**3**	**4**	**5**	**6**	**7**	**...**	**24**
sp1	AE	1	−90	0	0	0	0	0	0	...	0
sp2	AE	1	−95	0	0	0	0	0	0	...	0
sp3	AE	1	−80	0	0	0	0	0	0	...	0
sp4	AE	1	−70	0	0	0	0	0	0	...	0
sp5	MMF	1	−100	10	20	60	60	60	60	...	60
sp6	AE	1	−60	0	0	0	0	0	0	...	0
sp7	AE	1	−75	0	0	0	0	0	0	...	0
sp8	MMF	1	−110	50	100	250	250	250	250	...	250
sp9	MMF	1	−300	0	4	6	8	10	12	...	46
sp10	MMF	1	−210	5	7	9	11	13	15	...	49

be corroded by inflation and fluctuations in the foreign exchange market. As a result, in order to be properly operated on (add, subtract, divide, etc.), monetary values associated with different periods have to be adjusted using an interest rate (Gitman & Zutter, 2014).

In this respect, the financial value of a subproject is frequently given by the adjusted sum of its cash flow elements, which take into account the period in which a subproject starts. Such a sum is called its *net present value* or *NPV* for short. In more formal terms, the *NPV* of a subproject *sp*, which starts at period *t*, is given by

$$NPV(sp, t) = \sum_{k=t}^{wo} \frac{e_{k-t+1}}{(1+i)^k} \tag{19.1}$$

where *WO* is the subproject's window of opportunity, $e_{k \in \{1,2,\ldots,wo-t+1\}}$ is the *k*-th cash flow element of *sp* and *i* is an interest rate. For example, consider an interest rate of 1.5% per period, which is used in all the remaining examples presented in this chapter. If *sp5* is run at period 3, then

$$NPV(sp5, 3) = \frac{-\$100\,\mathrm{K}}{(1+1.5\%)^3} + \frac{\$10\,\mathrm{K}}{(1+1.5\%)^4} + \frac{\$20\,\mathrm{K}}{(1+1.5\%)^4} + \cdots + \frac{\$60\,\mathrm{K}}{(1+1.5\%)^{24}} = \$847\,\mathrm{K}$$

If *sp5* is run at period 4, its *NPV* decreases to $793 K. At period 5, its *NPV* decreases even further to $740 K and so on and so forth. Table 19.2 presents the *NPV* of subprojects *sp1*, *sp2*, ..., *sp10* according to the period in which they start running.

If a project is to be fully implemented, then all its subprojects have to be run. In these circumstances, the financial value of a project is the sum of the *NPV*s of its subprojects. On the other hand, if a project is only partly implemented, then its *NPV* is the sum of the subprojects that are actually going to be run. For example, consider the following running sequence of the subprojects described in Figure 19.1:

$$RS = sp1 \rightarrow sp2 \rightarrow sp6 \rightarrow sp7 \rightarrow sp8 \rightarrow sp3 \rightarrow sp4 \rightarrow sp5 \rightarrow sp10 \rightarrow sp9$$

TABLE 19.2
Subprojects' *NPV* according to the Period in Which They Start Running

	Period						
Subproject Id	**1**	**2**	**3**	**4**	**5**	**...**	**24**
sp1	−89	−87	−86	−85	−84	...	−63
sp2	−94	−92	−91	−90	−88	...	−66
sp3	−79	−78	−77	−75	−74	...	−56
sp4	−69	−68	−67	−66	−65	...	−49
sp5	957	902	847	793	740	...	−70
sp6	−59	−58	−57	−57	−56	...	−42
sp7	−74	−73	−72	−71	−70	...	−52
sp8	4315	4079	3847	3618	3392	...	−77
sp9	135	101	69	39	11	...	−210
sp10	282	244	208	174	142	...	−147

TABLE 19.3
Constraints That a Running Sequence Should Satisfy

Id	Condition
a	The first subproject is run in the first period
b	Only one project can be running at any given time
c	There is no delay between the completion of a subproject and the beginning of the next
d	Once a project starts it cannot be interrupted
e	All subprojects must be run within the window of opportunity

In addition, take into account the constraints established in Table 19.3.

In these circumstances,

$$\begin{aligned} & NPV(RS) \\ & = NPV(sp1 \rightarrow sp2 \rightarrow sp6 \rightarrow sp7 \rightarrow sp8 \rightarrow sp3 \rightarrow sp4 \rightarrow sp5 \rightarrow sp10 \rightarrow sp9) \\ & = NPV(sp1, 1) + NPV(sp2, 2) + NPV(sp6, 3) + NPV(sp7, 4) + NPV(sp8, 5) \\ & \quad + NPV(sp3, 6) + NPV(sp4, 7) + NPV(sp5, 8) + NPV(sp10, 9) + \text{NPV}(sp9, 10) \\ & = -\$89\,\text{K} - \$92\,\text{K} - \$57\,\text{K} - \$71\,\text{K} + \$3392\,\text{K} - \$73\,\text{K} - \$63\,\text{K} \\ & \quad + \$586\,\text{K} + \$32\,\text{K} - \$103\,\text{K} = \$3462\,\text{K} \end{aligned}$$

If the last constraint stated in Table 19.3 were waived, then one could consider running just the first five subprojects in running sequence *RS*, that is, $sp1 \rightarrow sp2 \rightarrow sp6 \rightarrow sp7 \rightarrow sp8$. In this case,

$$NPV(sp1 \rightarrow sp2 \rightarrow sp6 \rightarrow sp7 \rightarrow sp8)$$

would amount to

$$-\$89\,\text{K} - \$92\,\text{K} - \$57\,\text{K} - \$71\,\text{K} + \$3392\,\text{K} = \$3083\,\text{K}$$

19.2.3 Running Sequence Rollout

Table 19.4 presents the financial details of the rollout of running sequence *RS*. In that table, lines from *sp1* to *sp10* contain the undiscounted cash flow elements of each of the subprojects of project *P*. This takes into account the period in which each subproject is run. See Table 19.1 in this respect.

For example, the sixth column of line *sp3* contains the first nonzero value that is registered in that line. This arises from the fact that in *RS*, subproject *sp3* is run in the sixth period.

The line *Total* indicates the total contribution of the different subprojects to the cash flow of *RS* in each period. For instance, in period 7, line *Total* registers \$30 K, which is the result of \$100–\$70 K.

Line *PV*, which stands for *present value*, shows that the value at the beginning of period 1 is equivalent in worth to the value shown in the *Total* line. For example, in period 7, line *PV* registers \$27 K. This indicates that if one invests \$27 K at the beginning of period 1, obtaining an interest rate of 1.5%, by the end of the seventh period, one has $\$27\,\text{K} \times (1 + 1.5\%)^7 = \$30\,\text{K}$.

Moreover, the sum of the absolute value of all negative numbers in the *PV* line is *capital investment* (*CI*) required by the running sequence, that is, \$89 K + \$92 K + \$57 K + \$71 K + \$102 K + \$27 K + \$22 K = \$460 K. In other words, this is the amount of money that one has to have at one's disposal at the beginning of period 1 to pursue *RS*.

TABLE 19.4
Cash Flow of an Implementation Sequence

	Period											
Subproject	**1**	**2**	**3**	**4**	**5**	**6**	**7**	**8**	**9**	**10**	**...**	**24**
sp1	−90	0	0	0	0	0	0	0	0	0	...	0
sp2		−95	0	0	0	0	0	0	0	0	...	0
sp6			−60	0	0	0	0	0	0	0	...	0
sp7				−75	0	0	0	0	0	0	...	0
sp8					−110	50	100	250	250	250	...	250
sp3						−80	0	0	0	0	...	0
sp4							−70	0	0	0	...	0
sp5								−100	10	20	...	60
sp10									−210	5	...	33
sp9										−300	...	28
Total	−90	−95	−60	−75	−110	−30	30	150	50	−25	...	371
PV	−89	−92	−57	−71	−102	−27	27	133	44	−22	...	260
Rollout	−89	−181	−238	−309	−411	−438	−411	−278	−234	−256	...	3,462

Finally, the line *Rollout* contains the accumulated sum of the values introduced in the *PV* line. It should be noted that the last value of this line is the *NPV* of *RS*.

The *return on investment* (*ROI*) of running sequence *RS* is given by

$$ROI(RS) = \frac{NPV(RS) - CI(RS)}{CI(RS)} = \frac{3462 - 460}{460} = 653\%$$

See Finnerty (2013) for an introduction to project financing.

Table 19.5 presents several possible running sequences for the subprojects of the project *P* described in Figure 19.1 together with their respective *NPV*, *CI*, and *ROI*. These sequences have been generated taking into consideration the constraints established in Table 19.3.

TABLE 19.5
List of all Possible Running Sequences

Id	**Running Sequence**	***NPV*** **($1000 K)**	***CI*** **($1000 K)**	***ROI*** **(%)**
1	*sp1* → *sp2* → *sp6* → *sp7* → *sp8* → *sp3* → *sp4* → *sp5* → *sp10* → *sp9*	3462	460	653
2	*sp1* → *sp2* → *sp6* → *sp7* → *sp8* → *sp3* → *sp4* → *sp5* → *sp9* → *sp10*	3459	473	631
3	*sp1* → *sp2* → *sp6* → *sp3* → *sp7* → *sp8* → *sp4* → *sp5* → *sp10* → *sp9*	3238	524	518
4	*sp1* → *sp2* → *sp6* → *sp7* → *sp3* → *sp8* → *sp4* → *sp5* → *sp10* → *sp9*	3238	524	518
5	*sp1* → *sp2* → *sp3* → *sp6* → *sp7* → *sp8* → *sp4* → *sp5* → *sp10* → *sp9*	3236	526	515
⋮	⋮	⋮	⋮	⋮
40	*sp1* → *sp2* → *sp3* → *sp6* → *sp7* → *sp4* → *sp5* → *sp8* → *sp9* → *sp10*	2848	872	227

Note that the sequences in Table 19.5 have been ordered by their *ROI*. As a result, the sequence that comes first in that table is the logical choice to run the subprojects in *SP*. This is the running sequence that yields the highest return on the investment that is about to be made.

19.3 RELATED WORK

19.3.1 On Incremental Funding of Big Data Projects and Initiatives

In order to identify work that is related to the incremental funding of big data projects, several repositories of scientific and technological research were consulted using the search string introduced in Table 19.6. These repositories are presented in Table 19.7. The search for related work was carried out on March 18, 2015.

Note that altogether the repositories presented in Table 19.7 index the majority of significant computer-related research around the world. Table 19.8 shows the number of references yielded by each repository. It should be mentioned that one article was referred to in more than one repository. As a result, the redundant reference was eliminated from the search for related work.

Note the repository that returned the vast majority of potentially relevant references was Google Scholar. Nevertheless, more recently, Google Scholar has been criticized with respect to its usefulness as a repository of references to scientific and technical work (Delgado et al., 2014).

TABLE 19.6
String Used in the Search for Related Work

Search String
"big data" AND (("incremental funding" OR "step-by-step funding" OR "additive funding" OR "cumulative funding") OR ("incremental backing" OR "step-by-step backing" OR "additive backing" OR "cumulative backing") OR ("incremental financing" OR "step-by-step financing" OR "additive financing" OR "cumulative financing"))

TABLE 19.7
Repositories of Scientific and Technical Work

Repositories	Internet Address
ACM Digital Library	http://dl.acm.org/
Google Scholar	https://scholar.google.com
IEEE Xplore Digital Library	http://ieeexplore.ieee.org/Xplore/home.jsp
JSTOR	http://www.jstor.org/
Science Direct	http://www.sciencedirect.com/
Scopus	http://www.scopus.com/
Springer Link	http://link.springer.com/
Web of Science	http://wokinfo.com/webtools/searchbox/
DBLP Computer Science Bibliography	http://dblp.uni-trier.de/

TABLE 19.8
Hits per Repository of Scientific and Technical Work

Repositories	Hits
ACM Digital Library	0
Google Scholar	15
IEEE Xplore Digital Library	0
JSTOR	0
Science Direct	1
Scopus	0
Springer Link	0
Web of Science	0
DBLP Computer Science Bibliography	0
Total	16

However, Google Scholar is the only free access repository that contains references to books, technical reports, patent applications, dissertations, theses, and unpublished works. Furthermore, occasionally, it indexes journals and conference papers that are not currently indexed by other repositories. As a result, the use of Google Scholar tends to increase the coverage of any review of the existing literature. In particular, it enhances the range of the search for work that is related to the content of this chapter. Table 19.9 presents the type of the publications yielded by the search performed on the repositories introduced in Table 19.7.

All the references presented in Table 19.8 were written in English. In order to have their relevance to the incremental funding of big data projects determined, they had their titles, abstracts, and keywords carefully examined. In addition, whenever it was found necessary, the full text of these works was also analyzed. If the search for related work returned a reference to a book, its pertinent sections were examined with the help of Google book (https://books.google.com). More specifically, the keywords and expressions used to build the search string presented in Table 19.6 were used to feed the book search mechanism and locate the pertinent sections. All of this follows the ideas of Kitchenham et al. (2015) on the systematic review of the literature.

TABLE 19.9
Types of Reference Returned by the Search Performed on the Repositories of Scientific and Technical Work

Type of Publication	Quantity
Journal article	1
Conference article	2
Book chapter	2
Technical magazine article	2
Technical report	5
Books	1
Patent registration	1
Total	14

As a result, it was found that none of the references considered in Table 19.8 discusses the incremental funding of big data projects. Therefore, at this date, no proposal has considered the possibility of using the revenue generated by a big data subproject to fund the development of other system parts. Moreover, no proposal has considered the impact of incrementally funding big data projects on their financial value. In addition, so far, no one has recognized the impact of the incremental funding approach to project finance on the likelihood of a big data project being selected for implementation. Hence, it seems reasonable to claim that this chapter presents a new and meaningful contribution to the management of big data projects.

19.3.2 Related Work Summary

The systematic search carried out in Section 19.3.1 reveals that no proposals have been presented so far with respect to the incremental funding of big data projects. Nevertheless, extensive work has been performed on extending and perfecting the idea of incrementally funding IT-related projects.* This creates a basis that can be used to maximize the return on the investment made in big data projects.

For instance, if the number of subprojects is considerable, the ideas of Alencar et al. (2014) can be used to obtain an approximate solution with an arbitrary error margin and degree of confidence. In addition, if the cash flow elements are uncertain, the ideas of Schmitz et al. (2008) can be considered to select the running sequence that is likely to provide the highest return on investment.

Moreover, if one is interested in the efficiency of the investment that is about to be made in a big data project, one could use the proposal of Alencar et al. (2012b) to identify the running sequence that is efficient from the point of view of several financial performance indicators. See Alencar et al. (2012a) for a partial summary of the work that has been developed so far on the incremental funding of IT-related projects.

19.4 AN EXAMPLE

Consider a large health insurance company such as United Health, Kaiser Foundation, or Wellpoint in the United States or Boots, BUPA, or Capital Healthcare in Europe. Let us call this company Health Investment Corporation, or HIC.

Although the health insurance business can be traced back to late nineteenth-century England (Beik, 2014), the health insurance market has never been in such a difficult position (Brunoni et al., 2015). Lately, medical research has made incredible advances in the treatment of a number of disabling or potentially fatal diseases, such as cancer, diabetes, ischemic heart disease, stroke, acute asthma, and many others (Weaver & Bryce, 2015).

However, this has come at a price. Understandably, those who suffer from these diseases are determined to have access to these new treatments. As a result, they have been putting pressure on their representatives to strengthen legislation so that they are treated with the latest available technology. However, these new treatments tend to be expensive. Hence, the cost of health care has been escalating all over the world (Emanuel, 2012).

All of this has led to threats to increase taxation to fund public health, which no one wants. It has also led to private health insurance with reduced coverage that many would rather not have or to private health insurance with wide coverage that just a few can afford. Therefore, both government and private business are in a situation in which they have to do more with their existing resources (Auerbach & Kellermann, 2011).

The HIC is well aware of the challenges that private insurance faces in this day and age (Meier et al., 2013). Its managers believe that it should be possible to reduce its running costs considerably so that they can offer affordable wide coverage insurance. As a result, they have been considering

* A search in Google and the Google Academic can reveal the extension of these works.

a number of information technology-related projects. There is, however, one particular project that has caught the attention of the company's CEO, that is, the possibility of using the huge amount of data they have been storing in HIC's computerized information system to devise a cost reduction strategy (White, 2014).

19.4.1 Task Force

A task force composed of IT professionals, business consultants, and medical personnel has been put together to study the problem and come up with suggestions. Initially, they have identified in the literature the diseases that most strongly affect the running cost of health insurance plans. Among those, one can cite heart conditions, diabetes, hypertension, cancer, and asthma among others (Hu et al., 2015).

Moreover, according to the business and medical teams, the cost of the treatment of these diseases can be considerably reduced through managed care programs. These programs are designed to motivate people to be actively involved with the treatment of the diseases they have. This includes wide access to easy-to-read medical information, taking an active part in support groups, and medical, nursing, and psychological assistance. All of this is intended to commit policyholders to change their lifestyle so that their diseases are kept under control.

For example, some of the program's participants may be required to follow a strict diet while others have to agree to exercise regularly and reduce their daily workload. Moreover, some of them have to consent to visit their doctors on a regular basis, take their medicines exactly as they have been prescribed, and keep certain health indicator parameters within preestablished limits. This may include the amount of glucose, cholesterol, urea, creatinine, and calcium in their blood.

When a support group of their peers is made available, the participants' progress toward dealing with their illnesses has to be reported to the group. It is surprising what motivated and well-informed policyholders can do to improve their own health with the support of others.

Some disease management programs even inform medical doctors and patients on the existence of equally effective, but less expensive treatments, when they are available. It is believed that it is in everybody's best interest to keep the cost of health insurance as low as possible. See Kongstvedt (2015) for a thorough introduction to managed care programs. See Denham et al. (2013), Marton et al. (2014), and Wallasch and Hermann (2012) for reports on the success of managed care programs in different circumstances.

19.4.2 Program's Admission Criteria

Although HIC management has agreed to the idea of setting up a managed care program, there is still the question of selecting the diseases that are going to be dealt with by the program. In addition, the company has to identify the right people to invite to take part in the program.

According to the medical team that is advising the HIC, heart conditions and diabetes are the right diseases to start with. They are among those that most strongly affect the operational cost of health plans. Moreover, people who suffer from these diseases display a distinct behavior with respect to the use of health insurance plans that are not hard to track.

For example, people who have a heart condition tend to visit the cardiologist on a regular basis. In addition, they are required to take electrocardiograms and echocardiograms more frequently than those that have a healthy heart. The same can be said about people with diabetes. They tend to visit the endocrinologist several times a year and take blood tests that monitor their glucose level more frequently than others do.

Furthermore, when people join a health insurance plan, they are required to declare the existence of certain preexisting diseases. Otherwise, the coverage provided by the plan may be void in the

TABLE 19.10
Criteria to Be Used for Admission into the Managed Care Program

Criteria Id	Heart Condition	Diabetes
1	Visiting the cardiologist two or more times within a period of 12 months	Having appointments with the endocrinologist two or more times within a period of 12 months
2	Taking an electrocardiogram or echocardiogram two or more times within a period of 12 months	Taking a blood test that monitors glucose levels two or more times within a period of 12 months
3	Declaring a heart condition as a preexisting illness when joining the health insurance plan	Indicating diabetes as a preexisting illness when joining the health insurance plan
4	Being at least 60 years old	Being at least 60 years old
5	Being admitted to a medical unit with an ICD related to heart diseases	Being admitted to a medical unit with an ICD related to diabetes

event of medical developments related to these diseases. This includes heart conditions and diabetes (Green, 2014).

Finally, when a person is admitted to a medical unit, the health insurance plan is informed of the nature of the medical event via the international classification of disease codes or ICD codes. For example, the ICD codes for diabetes range from E10 to E14, depending on the type of diabetes one has. A full list of the ICD codes can be found in Bowie and Schaffer (2013).

The medical team that is advising HIC also indicates that the insurance cost of heart conditions and diabetes are greater among the elderly (Hu et al., 2015). Therefore, special attention may have to be given to people belonging to this age group. Table 19.10 summarizes the criteria devised by the medical team to admit HIC policyholders into the company's managed care program.

It should be noted that among the admission criteria presented in Table 19.10, the last two are of special interest. As indicated by the medical team, there are many studies showing that hospitalization is one of the most expensive events in the health insurance business. Moreover, the chances of being readmitted to a hospital after being discharged are much higher among the elderly population (Krumholz, 2013). Therefore, those who comply with criteria 4 and 5 can be considered extremely high-risk policyholders.

Although there is some evidence that managed care programs may not be the best way to deal with the risk of hospital readmission, some new reports have indicated that with some adjustments, these programs may become more effective in this respect (Donzé et al., 2013).

19.4.3 Managed Care Program

To facilitate understanding, planning, and running, the HIC-managed care program has been divided into a number of subprojects. These subprojects are described in Table 19.11.

It should be noted that as a result of the risk assessment subproject *sp2*, policyholders are divided into four groups in respect to the risk of incurring considerable insurance costs in the near future, that is, low, medium, high, and extreme.

According to the business and medical teams, the investment that would have to be made in the low- and medium-risk groups tends to yield a negligible return on investment. Therefore, people in these groups are not going to be invited to take part in the managed care program.

The remaining policyholders are to be persuaded to take part in different programs. These managed care programs are essentially different because people in the extreme high-risk group require stronger and more expensive actions. Otherwise, their health insurance costs can easily get out of control.

TABLE 19.11
Managed Care Program Subprojects

Id	Description
sp1	*Search and identification*—Use the vast amount of information that has been stored in the HIC's databases to find those who fit at least one of the admission criteria for the managed care programs
sp2	*Risk assessment*—Interview those who can be potentially invited to join the programs over the phone so that the severity of their conditions can be estimated. Record the results of the interviews and risk assessments in the HIC's databases
sp3	*Set up the managed care program for high-risk policyholders*—Design the services that the HIC's managed care program is going to provide for policyholders who have high risk of incurring considerable insurance costs
sp4	*Invite high-risk policyholders to join the program*—Invite those who qualify to join in the managed care program for high-risk policyholders. Record in the HIC's databases the invitation results
sp5	*Run the high-risk managed care program*—Get people to commit to the program's regulations and activities. Run the program and monitor the changes of the participants' lifestyle. Record in the HIC's databases every interaction between the program and its participants
sp6	*Set up the extreme high-risk disease managed care program*—Design the services that the managed care program is going to offer to policyholders that have extreme high risk of incurring considerable cost claims
sp7	*Persuade policyholders to join the extreme high-risk managed care program*—Persuade those who qualify to join in the extreme high-risk managed care program. Record the results of the invitation in the HIC's databases
sp8	*Run the extreme high-risk managed care program*—Get people to agree to the program's regulations and activities. Run the program and monitor the changes in the participants' lifestyle and health status. Register all the interactions between the program and its participants
sp9	*Advertising*—Advertise the existence of the managed care programs with the intention of getting new people to join the healthcare plan and to apply to the managed care programs. Use the information stored in the HIC databases to build the advertising strategy
sp10	*Make adjustments*—Exploit the information recorded in the HIC's databases to report on the results of both managed care programs. In addition, look for opportunities to make adjustments in the programs' eligibility criteria to make it more efficient. Moreover, use the same information to adjust the programs' services and activities to make it more attractive to policyholders. This is intended to reduce the program's dropout rate

19.4.4 Project Planning, Financing, and Implantation Constraints

The dependency relations that are required to hold true among the subprojects from *sp1* to *sp10* are presented in Figure 19.1. The cash flow of these subprojects is introduced in Table 19.1. Their *NPV* according to the period they start running are shown in Table 19.2. Table 19.5 presents the *NPV*, *CI*, and *ROI* for several possible implementation sequences.

The sequence that comes first in Table 19.5 is the one that yields the highest *ROI*. As HIC is a for-profit organization, this is the sequence that HIC's advisory team should select to implement the subprojects described in Table 19.11. This holds true if no restrictions have been imposed on the capital that is available to run those subprojects and a minimal value for *ROI* has not been preestablished.

However, it is not always the case that managers have at their disposal the required capital to implement the running sequence of their choice. Moreover, even if the capital is available, big data projects are usually compared with other investment opportunities before they are selected for implementation (Chandra, 2014).

In this respect, many companies tend to establish a *hurdle rate*, that is, a minimum return on investment that projects have to yield. If the *ROI* of a project falls below the acceptable hurdle rate, it should not be run. For example, if the hurdle rate for the managed care project were 700%, none of the running sequences in Table 19.5 would fulfill this requirement. As a result, the project would have to be abandoned (Calandro et al., 2015).

However, running all the subprojects in a portfolio may not always lead to the highest possible *ROI*. If a particular subproject sp_i requires considerable capital to be run and yields small financial returns, a higher *ROI* for a particular running sequence may be obtained by avoiding running sp_i. This is the case of subproject *sp9*, as it is the most expensive subproject in the portfolio. In addition, *sp9* is the subproject that yields the smallest financial returns across the window of opportunity of the managed care project. See Table 19.1 in this respect.

For example, consider the following running sequence, which *sp9* is not a part of

$$NRS = sp1 \rightarrow sp2 \rightarrow sp6 \rightarrow sp7 \rightarrow sp8 \rightarrow sp3 \rightarrow sp4 \rightarrow sp5 \rightarrow sp10$$

This particular running sequence yields an *NPV* of \$3565 K and requires a capital investment of \$438 K. As a result, its *ROI* is given by (\$3565 K–\$438 K)/\$438 K = \$714 K. Not only is the *ROI* of *NRS* considerably higher than the *ROI* of the sequence that comes first in Table 19.5, but it also requires less capital investment.

Although *NRS* does not consider running all subprojects presented in Table 19.11, this is the running sequence that yields the highest *ROI* among all possible implementation sequences. If HIC has made available the capital investment it requires, the managed care advisory team should select this sequence for implementation over all the other alternatives.

19.5 SUMMARY OF THE METHOD

Companies that consider running big data projects may benefit from taking the following steps:

1. *Project selection*—Let *P* be a big data project that has been divided into a portfolio of subprojects $SP = \{sp1, sp2, \ldots, sp10\}$.
2. *Dependency relations*—Define a graph $G = (V, E)$ that specifies the dependency relations that are required to hold true among the subprojects in *SP*. Note that

$$V = SP \quad \text{and} \quad E = \{(sp_i, sp_j) \mid sp_i, sp_j \in V\}$$

   In addition, if running sp_j depends on the completion of sp_i, then $(sp_i, sp_j) \in E$. The reverse also holds true.
3. *Network diagram*—Build the network diagram that corresponds to the information specified in *G*.
4. *The window of opportunity*—Determine the project's window of opportunity *WO*.
5. *Data flow elements*—For each $sp_k \in SP$, estimate the value of its cash flow component in period *i*, that is, $e_{sp_k,i}$. Note that $1 \leq i \leq WO$.
6. *Makespan*—Establish the makespan of every subproject in *SP*.
7. *The net present value*—Define the function *NPV(sp,t)* that returns the net present value of subproject *sp*, if it is run at period *t*. See Equation 19.1 in this respect.
8. *Running sequences*—Generate all possible running sequences. Take into account the constraints that may have been imposed on the running sequences that can be used to carry out project *P*. See Figure 19.1 and Table 19.3 in this respect. Take into account that running all the subprojects in the portfolio may lead to a suboptimal running sequence.
9. *The net present value*—Calculate the *NPV* of every possible running sequence. This is the sum of the *NPV*s of every subproject in the sequence according to the period in which they are run. See step 6 in this respect.

10. *The capital investment*—As everything costs something, it is important to figure out the capital investment *CI* required by each possible running sequence.
11. *The return on investment*—Calculate the return on investment of every possible running sequence. This is the ratio between their *NPV* minus *CI* and *CI*.
12. *Selecting the running sequence for implementation*—Among the running sequences that one has enough capital to run, select the one that has the highest *ROI*. Run this sequence and take advantage of the financial benefits it provides.

19.6 CONCLUSION

Although the term *big data* first appeared in a conference article written about 20 years ago by Michael Cox and David Ellsworth (Cox & Ellsworth, 1997), very little has been said so far on how the benefits of big data projects should be evaluated. This is unfortunate as the benefits of these projects are usually compared to the benefits of other competing initiatives before they are selected for implementation. As a result, big data project managers may find it difficult to gather the support they need to run their projects.

This chapter presents a method that goes toward filling this gap. The method allows project managers to evaluate big data projects from a financial point of view. Moreover, the method maximizes the return on investment yielded by these projects. This is achieved by identifying the subprojects' running sequence that provides the highest ratio between its net present value minus its capital investment, and its capital investment. As a result, big data projects tend to become more attractive and profitable.

The financial principles and techniques that are used by the method presented in this chapter are not difficult to understand. Although the calculations would be made easier with the support of automated tools, for small projects, they can be carried out with the help of a generic spreadsheet tool, such as MS Excel. All of this enables better decision making. Ultimately, this shall help to place big data projects at the center of initiatives that aim to extract more value from the data that organizations have at their disposal.

REFERENCES

Alencar, A. J., Doria Jr, J. V., Schmitz, E. A., Correa, A. L., & Vital Jr, I. M. 2012a. On the merits and pitfalls of the incremental funding method and its software project scheduling algorithms. *Communications in Computer and Information Science*, 292, 493–502.

Alencar, A. J., Franco, C. A., Schmitz, E. A., & Correa, A. L. 2014. A statistical approach for the maximization of the financial benefits yielded by a large set of MMFs and AEs. *Computing and Informatics*, 32(6), 1147–1169.

Alencar, A. J., Vital Jr, I. M., Schmitz, E. A., Correa, A. L., & Doria Jr, J. V. 2012b. Identifying the most efficient implementation sequence of IT projects broken down into MMFs and AEs. In *Wireless Networks and Computational Intelligence* (pp. 477–486). Springer, Berlin, Germany.

Auerbach, D. I., & Kellermann, A. L. 2011. A decade of health care cost growth has wiped out real income gains for an average US family. *Health Affairs*, 30(9), 1630–1636.

Bedeley, R., & Iyer, L. S. 2014. Big data opportunities and challenges: The case of banking industry. In *Proceedings of the Southern Association for Information Systems Conference* (pp. 1–6). Macon, GA, USA.

Beik, J. I. 2014. *Health Insurance Today: A Practical Approach* (5th edition). Saunders, Saint Louis, Missouri.

Bowie, M. J., & Schaffer, R. M. 2013. *Understanding ICD-10-CM and ICD-10-PCS: A Worktext* (2nd edition). Delmar Cengage Learning, Boston, MA.

Brunoni, J., Dolinger, T., Walker, I., Wood, D., & Coustasse, A. 2015. Is capitation an effective tool for reducing health care cost? *Insights to a Changing World Journal*, 2015(3), 85–106.

Calandro, J., Gates, D., Madampath, A., & Ramette, F. 2015. A practical approach to business unit hurdle rates, portfolio analysis and strategic planning. *ACRN Oxford Journal of Finance and Risk Perspectives*, 4(2), 75–90.

Chandra, P. 2014. *Projects: Planning, Analysis, Selection, Financing, Implementation, and Review*. McGraw Hill Education, New Delhi, India.

Chen, H.-M., Kazman, R., Haziyev, S., & Hrytsay, O. 2015. Big data system development: An embedded case study with a global outsourcing firm. In *Proceedings of the First International Workshop on Big Data Software Engineering* (pp. 44–50). Piscataway, NJ, USA: IEEE Press.

Chen, M., Mao, S., Zhang, Y., & Leung, V. C. 2014. Big data generation and acquisition. In *Big Data* (pp. 19–32). Springer, New York, NY.

Cox, M., & Ellsworth, D. 1997. Application-controlled demand paging for out-of-core visualization. In *Proceedings of the 8th Conference on Visualization'97* (pp. 235–244). IEEE Computer Society Press, Piscataway, NJ.

Delgado López-Cózar, E., Robinson-García, N., & Torres-Salinas, D. 2014. The Google Scholar experiment: How to index false papers and manipulate bibliometric indicators. *Journal of the Association for Information Science and Technology*, 65(3), 446–454.

Denham, A. C., Hay, S. S., Steiner, B. D., & Newton, W. P. 2013. Academic health centers and community health centers partnering to build a system of care for vulnerable patients: Lessons from Carolina Health Net. *Academic Medicine*, 88(5), 638–643.

Donzé, J., Aujesky, D., Williams, D., & Schnipper, J. L. 2013. Potentially avoidable 30-day hospital readmissions in medical patients: Derivation and validation of a prediction model. *JAMA Internal Medicine*, 173(8), 632–638.

Dutta, D., & Bose, I. 2015. Managing a big data project: The case of Ramco Cements Limited. *International Journal of Production Economics*, 165, 293–306. http://doi.org/10.1016/j.ijpe.2014.12.032

El-Mehalawi, M. 2010. The Pyramid Construction Schedule. Examiner.com. Retrieved from http://www.examiner.com/article/the-pyramid-construction-schedule

Emanuel, E. J. 2012. Where are the health care cost savings? *Journal of the American Medical Association*, 307(1), 39–40.

Finnerty, J. D. 2013. *Project Financing: Asset-Based Financial Engineering* (3rd edition). Wiley, Hoboken, NJ.

Fosso Wamba, S., Akter, S., Edwards, A., Chopin, G., & Gnanzou, D. 2015. How "big data" can make big impact: Findings from a systematic review and a longitudinal case study. *International Journal of Production Economics*, 165, 234–246.

Gitman, L. J., & Zutter, C. J. 2014. *Principles of Managerial Finance* (14th edition). Boston: Prentice Hall.

Green, M. A. 2014. *Understanding Health Insurance: A Guide to Billing and Reimbursement* (12th edition). Delmar Cengage Learning, Boston, MA.

Groves, P., Kayyali, B., Knott, D., & Van Kuiken, S. 2013. The "big data" revolution in healthcare (Technical Report). Center for US Health System Reform Business Technology Office.

Hampton, S. E., Strasser, C. A., Tewksbury, J. J., Gram, W. K., Budden, A. E., Batcheller, A. L. et al. 2013. Big data and the future of ecology. *Frontiers in Ecology and the Environment*, 11(3), 156–162.

Hodgson, D., & Cicmil, S. 2006. Are projects real? The PMBOK and the legitimation of project management knowledge. In Hodgson, D. & Cicmil, S. (eds.), *Making Projects Critical*. Palgrave, Basingstoke, UK, pp. 29–50.

Hu, Z., Hao, S., Jin, B., Shin, A. Y., Zhu, C., Huang, M. et al. 2015. Online prediction of health care utilization in the next six months based on electronic health record information: A cohort and validation study. *Journal of Medical Internet Research*, 17(9), 1–14.

Kelly, J. 2014. *Big Data Vendor Revenue and Market Forecast 2013–2017*. Wikibon. Retrieved from http://wikibon.org/wiki/v/Big_Data_Vendor_Revenue_and_Market_Forecast_2013-2017.

Kerzner, H. 2013. *Project Management: A Systems Approach to Planning, Scheduling and Controlling* (11th edition). Wiley, Hoboken, NJ.

Kitchenham, B. A., Budgen, D., & Brereton, P. 2015. *Evidence-Based Software Engineering and Systematic Reviews*. Chapman and Hall/CRC, Boca Raton, FL.

Kongstvedt, P. R. 2015. *Health Insurance and Managed Care: What They Are and How They Work* (4th edition). Jones & Bartlett Learning, Burlington, MA.

Krumholz, H. M. 2013. Post-hospital syndrome—An acquired, transient condition of generalized risk. *New England Journal of Medicine*, 368(2), 100–102.

Marton, J., Yelowitz, A., & Talbert, J. C. 2014. A tale of two cities? The heterogeneous impact of medicaid managed care. *Journal of Health Economics*, 36, 47–68.

Meier, C. A., Fitzgerald, M. C., & Smith, J. M. 2013. eHealth: Extending, enhancing, and evolving health care. *Annual Review of Biomedical Engineering*, 15, 359–382.

Melicher, R. W., & Norton, E. A. 2013. *Introduction to Finance: Markets, Investments, and Financial Management* (15th edition). Wiley, Hoboken, NJ.

Nuguti, E. 2015. *Project Management Scheduling: Bar Charts and Network Diagrams*. Amazon Digital Services, Nairobi, Kenya.

PMI. 2013. *A Guide to the Project Management Body of Knowledge: PMBOK* (5th edition). Newtown Square, PA: Project Management Institute.

Rao, K. V., & Ali, M. A. 2015. Survey on Big Data and Applications of Real Time Big Data Analytics. Retrieved from http://www.ijcea.com/wp-content/uploads/2015/09/20-K.Venkateswara-Rao.pdf.

Schmitz, E. A., Alencar, A. J., Fernandes, M. C., & de Azevedo, C. M. 2008. Defining the implementation order of software projects in uncertain environments. In *ICEIS* (pp. 23–29). Barcelona, Spain.

Shahzad, M., & Ahsan, A. 2014. Comparison of big data analytics tools: A bioinformatics case study. *FUUAST Journal of Biology*, 4(1), 113–118.

Shiffman, G. M., & Jochum, J. J. 2011. *Economic Instruments of Security Policy: Influencing Choices of Leaders* (2nd edition). Palgrave Macmillan, Basingstoke, Hampshire, UK.

Sullivan, B., & Mitra, S. 2014. Community issues in American Metropolitan Cities: A data mining case study. *Journal of Cases on Information Technology*, 16(1), 23–39.

Tien, J. M. 2015. An SMC perspective on big data: A disruptive innovation to embrace. *IEEE Systems, Man, and Cybernetics Magazine*, 1(2), 27–29. http://doi.org/10.1109/MSMC.2015.2442193.

Wallasch, T.-M., & Hermann, C. 2012. Validation of criterion-based patient assignment and treatment effectiveness of a multidisciplinary modularized managed care program for headache. *The Journal of Headache and Pain*, 13(5), 379–387.

Weaver, A., & Bryce, R. 2015. Technological advances in medicine: It's personal. *Computer*, (2), 21–23.

White, S. E. 2014. A review of big data in health care: Challenges and opportunities. *Open Access Bioinformatics*, 6, 13–18.

20 Parallel Data Mining and Applications in Hospital Big Data Processing

Jianguo Chen, Zhuo Tang, Kenli Li, and Keqin Li

CONTENTS

ABSTRACT

Most of the hospitals have accumulated a large amount of medical and treatment data after many years of operation. Moreover, data are still being generated in hospitals every day, which contain valuable information. How to extract and fully utilize the value of data from the massive historical hospital data is a key issue for both hospitals and society. With the arrival of the big data and cloud computing era, this issue has attracted considerable attention. In addition, the speed of data mining and analysis for large-scale data becomes a hot topic to researchers from both academia and industry. In this chapter, we focus on the optimization methods for parallel data-mining algorithms, and the applications of these algorithms in the field of large-scale hospital data processing. First, techniques of data mining and famous cloud computing platforms are considered. Then, different parallel optimization methods of the related data-mining algorithm are discussed, such as the parallel random forest algorithm based on an Apache Spark platform. Finally, applications of big data processing in hospitals are discussed, based on the optimized data-mining algorithms in the big data and cloud computing environment.

20.1 INTRODUCTION

20.1.1 Application Background

With the continuous emergence of a variety of new information dissemination methods and the rise of cloud computing and Internet of Things (IoT) technologies, the amount of data is increasing constantly at a high speed [1]. Almost every hospital has accumulated a large amount of medical and treatment data after many years of operation, and more data are being produced every day. There exists a large amount of valuable knowledge in the huge amounts of hospital data. More and more researchers and developers are concentrating on the issue of how to effectively extract and fully utilize the value of data from the large-scale historical hospital data.

Currently, most hospitals in many countries around the world are overcrowded and lack effective patient queue management. Patients are usually required to undergo examinations, inspections, or tests (referred to as "treatment tasks" in this chapter) according to their conditions. In such a case, more than one treatment task might be required for each patient. Some of the tasks are independent, whereas others might wait for the completion of dependent tasks. Most of the patients need to wait in queues for unpredictable but long periods of time, waiting for their turn to accomplish each treatment task.

In this chapter, we focus on helping patients complete their treatment tasks in a predictable time and helping hospitals schedule each treatment task queue to avoid overcrowded and ineffective queues. We propose a patient operation time consumption (POTC) model based on an optimized random forest (RF) algorithm, which is trained from the massive realistic data of various hospitals. The realistic hospital data are analyzed carefully and rigorously based on critical parameters, such as the start time and end time for each patient in a treatment task, the age and gender of a patient, and the detailed treatment content for each different task. Then, based on the POTC model, we implement a hospital treatment route recommendation (HTRR) system for hospitals. Time consumptions of different patients are calculated and predicted, which takes into account the patient's conditions and operations performed during the treatment. The total waiting time of each treatment task is predicted, which is the summation of the predicted time consumptions of all patients in the waiting queue of the task. Finally, an efficient and convenient treatment route is created and recommended to each patient to achieve intelligent triage.

20.1.2 Challenges for Hospital Big Data Processing

There exist various challenges in the process of constructing a high-quality and accurate POTC model from historical hospital data and the applications of HTRR:

1. Hospital data have the characteristics of mass and high dimensions and contain a lot of noisy data. The daily operation of hospitals draws up a huge amount of medical and treatment data. Depending on statistics, the number of patients in a medium-sized hospital is in the range of 8,000–12,000 per day, and the number of the corresponding treatment tasks records is between 120,000 and 200,000 per day. Each treatment task record contains a lot

of information, such as the information of a patient, the information of a treatment department and a doctor, the detailed contents of the treatment task, etc. Numerous unexpected events might exist during the treatments in the hospital every day, such as nonappointed tasks, treatment machine stoppage, etc. Meanwhile, most of the treatment tasks are participated by the hospital staff, such as the CT scan, payment, purchase, etc. All these conditions lead to a large proportion of noisy, incomplete, and inconsistent data in hospital data.

2. Because of the different treatment contents, the time consumptions for patients in different treatment departments are not in the same range. For instance, the time consumption for a patient in a CT scan task is greater than that in a payment task. What is more, owing to the different patient's conditions and different time periods, the time consumptions for patients in the same treatment department might also be different. For instance, in the case of a CT scan task, the time consumption for the elderly should be greater than a youngster. Hence, the operation time consumption for a patient in a treatment task is complex, which relates various parameters. Therefore, it is an opportunity that various POTC models are likely to be trained from massive historical hospital data that contain the necessary knowledge. Meanwhile, it is a problem obtaining the POTC auto-adaptively to match the conditions of different patients and different treatment tasks.
3. The speed of the data-mining process for the POTC model and the real-time requirement of HTRR are also critical. There are increasingly strict time requirements for HTRR applications. Fortunately, the development of parallel computing, cloud computing, distributed computing, and supercomputing provides such a high-speed computing power. Apache Hadoop and Spark are two famous cloud computing platforms, which are widely used in the fields of parallel computing and big data mining. Numerous parallel data mining algorithms and applications have been performed and implemented based on the Apache Hadoop and the Apache Spark platforms.

20.1.3 Chapter Organization

The rest of the chapter is structured as follows. Section 20.2 provides an overview of the cloud computing platforms and the parallel optimization methods of the related data-mining algorithm. A typical hospital application based on the big data and cloud environment is described in Section 20.3. The program deployment of the hospital application and the related experimental result analysis are shown in Section 20.4. Finally, Section 20.5 presents the conclusion and future work.

20.2 OVERVIEW OF OPTIMIZATION METHODS FOR PARALLEL DATA MINING

20.2.1 Related Work

Data mining and analysis for large-scale data has grown to be one of the hot research topics in the domains of both academia and industry currently. Because of the business demand and competitive pressure, almost every business holds higher demand on data processing in real time and validity than before [2]. Enormous data often have characteristics founded in various input variables in hundreds or thousands levels, while each one of them contains just a limited valuable knowledge. At the same time, big data have some characteristics such as high dimension, complexity, and much noisy data [3]. As a result, a critical challenge is the way to obtain valuable information and knowledge from massive data more efficiently and more accurately with data-mining methods.

On the one hand, many researchers proposed various special algorithms for data processing in each specific domain, and achieved great accuracy and performance. The RF algorithm [4] is an ensemble classifier algorithm based on numerous decision tree models, and is a suitable data-mining algorithm for big data. The RF algorithm is widely used in various fields, such as fast action detection via discriminative RF voting and Top-K subvolume search [5], and robust and accurate shape model matching using RF regression voting [6]. To improve the accuracy of the data analysis with continuous features, various optimization methods of classification and regression algorithms were proposed. A self-adaptive induction algorithm for the incremental construction of binary regression trees was presented in Reference 7. In Reference 8, a multibranch decision tree algorithm was proposed based on a correlation-splitting criterion.

On the other hand, various recommendation algorithms were presented and applied in different fields. Most existing recommendation algorithms were devoted to make use of the knowledge on the efficiency and correctness of algorithms. Gediminas et al. [9] introduced an overview of the current generation of recommendation methods, such as content-based, collaborative, and hybrid recommendation approaches. A travel recommendation algorithm that mines people's attributes and travel group types was discussed in Reference 10. Yang et al. [11] introduced a Bayesian-inference-based recommendation system for online social networks, in which a user propagates a content rating query along the social network to his direct and indirect friends.

However, to the best of our knowledge, there is no effective prediction and recommendation algorithm for POTC in the existing studies. Moreover, there is almost no existing study on hospital queuing management and treatment route recommendations.

20.2.2 Cloud Platform for Parallel Computing

With the popularity of the applications of parallel data analysis, researchers in various fields are seeking convenient technologies and tools to accomplish the computing tasks of the related realistic applications. The speed of data mining and analysis for big data is a very important factor [12] in practical project applications. Cloud computing, distributed computing, and supercomputing offer high-speed computing powers and provide an excellent opportunity for large-scale data processing. The Apache Hadoop and the Apache Spark are two famous cloud platforms that are widely used in parallel computing and massive data analysis. Numerous parallel data-mining algorithms were implemented based on the MapReduce [13] and RDD [14] models on these cloud platforms.

20.2.2.1 Apache Hadoop

Apache Hadoop is a distributed system infrastructure developed by the Apache Foundation. The core components of the Apache Hadoop platform are the Hadoop-distributed file system (HDFS) and the MapReduce programming model. HDFS serves as a storage system for massive amounts of data, and MapReduce provides a parallel and distributed programming model to compute and analyze the huge amount of data. The structure of the Apache Hadoop platform is illustrated in Figure 20.1.

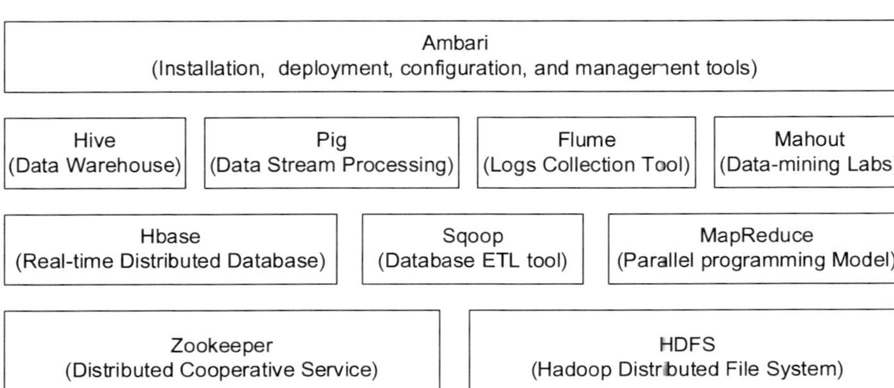

FIGURE 20.1 Structure of the Apache Hadoop platform.

In Figure 20.1, the structure of the Apache Hadoop platform contains a series of components. The functions of some of the core components are described as follows:

- *HDFS* is a basic data storage management in the Hadoop platform, which provides a solution for storing large-scale data files across multiple computing nodes.
- *ZooKeeper* is a large-scale distributed and reliable coordination system, which provides the functions, including configuration maintenance, name service, distributed synchronization, group services, etc.
- *HBase* is a scalable, high-reliability, high-performance, distributed, and dynamic model of column-oriented database. HBase uses HDFS as a file storage system, and uses Zookeeper as a collaborative service.
- *MapReduce* is a parallel and distributed programming model for large datasets. MapReduce contains a *Map* stage and a *Reduce* stage. In the *Map* stage, specified operations of independent elements on the dataset are performed, and produce the intermediate results in the form of $\langle key, value \rangle$. In the *Reduce* stage, the intermediate results in the same "*key*" are gathered in a reduce function, and get the final result after the corresponding computing.
- *Mahout* is a machine learning and math library based on MapReduce. Benefiting from the parallel computing programming model of MapReduce, Mahout has provided various data-mining algorithms, such as clustering, classification, and recommendation engine algorithms.

Various data-mining algorithms were presented based on the Apache Hadoop cloud platform in References 15 and 16. Focusing on large-scale data and the performance of classification algorithms, some studies on the intersection of parallel/distributed computing and learning of tree models were proposed. Panda et al. [17] proposed a scalable distributed framework based on MapReduce for parallel learning of decision tree models over large datasets. Besides, they developed and deployed a MapReduce-based tree learner, called PLANET, which can be scaled effectively. A parallel boosted regression trees algorithm was presented in Reference 18 for web search ranking, where a novel method for parallelizing the training of Parallel Boosted Regression Trees (GBRT) was performed based on data partitioning and distributed computing. Apache Mahout implemented various parallel machine-learning algorithms based on MapReduce, for example, the parallel RF algorithm and the parallel k-means algorithm.

20.2.2.2 Apache Spark

The Apache Spark platform is an open-source project that is contributed by numerical excellent developers from diverse organizations. Apache Spark is a popular parallel data-processing platform for interactive queries and iterative algorithms, and is suitable for computing and analysis of massive data. The structure of the Apache Spark platform is illustrated in Figure 20.2.

The Spark platform supports a lot of mechanisms for parallel computing and iterative computing, such as in-memory storage and efficient fault recovery. Spark's core programming model is the resilient distributed datasets (RDDs). RDDs represent a collection of distributed items, which can be manipulated in parallel across many computing nodes. The Spark platform provides various APIs for building and manipulating these collections. In the Spark platform, data are cached in memory before the processing phase, and iterations for the same data come directly from memory.

Apache Spark is an efficient cloud platform that is suitable for data mining and machine learning. Numeral achievements have been published in the field of data mining and machine learning based on Apache Spark.

Zaharia [19] presented a fast and interactive analytic over Hadoop data with Spark. Huang et al. [20] introduced an in-memory parallel processing algorithm for massive remotely sensed data based on the Apache Spark platform.

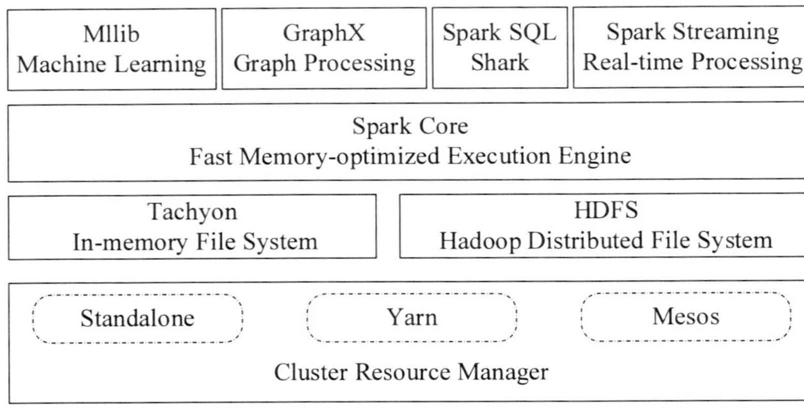

FIGURE 20.2 Structure of the Apache Spark platform.

20.2.3 Parallel Optimization of Random Forest Algorithm Based on Cloud Platform

The RF algorithm is an ensemble classifier algorithm based on decision tree, and is suitable for classification processing for big data. To train an RF model, first, k different training data subsets are generated from an original dataset with a bootstrap sampling approach. Then, k decision tree models are constructed as a C4.5 or CART algorithm by training these k subsets, respectively. Finally, an RF model is constructed by these k decision tree models. In the prediction process, each sample of the testing data is predicted by all decision tree models in the trained RF model, and the final classification result is returned depending on the vote of these tree models. The training and prediction process of the RF algorithm is presented in Figure 20.3.

However, the accuracy of the RF algorithm is affected by noisy data. As mentioned above, there are various conditions resulting in a large proportion of noise, incomplete, and inconsistent data in hospital data. The noisy data might lead to noisy decision trees and a noisy RF model, and decrease the accuracy of the RF model. Hence, it likely leads to a classification or regression error for the testing dataset.

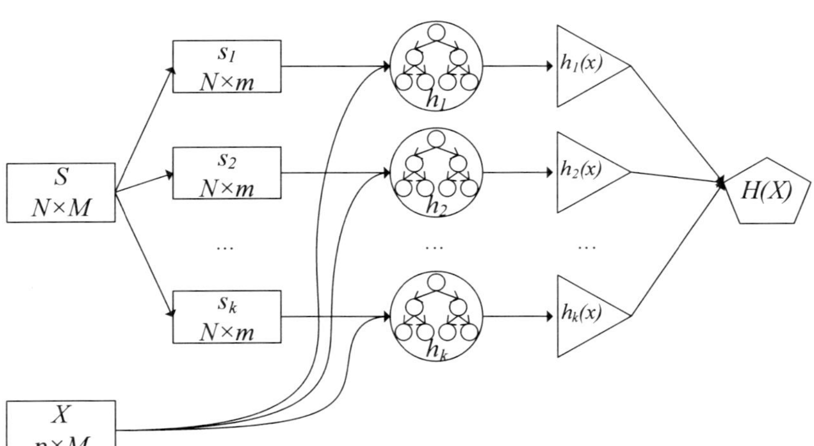

FIGURE 20.3 Training and prediction process of the random forest algorithm.

In this chapter, an innovative optimization approach of the RF algorithm is proposed to limit the above shortcut of the algorithm. First, a new margin distribution optimization method is introduced to reduce the influence of the algorithm accuracy for noisy data. Moreover, to improve the performance of the algorithm, we discuss a parallelization solution of the RF algorithm on the Apache Spark cloud platform.

20.2.3.1 New Margin Distribution Optimization Method for the RF Algorithm

To reduce the influence of the accuracy of the RF algorithm from noise and large-scale data, an innovative approach of the algorithm is introduced in this section by optimizing the margin distribution. We minimize classification intervals of margin distribution using the average classification interval measurement method instead of the traditional method. In the presence of noisy data, the optimization method can effectively narrow the effect of noisy data on the training process of RF.

As an important index to assess the performance of a classifier, the generalization ability refers to the ability of a classifier to correct classification of the training set outside of the sample. The generalization error relates to the error of judgment proportion classifier on the training set outside of the sample. In Reference 5, the class interval of RF function is defined as using the law of large numbers as the theoretical basis to prove the following conclusions are obtained: with the increase of the number of decision tree and RF in the generalization error, the RF model tends to a finite upper bound.

Margin function (also called classification interval function) is defined as the subtraction between the average number of sample that is divided into the correct class and the average number of samples that are divided into all error classes by the ensemble of classifiers, as described in Equation 20.1:

$$Mg(x, y) = AV_k(h_k(x, \Theta_k) = y) - AV_k(h_k(x, \Theta_k) = z), \quad (z \neq y), \tag{20.1}$$

where Θ_k is a random feature vector corresponding to a meta decision tree, $h(x, \theta_k)$ is the output of x and Θ_k, y is the correct classification vector, z is an error classification vector, and $AV_k(\cdot)$ is the average number of sample.

$Mg(x, y) < 0$ indicates that the sample x is classified into an error class by the classifier. The greater the value of the classification interval function $Mg(x, y)$, the better the classification performance of the current classifier, and the higher the classifier's confidence. The margin distribution optimization of the RF algorithm is shown in Figure 20.4.

In Figure 20.4, h_{min} is the minimum margin between two classifications, h_{mean} is the mean margin between two classifications, and h_{dist} is the optimized margin distribution by maximizing the margin mean and minimizing the margin variance simultaneously.

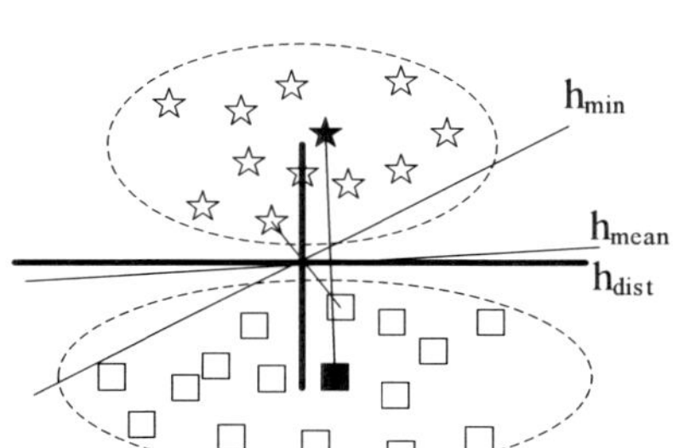

FIGURE 20.4 Margin distribution optimization of the random forest algorithm.

20.2.3.2 Parallelization of the RF Algorithm Based on the Apache Spark Cloud Platform

For the original RF algorithm, the construction progress of the decision tree models is in a serial way, in which each decision tree classifier is constructed one by one. To improve the speed of the RF algorithm, we parallelize the RF algorithm in the Spark cloud computing environment. Taking advantage of the cloud computing platform and the distributed memory management mechanism, the performance of the RF algorithm is improved by three parallel processes: the parallel training process of the RF model, the parallel splitting process of each decision tree, and the parallel prediction and voting process. The parallel training process of the decision trees of the RF model is shown in Figure 20.5.

1. *Parallel training process of k decision trees*: After the training data are loaded into the Tachyon system of the Spark platform, the training dataset has been sampled to k training subsets as k RDD objects at an action stage. In this approach, it will need more time consumption. Owing to the parallel training process of k decision trees, the training time of the RF algorithm reduces k times in theories. Therefore, we parallelize the training process of the algorithm. The k decision trees of the RF model are constructed at the same time.
2. *Parallel splitting process of the decision tree in the RF algorithm*: While parallelizing the training process of k decision trees, the splitting process of each decision tree can also

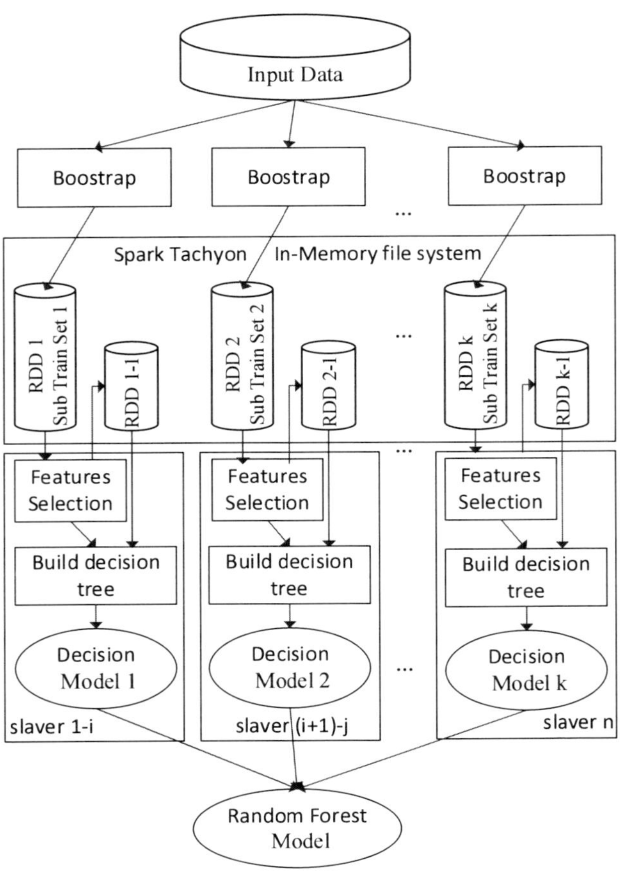

FIGURE 20.5 Parallel training process of the random forest model.

be parallelized. All the feature variables are calculated concurrently with the MapReduce model based on Spark. Thus, the training process of the RF model is a dual parallel process.

3. *Parallel prediction and voting process of the RF algorithm*: After the training process of the RF-algorithm, k-trained decision trees have been constructed. To increase the speed of prediction and voting process for the RF algorithm, this process is parallelized by a dual-layer parallel process on the Spark platform. In the first layer parallel process, the testing dataset is divided into a series of records. All records are predicted at the same time. In the second layer parallel process, each record is predicted by k decision trees concurrently.

20.3 APPLICATIONS IN HOSPITAL BIG DATA PROCESSING

In this section, we concentrate on the issue of how to extract and fully utilize the value of data from the massive historical hospital data. We focus on helping patients complete their treatment tasks in a predictable time and helping hospitals schedule each treatment task queue and avoid overcrowded and ineffective queues.

We use the improved RF algorithm to train a POTC model from massive realistic hospital data. Based on the trained POTC model, we develop an HTRR system. We identify and calculate different waiting times for different patients based on their conditions and operations performed during treatment. Consequently, an efficient and convenient treatment plan is created and recommended to each patient to achieve intelligent triage.

20.3.1 Preprocess for Large-Scale Hospital Data

Before training the POTC model, the large-scale hospital data are required to be preprocessed. Hospitals data from different processes of treatment are gathered. Then, some important features are selected and calculated, such as the operation time consumption of each treatment record, and the week and the time range of the treatment time. The detailed steps of the preprocess of the hospital data are summarized as follows:

1. *Gather hospital data from different treatment processes*: The daily business of the hospital produces a huge amount of treatment data. These data are gathered from different processes of treatment task, which include registration, medical examination, inspection, drug delivery, payment, and other treatment tasks.
2. *Choose the same dimensions of data*: Different contents and formats of the medical data and treatment data are generated in different processes of treatment, while the dimensions are also different. To train the operation time consumption model for each process of treatment, we choose the same features of data from these data, such as the patient information (e.g., patient card number, patient name, sex, and age), the treatment project information (e.g., project name, department name, doctor name, and doctor position), the active time information (e.g., start time and end time), and other related information of the patient.
3. *Calculate new features of data for model training*: To train the POTC model, some important features of the hospital data should be calculated, such as the operation time consumption of each treatment record, day of week for the treatment time, and the time range of treatment time. Other features that are not contributing to the model training are removed from the raw data, such as the patient card number, the patient name, telephone, etc. Here, for a single visit, we cite a single example of treatment operation records, which contains features such as the patient name, age, and gender. The detailed records of the treatment tasks on one patient's visit are shown in Table 20.1.

TABLE 20.1
Example of Treatment Data Records

Patient Number	Gender	Age	Task Name	Department Name	Doctor Name	Start Time	End Time
3278	Male	21	Checkup	Surgery	Dr. Li	2015-05-13 09:20:00	2015-05-13 09:32:14
3278	Male	21	Payment	Cashier-8	*Null*	2015-05-13 08:41:18	*Null*
3278	Male	21	CT scan	CT-1	Dr. Sun	2015-05-13 09:12:00	2015-05-13 09:26:00
3278	Male	21	MR scan	MR-3	Dr. Lin	2015-05-13 10:16:45	2015-05-13 10:23:52
3278	Male	21	Take medicine	TCM Pharmacy	*Null*	2015-05-13 10:36:14	2015-05-13 10:41:21
...	...	...	...	...	...	...	...

20.3.2 Patients Operation Time Consumption Model Based on Big Data

To predict the waiting time for each treatment task, we use the RF algorithm to train the POTC based on both patient and time characteristics, and then build the POTC model.

20.3.2.1 Training CART Regression Trees of the RF Model

Because the target variable of the RF model is the POTC, which is a continuous variable, a classification and regression tree (CART) model is used as a meta-classifier in the RF algorithm. Thus, a CART regression tree model is created for each training subset s_{traini}. The main process of building the regression tree of CART is described as follows:

Step 1. Calculate the best splitting features variables and the best split point. In each tree node's splitting process, each feature variable subspace y_j and each potential split point value v_p of y_j are chosen to calculate the loss function of (y_j, v_p), which is defined in Equation 20.2:

$$(y_j, v_p) = arg\min\left[\sum_{x\in R_L(y_j,v_p)} (y_i - c_L)^2 + \sum_{x\in R_R(y_j,v_p)} (y_i - c_R)^2\right], \tag{20.2}$$

where $R_L(y_j,\ v_p)$ is the first (left) subset of data split by v_p in the feature subspace y_j, and c_L is the average value in the $R_L(y_j,\ v_p)$ subset.

Step 2. Split the tree node and further grow the tree. Split the training dataset into two forks by v_p in the feature subspace y_j. $R_{L(y_j,\ v_p)}$ denotes the first (left) data subset and $R_{R(y_j,\ v_p)}$ denotes the second (right) data subset, which are defined in Equation 20.3:

$$R_{L(y_j,\ v_p)} = \{x|(y_j \le v_p)\},$$
$$R_{R(y_j,\ v_p)} = \{x|(y_j > v_p)\}. \tag{20.3}$$

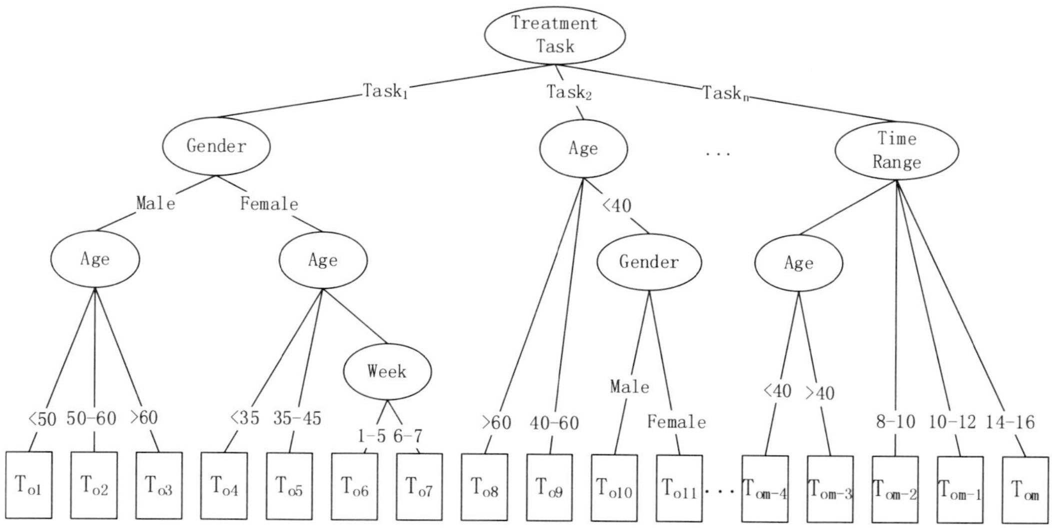

FIGURE 20.6 Meta CART tree of the POTC model.

Step 3. Construct multibranch for the CART model. Some independent variables of data are nominal data, which have different values, such as the time range (0–23) and day of week (Monday–Sunday). To construct the regression tree model felicitously, in this chapter, we introduce a multibranch regression tree model instead of two-fork tree model to construct the CART model. After the tree node splitting into two forks by variable y_j and value v_p in step 2, the same feature variable y_j continues to be selected to calculate the best split point v_{pL} for the data in the left branch and v_{pR} for the data in the right branch. A meta CART regression tree of the POTC model is shown in Figure 20.6.

These processes of construction of a meta CART tree are repeated to train *k* CART regression trees on *k* training subsets.

20.3.2.2 Collecting *k* CART Trees for an RF Model

After the construction of the *k* CART regression trees, these trees are gathered and combined into an RF model.

The original RF algorithm uses a traditional direct voting method in the voting process. In this case, if the RF algorithm contains some noisy decision trees, the accuracy of the algorithm is decreased. It likely results in a classification or regression error for the testing dataset. To mitigate this problem, in this chapter, a weighted voting method is applied to the RF algorithm in an innovative way. The weighted voting method can effectively improve the classification accuracy of the RF algorithm for testing dataset. The weighted regression result $H(X)$ of the RF model for the data X is the average value of k trees, as defined in Equation 20.4:

$$H(X) = \frac{1}{k}\sum_{i=1}^{k}[w_i \times h_i(x)], \tag{20.4}$$

where w_i is the weight of the tree h_i and $h_i(x)$ is a meta-classifier for a pruning regression tree constructed by the CART algorithm. The POTC model based on the RF algorithm is shown in Figure 20.7.

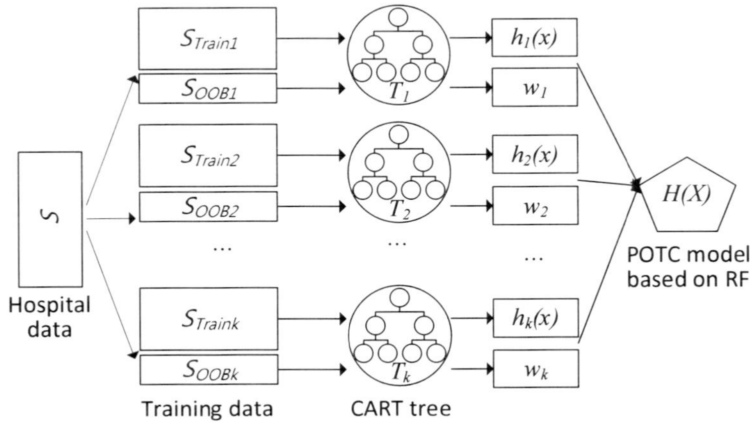

FIGURE 20.7 POTC model based on the RF algorithm.

20.3.3 Hospital Treatment Route Recommendation System Based on Big Data

Based on the trained POTC model, an HTRR system is developed. In the daily operation of every hospital, more than one treatment task might be required for most of the patients. As we all know, the best condition is that these patients can go to the task with the least waiting time for them. After the patients obtain the list of required tasks, the detailed information of the tasks, including the task id, task name, and the detailed information of patients in the waiting queue of the task, is sent to the HTRR system in real time. The HTRR system calculates and predicts the time consumption of each patient who is in the waiting queue of each task. Then, these tasks are re-sorted by the predicted waiting time in ascending order. Finally, an efficient and convenient treatment plan is created and recommended to each patient to achieve intelligent triage. The detailed steps of the HTRR system are described as follows:

1. *Predict the waiting time of all the treatment tasks for the current patient*: Assume that there exist various treatment tasks for each patient according to the patient's condition. Let $Tasks = \{Task_1, Task_2, \ldots, Task_n\}$ be a set of treatment tasks that the current patient needs to complete, and let $U_i = \{U_{i1}, U_{i2}, \ldots, U_{im}\}$ be a set of patients waiting in the queue for $Task_i$.

   For each patient U_{ik} waiting in the queue of $Task_i$, the POTC of each treatment task is predicted by the trained POTC model according to the patient's characteristics (such as gender and age), time factors (such as the week and month period of the treatment time), and other factors (such as treatment departments, available machines, and service windows). The patient treatment time consumption T_{ik} for patient U_{ik} in the queue of treatment task $Task_i$ is defined in Equation 20.5:

$$\begin{aligned} T_{ik} &= H(X_{ik}, \Theta j) \\ &= \frac{1}{k}\sum_{i=1}^{k}[CA_i \times h_i(x, \Theta j)], \end{aligned} \tag{20.5}$$

   where X_{ik} is the treatment data of patient U_{ik}, W_i is the accuracy weight of tree h_i, and $h_i(x)$ is a result of POTC predicted by a single CART regression tree.

   Then, all the predicted POTC of patients in the queue of the current treatment task is added to obtain the waiting time of $Task_i$, which is defined as T_i. The calculation formula of T_i is defined in Equation 20.6:

$$T_i = \frac{1}{W_i} \sum_{k=1}^{m} T_{ik}, \tag{20.6}$$

where W_i is the number of service windows or workbenches that can provide a service for treatment task $Task_i$ in parallel, m is the number of patients waiting in the queue of $Task_i$, and T_{ik} denotes the predicted waiting time for the patient-in-waiting $Patient_k$.

2. *Sort all the treatment tasks of the current patient in ascending order by waiting time*: All treatment tasks of the current patient are sorted in ascending order according to the waiting time. If there exists any task that is dependent on another task, these tasks should be sorted based on their dependencies rather than their waiting times.
3. *Provide an HTRR for the current patient*: Finally, an HTRR with the sorted treatment tasks is performed for each patient by a mobile application interface. Each patient can be invited to complete his treatment activities in the most convenient way with the least waiting time.

The parallel recommendation process of the HTRR system is shown in Figure 20.8.

Usually, more than one treatment task are required for each patient, and many patients waiting in the queue of each treatment task. Therefore, a parallel HTRR system is implemented for each patient if there is more than one treatment task for the patients.

Assume that there are n treatment tasks required for the current patient to complete and that there are a number of patients waiting in the queue of each treatment task. In the parallelization solution, n RDD objects are created to refer to the n treatment tasks. There exists a number of partitions in each RDD object that refer to patients waiting in the queue of each task. Let partition U_{ij} be the jth patient waiting for the ith treatment task.

Step 1. For each patient U_{ij} in a task $Task_i$, the time consumption of the patient might generate in the ith task, which is predicted by the trained POTC model. In this step, the

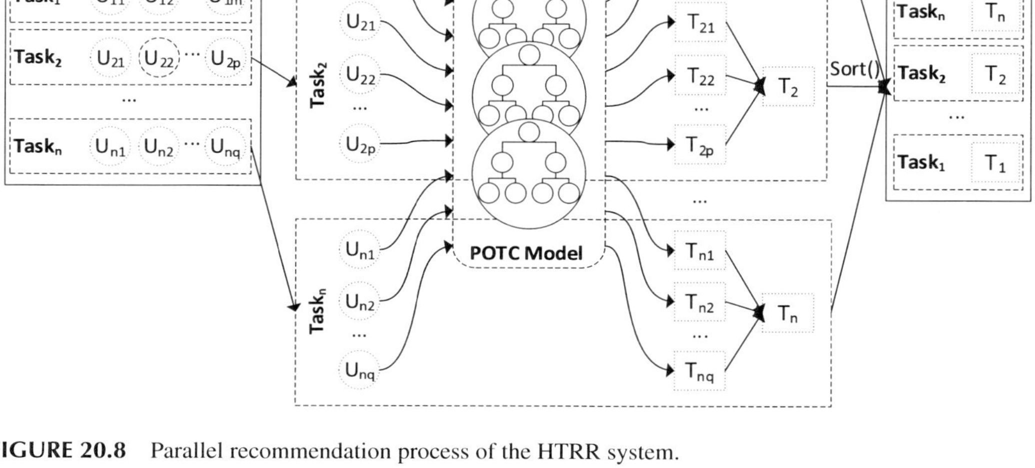

FIGURE 20.8 Parallel recommendation process of the HTRR system.

time consumption for each patient U_{ij} is calculated with the k-trained CART trees of the RF-based POTC model in a *shuffle*() function, and the predicted POTC T_{ij} of treatment task $Task_i$ is derived.
Step 2. The POTC of all the patients in each task is added in a *sum*() function, and the predicted waiting time T_i of each task is obtained. An RDD object $(Task_i, T_i)$ is created for each task.
Step 3. The predicted waiting times for all the tasks for the current patient are sorted in ascending order with a *sort*() function. A new RDD object T_s is created to save the sorted waiting times of all the treatment tasks. Hence, the parallel HTRR schema for the current patient is performed.

20.4 PROGRAM DEPLOYMENT AND APPLICATIONS RESULT ANALYSIS

The algorithms proposed in this chapter are applied to the actual project of a hospital in China. In the project, a data center and cloud platform are built at the National Supercomputing Center in Changsha (NSCC). Daily hospital treatment data are transmitted and stored in the HBase database of the data center. Then, treatment data are loaded into the Spark cluster regularly, and a POTC model of this hospital is trained with the POTC algorithm proposed. The tasks required for each patient and the current queue situations of the tasks are transmitted to the cloud platform in real time. The predicted waiting time of each task is calculated by the trained time prediction model. Finally, a real-time recommendation of hospital treatment route is available to each patient through the mobile system. The program deployment of the proposed system is introduced in Section 20.4.1. Numerous experiments and applications are performed and the experimental results are analyzed in Section 20.4.2.

20.4.1 Program Deployment

Almost every hospital has accumulated a large amount of medical and treatment data after many years of operation, and more data are being produced every day. These data are recorded in the database in the hospital, and then transported and stored in the HBase database in the data center of NSCC. Before the periodic training process of the POTC model, the hospital data are loaded from HBase into the Spark Tachyon system. Finally, applications of the POTC algorithm and the HTRR system are deployed and executed on the Spark cluster. The detailed steps of program deployment of the hospital application are described as follows:

1. *Store historical hospital data into HBase*: In our solution, the historical hospital data are stored in the HBase, which is a distributed storage system with high reliability, performance, and scalability. The HDFS is used as the file storage system of HBase. HDFS supports handling huge amounts of data in HBase with the MapReduce programming model.

   With the increase in the number of treatment data records in HBase, the data table will gradually split into multiple splits, and all the data are stored in corresponding regions that are managed by Zookeeper [21]. A uniform row key is created for each record, and each region stores the data on the row key in the range of [*startkey*, *endkey*]. Then, different regions are allocated to the corresponding region servers in the HBase cluster for management.

   Hospital treatment data are stored in a dictionary order of the row key. To load the same department and treatment task data efficiently in the training process of the POTC model, the row key of each treatment data is defined as follows:

$$rowkey = \{HospitalID + \text{``\_''} + DepartmentID + \text{``\_''} + TaskID + \text{``\_''} + ActionTime + \text{``\_''} + PatientID\}.$$

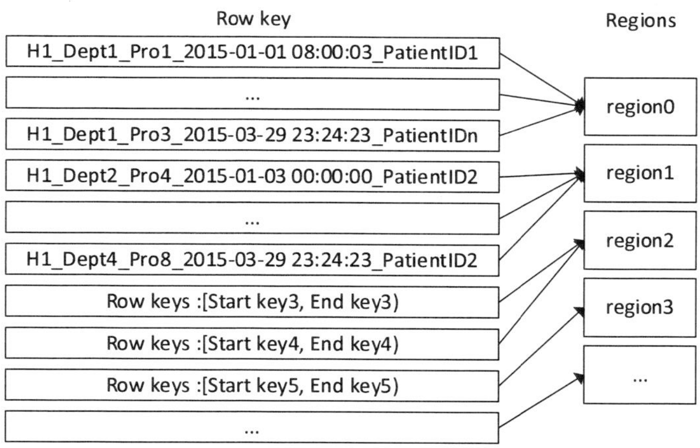

FIGURE 20.9 Row keys and regions in HBase for the hospital data.

Thus, the data in the same department and the same treatment task are stored near each other. An example of row keys and regions in HBase for the treatment data is shown in Figure 20.9.

2. *Load the hospital datasets into the Spark platform*: Before the training and prediction process, the large-scale hospital datasets are loaded into the Spark platform. Large-scale training data are stored in the Tachyon system of the Spark platform in the form of RDD objects. We create an RDD object $RDD_{original}$ to store the original training dataset S_o, which is stored in external files. The key code of this command is defined as follows:

$$RDD_{original} = SparkContext.textFile(S_o).$$

The process of loading massive hospital data to the Spark Tachyon memory system is shown in Figure 20.10. The RDD object $RDD_{original}$ supports two kinds of operations, *transformation* operation and *action* operation. *Transformation* operations include a series of operations on the RDD object, and a new RDD object will be returned. *Action* operations include a series of operations that compute a result based on the RDD object, and send it back to the driver program or save it to an external storage system.

At the *transformation* stage, k RDD objects are defined to save k training subsets, which are sampled from the original training dataset $RDD_{original}$ in a bootstrap sampling way. Because of the lazy fashion mechanism of Spark, the RDD objects are constructed and saved into the Tachyon memory system at the *action* stage with series operations. Extending from the MapReduce model, the Spark RDD model supports iterative computation. The intermediate data are stored in Spark cluster's memory as RDD objects, which are generated by the iterative processes of machine-learning algorithms. The mechanism of the Spark RDD model allows these RDD objects to be used repeatedly. Hence, it is suitable for the RF algorithm.

3. *Execute the application of the HTRR system on the Spark cluster*: Applications of parallel POTC model training and parallel HTRR system are deployed on a Spark cluster. The Spark cluster is constructed with a driver machine, a system master computing node, and a series of worker nodes. The process of job submit on the Spark cluster is shown in Figure 20.11.

First, the POTC and the HTRR system are submitted to the Spark driver after the Spark cluster startup. When an *action* function in the system is touched off, a new job is generated with a Spark

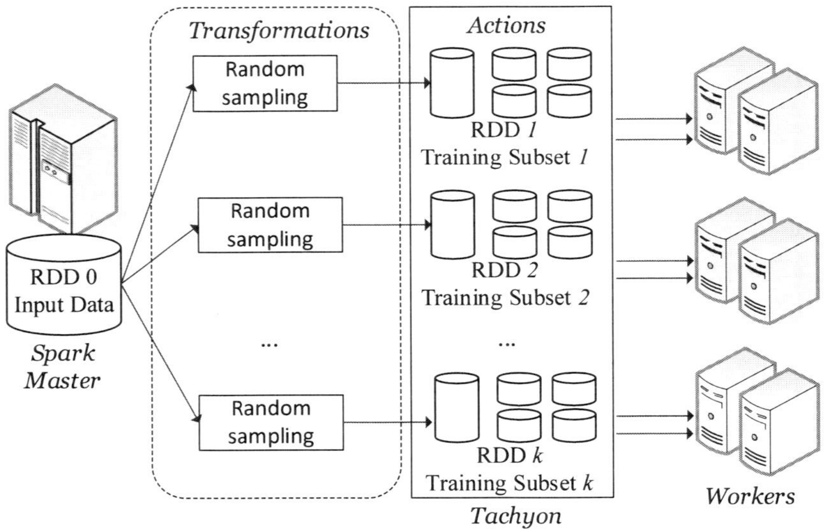

FIGURE 20.10 Process of loading hospital data to the Spark Tachyon.

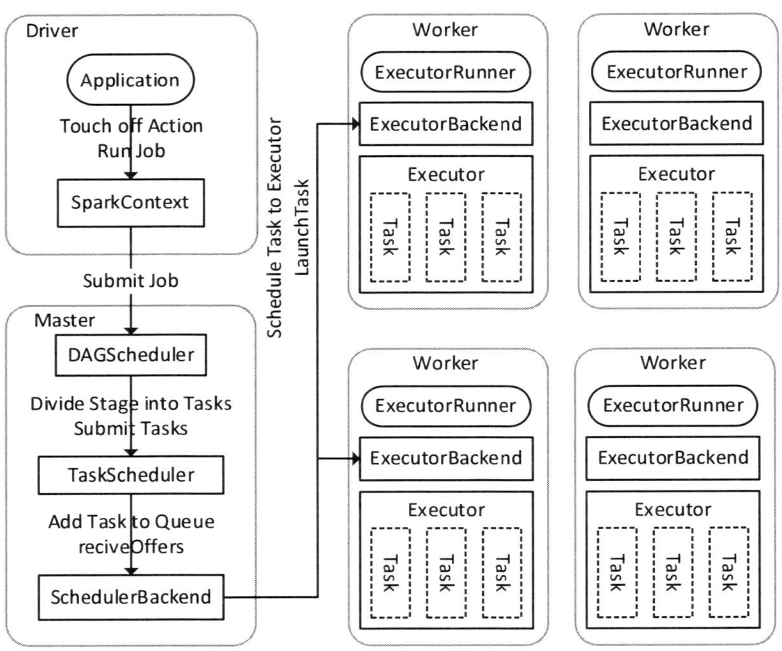

FIGURE 20.11 Process of job submit on the Spark cluster.

context. The job is submitted to the Spark master, and a DAG graph is produced by a DAG scheduler for each job, which will calculate various job stages and divide the stages into multiple tasks.

Second, the tasks are submitted to a task scheduler, which is responsible for scheduling these tasks to the corresponding executors on the worker nodes in the Spark cluster.

Finally, there exists one or more ExecutorBackend (EB) process in each worker node. Each process contains an executor object, and the executor object has one thread pool, and each thread will launch a task.

20.4.2 Applications Result Analysis

In this section, various experiments and applications of the proposed algorithm and the hospital system are performed. Sizable historical hospital data are selected from a hospital in China. Experimental results of pharmacy task are taken as examples to discuss in terms of the task quantities, the operation time consumption, and the average waiting time.

20.4.2.1 Experiment and Application Setup

All experiments are performed on a Spark cloud platform, which is built by one master computing node and 100 slave computing nodes. Each computing node executes in Ubuntu 12.04.4, with one Pentium® Dual-Core 3.20 GHz CPU and 8 GB memory. All nodes are connected by a high-speed Gigabit network, and are configured with Hadoop 2.6.0, Spark 1.4.0.

In our experiments, training data are chosen from a hospital in China, which covered 3 years (2013–2015). The data volumes are described in Table 20.2.

There are various treatment departments in the hospital and various treatment tasks in each department. Taking the data of the pharmacy task as an example, the quantities of the pharmacy task in all months in 2013–2015 are presented in Figure 20.12. Obviously, the data quantity is smooth and steady in each month except for February. Because it is the month of the Chinese New Year, many people are reluctant to go to the hospital in the new year.

20.4.2.2 Average Quantities of Pharmacy Task

A series of experiments of the proposed algorithm is performed, and experimental results of pharmacy task are taken as examples to discuss. At present, most hospitals in China consist of two types of pharmacies, namely, the Western medicine pharmacy and the traditional Chinese medicine pharmacy. More than one service window is available in each pharmacy department. Moreover, the dispensing medicines are mainly operated by the pharmacy staff. Medicines might be taken by a patient's family or companion rather than the patient himself.

In our experiments, the treatment time consumption of the pharmacy task for each patient is different, which is generally associated with the pharmacy staff, drug contents, and the time period factors. We analyze the quantities and time consumption of the pharmacy tasks in the time period factors in this section. The quantities of these two types of pharmacy tasks in each week period are presented in Figure 20.13.

As can be observed from Figure 20.13, there exist two peaks of the pharmacy treatment every day for both of the Western medicine pharmacy (shown in Figure 20.13a) and the traditional Chinese

TABLE 20.2
Datasets from an Actual Hospital Application

Years	Departments	Tasks	Instances	Data Size
2013	298	15,124	178,273,257	1.3 TB
2014	302	15,386	214,764,385	1.7 TB
2015	296	14,992	205,845,486	2.1 TB

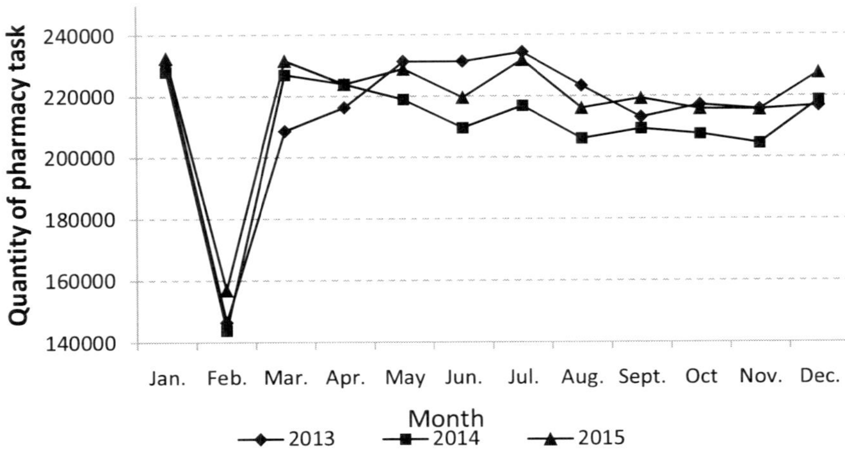

FIGURE 20.12 Average quantities of the pharmacy task in 2013–2015.

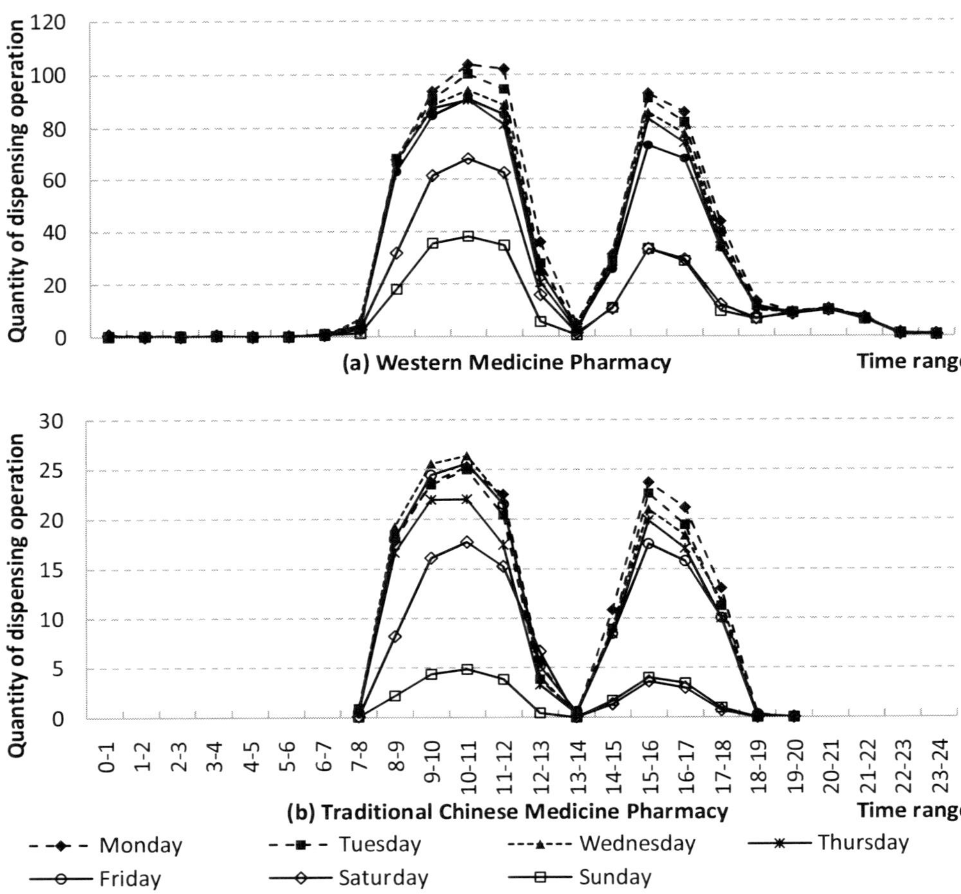

FIGURE 20.13 Quantities of the pharmacy task in each week period.

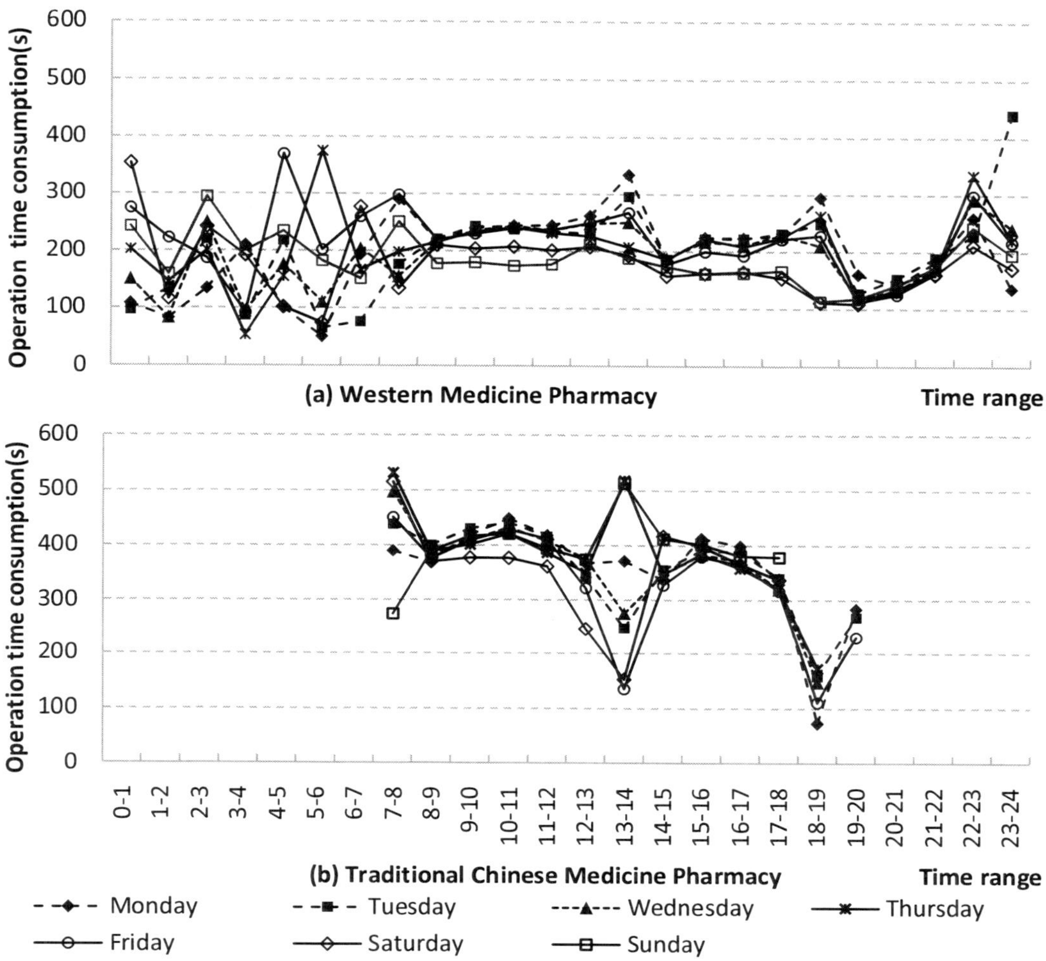

FIGURE 20.14 Operation time consumption of the pharmacy task.

medicine pharmacy (shown in Figure 20.13b). The first peak comes from 9 am to 12 am, and the second peak comes from 3 pm to 5 pm. Between 12 am and 3 pm, it is the rest time of most of the hospital staff; only the emergency department of the pharmacy is still open. Usually, the time period between 8 am and 6 pm every day is the work time for both of the Western medicine pharmacy and the traditional Chinese medicine pharmacy. Between 6 pm and 8 am, some service windows of the Western medicine pharmacies open, while all service windows of the traditional Chinese medicine pharmacy close.

In comparison with the traditional Chinese medicine pharmacy, there are more service windows for the Western medicine pharmacy, and less time consumption for each pharmacy operation. In addition, the overall number of patients on the weekend is less than that on weekdays. Taking the average quantity of pharmacy task in the first peak (9 am to 12 am) every day as an example, for the Western medicine pharmacy, there are 80–100 pharmacy tasks at the peak time in each weekday. The average quantity is 104 on Monday, 100 on Tuesday, 94 on Wednesday, 91 on Thursday, 91 on Friday, 68 on Saturday, and 38 on Sunday. For the traditional Chinese medicine pharmacy, the quantity of pharmacy at the peak time in each weekday is 15–25. The average quantity of pharmacy task is 25 on Monday, 25 on Tuesday, 26 on Wednesday, 22 on Thursday, 26 on Friday, 18 on Saturday, and 5 on Sunday.

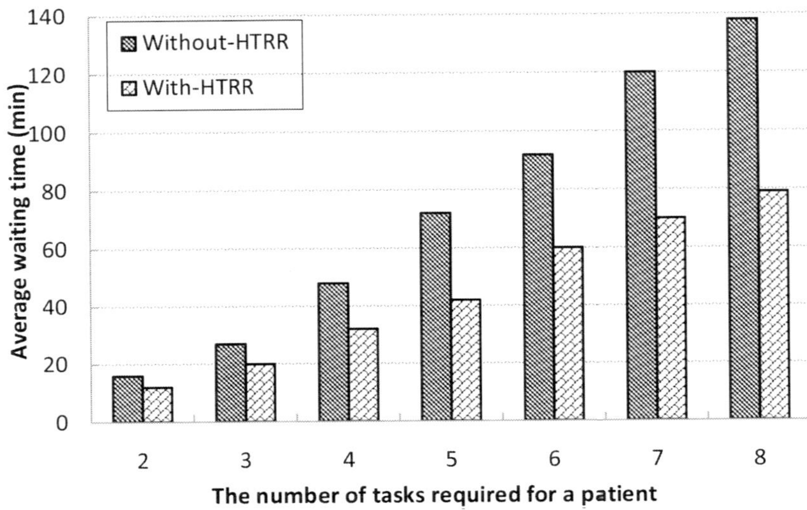

FIGURE 20.15 Average waiting time for patients.

20.4.2.3 Operation Time Consumption of the Pharmacy Task

After discussing the average quantity of the pharmacy task, we account and analyze the operation time consumption of the pharmacy task. The operation time consumptions of the pharmacy task under time factors are presented in Figure 20.14.

In Figure 20.14, each point in the charts refers to a value of one leaf node in the regression tree models of the POTC model. The average number of records at the leaf nodes of the peak-time case on weekdays is approximately 113,880 (= 104 × 365 days × 3 years). Obviously, in the peak-time case, because of the large number of records, the value of trained operation time consumption is smooth and steady in both the traditional Chinese medicine pharmacy and the Western medicine pharmacy. On the contrary, owing to the limited training samples, at the nadir point of two types of pharmacies, the average value of trained operation time consumption is undulating.

Taking 10.00 am on Monday of the Western medicine pharmacy as an example, the average quantity of pharmacy task is 104, namely, there are 113,880 (= 104 × 365 days × 3 years) records at the leaf node of the trained tree model. The operation time consumption is 180–240 s (approximately 3.0–4.0 min) for a Western medicine pharmacy task, and 380–440 s (approximately 6.3–7.3 min) for a traditional Chinese medicine pharmacy task. However, for nadir points of both weekday and weekend, there is 0 or 1 pharmacy treatment per hour on average, namely, there are 0–1095 (= 1 × 365 days × 3 years) records at the leaf node of the trained tree model. With the number of records of each leaf node reduced, the accuracy of operation time consumption of each leaf node is decreased.

20.4.2.4 Average Waiting Time for Patients

To evaluate the efficiency of the HTRR system, various experiments about the average waiting times for patients in the with-HTRR case with that in the without-HTRR case are performed. Each case is under treatment data with 8000 patients and 35,480 treatment records. We accounted and compared the average waiting times of patients in the with-HTRR case with that in the without-HTRR case. The results of comparison are presented in Figure 20.15.

It is easy to observe from Figure 20.15 that the advantage of the average waiting time of patients in cases of with-HTRR is greater than that in cases of without-HTRR. When the number of tasks required for each patient is equal to 2, the average waiting time of each patient is approximately 16 min in the without-HTRR case (the original case), while 12 min in the with-HTRR case. When there are four treatment tasks required for each patient, the average waiting time is approximately

48 min in the former case, while it is 32 min in the latter case. When there are eight treatment tasks required for each patient, the average waiting time is approximately 138 min in the former case, while it is 79 min in the latter case.

20.5 CONCLUSIONS

In this chapter, we discussed the parallel optimization of data-mining algorithms in the big data and cloud computing environment and its applications in hospitals. The parallel optimization methods of the parallel RF algorithm based on an Apache Spark platforms are introduced. Then, to utilize the large-scale hospital data fully and effectively, we developed applications of hospitals based on the optimized data-mining algorithms, which are implemented in a cloud computing environment. Abundant experimental results and applications indicated that the optimized data-mining algorithms achieve a high accuracy and performance and the hospital applications reach the requirements of hospitals and society.

In addition, there are many interesting issues about data-mining algorithms and applications in hospitals in a big data environment. As the amount of data in hospitals are increasing every day, various incremental data-mining algorithms based on streaming data and real-time applications of hospitals will be our future work.

REFERENCES

1. Shunmei Meng, Wanchun Dou, Xuyun Zhang, and Jinjun Chen. Kasr: A keyword-aware service recommendation method on MapReduce for big data applications. *Parallel and Distributed Systems, IEEE Transactions on*, 25(12):3221–3231, 2014.
2. Rajeev Gupta, Himanshu Gupta, and Mukesh Mohania. Cloud computing and big data analytics: What is new from databases perspective. *Big Data Analytics*, 7678:42–61, 2012.
3. Liwei Kuang, Fei Hao, Laurence T. Yang et al. A tensor-based approach for big data representation and dimensionality reduction. *Emerging Topics in Computing, IEEE Transactions on*, 2(3):280–291, 2014.
4. Leo Breiman. Random forests. *Machine Learning*, 45(1):5–32, 2001.
5. Gang Yu, Norberto A. Goussies, Junsong Yuan, and Zicheng Liu. Fast action detection via discriminative random forest voting and top-k subvolume search. *Multimedia, IEEE Transactions on*, 13(3):507–517, 2011.
6. Claudia Lindner, Paul A. Bromiley, Mircea C. Ionita, and Tim F. Cootes. Robust and accurate shape model matching using random forest regression-voting. *Pattern Analysis and Machine Intelligence, IEEE Transactions on*, 25(3):1–14, 2014.
7. Raul Fidalgo-Merino and Marlon Nunez. Self-adaptive induction of regression trees. *Pattern Analysis and Machine Intelligence, IEEE Transactions on*, 33(8):1659–1672, 2011.
8. Nima Salehi-Moghaddami, Hadi Sadoghi Yazdi, and Hanieh Poostchi. Correlation based splitting criterionin multi branch decision tree. *Central European Journal of Computer Science*, 1(2):205–220, 2011.
9. Gediminas Adomavicius and Alexander Tuzhilin. Toward the next generation of recommender systems: A survey of the state-of-the-art and possible extensions. *Knowledge and Data Engineering, IEEE Transactions on*, 17(6):734–749, 2005.
10. Yan Ying Chen, An-Jung Cheng, and Winston H. Hsu. Travel recommendation by mining people attributes and travel group types from community-contributed photos. *Multimedia, IEEE Transactions on*, 15(6):1283–1295, 2013.
11. Xiwang Yang, Yang Guo, and Yong Liu. Bayesian-inference based recommendation in online social networks. *Parallel and Distributed Systems, IEEE Transactions on*, 24(4):642–651, 2013.
12. Xindong Wu, Xingquan Zhu, and Gongqing Wu. Data mining with big data. *Knowledge and Data Engineering, IEEE Transactions on*, 26(1):97–107, 2014.
13. Jeffrey Dean and Sanjay Ghemawat. MapReduce: Simplified data processing on large clusters. *Communications of the ACM*, 51(1):107–113, 2008.

14. Matei Zaharia, Mosharaf Chowdhury, Tathagata Das, Ankur Dave, Justin Ma, Murphy McCauley, Michael J. Franklin, Scott Shenker, and Ion Stoica. Resilient Distributed Datasets: A fault-tolerant abstraction for in-memory cluster computing. In *USENIX NSDI, 2012*, San Jose, pages 1–14. USENIX, 2012.
15. Sara del Rio, Victoria Lopez, Jose Manuel Benitez, and Francisco Herrera. On the use of MapReduce for imbalanced big data using random forest. *Information Sciences*, 285:112–137, 2014.
16. Lena Mashayekhy, Mahyar Movahed Nejad, Daniel Grosu, Quan Zhang, and Weisong Shi. Energy-aware scheduling of MapReduce jobs for big data applications. *Parallel and Distributed Systems, IEEE Transactions on*, 26(3):1–10, 2015.
17. Biswanath Panda, Joshua S. Herbach, Sugato Basu, and Roberto J. Bayardo. Planet: Massively parallel learning of tree ensembles with MapReduce. *Proceedings of the VLDB Endowment*, 2(2):1426–1437, 2009.
18. Stephen Tyree, Kilian Q. Weinberger, and Kunal Agrawal. Parallel boosted regression trees for web search ranking. In *International Conference on World Wide Web*, pages 387–396, 2011.
19. Matei Zaharia, Mosharaf Chowdhury, Tathagata Das, Ankur Dave, Justin Ma, Murphy McCauley, Michael J. Franklin, Scott Shenker, and Ion Stoica. Fast and interactive analytics over Hadoop data with Spark. In *USENIX NSDI, 2012*, pages 45–51. USENIX, San Jose, Chicago, 2012.
20. Wei Huang, Lingkui Meng, Dongying Zhang, and Wen Zhang. In-memory parallel processing of massive remotely sensed data using an Apache Spark on Hadoop yarn model. *IEEE Journal of Selected Topics in Applied Earth Observations and Remote Sensing*, 99:1–17, 2016.
21. Patrick Hunt, Mahadev Konar, Flavio P. Junqueira, and Benjamin Reed. Zookeeper: Wait-free coordination for Internet-scale systems. In *Proceedings of 2010 USENIX Annual Technical Conference (USENIX ATC'10)*, pages 1–14. USENIX, San Jose, Chicago, 2010.

21 Big Data in the Parking Lot

Ryan Florin, Syedmeysam Abolghasemi, Aida Ghazi Zadeh, and Stephan Olariu

CONTENTS

ABSTRACT

One of the significant research challenges in the realm of vehicular clouds is to identify conditions under which these clouds can support big data applications. It is clear that big data applications, with stringent data-processing requirements, cannot be supported by ephemeral vehicular clouds, where the residency time of vehicles in the cloud is too short for supporting virtual machine setup and migration. Similarly, it turns out that vehicular cloud implementations relying on bandwidth-constricted interconnection topologies are not suitable for big data applications. Unfortunately, this is the case of the vast majority of vehicular clouds proposed thus far in the literature that rely on a wireless interconnection fabric.

Our main contribution is to identify sufficient conditions under which big data applications can be effectively supported by datacenters built on top of vehicles in a parking lot. This is pioneering work: to the best of our knowledge, this is the first time researchers are looking at evaluating the feasibility of the vehicular cloud concept and its suitability for supporting big data applications. One of our main findings is that (1) if the residency times of the vehicles are sufficiently long and (2) if the interconnection fabric has a sufficient amount of bandwidth, then big data applications can be supported effectively by such datacenters.

21.1 INTRODUCTION AND MOTIVATION

The past decade has witnessed the emergence and incredible success of *cloud computing* (CC), a paradigm shift adopted by information technology (IT) companies with a large installed infrastructure base that often goes underutilized [1–6]. The unmistakable appeal of CC is that it provides scalable access to computing resources and to a multitude of IT services. Not surprisingly, CC and cloud IT services have seen and continue to see a phenomenal adoption rate around the world [7]. In order to achieve almost unbounded scalability, availability, and security, CC requires substantial architectural support ranging from virtualization, to server consolidation, to file system support, to memory hierarchy design [8,9].

The National Institute of Standards [10] has defined CC as "*A model for enabling convenient, on-demand network access to a shared pool of configurable computing resources (e.g., networks, servers, storage, applications, and services) that can be rapidly provisioned and released with minimal management effort or service provider interaction.*"

As it turns out, CC is a catchy metaphor for *utility computing* implemented through the provisioning of various types of *hosted services* over the Internet [1]. Indeed, it has been argued [11] that CC was inspired by the concept of utility computing and was enabled by the availability of infrastructure providers whose surplus computational resources and storage can be rented out to users. In this context, a user may purchase the amount of compute services they need at the moment. They also need not be concerned with over-provisioning for services whose popularity does not meet their predictions and market analysis, thus wasting costly resources, or under-provisioning for one that becomes wildly popular, and missing potential customers and revenue. As a result, the underlying business model of CC is the familiar *pay-as-you-go* model of metered services, where a user pays for whatever he or she uses and no more, and where additional demand for service can be met in real time [1,9].

In time, this state of affairs has led naturally to the establishment of a global compute-power marketplace [8]. In turn, the availability of the compute-power marketplace has a number of important corollaries. For example, instead of investing in infrastructure, businesses and individual entrepreneurs may find it useful to rent the infrastructure and oftentimes the software required to run their applications. This powerful idea has been suggested, at least in part, by the pervasive presence of relatively low-cost high-speed Internet, a good handle on virtualization, and advances in parallel and distributed computing [9,12].

21.1.1 A First Look at Vehicular Clouds

This subsection provides an introduction to the ideas that underlie vehicular cloud (VC) computing and investigates some of its ramifications, challenges, and opportunities.

A few years ago, inspired by the success and promise of conventional CC, a number of papers [13–17] have introduced the concept of VC, a nontrivial extension of the conventional CC paradigm. VCs were motivated by the realization that present-day vehicles are endowed with powerful onboard computers, powerful transceivers, and an impressive array of sensing devices. As it turns out, most of the time the computing, storage, and communication resources available in our vehicles are chronically underutilized. Putting these resources to work in a meaningful way is poised to have a significant societal impact.

It is very likely that, given the right incentives, the owners of vehicles will decide to rent out their onboard capabilities just as the owners of large computing or storage facilities find it economically appealing to rent out their excess capacity. For example, we anticipate that in the near future air travelers will park and plug their vehicles in airport long-term parking lots. In return for free parking and other perks, they will allow their vehicles to participate, during their absence, in the airport datacenter as suggested by [14].

More generally, we expect that in a VC the underutilized vehicular resources including compute power, storage, and Internet connectivity can be shared between drivers or rented out over the Internet to various customers, very much as conventional cloud resources are. In [16], it was suggested that, even under current technology, many forms of VCs are technologically feasible and economically viable. They predicted that, once adopted, the VCs will be *the next paradigm shift* with a lasting technological and societal impact [16].

One of the fundamental ways in which VCs differ from conventional clouds is in the ownership of resources. In VCs, the ownership of the computational resources is distributed over a large vehicle-owner population as opposed to a single owner as is the case of conventional clouds run by Amazon, Google, IBM, Microsoft, Facebook, Yahoo!, Oracle, and other players. A first corollary of this is that the resources of the VC are likely to be highly dynamic. As vehicles enter and leave the parking lot, new computational resources become available while others depart, creating a volatile environment where the task of promoting reliability, dependability, and availability becomes very challenging. A second corollary is that in VCs, the distributed ownership of computational resources makes it very challenging to promote reliability, dependability, and availability. To get a feel for the problem, assume that we just assigned a user job to a vehicle currently in the parking lot. If the vehicle remains in the parking lot until the job terminates, all is well. Difficulties arise when the vehicle departs before job completion. In such a case, unless special precautions are taken, the entire work done is lost and we have to restart the entire job again, taking chances on another vehicle, and so on until eventually the job is completed.

21.1.2 Big Data Applications

The volume of data that has to be collected and analyzed on a daily basis is growing rapidly, in fact exponentially, because data is collected by all sorts of sensing devices embedded in our sensor networks, smartphones, smart glasses, smart cars, various RFID readers, and so on [18]. Similarly, huge amounts of data are produced by social networks, various flavors of vehicular networks, and by devices forming what has been called the *Internet of Things* (IoT) [19,20].

Arguably, we are approaching a fundamental paradigm shift in computing as the number of smart device (e.g., smartphone and tablet) users is expected to exceed 3 billion (40% of the global population) by the end of 2016 and to swell to more than 4 billion in the next 3 years [21,22]. In addition, given the recent advances in microprocessors and the development of more types of connected smart devices (e.g., smart watches, smart glasses, smart meters, connected vehicles, etc.), we are seeing the next phase of the Internet, populated by traffic originating primarily from IoT devices. Cisco predicted that the number of connected IoT devices will reach 50 billion by 2020 [23,24].

By 2017, it is expected that the amount of monthly data generated by devices such as smartphones, wearables of all sorts, and vehicles will reach 14 exabytes and will surpass 24.3 exabytes by 2019 [25]. With the widening gap between bandwidth capacity and data volumes, more and more useful data will be thrown away for the lack of processing capability. Besides its mere size, the data collected by various smart devices is incredibly rich in contextual information and, if properly harvested, could contribute tremendously to enhancing our understanding of our environment and daily experience.

Given the ephemeral nature of context and context-sensitive needs of individuals and enterprises, the highest value from data can be extracted only by processing it in *near real-time*. However, due to latency and costs involved in moving data to and from a distant cloud facility, cloud-based real-time processing huge amounts of data in near real-time remain a big challenge. Until new data-processing technologies are developed, the processing of huge volumes of data with stringent time constraints is neither technologically feasible nor economically viable [26].

Yet another example of large data sets that need to be processed not only fast but also reliably is provided by the type of processing dealing with customer experience in e-commerce applications. In this context, the most prevalent workloads are searches and many other services that support and enhance a customer's experience. Managing the contents of a shopping cart and various queries launched by a prospective customer requires the ability to store and recover efficiently customer preferences, a history of previous purchases, returns, personal data, and so on. This information must be maintained reliably and must be made available in a fraction of a second. The common wisdom is that unhappy customers will not be return customers [27].

Another type of workload is associated with queries launched by a customer and involves composite services. For example, a customer may be interested in restaurants in New York. The search algorithm must traverse all available postings of each such item and must return the answers in a given, often customer-aware, way. A successful search service presupposes that the data is stored reliably and that it is accessible in a fraction of a second irrespective of how many servers are down at the moment [1].

Importantly, in the examples above, the total user-perceived latency needs to be a fraction of a second. Consequently, any file system in support of such applications must support latency reduction. However, high throughput is also an important performance metric because a highly popular service needs to support many thousands of simultaneous queries. The high availability requirements in such a system can only be supported through redundancy of storage (in addition to execution redundancy, where each user query may be executed by two or more servers). Storage redundancy implies that virtually each data item must be stored at several locations in the network.

More generally, *big data* is a commonly used term for describing data collections, both structured and unstructured (as discussed above), that are so large and so complex that traditional data-processing applications are inadequate for handling them effectively. And yet, this data needs to be analyzed for the purpose of decision making in such relevant areas as identifying trends in customer behavior, weather patterns, computer vision, medical sciences, terror attack prevention, nanotechnology, microbiology, robotics, and massively parallel processing, to name just a few [28–37]. The challenges involved in handling these large amounts of data in a timely and secure and privacy-preserving fashion range from data collection, to data transfer, to data storage, to data analysis, to data visualization, to many others.

As it turns out, emerging *big data applications* involve sophisticated multiphase data processing [26]. Many of these applications rely on MapReduce [12,38] and on its open-source twin Hadoop [39–41]. Since our simulations use MapReduce, we now provide a succinct review of how MapReduce works.

MapReduce was introduced by Google in 2004 and is suitable for processing semistructured and unstructured data [2]. MapReduce was inspired by the Lisp functions with the same name and same functionality. The processing performed by MapReduce has two sequential stages: *Map* and *Reduce*. In the Map phase, a user-defined function is applied to every logical input record to produce an intermediate result of key–value pairs; the Reduce stage collects all the key–value pairs produced by the Map stage and collapses them using yet another user-supplied function [12].

21.1.3 Our Contributions

The conception of VC is novel and so are the myriad of potential applications and significant research challenges facing the VC research community. While a good number of papers were written about various flavors of VCs, there are virtually no studies concerning the practical feasibility of VCs. Some of these papers proposed VCs built on top of moving vehicles interconnected by some form of wireless communication fabric; some other authors consider a mix of moving and stationary vehicles. Our extensive simulations show that VCs based on wireless communications do not appear to be able to support big data applications effectively. It is our hope that this negative result might serve as a wake-up call to the VC community.

One of the significant research challenges in the realm of VCs is to *identify* conditions under which the VCs can support big data applications. It is clear that such applications, with stringent data-processing requirements, cannot be supported by *ephemeral* VCs, that is to say, VCs where the residency time of vehicles in the cloud is too short for supporting VC setup and VM migration. Similarly, VC implementations with bandwidth-constricted interconnection topologies are not suitable for big data applications. Unfortunately, so are the vast majority of VCs that rely on a wireless interconnection fabric.

Our main contribution is to identify sufficient conditions under which big data applications can be effectively supported by datacenters built on top of vehicles in a parking lot. This is pioneering work: to the best of our knowledge, this is the first time researchers are looking at evaluating the feasibility of the VC concept and its suitability for supporting big data applications. One of our main findings is that if the residency times of the vehicles are sufficiently long and if the interconnection fabric has a sufficient amount of bandwidth, then big data applications can be supported effectively by such datacenters. The extensive details of our findings are spelled out in Section 21.7.

At this point, it is appropriate to give the reader a synopsis of the chapter. Section 21.2 offers a succinct synopsis of cloud services, followed by, in Sections 21.3 and 21.4, a taxonomy of VCs and a survey of relevant work on VCs, respectively. In Section 21.5, we review, respectively, the assumptions we make about the architecture and services provided by the VC, the strategy for VM migration, and the capabilities of vehicles. Specifically, in Section 21.5.1, we discuss VM migration and data replication strategies, while in Section 21.5.2, we discuss our assumptions about the onboard capabilities of vehicles. Next, Section 21.6 discusses a particular instance of a realistic VC that will be used in our simulation section. Section 21.7 presents the details of our empirical evaluation of the conditions that allow a VC-based datacenter to support big data applications effectively. Specifically, Section 21.7.1 introduces our simulation model; Section 21.7.2 presents the interconnection model used in our empirical evaluation; Section 21.7.3 presents our interpretation of the results we have obtained; Section 21.7.4 presents a critical look at two strategies for setting the VM migration offset; Section 21.7.5 contrasts the performance of a VC-based datacenter with that of a conventional datacenter. Finally, Section 21.8 offers concluding remarks and directions for future work.

21.2 A REVIEW OF CLOUD SERVICES

Hand in hand with CC go cloud IT services where not only computational resources and storage are rented out, but also specialized services are provided on demand. In this context, users may purchase the amount of services they need at the moment. As their IT needs grow and as their services and customer base expand, the users will be in the market for more and more cloud services and more diversified computational and storage resources [26]. As a result, developers with innovative ideas for new applications are no longer required to immobilize capital in hardware and software to test their ideas. They also need not be concerned with over-provisioning for services whose popularity does not meet their predictions, or under-provisioning for those that become wildly popular [11].

Three aspects are novel in CC: first, it gives users the illusion of having infinite computing resources available on demand, thus eliminating the need for them to plan far ahead for resource provisioning. Second, it eliminates the up-front financial commitment by cloud users, allowing companies to start small and to increase hardware resources only when there is an increase in their needs because of their applications getting more popular. Third, it gives users the ability to pay for computing resources on a short-term basis as needed (e.g., processors by the hour and storage by the day) and release them as needed, thereby rewarding conservation by releasing resources (e.g., machines and storage) when they are no longer useful.

There are three basic types of conventional cloud services:

Infrastructure as a Service (IaaS): Here the cloud provider offers its customers computing, network, and storage resources. A good example is Amazon Web Services (AWS), where Amazon provides its customers computing resources through its Elastic Compute Cloud

(EC2) service and storage service through both Simple Storage Service (S3) and Elastic Book Store (EBS) [42].

Platform as a Service (PaaS): PaaS solutions are development platforms for which the development tool itself is hosted in the cloud and accessed through a browser. With PaaS, developers can build Web applications without installing any tools on their computers and then deploy those applications without any specialized systems administration skills. Google AppEngine [43] and Microsoft Azure [44] are good examples of this category.

Software as a Service (SaaS): With SaaS, a provider licenses an application to customers as a service on demand, through a subscription, in a "pay-as-you-go" model. This allows customers to use expensive software that their applications require, without the hassle of installing and maintaining that software. GoogleAppEngine and IBM [45] are good examples of this category.

21.3 A TAXONOMY OF VCs

The huge fleet of vehicles that crisscross our roadways and city streets feature an impressive array of onboard computational, storage, and sensing capabilities. It is common knowledge that many of these vehicles spend hours each day in a parking garage, parking lot, or driveway. The computational and storage capabilities of these parked vehicles are a vast untapped resource that, at the moment, is wasted. These attributes make vehicles ideal candidates for servers in a datacenter. As mentioned in Section 21.1, the CC paradigm has worked well for enabling the exploitation of excess computing capacity.

We believe it is only a matter of time before the potential of the huge vehicular fleet on our roadways, streets, and parking lots will be recognized as an abundant and underutilized computational resource that can be tapped into for the purpose of providing third-party or community services.

As already mentioned, it is reasonable to expect that, given the right incentives, the owner of a vehicle will decide to rent out excess onboard capabilities, just as the owners of large computing or storage facilities find it economically appealing to rent out their excess capacity. For example, it is quite natural to assume that, while on travel, travelers will park and plug their cars in airport long-term parking garage. While in the parking garage, the airport will power the vehicles' computing resources and will allow for on-demand access to this parking garage datacenter. Likewise, it is easy to infer that the drivers of vehicles stuck in congested traffic will be more than willing to volunteer their onboard computing resources so that municipal traffic management centers can run complex simulations designed to help alleviate the effects of congestion by city-wide rescheduling of traffic lights.

Recall that what distinguishes vehicles in a VC from servers in a conventional cloud is the dynamic availability of resources. Clearly, some vehicles are parked for unpredictable periods of time (think of the parking lot of a convenience store) while others are stuck in congested traffic and move at very low speed changing their points of attachment to some wireless network. Finally, some of our vehicles spend substantial amounts of time on the road and may be involved in dynamically changing situations; in such situations, the vehicles have the potential to cooperate with local authorities to solve, in a timely fashion, traffic-related problems that cannot be addressed by the municipal traffic management centers alone for the lack of adequate computational resources. Eltoweissy et al. [46] and Olariu et al. [17] have argued that in many such situations, the vehicles have the potential to cooperatively solve problems that would take a centralized system an inordinate amount of time, rendering the solution useless.

More significantly, Eltoweissy et al. [46] have postulated that, in the near future, the vehicles will autonomously self-organize into VCs utilizing their corporate resources on-demand and largely in real-time in resolving critical problems that may occur unexpectedly. The new VCs will also contribute to unraveling some technical challenges of the increasingly complex transportation systems with their emergent behavior and uncertainty.

With this in mind, Eltoweissy et al. [46] have proposed to think of a VC as *a group of largely autonomous vehicles whose corporate computing, sensing, communication, and physical resources can be coordinated and dynamically allocated to authorized users.*

In our vision, the VC concept is the next natural step in meeting the computational and situational awareness needs not only of the driving public but also of a much larger segment of the population. A primary goal of the VC is to provide on-demand solutions to events that have occurred but cannot be met reasonably with preassigned assets or in a proactive fashion.

It is important to delineate the structural, functional, and behavioral characteristics of VCs. As a step in this direction, Olariu et al. [16] have identified autonomous cooperation among vehicular resources as one of the distinguishing characteristics of VCs. Another important characteristic of VCs is the ability to offer a seamless integration and decentralized management of their onboard resources. We anticipate that a VC can dynamically adapt its managed vehicular resources allocated to applications according to changing application-level requirements and environmental and systems conditions.

As far as a simple taxonomy goes, VCs can be public, private, or various hybrids thereof. The public VC will provide (typically short-term) services on the Internet, whereas a private VC is proprietary and provides (typically long-term) services to a limited set of users and would belong to specific vehicle fleets such as FedEx, UPS, Costco, or Wal-Mart. Private VCs may be of interest to military units as discussed by Florin et al. [47]. As an example of a hybrid VC, one may consider an inter-VC cooperation.

We believe it is not too far-fetched to imagine, in the not-so-distant-future, a large-scale federation of VCs established ad hoc in support of mitigating large-scale emergencies. One of these large-scale emergencies could be a planned evacuation in the face of a potentially deadly hurricane or tsunami that is expected to make landfall in a coastal region [48–53]. Yet another such emergency would be a natural or man-made disaster apt to destroy the existing infrastructure and to play havoc with cellular communications. In such a scenario, a federation of VCs could provide a short-term replacement for the infrastructure and also provide a decision-support system.

While a static VC (e.g., vehicles in a parking lot) may mimic the behavior of a conventional CC facility, many of our vehicles spend a substantial amount of time on the road and may be involved, on a daily basis, in various dynamically changing situations, ranging from normal traffic to congestion, to accidents, to other similar traffic-related events.

Under present-day practices, the vehicles are mere spectators that witness traffic-related events without being able to participate in the mitigation of their effect. We suggest that in such situations the vehicles have the potential to cooperate with various authorities to solve problems that otherwise will either take an inordinate amount of time to solve (traffic jams) or cannot be solved for the lack of adequate resources that can be brought to bear.

The mobility attribute of the VC, combined with the fact that the presence of vehicles in close proximity to an event is very often an unplanned process, implies that the pooling of the resources of those vehicles that for a VC in support of mitigating the event must occur spontaneously by the common recognition of a need for which there are no preassigned or dedicated resources available. This option does not exist in conventional clouds and turns out to be an important defining characteristic of VCs.

21.4 A SURVEY OF RECENT WORK ON VCs

The main purpose of this section is to offer a succinct survey of recent papers dealing with VCs. The first papers that have introduced the concept of VC were Eltoweissy et al. [46] and Olariu et al. [15,17]. These early papers have defined various possible versions of VCs, have pointed out their multifold applications, and have identified a number of research challenges. For example, *autonomous clouds* were proposed for the first time by Olariu et al. [15], where they also surveyed a number of important applications and interesting research challenges.

Actually, some researchers have pointed out that, even under present-day state of the practice, many implementations of VCs are feasible and economically viable [15,17,54,55]. Olariu et al. [16] argued that, once adopted, VCs will be the next paradigm shift, taking vehicular networks to the next level of relevance and innovation.

Recently, Gu et al. [56] published a survey paper where they reviewed key issues in VC mostly concerning its architecture, inherent features, service taxonomy, and potential applications. Not long afterwards, Whaiduzzaman et al. [55] offered an updated perspective of various research topics in VCs.

Arif et al. [14] have looked at datacenters run on top of the vehicles parked at a major airport. In that context, they proposed a stochastic prediction model for the parking occupancy given time-varying arrival and departure rates. They provided closed forms for the probability distribution of the parking lot occupancy as a function of time, for the expected number of vehicles in the parking lot and its variance, and for the limiting behavior of these parameters as time increases. In addition to analytical results, they have obtained a series of empirical results that confirm the accuracy of their analytical derivations.

Vignesh et al. [57] suggested potential new services that could be offered in VCs. A dynamic group of vehicles in a parking lot is considered where the vehicles are typically parked for several days and can form a stationary VC (SVC). The vehicle that controls the allocation of resources is called the SVC Master (SVC-M). The other vehicles in SVC are called SVC Participants (SVC-P). Once a vehicle wishes to join the SVC, it broadcasts an Association Request message. If it does not receive any ACK within a certain interval, it assumes that there is no SVC yet formed and acts as the SVC-M. If there is already an SVC-M, it will receive an association ACK. In *Computation as a Service* (CaaS), the client sends a request for computation to the SVC-M. The SVC-M selects the node with the maximum processing power and the longest parking history, then contacts the selected node through a request, and thereby hands over the computational data. In *Storage as a Service* (StaaS), the client initiates a storage request to the SVC-M along with the content to be stored. SVC-M finds the node with the maximum memory and availability using the information in the resource table and contacts that respective node and sends the associated storage files to the SVC-P. In StaaS retrieval, the client that stored data in the SVC initiates a storage retrieval request to the SVC-M. The SVC-M finds the SVC-P that currently holds the requested content and contacts that SVC-P and sends the names of the files to be retrieved. The SVC-P returns the stored file contents to the SVC-M, and the SVC-M then sends the stored content to client.

Hussain et al. [54] proposed a network model with an architecture divided into two networks (i.e., VANET and CC) connected through gateway terminals (GTs). Vehicles moving on the road serve as both producers and consumers. Roadside units (RSU) serve as GTs between vehicles and cloud infrastructure. Vehicles with onboard 3G/4G Internet access can serve as a secondary GTs to the cloud. Cloud architecture also consists of Authenticator, CPM (Cloud Processing Module), CKB (Cloud Knowledge Base), and vehicles CDM (Cloud Decision Module). This system uses the message lifetime, which defines the message validity period, to prevent stale messages from cluttering the network.

He et al. [58] proposed a novel software architecture for the vehicular data clouds in the IoT environment. A new generation of IoT-based vehicular data clouds can be developed to bring many benefits, such as predicting increasing road safety, reducing road congestion, managing traffic, and recommending vehicle maintenance or repair. The proposed IoT-based vehicular data cloud contains various devices such as sensors, actuators, controllers, GPS devices, mobile phones, networking technologies (wireless sensor network, cellular network, satellite network), CC, IoT, and middleware. It supports V2V and V2I communications and is able to collect and exchange data among drivers, vehicles, and roadside infrastructure such as cameras and street lights. This paper explains intelligent parking cloud service. Finding available parking is challenging in many cities, so a system to find available parking spots is necessary [59,60]. In this architecture, a vehicle is equipped with a processor and a transceiver such as Bluetooth devices and infrared devices. When a vehicle is about to enter a parking lot, the entrance booth validates the reservation and, if it is valid, a direction for finding the spot is sent to the driver. Sensors connected to the computer center report the status of every parking spot on an ongoing basis. This mechanism can be used for advertisement of a particular parking spot. IoT-based vehicular data clouds must be efficient, scalable, secure, and reliable before they could be deployed at a large scale. Existing algorithms and mechanisms are unsatisfactory to meet all these requirements at the same time. Some of the challenges include performance, reliability and quality of service, security and privacy, and integration of IoT with new and existing devices and technologies.

In order to be able to schedule resources and to assign computational tasks to the various vehicles in the VC, a fundamental prerequisite is to have an accurate picture of the number of vehicles that are expected to be present in the parking lot as a function of time. What makes the problem difficult is the time-varying nature of the arrival and departure rates. Arif et al. [14] have proposed a stochastic prediction model for the parking occupancy given time-varying arrival and departure rates. They provided closed forms for the probability distribution of the parking lot occupancy as a function of time, for the expected number of vehicles in the parking lot and its variance and for the limiting behavior of these parameters as time increases. In addition, they have obtained a series of empirical results that confirm the accuracy of their analytical predictions.

Recently, Ghazizadeh et al. [61] have studied the problem of task scheduling in VCs and presented a near-optimal solution based on mixed integer linear programming. Being integer programming-based, their solution has the disadvantage that it does not scale to a large number of vehicles.

Fault tolerance and availability are important issues in CC and, therefore, also in VCs. Of the papers cited above, the only one that even recognizes fault tolerance and availability being important is He et al. [58]; however, they have not provided any solution. Recently, Ghazizadeh [62] has started to look at the strategies for improving the mean time to failure (MTTF) in VCs. His work was continued by [63,64] and also by Florin et al. [47].

Other important topics related to VC management are also getting attention. For example, Baron et al. [65] and Refaat et al. [66] are addressing the important topic of virtual machine (VM) migration in VCs. Strategies for VM migration are essential in conventional CCs. Due to the dynamic nature of VCs, VM migration becomes even more important here.

Finally, Yan et al. [67] have investigated the problem of providing security and privacy in VCs. They have shown that many of the insecurities found in conventional CC carry over to VCs. In addition, they have identified a number of VC-specific security problems and have proposed preliminary solutions.

21.5 A HIGH-LEVEL VIEW OF THE DATACENTER AND VC MODEL

The main goal of this section is to present a bird's-eye view of the datacenter and VC model assumed in this chapter. Both the datacenter and VC model will be presented in much more detail in Sections 21.6 and 21.7.

Throughout this chapter, we deal with a datacenter supported by a (static) VC built on top of vehicles parked in a sufficiently large parking lot, similar to the long-term parking lot at a major airport, or to the parking lot of a large corporation that employs thousands of people and operates around the clock 24/7. To be more specific, we consider a variant of the latter scenario, which we describe in some detail in Section 21.6. For obvious reasons, such a parking lot is almost always nearly full and, in particular, it is always possible to find a vehicle that can be assigned to an incoming user job.

The resulting VC will harvest the corporate computational and storage resources of the participating vehicles sitting in the parking lot for the purpose of creating a VC-based datacenter and a huge distributed data storage facility that, with proper security safeguards in place, will turn out to be an important computational asset that the corporation cannot afford to waste. In the scenario above, the architecture of the VC will be almost identical to the architecture of a conventional cloud [1,6,68,69],

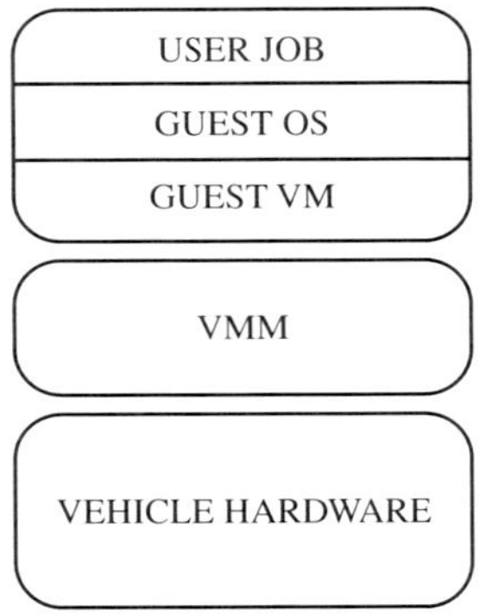

FIGURE 21.1 Illustrating the virtualization model assumed in this chapter.

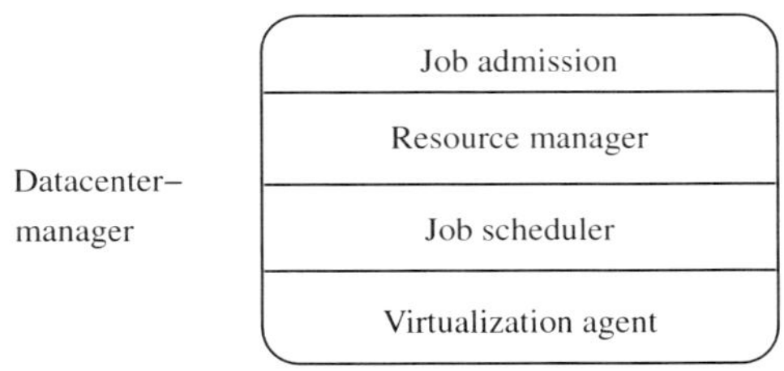

FIGURE 21.2 Illustrating the functional view of the datacenter manager assumed in this chapter.

with the important difference that the VC is far more dynamic than a conventional datacenter. Indeed, imagine what happens when a large number of workers end their workday and depart, only to be replaced by the folks working the next shift.

To keep things relatively simple, we assume that the VC offers only IaaS cloud services. Recall that in IaaS, the users request a hardware platform and specify their preferred OS support. As illustrated in Figure 21.1, the VC offers the user a virtualized instance of the desired hardware platform and operating system bundled as a VM and guest OS hosted by one of the vehicles in the parking lot. For fault-tolerance purposes, each user job may be assigned to multiple vehicles. When the VM running the user job in a specific vehicle terminates execution, the result is uploaded to the datacenter. In this scenario, the datacenter waits for the prescribed number of instances of the user job to terminate and makes a final determination by using, for example, a quorum-based algorithm or voting mechanism [70–73].

To get an idea of the type of processing that is going on, consider a user job submitted for execution by the datacenter and refer to Figure 21.2 that offers a functional view of the datacenter manager module. The requirements of the submitted user job, in terms of the hardware platform that needs to be emulated, the requested OS, and the user-specified input data, are evaluated by the *Job Admission* daemon. If these requirements can be met by the datacenter, the job is admitted and gets inserted into a queue of jobs awaiting execution. Otherwise, the job is rejected.

Once the job makes it to the front of the queue, control passes to the *virtualization agent* that bundles the resources specified by the user job into a VM, specific OS, and the input data to the VM. Finally, the virtualization agent passes control to the *job scheduler* that identifies one vehicle (or a group of vehicles) on which the job is to be executed. For simplicity, in this chapter, we assume that each user job is assigned and executed on a single vehicle. The extension to the case where, for the sake of redundancy, each user job is run on several vehicles will be investigated in an upcoming work.

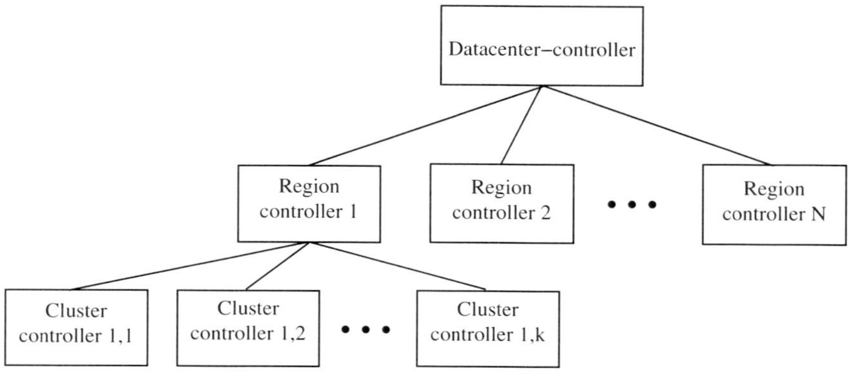

FIGURE 21.3 Illustrating the logical view of the datacenter communications assumed in this chapter.

Next, Figure 21.3 presents the logical view of the communication structure of the datacenter. This communication structure is, conceptually, very similar to that of a standard datacenter (see Barroso et al. [1]). The analogy is better understood if one bears in mind that a vehicle in the parking lot is just like a server in a rack of servers. Accordingly, the parking lot is partitioned logically into clusters of parking spots, regions of clusters, and so on. The communication in each cluster is under the control of a switch called the *cluster controller*. Similarly, the communication in a region is under the control of a switch called a *region controller*. Referring to Figure 21.3, the parking lot is partitioned into N regions. Each such region consists of k clusters. The datacenter manager discussed above is in control of assigning user jobs to various vehicles in the parking lot.

21.5.1 VM Migration and Data Replication

Once a vehicle is ready to leave the parking lot, a number of actions need to be undertaken. First and foremost, if the vehicle is hosting a guest VM, the VM and all intermediate data stored by the departing vehicle must be *migrated* to an available vehicle in the parking lot. There are several known strategies for VM migration [65,66,74,75]. For the purpose of this chapter, we have not implemented a specific migration discipline. We have estimated the average time such a migration should take for a given VM size and available network bandwidth.

Inspired by the data replication strategies adopted by the Google File System (GFS) [76] and the Google record storage system Bigtable [77], in support of reliability, dependability, and availability, the datacenter will mandate data replication for multistage big data applications.

As an example, at the end of the Map stage, the intermediate result, in the form of a set of key–value pairs, will be stored by a number of vehicles in the parking lot. Likewise, when a VM belonging to a multistage user job has to be migrated, it will go (if at all possible) to one of the vehicles that stores relevant intermediate data for that job. More details on this are discussed in Sections 21.6 and 21.7.

21.5.2 The Vehicle Model

The past 10 years have seen an unmistakable trend toward making the vehicles on our roads and city streets smarter and the driving experience safer, less stressful, and, as a result, more enjoyable [78]. A typical vehicle today is likely to contain at least some of the following devices: an onboard computer, a GPS device coupled with a digital map, a radio transceiver, a short-range rear collision radar device, and a camera. These are supplemented, in high-end models, by sophisticated sensing devices that can alert the driver to all manner of mechanical malfunctions and road conditions [78,79].

We assume that each vehicle has a virtualizable onboard computer similar, but not necessarily identical, to the Intel Itanium [80], AMD Athlon, or Opteron lines of processors. The vehicles are assumed to have been preloaded with a suitable VM monitor (VMM) that is in charge of mapping between the guest VM and the host car's resources (see Figure 21.1). In this chapter, we assume that each vehicle runs a single VM. This restriction is nonessential and is made only to streamline the presentation. Because of their sophisticated compute capabilities and ample storage, our vehicles are good candidates for servers in a warehouse-scale computer [2].

We assume that the datacenter has implemented a mechanism that identifies available vehicles in the parking lot. Such a mechanism can be implemented by assigning to each vehicle a status bit. When a vehicle is about to leave the parking lot, the datacenter alerts all the other vehicles assigned to the same user job of the imminent departure. When a vehicle enters the parking lot and joins the VC, it will initiate communication with the *resource manager* component of the datacenter manager. We assume that the drivers of the vehicle will select an available parking spot at random. The resource manager identifies the cluster and region where the vehicle is parked. Finally, the job scheduler can select, using some form of locality criteria, one or several available vehicles that can be assigned to a job.

21.6 DETAILS OF THE DATACENTER ARCHITECTURE

The goal of this section is to spell out the details of our datacenter implemented on the vehicles in the parking lot of a plant that operates 24 hours a day, 7 days a week.* The patrons of the parking lot are working at the plant in staggered 8-hour shifts, providing a pool of vehicles that can serve as the basis for a datacenter. We assume that the vehicles in the parking lot are plugged into a standard power outlet and are provided Ethernet connection to the datacenter. The challenge facing the implementation of the datacenter is to maintain high availability and reliability in the face of the dynamically changing resources. Trade-offs will be identified and analyzed and several possible solutions will be contrasted.

Imagine a medium-size plant that employs 7680 people and that operates around the clock, 7 days a week. For simplicity, assume that all the workers drive their own vehicle to work. In order to avoid bottlenecks at the entrance to the parking lot, the plant has implemented staggered 8-hour shifts. This is to say, at the top of each hour, 320 people end their workday and leave the plant, only to be replaced by 320 fresh workers that start their 8-hour workday.

- The parking lot has a capacity of 2560 vehicles and is assumed to be nearly always full.
- We assume that all the 320 vehicles belonging to departing workers leave the parking lot before the 320 new vehicles pull in.
- An arriving vehicle picks one of the available parking spots at random.
- For each vehicle, the datacenter keeps track, among others, of its status (available or busy), of its arrival time, and of its departure time.

Services: The datacenter offers its users a virtualized instance of their desired hardware platform and operating system bundled as a VM and guest OS, hosted by some vehicle in the parking lot.

- The vehicles are assumed to have been preloaded with a suitable VMM that maps between the guest VM and the host vehicle's resources.
- Each vehicle hosts at most one VM and has ample disk space. The size of a VM is uniformly 500 MB.

* A good example of such a plant is Newport News Shipbuilding located in Hampton Roads, Virginia, that employs well over 20,000 people.

- The users are assumed to run jobs whose durations are uniformly distributed in the interval [1,5] hours. The duration of a job is taken to be the amount of time it takes the job to execute in the absence of any overhead.
- Each user runs a MapReduce job with an input of 50 GB and generates intermediate data (at the end of the Map stage) of 25 GB.

Network support: The network fabric that interconnects the vehicles in the datacenter is described next.

- At the logical level, the parking lot is organized as a quadtree as illustrated in Figure 21.4.
- The root of the tree is a 64 Gb switch* called the *datacenter controller* (DC) collocated with the datacenter manager. The DC is in charge of the communication between the parked vehicles and the datacenter.
- The DC has four children, termed *region controllers* (RC). Each RC is a 16 Gb switch in charge of the communication within its own region.
- Each RC has four children, termed *group controllers* (GC). Each GC is a 4 Gb switch in charge of the communication within its own group.
- Finally, each GC has four children, termed *cluster controllers* (CC). Each CC is a 1 Gb Ethernet switch in charge of a *cluster* of 40 parking spots (vehicles). The vehicles in a cluster communicate uniquely through the local CC. The CC also acts as a gateway to other members of the communication hierarchy described above.

Dependability and availability support: The datacenter strives to ensure a high level of dependability and availability as described next.

- In support of availability and reliability, vehicles are expected to store data belonging to various users, as explained next.
- Three replicas of all intermediate data produced by a job must be saved. To minimize latency, the first copy is stored in the hard drive of the host vehicle; the second copy is stored on a vehicle in the same cluster; and the third copy is stored on a vehicle anywhere in the parking lot.
- The datacenter also keeps track of the various jobs that use a given vehicle's hard drive as a repository.
- When a vehicle is about to depart, its guest VM as well as the data it stores need to be migrated to a suitable vehicle. This operation takes time and several migration strategies have been explored.
- When a vehicle departs without having migrated its guest VM, the corresponding user job will have to be restarted from scratch.
- If it becomes apparent that a vehicle is about to depart, the datacenter must attempt to relocate the data stored in its hard drive.

Statistical data we are interested to collect: In order identify sufficient conditions for our VC-based datacenter to support big data applications, we intend to collect statistical data as described next.

Before we discuss these statistical data, a definition is necessary. We define *job completion time* as the total amount of time it takes a job to complete. Observe that job completion time is the sum of *job duration time*† and the various overheads incurred, such as downloading the initial data on which the job is to run, migrating the corresponding VM, replicating the intermediate data produced, and transferring the job output to the datacenter manager.

---

* We assume that the link connecting the DC with its four children (see below) has a bandwidth of 16 GB.

† This is the time that takes the user job to execute in the absence of any overhead.

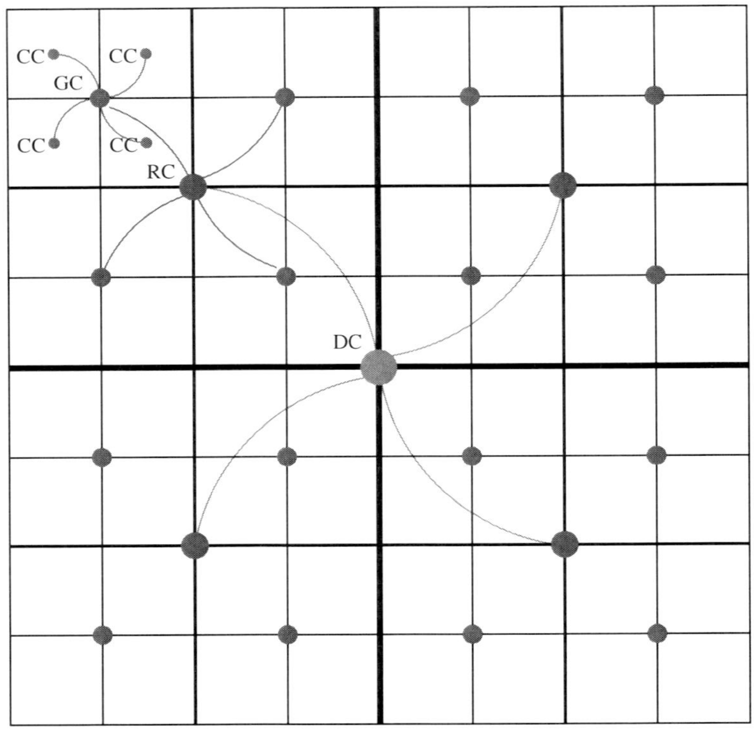

FIGURE 21.4 Illustrating the logical partition of the parking lot.

The goal is to minimize job completion time. In order to do this, we wish to evaluate strategies for various VM migration and data replication strategies.

Job completion time overhead: When a job is first assigned to a vehicle from the job queue, a job start time is set on the job. This is not reset if the job fails and is sent back to the job queue. When the job completes, the time span is recorded. This value is the total job completion time. To get the overhead, the job processing time defined by the parameter is subtracted. The overhead may include time due to sending data or VMs, VM migrations, or if the job fails, additional job processing time. At the end of the simulation, the average is saved.

Average jobs in parking lot: At each time point, the number of the jobs currently assigned in the parking lot is counted and saved by the datacenter. At the end of the simulation, the average is saved.

Total jobs completed: Every time a job completes, the datacenter increments a counter representing the number of jobs completed. At the end of the simulation, the average is saved.

Failures per job: Upon a job failure, the datacenter increments a counter representing the number of failed jobs. At the end of the simulation, this number is divided by the number of completed jobs.

VM migrations per job: Every time a VM migration is started, the datacenter increments a counter representing the number of VM migrations. This is divided by the number of jobs completed to give the number of VM migrations per job.

MTTF: MTTF is defined in the parking lot as the average of the total amount of processing time completed across all jobs before a failure occurs. After the simulation, the average job completion time, total jobs completed, and the number of job failures are all known. To get the MTTF, the average job completion time is multiplied by the jobs completed and then divided by the number of job failures. This value is saved.

21.7 EMPIRICAL PERFORMANCE EVALUATION

Given the pioneering nature of the parking lot datacenter and our interest in reporting the feasibility of delivering big data applications in VC-based datacenters, in our simulations we have varied our parameters widely to get a good understanding of how the model acts. In doing so, we made a choice for this baseline simulation to run a large number of varying experiments a few number of times, rather than a few experiments several times. This gives us a full view over a wide variety of input parameters, at the expense of not having the smoothing effects of averaging several runs.

Recall that the datacenter offers IaaS cloud services and that, to fix the ideas, the user jobs are assumed to be two-stage MapReduce tasks each involving an input of size 50 GB, consistent with big data-processing needs.

21.7.1 Simulation Model

Each experiment is run for 1 week (10,080 minutes) with time stepping each minute. Vehicle arrivals are set such that the parking lot is nearly always full. We assume that vehicle residency is exponentially distributed with a mean of 480 minutes. As a vehicle arrives, it is assigned to a random empty spot in the parking lot. Immediately upon arrival in the parking lot, the vehicle is assumed to be available for job assignment.

Incoming user jobs are placed into a job queue run by the datacenter and are only assigned if the following conditions are met:

- Only u, vehicle utilization percentage, of the vehicles in the parking lot may be assigned a job at any given time.
- Only i vehicles may be in the initial job setup status at any given time.
- A vehicle may have at most one VM assigned to it at any given time.

In each of our simulations, u is set to 0.8 and i varies between 100, 200, and 300, meaning only 80% of cars in the parking lot may be assigned jobs and, depending on the value of i, only 100, 200, or 300 cars may be in the initial setup task of the job. Both u and i act as a *throttle* that limits the number of jobs being assigned from the job queue.

Incoming jobs arrive according to a Poisson distribution with parameter λ, varying from 0.05 to 1 minute every 0.05 minutes. λ represents the job inter-arrival time, meaning that jobs will arrive from once every 3 seconds to once every 60 seconds.

Upon arrivals, jobs are assigned to the job queue, organized as a priority queue. The job with the earliest arrival time is assigned first to the vehicle in the parking lot that has the latest departure time. Each job has a VM size, input data size, and processing time. The VM and data size are both static, set to 500 and 50,000 MB (i.e., 50 GB), respectively. Processing time varies starting from 30 to 300 minutes, in increments of 30 minutes.

Upon assignment, the job starts the first of five tasks. The first task is the initial job setup. In this task, the datacenter sends the VM, assumed to be of size 500 MB, and the input data, of size 50 GB, to the vehicle over the network, as explained in Section 21.7.2. Processing may not begin until this step is complete.

The next three tasks are the Map, backup, and Reduce tasks. In the Map and Reduce tasks, half the job processing is completed, meaning each Map and Reduce tasks lasts for half the processing time. Between the Map and Reduce task is the backup task. In this task, the intermediate data, assumed to be of size 25,000 MB (i.e., 25 GB), is copied from the host vehicle to three backups hosts: two of

Simulation Parameters

Parameter	Description	Values
Simulation length	Length of the simulation in minutes	10,080 minutes
Car residency distribution	Distribution of the amount of time a car spends in the parking lot	Exponential
Car residency mean	Mean time of residency for a car	Mean 480 minutes
Incoming job distribution	Distribution of incoming jobs	Poisson
λ	Inter-job arrival time of incoming jobs	Varies between 0.05 and 1
u	Fraction of total vehicles that may have a job assigned	0.8
i	Number of jobs in initial setup	Varies between 100, 200, and 300
VM size	Size, in MB, of the VM	500 MB
Data size	Size, in MB, of the data	50,000 MB
Job-processing time	Length of time it takes a job to complete processing	Varies between 30 and 300 minutes
τ	Length of time prior to the car leaving that the VM migration will be started	30 and 60 minutes

these backup hosts are sent to the same cluster, and an additional backup host is a vehicle in the same group, but a different cluster. Upon job failure, the job can be restarted at the Reduce task using the backup. Backups are also sent over the network.

The final task is the job finalization task. The results of the Reduce task must be sent to the datacenter over the network.

We assume that we know when the vehicles leave. Given this information, we are able to mitigate job failure due to vehicles leaving. If a backup exists, the job VM can be migrated to the vehicle with the backup, and the job can restart. The datacenter will start this VM migration at a set time, τ, prior to the vehicle leaving. This gives the datacenter time to find a new vehicle to assign the job to, and then to migrate the VM to that vehicle. If a backup exists, the new host will be chosen as the vehicle that does not already have a job. If there are multiple, then the one with the latest departure time is chosen. If no backup exists, or no new host is available, then the vehicle will continue its current task until either a backup host becomes available or the vehicle leaves. If a new host is found, the VM must be sent via the network to the new host. If the vehicle leaves before the job is complete or before the VM is migrated, then the job fails and is reinserted into the job queue. Since, as already mentioned, the job queue is organized as a priority queue based on the job arrival time into the system, a failed job takes precedence over newly arrived jobs and will be assigned to the next available vehicle.

21.7.2 Network Model

In our simulation, there are four types of messages that are being sent via the network: initial setup data, backup data, VM migration data, and job finalization data. To simplify our model, we chose to simulate the network by giving each message an equal share of the bandwidth at each link. This choice leads to an easier understanding of what is happening in the datacenter, rather than introducing the intricacies of a certain protocol. We assume that a message sent in the current time unit is sent and received in the same time unit and the available bandwidth can be fully utilized. Each of the routes of the messages are first determined and the bandwidth at each link is divided among all messages on the link. Then for each individual message, the lowest link bandwidth is used, which represents the bandwidth available for the message.

21.7.3 Interpreting Our Results

Each graph has a distinct separation in the features of the graphs. Near a value of 0.6 for λ, each graph in Figure 21.5 shows a distinct divide. When this point is reached, no additional jobs can be assigned until one in initial setup state moves into the next state. This plays the role of the admission control daemon and acts as a throttle to the datacenter in order to ensure that the network does not get too congested. When i is 100, as is shown in the first column of Figure 21.5, the divide is near a value for λ of 0.65. Similarly, for i of 200, the divide is near a value of λ of 0.6, and for i of 300, the divide is near a value for λ of 0.55. This divide represents the point at which the value of i is met. To the right, those with lower incoming job rates, the datacenter is able to run the jobs that have been assigned more efficiently as the job rate decreases or λ increases. This is to be expected that if there are fewer jobs assigned to the datacenter, it will be able to handle them more efficiently.

This efficiency is clearly seen in the first row of plots in Figure 21.5 that show job completion time overhead. This shows the job completion time minus the job-processing time. This represents the overhead due to the network and VM migrations. To the far right, for lower incoming job rates, the overhead is low representing the amount of time sending data over the network is quite low. As the job rate increases, the traffic in the network increases, leading to higher job completion time. At the point of the divide, the number of incoming jobs is limited by the number of jobs in the initial job setup state.

As can be seen in the middle row of plots in Figure 21.5, the number of jobs assigned at any point in the parking lot stays nearly constant to the left of this divide. To the right of the divide, it drops off sharply and eventually flattens out. Each job must take at minimum the job processing time to complete, as would be the case with a network with infinite bandwidth. As more jobs are added to the datacenter, the load on the network increases, adding more overhead to the job completion time, as is also seen in the top row of plots. This leads to a sharp increase in the number of jobs in the parking lot up to the point they are throttled by the value i. To the left of the divide, the number of jobs in the parking lot is nearly constant. This shows that the datacenter is able to complete jobs at the same rate as jobs are accepted.

The third row of plots in Figure 21.5 shows the number of jobs completed. As expected, the number of jobs completed increases as the throttle i increases from 100 jobs to 200 jobs. This trend does not continue as it is increased to 300 jobs; instead, the opposite is true for some values of job processing time. This is due to an increasing number of job failures occurring with low values of λ and high values of job processing time.

We now look at the plots in Figure 21.6. These plots show statistics relating to the vehicles leaving the datacenter. In these figures, the same divide as in the plots in Figure 21.5 still exists, but is not as clear. The failures typically occur to the left of the λ divide and for higher job completion times. This agrees with intuition, as if there are more jobs and the jobs are longer, then the jobs will increase the load on the network until the point the job takes longer than the residency time of the vehicle. This is exactly what the plots in the first row of Figure 21.6 show. These are the failures per job. As the incoming job rates increase and the job completion time increases, there are more job failures. Also, as the throttle i increases, there are more and more failures.

The middle row of plots in Figure 21.6 shows the number of VM migrations per job. The shape of these plots reflects that of the first row. In an ideal set of plots, the shape representing the number of VM migrations per job should be larger and more prominent than that of the failures. This would show that the VM migrations essentially keep failures from occurring. We do not see this in our graphs leading us to assume that we are not handling VM migrations in an optimal way.

Finally, we look at the MTTF in the bottom row of plots in Figure 21.6. To get the value of MTTF, we take the number of completed jobs multiplied by average job completion time and divided by the number of job failures. For lower values of the throttle i, the MTTF is high and it decreases as i increases. At i equal to 100, the worst MTTF is above 60,000 minutes (10 hours). For i equal to 200,

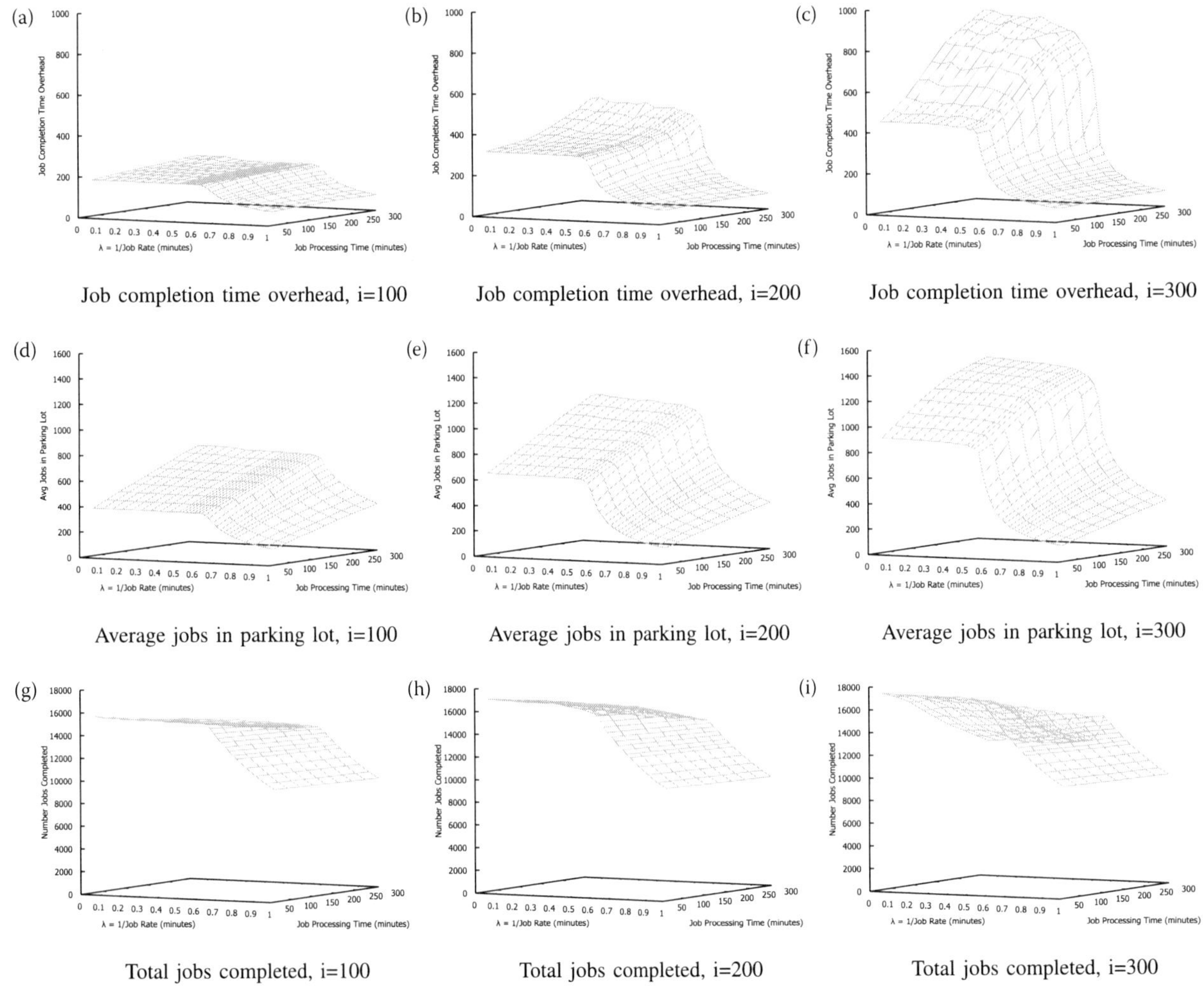

FIGURE 21.5 Job statistics for $\tau = 60$. Job completion time overhead: (a) $i = 100$, (b) $i = 200$, and (c) $i = 300$. Average jobs in parking lot: (d) $i = 100$, (e) $i = 200$, and (f) $i = 300$. Total jobs completed: (g) $i = 100$, (h) $i = 200$, and (i) $i = 300$.

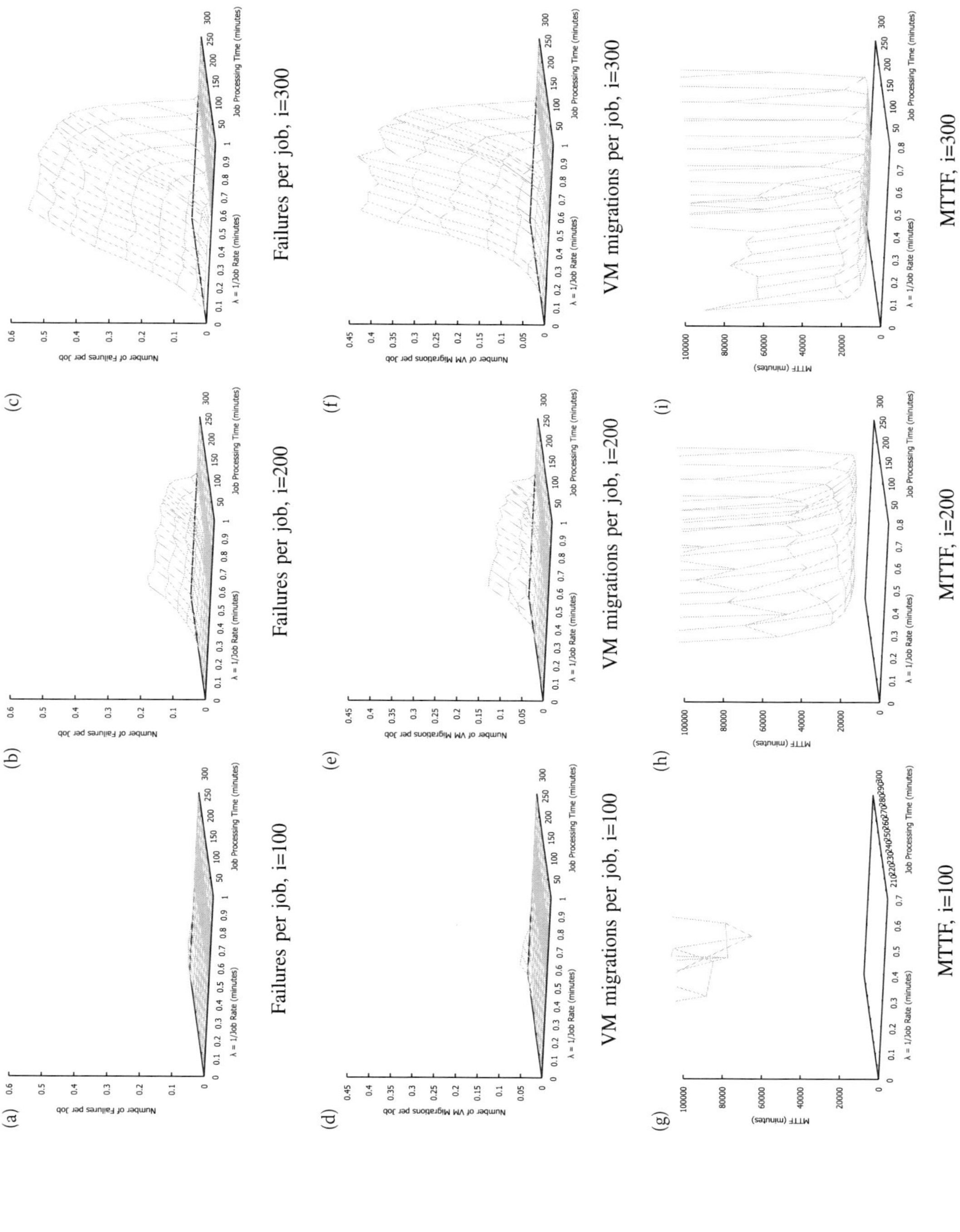

FIGURE 21.6 Job failure statistics for $\tau = 60$. Failures per job: (a) $i = 100$, (b) $i = 200$, and (c) $i = 300$. VM migrations per job: (d) $i = 100$, (e) $i = 200$, and (f) $i = 300$. MTTF: (g) $i = 100$, (h) $i = 200$, and (i) $i = 300$.

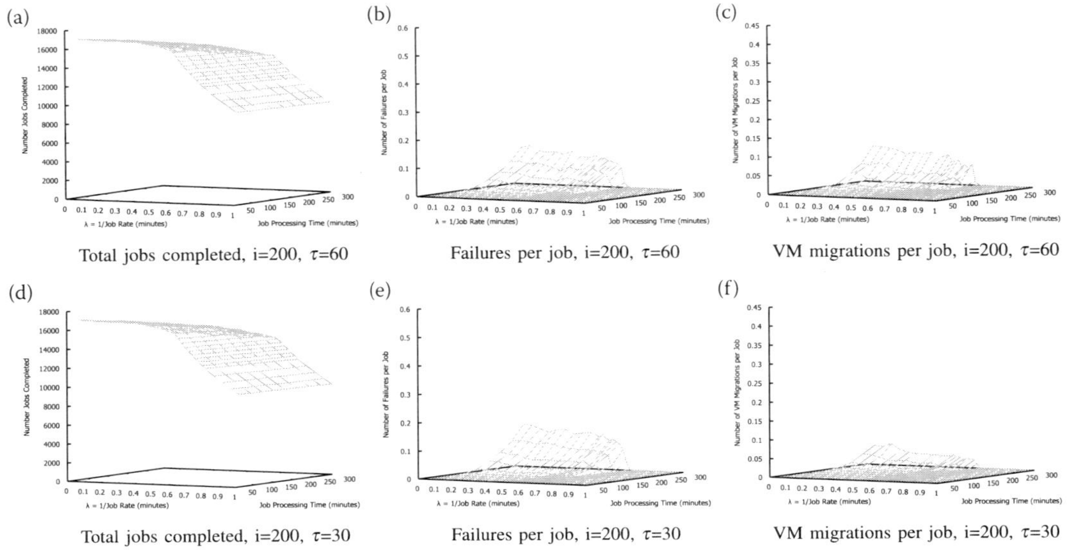

FIGURE 21.7 Comparison of $\tau = 60$ and $\tau = 30$. Total jobs completed: (a) $i = 200$, $\tau = 60$; (d) $i = 200$, $\tau = 30$. Failures per job: (b) $i = 200$, $\tau = 60$; (e) $i = 200$, $\tau = 30$. VM migrations per job: (c) $i = 200$, $\tau = 60$; (f) $i = 200$, $\tau = 30$.

the worst MTTF is above 15,000 minutes (4.16 hours), and for *i* equal to 300, the worst MTTF is only above 7600 minutes (2.1 hours).

21.7.4 Comparing VM Migration Offset

The plots in Figure 21.7 show the differences in our plots or VM migration offsets of 30 and 60 minutes. We expected the VM migration offset of 30 minutes to show much better results than that of the 60-minute setting. This intuition came from our observation that a VM migration does not take very long since its size is low and that by starting the VM migration at 60 minutes, we essentially cut short the length of time each vehicle is able to process.

In Figure 21.7, each plot has a value of *i* equal to 200 and τ is 60 minutes in the top row and 30 minutes in the bottom row. The first column of plots shows the number of jobs completed, the second column shows the number of failures per job, and the third column shows the number of VM migrations per job. The difference in job completion time is very slight, but the values are slightly better for a VM migration offset of 60 than for 30. The difference is at its maximum less than 100 jobs more completed. The difference in values increases as the λ decreases and the job completion time increases. The number of VM migrations for a VM migration offset of 60 is roughly double that of 30. Finally, we see that there are slightly less job failures for a VM migration offset of 60 than that of 30. Each of these again shows us that our VM migrations are less than ideal.

21.7.5 Comparison with a Conventional Datacenter

Finally, to compare our VC with a conventional datacenter with similar bandwidth and servers, we keep all our input parameters the same, except for the residency time of vehicles, which we set to be infinite. The difference in the results will represent the overhead caused by vehicles leaving the datacenter. These are shown in Figures 21.8 and 21.9.

First we look at Figure 21.8 that shows the number of jobs completed for *i* equal to 100, 200, and 300, the first, second, and third columns, respectively, for both the VC and the conventional

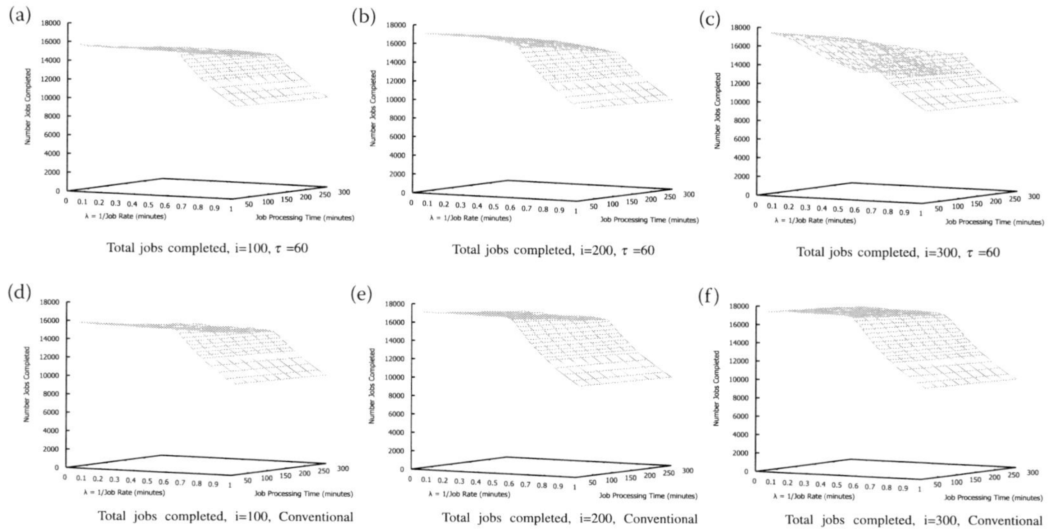

FIGURE 21.8 Comparison of vehicular and conventional datacenter. Total jobs completed: (a) $i = 100$, $\tau = 60$; (b) $i = 200$, $\tau = 60$; (c) $i = 300$, $\tau = 60$; (d) $i = 100$, conventional; (e) $i = 200$, conventional; (f) $i = 300$, conventional.

datacenter. For comparison, we used 60 as the value for τ. This value will not matter in the results for the conventional datacenter since these servers will not leave. As expected, in all cases, the number of jobs completed in the VC is less than that of the datacenter. In both, for i equal to 100, there is very little difference. As the values of i increase, this difference becomes much more significant, especially as the job completion time increases. This is most pronounced with i equal to 300. The overhead due to vehicles leaving leads to many more jobs being completed in the conventional datacenter than our VC-based datacenter.

Next, we look at Figure 21.9 showing the job completion time overhead for VC-based and conventional datacenters. Again, the columns show values of i equal to 100, 200, and 300, and the top row shows the VC-based datacenter while the bottom row shows the conventional datacenter. As expected, the overhead in the VC-based datacenter is more than that of the conventional datacenter in all cases. Again, as i increases and the job completion time increases, the VC-based datacenter fares worse as the job completion time increases. The difference of the two represents the overhead in job completion time due to vehicles leaving the parking lot.

21.8 CONCLUDING REMARKS AND DIRECTIONS FOR FUTURE WORK

A few years ago, inspired by the success of conventional cloud services, a number of papers have introduced the concept of VC, a nontrivial extension of the conventional CC paradigm.

In this pioneering work, we investigated sufficient conditions under which big data applications can be effectively supported by datacenters built on top of vehicles in a medium-sized parking lot and we have determined a baseline solution for implementation of such VCs. This paper is only a groundwork and the first step for our future works.

Inspired by the data replication strategies adopted by the GFS, we proposed and studied the effects of data storage redundancy on vehicles of a parking lot. In our simulation, at the end of the Map stage, two instances of the data were replicated on vehicles in the same cluster as the original vehicle and an instance was replicated on a vehicle in the same group, but a different cluster. In future work, we will look at more scenarios for data replication and we will take into consideration the jobs with fewer or more stages than a MapReduce job. As a baseline, the assumption is that each vehicle can

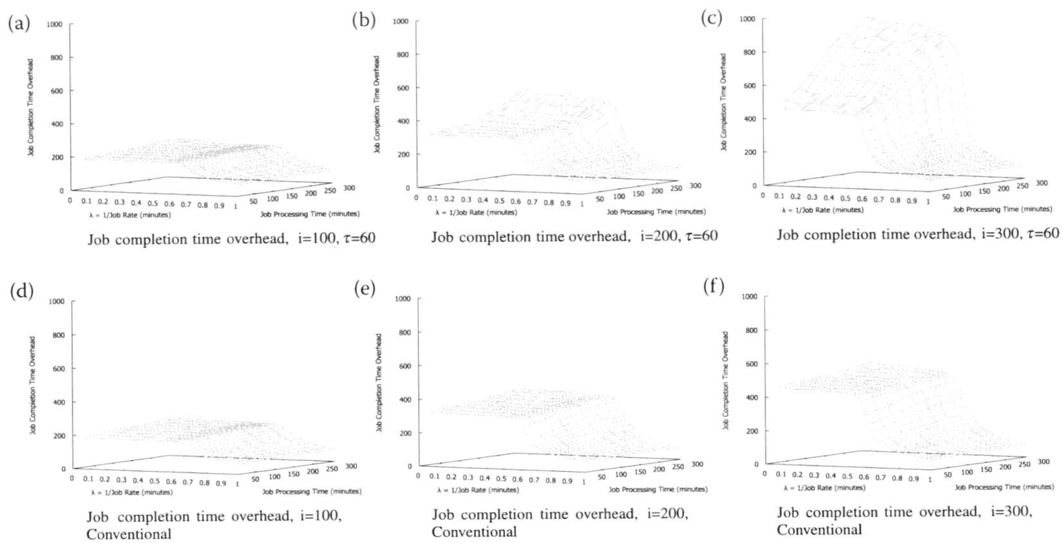

FIGURE 21.9 Comparison of vehicular and conventional datacenter. Job completion time overhead: (a) $i = 100, \tau = 60$; (b) $i = 200, \tau = 60$; (c) $i = 300, \tau = 60$; (d) $i = 100$, conventional; (e) $i = 200$, conventional; (f) $i = 300$, conventional.

run one VM at a time and the VM migration is attempted 30 or 60 minutes before the vehicle departs, to vehicles that contain an instance of the data. We need to find optimized solutions for this matter by studying more VM migration strategies such as double migration strategy.

We also looked at a job assignment strategy that selects vehicles with the longest residency time for assignment of new jobs. This approach for vehicle selection can lead to issues like unbalanced clusters, where a cluster has more jobs than its neighbor clusters. This can be optimized with load balancing and more sophisticated job assignment algorithms. We need to find better ways to utilize the datacenter to its fullest potential since currently only less than half of the vehicles in the parking lot have jobs at any time.

Our other interest relies on analyzing possibilities of having a fully wireless architecture as opposed to a combination of links as it was described in the network support in Section 21.6. Given the fact that the datacenter should support big data, the task of promoting reliability, dependability, and availability is a challenge in such networks.

In the future work, we will also investigate the case which a job starts on several vehicles to enhance the reliability of the VC. Improving the accuracy and reliability might come with the cost of stalling in the system, which should be studied. This promises to be an exciting area of investigation.

REFERENCES

1. L. A. Barroso, J. Clidaras, and U. Hölzle. *The Datacenter as a Computer: An Introduction to the Design of Warehouse-Scale Machines* (2nd edition). Morgan & Claypool, San Rafael, CA, 2013.
2. L. A. Barroso and U. Hölzle. *The Datacenter as a Computer: An Introduction to the Design of Warehouse-Scale Machines*. Morgan & Claypool, San Rafael, CA, 2009.
3. J. Foley. Private clouds take shape. *Information Week*, August 2008.
4. J. N. Hoover and R. Martin. Demystifying the cloud. *InformationWeek Research and Reports*, pp. 30–37, June 2008.
5. W. Kim. Cloud computing: Today and tomorrow. *Journal of Object Technology*, 8(1):65–72, January–February 2009.

6. D. Nurmi, R. Wolski, C. Grzegorczyk, G. Obertelli, S. Soman, L. Youseff, and D. Zagorodnov. The Eucalyptus open-source cloud-computing system. In *Proceedings of IEEE/ACM International Symposium on Cluster Computing and the Grid (CCGRID)*, pp. 124–131, May 2009.
7. National Institute of Standards and Technology (NIST). DRAFT cloud computing synopsis and recommendations. http://csrc.nist.gov/publications/ drafts/800-146/Draft-NIST-SP800-146.pdf, May 2011.
8. R. Buyya, C. Vecchiola, and S. Thamarai Selvi. *Mastering Cloud Computing: Foundations and Applications Programming*. Morgan Kaufmann, Elsevier, 2013.
9. D. C. Marinescu. *Cloud Computing, Theory and Applications*. Morgan Kaufman, Elsevier, 2013.
10. National Institute of Standards and Technology (NIST). NIST definition of Cloud Computing, http://nvlpubs.nist.gov/nistpubs/Legacy/SP/nistspecialpublication800-145.pdf, accessed 01/17/2017.
11. M. Armbrust, A. Fox, R. Griffith, A. D. Joseph, R. H. Katz, A. Konwinski, G. Lee et al. Above the clouds: A Berkeley view of cloud computing. In *Technical Report No. UCB/EECS-2009-28*, U.C. Berkeley, February 2009.
12. J. L. Hennessy and D. A. Patterson. *Computer Architecture: A Quantitative Approach*. Morgan Kaufman, Elsevier, 2012.
13. M. Abuelela and S. Olariu. Taking VANET to the clouds. In *Proceedings of Eighth ACM International Conference on Advanced in Mobile Computing, (MoMM'2010)*, Paris, France, December 2010.
14. S. Arif, S. Olariu, J. Wang, G. Yan, W. Yang, and I. Khalil. Datacenter at the airport: Reasoning about time-dependent parking lot occupancy. *IEEE Transactions on Parallel and Distributed Systems*, 23(11):2067–2080, 2012.
15. S. Olariu, M. Eltoweissy, and M. Younis. Towards autonomous vehicular clouds. *ICST Transactions on Mobile Communications and Computing*, 11(7–9):1–11, July–September 2011.
16. S. Olariu, T. Hristov, and G. Yan. The next paradigm shift: From vehicular networks to vehicular clouds. In Basagni, S. et al. (Eds), *Mobile Ad Hoc Networking Cutting Edge Directions*, pp. 645–700. Wiley and Sons, New York, NY, 2013.
17. S. Olariu, I. Khalil, and M. Abuelela. Taking VANET to the clouds. *International Journal of Pervasive Computing and Communications*, 7(1):7–21, February 2011.
18. M. Hilbert and P. Lpez. The world's technological capacity to store, communicate, and compute information. *Science*, 332(6025):60–65, 2011.
19. A. F. Mohammed, V. T. Humbe, and S. S. Chowhan. A review of big data environment and its related technologies. In *Proceedings of 2016 International Conference on Information Communication and Embedded Systems (ICICES)*, pp. 1–5, Chennai, India, 2016.
20. A. B. Patel, M. Birla, and U. Nair. Addressing big data problem using Hadoop and MapReduce. In *Proceedings of 2012 Nirma University International Conference on Engineering (NUiCONE-2012)*, December 2012.
21. eMarketer. Worldwide smartphone usage to grow 25% in 2014. http://www.emarketer.com/Article/Worldwide-Smartphone-Usage-Grow-25-2014/1010920, June 2014.
22. eMarketer. Tablet users to surpass 1 billion worldwide in 2015. http://www.emarketer.com/Article/Tablet-Users-Surpass-1-Billion-Worldwide-2015/1011806, January 2015.
23. S. Amyx. Why the internet of things will disrupt everything. http://innovationinsights.wired.com/insights/2014/07/internet-things-will-disrupt-everything/, July 2014.
24. C. Chase. The Internet of Things as the next big thing. http://www.directive.com/ blog/item/the-internet-of-things-as-the-next-big-thing.html, June 2013.
25. A. N. Systems. Global mobile data traffic forecast update, 2014–2019. http://www.getadvanced.net/global_mobile_data_traffic_forecast_update_20142019, March 2015.
26. D. C. Marinescu. *Complex Systems and Clouds: A Self-Organization and Self-Management Perspective*. Morgan Kaufman, Elsevier, 2016.
27. G. DeCandia, D. Hastorun, M. Jampani, G. Kakulapati, A. Lakshman, A. Pilchin, S. Sivasubramanian, P. Vosshall, and W. Vogels. Dynamo: Amazons highly available key-value store. In *Proceedings of 23rd ACM Symposium on Operating Systems Principles (SOSP07)*, Stevenson, WA, October 14–17, 2007.
28. D. Bhagavathi, P. J. Looges, S. Olariu, and J. L. Schwing. A fast selection algorithms on meshes with multiple broadcasting. *IEEE Transactions on Parallel and Distributed Systems*, 5(7):772–778, 1994.
29. T. H. Ibrahim, Y. Abaker, B. A. Ibrar, M. Nor, G. Salimah, and U. K. S. Abdullah. The rise of "big data" on cloud computing: Review and open research issues. *Information Systems*, 47:98–115, 2015.
30. R. Lin and S. Olariu. Reconfigurable buses with shift switching: Concepts and applications. *IEEE Transactions on Parallel and Distributed Systems*, 6(1):93–102, 1995.

31. K. Nakano and S. Olariu. Randomized leader election protocols in radio networks with no collision detection. In *Algorithms and Computation*, pp. 362–373, 2000.
32. S. Olariu, M. Eltoweissy, and M. Younis. ANSWER: AutoNomouS netWorked sEnsoR system. *Journal of Parallel and Distributed Computing*, 67:114–126, 2007.
33. S. Olariu, J. L. Schwing, and J. Zhang. Fundamental algorithms on reconfigurable meshes. In *Proceedings of 29th Allerton Conference on Communications, Control and Computing*, pp. 811–820, Monticello, IL, September 1991.
34. S. Olariu, J. L. Schwing, and J. Zhang. Fast computer vision algorithms for reconfigurable meshes. *Image and Vision Computing*, 10(9):610–616, 1992.
35. O. J. Reichman, M. B. Jones, and M. P. Schildhauer. Challenges and opportunities of open data in ecology. *Science*, 332(6018):73–75, 2011.
36. C. Snijders, U. Matzat, and U.-D. Reips. Big data: Big gaps of knowledge in the field of Internet. *International Journal of Internet Science*, 7:1–5, 2012.
37. A. Zomaya, M. Clements, and S. Olariu. A framework for reinforcement-based scheduling in parallel processor systems. *IEEE Transactions on Parallel and Distributed Systems*, 9(3):249–260, 1998.
38. J. Dean and S. Ghemawat. MapReduce: Simplified data processing on large clusters. *Communications of the ACM*, 51(1):107–113, January 2008.
39. C. J. Shafer, S. Rixner, and A. L. Cox. The Hadoop distributed file system. In *Proceedings of 25th IEEE Symposium on Mass Storage Systems and Technologies (MSST10)*, pp. 1–10, Lake Tahoe, Nevada, May 2010.
40. B. K. Shvachko, H. Kuang, S. Radia, and R. Chansler. The Hadoop distributed file system: Balancing portability and performance. In *Proceedings of IEEE International Symposium on Performance Analysis of Systems and Software (ISPASS10)*, pp. 122–133, White Plains, NY, March 2010.
41. T. White. *Hadoop: The Definitive Guide* (1st edition). O'Reilly Media, Inc., 2009.
42. Amazon Inc. Amazon web services. http://aws.amazon.com, 2010.
43. Google, Inc. Google app engine. http://code.google.com/appengine/, 2010.
44. Microsoft Corporation Windows azure. https://azure.microsoft.com/en-us/, accessed 01/17/2017.
45. IBM Inc. IBM smart cloud. http://www.ibm.com/cloud-computing, 2010.
46. M. Eltoweissy, S. Olariu, and M. Younis. Towards autonomous vehicular clouds. In J. Zheng, D. Simplot-Ryl, V.C.M. Leung (eds), *Ad Hoc Networks. ADHOCNETS*. Lecture Notes of the Institute for Computer Sciences, Social Informatics and Telecommunications Engineering, vol 49. Springer, Berlin, Heidelberg, 2010.
47. R. Florin, P. Ghazizadeh, A. Ghazi Zadeh, and S. Olariu. Enhancing dependability through redundancy in military vehicular clouds. In *Proceedings of IEEE MILCOM'2015*, Tampa, FL, October 26–28, 2015.
48. M. K. Lindell and C. S. Prater. Critical behavioral assumptions in evacuation time estimate analysis for private vehicles: Examples from hurricane research and planning. *Journal of Urban Planning and Development*, 133(1):18–29, March 2007.
49. T. Litman. Lessons from Katrina and Rita: What major disasters can teach transportation planners. *ASCE Journal of Transportation Engineering*, 132(1):11–18, 2006.
50. P. Murray-Tuite and H. Mahmassani. Transportation network evacuation planning with household activity interactions. *Transportation Research Record: Journal of Transportation Research Board*, 1894:150–159, 2004.
51. US Department of Transportation. Intelligent transportation systems for planned special events: A cross-cutting study. In *Technical Report FHWA-JPO-08-056*, Federal Highway Administration, Washington, DC, 2008.
52. M. C. Weigle and S. Olariu. Intelligent highway infrastructure for planned evacuations. In *Proceedings of the First International Workshop on Research Challenges in Next Generation Networks for First Responders and Critical Infrastructures (NetCri)*, pp. 594–599, New Orleans, LA, April 2007.
53. S. Wilson-Goure, N. Houston, and A. V. Easton. Case studies: Assessment of the state of the practice and state of the art in evacuation transportation management. In *Technical Report FHWA-HOP-08-014*, Federal Highway Administration, Washington, DC, 2006.
54. R. Hussain, F. Abbas, J. Son, and H. Oh. TIaaS: Secure cloud-assisted traffic information dissemination in vehicular ad hoc networks. In *2013 13th IEEE/ACM International Symposium on Cluster, Cloud and Grid Computing (CCGrid)*, pp. 178–179, May 2013.

55. M. Whaiduzzaman, M. Sookhak, A. Gani, and R. Buyya. A survey of vehicular cloud computing. *Journal of Network and Computer Applications*, 40:325–344, 2014.
56. L. Gu, D. Zeng, and S. Guo. Vehicular cloud computing: A survey. In *Proceedings of IEEE Globecom Workshops*, pp. 403–407, December 2013.
57. N. Vignesh, R. Shankar, S. Sathyamoorthy, and V. M. A. Rajam. Value added services on stationary vehicular cloud. In Natarajan R. (eds), *Distributed Computing and Internet Technology*, ICDCIT 2014. Lecture Notes in Computer Science, vol. 8337. Springer.
58. W. He, G. Yan, and L. D. Xu. Developing vehicular data cloud services in the IoT environment. *IEEE Transactions on Industrial Informatics*, 10(2):1587–1595, May 2014.
59. A. Schlote, C. King, E. Crisostomi, and R. Shorten. Delay-tolerant stochastic algorithms for parking space assignment. *IEEE Transactions on Intelligent Transportation Systems*, 15(5):1922–1935, 2014.
60. J. K. Suhr and H. G. Jung. Sensor fusion-based vacant parking slot detection and tracking. *IEEE Transactions on Intelligent Transportation Systems*, 15(1):21–36, 2014.
61. P. Ghazizadeh, R. Mukkamala, and S. El-Tawab. Scheduling in vehicular cloud using mixed integer linear programming. In *Proceedings of First International Workshop on Mobile Sensing, Computing and Communication*, pp. 7–12, New York, NY, 2014.
62. P. Ghazizadeh. Resource allocation in vehicular cloud computing. PhD Thesis, Old Dominion University, July 2014.
63. P. Ghazizadeh, R. Florin, A. Ghazi Zadeh, and S. Olariu. Reasoning about the mean-time-to-failure in vehicular clouds. *IEEE Transactions on Intelligent Transportation Systems*, 17(3):511–521, 2016.
64. P. Ghazizadeh, S. Olariu, A. Ghazi Zadeh, and S. El-Tawab. Towards fault-tolerant job assignment in vehicular cloud. In *Proceedings of IEEE SCC*, pp. 17–24, June 2015.
65. B. Baron, M. Campista, P. Spathis, L. H. Costa, M. Dias de Amonim, O. C. Duarte, G. Pujolle, and Y. Viniotis. Virtualizing vehicular node resources: Feasibility study of virtual machine migration. *Vehicular Communications*, 4:39–46, April 2016.
66. T. K. Refaat, B. Kantarci, and H. T. Mouftah. Virtual machine migration and management for vehicular clouds. *Vehicular Communications*, 4:47–56, April 2016.
67. G. Yan, D. Wen, S. Olariu, and M. C. Weigle. Security challenges in vehicular cloud computing. *IEEE Transactions on Intelligent Transportation Systems*, 4(1):6–16, January 2013.
68. Citrix. Virtualization, networking and cloud computing. http://www.citrix.com, 2009.
69. VMware. Vmware virtualization software for desktops, servers & virtual machines for virtual and public cloud. http://www.vmware.com, 2009.
70. L. F. Sarmenta. Sabotage-tolerance mechanisms for volunteer computing systems. *Future Generation Computer Systems*, 18(4):561–572, 2002.
71. K. Watanabe, M. Fukushi, and S. Horiguchi. Expected-credibility-based job scheduling for reliable volunteer computing. *IEICE Transactions on Information and Systems*, 93(2):306–314, 2010.
72. Y. Zuev and S. Ivanov. The voting as a way to increase the decision reliability. *Journal of the Franklin Institute*, 336(2):361–378, 1999.
73. Y. A. Zuev. On the estimation of efficiency of voting procedures. *Theory of Probability & Its Applications*, 42(1):73–81, 1998.
74. D. Kapil, E. S. Pilli, and R. Joshi. Live virtual machine migration techniques: Survey and research challenges. In *Proceedings of Third International IEEE Advance Computing Conference (IACC)*, Ghaziabad, India, February 2013.
75. P. Kaur and A. Rani. Virtual machine migration in cloud computing. *International Journal of Grid Distribution Computing*, 8(5):337–342, 2015.
76. A. S. Ghemawat, H. Gobioff, and S.-T. Leung. The Google File System. In *Proceedings of 19th ACM Symposium on Operating Systems Principles (SOSP03)*, pp. 29–43, Bolton Landing, NY, October 2003.
77. F. Chang, J. Dean, S. Ghemawat, W. C. Hsieh, D. A. Wallach, M. Burrows, T. Chandra, A. Fikes, and R. E. Gruber. Bigtable: A distributed storage system for structured data. In *Proceedings of Seventh USENIX Symposium on Operating Systems Design and Implementation (OSDI06)*, Seattle, WA, November 2006.
78. R. Roess, E. Prassas, and W. McShane. *Traffic Engineering* (4th edition). Pearson, Boston, MA, 2011.
79. Texas Transportation Institute. 2012. Mobility Report, http://www.pagregion.com/Portals/0/documents/HumanServices/2012MobilityReport.pdf, accessed 01/17/2017.
80. G. Neiger, A. Santoni, F. Leung, D. Rodgers, and R. Uhlig. Intel virtualization technology: Hardware support for efficient processor virtualization. *Intel Technology Journal*, 10(3):167–178, 2006.

Index

A

B

C

D

E

F

G

J

K

L

M

N

Q

R

S

T

U

V

W

X

Y

Z